THE HANDBOOK OF CLINICAL PSYCHOLOGY
Theory, Research, and Practice
Volume I

VOLUME I

The Handbook of Clinical Psychology:

Theory, Research, and Practice

Edited by:

C. Eugene Walker, *Ph.D.*
University of Oklahoma
Medical School

Consulting Editors:

Frederick Kanfer, *Ph.D.*
University of Illinois

Alan Kazdin, *Ph.D.*
Western Psychiatric Institute,
Pittsburgh

Joseph Matarazzo, *Ph.D.*
University of Oregon
Health Sciences Center

Eliot Rodnick, *Ph.D.*
University of California,
Los Angeles

Julian Rotter, *Ph.D.*
University of Connecticut

DORSEY
PROFESSIONAL
SERIES

DOW JONES-IRWIN
Homewood, Illinois 60430

© DOW JONES-IRWIN, 1983

All rights reserved. No part of this publication may be
reproduced, stored in a retrieval system, or transmitted,
in any form or by any means, electronic, mechanical,
photocopying, recording, or otherwise, without the prior
written permission of the publisher.

ISBN 0-87094-319-7

Library of Congress Catalog Card No. 82–73409

Printed in the United States of America

1 2 3 4 5 6 7 8 9 0 MP 0 9 8 7 6 5 4 3

Preface

Clinical psychology today represents one of the most stimulating and rapidly developing areas of professional and scientific endeavor. The swift pace of developments in the field and the staggering weight of literature produced each year make compendia and handbooks essential tools for the student, the researcher, and the practitioner.

This handbook attempts to strike a balance between scholarly review of current research literature and enlightened suggestions toward the best clinical practice. The chapters have all been prepared by highly competent individuals in the area under consideration. Sincere appreciation is expressed to the Consulting Editors who assisted in selecting topics to be covered, suggesting qualified authors, and, when called upon, editorial advice. The authors and editor owe a great debt of gratitude to Leanne Ware, research assistant, who assisted in every stage of the development of the present project, giving dedicated personal attention and much time beyond the hours for which she was paid in order for the manuscript to be completed. Special appreciation is also due Donna Hill who worked long hours typing and coordinating the preparation of the manuscript. Needless to say, however, any remaining flaws in the volume are the responsibility of the editor and the chapter authors. We hope that this handbook will prove a rewarding and useful reference.

C. Eugene Walker

Contributing authors

David Ametrano
University of Michigan
Ann Arbor, Michigan

Irene Mass Ametrano
Eastern Michigan University
Ypsilanti, Michigan

Anne Anastasi
Fordham University
Bronx, New York

Frank Andrasik
State University of New York, Albany
Albany, New York

John W. Baker II
Private Practice
New Windsor, New York

Rodney R. Baker
Veterans' Administration Medical Center
San Antonio, Texas

Alan Barclay
Wright State University
Dayton, Ohio

E. Edward Beckham
University of Oklahoma Medical School
Oklahoma City, Oklahoma

Allen E. Bergin
Brigham Young University
Provo, Utah

Stephen N. Berk
Temple University
Philadelphia, Pennsylvania

Edward B. Blanchard
State University of New York, Albany
Albany, New York

Jenny Boyer
University of Oklahoma Medical School
Oklahoma City, Oklahoma

Paul W. Clement
Fuller Theological Seminary
Pasadena, California

Nicholas A. Cummings
Biodyne Institute
San Francisco, California and
Honolulu, Hawaii

Lynnda M. Dahlquist
West Virginia University
Morgantown, West Virginia

Douglas R. Denney
University of Kansas
Lawrence, Kansas

Robert E. Doan
University of Oklahoma
Norman, Oklahoma

Jay S. Efran
Temple University
Philadelphia, Pennsylvania

Charles H. Elliott
University of Oklahoma Medical School
Oklahoma City, Oklahoma

Ian M. Evans
State University of New York,
Binghamton
Binghamton, New York

Ian R. H. Falloon
Mental Health Clinical Research Center
for the Study of Schizophrenia;
Rehabilitation Research and
Training Center for Mental Illness
Los Angeles, California

John W. Fantuzzo
Fuller Theological Seminary
Pasadena, California

Douglas S. Faust
Eastern Virginia Medical School
Norfolk, Virginia

Anitra S. Fay
Psychological Consultants
Fort Smith, Arkansas

Stephen Flanagan
Mental Health Clinical Research Center
for the Study of Schizophrenia;
Rehabilitation Research and
Training Center for Mental Illness
Los Angeles, California

David Foy
Mental Health Clinical Research Center
for the Study of Schizophrenia;
Rehabilitation Research and
Training Center for Mental Illness
Los Angeles, California

Lawrence Glanz
University of Pittsburgh
School of Medicine
Pittsburgh, Pennsylvania

Daniel C. Goldberg
Jefferson Medical College
Philadelphia, Pennsylvania

Solomon C. Goldberg
Medical College of Virginia
Richmond, Virginia

Leslie S. Greenberg
University of British Columbia
Vancouver, British Columbia

Robert M. Hamer
Medical College of Virginia
Richmond, Virginia

Sandra L. Harris
Rutgers, The State University
New Brunswick, New Jersey

Don M. Hartsough
Purdue University
West Lafayette, Indiana

Stanley D. Imber
University of Pittsburgh School of Medicine
Pittsburgh, Pennsylvania

Phillip C. Kendall
University of Minnesota
Minneapolis, Minnesota

Irving Kirsch
University of Connecticut, Storrs
Storrs, Connecticut

Walter G. Klopfer
Portland State University
Portland, Oregon

Sheldon J. Korchin
University of California, Berkeley
Berkeley, California

Margaret R. Kriss
University of Minnesota
Minneapolis, Minnesota

Michael J. Lambert
Brigham Young University
Provo, Utah

Craig W. LeCroy
University of Wisconsin—Madison
Madison, Wisconsin

Mark H. Lewin
Upstate Psychological Service Center, P.C.
Rochester, New York

Robert Paul Liberman
Mental Health Clinical Research Center
for the Study of Schizophrenia;

Rehabilitation Research and
Training Center for Mental Illness
Los Angeles, California

David Lukoff
Mental Health Clinical Research Center
for the Study of Schizophrenia;
Rehabilitation Research and
Training Center for Mental Illness
Los Angeles, California

Stephen Marder
Mental Health Clinical Research Center
for the Study of Schizophrenia;
Rehabilitation Research and
Training Center for Mental Illness
Los Angeles, California

William P. Milberg
Veterans' Administration Hospital
Boston, Massachusetts

Brendan A. Maher
Harvard University
Cambridge, Massachusetts

Peter E. Nathan
Rutgers, The State University
New Brunswick, New Jersey

Ted D. Nirenberg
Veterans' Administration Medical Center
and Brown University
Providence, Rhode Island

Roberta A. Olson
University of Oklahoma Medical School
Oklahoma City, Oklahoma

Steven C. Parkison
Walter Reed Army Medical Center
Washington, D.C.

Paul A. Pilkonis
University of Pittsburgh School of Medicine
Pittsburgh, Pennsylvania

Benjamin Pope
The Sheppard and Enoch Pratt Hospital
Towson, Maryland

Julian Rappaport
University of Illinois
Urbana-Champaign, Illinois

Sheldon D. Rose
University of Wisconsin—Madison
Madison, Wisconsin

Joseph R. Sanders
American Board of Professional Psychology
Washington, D.C.

Susan H. Sands
University of California, Berkeley
Berkeley, California

Lee Sechrest
University of Michigan
Ann Arbor, Michigan

Edward Seidman
University of Illinois
Urbana-Champaign, Illinois

Aaron Smith
University of Michigan
Ann Arbor, Michigan

Clifford H. Swensen
Purdue University
West Lafayette, Indiana

Fernando Tapia
University of Oklahoma Medical School
Oklahoma City, Oklahoma

Gary R. VandenBos
American Psychological Association
Washington, D.C.

Helen H. Watkins
University of Montana
Missoula, Montana

John G. Watkins
University of Montana
Missoula, Montana

John T. Watkins
University of Oklahoma Medical School
Oklahoma City, Oklahoma

R. Douglas Whitman
Wayne State University
Detroit, Michigan

Christine Winter
Counseling Associates
Mystic, Connecticut

Byron Wittlin
Mental Health Clinical Research Center
for the Study of Schizophrenia;

Rehabilitation Research and
Training Center for Mental Illness
Los Angeles, California

Robert Henley Woody
University of Nebraska at Omaha
Omaha, Nebraska

Contents

Volume I

within treatment variability. Multiple covariates. Heterogeneous regressions. Large treatment differences on covariate. Comparison of change in intact groups. Measurement of change. Cross-over designs. Analysis of dropouts. Multiple regression and correlation: *Pitfalls in using multiple correlation and regression. Cross validation instead of significance. Interaction terms as predictors. The art of predictor selection.* Factor analysis. Multidimensional scaling. Single-case analysis.

How much should an evaluation cost? Design issues in evaluation: *Validity. True experiments. Threats to internal validity. Quasi-experimental designs.* Role of the evaluator: *Changing programs. Planning. Program implementation. Program monitoring. Outcome assessment. Data collection and management. Measuring change. Benefits and costs of interventions.* Coda.

PART II: PSYCHOTHERAPY RESEARCH

A view of the field. Prediction—Relating process to outcome: *Activity. Experience. Dramatic interpretation. Association.* Explanation—Pattern identification: *Intervention effects. In-therapy behavior. Experience. Organized patterns.* Description—Development of process systems: *Interactional. Therapist behavior. Client behavior.*

Toward a taxonomy of therapist influence. Static therapist traits and psychotherapy outcome: *Race. Gender. Qualifications and experience. Personal adjustment. Expectancies.* SES: *Personality variables.* Therapist process variables and psychotherapy outcome: *Therapist style and related in-therapy behavior. Therapist intervention or operation. Relationship variables.* Future directions for research on the therapist's contribution: *1. The study of process variables (those derived from the in-therapy behavior of therapists) should be emphasized over personality and other static traits. 2. The therapist's contribution to effective psychotherapy might best be studied through the simultaneous examination of multiple therapist variables. 3. The therapist's contribution must be studied in interaction with patient and contextual variables. 4. The importance of therapist variables in the behavior therapist needs to be more carefully explored.*

Rapprochement. Efficacy and accountability: Secondary and aggregated techniques of analysis. Durability of psychotherapy effects. Comparative outcomes with drug therapy and psychotherapy. Psychotherapy and outcomes in physical health: *Psychotherapy for psychosomatic disorders. Behavioral medicine. Preparation for surgery. Psychological interventions in chronic disease and with geriatric patients. The effects of psychological care on medical utilization.* Negative effects of psychotherapy. Relationship between process and outcome: *Difficulty of predicting outcome from pretreatment measures. Lack of comparative outcome effects. Similarities and differences between naturally occurring, helpful relationships and formal psychotherapy.*

What is psychotherapy? Essential ingredients of psychotherapy: *The therapeutic climate. The therapeutic alliance. The therapeutic climate: A brief overview. Specific therapeutic processes. A brief recapitulation.* The movement toward rapprochement among theories of psychotherapy. To avert some misunderstanding.

PART III: DIAGNOSIS AND ASSESSMENT

History. The manuals: *DSM-III* and its predecessors: *Multiaxial diagnosis. Operational criteria. Consultation/liaison and field trials. The Diagnostic Manual.* The syndromes: *Disorders usually first evident in infancy, childhood, or adolescence. The disorders. Overall. Organic Mental Disorders. Substance Use Disorders. Schizophrenic Disorders. Paranoid Disorders. Psychotic disorders not elsewhere classified. Affective Disorders. Anxiety Disorders. Somatoform Disorders. Dissociative Disorders. Psychosexual Disorders. Factitious Disorders. Disorders of impulse control not elsewhere classified. Adjustment Disorder. Psychological factors affecting physical condition. Personality Disorders. V codes.* The present and the future.

Introduction. Communication in the interview: *Verbal content. Control and direction of verbal content. Verbal style in interview communication. Expressive aspects of interview communication. Sequence effects in the interview.*

Purposes of behavioral assessment: *Screening and needs assessment. Problem identification and goal definition. Hypothesis testing and the functional analysis. Network analysis for design or choice of therapy. Monitoring key outcomes. Evaluating general outcomes.* Measurement procedures: *Self-ratings. Direct behavioral observation in contrived settings. Naturalistic behavioral observation. Measures of psychological and psychophysiological functioning.* New developments in clinical assessment: *Assessing the physical environment. Assessing social interactions. Assessing behavioral interrelationships. Differentiation of skill and motivation.* Conclusions and future directions.

Intelligence in context: *Population changes in intelligence test performance. Interpreting present performance against antecedent background. Predicting competence in specified environments.* Comprehensive assessment of the handicapped: *Physical handicaps. Mental retardation. Learning disabilities.* Diagnostic interpretations of test performance: *Intelligence tests. Projective techniques.* Self-report personality inventories: Evolving methodology: *Empirical item selection. Construct validation. Traits and situations. Traits and states.* Health-related inventories: *Jenkins Activity Survey. Millon Behavioral Health Inventory. Health status measures.*

Diagnostic considerations: *The "brain-damaged" patient.* The evolution of current psychological and neuropsychological testing techniques. Current tests of organicity in clinical psychological assessments: The Wechsler scales: *Do V-PIQ differences provide reliable lateralizing indices? Hierarchy of cerebral functions and the Wechsler subtests. The Bender-Gestalt test. Other individual psychological tests and neuropsychological test batteries.* "Appraising the literature correctly": The rationale in selection and construction of tests and batteries for neuropsychological assessment: *The Halstead-Reitan battery (HRB). Luria's theories and the Luria-Nebraska battery (L-N). Quo Vadis?* Comparisons of functional psychiatric versus organic patients. Suggested contexts and guidelines for evaluating neuropsychological tests: *The concept of brain damage as a unitary disorder in a single psychological test function. General versus specific defects.* Suggested guidelines for evaluation of Wechsler subtest performances. Brief supplemental screening tests: *The Symbol Digit Modalities Test (SDMT). Single and Double Simultaneous Stimulation (Face-Hand) Test (SDSS). Purdue Pegboard Tests of Manual Dexterity. Benton Visual Retention Test. Other memory tests.* Sex and brain damage. Appendix: Guidelines for evaluation of individual measures of the Michigan Neuropsychological Test Battery: *1. Human Figure Drawing. 2. WAIS or WISC. 3. VOT, RCPM, and VRT. 4. Purdue Pegboard. 5. Symbol-Digit Written and Oral Substitutions. 6. Single and Double Simultaneous Stimulations. 7. Memory for Unrelated Sentences.* General principles and implications.

Introduction. How influential is the psychological report? Barriers to communication and their resolution. Importance of specifying level of behavior. How to write a psychological report. Feedback: False and true: *False feedback. True feedback.* Illustrative reports.

Volume II

PART IV: RECENT DEVELOPMENTS IN TREATMENT MODALITIES

PART V: THE PRACTICE OF PSYCHOLOGY

Continuing professional development of the profession. Continuing professional development of the individual psychologist: *Self-assessment. Continuing education. Peer review. Public issues and policy.*

Introduction and overview. Education, training, and research issues. Health
psychology and related issues. Federal health insurance programs. Federal
Trade Commission. Medicare and Medicaid. Criminal code reform and
the not guilty by reason of insanity plea. Training in professional psychology.
Concluding observations.

PART VI: FORENSIC PSYCHOLOGY

The diagnostic arena: *State civil commitment for the mentally ill. State criminal commitment for the mentally ill who have allegedly committed a crime.
State commitment of juveniles. Family law. Adult guardianship.* The treatment
arena: *Contractual agreements for treatment. Consent for treatment. Privileged communication and duty to warn third parties.* The expert witness:
*The adversary system. Qualifications. The time of referral. Subpoenas and
depositions. The preparation and giving of testimony.* Malpractice.

Forensic psychology. The psychologist-attorney relationship. Understanding
the law. Psychological information. Privileged communication. Duty to warn.
Malpractice. Apostolic zeal.

PART I

Theoretical and experimental foundations

1

A history of clinical psychology

Irving Kirsch*
and
Christine Winter†

If, until recently, psychologists have remained indifferent to their professional history (Watson, 1960), this has been particularly true of clinical
psychologists. Our most important historical text is titled *A History of
Experimental Psychology* (Boring, 1950), and except for a chapter
on psychoanalysis—which in any case has remained more or less firmly
entrenched within psychiatry—clinical psychology has been largely ignored in our histories. Yet surely, history should be as important to clinicians as to other psychologists. Without knowing our history, we cannot
fully understand our present nor anticipate our future.

The years 1896 and 1946 stand out as the major landmarks in the
history of clinical psychology. In 1896, Lightner Witmer established the
first psychological clinic at the University of Pennsylvania, thereby founding clinical psychology as a profession. Fifty years later, the Veterans
Administration launched a fundamental transformation of the field—a
transformation so profound that one might well think of clinical psychology
as two separate professions.

Originally, clinical psychology was a small field commanding little
respect within psychology as a whole. Diagnostic assessment of the problem child was the primary professional activity of its often poorly trained
practitioners. The minority of clinicians who practiced psychotherapy at
all did so under psychiatric supervision. Private practice was relatively
rare, and those who did earn their living in this manner were known as
consulting rather than *clinical* psychologists. To their constant consterna-
tion, the early clinicians found themselves referred to as *mental testers*
by other professionals.

* University of Connecticut, Storrs.
† Counseling Associates, Willimantic, Connecticut.

Since 1946, psychotherapy has become the defining professional activity of clinical psychologists. During the 1970s, more professional time was devoted to the practice of therapy than to any other task. In contrast, diagnosis and assessment accounted for less than 10 percent of professional time (Garfield & Kurtz, 1976). Along with this change in activity has come a dramatic increase in size and prestige. Clinical psychology has become the largest area of specialization within American psychology.

These events—the founding of clinical psychology in 1896, its development as a profession primarily identified with the task of psychological assessment, and the professional revolution through which clinical psychologists became psychotherapists—constitute a skeletal outline of the professional history of clinical psychology. They are the events that dictated the form and content of this chapter. Before examining these developments in greater detail, we will consider the early history of mental testing. The early developers of mental tests would not have identified themselves as clinical psychologists, but their work provided a foundation upon which early clinical psychology was built. This will be followed by a section on the founding and professional development of clinical psychology. When psychologists became psychotherapists, the history of psychotherapy became an important aspect of the history of clinical psychology. This history,with its roots in antiquity, will be taken up in the third section of this chapter. Finally, we will turn to some of the more recent trends developing in the field.

In addition, there is one event to which clinical psychology, the psychology of individual differences, and indeed all areas of modern psychology owe their existence. That event is the founding of psychology as an independent discipline by Wilhelm Wundt. Kuhn (1970) has argued that a science reaches maturity through an "achievement [that is] sufficiently unprecedented to attract an enduring group of adherents away from competing modes of scientific activity [and] sufficiently open-ended to leave all sorts of problems for the redefined group of practitioners to resolve" (p. 10). The program of experimental research emanating from the psychological laboratory established by Wundt at Leipzig between 1875 and 1879 was exactly this sort of paradigmatic achievement. Scholars from all over the world flocked to Leipzig to study under Wundt, many of them subsequently returning to their own countries to establish laboratories and university departments of psychology.

Among Wundt's many students were Emil Kraepelin, who applied Wundt's experimental methods to the field of psychopathology and developed the first modern psychiatric nosology; James McKeen Cattell, whose doctoral dissertation, supervised by a somewhat reluctant Wundt, was one of the first empirical investigations of individual differences; and Witmer, the founder of clinical psychology. Wundt's interest was the study of the normal, generalized adult human mind, and as such was the antithesis of the clinical perspective. Nevertheless, the work of clinicians has always contained a Wundtian influence. Diagnosticians of the problem child brought an experimental attitude with them to their task, and one of the chief contributions of psychology to the field of psychotherapy has been the controlled empirical investigation of therapeutic outcome.

THE RISE OF INDIVIDUAL PSYCHOLOGY

An orthodox history of psychological testing

The first attempts at the psychological measurement of individual differences occurred in an effort to resolve a problem in astronomy. In August 1795, Nicholas Maskelyne, the astronomer royal at the Royal Observatory at Greenwich, noticed that his assistant's estimates of the times of stellar transits were $\frac{5}{10}$ of a second later than his own. The anomalous results were handled in the manner in which anomalies are usually initially treated: they were blamed on the ineptitude of the individual scientist. The assistant, David Kinnebrook, was cautioned to take greater care in the accuracy of his observations. But despite Kinnebrook's best efforts, the discrepancy between him and his supervisor increased rather than decreased. By January 1796, it had increased to $\frac{8}{10}$ of a second, and Kinnebrook was dismissed from his position.

This incident might have gone by as less than a minor footnote in the history of science had not a young German astronomer, Friedrich Wilhelm Bessel, taken notice of it some 20 years later. Bessel hypothesized that Kinnebrook's "error" was not due to ineptitude or sloppiness but that it might instead be due to involuntary individual differences which could be found even between the most capable observers. Testing this proposition by comparing his own observations with those of other astronomers, he determined that these differences did exist. Bessel represented the average difference between any two observers of stellar transits as a "personal equation," taking the form $A - B = t$, in which A and B are the estimates of particular astronomers and t is the average discrepancy between them.

During the 1860s, the personal equation attracted the attention of physiologists. Among others, it attracted the attention of Wundt, who at that time was a *Dozent* (lecturer) in physiology at the university in Heidelberg. Using the personal equation as a model, Wundt developed the complication experiment, an antecedent to the more influential reaction-time experiment (Kirsch, 1976). In Wundt's hands, these experimental procedures were placed in the service of general psychology; it remained for his student, Cattell, to restore them to individual psychology.

Credit for the first systematic study of individual differences in intellectual ability must be granted to Francis Galton. Inspired by the evolutionary theory of his half cousin, Charles Darwin, Galton needed to measure these differences in order to investigate their heritability. Hypothesizing that acuity of sensory discrimination would be correlated with intelligence, he adapted the psychophysical methods of Weber and Fechner to the task of measuring individual differences in sensitivity (Galton, 1883). Galton's measures of weight discrimination, pitch threshold, and mental imagery were thus the first mental tests.

In the United States, mental testing was pioneered by Cattell, who was influenced more by a brief association with Galton than by his studies with Wundt. Cattell (1890) coined the term *mental test* in an article describing the series of 10 tests used in his research at the University of Pennsylvania. These included measures of reaction time and of sensory discrimination and judgment. More or less similar test batteries were developed by Jastrow (1891–1892) and Gilbert (1894). A somewhat different approach to testing was taken in France by Alfred Binet. Instead of testing such simple functions as sensory discrimination and reaction time, Binet and Henri (1896) proposed that complex mental processes—including memory, imagination, attention, and comprehension—be tested directly. They argued that although simple tests yielded more precise and reliable scores, the more complex tests tapped functions in which there were greater individual differences and which were more significant to daily life. Series of tests involving more complex processes than those tested by Galton, Cattell, and Jastrow were developed by Münsterberg (1891), Kraepelin (1895) and his student Oehrn (1895), Guiccardi and Ferrari (1896), Ebbinghaus (1897), and Thorndike (1903).

The early optimism in the promise of mental testing was dampened somewhat by disappointing results from attempts to evaluate the tests. In the first of these efforts, Bolton (1891–1892) reported a lack of correspondence between students' scores on the digit span test devised by Jacobs (1887) and teachers' ratings of their intelligence. Similar results were reported by Gilbert (1897) for all but two of the tests in his array. Though supportive of Binet's strategy of testing complex processes, Stella Sharp (1898–1899), working with Titchener at Cornell, reported "a lack of correspondences in the individual differences observed in the various tests . . . [indicating] a relative independence of the particular mental activities under investigation" (p. 389). The most serious blow to the early testing movement came from Clark Wissler's (1901) correlational analysis of test data from Cattell's laboratory. He reported that neither the correlations between pairs of psychological tests nor those between academic grades and the various tests differed significantly from what would be expected by chance.

The publication of the first Binet-Simon Scale (Binet & Simon, 1905b), developed for the purpose of diagnosing mental retardation in school children, provided a second start to the testing movement. The 1905 scale was composed of a series of 30 tests arranged in order of increasing difficulty. The tests measured a wide variety of complex mental functions, with particular emphasis on judgment, comprehension, and reasoning, which Binet and Simon considered to be the essentials of intelligence. Preliminary norms were obtained by testing normal children in the primary schools and retarded children in the Salpêtrière hospital (Binet & Simon, 1905a). Children's intellectual levels could then be described in terms of the number of years by which they deviated from the norm for their age.[1]

When a revised scale was published in 1908 (Binet & Simon, 1908), the response was overwhelmingly positive. The 1908 scale was soon in use in the United States, Belgium, England, Italy, and Germany. In 1916, Lewis M. Termin published the Stanford Revision of the Binet-Simon Scale—the Stanford-Binet, as it has come to be known. The Stanford-Binet, utilizing the intelligence quotient (IQ) earlier suggested by William Stern (1912), gained worldwide recognition and stood without serious challenge in the field of intelligence testing until the introduction of the first of the Wechesler scales (1939).

The next major impetus to the psychological testing movement came by way of World War I. When the United States entered the war in 1917, APA president Robert Yerkes organized a Committee on Methods of Psychological Examining of Recruits for the Army's medical department. The committee, which included Henry H. Goddard and Termin among its members, produced two intelligence tests designed for group administration: the Army Alpha and the Army Beta. Samelson (1979) has persuasively argued that the army testing program was not, in fact, very successful. Nevertheless, it was certainly perceived as such at the time. Among the effects on psychology attributed to the favorable publicity that the war work received are increased respectability within the larger scientific community, foundation support for psychological research, and employment opportunities for psychologists. Cattell claimed that "the army testing put psychology on the map of the United States," and historian Thomas M. Camfield concluded that "if psychology had not in fact contributed significantly to the war, the war had contributed significantly to psychology" (Quoted in Samelson, 1979, p. 154).

The success of intelligence testing gave rise to a proliferation of a wide variety of psychological tests. By 1933, there were more than 3,000 tests listed by the Psychological Corporation (Hildreth, 1933)—tests of educational achievement, aptitude, personality traits, social adjustment, and so on. These were the tools of the trade for the fledgling profession of clinical psychology.

---

[1] The commonly held impression that the concept of mental age was first introduced in the 1908 revision is inaccurate in two respects. First, the term *mental age* is a product of the various translations and subsequent revisions of the Binet tests. A more accurate translation of Binet's term is *mental level* (Wolf, 1973). Second, the concept of an age-related mental level was clearly introduced in the original 1905 scale. "We have wished simply to show that it is possible to determine in a precise and truly scientific way the mental level of an intelligence, to compare this level with a normal level, and consequently to determine by how many years a child is retarded" (Binet & Simon, 1905a, p. 336).

A critical history of mental testing

The history presented above is a "Whig" history of the origins and early development of mental testing, chronicling the positive achievements of great pioneers in a steady stream of progress toward the present. There is also, however, a less-comfortable, though not less-important, side to the history of mental testing, a critical history in which events are examined in relation to their social and political contexts (e.g., Buss, 1976; Kamin, 1974; Norton, 1979; Samelson, 1978, 1979). The dominant theme of critical historiography in this area has been the close relationship between mental testing and the eugenics movement. This aspect of the history of individual psychology is particularly important as a context for the more recent controversies over race and intelligence.

Mental testing and eugenics were given birth by the same author in the same book. The term *eugenics* was coined by Galton (1883) in the *Inquiries*, where he defined it as

> the science of improving stock, which is by no means confined to questions of judicious mating, but which, especially in the case of man, takes cognisance of all influences that tend in however remote a degree to give to the more suitable races or strains of blood a better chance of prevailing speedily over the less suitable than they otherwise would have had. (p. 25)

Two preliminary suggestions were made as to the means by which this "better chance" could be provided. First, public endowments would be made to promote early marriages among members of "superior races," and second, bonus marks would be given for family merit in competitive examinations for employment. Galton delayed discussion of additional measures because of the popular sentiment, "for the most part quite unreasonable, against the gradual extinction of an inferior race" (p. 308). The central purpose of the *Inquiries* was propagandistic; it was intended to establish the possibility and the importance of eugenics. The first mental tests were developed as a means to that end.

Eugenics and mental testing developed as two streams from a common source and remained connected by numerous branches. Many of the pioneer intelligence theorists and test developers (e.g., Cattell, Termin, Yerkes, Charles Spearman, Edward Lee Thorndike, and Cyril Burt) played active roles in eugenics organizations. Perhaps the strongest connection between these two fields was provided by Henry Goddard, whose importance to the American eugenics movement is regarded by historian Mark Haller (1963) as second only to that of Charles Davenport, the biologist who formally established the movement in 1910.

In 1906, Goddard was appointed director of the research laboratory at the Vineland Training School, a private institution for the mentally retarded. While in that position, he introduced the Binet scales to the United States (Goddard, 1908, 1910) and produced a revision which for a period of five years was the standard American version of the test (Goddard, 1911). In addition, Goddard successfully promoted the idea that the Binet scale measured an unchangeable innate ability—an idea that Binet (1909) had condemned as "brutal pessimism."

Goddard's most influential work was his book *The Kallikak Family* (1912), tracing the descendants of Old Horror, the illegitimate son of a soldier in the American Revolution, and a retarded woman. Of Old Horror's 480 traceable descendants, 143 were determined to be mentally retarded, and only 46 were considered normal. Of equal importance, many of the retarded descendants were also paupers, alcoholics, epileptics, criminals, and sexual "degenerates." This latter finding established feeblemindedness as "the greatest of all eugenical problems" (Laughlin, 1914, p. 18).

When the Eugenics Records Office, the leading eugenics organization in the United States, commissioned a study on the best practical means for cutting off the supply of defective genes, Goddard was appointed to the important role of expert advisor representing the field of psychology. The report of this study (Laughlin, 1914) reveals the overall thrust of the eugenics movement during its period of greatest influence. It concluded that 10 percent of the American population was genetically defective and that the breeding capacity of those defectives could best be eliminated through a program of institutionalization and sterilization. This could be accomplished, the report maintained, within two generations, during which time the institutions could be made self-supporting, "due to continually receiving a higher class of inmates" (p. 58) whose labor would support the program. Since feeblemindedness was regarded as a cause of many traits that the eugenicists wished to eliminate (i.e., poverty, crime, alcoholism, and epilepsy), Goddard's revision of the Binet test would provide the most important means of selecting candidates for the sterilization program. Although nothing as sweeping as the Eugenics Records Office proposals were adopted, by 1931 30 states had adopted sterilization laws of one kind or another (Landman, 1932).

The eugenicist/mental tester collaboration had its greatest social impact in dealing with the issue of immigration. It is also in this area that the racist implications of eugenics first became clear. In 1912, Goddard administered the Binet test to immigrants at Ellis Island and concluded that between 79 and 87 percent of the immigrant Jews, Hungarians, Italians, and Russians were mentally retarded (Goddard, 1917). But the data with the greatest influence was produced by the Army testing program. The most startling finding of the Army testing was that nearly half of the soldiers tested could be classified as feebleminded (Yerkes, 1921). In addition, it was reported that blacks scored lower than whites, immigrants scored lower than native-born whites, and immigrants from Latin and Slavic countries scored well below those from Scandinavian and English-speaking countries. Finally, it was noted that intelligence scores were positively associated with length of residence in the United States. Of these findings, it was suggested that only the latter might be "an artifact of the method of examination" (Yerkes, 1921, p. 704).

These data were then further analyzed by Carl C. Brigham (1923), who later contributed to the development of the Scholastic Aptitude Test for the College Entrance Examination Board. Using a racial classification scheme proposed by William Ripley in 1899, Brigham estimated the proportion of "Nordic, Alpine, and Mediterranean blood" in each European country and compared these figures to the number of immigrants arriving from each country in successive time periods. Finding that between 1890 and 1910 Nordic immigration had declined while Alpine and Mediterranean immigration had increased, he concluded that the association between intelligence and length of residence was due to "a progressive decrease in the intellectual level of immigrants coming to this country in each succeeding five year period" (p. 199). To prevent the decline of American intelligence, Brigham urged the adoption of highly selective immigration and naturalization laws. In addition, warning of special problems associated with the presence of blacks in the United States, he advocated measures "looking toward the prevention of the continued propagation of defective strains in the present population" (p. 210).

In 1923, the Army data, as interpreted by Brigham, were presented to congressional committees on immigration. The result of the committee hearings was the Johnson-Lodge Immigration Act of 1924, which established permanent immigration quotas favoring the preferred Nordic stock. "National origin" quotas remained in effect until 1968, when they were replaced by an overall quota of 190,000 per year, with a limit of 20,000 from any one country.

During the 1930s, there occurred a shift in American psychological thinking away from the theory of racial differences in innate intelligence. Simultaneously, there was a rapid decline in the strength of the eugenics movement. It seems reasonable to suggest two common causes of these trends. The first was the general leftward shift in American political opinion that occurred during the Depression, a shift that occurred within psychology as well (Samelson, 1978). A second factor was the rise of Naziism, which "demonstrated the uses that might be made of some of the eugenics doctrines" (Haller, 1963, p. 7).

THE PROFESSIONAL DEVELOPMENT OF CLINICAL PSYCHOLOGY

The birth of clinical psychology

Lightner Witmer was born in Philadelphia on June 28, 1867. Following a year at the Law School of the University of Pennsylvania (1888–1889), he transferred to the philosophy department, where he came under the influence of Cattell, who had returned from Europe in 1889 to found a psychology laboratory at Pennsylvania. After earning a Master of Arts in 1891, Witmer traveled to Leipzig, where he attempted to emulate Cattell's example by expressing his desire to choose an applied problem for his dissertation. However, the suggestion was rejected by Wundt, who insisted on a more traditionally acceptable topic. Witmer returned to Pennsylvania in 1892, where he replaced Cattell as director of the psychological laboratory. Four years later, he established a clinic at the university, thereby inaugurating clinical psychology as a profession.

The most complete description of the incident that led directly to the founding of the Psychological Clinic at the University of Pennsylvania was provided by Arthur Holmes (1912), the clinic's first assistant director.

> In 1896 a supervising principal in a Philadelphia grammar school, and at that time also a student in the Psychological Department of the University of Pennsylvania, had under her instruction a boy known to the teaching profession as a chronic bad speller. Being a student of psychology and seeing quite naturally that the science of the processes of consciousness was the one most closely related to the case, this teacher turned to Dr. Lightner Witmer, Professor of Psychology at the University of Pennsylvania, who undertook to ascertain the cause of this deficiency and the proper treatment for its elimination.
>
> Briefly, he soon discovered that the boy saw double. Glasses were fitted to his eyes and special instruction was begun which soon brought about a marked improvement both in the boy's reading and spelling. Unfortunately his early death from a lingering disease cut short the possibilities of observation and training, but since that time Dr. Witmer has been receiving children for all manner of mental and moral difficulties and treating them at his Psychological Clinic. (pp. 28–29)

This first case set the pattern for Witmer's clinic. Children with a variety of learning difficulties and behavior problems were referred for assessment by the school system. Diagnosis was carried out by a clinical team consisting of a physician, a social worker, and a psychologist. The physician would complete a medical examination of the problem child and the social worker would prepare a social case history. The psychologist would provide anthropometric, optometric, and psychometric examinations, the latter utilizing instruments from the experimental laboratory. Following this elaborate assessment, a treatment program would be designed and implemented. The degree of improvement was then documented by retesting.

Witmer's (1896, 1897) description of his clinical methods encountered somewhat less-than-enthusiastic reception from his colleagues in the American Psychological Association (Collins, 1931). Nevertheless, in 1907 the clinic was expanded and a new journal, *The Psychological Clinic,* published until 1935, was established. In 1908, Carl Seashore founded a psychological clinic at the University of Iowa modeled after Witmer's clinic at Pennsylvania. In 1914, there were at least 19 psychological clinics in operation (Wallin, 1914), and by 1935, the number had grown to 87 (Louttit, 1939).

The list of Witmer's contributions to clinical psychology is impressive. In addition to establishing the first psychological clinic, he gave the new profession its name (Witmer, 1907), defined it as the application of psychological techniques to the diagnosis and treatment of individual cases, invented the modern interdisciplinary team, established the first journal devoted to clinical psychology, and even campaigned for a prevention-oriented field of community psychology (Witmer, 1909). Despite these accomplishments, Witmer has never been afforded widespread recognition in the field. Even during the height of his career, he failed to achieve fame among his professional colleagues. One reason for the lack of recognition given to Witmer is that psychological clinics were soon overshadowed by the development of the child guidance movement under the leadership of William Healy. Child guidance clinics were psychiatric rather then psychological establishments, but they were far more numerous than psychological clinics and therefore provided more employment opportunities for members of the new profession. The fact that Witmer's clinic served as a model for the first child guidance clinic was somehow lost in the shuffle.

Psychology and psychotherapy

The practice of psychotherapy by psychologists developed slowly. From the very beginning, Witmer (1896) had involved himself in remedial treatment as well as diagnosis, an interest later shared by clinicians in other settings as well. The treatment offered by psychologists was not psychotherapy; it was the provision of special tutoring aimed at helping children overcome deficits in reading or speech. At times, emotional factors were seen to be involved in a child's academic impediments, and in such instances, the boundary between remedial teaching and psychotherapy became blurred. Dissatisfied with their limited professional role, psychologists began proposing that "while ostensibly tutoring," they extend their responsibilities to the treatment of behavior and personality problems (Tulchin, 1930).

The development of clinical psychologists from mental testers to diagnosticians and from diagnosticians to therapists occurred against considerable resistance. Members of the medical profession had expressed alarm at the idea that psychologists might be allowed to diagnose children as retarded (New York Psychiatrical Society, 1917). Certainly, psychotherapy was out of the question. Similar objections to the idea of psychologists as therapists were voiced within psychology as well. Nevertheless, by the time the United States was entering World War II, approximately one third of all clinical psychologists included psychotherapy as part of their professional activities (Louttit, 1939).

During the war, there occurred a tremendous surge of popular and professional interest in psychotherapy. The causes of this psychotherapeutic revolution in America are not altogether clear, although the influx of a number of eminent psychoanalysts fleeing Naziism in Europe was certainly an important factor. In any case, psychology was only one area in which the shift toward therapy was discernable. Psychiatry, which had been primarily concerned with diagnosis and institutional care, adpoted therapy as its main professional interest after the war. Similar, if somewhat less pronounced, shifts occurred within social work and psychiatric nursing.

The new interest in therapy and psychological adjustment was evident in popular culture as well. *Lady in the Dark,* a Kurt Weill-Moss Hart musical comedy about a patient in psychoanalysis, was a Broadway hit in 1941 and a moderately successful movie in 1944. It was followed by Alfred Hitchcock's *Spellbound* (1945), *The Dark Mirror* (1946), and *Possessed* (1947), all dealing seriously with psychological problems.

The increased interest in therapy was matched by an increase in the perceived need for therapy. Selective Service rejection rates suggested that one out of three young adults suffered from neurotic problems (Rowntree, 1944). In addition, the Army reported that almost 45 percent of its first 1.5 million medical discharges were due to neuropsychiatric disabilities and estimated that at least 2 million veterans would need psychiatric treatment by the end of the war. To meet this perceived need, there were less than 3,000 active members and fellows in the American Psychiatric Association. Thus, with psychologists declaring therapy to be a legitimate part of their professional role, second only to assessment, it is no wonder that the Veterans Administration took the step that would complete the transformation of clinical psychologists from mental testers to psychotherapists and from technicians to independent professionals.

In 1946, the Veterans Administration created modern clinical psychology. This may seem a rash statement, and it is perhaps somewhat of an oversimplification. Yet, in a sense, it is an accurate assessment of the impact that the VA had on the field after the war. For two decades, clinicians had been moving toward incorporating psychotherapy into their profession and had been pressing for the establishment of higher standards of training, but the VA was the force that transformed that ambition into reality. It did so by providing paid traineeships for clinical graduate students and jobs for the graduates, by establishing the Ph.D. as the minimum educational requirement for clinical psychologists, and by defining the psychologist's role to include the practice of individual and group therapy (Miller, 1946).

In response to the VA program, psychology departments throughout the country established clinical training programs. At the same time, the

U.S. Public Health Service announced the availability of funds to support training in clinical psychology. By September 1946, 22 clinical doctoral programs had been established, and within a year, that number had nearly doubled (Sears, 1947). By the end of the decade, nearly 1,500 clinical graduate students were being trained in some 60 doctoral programs.

In 1949, the APA sponsored a conference on training in clinical psychology at Boulder, Colorado. It was at the Boulder Conference—as it has come to be known—that the scientist-professional model was formally established (Raimy, 1950). Clinical psychologists were to be simultaneously trained as scientists and as service providers and were expected to combine both roles in their postgraduate professional activities. It was agreed that all clinical doctoral students should be trained in psychotherapy, but independent private practice was opposed by most of those present. Despite the persistance of negative attitudes toward private practice on the part of academic psychologists, by the mid-1970s, nearly one in four clinicians were primarily private practitioners, and almost half were engaged in part-time private practice (Garfield & Kurtz, 1976).

THE ORIGINS OF PSYCHOTHERAPY

The history of modern psychotherapy begins, of course, with Freud. Yet psychotherapy, defined as the psychological treatment of psychological problems, has been widely practiced for tens of thousands of years. In most of these historical instances, the practitioners and their clients thought they were doing something very different than psychotherapy. When shamans and priests treated what we now believe to be psychological maladies, they believed that they were treating supernatural disorders by supernatural means. Similarly, physicians utilizing treatments that we now consider placebos to treat psychological disorders were unwittingly using a form of psychotherapy as their method of treatment.

Throughout the history and prehistory of humanity, the predominant approach to understanding and treating psychological difficulties has been based on supernatural ideas. Abnormal behavior was universally explained as due to the influence of spirits, and rites of exorcism were the most common forms of treatment. Modern psychotherapy came into being through a gradual rationalization of these magical beliefs. One of the earliest steps in this process is recorded in the First Book of Samuel. Here, Saul is described as suffering from a behavorial disorder caused by spiritual possession, but the treatment that is successfully employed to cure his disorder is purely psychological:

> The Spirit of the Lord had forsaken Saul, and at times an evil spirit from the Lord would seize him suddenly. His servants said to him, "You see, sir, how an evil spirit from God seizes you; why do you not command

your servants here to go and find some man who can play the harp?—
then, when an evil spirit from God comes on you, he can play and you
will recover." Saul said to his servants, "Find me a man who can play
well and bring him to me." . . . And whenever a spirit from God came
upon Saul, David would take his harp and play on it, so that Saul found
relief; he recovered and the evil spirit left him alone. (I Samuel 16:14–
23)

The development of rational philosophy in the classical world gave
birth to a rationalist tradition of psychological treatment. The Greek philos-
opher Epicurus (341–270 B.C.) was the world's first rational therapist.
In the thoroughly materialist Epicurean philosophy, the entire universe,
including the human soul, was seen as composed of atoms in motion.
Epicurus believed that "diseases of the mind"—particularly ambition for
wealth, power, and glory, and fear of death and of the gods—were the
principal causes of human misery. These mental diseases were to be
treated by philosophers by means of rational arguments. The following
passages written by Epicurus might, with little alteration, stand as an
introduction to Ellis's rational emotive therapy:

> How comes it, that a Father whose Son is killed, is not a whit less cheerful
> or merry, if he know not of the death of his Son, than if he were yet alive
> and in health? . . . Certainly, if Nature itself were the Author of that sadness,
> the Father's mind would be struck with a sense of loss of his Son in the
> same moment wherein he was slain. . . .
>
> Hence it is a perspicuous Truth, that those things, for which the mind
> becomes malcontent and contristate, are not Real Evils to us; forasmuch
> as they are without the orb of our Nature, and can never touch us immedi-
> ately or of themselves, but by the mediation of our own Opinion. . . . It
> is Reason alone which makes life happy and pleasant, by expelling all
> such false Conceptions or Opinions, as may any way occasion perturbation
> of mind. (From excerpts in Ehrenwald, 1976, pp. 167–168)

The rational tradition in psychotherapy was continued in Rome by
Cicero (106–43 B.C.). Believing that the neglect of reason was the cause
of all mental disorders, Cicero wrote in the *Tusculan Disputations:*

> The cure of grief, and of other disorders, is one and the same, in that
> they are all voluntary, and founded on opinion; we take them on ourselves
> because it seems right so to do. Philosophy undertakes to eradicate this
> error as the root of all our evils: let us therefore surrender ourselves to
> be instructed by it, and suffer ourselves to be cured; for whilst these evils
> have possession of us, we not only cannot be happy, but cannot be right
> in our minds. (Quoted in Alexander and Selesnick, 1966, p. 73)

In the 12th century, Moses Maimonides, a Jewish physician born in
Spain, advised moderation as a cure for "diseases of the soul." His strategy
for overcoming resistance on the part of his patients consisted of urging
them to exaggerate the opposite of the behaviors that had caused their
disorders. Thus, misers were induced to squander their wealth, and when

they reached the point where they were about to become squanderers, were advised to moderate their generosity.

In general, rationalist approaches to psychotherapy have been the exception rather than the rule. Nevertheless, rationalism remains an important tradition in therapy. It is laid to rest in one generation only to spring up in the next as a challenger to the dominant trend. Rationalism was the basis of Paul Charles Dubois' (1913) persuasion therapy, an early alternative to psychodynamic approaches. It is alive today in the cognitive therapies of Albert Ellis and Aaron Beck.

The discovery of the unconscious and the birth of insight therapy

It comes as a surprise to many to learn that the height of the belief in the power of demons occurred not in the Dark or Middle Ages, but during the Renaissance and the scientific revolution (Kirsch, 1978, 1980). It may also come as a surprise that from this magical tradition, rather than from the rationalist trend, the mainstream of modern psychotherapy developed. Freud laid the foundations for modern therapy by declaring insight into the unconscious as the goal of treatment. Thus, the discovery— or invention, depending on one's point of view—of the unconscious was the cornerstone of psychodynamic therapy. There is a direct line of descent from the rites of exorcism, through mesmerism and hypnosis, to modern conceptions of the unconscious.

It is now well known that the concept of the unconscious was not discovered by Freud, and it has become traditional to credit Leibniz, Herbart, and Fechner with its development. In fact, a clear conception of unconscious ideas are contained in a work written some 200 years prior to Leibniz's discussion of "changes in the soul of which we are not conscious." The *Malleus Maleficarum* or *Witches' Hammer*, the earliest official manual of the inquisition against supposed witches, contains the following description of the process by which ideas are drawn into consciousness from an unconscious storage system:

> The apparitions that come in dreams to sleepers proceed from the ideas retained in the repository of their mind. . . . Also such things happen not only to the sleeping, but even to those who are awake. For in these also the devils can sit up and excite the inner perceptions and humours, so that ideas retained in the repositories of their minds are drawn out and made apparent to the faculties of fancy and imagination, so that such men imagine these things to be true. And this is called interior temptation.
>
> And it is no wonder that the devil can do this by his own natural power; since any man by himself, being awake and having the use of his reason, can voluntarily draw from his repositories the images he has retained in them; in such a way that he can summon to himself the images of whatsoever things he pleases. (Kramer & Sprenger, 1928, p. 129 originally published 1484)

Freud had studied the *Malleus* and was quite familiar with the works of Leibniz, Herbart, and Fechner. It is important, however, to note the differences between these notions of unconscious ideas or perceptions and the modern concept of the unconscious. When academics employed the term *unconscious,* it was generally used as an adjective. In modern clinical theories, it is generally used as a noun. The nominalized unconscious is a separate personality, with its own wishes and desires and its own stream of emotions that are stirred up and then laid to rest. The first use of the unconscious as a noun occurred in Eduard von Hartmann's (1868) three-volume *Philosophy of the Unconscious.* Using Kant's discussion of unconscious ideas as a starting point, von Hartmann developed a philosophy involving three levels of unconscious processes. In addition to the individual physiological and psychological unconscious, he postulated a collective unconscious (anticipating Jung) and a metaphysical absolute unconscious. Given the considerable popularity of Hartmann's work in the late-19th century, it is unlikely that Freud would not have been aware of it. But Hartmann's unconscious was very different from the unconscious of psychodynamic theory.

The most important antecedents to Freud's theory of the unconscious were not contained in the work of academic psychologists and philosophers, but rather in the French clinical tradition that stemmed from the work of the Viennese physician, Franz Anton Mesmer (1734–1815). Mesmerism provided the link between Freud's natural demons and the supernatural demons that preceded them. The phenomena of hypnosis generated the theories of unconscious personalities upon which Freud's theory of the unconscious was based.

Mesmer, whom Buranelli (1975) has called "the wizard from Vienna," was a flamboyant healer who used a magnetic wand and a dramatic procedure to cure his patients. His quasi-astrological theory postulated the existence of a magnetic fluid through which the stars and planets affect human bodies. Nervous disorders, he maintained, were caused by an imbalance of "animal magnetism." Mesmer's method of treatment was as follows: patients were brought into a richly carpeted and dimly lit room, ornately decorated with astrological symbols. Soft music and sweet incense filled the air as they sat around a *baquet* or tub filled with magnetized water. Into the midst of this scene strode Mesmer, decked in a lilac taffeta robe and carrying a magnetic wand. A pass of the wand produced a convulsive "crisis," the exact nature of which was specific to the disease being treated. With each magnetic treatment the crisis would be less intense, finally disappearing when the patient was cured.

The close connection between mesmerism and demonology was revealed in 1775, when Mesmer was invited to Munich by an official commission of inquiry formed to investigate the work of an exorcist, Father Johann Joseph Gassner. Gassner's procedure involved solemnly intoning: "If there is anything preternatural about this illness, I command it, in

Jesus' name, to manifest itself now." If symptoms specific to the disease appeared, it was taken as evidence that the illness was caused by possession, and Gassner would command the demon to depart. Given the evident similarity in their methods, Mesmer could hardly conclude that Gassner was a fraud. Instead, he proclaimed that Gassner was a gifted magnetist unaware of the real cause of his altogether genuine cures. Gassner, of course, had not used magnets in his exorcisms, and Mesmer soon dispensed with their use as well. Gassner had proved that a human being could act as an animal magnet without resort to other magnetic objects.

Mesmer sought to provide a naturalistic theory for the phenomena of possession and exorcism, but with its emphasis on the effects of a universal fluid, Mesmer's theory was physical rather than psychological. The first step in providing a psychological theory of mesmerism was taken by Mesmer's disciple, the Marquis de Puységur. Instead of displaying the usual convulsions upon being magnetized, one of Puységur's patients fell into what is now termed a hypnotic trance. In this "perfect crisis," patients retained the ability to talk and often aided the therapist in diagnosing and prescribing treatments for their disorders. Puységur's discovery of "artificial somnambulism"—given the name *hypnosis* by James Braid in 1843—led him to discard Mesmer's theory of a magnetic fluid and to replace it with a purely psychological theory based on expectancy and motivation. It also led to the discovery of spontaneous posthypnotic amnesia upon which theories of the clinical unconscious were based.

By the beginning of the 19th century, posthypnotic amnesia had generated a widely held theory of the splitting of consciousness into two or more separate personalities. The logic behind the theory of dissociation was described by Charles Richet in 1875:

> [Posthypnotic amnesia] is absolutely characteristic, and I have seen no exceptions to this. But, and this is the strange thing, that which happens during [hypnotic] sleep has not completely disappeared, since the reproduction of [hypnosis] recalls the memory. It is this which accounts, I believe, for the division of consciousness of which so many magnetizers speak. The ego consists of the collection of our memories; and when it is limited to a special physical state, it is almost correct to say, theoretically speaking, that the person is different, since she recalls in [hypnotic] sleep an entire series of acts which she ignores completely while awake. (Quoted in Levin, 1978, p. 98)

Jean Martin Charcot (1887), whose demonstrations first convinced Freud of the possibility of powerful unconscious mental processes, appears to have been the first to attempt an explanation of hysteria in terms of dissociation. He suggested that in hysteria a fragment of the mind spontaneously dissociated from the rest of consciousness. Dissociation theory was further developed by two of Charcot's students. Alfred Binet

(1892) and Pierre Janet (1889). The latter attributed hysteria to "subconscious fixed ideas" which were dissociated from consciousness due to traumatic events in the past. In one case study, Janet (1889) demonstrated the treatment of hysteria by having the patient relive the traumatic events under hypnosis while he introduced certain therapeutic modifications to the memory. Freud and Joseph Breuer (1893) added their own modifications to dissociation theory, suggesting that a splitting of consciousness occurs when a person fails to discharge the feelings associated with a traumatic event and instead intentionally suppresses its memory.

The connection between demonology and the modern concept of the unconscious is conceptual as well as circumstantial. Theories of demonic possession and theories of the unconscious share the common conception of a hidden personality within the individual causing behavior alien to the ego. In modern theories, the demons of antiquity have merely lost their supernatural characteristics. In defending dissociation theory, Freud noted this conceptual similarity:

> Let no one object that the theory of dissociation of consciousness as a solution of the enigma of hysteria is too far-fetched to suggest itself to the untrained and unprejudiced observer. In fact, the Middle Ages had chosen this very solution, in declaring possession by a demon to be the cause of hysterical manifestations; all that would have been required was to replace the religious terminology of those dark and superstitious times by the scientific one of today. (Freud, 1893, p. 20)

The theory to which Freud was referring here was very different than his later psychoanalytic theory. The idea of repression had not yet been developed, and it would be another four years before Freud would reach the conclusion that the symptom-producing unconscious ideas were wishes rather than memories of actual occurrances. Nevertheless, Freud and Breuer's prepsychoanalytic dissociation theory has proven to be highly influential. A number of new therapies (e.g., reevaluation counseling, bioenergetics, and primal therapy) are justified with theories closely resembling the Freud-Breuer theory. Indeed, the idea that it is psychologically—and perhaps physically—harmful to suppress rather than express one's feelings may be one of the few ideas around which a majority of therapists have developed a consensus.

PSYCHOLOGY'S CONTRIBUTIONS TO PSYCHOTHERAPY

In the dissociation theories of the 19th century, the splitting of consciousness into two or more personalities was generally regarded as an abnormal condition. In contrast, psychoanalytic theory regards the division of mental functioning into conscious and unconscious as an aspect of normal development. This characteristic of psychoanalytic theory is one reflection of Freud's ambition to develop psychoanalysis as a general psychology, rather than a medical or abnormal psychology—an ambition also apparent in his *Project for a Scientific Psychology*. This view of psychoanalysis was most clearly expressed by Freud in his defense of Theodor Reik, a lay analyst, against a charge of quackery:

> Psycho-analysis is not a specialized branch of medicine. I cannot see how it is possible to dispute this. Psycho-analysis falls under the head of psychology; not of medical psychology in the old sense, nor of the psychology of morbid processes, but simply of psychology. It is certainly not the whole of psychology, but its substructure and perhaps even its entire foundation. (Freud, 1927, p. 207)

Despite Freud's attitude, psychoanalysis has largely remained within the medical profession, especially in the United States, where opposition to lay analysis was strongest. Following an early interest in dissociation theory and Janet's dynamic psychiatry (James, 1890; Jastrow, 1906; Prince, 1906), American psychologists became aware of psychoanalysis. Academic psychology's flirtation with psychoanalytic theory began when G. Stanley Hall brought Freud and Jung to Clark University for the 20th-anniversary celebrations in 1909. It was continued by Holt (1915) and by Dollard and Miller (1950), both of these works attempting an integration of psychoanalytic concepts with behaviorist learning theory. Nevertheless, psychoanalysis remained a more or less sympathetically viewed doctrine that stood separate from the mainstream of academic psychology. Psychology's best-known contributions to psychotherapy came in the form of alternatives to the psychoanalytic approach, first in the work of Carl Rogers and second in the development of behavior therapy.

Client-centered therapy and psychotherapy research

Carl Rogers, a scientist-professional a decade before the Boulder Conference, was responsible for two major achievements, either of which alone would have earned him a lasting place in the history of psychotherapy. Though there had been a number of dissidents within the psychoanalytic movement who developed their own theories and methods of therapy, Roger's client-centered therapy proved to be the first major alternative to psychodynamic therapies. In addition, Rogers pioneered the systematic empirical study of psychotherapy process and outcome.

The initial impetus for the development of client-centered therapy came from the work of Otto Rank. Rank abandoned the psychoanalytic technique of free association and deemphasized interpretation. In place of these methods, Rank emphasized the development of a therapeutic relationship based on the warm and accepting attitude of the therapist. With this attitude, the therapist could act as a sympathetic sounding board for patients struggling with the problems of developing more satisfying interpersonal relationships. Rank's student, Jessie Taft (1933), through whom Rogers became familiar with the principles of relationship therapy, took the step of abandoning interpretation altogether.

There were three stages in the development of client-centered therapy. During the first stage (Rogers, 1942), the emphasis was on reflection and clarification of feelings as a therapeutic technique leading to the gaining of insight by the client. The second stage was a period of transition (e.g., Rogers, 1951) during which the specific technique of reflection was gradually deemphasized and greater stress was placed on the attitudes of the therapist. Eventually, three therapist attitudes—unconditional positive regard, empathy, and congruence—were hypothesized as the necessary and sufficient conditions of therapeutic change (Rogers, 1957). Underlying Rogers's theory and practice of psychotherapy during all three stages was what he referred to as *the basic hypothesis*, the hypothesis that "the individual has a sufficient capacity to deal constructively with all those aspects of his life which can potentially come into conscious awareness" (Rogers, 1951, p. 24).

Psychology achieved its independence from philosophy by applying experimental methods to questions of mental structure and function. It is therefore fitting that clinical psychology should distinguish itself from other helping professions by its commitment to research. Although the idea of bringing an experimental attitude to questions of clinical treatment can be traced to Witmer, the first coherent research program concerned directly with psychotherapy was begun by Rogers (1942) at Ohio State University. Beginning with "The Case of Herbert Bryan," Rogers provided data for research in therapy by recording, transcribing, and, in some instances, publishing the verbatim transcripts of several complete series of therapeutic sessions.

Rogers' research program has been summarized in Kirschenbaum's (1979) biography. Through most of the 1940s, there was an emphasis on describing therapeutic process, with a variety of methods devised for assessing and categorizing counselor and client communication. Outcome was assessed, first through therapist evaluation and later by means of the Minnesota Multiphasic Personality Inventory (MMPI), various projective tests, and, in some instances, galvanic skin response and heart rate. Later, in an extensive and ambitious research program at the University of Chicago, Rogers introduced such innovations as no-treatment and waiting-list controls (Rogers & Dymond, 1954). Much of contemporary psychotherapy research is built upon the foundation of Rogers's work.

Behavior therapy

Psychology's second major contribution to psychotherapy has been the development of behavior therapy. When psychologists turned their attention to therapy, it was quite natural for them to regard it as a problem of relearning. Prior to the introduction of behaviorism, Morton Prince (1909–1910) described psychotherapy as a process in which maladaptive systems of ideas are replaced by new and more adaptive associations. With the triumph of behaviorism, conditioning models were applied to clinical problems, first by experimentalists and later by clinicians.

The most famous precursor of behavior therapy was Mary Cover Jones's (1924a) report of her work on the elimination of children's fears. Although Jones tried seven different fear-reduction methods with a variety of children, it is her successful use of an in vivo conditioning procedure to treat a 34-month-old boy named Peter for a fear of rabbits that is most often cited. The essence of Jones's treatment was to have the rabbit gradually brought closer to Peter while he was eating a food that he liked. However, deconditioning was only one of two treatments that Jones reported as leading to a successful outcome. She also reported several cases in which children's fears were overcome through the method of "social imitation" or *modeling*, as we call it today. Indeed, her extended report of her work with Peter reveals that he was treated with a combination of modeling and in vivo desensitization (Jones, 1924b).

Yates (1970) has documented a surprisingly large number of instances of behavioral treatments prior to the emergence of modern behavior-therapy as a formal movement in the 1950s. These include applications of conditioning procedures for the treatment of enuresis, hysteria, anxiety, depression, sexual deviation, alcoholism, morphine addiction, tics, stuttering, allergy, and anorexia. In addition, the development of "negative practice" as a treatment technique (Dunlap, 1932) was a forerunner, not only of behavior therapy, but of paradoxical strategies as well.

Behavior therapy as a self-conscious movement came into being as a convergence of three major trends: (1) the development of systematic desensitization and related techniques by Joseph Wolpe (1958) in South Africa, (2) the independent development of behavior therapy at Maudsley Hospital in England (Eysenck, 1959), and (3) the application of operant conditioning to the behavior of children (Bijou, 1955) and psychotic adults (Skinner, Solomon, & Lindsley, 1953; Ullmann & Krasner, 1965). The unprecedented growth of the new movement may have been related to Eysenck's (1952) report that approximately two-thirds of all neurotics show substantial improvement within two years whether they enter therapy or not. The ensuing debate, which had not been fully laid to rest some 30 years later (Erwin, 1980), led to a crisis in confidence for many therapists and thus helped to create a receptive audience for the behavioral approach. Behavior therapy offered more easily specifiable objective criteria for improvement and the promise of experimental documentation of effectiveness.

It is ironic that behavior therapy developed just when experimentalists were abandoning behaviorism and becoming cognitive psychologists.

In large measure, the cognitive revolution in experimental psychology involved a shift in focus from the subject of learning to perception and memory, but even in the field of learning, neo-Hullians (e.g., Spence, 1966) were abandoning strict stimulus-response (S-R) formulations in favor of the inclusion of cognitive variables as had been championed by Tolman (1932). Thus it is not surprising that within a decade of its founding, behavior therapy was going cognitive.

The cognitive trend in behavior therapy began with the publication of Albert Bandura's (1969) *Principles of Behavior Modification,* which emphasized the cognitive factors in human learning. Two years later, Arnold Lazarus's (1971) *Behavior Therapy and Beyond* was published. Working directly with Wolpe in South Africa, Lazarus had been a pioneer in the development of behavior therapy. A decade later, he was conceding that only a small part of what occurred when he practiced therapy could strictly be referred to as behavioral. In particular, Lazarus combined the cognitive techniques of Albert Ellis's (1962) rational emotive therapy with behavioral strategies in treating his clients. Together with *Principles of Behavior Modification, Behavior Therapy and Beyond* signaled the beginning of a convergence between cognitive and behavioral approaches to therapy, a merger with theoretical roots in Julian B. Rotter's (1954) social learning theory.

CLINICAL PSYCHOLOGY TODAY

Though the scientist-professional model still dominates clinical training, in practice there continues to be a considerable cleavage between the two roles. Doctor of psychology programs suggested by Poffenberger (1938) have become a reality in the 1970s, lending a degree of formal recognition to this separation of roles.

In recent years, humanistic therapies (though not client-centered therapy) and cognitive behavioral therapies have increased in influence. Simultaneously, the number of clinical psychologists expressing allegiance to traditional psychodynamic approaches has decreased. A majority of therapists have come to adopt the designation *eclectic* (Garfield and Kurtz, 1976). Though therapists with divergent therapeutic styles are undoubtably classified under this rubric, the growth of eclecticism surely reflects the development of a largely atheoretical convergence of psychodynamic, humanistic, behavioral, and cognitive techniques.

The absence of reliable evidence favoring one form of treatment over another in a competitive market has produced a plethora of new therapies. Hardly a year passes without some new therapeutic approach attracting attention as the newest candidate for a universal panacea. If anything, the claims that are made are becoming even more extravagant, though they remain unsupported by reliable data. The mainstream of psychotherapy research stands in marked contrast to the cure-all approach of many fads. Researchers are focusing on therapist-client-method matches or on investigating the elements common to all psychotherapies.

As the field has matured, the range of activities that constitutes the professional role of clinical psychologist has grown wider. Neuropsychological assessment has been added to the diagnostic tasks of clinicians. Treatment modalities that have gained widespread acceptance include group therapy, family therapy, crisis intervention, and sex therapy. The wider acceptance of new treatment modalities than new schools of therapy is due to the fact that the former do not require any particular theoretical orientation. The theoretical foci of therapists working in these modalities range from intrapersonal to systemic.

The sharpest breaks with tradition have been the creation of professional roles that do not involve diagnosis or psychotherapy. The community mental health movement, which developed out of the liberal political climate of the 1960s, encompassed an ideological focus on prevention rather than treatment. The fiscal and political conservatism that ushered in the 1980s portends lean years for community psychology in general and its more inovative aspects in particular. Nevertheless, one result of the community movement has been an expansion of the settings in which clinicians provide services. The consultation and education staff of community mental health centers have brought services into a variety of public agencies (e.g., school systems, police departments, and public health nursing agencies, etc.) and into private industry as well. With cutbacks in public funding, the proportion of programs directed toward industry is likely to increase.

Behavorial medicine, currently the most rapidly growing specialty within clinical psychology, involves the application of behavioral treatment to physical disorders (Schwartz & Weiss, 1977). The techniques of behavior therapy, supplemented by hypnosis and biofeedback, are being applied to a variety of problems, including obesity, smoking, compliance with medical treatments, pain management, headaches, and cardiovascular disorders. Programs aimed at altering type A behaviors are likely to become an important focus of behavioral medicine during the next few years. Behavioral medicine brings to behavior therapy a large number of serious, well-defined problems, with easily specifiable criteria for success (e.g., mortality rates). It will undoubtably continue to grow during the 1980s with its ultimate fate depending on the results of outcome research.

Given the diversity of professional activities and the considerable overlap with other professions, the question "What is a clinical psychologist?" is not easy to answer. Diagnostic testing is one skill that sets our field apart from others, but it is also a professional identity from which we have long struggled to escape. Clinical psychology is also distinguished by its roots in the experimental laboratory. The design and implementation of therapeutic and preventive interventions may be accomplished by members of any of the helping professions. The evaluation of these interventions is a specialty of psychology. Furthermore, the increased involvement of third party payers has given rise to new demands for evaluation research. Thus the scientist-professional combination may continue to be the relevant thread of the fabric of our professional identity.

SUMMARY

In 1896, Lightner Witmer founded the field of clinical psychology by establishing the world's first psychological clinic at the University of Pennsylvania. During its first 50 years of existence, clinical psychology was a relatively small field concerned primarily with the diagnostic assessment of the problem child. Psychological tests were the most important tools of clinical psychologists during this period, and although clinicians objected to the label, they were widely known as "mental testers." The mental testing movement developed in tandem with the eugenics movement and has, throughout its existence, been surrounded by controversy.

During World War II, psychiatric disability came to be seen as one of the nation's greatest health problems. In 1946, the Veterans Administration established the clinical training programs that transformed clinical psychology into a profession dominated by the practice of psychotherapy. The first modern psychotherapy was developed by Freud at the turn of the century, but the theory of the unconscious upon which it was based can be traced to 17th-century theories of demonic possession and to the theories of 18th-century mesmerists. Psychology's major contributions to psychotherapy have been the development of humanistic therapy by Carl Rogers, the development of behavior therapy, and the experimental study of therapy outcome and process, which has been a hallmark of the work of Rogers and the behavior therapists.

Recent trends have included a shift toward cognitive and cognitive behavioral approaches to treatment, a shift which is undoubtedly connected to the cognitive revolution within psychology as a whole. At the same time, there has been a search for new professional roles that go beyond the traditional areas of psychological assessment and therapy. During the 1960s, community psychology developed as an offshoot of clinical psychology, with an emphasis on prevention rather than treatment. In the 1980s, behavioral medicine appears to be among the most rapidly growing specialty areas in the field.

REFERENCES

Alexander, F. G., & Selesnick, S. T. *The history of psychiatry.* New York: New American Library, 1966.

Bandura, A. *Principles of behavior modification.* New York: Holt, Rinehart & Winston, 1969.

Bijou, S. W. A systematic approach to an experimental analysis of young children. *Child Development,* 1955, *26,* 161–168.

Binet, A. *Les altérations de la personnalité.* Paris: Alcan, 1892.

Binet, A. *Les idées modernes sur les enfant.* Paris: Flammarion, 1909.

Binet A., & Henri, V. La psycholgie individuelle. *L'Année Psychologique,* 1896, *2,* 411–465.

Binet, A., & Simon, T. Application des Méthodes nouvelles au diagnostic du niveau intellectuel chez des enfants normaux et anormaux d'hospice et d'école primaire. *L'Année Psychologique,* 1905, *11,* 245–366. (a)

Binet, A., & Simon, T. Méthodes nouvelles pour le diagnostic du niveau intellectuel des anormaux. *L'Année Psychologique,* 1905, *11,* 191–244. (b)

Binet, A., & Simon, T. Le developpement de l'intelligence chez les enfants. *L'Année Psychologique,* 1908, *14,* 1–94.

Bolton, T. L. The growth of memory in school children. *American Journal of Psychology,* 1891–1892, *4,* 362–380.

Boring, E. G. *A history of experimental psychology.* New York: Appleton-Century-Crofts, 1950.

Brigham, C. C. *A study of American intelligence.* Princeton, N.J.: Princeton University Press, 1923.

Buranelli, V. *The wizard from Vienna.* New York: Coward, McCann & Geoghegan, 1975.

Buss, A. R. The historical context of differential psychology and eugenics. *Journal of the History of the Behavorial Sciences,* 1976, *12,* 47–58.

Cattell, J. M. Mental tests and measurements. *Mind,* 1890, *15,* 373–381.

Charcot, J. M. (1887). *Clinical lectures on diseases of the nervous system,* Vol. 3. London: New Sydenham Soc., 1889.

Collins, J. Lightner Witmer: A biographical sketch. In R. A. Brotemarkle (Ed.), *Clinical psychology: Studies in honor of Lightner Witmer to commemorate the 35th anniversary of the founding of the first psychological clinic.* Philadelphia: University of Pennsylvania Press, 1931.

Dollard, J., & Miller, N. E. *Personality and psychotherapy: An analysis in terms of learning, thinking, and culture.* New York: McGraw-Hill, 1950.

Dubois, P. *The pyschological origin of mental disorders.* New York: Funk & Wagnalls, 1913.

Dunlap, K. *Habits, their making and unmaking.* New York: Liveright, 1932.

Ebbinghaus, H. Über eine neue Methode zur Prüfung geistiger Fähigkeiten und ihre Anwendung bei Schulkindern, *Zeitschrift für angewandte Psychologie,* 1897, *13,* 401–459.

Ehrenwald, J. (Ed.) *The history of psychotherapy: From healing magic to encounter.* New York: Jason Aronson, 1976.

Ellis, A. *Reason and emotion in psychotherapy.* Secaucus, N.J.: Lyle Stuart, 1962.

Erwin, E. Psychoanalytic therapy: The Eysenck argument. *American Psychologist,* 1980, *35,* 435–443.

Eysenck, H. J. The effects of psychotherapy: An evaluation. *Journal of Consulting Psychology,* 1952, *16,* 319–324.

Eysenck, H. J. Learning theory and behaviour therapy. *Journal of Mental Science,* 1959, *105,* 61–75.

Freud, S. (1893). Charcot. *Collected papers* (Vol. 1.). New York: Basic Books, 1959.

Freud, S. (1927). Postscript to a discussion on lay analysis. *Collected papers* (Vol. 5.). New York: Basic Books, 1959.

Freud, S., & Breuer, J. (1893). On the psychical mechanism of hysterical phenomena. *Collected papers* (Vol. 1.). New York: Basic Books, 1959.

Galton, F. *An inquiry into human faculty and its development.* London: Macmillan, 1883.

Garfield, S. L. & Kurtz, R. Clinical psychologists in the 1970s. *American Psychologist,* 1976, *31,* 1–9.

Gilbert, J. A. Researches on the mental and physical development of school children. *Studies of Yale Psychological Laboratory,* 1894, *2,* 40–100.

Gilbert, J. A. Researches on school children and college students. *University of Iowa Studies in Psychology,* 1897, *1,* 1–39.

Goddard, H. H. The Binet and Simon tests of intellectual capacity. *The Training School Bulletin,* 1908, *5,* 3–10.

Goddard, H. H. A measuring scale for intelligence. *The Training School Bulletin,* 1910, *6,* 146–155.

Goddard, H. H. A revision of the Binet scale. *The Training School Bulletin,* 1911, *8,* 56–62.

Goddard, H. H. *The Kallikak family: A study in the heredity of feeblemindedness.* New York: Macmillan, 1912.

Goddard, H. H. Mental tests and the immigrant. *Journal of Delinquency,* 1917, *2,* 243–277.

Guiccardi, G. & Ferrari, G. C. I testi mentali per persame deli alienati. *Revista Sperimentale di Freniatria,* 1896, *22,* 297–314.

Haller, M. H. *Eugenics: Hereditarian attitudes in American thought.* New Brunswick, N.J.: Rutgers University Press, 1963.

Hartmann, E. (1886). *Philosophy of the unconscious.* London: Trubner, 1884.

Hildreth, G. *A bibliography of mental tests and rating scales.* New York: Psychological Corporation, 1933.

Holmes, A. *The conservation of the child.* Philadelphia: J. B. Lippincott, 1912.

Holt, E. B. *The Freudian wish and its place in ethics.* New York: Holt, Rinehart & Winston, 1915.

Jacobs, J. Experiments in "prehension." *Mind,* 1887, *12,* 75–79.

James, W. *Principles of psychology.* New York: Holt, Rinehart & Winston, 1890.

Janet, P. *L'automatisme psychologique.* Paris: Alcan, 1889.

Jastrow, J. Some anthropological and psychologic tests on college students—A preliminary survey. *American Journal of Psychology,* 1891–1892, *4,* 420–427.

Jastros J. *The subconscious.* Boston: Houghton Mifflin, 1906.

Jones, M. C. The elimination of children's fears. *Journal of Experimental Psychology,* 1924, *7,* 382–390. (a)

Jones, M. C. A laboratory study of fear: The case of Peter. *Pediatrics Seminar,* 1924, *31,* 308–315. (b)

Kamin, L. J. The science and politics of IQ. *Social Research,* 1974, *41,* 387–425.

Kirsch, I. The impetus to scientific psychology: A recurrent pattern. *Journal of the History of the Behavorial Sciences,* 1976, *12,* 120–129.

Kirsch, I. Demonology and the rise of science: An example of the misperception of historical data. *Journal of the History of the Behavioral Sciences,* 1978, *14,* 149–157.

Kirsch, I. Demonology and science during the scientific revolution. *Journal of the History of the Behavioral Sciences,* 1980, *16,* 359–368.

Kirschenbaum, H. *On becoming Carl Rogers.* New York: Dell Publishing, 1979.

Kraepelin, E. Der Psychologische versuch in der Psychiatrie. *Psychologische Arbeiten,* 1895, *1,* 1–95.

Kramer, H., & Sprenger, J. (1484). *Malleus Maleficarum.* London: Arrow, 1928.

Kuhn, T. S. *The structure of scientific revolutions.* Chicago: University of Chicago Press, 1970.

Landman, J. H. *Human sterilization: The history of the sexual sterilization movement.* New York: Macmillan, 1932.

Laughlin, H. H. Report of the committee to study and to report on the best practical means of cutting off the defective germ-plasm in the American population: I. The scope of the committee's work. *Eugenics Records Office Bulletin,* 1914, *10A,* 1–64.

Lazarus, A. P. *Behavior therapy and beyond.* New York: McGraw:Hill, 1971.

Levin, K. *Freud's early psychology of the neurosis: A historical perspective.* Pittsburgh: University of Pittsburg Press, 1978.

Louttit, C. M. The nature of clinical psychology. *Psychological Bulletin,* 1939, *36,* 361–389.

Miller, J. G. Clinical psychology in the Veterans Administration. *American Psychologist,* 1946, *1,* 181–189.

Münsterberg, H. Zur individval Psychologie. *Centralblatt für Nervenheilkunde und Psychiatrie,* 1891, *14,* 196–198.

New York Psychiatrical Society. Activities of clinical psychologists. *Psychological Bulletin,* 1917, *14,* 224–225.

Norton, B. Charles Spearman and the general factor in intelligence: Genesis and interpretation in the light of sociopersonal considerations. *Journal of the History of the Behavioral Sciences,* 1979, *15,* 142–154.

Oehrn, A. Experimentelle Studien zur individual Psychologie. *Psychologischen Arbeiten,* 1895, *1,* 92–152.

Poffenberger, A. T. The training of a clinical psychologist. *Journal of Consulting Psychology,* 1938, *2,* 1–6.

Prince, M. *The dissociation of a personality.* New York: Longmans, Green, 1906.

Prince, M. The psychological principles and field of psychotherapy. *Journal of Abnormal Psychology,* 1909–1910, *4,* 72–98.

Raimy, V. C. (Ed.). *Training in clinical psychology.* Englewood Cliffs, N.J.: Prentice-Hall, 1950.

Rogers, C. R. *Counseling and psychotherapy: New concepts in practice.* Boston: Houghton Mifflin, 1942.

Rogers, C. R. *Client-centered therapy: Its current practices, implications, and theory.* Boston: Houghton Mifflin, 1951.

Rogers, C. R. The necessary and sufficient conditions of therapeutic personality change. *Journal of Counseling Psychology*, 1957, *21*, 95–103.

Rogers, C. R., & Dymond, R. F. (Eds.). *Psychotherapy and personality change*. Chicago: University of Chicago Press, 1954.

Rotter, J. B. *Social learning and clinical psychology*. Englewood Cliffs, N.J.: Prentice-Hall, 1954.

Rowntree, L. G. National program for physical fitness revealed and developed on the basis of thirteen million physical examinations of Selective Service registrants. *Journal of the American Medical Association*, 1944, *125*, 821–826.

Samelson, F. From "race psychology" to "studies in prejudice": Some observations on the trematic reversal in social psychology. *Journal of the History of the Behavioral Sciences*, 1978, *14*, 265–278.

Samelson, F. Putting psychology on the map. In A. R. Buss (Ed.). *Psychology in social context*. New York: Irvington Publishers, 1979.

Schwartz, G. E., & Weiss, S. M. *Preceedings of the Yale conference on behavioral medicine*. Washington, D.C.: Department of Health, Education and Welfare, 1977.

Sears, R. R. Clinical training facilities: 1947. *American Psychologist*, 1947, *2*, 199–205.

Sharp, S. E. Individual psychology: A study in psychological method. *American Journal of Psychology*, 1898–1899, *10*, 329–391.

Skinner, B. F., Solomon, H. C. & Lindsley, O. R. Studies in behavior therapy: Status report I. Waltham, Mass., Metropolitan State Hospital, November 30, 1953.

Spence, K. W. Cognitive and drive factors in the extinction of the conditioned eyeblink in human subjects. *Psychological Review*, 1966, *73*, 445-458.

Stern, W. L. (1912). The psychological methods of testing intelligence. *Educational Psychology Monographs*, No. 13. Baltimore: Warwick & York, 1914.

Taft, J. *The dynamics of therapy in a controlled relationship*. New York: Macmillan, 1933.

Thorndike, E. L. *Educational psychology*. New York: Lemcke & Buechner, 1903.

Tolman, E. C. *Purposive behavior in animals and men*. New York: Appleton-Century-Crofts, 1932.

Tulchin, S. H. The psychologist. *American Journal of Orthopsychiatry*, 1930, *1*, 39–47.

Ullmann, L. P., & Krasner, L. (Eds.). *Case studies in behavior modification*. New York: Holt, Rinehart & Winston, 1965.

Wallin, J. E. W. *The mental health of the school child*. New Haven: Yale University Press, 1914.

Watson, R. I. The history of psychology: A neglected area. *American Psychologist*, 1960, *15*, 251–255.

Wechsler, D. *The measurement of adult intelligence*. Baltimore: Williams & Wilkins, 1939.

Wissler, C. The correlation of mental and physical tests. *Psychological Review, Monograph Supplement*, 1901, *3*, no. 16.

Witmer, L. Practical work in psychology. *Pediatrics*, 1896, *2*, 462–471.

Witmer, L. The organization of practical work in psychology. *Psychological Review*, 1897, *4*, 116–117.

Witmer, L. Clinical psychology. *The Psychological Clinic*, 1907, *1*, 1–9.

Witmer, L. The restoration of children of the slums. *The Psychological Clinic,* 1909, *3,* 266–280.

Wolf, T. H. *Alfred Binet.* Chicago: University of Chicago Press, 1973.

Wolpe, J. *Psychotherapy by reciprocal inhibition.* Stanford: Stanford University Press, 1958.

Yates, A. J. *Behavior therapy.* New York: John Wiley & Sons, 1970.

Yerkes, R. M. (Ed.). Psychological examining in the United States army. *Memiors of the National Academy of Sciences,* 1921, *15.*

2

Experimental psychology for the clinical psychologist

William P. Milberg*
R. Douglas Whitman†
and
Brendan A. Maher‡

The difficulty in writing a chapter on experimental psychology for the clinical psychologist is in deciding what to exclude. Virtually all of experimental psychology is of some relevance. We chose to review all articles which have appeared in the past five years in *The Journal Of Abnormal Psychology, The Journal Of Consulting And Clinical Psychology, The British Journal Of Psychiatry,* and *The Archives Of General Psychiatry.* The topics included in this survey represented those experimental procedures or paradigms which were used in at least 10 studies reported in journals surveyed.

The following areas are reviewed below: reaction time, dichotic listening, memory research, physiological measures including biofeedback, attribution theory, and hypnosis.

REACTION TIME

Reaction time measures have been so widely used in schizophrenia research that the "cross-over effect" (See Chapter 3) may be the most replicated finding in the experimental psychopathology literature. More recently, however, reaction time procedures have been finding their way into the clinical literature in a wider number of areas. Researchers in the areas of learning disabilities, amnesia, depression, and information processing in schizophrenia have been utilizing a variety of reaction time

* Veteran's Administration Outpatient Clinic, Boston.
† Wayne State University, Detroit.
‡ HarvardUniversity,Cambridge,Mass.

procedures. The first systematic use of reaction time as a means of looking into the black box is attributed to F. C. Donders who employed it in the study of the "speed of mental processes." Donders organized reaction time tasks into three categories. *Donders' A* task was a simple reaction time in which a subject responded to a single stimulus as quickly as possible. *Donders' B* task was a choice reaction time in which one of several possible responses was appropriated for one of many possible stimuli presented to the subject. *Donders' C* task required a response to one correct stimulus and no response to any other stimuli.

A partitioning of information processes is theoretically possible through the comparison of reaction times obtained from each of Donders' tasks. Reaction time in a Donders' B task is longer than in either of the other tasks. Donders concluded that this was due to extra cognitive processes involved in the B task. Predating the stage analysis approach to information processing, Donders proposed that the B task was composed of: (1) the time required to respond to a stimulus (Donders' A); (2) the time needed to categorize the stimulus, and; (3) the time needed to select a response. Donders' C task, in this paradigm, was a B task without the need to engage in response selection. Thus, by subtracting the time needed for one task from that needed for another, the time needed for each of the three types of decision-making processes could be estimated.

The Sternberg task.   Sternberg in 1963 presented results using a procedure simple in design but with unexpected power. It has been so widely used that it is now simply referred to as the Sternberg task. A subject is first presented with a list of items to memorize, called the positive set, followed by a probe item, called the negative set. The subject's task is to identify whether the probe item appeared in the positive set. Sternberg reported that the choice reaction time *increased* linearly as a function of the size of the stimulus list. Assuming that an individual scans his "internal list" one item at a time (serially) a no response requires checking the entire list. Since yes responses took the same amount of time, Sternberg hypothesized subjects must exhaustively scan the entire list each time.

At first glance this result is puzzling. Why should the entire list be scanned when the correct item is encountered early in the list? Sternberg's answer is related to the speed of scanning. Calculating the time required to scan a single item results in an estimate of 25 items scanned per second. Sternberg (1966) argued that this was faster than the time necessary to decide whether a single test item matched another. Thus, he concluded, the information processing system exhaustively scans the entire list and then makes a matching decision.

The estimate for the scanning speed was estimated using the Donders' subtraction method. By adding a new item to the list and then subtracting the time required for the entire list, the amount of time needed for an additional item is estimated. However, Sternberg (1969a, 1969b) argued that this method assumes that the experimental manipulation (the addition of one item) affects only one part of the information processing.

Sternberg's analysis requires the assumption of item-by-item serial processing. However, Townsend (1971; 1974) has argued that the same results can be generated by several different models, one of which assumes parallel (simultaneous) processing of items.

The Donders' reaction time paradigm is an example of what is called the subtraction method. Basically, the experimenter identifies a sequence of processing events and estimates the time taken to process one of these by comparing a sequence including the event with one in which the processing stage has presumably been subtracted. The Sternberg task is an example of the additive method.

Both the additive and subtractive methods require that the experimenter knows the sequence of information processing stages involved with the experimental task. However, often the stages are intuitively derived and difficult to demonstrate empirically. Further, both methods make a basic assumption that the comparison task, which has one "added" or "subtracted" step, is indeed comparable. But even a minor change in task may theoretically change—in unknown ways—the entire information process. The stages involved, the number of stages, and the interaction of stages may change as a function of task change. These criticisms are discussed in detail in a highly sophisticated review of reaction time methods by Pachella (1974). The interested reader should consult this source.

MEMORY

A large number of articles have appeared in the past five years focusing attention on memory processes in amnesia, alcoholism, and schizophrenia. Though memory has attracted the attention of psychologists for decades, the three-stage model proposed by Atkinson and Shiffrin (1968) generated a renewed interest in the topic. Theirs was the first significant model of human memory utilizing a computer analogy and shifting significantly away from the associationist tradition. They proposed three stages of memory called the *sensory register*, the *short-term store*, and the *long-term store*. These different stores were hypothesized not only to differ in functional characteristics but also to have different anatomical underpinnings.

The sensory register served as a passive storage buffer for sensory information. Here it simply sat and decayed (became unavailable) very rapidly or was erased by new stimulation. The purpose of the register was to permit the information processing system time to code the information for later processing. The original model proposed only a visual register though theorists felt that evidence would be found for other modalities as well. The evidence for the sensory register was based on research on iconic storage, largely stimulated by the research of Sperling (1960) and Averbach and Coriell (1961), and the visual masking literature. Sperling demonstrated that subjects could report any part of a rapidly presented stimulus display even when the entire display exceeded their capacity and when the cue indicating which part to report occurred after the display had terminated.

The ability to access any part of a stimulus after its termination indicated the existence of what Sperling called an iconic store. A variety of techniques (Haber & Standing, 1969; Eriksen, 1966; Smith & Schiller, 1966) were used to estimate the duration of this sensory store, generally arriving at a figure around 25 msec. Evidence for an auditory sensory store was provided by a number or researchers (Darwin, Turvey, & Crowder, 1972; Effron, 1970; Glucksberg & Cohen, 1970; Massaro, 1970), but a wide range of register durations were obtained ranging from 130 msec. to 5 sec.

The short-term store was conceptualized as a working memory where cognitive processing is consciously performed. Subsequent research demonstrated that the short-term store was both space (Miller, 1956) and time limited (Peterson & Peterson, 1959; Murdock, 1961). By first presenting subjects with trigrams and then having them count backwards by threes immediately, thereby preventing rehearsal, Peterson and Peterson demonstrated that the nature of the stimuli to be remembered did not affect the duration of the short-term store. Thus, the short-term store appeared to be both space and time limited.

Atkinson and Shiffrin had originally proposed that the short-term store was auditory in nature. Conrad (1964) found that recalling visually presented letters resulted in acoustic errors (errors more similar to the stimulus in sound than in orthography) suggesting a similar store for visual material (Brooks, 1968; Shepard and Metzler, 1971).

The multistore models have now been replaced by a number of more flexible multiple processing models. Lachman, Lachman, and Butterfield (1979) have identified a number of reasons why the multistage models are currently viewed as inadequate. They point out that although the multistage models were supposed to operate via a unique code, research indicated a variety of codes (transformations of the stimuli) operating in the processing of information. Several researchers reported evidence for visual codes in short-term memory (Kroll, et al., 1970; Kroll, 1975), semantic codes (Shulman, 1970, 1972) and articulatory codes (Levy, 1971; Peterson and Johnson, 1971).

Also, estimates of the duration of information in the sensory register and short-term memory were variable. Estimates for the icon ranged from .25 sec. (Averbach & Coriel, 1961) to several seconds in length (Posner, 1969; Murdock, 1971). Further, if visual imagery were involved, estimates considerably longer were produced (Phillips & Baddeley, 1971; Kroll et al., 1970).

Similarly, estimates of the duration of the short-term store also varied.

Further, the capacity of the short-term store remained difficult to identify. Craik and Lockhart noted that various estimates place the capacity at anywhere from 2 to 20 words, depending upon the nature of the material.

Lachman, Lachman, and Butterfield concluded, however, that these specific problems with the multistore models were not as critical as more general concerns in the ultimate rejection of the stage models. At the core of the conceptual objections in the minds of many researchers was the absence of a consideration of "meaning" in the model. The contents of experience—in long-term memory—were not taken into account in early forms of the memory models. Thus, these models did not take into account the advantage of experience and remained inflexible. Further, they made no significant statements about the nature of the long-term store. As such, they were tied to very limited laboratory situations.

In response to these objections a number of alternate models have been proposed. Chief among these have been the dual processing model of Pavio, (1971) and the levels of processing model of Craik and Lockhart.

Pavio (1969, 1971) has proposed a "dual processing" model which hypothesizes spearate coding systems for verbal and nonverbal visual imagery. There are three types of evidence for this hypothesis. First, recognition memory for pictures is better than that for words (Shepard, 1967; Standing, 1973). Second, a number of studies have demonstrated the incidental learning of visual characteristics of verbal material (Kohlers, 1978). Finally a number of researchers have reported that the retention of visual material is more disrupted by a concomitant visual task than a concomitant verbal task, and vice versa (Baddeley, Grant, Wight, & Thompson, 1975; Brooks, 1968).

Craik and Lockhart's levels of processing model. Currently, one of the more influential models of human memory is the levels of processing model proposed by Craik and Lockhart (1971). They have refocused the field not on the underlying structure of some theoretical model but on the processes of memory. Their model carries with it many similarities to the Atkinson and Shiffrin model. Information, in their model, is available for only a short period of time unless it is "recycled." But their model is more dynamic in the sense that what is coded from the input is determined by the intentions of the individual. If the subject is asked to identify nouns in a list of words, they will tend not to code other information about the list.

The prototypic experiment in this area (Craik & Tulving, 1975) involved an incidental learning task in which subjects were presented a list of words and were instructed to answer a question about each word as it was presented. They were not told that it was a memory experiment but were asked to recall all words at a later time. The questions asked about each word ranged from references to the physical characteristics of the word (such as, "Is the word in capital letters?") to questions presumably requiring deeper processing (such as, "Does the word fit the following sentence. . . He met a ———— on the street." The results confirmed that the deeper a word was processed, the better it was recalled. These results have been widely supported.

A number of researchers have argued, however, that the levels of processing model applies only to the incidental learning task employed by Craik and Lockhart (Bransford, Franks, Morris, & Stein, 1978a,b; and Tulving, 1978). They have reported that the depth of processing argument seen in the Craik and Tulving study applies only to the free recall task. If the subject is asked to select from a second list of words, for example, those which rhymed with words presented in the first task, subjects were able to do so. Thus, despite the fact that these words were not as easily recalled, the rhyming dimension was still available.

Tulving and his colleagues (Tulving & Osler, 1968; Thomson & Tulving, 1970) have demonstrated in several studies that the extent to which information is available to a subject regarding a previous event is dependent upon the extent to which there is some correspondence between the encoding of the original material, which in turn is dependent upon the task, intentions, and the type of information required for the recall task. Some researchers argue that cues which match a part of the encoded message permit retrieval of the entire input. However, others have demonstrated that certain features of stimuli are more powerful as cues.

Glanzer and Koppenaal (1977) have argued that the levels of processing model does not replace the stage models but merely elaborates on them with a better discussion of the influence of long-term memory processes. Other researchers have echoed Tulving's views regarding encoding specificity and demonstrated effective retrieval of material presented at a "low" level of processing when the retrieval task was appropriate for the encoding. (Bransford, et al., 1978a,b; Morris, et al., 1977b; Tulving, 1978). Craik himself has pointed out that the greatest criticism of the levels of processing model is the theoretical circularity (Baddeley, 1978; Eysenck, 1978; Nelson, 1977). The evidence of levels of processing is indexed by its very effect in memory. The only objective criterion for the depth of processing is its effect upon memory.

Extensions of the Atkinson and Shiffrin model. Two major elaborations of the Atkinson and Shiffrin model have appeared. Neither has stimulated significant research in clinical psychology, but both are attempts to expand the original multistore model in directions which make it more flexible and capable of integrating long-term memory processes with short-term memory processes.

Atkinson and Juola (1974, p. 287) have proposed two kinds of memory recoding: perceptual and conceptual. Their description of their functioning is reminiscent of Hebb's "cell assemblies" (1949). The perceptual codes serve the function of encoding the basic perceptual attributes of incoming sensory information—lines, curves, and the like. The conceptual codes consist of sets of interconnected perceptual codes, which together make up a concept. Thus, the perceptual codes for an animal consist of all the perceptual codes used for the actual animal, its name, associations, higher level categorical names, etc. All these interconnected codes form the long-term semantic store. A second part of long-term memory is an episodic memory, useful for list learning and the like. Short-term memory in the new model has become less fixed to a particular coding scheme (unlike the acoustic articulatory code of the original model) but otherwise corresponds to the original model. Clearly the emphasis in the revision has shifted from the perceptual and short-term processes.

Indeed, as Craik (1979) has pointed out, there is a growing recognition of the value of "schema" as a theoretical construct hypothetical device. The schema, as used by a number of researchers, (Anderson & Reder, 1978; Rummelhart & Ortony, 1977) are long-term memory conceptual frameworks which permit the rapid processing of stimuli which fit neatly into them. Activation of a schema causes a spreading activation of a network of associated words and ideas thus permitting a top-down richer perception and encoding and restructuring of memories. Here the processes of long-term memory are taken into account, and the concerns raised by a number of researchers regarding the effects of context and the importance of the correspondence between the type of task in which material is first presented and the manner in which it is retrieved is given full play.

A less dynamic extension of the Atkinson and Shiffrin model has been proposed by Schneider and Shiffrin (1977; Shiffrin & Schneider, 1977), largely in response to the Sternberg challenge to the original model. They propose two underlying processes: automatic and controlled search. Automatic processes are involved when the information processing demands are so well learned that they can be carried out immediately without any conscious effort. Controlled processes, on the other hand, are not handled in long-term memory. They require the use of short-term working memory and, when the task becomes difficult, may require conscious control on the part of the subject. Again, this model is consistent with the general movement towards a working, short-term, conscious, articulating memory which expands the efficiency of the automatic processing of the central processor.

ATTRIBUTION THEORY

For a period of time George Kelly's (1955a, 1955b) application of his perspectives on attribution theory to his theory of personal constructs influenced clinical psychology. Interest in Kelly's theories appears to have waned. Interest in attribution theory, however, has increased greatly among clinical psychologists because of the recent revision of the "learned helplessness" model of depression (Abramson, Seligman, & Teasdale, 1978). Though person perception has been a focus of attention for psychologists for quite some time the roots of modern attribution theory can clearly be traced to the work of Fritz Heider (1944, 1958). Heider was interested in understanding the relationship between the stimulus conditions external to the individual—the environment, including other persons—and the way in which the individuals perception of them affect his or her choice of action.

Agreeing with Brunswik's (1934) contention that the objects of social and nonsocial perception could be modeled by the same perceptual processes, and remaining faithful to the general orientation of gestalt psychology, Heider sought the common organizational principles underlying the individual's construction of both object and person events.

This general approach was best illustrated by a classic study by Fritz Heider and Marianne Simmel (1944). Simmel constructed a film in which three geometric patterns, a large and a small triangle, a small dot, and a square with a moveable side moved about the screen in a somewhat orderly fashion. Subjects viewing the film attributed personal motivations and intentions to the movements of the shapes. Usually the interpretations centered around a "fight and chase" between two of the elements concluding with one of them "tricking" the other into entrappment in the "house."

Orne (1962) has suggested that Heider and Simmel's instructions produced a bias on the part of the subject towards the personification of the action. However, the reasons for the bias in the instructions were, as pointed out by Shaver (1975), similar in at least one respect to the reasons the subjects attributed intentions to the moving geometric patterns. A description of the events without such structuring would be difficult and confusing. Describing the simultaneous movements of nonrelated geometric shapes without reference to motivation and intention would be chaotic. However, description of part of the otherwise meaningless events in terms of attributions, such as "the large triangle chased the small one around the box," summarizes the action into a person form which conveys the otherwise arbitrary and unconnected events in a meaningful way.

Attribution thus becomes an efficient way to organize the world, to construct it in a meaningful way permitting interpretation and prediction. This is, in Heider's terms, "common sense psychology." It is the way in which the individual makes an understandable world.

In Heiders words: "it is an important principle of common sense psychology, as it is of scientific theory in general, that man grasps reality, and can predict and control it, by referring transient and variable behavior and events to relatively unchanging underlying conditions, the so-called dispositional properties of his world." (Heider, 1958, p. 79.)

According to Heider's common sense psychology, an action of another individual is understood in terms of *personal* and *environmental* components of the action. The extent to which an individual attributes the actions of another to personal versus environmental factors is most obviously seen in the language of description. Consider an observer commenting upon an individual rowing a boat across the lake, "he is *trying* very hard," infers personal factors, whereas, "it is *difficult* to row the boat," implies environmental factors.

Heider further divided the personal factors into a power factor and a motivational factor. The power factor is represented by ability and skill while the motivation factor refers to the individuals intention (does he intend to row across the lake) and exertion (how hard is he trying). According to Heider, the naive psychologist views the two personal factors, power and motivation, as so orthogonal that power is regrouped, in his conceptualization, with environmental factors (skill + task difficulty) to form the concept of "can" in the individuals mind.

The correspondent inference theory of Jones and Davis. One major extension of Heider's model has been proposed by Jones and Davis (1965). Jones and Davis' theory of correspondent inferences attempted to determine the dispositions presumed to be inherent in an individual's actions. Clearly, this subtheory applies only to those situations in which the observer is attempting to understand the dispositions of another person—not the underlying factors determining their own actions.

Jones and Davis began their analysis by assuming that each observer recognizes that each action carries with it certain predictable effects. The observer, by comparing these potential effects with those of alternative actions can infer the intentions of the actor. Consider, for example, working on a paper with the doors to your office open versus closed. The door closed option produces certain effects—paper writing, reading, low probability of disturbance by others. The door open option produces many of the same effects but increases the probability of being disturbed by a chance visitor. This difference can be used to infer intention by an observer. In the closed door situation, this effect is not likely. The *difference* in corresponding effects provides the critical information for the inference of intention.

PSYCHOPHYSICS

The fundamental question of the relationship between physiological systems and behavior has its roots in the earliest traditions of Western philosophy and lies at the foundation of modern experimental psychology. However, until the 1940s when improved electronic recording techniques began to appear, the relationship between functional physiological systems and behavior were primarily within the realm of philosophical speculation rather than empirical investigation.

Psychophysiological methods have been of great interest to experimental psychopathologists and psychotherapists mainly because of the apparent relationship between these measures and emotional behavior. The current literature also indicates a continued interest in "biofeedback" as both an experimental tool and as a clinical technique. There is also a considerable amount of current research devoted to psychophysiological factors or measures in schizophrenia research. Also a number of psychologists interested in the growing area of "behavioral medicine" are interested in physiological parameters. Although psychophysiology may in theory be concerned with the measurement of any biological process, in practice most research has concerned itself with functioning the measurement of electrical activity associated with the cerebral cortex, skeletal muscles, heart peripheral vasculature, blood pressure, electrodermal activity, and eye movements. In this section the major experimental paradigms, questions, and methods used in experimental psychophysiology as the discipline applies to clinical psychology will be discussed.

The techniques of psychophysiology

Most psychophysiological research has been dependent on the fact that many biological systems produce activity that is detectable as a change in electrical potential or of the resistance of an electrical circuit between two conductors. The equipment needed for the measurement of this activity is relatively straight forward and varies little as a function of physiological site (Brown, 1972).

In order to measure the activity at the site of measurement, a conductor, in the form of a disc clip (to attach to ears, tongues, and other like surfaces), or needle (to record from muscles, nerve cells, etc.), must be attached. Disc electrodes are most commonly used. They vary in size and shape but are usually disk shaped and may be flat or slightly cupped and are composed of a highly conductive material, such as silver. Contact with the skin is enhanced with an electrically conductive paste, and rubbing off the upper layer of epidermis all contributes to the establishment of a good electrical contact. Optimally a circuit with less than a 5,000 Ohms K resistance is desired (Venables and Christie, 1980).

The next component needed is a device sensitive to electrical activity. Originally this was a needle attached to an electromagnet that rotated when electrical activity went through the magnetic coil. This device (called the galvanometer after its inventor, Luigi Galvani) was limited in sensitivity but could be used to record muscle activity, some neural activity, and, with the help of a small electrical current, the conductance of the skin. The sensitivity of this device was greatly enhanced by the invention of the vacuum tube amplifier which enabled the recording of even the most minute signals. Sensitive recording of muscle (striated and smooth), nerve, and vascular activity was then facilitated.

The third component of the system, of course, is something that makes the electrical activity visible to human observation and keeps a record of this information. This device may simply be the needle of the galvanometer. A record may be kept by placing a moving piece of paper under the needle or by attaching the amplifier output to an electromagnetic tape recorder.

The most recent addition to the technology of the psychophysiological experiment has been the computer. Most biological electrical activity is noisy; i.e., there is much information present in the signal that is not directly under the control or easily explained by the experimenter. The computer has been used to enhance the measurement of subtle physiological changes by averaging physiological responses that have a constant temporal relationship to an experimentally controlled stimulus over many trials.

The psychophysiological experiment

Psychophysiological investigations employ, in a broad sense, one of two experimental paradigms—correlational and manipulative. It is safe to say that the majority of all research in this areas used what we shall call the Correlational Paradigm. In this paradigm physiological measurements are made while the subject is presented with a stimulus. The stimulus has presumably been chosen because of its relationship to some psychological response process and the biological measure chosen to be a correlate of that process. Hence the chosen stimulus may be "scary" so that the physiological correlate of fear might be measured. The stimulus may be a problem that requires concentration so that a biological measure of attention or concentration might be measured. There is some research that identifies the physiological measures with the hypothetical psychological processes (for example, subvocal motor activity measuring thinking, McGuigan, 1973, or GSR being equated with anxiety), but most researchers view the biological responses as part of a complex response system interacting with various experimental demands.

We will call the other major paradigm the manipulative paradigm. In these studies research is directed at manipulating the physiological variable, usually via operant or classical conditioning procedures, with no particular assumption about the relationship between the stimulus and the biological response. In this case the psychology of the control of the physiological measure variable is studied. Hence, in these experiments it is the mastery of the physiological response which is of interest. Examples of these experiments include those involving the teaching of control of heart rate, blood pressure, temperature of the testicles, etc.

The electrical activity of the brain. Measurement of the electrical activity of the brain has its origins in the work of Caton (1875) who reported the spontaneous changes in the electrical potentials recorded from the surface of brains of live animals. Later Berger (1929) discovered that in humans this activity could be subtyped into various rhythmic patterns that he designated Alpha and Beta. He also discovered that patients with epileptic seizures often did not show the same organized activity as did normals. Other patterns of activity and their significance have been a major focus of attention in subsequent research.

The electrical activity of the brain, the electroencephalogram (EEG), is recorded by placing electrodes over various sites on the skull. These sites are chosen to best record activity from the major anatomical structures of the cerebral cortex (frontal, parietal, occipital, and temporal lobes).

The EEG usually has a frequency of 2 to 50 Hz, permitting the filtering out of higher frequency signals, such as EMG activity, which would otherwise interfere with the EEG interpretation. The power of these waves is quite small, ranging from only a few uVs to 200 uVs, so that extensive amplification is needed.

A normal EEG record contains clusters of waves of moderate amplitude with frequencies between 8 to 13 Hz called Alpha. A background of higher frequency activity, at 14 to 30 Hz, called Beta is also present. Alpha usually increases when the subject's eyes are closed and he or she is relaxed. When aroused with eyes open the record consists almost exclusively of Beta waves. Slower waves, called Delta, at less than 4 Hz are usually associated with destructive changes in brain tissue.

The use of the EEG in research has utilized both correlative and manipulative paradigms. In manipulative paradigms, it is difficult to use the raw EEG because of the complexity of the signal. The development of computer averaging of event-related potentials must be considered a great advance for psychophysiological research.

The principle of Evoked Potentials (EPs) is simple though the actual implementation of the technique is complex and requires specialized computer technology. To obtain an EP a sensory stimulus (visual, auditory, somatosensory) that may vary in complexity from a click to a word or a light flash to a geometric design is delivered to the subject while his EEG is sampled at a fixed time interval after the stimulus onset. This process is repeated many times and the data from this time-locked recording is then summed together. That part of the EEG record which has not been time locked has a random relationship with the stimulus and will cancel itself out (producing a straight line) when summed over many trials. However, the time-locked portion of the signal is converted to an enhanced wave which is reliably related to the stimulus. The physiological correlates of relatively complex psychological processes can thus be studied. The experimenter may examine the effect of instructions to the subject to attend to certain stimuli, to particular aspects of a stimulus, etc.

Most sensory information passes through a fixed sequence of information processing structures in the nervous system beginning with the peripheral sensory receptors proceeding to the sensory nuclei in the spinal cord and brain stem before proceeding to the higher processing centers of the cortex. By varying the time interval between the stimulus and the EP, the participation of these various neuroanatomical structures in psychological functions may be examined.

Evoked potentials recorded in the first 150 msec probably reflect the processing of the sensory stimulus at relatively low levels of the nervous system (Regan, 1972). These responses are only minimally affected by voluntary alterations in attention by the subject and in fact are the most reliable evoked potentials made. The evoked potentials recorded in the first 50 msec may not differ whether the subject is awake or unconscious (see Sutton, Braren & Zubin, 1965, Sutton, Tuetling & Zubin, 1967; Regan, 1972). Evoked potentials collected in the first 20 to 30 msec after the stimulus are reflective of the brain stems sensory information processing and have been found to be quite useful in the precise diagnosis of brain stem lesions. This method has also been used to test hearing in infants, retarded adults, and patients not capable of cooperating with traditional audiometric procedures (Coats & Martin, 1977). Evoked potentials collected after 200 msecs are thought more important for the study of psychological processes. These are thought to reflect cortical information processing and are quite readily affected by subject's alertness, expectancies, memory, and attention (Hillyard & Picton, 1979).

The two most widely studied late evoked potential phenomena are *contingent negative variation* and the *wave deflection evoked potential* recorded approximately 300 msecs after the stimulus onset known as the P300 wave.

Contingent negative variation. If a subject is presented with a standard reaction time task in which a ready signal is followed at some time interval by an imperative signal for the subject to produce a simple key press or finger lift a very dramatic change in the EEG can be observed. Approximately 1 second after the ready signal, the evoked potential shows a negative shift in voltage which returns to baseline level when the subject responds. This phenomenon, first described by Walter et al. (1964), has been descriptively called contingent negative variation and is considered a correlate of subject expectancy or preparation for an upcoming event that will be informationally relevant to the subject (Walter, 1965; Low et al., 1966).

P300. This later evoked potential has been related in many interesting ways to higher mental activity. For example, Tueting and Sutton (1973) used a task in which subjects had to detect a click presented just above threshold. The click was always preceded by a loud and clearly audible click that subjects were told was irrelevant to the experiment. The subjects correct detections, misses, false alarms and correct misses, and false alarms were recorded as was the P300 wave locked to the test clicks and the supposedly irrelevant but loud click. The largest evoked potentials were observed for correctly detected test clicks with almost no responses observed for the missed test clicks. Interestingly the loud but irrelevant click resulted in only a small evoked potential.

The EEG also showed a small but reliable P300 for false positive alarms (subject reports that a click is present when it is not) that the subject felt occuring with great confidence. Hence the P300 seems to be related to conscious experience of a stimulus rather than the simple physical magnitude of the stimulus. Another important dimension apparently affecting the magnitude of the evoked potential is the probability that a stimulus will occur when the subject expects it. The more surprising the stimulus, the larger the P300 (Sutton, Braren, & Zubin, 1965). The P300 appears to decrease in magnitude or habituates when a test stimulus is repeated frequently with a high degree of certainty. The P300 has been interpreted to be an important correlate of subject selection of environmentally relevant information. These characteristics have made the P300 a frequent focus of study in populations such as schizophrenics and children with learning disabilities in which deficits in attention appear to be central to the disorder.

Since the basic physiological mechanism underlying the P300, as well as its relation to the many variables by which it is affected, are unknown, interpretation of the results obtained with non-normal populations is difficult. For example a diminished evoked potential in a patient population in whom difficulties with attention appear to be an important and empirically observable symptom may suggest that some underlying attentional mechanism is faulty—or, more simply, it may confirm that the subject does not pay attention well.

Manipulative experiments.   The voluntary control of EEG was once a very popular topic of research, particularly the control of the Alpha rhythm. It was thought that Alpha control could produce highly relaxing states of heightened self-awareness similar to those reported to accompany meditative states (Kamiya, 1968). The issue was found to be more complex than originally thought when it was discovered that the act of trying to control Alpha and subject motivation were perhaps more important than Alpha control per se (Walsh, 1979). The basic paradigm for Alpha control involved the delivery of a visual or auditory signal to the subject every time Alpha was produced. The subject's task was to maximize the occurrence of the signal. In many studies the subject's introspections about the experience were elicited; in other cases performance on psychological measures were observed. In several studies it was found that subjects could achieve heightened states of relaxation with false Alpha feedback and that heightened relaxation, or other special feelings, were not necessarily reported when large amounts of Alpha were produced. The topic is no longer popular in the standard psychophysiological journals, but the interested reader is referred to Lynch, Paskewitz, and Orne (1974) for a more extensive review of the topic.

Cardiovascular system. The electromagnetic signal recorded from the heart is known as the electrocardiogram. The wave form of the EEG provides information about heart rate, periodicity and amplitude, as well as the integrity of the various components of the heart. Perhaps because of its importance in physical health, a great deal of effort has been made to study the psychophysiology of the heart, vascular system, and blood pressure. In the last five years the greatest proportion of research has been conducted examining subjects ability to control cardiovascular functions rather than attempting to correlate them with complex psychological processes.

Although there has been some work examining changing heart rate, blood pressure, and other cardiovascular variables while subjects perform mental tasks (see McGuigan, 1973 for review), these studies have not resulted in the specificity that was discovered with the EEG. The exception to this may be the description of a phenomenon called the "orienting reflex" usually associated with Sokolov (1963), in which heart rate appears to decelerate when a subject is presented with a novel stimulus. Much of the work with the so-called orienting reflex was performed with animals, and the effects do not appear to be as reliable when similar experiments are conducted with humans. Also the orienting reflex, when it is observed, does not appear to have the subtle, rapid relations relationship to information presentation as does the EEG. This may, of course, simply be a measurement problem. A good method of eliminating physiological noise in the cardiovascular system may not be available. Alternatively, the cardiovascular system may not be available. Alternatively, the cardiovascular system may not be a good index of higher nervous activity in humans.

Heart rate and blood pressure were among a set of responses not considered to be under voluntary control in the early history of experimental psychology of learning. Pavlov (1927) and Skinner (1938) distinguished between conditioning involving the skeletal musculature that was considered to involve adaptive responses to the environment largely under the "voluntary" contol of the organism, and the more primitive conditioning of the smooth muscles and glands that were considered to involve only simple "reflex arcs" in the nervous system and not to be under the direct control of the organism.

It is largely the work of N. E. Miller (1974) and his students that has been responsible for a change in this view. They demonstrated that autonomic responses such as heart rate and blood pressure could under certain circumstances be controlled by the subject if appropriate information about the state of these response systems was made available to the subjects. In humans much research has been directed towards optimizing these effects.

The most consistent finding which has emerged from this immense literature is that the feedback used must be relevant to the response system in question. For example, (Lang & Twentyman, 1974) allowed subjects either binary feedback (success or failure) or analogue feedback (a line whose length was determined by heart rate). They found that subjects could use analogue and binary feedback equally well to slow heart rate but that analogue feedback was superior for training heart rate acceleration. After training, subjects could sustain changes in heart rate even without feedback.

These results prompted the authors to hypothesize different psycho-physiological mechanisms for cardiac speeding and slowing. Heart rate acceleration learning proceeded relatively rapidly for subjects, and it was proposed that subjects needed only to use behaviors already in their repertoire to increase heart rate. The analogue feedback provided the best feedback for this purpose.

Heart rate slowing was acquired with greater difficulty and with more frequent return to the baseline between training sessions. They concluded that slowing involves true "visceral learning" that could not be acquired over a few training sessions.

LATERALIZATION IN THE NERVOUS SYSTEM

In the five years preceding this review there has been a growing trend in the literature on psychopathology and normal personality to utilize the concept of structural or functional differences in the brain as an explanatory construct. In particular the concept of lateral specialization of function of the two cerebral hemispheres has been the focus of extensive examination. The development of the concept of laterality and issues concerning measurement will be discussed below.

The cortex is generally presumed to subserve the higher mental processes such as language, perception, and memory. This large structure consists of two roughly symmetrical hemispheres consisting of a number of convoluted layers of neurons and numerous tracts of fibres connecting areas within each hemisphere. Homologous areas of each hemisphere are interconnected via a large bundle of fibres known as the corpus callosum.

In 1861 Paul Broca presented the clinical findings and a post-mortem report of a patient to a meeting of anthropologists in Paris. The patient had apparently become "speechless" shortly before he died. The post-mortem examination of the brain revealed a large lesion in the patient's left frontal lobe. In 1865 Broca reported to the society the findings in a series of cases indicating that only patients with lesions in the left hemisphere lost their ability to use language. Though this hypothesis was widely debated, hundreds of additional case reports and experimental investigations have confirmed the general case (Wernicke, 1874; Benson, 1979; Goodglass & Kaplan, 1972).

It is now generally agreed that in right-handed adults aphasia (the acquired loss of language ability due to neurological disorder) occurs primarily with lesions of the left hemisphere. This correlation is not nearly as great for patients who are left-handed, but still a majority of left-handers become aphasic when their left hemisphere sustains damage. The relationship between handedness and lateralization of other higher processes is an important one and the subject of a great deal of speculation, but it is beyond the scope of this chapter.

Most of the clinical case material used to make the association between the left hemisphere and language was based on patients whose brains were damaged by strokes, penetrating missile wounds of war, or tumors. From this data the concept of the major and minor hemisphere emerged. The left hemisphere was considered the most important for higher mental activity (which was largely considered to be verbally based). Several sources of data helped change the concept of cerebral dominance as it was held even into the 1960s by much of the behavioral neurology literature. One source of change was that the importance of nonverbal processes were beginning to receive attention in the mainstream of American experimental psychology (e.g., Pavio, 1971). More important, however, was the work of Roger Sperry and his colleagues and students (e.g., Sperry & Gazzaniga, 1967; Bogen, 1969; Zaidel & Sperry, 1973). They took advantage of the unique opportunity to study patients in which the cerebral hemispheres had been surgically separated to prevent the propagation of seizure activity. The important component of this operation was the severing of the corpus callosum. With these patients one could present material to one hemisphere by placing it in the relevant sensory field contralaterally to the hemisphere of interest. Hence, visuospatial, musical, symbolic, or verbal material could be presented to one hemisphere or the other in the visual, auditory, or somatosensory modalities. The main result of their research may be summarized simply: each hemisphere is primarily responsible for the processing of verbal information, while the right hemisphere is responsible for the processing of visuospatial and other nonverbal information. Some writers have argued that this case material may be misleading because the data was collected from patients with epilepsy whose brains may not have the same patterns of lateralization as non-brain-damaged patients. No technique was available for the study of hemispheric lateralization in intact, normal subjects.

This situation changed with the publication in 1961 of a now classic experiment by Doreen Kimura. Kimura used a technique that had been developed by Broadbent (1954) to study selective listening to demonstrate perceptual asymmetries in the auditory system that appeared to be related to the specialized language information processing capabilities of the left hemisphere. The dichotic listening procedure, as it is called, involved the simultaneous presentation of different auditory stimuli to the two ears of the subject. Broadbent originally used widely spaced speakers to achieve ear by ear separation, but most later studies have employed earphones for this purpose. In the Kimura experiment subjects heard two different sets of recorded digits presented simultaneously, one digit to each ear. Their task was to report as many digits as possible. Subjects were demonstrated to reliably report digits presented to the right ear more accurately than the digits presented to the left ear.

Kimura later showed that dichotically presented backwards speech showed a right ear advantage (Kimura & Folb, 1968) and that dichotic musical melodies produce a left ear advantage (Kimura, 1964). These relatively simple findings represented a small methodological revolution in the study of the psychology of hemispheric functioning. Literally hundreds of studies followed studying the linguistic boundary conditions for the occurrence of the effect (Zurif & Sait, 1970; Blumstein & Cooper, 1974; Studdart-Kennedy, Shankweiler & Shulman, 1970) and the strategic factors that determined the degree (Bryden, 1964) and direction (Milberg et al., 1981) of the observed advantage. Dichotic listening and related techniques in the visual modality are the primary methods that have been used to explore hemispheric differences in information processing in patients with psychiatric disorders. It is for this reason that it is important to understand Kimura's interpretation and explanation of her original results as well as the questions of logic and methodology that have arisen regarding dichotic listening and other procedures that purport to measure cerebral asymmetries in intact humans.

Kimura made several assumptions about neuroanatomy and function to explain her observation of the right ear advantage for digit recall. The cornerstone of her explanation lies in the fact that much of the higher nervous system is wired in a crossed or contralateral manner; motor and sensory functions of the left side of the body are primarily controlled by the right cerebral hemisphere, and the converse is true for the left hemisphere. This situation is somewhat true for the auditory system although the ears do have some functional communication with the ipsilateral hemisphere (Carpenter, 1973). It was assumed that under the conditions of dichotic listening the contralateral pathways predominate; i.e., the right ear to the left hemisphere such that the right ear has preferred communication with the left hemisphere, and vice versa. Verbal information, dichotically presented, has direct access to the "language" processing mechanism of the left hemisphere, while information presented to the left ear must first be processed by the right hemisphere (that does not have the same verbal processing capabilities as does the left) before it can reach the left hemisphere via the corpus callosum. This hard wiring explanation is not universally accepted for several reasons. First, the procedure used by Kimura does not have high test-retest reliability: subjects who show a right ear advantage on one occasion may show a left ear advantage or, more commonly, no advantage on another (Blumstein, Goodglass, & Tarter, 1975). Also, within a sample of subjects, the incidence of the right ear advantage does not correspond well to the distribution of left hemisphere dominance that is obtained by examination of the incidence of aphasias with brain lesions. Ninety-five percent of patients with aphasias have left hemisphere lesions (right-handers) while estimates of right ear advantage vary from 65 percent to 85 percent. Finally, such strategic factors as direction of attention (Bryden, 1964) and sub-vocalization (Milberg et al., 1981) can influence the degree and even the direction of the observed asymmetry for verbal material.

Kinsbourne has suggested the concept of hemispheric activation as an alternative to Kimura's hard wiring model. In Kinsbourne's view (Kinsbourne, 1970), perceptual asymmetries arise because attention is directed to the side of space contralateral to the hemisphere used to process the incoming stimulus. "Verbal" information, or a verbal response set, activates the left hemisphere resulting in an attentional bias towards the right side of space. Hence, information occurring in the right side of space (e.g., right ear) will be preferentially processed. As long as the left hemisphere is activated, both verbal and nonverbal information will be better attended to if it originates to the right of the midline. Kinsbourne and others have attempted to examine this prediction from both models experimentally, and the results are thus far debatable.

SUMMARY

Five areas representing areas of interest prevalent in the clinical literature are briefly reviewed. The classic reaction time procedure of Donders is described as a method of partitioning mental processes. This approach has been particularly useful as a tool in the development of a variety of stage analyses of cognitive activity. The additive and subtractive methods are discussed as complimentary approaches to this research.

The classic stage conceptualization of memory is still used in some form but has evolved into a more complex conceptualization. During the 1960s, the addition of a sensory store to the stages of memory was demanded by the findings of Sperling and Averbach and generated an exciting decade of research. More recently, however, the literature has reflected a growing disatisfaction with the stage models. Pavio's dual-processing model and Craik and Lockhart's levels of processing approach have represented the reaction of the field to the static nature of the stage models. Recent stage models have attempted to combine the features of both approaches to modeling memory processes in order to produce a more dynamic and realistic conceptualization.

Attribution theory has changed little since its original conceptualization by Heider. Its position as an essential part of the reformulation of the learned helplessness theory of depression is reviewed, and the research surrounding this research is reviewed.

In view of the continued interest in biofeedback and a growing interest in psychophysiological techniques as they are used in behavioral medicine and schizophrenia research, the history of the development of this area is briefly reviewed. Also, the basic experimental paradigms used in this area are described. Finally, some of the current research directions are identified.

Interest in lateralization of the nervous system and cognitive processes has continued to grow rapidly, and the field is gaining some experimental sophistication as researchers proceed from the identification of phenomenon to the modeling of the parameters under which they occur. The development of this area and a consideration of some of the remaining issues is presented.

REFERENCES

Abramson, L., Seligman, M. E. P., & Teasdale, J. D. Learned helplessness in humans: Critique and reformulation. *Journal Of Abnormal Psychology,* 1978, *87*(1), 49–74.

Anderson, J. R., & Reder, L. An elaborate processing explanation of depth of processing. In L. S. Cermak & R. M. Craik (Eds.), *Levels of processing in human memory.* Hillsdale, N.J.: Erlbaum, 1978.

Atkinson, R. C., & Juola, J. F. Search and decision processes in recognition memory. In D. H. Kranz, R. C. Atkinson, R. D. Luce, & P. Suppes (Eds.), *Contemporary developments in mathematical psychology.* San Francisco: W. H. Freeman, 1974.

Atkinson, R. C., & Shiffrin, R. M. Human memory: A proposed system and its control processes. In K. W. Spence & J. T. Spence (Eds.), *Advances in the psychology of learning and motivation research and theory* (Vol. 2). New York: Academic Press, 1968.

Averbach, I., & Coriell, A. S. Short-term memory in vision. *Bell System Technical Journal,* 1961, *40,* 309–328.

Baddeley, A. D. The trouble with levels: A re-examination of Craik and Lockhart's framework for memory research. *Psychological Review,* 1978, *85,* 139–152.

Baddeley, A. D., Grant, S., Wight, E., & Thompson, N. Imagery and visual working memory. In P. M. Rabbitt & S. Dornic (Eds.), *Attention and performance* (Vol. 5). New York: Academic Press, 1975.

Benson, D. F. Aphasia. In Kenneth M. Heilman & Edward Valenstein (Eds.), *Clinical neuropsychology.* New York: Oxford, University Press, 1979.

Berger, H. Uber das Elektren kephalogramm des Menschen. *Arch. Fur Psychiatrie Und Nervenkrankheiten,* 1929, *87,* 527–570.

Blumstein, S., & Cooper, W. E. Hemispheric processing of intonation contours. *Cortex,* 1974, *10,* 146–158.

Blumstein, S., Goodglass, H., & Tarter, V. The reliability of ear advantage in dichotic listening. *Brain And Language,* 1975, *2,* 226–236.

Bogen, J. E. The other side of the brain: Dysgraphia and dyscopia following cerebral commissurotomy. *Bulletin of The Los Angeles Neurological Society,* 1969, *34,* 73–105.

Bransford, J. D., Franks, J. J., Morris, C. D., & Stein, B. S. An analysis of memory theories from the perspective of problems of learning. In L. S. Cermak & F. I. M. Craik (Eds.), *Levels of processing and human memory.* Hillsdale, N.J.: Erlbaum, 1978. (a)

Bransford, J. D., Franks, J. J., Morris, C. D., & Stein, B. S. Some general constraints on learning and memory research. In L. S. Cermak & F. I. M. Craik (Eds.), *Levels of processing and human memory.* Hillsdale, N.J.: Erlbaum, 1978. (b)

Broadbent, D. E. The role of auditory localization in attention and memory span. *Journal Of Experimental Psychology,* 1954, *47,* 191–196.

Broca, P. Remarques sur le siege de la faculte du langage articule suivie d'une observation d'aphemie. *Bull. Soc. Anat., Paris,* 1861, *6,* 330.

Broca, P. Sur la faculte du langage articule. *Bull. Soc. Anthr., Paris,* 1865, *6,* 337–393.

Brooks, L. R. Spatial and verbal components in the act of recall. *Canadian Journal Of Psychology,* 1968, *22,* 349–368.

Brown, C. Instruments in psychophysiology. In Norman S. Greenfield & Richard A. Sternbach (Eds.), *Handbook of psychophysiology,* New York: Holt, Rinehart & Winston, 1972.

Brunswik, E. *Wahrnehmung und Gegerstandswelt.* Leipzip and Weir: Deutick, 1934.

Bryden, M. P. The manipulation of strategies of report in dichotic listening. *Canadian Journal Of Psychology,* 1964, *18,* 126–138.

Carpenter, M. B. *Core text of neuroanatomy.* Baltimore, Md.: Williams & Wilkins, 1973.

Caton, R. The electric currents of the brain. *British Medical Journal,* 1875, *2,* 278.

Coats A., & Martin, J. L. Human auditory nerve action potentials and brainstem evoked responses. *Archives Of Otolaryngology,* 1977, *103,* 605–622.

Conrad, R. Acoustic confusions in immediate memory. *British Journal Of Psychology,* 1964, *55,* 75–84.

Craik, F. I. M. Human memory. *Annual Review Of Psychology,* 1979, *30,* 63–102.

Craik, F. I. M., & Lockhart, R. S. Levels of processing: A framework for memory research. *Journal of Verbal Learning and Verbal Behavior,* 1971, *11,* 671–684.

Craik, F. I. M., & Tulving, E. Depth of processing and the retention of words in episodic memory. *Journal of Experimental Psychology: General,* 1975, *104,* 268–294.

Darwin, C. J., Turvey, M. T., & Crowder, R. G. An auditory analogue of the Sperling partial report procedure. *Cognitive Psychology,* 1972, *3,* 255–267.

Donders, F. C. Over de snelheid van psychische processen. On derzoekingen gedaan in Let Psyiologish Laboratorium der U trechtsche Hoogeschool: 1868–1869. *Tweede Reeks, 11,* 92–120. Translated by W. G. Koster in W. G. Koster (Ed.), *Attention and Performance II., Acta Psychologia,* 1969, *30,* 412–431.

Effron, R. The minimum duration of a perception. *Neuropsychologia,* 1970, *8,* 57–63.

Eriksen, C. W. Temporal luminance summation effects in backward and forward masking. *Perception And Psychophysics,* 1966, *1,* 87–92.

Eysenck, M. W. Levels of processing: A critique. *British Journal Of Psychology,* 1978, *69,* 157–169.

Glanzer, M., & Koppenaal, L. The effect of encoding tasks on free recall: Stages and levels. *Journal Of Verbal Learning And Verbal Behavior,* 1977, *16,* 21–28.

Glucksberg, S., & Cohen, G. N. Memory for nonattended auditory material. *Cognitive Psychology,* 1970, *1,* 149–156.

Goodglass, H., & Kaplan, E. *The assessment of aphasia and related disorders.* Philadelphia: Lea & Febiger, 1972.

Haber, R. N., & Standing, L. G. Direct measure of short-term visual storage. *Quarterly Journal Of Experimental Psychology,* 1969, *21,* 43–54.

Hebb. D. O. *The organization of behavior.* New York: John Wiley & Sons, 1949.

Heider, F. Social perception and phenomenal causality. *Psychological Review,* 1944, *51,* 358–374.

Heider, F. *The psychology of interpersonal relations.* New York: John Wiley & Sons, 1958.

Heider, F., & Simmel, M. An experimental study of apparent behavior. *Journal Of Psychology,*1944, *57,* 243–259.

Hillyard, S. A., & Picton, T. W. Event-related brain potentials and selective information processing in man. In J. E. Desmedt (Ed.), *Progress in clinical neurophysiology* (Vol. 6). Karger: Basel, 1979.

Jones, E. E., & Davis, K. E. From acts to dispositions: The attribution process in person perception. In L. Berkowitz (Ed.), *Advances in experimental social psychology* (Vol. 2). New York: Academic Press, 1965.

Kamiya, J. EEG operant conditioning and the study of states of consciousness. In D. Freedman (Ed.), *Laboratory studies of altered psychological states.* Symposium at the American Psychological Association, Washington, D.C., 1968.

Kelly, George A. *The psychology of personal constructs* (Vol. 1). New York: W. W. Norton, 1955. (a)

Kelly, George A. *The psychology of personal constructs* (Vol. 2). New York: W. W. Norton, 1955. (b)

Kimura, D. Cerebral dominance and the perception of verbal stimuli. *Canadian Journal of Psychology,* 1961, *15,* 166–171.

Kimura, D. Left-right differences in the perception of melodies. *Quarterly Journal of Experimental Psychology,* 1964, *16,* 355–358.

Kimura, D., & Folb, S. Neural processing of backwards speech sounds. *Science,* 1968, *161,* 395–396.

Kinsbourne, M. The cerebral basis of lateral asymmetries in attention. *Acta Psychologia,* 1970, *33,* 193–201.

Kohlers, P. A. A pattern analyzing basis of recognition. In L. S. Cermak & F. I. M. Craik (Eds.), *Levels of Processing and human memory.* Hillsdale, N.J.: Erlbaum 1978.

Kroll, N. E. A. Visual short-term memory. In J. A. Deutsch (Ed.), *Short term memory.* New York: Academic Press, 1975.

Kroll, N. E.A., Parks, T., Parkinson, S. R., Bieber, S. L., & Johnson, A. L. Short-term memory while shadowing: Recall of visually and aurally presented letters. *Journal Of Experimental Psychology,* 1970, *85,* 220–224.

Lachman, R., Lachman, J. L., & Butterfield, E. C. *Cognitive psychology and information processing.* Hillsdale, N.J.: Erlbaum, 1979.

Lang, P., & Twentyman, C. Learning to control heart rate: Binary vs. analogue feedback. *Psychophysiology,* 1974,*11*(6), 616–629.

Levy, B. A. Role of articulation in auditory and visual short-term memory. *Journal Of Verbal Learning And Verbal Behavior,* 1971, *10,* 346–354.

Low, M., Borda, R., Frost, J., & Kellaway, P. Surface negative slow potential shift associated with conditioning in man. *Neurology (Minneapolis)*, 1966, *16*, 771–782.

Lynch, J., Paskewitz, D., & Orne, M. Some factors in the feedback control of human alpha rhythm. *Psychosomatic Medicine*, 1974, *36*(5), 399–410.

Massaro, D. W. Preperceptual auditory images. *Journal Of Experimental Psychology*, 1970, *85*, 411–417.

McGuigan, F. J. Electrical measurement of covert processes as an explication of "higher mental events." In F. J. McGuigan & R.A. Schoonover (Eds.), *The psychophysiology of thinking*. New York: Academic Press, 1973.

McGuigan, F. J. *Cognitive psychophysiology: Principles of covert behavior*. Englewood Cliffs, N.J.: Prentice-Hall, 1978.

Milberg, W. P., Whitman, R. D., Rourke, D., & Glaros, A. Role of subvocal motor activity in dichotic speech perception and selective attention. *Journal Of Experimental Psychology: Human Perception And Performance*, 1981, *7*(1), 231–239.

Miller, G. A. The magical number seven, plus or minus two: Some limits on our capacity for processing information. *Psychological Review*, 1956, *63*, 81–97.

Miller, N. Biofeedback: Evaluation of a new technic. *New England Journal Of Medicine*, 1974, *290*, 684–685.

Morris, C. D., Bransford, J. D., & Franks, J. J. Levels of processing versus transfer appropriate processing. *Journal Of Verbal Learning And Verbal Behavior*, 1977, *16*, 21–28.

Murdock, B. B. The retention of individual items. *Journal Of Experimental Psychology*, 1961, *62*, 618–625.

Murdock, B. B. Four channel effects in short-term memory. *Psychonomic Science*, 1971, *24*, 197–198.

Nelson, T. O. Repetition and depth of processing. *Journal Of Verbal Learning And Verbal Behavior*, 1977, *16*, 151–171.

Orne, M. T. On the social psychology of the psychological experiment: With particular reference to demand characteristics and their implications. *American Psychologist*, 1962, *17*, 776–783.

Pachella, R. G. The interpretation of reaction time in information processing research. In B. Kantowitz (Ed.), *Human information processing: Tutorials in performance and cognition*. Hillsdale, N.J.: Erlbaum, 1974.

Pavio, A. Mental imagery in associative learning and memory. *Psychological Review*, 1969, *76*, 241–263.

Pavio, A. *Imagery and verbal processes*. New York: Holt, Rinehart & Winston, 1971.

Pavlov, I. *Conditioned reflexes*. New York: Oxford University Press, 1927.

Peterson, L. R., & Johnson, S. T. Some effects of minimizing articulation on short-term retention. *Journal Of Verbal Learning And Verbal Behavior*, 1971, *10*, 346–354.

Preterson, L. R., & Peterson, M. J. Short-term retention of individual verbal items. *Journal Of Experimental Psychology*, 1959, *58*, 193–198.

Phillips, W. A., & Baddeley, A. D. Reaction time and short-term visual memory. *Psychonomic Science*, 1971, *22*, 73–74.

Posner, M. I. Abstraction and the process of recognition. In G. H. Bower and J. T. Spence (Eds.), *The psychology of learning and motivation: Advances in research and theory* (Vol. 3). New York: John Wiley & Sons, 1972.

Regan, D. *Evoked potentials.* New York: John Wiley & Sons, 1972.

Rummelhart, D. E., & Ortony, A. The representation of knowledge in memory. In R. C. Anderson, R. J. Spiro, & W. E. Montague (Eds.), *Schooling and the acquisition of knowledge.* Hillsdale, N.J.: Erlbaum,1977, pp. 99–136.

Schneider, W., & Shiffrin, R. M. Controlled and automatic human information processing: I. Detection, search and attention. *Psychological Review.* 1977, *84*, 1–66.

Shaver, K. G. *An introduction to attribution processes.* Cambridge, Mass.: Winthrop, 1975.

Shepard, R. N. Recognition memory for words, sentences, and pictures. *Journal Of Verbal Learning And Verbal Behavior,* 1967, *6*, 156–163.

Shepard, R. N., & Metzler, J. Mental rotation of three-dimensional objects. *Science,* 1971, *171*, 701–703.

Shiffrin, R. M., & Schneider, W. Controlled and automatic human information processing: II. *Psychological Review,* 1977, *84*, 127–190.

Shulman, H. G. Encoding and retention of semantic and phonemic information in short-term memory. *Journal Of Verbal Learning And Verbal Behavior,* 1970, *9*, 499–508.

Shulman, H. G. Semantic confusion errors in short-term memory. *Journal Of Verbal Learning And Verbal Behavior,* 1972, *11*, 221–227.

Skinner, B. F. *The behavior of organisms: An experimental analysis.* New York: Appleton-Century-Crofts, 1938.

Smith, M. C., & Schiller, P. H. Forward and backward masking: A comparison. *Canadian Journal Of Psychology,* 1966, *20*, 191–197.

Sokolov, E. N. *Perception and the conditioned reflex.* New York: Macmillan, 1963.

Sperling, G. The information available in brief visual presentations. *Psychological Monographs,* 1960, *74*(Whole No. 11).

Sperry, R. W., & Gazzaniga, M. S. Language following surgical disconnection of the commissures. In F. L. Darley (Ed.), *Brain mechanisms underlying speech and language.* New York: Grune & Stratton, 1967.

Standing, L. Learning 10,000 pictures. *Quarterly Journal Of Experimental Psychology,* 1973, *25*, 207–222.

Sternberg, S. *Retrieval from recent memory. Some reaction time experiments and a search theory.* Paper presented at the meeting of the Psychonomic Society, Bryn Mawr, August 1963.

Sternberg, S. High-speed scanning in human memory. *Science,* 1966, *153*, 652–654.

Sternberg, S. The discovery of processing stages: Extensions of Donders' method. *Acta Psychologia,* 1969, *30*, 276–315. (a)

Sternberg, S. Memory scanning: Memory processes revealed by reaction time experiments. *American Scientist,* 1969, *57*, 421–457. (b)

Studdert-Kennedy, M., Shankweiler, D., & Schulman, S. Opposed effects of a delayed channel on perception of dichotically and monotically presented CV syllables. *Journal Of The Acoustic Society Of America,* 1970, *48*, 599–602.

Sutton, S., Braren, M., & Zubin, J. Evoked-potential correlates of stimulus uncertainty. *Science,* 1965, *150*, 1187–1188.

Sutton, S., Tueting, P., Zubin, J., & John, E. R. Information delivery and the sensory evoked potential. *Science,* 1967, *155*, 1436–1439.

Thomson, D. M., & Tulving, E. Associative encoding and retrieval: Weak and strong cues. *Journal Of Experimental Psychology,* 1970, *86,* 255–262.

Townsend, J. T. A note on the identifiability of parallel and serial processes. *Perception & Psychophysics,* 1971, 163.

Townsend, J. T. Issues and models concerning the processing of a finite number of inputs. In B. H. Kantowitz (Ed.), *Human information processing: Tutorials in performance and cognition.* Hillsdale, N.J. Erlbaum, 1974.

Tueting, P. & Sutton, S. The relationship between pre-stimulus negative shifts and post stimulus components of the averaged evoked potential. In S. Kornblum (Ed.), *Attention and performance IV.* New York: Academic Press, 1973.

Tulving, E. Relation between encoding specificity and levels of processing. In L. S. Cermak & F. I. M. Craik (Eds.), *Levels of processing and human memory.* Hillsdale, N.J.: Erlbaum, 1978.

Tulving, E., & Osler, S. Effectiveness of retrieval cues in memory for words. *Journal Of Experimental Psychology,* 1968, *77,* 593–601.

Venables, P. H., & Christie, M. J. Electrodermal activity. In I. Martin & P. H. Venables (Eds.), *Techniques in Psychophysiology,* New York: John Wiley & Sons, 1980.

Walsh, David H. Interactive effects of alpha feedback and instructional set on subjective state. *Psychophysiology,* 1979, *11*(4), 428–435.

Walter, W. G. Brain responses to semantic stimuli. *Journal Of Psychosomatic Research,* 1965, *9,* 51–91.

Walter, W. G., Cooper, R., Aldridge, V., McCallum, W., & Winter A. Contingent negative variation: An electrical sign of sensori-motor association and expectancy in the human brain. *Nature,* 1964, *203,* 380–384.

Wernicke, C. *Der Aphasische Symptomerkomplex.* Breslau: Cohen & Weigart, 1874.

Zaidel, D., & Sperry, R. W. Performance on the Raven's Coloured Progressive Matrices by subjects with cerebral commissurotomy. *Cortex,* 1973, *9,* 34–39.

Zurif, E. B., & Sait, P. E. The role of syntax in dichotic listening. *Neuropsychologia,* 1970, *8,* 239–244.

3

Experimental psychopathology

R. Douglas Whitman *
William P. Milberg†
and
Brendan A. Maher ‡

In reviewing the literature in preparation for this book, it became clear that the preponderance of systematic research reported in the psychopathology literature is devoted to either schizophrenia or depression. Though a number of other areas are attracting attention, this review, because of space limitations, will be restricted to these major areas.

SCHIZOPHRENIA

Kraepelin's (1896) description of schizophrenia has survived as one of the most accurate and rich descriptions of the clinical symptoms of the schizophrenic. The experimental investigation of the psychology of this disorder has historically been the greatest challenge to the psychopathologist. Although it has been the focus of more pages of journal space than any other topic, its study has led to as many contradictions and blind alleys as to reliable, useful findings. The fundamental objective of the experimental psychopathologist in this area has been to develop measures that are related to the clinical picture of schizophrenia while providing an account of the psychosocial processes involved in the etiology and content of the schizophrenic syndrome. It is generally assumed that the behavioral symptoms are excesses or deficits in normally occurring psychological functions and/or the interaction of deficient processes with ones which are normally functioning. As Bleuler noted (1911) some

* Wayne State University, Detroit.

† Veteran's Administration Hospital, Boston.

‡ Harvard University, Cambridge, Mass.

symptoms may be amplifications of a basic deficit and others may be compensatory changes in normal functioning. Thus, the psychopathologist is faced with a complex behavioral phenomenon and must infer what in the clinical picture is "primary and fundamental" and what is "secondary and accessory." Some of the symptoms are those affected when any of the components of human information processing are disabled (e.g., IQ, social withdrawal, etc.), and others may be specific to schizophrenia.

Hence, some symptoms may represent stable, basic subject characteristics which are central to the specific pathology of schizophrenia, and other deficits may be present because of the interaction of the pathology with intact functions.

Consider the case of a bacterial infection which produces skin lesions by destroying cells at the infected site with a toxin. The presence of the bacteria mobilizes white blood cells which release pyrogens as they attack the foreign matter. These pyrogens, in turn, signal the central nervous system structures responsible for temperature regulation, and the body temperature is raised. This temperature change kills bacteria but also creates discomfort. The fever and malaise which result are a normal response to an infection and ultimately may be worse for the organism than the destructive effects of the original bacteria.

Meehl (1962) suggested that individuals who were likely to become schizophrenic had inherited a basic neural integrative defect, which he labled "schizotaxia." Such individuals developed personality types that reflected this basic neural deficit. He called these individuals "schizotypic." Under conditions of stress these individuals were at high risk for the development of the full psychotic disorder. Recently Spring and Zubin (1977, 1978) restated this position, separating "diasthesis," that is, "vulnerability," to the disease from other characteristics of the person and exposure to environmental stresses that may precipitate the disorder. The primary difference between the Zubin and Spring position and the Meehl position is that the former authors postulate that vulnerability is inherited along a continuum that is orthogonal to other inherited traits that may also mediate the development of the disorder. Hence, persons with different intelligence levels, coping syles, etc., may inherit similar levels of vulnerability. They suggest that even persons with low vulnerability have some probability of developing schizophrenia if the environmental stressors are sufficient. What differentiates these individuals from those who are highly vulnerable is that the latter are more likely to show relapses and become chronic than are the former. They suggest that vulnerability represents a stable trait that can be measured behaviorally in individuals even when they are not psychotic. The development of schizophrenia is a "state" which can be attained by people with the "trait."

A related concept developed by Chapman and Chapman (1973) is that of generalized and specific deficits. They have suggested that the task of the experimental psychopathologist is the demonstration of specific deficits in functioning rather than merely reconfirmation that the schizophrenic has a general problem solving tasks given by psychologists. Across large groups of individuals, most psychological tasks share some variance. A loss of efficiency in performance may be expected to result in some deficit on any task presented the subject. The better the discriminating power of the test or the better the reliability of the test, the greater are the differences which can be expected between clinical and control groups.

Hence, the concepts of schizotypy, vulnerability, and specific deficit are quite similar, though in the former two cases the emphasis is on inherited traits that may be reflected in basic behavioral deficits. The concept of specific deficit is more purely a behavioral concept.

The enterprise of developing reliable measures of "state" or general deficit is legitimate since these measures can be helpful in predicting performance in other situations dependent upon these functions. For example, the score on an IQ test may be the best predictor of school performance. An actively psychotic person who scores low on an IQ test may be expected to do poorly in school. However, this score may not tell us the specific reasons why the person fails, what kind of psychosis he is suffering from (manic depressive, schizophrenia, senile dementia), or how to treat the patient. This measure, however, may be the best indicator of clinical improvement and ultimate ability to function. The purported goal of most psychopathology research, however, is not the identification of these general indicators of psychopathology but the development of measures that are sensitive to specific, trait-based measures of schizophrenia. These studies attempt to somehow eliminate the effect of the general psychotic state of the subject and measure the possible sources of the deficit.

There are several experimental paradigms that have been used to isolate or separate the effects of trait or specific deficits underlying the schizophrenic disorder and psychological deficits that are related to severe psychopathology in general. The ultimate task, of course, is to explain how these deficits produce the symptoms that are observed clinically.

1. Matched subjects. The most common method of specifying deficits in schizophrenics is to compare them with nonschizophrenics who would be expected to show the same level of impairment. Typical subject groups used have been nonschizophrenic psychotic patients, such as manic-depressives, nonpsychotic mixed groups with psychiatric diagnoses, alcoholics, and the elderly. In each case it is hoped that the groups have equally severe disorders of general functioning.

2. Matched tasks. A second strategy (often used in conjunction with the first) is to employ two tasks both of which are equally correlated with general levels of functions but with one of the tasks related to the specific deficit of interest. For example, Rosenbaum (1971) employed a weight discrimination task matched in difficulty with an auditory intensity discrimination task. Matching for difficulty was accomplished with normal subjects. These tasks were then administered to normals and schizophrenics. They found that schizophrenics performed more poorly than normals on the weight discrimination task as difficulty increased, but not differentially worse than normals on the auditory task as difficulty increased.

3. High Risk. In this paradigm first-degree relatives of schizophrenics are tested with measures thought to reflect basic deficits in schizophrenia. These subjects are compared to demographically similar but nonpsychotic subjects. These individuals may be tested before they become actively psychotic. If they show psychological deficits different from those seen in the controls, this is considered evidence for a specific marker deficit. Further, if the severity of these deficits (or even the presence of these deficits within the schizophrenic relatives) is predictive of the development of the full-blown disorder, then this is even stronger evidence for these deficits being basic to schizophrenia.

4. Stability of deficits within subjects. A paradigm that is little used but nevertheless potentially useful in the identification of or separation of trait- and state-related psychological deficits is the examination of the stability of these measures over many different occasions. It has been noted by several writers that many schizophrenic symptoms seem to wax and wane, whereas others seem to be more reliably present (Manschreck, 1981). For example, ratings of thought disorder may change dramatically from day to day. Presumably, over many test trials trait variables will remain more stable than state variables. The larger the sample of behavior, the more accurately the stability of these measures will be estimated. Several statistical techniques are available for the analysis of this time series data including autocorrelation and ANOVAS with error terms that have taken the repeated nature of the data into account. The data from this type of study will not necessarily yield definitive information about trait versus state symptons since trait symptoms also vary in their manifestation. However, by understanding the stability of various symptoms, a more dynamic picture of schizophrenia can be obtained than with a single, static cross-sectional slice.

5. Manipulation of state. A related paradigm to the former is the utilization of methods expected to affect the state of the subject and perhaps to a lesser extent the trait symptoms. For example, in a series of studies Braginsky, Braginsky, and Ring (1969) found that the demand characteristics of the interview situation in which the patient was examined could dramatically alter the presence of thought disorder. In situations where the patient was threatened with discharge if they were not sick enough, they produced significantly higher thought disorder ratings than when they were told that the interview was for the purpose of determining suitability for increased ward privileges. Also, the effects of medications may be used to differentiate trait from state symptoms. Symptoms that change dramatically with antipsychotic medication are more likely to be state symptoms than those that are not affected. In both cases multiple measurements are needed.

These paradigms are by no means mutually exclusive and could be used conjunctively. Historically, however, the first two paradigms have been the most popular with the high-risk paradigm a distant third. Very few studies have been conducted examining the stability of various psychological deficits in schizophrenia. Experimental research has primarily been concerned with cognitive symptoms in the areas of memory, attention, performance, and perception. However, in few of these studies can the differentiation be made between trait- or state-related symptoms. In the remainder of this section some of these content areas will be examined in light of the above paradigms.

Attention.   Attention is a construct in psychology that has many different referents and probably can be said to be representative of several different psychological functions rather than a single entity. Not surprisingly, then, many seemingly unrelated experimental procedures have been used with schizophrenics all of which have been interpreted as measuring "attention." These procedures have been as disparate as dichotic listening, the continuous performance task and simple reaction time tasks in which the subject has to lift their finger off a key when a signal occurs, and even the ability to track the movements of a pendulum with smooth eye movements.

The procedure with perhaps the longest history in the study of schizophrenia is the simple reaction time procedure first applied to schizophrenics by Shakow and his students (Rodnick & Shakow, 1940). In this paradigm subjects see a ready signal (usually a light) that signals them to depress a key. A few seconds later an imperative signal occurs (usually a buzzer but sometimes another light) after which the subject must lift his finger off the key as quickly as possible. Preparatory intervals between 1 and 25 seconds are typically used. The time interval between the ready and the imperative signal may be repeated over many trials (regular series) or may be varied randomly (irregular series).

Normal subjects typically have shorter reaction times when the preparatory interval between signals is repeated in blocks. This is true except for very long preparatory intervals (PIs) where no difference is observed between regular and irregular series of PIs. Schizophrenic overall reaction time (RT) performance is considerably slower than that of normals whether long or short, regular or irregular PIs are used. However, the interesting finding is that the effect of regularity differs for schizophrenics. They also appear to respond faster with regular than irregular PIs but only when very short PIs are compared (often four seconds or less). With longer PIs, however, the schizophrenic performance with the regular PIs actually deteriorates until there is no difference between their regular and irregular PI performance. In fact, their performance may actually be worse with the regular PI than with the irregular PI. This effect has been called the reaction time cross-over effect. More recently, the deleterious effect of repetition itself has been amply demonstrated. Bellissimo and Steffy (1975) demonstrated that repeating an interval more than two times resulted in significant increases in RT for the schizophenics and a decrease for normals. There is evidence that this cross-over effect may represent a schizophrenic trait variable or a specific deficit using some of the paradigms described earlier. For example, by encouraging schizophrenic subjects to respond quickly, their RTs decrease to near normal levels. However, the cross-over effect remains. Also, this phenomenon has been observed in first-degree relatives of schizophenics.

Another measure that was originally developed to test attentional performance in schizophrenics as well as to provide a possible measure of a psysiological deficit is the eye tracking procedures used by Holtzman and his colleagues (Holtzman, Proctor, & Hughes, 1973; Holtzman, Proctor, & Levy, 1974; Holtzman et al., 1978; Latham et al., 1981). In these experiments subjects are presented with a swinging pendulum that they must track with eye movements. The facility with which they track the pendulum is measured with electrodes attached over the extraocular muscles. In normal subjects, after only a few swings, subjects are able to track the pendulum with smooth eye movements. This activity becomes rather automatic and thus is different from the rapid eye fixations (saccades) of normal reading. Schizophrenics break into saccadic eye movements, showing cogwheeling or a stop-and-start pattern and general shakiness when they must track a pendulum smoothly. This performance is improved considerably when the subject must read numbers written on the pendulum. This could, of course, represent a general rather than a specific deficit. Nonschizophrenic psychotic patients are also reported to have eye tracking difficulties. Interestingly, Holtzman et al. (1978) found that first-degree relatives of schizophrenics who were never themselves psychotic also show similar eye tracking abnormalities.

Both reaction time cross-over and eye tracking may represent schizophrenic trait variables. Unfortunately, a good account of the explanation for these phenomena has not been proposed.

Additional studies of attentional performance in schizophrenics have employed dichotic listening techniques (Wishner & Wall, 1974) and the visual span of apprehension technique (Neale, 1971). On both of these tasks schizophrenics perform more poorly than normals. However, in neither case has it been demonstrated that these deficits are specific to

schizophrenics or represent basic pathology. With both of these paradigms schizophrenics are found to be more vulnerable to distracting stimuli, whether auditory or visual, than are nonschizophrenics.

Memory. Many studies have reported that schizophrenics perform
more poorly on memory tasks than do normals. Lawson, McGhie, and
Chapman (1964), for example, reported that schizophrenics' performance
on a task requiring the learning of word strings that varied in the random-
ness of the sentential relationships between words was no different from
normals when random word strings were presented, but their performance
did not improve as much as normals when presented with ordered word
strings approximating English sentences. The authors suggest that this
is evidence that schizophrenics simply do not take advantage of redundancy in language as well as normals. An alternative explanation is that
their overall verbal memory is simply worse than normals (a general
deficit) which would be related to their general state of psychosis rather
than to their inability, in particular, to utilize redundancy. Further, it is
possible that the failure to utilize redundancy is merely correlated with
psychosis since the normals appear to show a ceiling effect. These studies
have not met any of the criteria set forth in the introduction to this section.

Bauman (1971) presented schizophrenics and normals with a consonant trigram (e.g., Arp, cuk) learning task. She tested both recall and
recognition. Some subjects were told that the list was organized alphabeti-
cally and this organizational cue could be used to facilitate recall. No
differences were found between subject groups on the recognition task,
but schizophrenics showed poorer recall than normals. The effect of cuing
helped improve the performance of normals on the recall task but did
not change the performance of the schizophrenics. These results were
interpreted as showing an inability to organize material on the part of
the schizophrenics.

Koh, Kayton, and Berry (1973) presented lists of nouns for recall composed of either unrelated nouns or lists with nouns within superordinate
semantic categories (e.g., furniture). Schizophrenic performance was
worse than normals or nonschizophrenic controls, particularly in the categorized list condition. Furthermore, they demonstrated much poorer organization of the stimulus list. The reason for this finding is unclear since
their performance is usually benefited by category cues for recall (Marusarz & Koh, 1980). Traupmann (1980) also recently demonstrated that
schizophrenics are sensitive to category information. Again there is the
possibility that failure to show category effects when tested in a free recall
situation (as opposed to memory probe procedures used in the Marusarz
and Traupmann study) may simply reflect the general level of pathology
rather than specific deficits of schizophrenics. Although schizophrenics
have been compared to other patient groups in these studies, none has
independently compared the subjects on clinical status or deterioration

from premorbid status in relation to these functions. These studies have also not met the other criteria set forth in the introduction.

The accuracy of recall for a rapidly presented visual pattern is reduced by the presentation of a visual noise mask if that mask is presented with a critical period of time (Tulving, 1972). There is some evidence that this critical time period during which the mask is effective is longer in schizophrenics (Saccuzzo & Miller, 1977). Subjects were presented with either a T or an A followed by a visual mask. The critical interval between stimulus and mask needed for accurate identification was longer for schizophrenics than for normals. This technique has also been used with the relatives of schizophrenics (Asarnow & MacCrimmon, 1981) with similar results for nonschizophrenic relatives. These results suggest that schizophrenics may have an information processing deficit prior to the categorical encoding of material needed for long-term storage. They also suggest that schizophrenic information processing may be slower than normal. The stability of these results over time and evidence of a relationship between these findings and clinical states have not been forthcoming.

Conclusions. The specification of the nature and reliability of attentional and memory deficits in schizophrenia is in its infancy. Few of the findings permit the separation of trait versus state and specific versus general deficits.

DEPRESSION

Over the past decade the number of studies devoted to the study of depression has expanded geometrically, largely due to a number of specific theories which have been proposed. Most of the research has been stimulated by three theoretical models of depression: those of Seligman (1972, 1975, 1978); Beck (1967, 1974, 1976) and Lewinsohn (1974). All of these models have a strong cognitive flavor, though Lewinsohn's is more in line with traditional reinforcement perspectives. Many authors have pointed out that these theories are either predated or contemporary with similar proposals put forth by others. Blaney (1977), for example, notes the general similarity between Seligman's model of depression and Bannister's theory of schizophrenia (1963), Schwartz's (1964) theory of paranoia, and Ullman and Krasner's (1969) theory of psychopathy. For whatever reason, however, these three models have influenced the field more than any others.

Seligman's learned helplessness model. Seligman's learned helplessness model (and its various reformulations) has been the most influential perspective on depression over the past decade. It has generated a tremendous volume of research and has had an impact not only on the research on depression but also on several related areas. It has been largely rejected by most researchers in the field and, more recently, even by its originator (Abramson, Seligman, & Teasdale, 1978) in its original formulation, and yet it continues to stimulate new studies. It seems obvious that its influence is, in part, a function of the general trend towards the rediscovery of cognitive processes which is influencing the entire field of psychology. However, as Huesmann has pointed out (1978), other theories utilized mediating processes without the same success. The influence must also be attributed to the specificity and subsequent testability of the learned helplessness model. In reflecting the trend of the field while at the same time operationalizing its premises, the model, by its very failure, has significantly advanced the area.

The original model was derived from analogue research in the laboratory using infrahuman species. In a series of experiments Seligman and his colleagues demonstrated that naive animals subjected to periods of stress during which their responses had no obvious contingent relationship to the stressful events would subsequently act "helpless" in other learning situations (i.e., Overmier & Seligman, 1967; Seligman & Maier, 1967; Seligman & Geer, 1968; Seligman et al., 1975). Seligman argued that the subjects had learned response outcome independence, "learned helplessness." A number of methodological attacks on these early studies appeared and were largely dealt with.

Seligman proposed that this animal model applied equally well to depressed persons, largely referring to those suffering from a reactive depression, though he did generalize his findings to a wide variety of pathological states. The generalization of the model was strengthened by the work of Hiroto (Hiroto, 1974; Hiroto & Seligman, 1975). In studies using parallel procedures to those employed in the animal studies, he first exposed subjects to inescapable noise and then tested their learned helplessness in a finger shuttle box and in an anagram-solving task. In the Hiroto and Seligman study it was also reported that depressed subjects who had not been placed in a helpless situation performed on the learning tasks in a manner similar to the learned helplessness subjects. Extensions of the animal model to human and clinical populations strengthened and extended its influence. One of the first reformulations of the model resulted from a study reported by Miller and Seligman (1973). They reported that depressed college students showed reduced expectancy for success for skilled tasks than for chance tasks than did nondepressed college students. Thus, the emphasis shifted from experimenter perceived noncontingency of response and reinforcement as defined in the animal studies to the attribution of different "perceptions" of noncontingency on the part of the subjects. These early studies also suggested that Rotter's conceptualization of locus of control might provide a supportive framework for the understanding of the nature of learned helplessness. (This had been suggested in the early studies of Hiroto, 1974, and Naditch, Gargan, and Michael, 1975.) Indeed, a number of studies reported a correlation between depression and perceived locus of control (e.g., Calhoun, Cheney, & Dawes, 1974), thought these reports have not gone without challenge (Lamont, 1972a, 1972b). Not only have a number of studies failed to find a correlation between helplessness and the attribution of external control, but depressed subjects appeared to make an accurate assessment of the degree of internal versus external control involved with any task.

A number of problems were noted in the literature, and researchers gradually became dissatisfied with the learned helplessness model. Abramson and Sackheim (1977) noted an essential paradox in the model (and also in Beck's model discussed later). They pointed out that uncontrollability and self-blame should not occur simultaneously. That is, if an individual is helpless because their behaviors are perceived to have no causal relationship to outcome, they should not feel compelled to blame themselves. In fact, the act of blaming themselves seems to argue against the universal feeling of helplessness. Peterson (1979) confirmed the correlation between self-blame and feelings of helplessness using self-report ratings. Blaney (1977) offered the alternative point of view that though control, feelings of control, and rates of reinforcement were clearly important in depression, not only for Seligman's theory but also for Lewinsohn's, none of them had been demonstrated to have a causal relationship with depressed state. He suggested that many of the results could just as easily be explained by the assumption that failure on the tasks led to low feelings of self-esteem (Coyne et al., 1980). In a later paper (Willis & Blaney, 1978), no support was found for the relationship between depression and the perception of control (see also Garber & Hollon, 1980).

The most recent reformulation of the theory identifies a number of inadequacies in the original model and attempts to remedy these with the addition of an attributional framework. The first inadequacy focuses on the failure of the learned helplessness model to distinguish between personal inability to influence the outcome of events and universal helplessness (the case in which no one can control the outcome). Abramson et al. (1978) contend that feelings of helplessness in the face of either of these perceptions result in either personal or universal helplessness, respectively. The authors argue that this modification results in a number of improvements in the original theory. It answers the deficiency noted above and permits a distinction to be made between the perception of uncontrollability and the perception of failure. And it suggests that a loss of self-esteem may result in conditions of perceived personal helplessness since this involves a comparison of self with others.

The original model also failed to specify the conditions under which an individual exposed to a helplessness situation would generalize their perceptions and respective helplessness to other situations. It failed to specify the parameters which would affect the chronicity of the helplessness condition. To answer these problems Abramson et al. (1978) proposed two additional dimensions of stability-instability and specificity-globality. First, they suggested that an individual, once making the judgment that certain outcomes are independent of their actions, attribute the cause of this condition to either a stable, relatively long-lasting cause or to an unstable, short-lived cause. They further suggest that the second dimension, specificity-globality, is necessary to completely specify the conditions under which an attribution of helplessness might remain chronic and/or generalized. On this dimension the individual makes a judgment as to whether the perceived causes of the noncontingent condition affect all behavior or only specified behaviors.

Thus, the revised model proposes that an individual first perceives that his behavior is unrelated to outcomes. The individual then attributes this condition to causes perceived to be characterized along the three dimensions (internal-external, stable-unstable, global-specific). Thus, if an individual fails at a task (for example, an examination) and that individual attributes the failure to his or her own innate stupidity, then the individual is making an internal, stable, and generally global attribution. This condition is difficult to change and pervasive in its effect on the individual's perception of control over outcomes. Attributing the failure to the flu, on the other hand (internal, global, but unstable), or to the instructor's failure to effectively communicate what the exam would cover (external, specific, probably unstable) should leave the individual with higher feelings of self-esteem and less helplessness.

In general, attributions of globality should result in helplessness across a wide range of situations. An attribution to a stable cause should result in feelings of helplessness over longer periods of time. Thus, broad transfer of learned helplessness occurs when individuals attribute their failures to causes which are perceived as stable and global.

The modifications of the learned helplessness model have so altered the original model that it can be considered as an entirely new model. The attributional model is more flexible. It permits a wider range of factors to affect the predictions possible with the model. Individual differences in attributional tendencies are now more critical. The entire body of research on attribution theory now bears upon the prediction of what will be made by an individual in a learned helplessness situation (Harvey, 1981). Some general correlations will be relevant. For example, Abramson et al. point out that research on attribution theory indicates that females are more likely to attribute failure to lack of ability (global and stable) and males to lack of effort (specific and unstable) (Dweck, Goetz, & Strauss, 1977) and that this corresponds to the greater proportion of reported depression in females. But if this model proves viable, the factors contributing to the development of individual styles of attributional behavior become critical.

Further, the revised model permits the continual addition of new attributional dimensions. For example, Wortman and Dintzer (1978) propose

that the dimensions of "controllability" and "foreseeability" may be relevant to depression. Each proposed dimension can be examined empirically to determine its relevance to depression.

A large number of studies have pursued the implications of the attributional model, and it is only possible to sample representative studies
here. Gong-Guy and Hammen (1980) found that though people described their most upsetting personal events as internal, intended, global,
expected, and stable, they found no differences between depressed and
nondepressed persons. Hammen and Cochran (1981) also found no differences between depressed and nondepressed persons in terms of attributions but did find that depressed people reported more upset and
uncertainty in their lives. This, of course, is not specific enough to support
the revised model. Miller and Norman (1981), using clinically depressed
patients, assigned subjects to acute or chronic groups and subjected
them to a task identified as reflecting "social intelligence" but with either
internal or external attributions supplied by the experimenter. They were
then given an anagram task. The recovered group was subjected to a
learned helplessness condition. Both the helplessness and depressed subjects who received internal attributions expressed less depression than
did those receiving external attributions.

Golin, Sweeney, & Shaeffer (1981) tested Beck depression scores and
attributions in 206 college students at two times separated by one month.
Internality, stability, and globality were correlated with depression. Testing
the causal role using cross-lag analysis indicated that stable and global
attributions for bad outcomes might be the cause of depression. Internal
attributions were not related to subsequent occurrence of depression.
But, unexpectedly, unstable attributions for good outcomes did correlate
with later depression. This study represents the type of studies, with both
normal and clinical populations—and over longer periods of time—which
must be conducted in order to trace the causal relationships implied
by Seligman's, Beck's, and Lewinsohn's models of depression.

Beck (1967, 1974), drawing upon clinical observations and a comprehensive consideration of the literature on depression, proposed that cognitive distortions, negative in direction, were critical to the development
of depression. Though recognizing the importance of negative life experiences in the occurrence of depression, Beck argued that it was the perception of the events that was critical to the occurrence of depression and
that the affective component was a concomitant of the thinking of the
depressed individual. Beck developed a symptom list (1967) originally
using 50 depressed and 30 nondepressed patients in psychotherapy,
and then developed the inventory further with a larger sample of
966 psychiatric patients. His inventory supported the observation that
depressed persons expressed negative self-evaluations and expectations.

A number of studies have substantiated the occurrence of these negative perceptions in depression (Hammen & Krantz, 1976; Hammen & Podesky, 1977; Laxer, 1964a, 1964b; Derry & Kuiper, 1981). Krantz and Hammen (1979) presented subjects with stories and then a question-naire about the stories and found a consistent relationship between high depression scores and negative cognitive distortions. The high scorers on cognitive distortion were also more likely to be depressed eight weeks later.

Lewinsohn's model of depression proposes that depression results from an interaction between few reward-producing responses on the part of the individual and unavailability of reinforcing events in the environment. In general, the model argues that individuals who are depressed do not interact with the environment in a manner which produces a sufficient density of rewards. This may occur after the death of a loved one or because depressed people do not have the prerequisite social skills neces-sary to interact effectively with the environment. The majority of the sup-portive studies have been correlational in nature (as is true of Beck's model and somewhat less true of Seligman's). In general, Lewinsohn and his co-workers reported a correlation between the participation of individuals in pleasant events and their level of depression (Lewisohn & Amenson, 1978). As has been pointed out (Blaney, 1977), however, this is a highly predictable finding. It would certainly be more surprising to find the opposite relationship.

One answer to this objection is longitudinal studies in which the time course of reward-producing activities and depression could be uncov-ered. A number of studies (Lewinsohn & Libet, 1972; Lewinsohn & Graf, 1973) have failed to strongly support the Lewinsohn model. A number of studies have also examined the relationship between increasing the reward-producing activities of depressed individuals, since Lewinsohn's theory predicts therapeutic effects resulting from this manipulation. These studies, too, have been largely nonsupportive.

Lewinsohn has responded to these studies by broadening his research focus. His research has been redirected toward the relationship between social skills and depression. A number of studies have reported that de-pressed individuals as a group manifest poor social skills. Indeed, Lewin-sohn et al. (1981; Amenson & Lewinsohn, 1981) have proposed that deficits in social skills are antecedent conditions for depression.

Effort has also been directed towards the examination of the relationship between depression-related cognitions. In general, depressed patients are reported to show less expectation of success and to reward themselves less than do others. Though these studies have typically used self-report indices of social effectiveness, others also rate them as less socially effec-tive. However, these correlations are again not causally tied to the devel-opment of depression.

In general, the cognitive models of depression, by relying primarily on correlational studies, may have provided a more adequate description of the cognitive manifestations of depression without providing convincing evidence of any causal relationships. Each theory is only generally supported by the research, and a significant body of negative or contradictory findings exist. The revised attributional theory of Seligman remains more specific and predictive than the others, but it, too, suffers from the same chicken-and-egg problem. Future research will undoubtedly concentrate on longitudinal studies and the experimental manipulation of mood, reinforcement rates, etc., in order to tease out the time course of the cognitive features of depression.

A second major problem with the main models of depression discussed here is the general lack of concern for possible qualitative differences in depressives and how these different "types" might relate to the various models. Though early objections to some of the research focused on the generalization of findings from depressed college students to clinically depressed populations, Depue and Monroe and their colleagues (Depue & Monroe, 1978a, 1978b: Depue et al., 1981) have focused on the heterogeneity of depressives within clinical populations. Their research has focused on the development of an inventory, the General Behavior Inventory, designed to discriminate individuals at risk for bipolar depression. This approach, consistent with the tendency to use behavioral indicators of high risk that is now popular in schizophrenia research, represents the other trend in psychopathology research. A meeting of these two areas in the identification of the particular cognitive styles of persons at risk for depression is likely in the future.

SUMMARY

Two areas of research interest, schizophrenia and depression, are identified as predominant in the current clinical literature. The development of the concept of psychological deficit is outlined, and the emergence of the more complex concept of vulnerability is traced in the current literature. The major experimental paradigms used in schizophrenia research are described, and the advantages and disadvantages of each are indicated. Three major theories of depression, those of Seligman, Beck, and Lewinsohn, provide the framework for the majority of the current research on depression. The development of these theories, the issues surrounding them, and the current research directions are indicated.

REFERENCES

Abramson, L. Y., Garber, J., Edwards, N. B., & Seligman, M. E. P. Expectancy changes in depression and schizophrenia. *Journal of Abnormal Psychology*, 1978, *87*(1), 102–109.

Abramson, L. Y., & Sackheim, H. A. A paradox in depression: Uncontrollability and self-blame. *Psychological Bulletin*, 1977, *84*(5), 838–851.

Abramson, L. Y., Seligman, M. E. P., & Teasdale, J. D. Learned helplessness in humans: Critique and reformulation. *Journal of Abnormal Psychology*, 1978, *87*(1), 49–74.

Amenson, C. S., & Lewinsohn, P. M. An investigation into the observed sex difference in prevalence of unipolar depression. *Journal of Abnormal Psychology*, 1981, *90*(1), 1–13.

Asarnow, R. F., & MacCrimmon, D. J. Residual performance deficit in clinically remitted schizophrenics: A marker of schizophrenia? *Journal of Abnormal Psychology*, 1978, *87*(6), 597–608.

Asarnow, R. F., & MacCrimmon, D. J. Span of apprehension deficits during postpsychotic stages of schizophrenia. *Archives of General Psychiatry*, 1981, *38*, 1006–1009.

Bannister, D. The genesis of schizophrenic thought disorder: A serial invalidation hypothesis. *British Journal of Psychiatry*, 1963, *109*, 680–686.

Bauman, E. Schizophrenic short-term memory: A deficit in subjective organization. *Canadian Journal of Behavioral Science*, 1971, *3*, 55–68.

Beck, A. T. *Depression: Clinical, experimental and theoretical aspects.* New York: Hoeber, 1967.

Beck, A. T. The development of depression: A cognitive model. In P. J. Freidman & M. M. Katy (Eds.), *The psychology of depression.* Washington, D.C.: Winston, 1974.

Beck, A. T. *Cognitive therapy and emotional disorders.* New York: International Universities Press, 1976.

Bellissimo, A., & Steffy, R. A. Contextual influences on crossover in the reaction time performance of schizophrenics. *Journal of Abnormal Psychology*, 1975, *84*, 210–220.

Blaney, P. H. Contemporary theories of depression: Critique and comparison. *Journal of Abnormal Psychology*, 1977, *86*(3), 203–223.

Bleuler, E. [*Dementia praecox or the group of the schizophrenias*] (J. Zinkin, trans.). New York: International Universities Press, 1950. (Originally published, 1911.)

Braginsky, B., Braginsky, D., & Ring, K. *Methods of madness: The mental hospital as a last resort.* Holt, Rinehart & Winston: New York, 1969.

Calhoun, L. G., Cheney, T., & Dawes, A. S. Locus of control, Self-reported depression and perceived causes of depression. *Journal of Consulting and Clinical Psychology*, 1974, *42*, 736–741.

Chapman, L. J., & Chapman, J. P. *Disordered thought in schizophrenia.* New York: Appleton-Century-Crofts, 1973.

Coyne, J. C., Metalsky, G. I., & Lavelle, T. L. Learned helplessness as experimenter-induced failure and its alleviation with attentional redeployment. *Journal of Abnormal Psychology*, 1980, *89*(3), 350–357.

Depue, R. A., & Monroe, S. M. Learned helplessness in the perspective of the depressive disorders: Conceptual and definitional issues. *Journal of Abnormal Psychology*, 1978, *87*(1), 3–20. (a)

Depue, R. A., & Monroe, S. M. The unipolar-bipolar distinction in the depressive disorders. *Psychological Bulletin*, 1978, *85*(5), 1001–1029. (b)

Depue, R., Slater, J., Woldstetter-Kausch, H., Klein, D., Goplerud, E., & Farr, D. A. Behavioral paradigm for identifying persons at risk for bipolar depressive disorder: A conceptual framework and five validation studies. *Journal of Abnormal Psychology*, 1981, *90*(5), 381–437.

Derry, P. A., & Kuiper, N. A., Schematic processing and self-reference in clinical depression. *Journal of Abnormal Psychology*, 1981, *90*(4), 286–297.

Dweck, C. S., Goetz, T., & Strauss, N. *Sex differences in learned helplessness.* Unpublished manuscript, University of Illinois, 1977.

Garber, J., & Hollon, S. Universal versus personal helplessness in depression: Belief in uncontrollability or incompetence. *Journal of Abnormal Psychology,* 1980, *89*(1), 56–66.

Golin, S., Sweeney, P. D., & Shaeffer, D. E. The casuality of causal attributions in depression: A cross-lagged panel correlational analysis. *Journal of Abnormal Psychology,* 1981, *90*(1), 14–22.

Gong-Guy, E. & Hammen, C. Causal perception of stressful events in depressed and nondepressed outpatients. *Journal of Abnormal Psychology,* 1980, *89*(5), 662–669.

Gotlieb, I. H. Self-reinforcement and recall: Differential deficits in depressed and nondepressed psychiatric inpatients. *Journal of Abnormal Psychology,* 1981, *90*(6), 521–530.

Hammen, C. L., & Cochran, S. D. Cognitive correlates of life stress and depression in college students. *Journal of Abnormal Psychology,* 1981, *90*(1), 23–27.

Hammen, C. L., & Krantz, S. Effect of success and failure on depressive cognitions. *Journal of Abnormal Psychology,* 1976, *85*(6), 577–586.

Hammen, C. L., & Podesky, C. A. Sex differences in the expression of depressive responses on the Beck Depression Inventory. *Journal of Abnormal Psychology,* 1977, *86*(6), 609–614.

Harvey, D. M. Depression and attributional style: Interpretations of important personal events. *Journal of Abnormal Psychology,* 1981, *90*(2), 134–142.

Hiroto, D. S. Locus of control and learned helplessness. *Journal of Abnormal Psychology,* 1974, *102,* 187–193.

Hiroto, D. S., & Seligman, M. E. P. Generality of learned helplessness in man. *Journal of Personality and Social Psychology,* 1975, *31,* 311–327.

Holtzman, P. S., Kringlen, E., Levy, D., & Haberman, S. Smooth pursuit eye movements in twins discordant for schizophrenia. In L. C. Wynne, R. Cromwell, & S. Matthysse (Eds.), *The nature of schizophrenia.* New York: John Wiley & Sons, 1978.

Holtzman, P. S., Levy, D. L., & Proctor, L. R. The several qualities of attention in schizophrenia. In L. C. Wynne, R. Cromwell, & S. Matthysse (Eds.), *The nature of schizophrenia.* New York: John Wiley & Sons, 1978, pp. 295–306.

Holtzman, P. S., Proctor, R. L., & Hughes, D. W. Eye tracking patterns in schizophrenia. *Science,* 1973, *181,* 179–181.

Holtzman, P. S., Proctor, L. R., & Levy, D. L. Eye tracking dysfunction in schizophrenia patients and their relatives. *Archives of General Psychiatry,* 1974, *31,* 143–151.

Huesmann, L. Cognitive processes and models of depression. *Journal of Abnormal Psychology,* 1978, *87*(1), 194–198.

Koh, S. D., Kayton, L. & Berry, R. Mnemonic organization in young nonpsychotic schizophrenics. *Journal of Abnormal Psychology,* 1973, *81*(3), 299–310.

Kraepelin, E. *Dementia praecox and paraphrenia.* Edinburgh: Livingston, 1896.

Krantz, S. & Hammen, C. Assessment of cognitive bias in depression. *Journal of Abnormal Psychology,* 1979, *88*(6), 611–619.

Lamont, J. Depression, locus of control, and mood response set. *Journal of Clinical and Consulting Psychology,* 1972, *28,* 342–345. (a)

Lamont, J. Item mood-level as a determinant of I-E test responses. *Journal of Clinical Psychology*, 1972, *28*, 190. (b)

Latham, C., Holtzman, P.S., Manschreck, T., & Tole, J. Optokinetic nystagmus and pursuit eye movements in schizophrenia. *Archives of General Psychiatry*, 1981, *318*, 997–1003.

Lawson, J., McGhie, A., & Chapman, L. Perception of speech in schizophrenia. *British Journal of Psychiatry*, 1964, *110*, 375–380.

Laxer, R. M. Relation of real self-rating to mood and blame and their interaction in depression. *Journal of Consulting and Clinical Psychology*, 1964, *28*, 538–546. (a)

Laxer, R. M. Self-concept changes of depressive patients in general hospital treatment. *Journal of Canadian Psychology*, 1964, *28*, 214–219. (b)

Lewinsohn, P. M. A behavioral approach to depression. In R. J. Friedman & M. M. Katz (Eds.), *The psychology of depression*. Washington, D.C.: Winston, 1974.

Lewinsohn, P. M., & Amenson, C. S. Some relations between pleasant and unpleasant mood-related events and depression. *Journal of Abnormal Psychology*, 1978, *87*(6), 644–654.

Lewinsohn, P. M., & Graf, M. Pleasant activities, activity schedules, and depression. *Journal of Abnormal Psychology*, 1973, *41*, 261–268.

Lewinsohn, P. H., & Libet, J. M. Pleasant events, activity schedules and depression. *Journal of Abnormal Psychology*, 1972, *79*, 291–295.

Lewinsohn, P. M., Mischel, W., Chaplin, W., & Barton, R. Social competence and depression: The role of illusory correlation. *Journal of Abnormal Psychology*, 1981, *89*(2), 203–212.

Lewinsohn, P. M., Steinmetz, J. L., Larson, D. W., & Franklin, J. Depression-related cognitions: Antecedents or consequence? *Journal of Abnormal Psychology*, 1981, *90*(3), 213–219.

Lobitz, W. & Post, R. D. Parameters of self-reinforcement and depression. *Journal of Abnormal Psychology*, 1979, *88*(1), 33–41.

Manschreck, T. C. Schizophrenic disorders. *New England Journal of Medicine*, 1981, *305*, 1628–1630.

Marusarz, T. Z., & Koh, S. D. Contextual effects on the short-term retrieval of schizophrenic young adults. *Journal of Abnormal Psychology*, 1980, *89*(6), 6, 683–696.

Meehl, P. E. Schizotaxia, schizotypy, and schizophrenia. *American Psychologist*, 1962, *17*, 827–838.

Miller, I. W., & Norman, W. H. Effects of attributions for success on the alleviation of learned helplessness and depression. *Journal of Abnormal Psychology*, 1981, *90*(2), 113–114.

Miller, W. R., & Seligman, M. E. P. Depression and the perception of reinforcement. *Journal of Abnormal Psychology*, 1973, *82*, 62–73.

Naditch, M. P., Gargan, M. A., & Michael, L. Denial, anxiety, locus of control, and the discrepancy between aspiration and achievements as components of depression. *Journal of Abnormal Depression*, 1975, *84*, 1–9.

Neale, J. M. Perceptial span in schizophrenics. *Journal of Abnormal Psychology*, 1971, *77*, 196–204.

Overmeir, J. B., & Seligman, M. E. P. Effects of inescapable shock upon escape and avoidance learning. *Journal of Comparative and Physiological Psychology*, 1967, *63*, 28–33.

Peterson, C. Uncontrollability and self-blame in depression: Investigation of the paradox in a college population. *Journal of Abnormal Psychology,* 1979, *88*(6), 6, 620–624.

Rodnick, E., & Shakow, D. Set in the Schizophrenia as measured by a composite reaction time index. *American Journal of Psychiatry,* 1940, *97,* 214–225.

Rosenbaum, G. Feedback mechanisms in schizophrenia. In E. R. Luby & J. Gottlieb (Eds.), *The Lafayette Clinic studies in schizophrenia.* Detroit: Wayne State University Press, 1971.

Saccuzzo, D., & Miller, S. Critical interstimulus interval in delusional schizophrenics and normals. *Journal of Abnormal Psychology,* 1977, *86*(3), 261–266.

Schwartz, D. A. The paranoid-depressive existential continuum. *Psychiatric Quarterly,* 1964, *38,* 690–706.

Seligman, M. E. P. Learned helplessness. *Annual Review of Medicine,* 1972, *23,* 407–412.

Seligman, M. E. P. *Helplessness: On depression, development and death.* San Francisco: W. H. Freeman, 1975.

Seligman, M. E. P. Comment and integration. *Journal of Abnormal Psychology,* 1978, *87*(1), 165–179.

Seligman, M. E. P., Abramson, L. Y., Semmel, A., & Baeyer, C. Depressive attribution style. *Journal of Abnormal Psychology,* 1979, *88*(3), 242–247.

Seligman, M. E. P., & Beagler, G. Learned helplessness in the rat. *Journal of Comparative and Physiological Psychology,* 1975, *88,* 534–541.

Seligman, M. E. P., & Geer, J. The alleviation of learned helplessness in the dog. *Journal of Abnormal and Social Psychology,* 1968, *73,* 256–262.

Seligman, M. E. P., & Maier, S. F. Failure to escape traumatic shock. *Journal of Experimental Psychology,* 1967, *74*(1), 1–9.

Seligman, M. E. P., Rossellini, R., & Kozak, M. Learned helplessness in the rat: Reversibility, time course, and immunization. *Journal of Comparative and Physiological Psychology.* 1975, *88,* 542–547.

Spring, B. & Zubin, J. Reaction time and attention in schizophrenia. *Psychological Bulletin.* 1977, *3*(3), 437–444.

Spring, B. & Zubin, J. Attention and information processing as indicators of vulnerability to schizophrenic episodes. In L. C. Wynne, R. Cromwell, & S. Matthysse (Eds.), *The nature of schizophrenia.* New York: John Wiley & Sons, 1978, pp. 366–375.

Townsend, J. T. A note on the identifiability of parallel and serial processes. *Perception and Psychophysics,* 1971, 163.

Traupmann, K. L. Encoding processes and memory for categorically related words by schizophrenic patients. *Journal of Abnormal Psychology,* 1980, *89*(6), 704–716.

Tulving, E. Episodic memory. In E. Tulving, & W. Donaldson (Eds.), *The organization of memory.* New York: Academic Press, 1972.

Ullman, L. P., & Krasner, L. *A psychological approach to abnormal behavior.* Engelwood Cliffs, N.J.: Prentice-Hall, 1969.

Willis, M. H., & Blaney, P. Three tests of the learned helplessness model of depression. *Journal of Abnormal Psychology,* 1978, *87*(1), 131–136.

Wishner, J., & Wahl, O. Dichotic listening in schizophrenia. *Journal of Consulting and Clinical Psychology,* 1974, *42,* 538–546.

Wortman, C., & Dintzer, L. Is an attributional analysis of the learned helplessness phenomenon viable? A critique of the Abramson-Seligman-Teasdale reformulation. *Journal of
Abnormal Psychology,* 1978, *87*(1), 75–90.

Youngren, M., & Lewinsohn, P. The functional relation between depression and problematic
interpersonal behavior. *Journal of Abnormal Psychology,* 1980, *89*(3), 333–341.

4

Problems in statistics and experimental design in clinical psychopathology

Solomon C. Goldberg, Ph.D.*
and
Robert M. Hamer, Ph.D.†

PREFACE

In the limited space of this chapter, it is impossible to present materials at the same level of detail that appears in textbooks and reference works. We assume that the reader has already had at least one course covering a wide variety of statistical techniques. The orientation of this chapter will be on special problems that arise in statistics and experimental design as applied to issues and problems of clinical research. Statistics have generally been devised in the attempt to address specific scientific problems, and clinical research is no exception. Hence, our orientation will always be one of determining the most appropriate statistic for any particular question.

CLINICAL SCIENCE AND RELATIONSHIPS AMONG VARIABLES

The behavioral and clinical sciences set as their task the establishment of lawful relationships among two or more variables. To go a step further, when possible, we as clinical researchers are interested in the causes of clinical phenomena. Why do some people hallucinate and others not? Can psychotherapy reduce hallucinations? The only way to establish

* Professor and Director of Research, Department of Psychiatry, Medical College of Virginia, Virginia Commonwealth University, Richmond.

† Assistant Professor and Chief of the Section on Data Analysis, Department of Psychiatry, Medical College of Virginia, Virginia Commonwealth University, Richmond.

cause with any certainty is to place one of the putatively causative variables under experimental control. Thus, if the patient's level on the causative variable can be manipulated by the experimenter, and there are
differences in outcome as a result of having different levels of the causative
agent, we can say with some certainty that the manipulated variable was
the cause of the outcome. One good example is in a study of the effectiveness of cognitive therapy on depression. Experimental control of the puta-
tive cause is achieved by assigning depressed patients consecutively
and randomly to receive cognitive therapy or not. If there are differences
between the two groups in reduction of depression favoring cognitive
therapy, we may say with some certainty that the difference in outcome
was produced by or caused by our experimental manipulation (the cognitive therapy). Consider, however, another study of a group of depressed
patients, wherein some of them happened to receive cognitive therapy
while others did not, but there was no random assignment to treatment.
Instead, the therapy received by the patient was the clinician's choice
according to what he felt was most appropriate. Any difference in outcome
between cognitive therapy and its absence in this study could not really
be said to be caused by the cognitive therapy because there might well
have been the opportunity for patients with naturally better prognoses
to have been assigned to the cognitive therapy. Hence, differences in
outcome could be because of better prognoses in the group rather than
because of the therapy, although it is probably a confounding of both.
This latter kind of study shows a relationship between two variables (cognitive therapy and outcome) but because the causative variable was not
under experimental control by the investigator, causation can never be
ascribed. There are those in the world of behavioral science who have
come to believe that, therefore, the only credible studies are experimental
and that correlational studies, which only observe but do not manipulate
any of the variables, are of no value. Sometimes it is impractical to use
experimental methods because actual manipulation of the relevant variable may be impossible (e.g., sex), impractical (wealth), immoral (giving
someone the experience of being raped), or illegal (withholding needed
treatment). In such a situation, we must do the best we can with correlational studies. The position of this chapter is that correlational studies
must make more limited and more tentative statements but have definite
value. The reader should keep in mind a number of other nonexperimental
sciences that the world is not yet prepared to discard, such as astronomy,
geology, and meteorology. Because of different analytic techniques involved, the chapter is divided, perhaps unevenly, into experimental and
nonexperimental studies.

EXPRESSIONS OF RELATIONSHIPS

Relationships between variables can be expressed by a number of
statistical indices. The appropriateness of each depends on the nature

of the variable. Generally, we may classify the data a researcher collects into one of a number of types. Usually, data scales are described as being nominal, ordinal, interval, or ratio; quantitative scales indicating amounts are either continuous or discrete.

Nominal data (also called *qualitative* or *categorical*) are classification data. An example of nominal data is psychiatric classification (i.e., the labeling of patients as schizophrenics, affective disorders, substance abusers, etc.). Sex (male or female) and marital status (single or married) are also nominal data. Being male is neither more nor less than being female. Being single is neither more nor less than being married.

Ordinal data are ranks. For ordinal data, we know the order in which we can arrange the observations on the attribute or variable and can say that one rank is more than another but not how much more. Data in which someone is asked to rate a subject or stimulus on a 1-to-5 scale, or on a 1-to-7 scale, are ordinal. Sometimes we behave as if they were interval, but in reality they are ordinal.

Interval-level data are those in which we know not only the order of the data, but that the difference between adjacent scale points are equal regardless of position on the scale, but there is no true zero. An example of interval-level data is temperature, in which the difference between 96 and 98 is the same as the difference between 98 and 100, but 0 degrees Fahrenheit does not mean the absence of heat.

Ratio data are very much like interval data but, in addition, have a useful zero point. Blood levels of a drug or the number of abnormal behaviors exhibited are ratio-level data because zero means absolute absence.

Quantitative data may also be continuous or discrete. Continuous data do not fall into natural categories, while discrete data do. If, for example, we collected data on the number of psychotic breaks a patient had, we would have discrete data. A patient cannot have 4.6 psychotic breaks; he or she would have either 4 or 5. On the other hand, a person can have a lithium level of .77. If we were able to measure more precisely, it might be .776 or .7752, but there are no numerical categories into which blood lithium levels must fall.

Finally, data may have statistical distributions. Some variables are normally distributed, some according to other distributions. Most classic parametric statistical techniques require data that are interval or ratio level and normally distributed. In practice, we have found that the parametric techniques work reasonably well when the variable has at least 5 or 7 discrete points (which can be roughly equally ordered) and approximates a bell-shaped curve. In practice, violations of these conditions frequently result in loss of power in the statistic and sometimes in an overstatement of significance. For instance, a significant product-moment correlation can be obtained on the basis of a few fortuitously placed outliers; a nonparametric rank correlation on the same data would produce a near-zero correlation. Does this argue for exclusive use of nonparametric methods to be on the safe side? Not necessarily. Parametric methods are desired for their greater power but should be disregarded only in those few instances in which the nonparametric methods produce *markedly* different results. In behavioral variables, ratio and interval scales are rare. Countable behaviors (e.g., the number of times the patient hallucinated during the day) provides a zero point and equal intervals between each discrete point. However, the frequency distribution of this symptom in a sample of patients is far from bell-shaped.

Ratings of hallucinations, as opposed to an actual count, provide a zero point, but we are less certain of having equal intervals between scale points. At the same time, the quality of the data seems to be somewhere between a rank order and an interval scale. The requirement of normality poses more of a problem, as in many variables there is a pileup at the zero point. Data transformations may do little to normalize such a distribution. One practical solution might be to do both parametric and nonparametric analyses on the most nonnormally distributed variables. If the results are not markedly different, accept the parametric analysis because of its greater power. If markedly different, accept the nonparametric solution.

To most readers, it is intuitively plausible to find a relationship, for example, between social class and community adjustment. The expression of a relationship will most likely be in terms of the Pearson product-moment correlation coefficient. It is not so clear that we are dealing with a relationship when we ask about sex differences and differences in marital status with regard to community adjustment. If we were to find that females had better community adjustment or that married individuals had better community adjustment, we would be able to say, in the generic sense, that we have found a relationship between sex and community adjustment or marital status and community adjustment. The same would apply to categorical variables with a greater number of categories, such as clinical diagnosis, which might very well contain a half-dozen or more categories. If a one-way analysis of variance showed differences among the diagnoses with respect to community adjustment, we may think of this result as the expression of a relationship between a categorical variable (diagnosis) and a quantitative variable (community adjustment). Relationship does not necessarily mean correlation coefficient, although in many cases the result is expressed as a correlation coefficient. In finding sex differences in community adjustment, although many investigators might analyze these data by means of a *t*-test between the two means, that same relationship could be expressed by a point biserial correlation, in which case we would know not only the significance of the relationship but its strength as well. Even the differences in community adjustment among five clinical diagnoses can be translated into an expression of strength of relationship. Both significance and strength of relationship, in terms of variance accounted for, need to be reported. We might also have other questions

Table 1

Appropriate expressions of relationship between types of variables

	1	2	3
1. Interval scale (e.g., age)	Pearson correlation; intraclass correlation		
2. Rank order scale (e.g., sociometric choice)	Rank correlation or Pearson correlation	Rank correlation	
3. Two categories (e.g., sex)	t-test of means; point biserial correlation	Mann-Whitney U-test; point biserial correlation	Chi-square; phi coefficient; kappa

concerning sex differences in marital status or sex differences in clinical diagnoses, which are all to be interpreted generically as relationships between two categorical variables. Table 1 presents a rough outline of the kinds of statistics appropriate in expressing the relationship between any two kinds of variables.

When assessing the association between two nominal-level or categorical variables, a chi-square is often the measure used (Hays, 1963, p. 336). This measure tests the hypothesis that the distribution of responses among the categories of one variable (e.g., diagnosis versus blood type) is independent of the distribution of responses among the categories of the other variable. This test is only an approximation, and with less than five responses per cell, the approximation is not very good. It is also not very good for the special cases where each of the two variables has only two categories; there are a variety of controversial correlations which have been proposed for the two-by-two situation, but what is known as *Yate's correction* is usually performed. Chi-square can be expressed as a phi coefficient to indicate correlational value.

If one is trying to assess the extent to which two rank order (ordinal) variables are related to each other (e.g., ranked severity of illness in the ward versus relative production in occupational therapy), some type of rank order correlation is often appropriate. The most common rank order correlation is Spearman's rank order correlation, whose distribution is well known. There are other rank order correlations (namely, tau, due to Kendell), but these are not widely used.

For two variables measured at the interval or ratio level (or close approximations), an appropriate measure is the Pearson product-moment correlation coefficient (Hayes, 1963, p. 490), hereafter called the *correlation coefficient*. Because correlation is popular and useful, it has been studied at length.

A linear relationship, which the correlation measures, is of the form $y = ax + b$, where y is one variable, x is the other variable, and a and b are constants. The equation says that one variable is a multiple of another, plus an additive constant. Of course, not all relationships are linear. However, even if a relationship is nonlinear, a linear formula may be useful in approximating it, because over some range the relationship may be close to linear. An analogy is that the surface of the earth appears flat, even though it is curved, because the earth is so large that in any local area, the difference between flat and curved is small.

The range of the correlation coefficient is between -1 and 1, inclusive. A correlation of -1 indicates large scores on one variable associated with small scores on the other, and vice versa. A correlation of 0 indicates there is no particular association between high or low scores on the two variables, and a correlation of $+1$ indicates high scores on one variable associated with high scores on the other.

In most psychological situations, correlations rarely rise above .60 or .70 in absolute value. Thus, a correlation of .60 or .70 should be considered substantial, useful, and interesting. However, when assessing reliability, often higher correlations are required. Interrater reliabilities and test-retest reliabilities often are in the .80 or .90 range. Except for reliabilities, one might be suspicious when finding overly high correlations.

Reliability

Suppose that two psychologists were interested in the extent to which they agreed on the diagnoses of incoming patients. Their diagnoses would be confined to one of the five types of schizophrenic disorders: (a) disorganized, (b) catatonic, (c) paranoid, (d) undifferentiated, and (e) residual. Thus, each diagnostician will attach one of five labels to a patient.

One way to arrange the data is in a two-way table, where the numbers in the i, ith cell represent the number of cases judged to be type 1 by both raters and the numbers in the i, jth cell represent the number of patients judged to be type i by rater 1, and type j by rater 2. When one sees a table like this, chi-square immediately suggests itself as a means of measuring reliability or agreement. Unfortunately, chi-square is not a good measure of agreement because it measures independence, which is vastly different than agreement.

A product-moment correlation might be a candidate if the data were quantitative (interval or ratio level) or a rank-order correlation if the data were ordinal, but the data in this case are nominal. An intraclass correlation, too, requires that the data be quantitative.

The correct index of agreement for this situation is called kappa (Cohen, 1960) and is a measure of percent agreement, corrected for chance agreement, and scaled to fall between 0 (no agreement) and 1 (perfect agreement). The sampling distribution of kappa has been worked out so that statistical tests of significance can be performed.

Suppose that the two psychologists were not making diagnostic judgments but, having already decided that the patient was a schizophrenic disorder, paranoid type, were judging the ranked severity of the disorder. In this case, the result is of ordinal level, and a modification of kappa called *weighted kappa* is appropriate (Cohen, 1968). Weighted kappa not only measures agreement but also addresses the issue that some disagreements may be worse than others. A rank order correlation is not acceptable because it is invariant to changes in scale. If two raters rated patients on a 1-to-7 scale, and one only used points 1, 2, and 3, while the other only used points 5, 6, and 7, it would be possible to still have a perfect rank correlation.

Finally, suppose that the data are two psychologist's scores of each patient on a scale such as the Hamilton Depression Scale. In this case, the data are more than ranked although not strictly interval. In this case, a product-moment correlation might be appropriate, but because the product-moment correlation is invariant with respect to additive or multiplicative transformation, one set of scores can be very different than the others and still produce a high correlation as long as the pattern is the same. A measure sensitive to not only the pattern but also to the actual levels of the responses is the intraclass correlation (Winer, 1971, p. 124), and this should be used for measuring agreement on quantative data.

RESEARCH QUESTIONS

In forming clinical research questions or hypotheses, we are not asking about an individual case. We are not asking whether this patient will ultimately show a good or bad community adjustment. While this is a question of sorts, the research question inquires about a relationship between at least two series of observations. Whether the inquiry is stated in terms of a research question or of a research hypothesis is immaterial and often a matter of taste. We could say, for example, that our research question asks whether there are sex differences in community adjustment or that our research hypothesis is that there are sex differences in community adjustment. In either of them, a relationship between at least two variables is being posited.

More than any other aspect of research, it is probably most important to ask the right question. Asking the right question comes from being aware of the major issues in a field and knowing the kinds of results different analyses can yield. Many clinical questions revolve around the perennial one of how the varieties of psychopathology come to be; that is, what caused them, and what events, controlled and uncontrolled, have a bearing on (are related to) their course over time?

Types of research questions and the strategies to answer them

The framing of the research question is possibly the most important aspect of the research enterprise. All of our measures, procedures, selection of subjects, designs, and data analysis must be appropriate to the research question being posed. At the risk of some oversimplification, we shall classify research questions into those which ask (a) about the etiology of psychopathology (e.g., what are the conditions that produce schizophrenia?), (b) what is the naturalistic course over time of individuals who have a certain kind of psychopathology, and (c) if there are any interventions which have an effect on clinical course. In most research, there are always variations and combinations of these fundamental questions. Asking the right question depends on knowing what really is not yet firmly established. Too often the less-experienced investigator feels that the question he can think of is so obvious that it must have been answered many times over. Several examples will be given in terms of research on the etiology, course, and treatment of schizophrenia.

Etiology.   Through the 1950s there had been much controversy but scant evidence as to whether schizophrenia was a disorder with a genetic or an environmental etiology (nature-nurture controversy). The double-bind theory of Gregory Bateson (1956) contended that a person became schizophrenic as a result of receiving conflicting communications from his parents. Theodore Lidz (1965) held that faulty communication within the family was at the root of schizophrenia, while Frieda Fromm-Reichmann (1952) offered primarily psychodynamic interpretations. At the same time, the epidemiological studies of Franz Kallmann (1938) showed a greater concordance for schizophrenia the closer one was in blood ties to an index case. Thus, the highest concordance was between monozygotic twins, the next with dizygotic twins and siblings, and the least with half-siblings. Kallmann's interpretation was in genetic terms, but his critics pointed out that monozygotic twins share not only the same genetics but a more similar environment as well (a problem with all twin-based theories of heritability).

It occurred to Seymour Kety and David Rosenthal (1968), at the National Institute of Mental Health, to design a study that would disentangle nature from nurture and to ask if there were any genetic basis for schizophrenia at all. If there were, children whose biological parents were schizophrenic but who were reared from birth by someone else should suffer a higher incidence of this disorder than adopted children without schizophrenic parents.

The study was done in Denmark because of the excellent Danish record system through which they identified documented cases of schizophrenic parents whose newborns were adopted by normal parents within the first three months of life. These newborns were to be compared with another set of newborns of normal parents who were adopted by other normal parents. This was to control for the possible effect of being adopted. Members of this control group were also selected so that they were adopted during the same year and lived in the same neighborhood as those in the group with schizophrenic parents. The results generally tended to confirm the genetic hypothesis in that newborns with schizophrenic parents eventually had a higher rate of schizophrenic and other breakdowns.

Could this study have been done in the United States? It probably could have been but with a great deal more effort. One could attempt to identify schizophrenic parents, verify their diagnosis by actual interview, and then follow their adopted-out newborns into the age of risk throughout the United States. It is obviously less difficult to do this in a small country such as Denmark with relatively little emigration. In doing such a study, does one begin with a group of schizophrenic patients and determine (a) who had schizophrenic parents and (b) who was reared by normal parents? If records contained all the information on diagnosis and adoption, this could be done but at great expense. Or, one could begin with the schizophrenic parents and go to the smaller proportion who adopted out their children. The most efficient way was to begin with the adoption records as adoption defines the separation of the two etiological variables. Then we do not have to deal with the large number of parents or children who were not involved in adoption.

Another important aspect of the study was designating the criteria for schizophrenia and demonstrating that the diagnosis was reliably ascertained. Do we trust what is on the record, and can we confirm the diagnosis ourselves? Do we have the time and the labor force to follow the newborns for 15 years into the age of risk? Often studies are done which find a disproportionate number of abnormalities of various kinds in currently schizophrenic individuals, with the implication that these abnormalities have etiological significance. However, because one does not know whether these abnormalities existed prior to the onset of the clinical disorder, they may very well have been produced by the disorder. An example is the current research interest in obtaining samples of children who are at high risk for schizophrenia by virtue of having schizophrenic parents but who are not yet clinically schizophrenic themselves, in the hope of identifying abnormalities which may presage the clinical disorder.

Etiological agents (especially nature and nurture) may be interactive rather than additive. According to this model, one cannot become schizophrenic without being a schizophrenic genotype and without experiencing a particular kind of environmental stress. The genotype or the stress alone is not sufficient. Individuals experiencing the stress but without the genotype or those with only the genotype and not the stress will not become schizophrenic. A simple correlation between stress and development of schizophrenia is bound to be weak, as would also a correlation between having the genotype and developing schizophrenia. What is necessary to test the interactive hypothesis is the generation of an interaction between diathesis and stress.

The adoption studies by Kety and Rosenthal are correlational because it is impossible to randomly assign individuals to having or not having a schizophrenic biological parent. Are we entitled to attribute causation to the genetic variable? Although the study supports the contention of a genetic etiology, it does not rule out the possibility of there being an environmental etiological agent as well. It simply has not tested for it. Additionally, it was not necessary (because of excellent records for the study) to be entirely prospective in the sense of beginning to follow the newborns at the very moment they were adopted into the succeeding 15 to 20 years as they entered the age of risk. The main difficulty of retrospectively ascertained variables is that usually they cannot be reliably obtained. With a prospective study, one can take steps (e.g., do a diagnostic interview on the parents to determine whether they are schizophrenic) to make certain that the crucial variables are reliable.

Clinical course.   The clinical course of dementia praecox was originally described by Kraepelin (1919) as one of deterioration over time. Bleuler (1911) later identified a number of patients whose course was more benign. The question naturally arose as to what characteristics of the patient and his history might be associated with better versus worse clinical outcome over time. There is now a sizable body of research which has identified aspects of premorbid social and sexual adjustment as being associated with long-term course. Poor outcome has an insidious onset and is found to be associated with childhood asociality, having poor heterosexual relationships, and being single. Such studies employ correlational analyses between the premorbid-adjustment variables and measures of long-term outcome such as judgments of recovery, symptom remission, community adjustment, and number of days spent in the hospital. There is also the question of case definition in deciding the criteria for schizophrenia. Do we trust the diagnosis or do we have to interview the patient? As most of the predictor variables are retrospectively obtained, they are based on faulty memory or unreliable observations. A prospective study would not have these problems. Time in the community is not constant among patients; some have been out longer than others and have had more opportunity to adjust. As a compromise, some investigators have controlled for time in the community statistically by partialling it out of the other relationships. A more idealized study would follow up at a constant time after discharge. The results of this body of research with all its faults has led to two theoretical groups of schizophrenia, the good versus the poor premorbid personalities, which have figured importantly in studies of treatment and etiology as well. (Philips, 1953).

Treatment studies.   Electroconvulsive therapy (ECT) had been originally developed as a therapy for schizophrenia on the faulty supposition that schizophrenics tended not to have concurrent epilepsy. The simplistic theory was that somehow the convulsions of epilepsy would protect

against the development of schizophrenia. Also, schizophrenics have traditionally been treated with various forms of psychotherapy, and in the
mid-1950s, the modern era of drug treatment for schizophrenia began.
All three of these therapies were commonly accepted as being efficacious
without benefit of a formal test of their efficacy because the judgment
of efficacy resulted from the fact that the therapies were tried on a number
of patients with good results. However, a good test of efficacy requires
that some patients also be assigned to a group that does not get the
therapy so that they may be compared with those who do.

Phillip May (1968) conducted such a study. He randomly assigned
schizophrenic patients who met certain diagnostic criteria to one of five
treatments: (1) individual psychotherapy alone, (2) drugs alone, (3) individual psychotherapy plus drugs, (4) ECT, and (5) milieu therapy as a
control group. This is an interesting design in that part of it (the drugs
and psychotherapy) are in the form of a two-by-two factorial of all possible
combinations of drugs and psychotherapy versus their absence. The results indicated that the only effective treatment was drug. Psychotherapy
was no more effective than simply being immersed in the milieu of the
ward. There was some suggestion that ECT was effective but not strongly
so. The study is prospective, and with random assignment, we may attribute a causative effect to drugs.

Strategy and logistics

What are the strategic considerations in constructing a study of this
kind? If the study is on schizophrenic patients, how do we know one
when we see one, so that we may accept the eligible and reject the
ineligible (inclusion/exclusion criteria)? In deciding on diagnostic eligibil-
ity, would two equally well-trained diagnosticians agree with each other
(reliability)? If these two diagnosticians would not agree, and they were
to do the studies separately, they might come up with totally different
results. How does one define the treatment procedures that will be used
(manipulation)? Which drug, how much of it, and in what duration of
treatment represents drug therapy? What procedures are considered appropriate psychotherapy for these patients? Are we to say that psychotherapy is whatever is given here at this institution or is there some way of
judging its quality so that in the event of no effect, there cannot be the
criticism that poor psychotherapy was given? What will indicate to us
whether the patient has worsened or improved? If the latter are to be
judged by a clinician employing standard rating scales, what is the rater
agreement reliability on each of these scales? If scales are not sufficiently
reliable and there is no effect of a treatment, the lack of effect might
be due to the unreliability. Because the clinical rater of improvement
might be influenced by his knowledge of which treatment the patient
was getting, what steps can be taken to eliminate or minimize this possible

bias? In May's study, for example, the clinical raters knew who was receiving the psychotherapy and who was only getting the milieu. Nonetheless, they failed to observe a difference in improvement between the two groups, even though they were possibly biased in favor of psychotherapy. Hence, the negative results with regard to the efficacy of psychotherapy are more credible than if they had been positive. What duration should the treatments be? In the case of drug or shock treatment, the expectation for action is relatively shorter than for psychotherapy. Drugs might be expected to act within four to six weeks, while this time would be much too short for almost any psychotherapy. Drug and shock treatment would be expected to have their effects mainly on schizophrenic symptomatology, such as auditory hallucinations, loose associations, ideas of persecution, ideas of reference, inappropriate affect, or blunted affect. Several reliable and valid scales, which were not in wide use at the time that May began his study, are currently available for these symptom dimensions. A review must be made of the dimensions of psychopathology that one would hope to change. A more realistic expectation for psychotherapy would be that it would have more of an effect on aspects of community adjustment such as interpersonal compatibility and assumption of adult responsibilities, rather than on the reduction of schizophrenic symptoms. Drugs may reduce symptoms but they cannot create social skills. Thus, the analysis of drug and psychotherapy probably ought to be with regard to different dependent variables.

Are there any variables other than treatments which could influence the amount of change shown by a patient? If so, we ought to control or rule them out by experimental or statistical means. What should we do about all the other treatments the hospital has to offer which are available to the study patients, such as occupational therapy, dance therapy, attendance at patient government, etc.? In most cases, it is too difficult to prevent study patients from participating in these even though their effects are unknown. Most studies assume that patients in both study treatments will have an equal amount of the other uncontrolled therapies. It is always possible that a study patient doing poorly in one of the treatments will receive compensatory attention from ward personnel, hence diluting our treatment effect. In the flow of patients through the study, what kind of evaluation case load can be managed by the research team of a given size? The number of beds available for study patients can determine the maximum case load. Have the nonstudy personnel (nurses, orderlies, residents, and interns) who have some contact with the study patients been thoroughly briefed? Are the nurses comfortable with the idea that schizophrenic patients might receive a placebo? In being briefed on the nature of the study, they should be assured that any study patient beginning to worsen will be removed from the study and will not be carried through heroically in a deteriorating condition. If any patients worsen, that is their answer to their study treatment.

Periodic public relations activities with nonstudy personnel are essential to forestall passive resistance and the spoiling of study patients by giving them treatments which are not allowed. A "professional compulsive" should be engaged to make certain that all relevant assessments have been collected at the appropriate times and correctly completed. If possible, data should be entered on the computer or on punch cards on the premises. Although the chances are small that raw data would be lost if sent elsewhere for data entry, it is too great a risk for data obtained by such great efforts.

What are the appropriate analyses of the data to answer the specific research questions?

ARTIFACTS IN OBSERVED RELATIONSHIPS

Any observed relationship between two variables, whether the relationship is expressed as a correlation coefficient or not, is obtained on a limited sample of patients. The hope is that the sample results are true as well of the population from which the sample was drawn. In this section, we describe some sampling and measurement problems which may produce spurious results. The first is unreliability of measurement. The strength of relationship between any two variables will be attenuated to the extent that either or both of the variables suffers from unreliability. Thus, if the true correlation between two variables in the population is .60, if either or both of the variables has not been measured perfectly reliably, the obtained relationship in the sample will be something less than .60. Unreliability of measurement *cannot* be responsible for a spuriously high relationship, only a spuriously low one. If a significant relationship is obtained between two variables despite known low reliability, the result is quite credible as an underestimate of the relationship that would be obtained with perfect reliability. To have a nonsignificant relationship be credible, one needs high reliability of measurement.

Spuriously high relationships can be obtained when there are systematic or constant errors rather than variable errors in those variables being related. One example of constant error is a halo effect. Suppose that the same clinician rated 100 patients with regard to anxiety and depression. If a significant relationship is obtained, part of it may be due to the same mental set being used when rating both anxiety and depression because that set resides in the skull of the rater. Unfortunately, we do not know whether all or only part of the observed relationship is accounted for by halo. One solution is to use two experimentally independent observers to rate anxiety and depression. If the correlation between scales *within* raters exceeds the correlation between scales *between* raters, there is evidence of halo. Another example of constant systematic error leading to spuriously high relationships is what has been referred to as *technique contamination*. That is, there may be a relationship observed between an arithmetic test and a spatial visualization test because both were obtained as paper and pencil tests. To overcome this difficulty, different measurement techniques need to be used to measure the different variables. (For example, use of the TAT to measure achievement motivation and the MMPI to measure depression.)

Suppose that you measure the blood levels of an antidepressant in two groups, and there are two lab technicians performing the analyses. If it happens that one finds consistently higher levels than the other, and it happens that one gets a disproportionate number of patients in one of the comparison groups, the lab technician differences as constant error will be confounded with the group differences. That is, the relationship between group membership and blood level is a function of constant-technician error.

Sampling biases may artificially alter the observed strength of the relationship. The failure to sample extreme scores on either or both of the variables will result in a lower relationship than is true of the general population. If two variables have a moderate-to-high correlation and if you discard the data from everyone who scores below some level on one or both variables, the correlation calculated from the remaining sample will be much lower. You might ask, Why would anyone do such a thing? But this is exactly what happens with tests like the Scholastic Aptitude Test (SAT). People of a wide range of ability take the SAT, but people from the higher end of the distribution tend to be the ones that go on to college. Thus, when SAT scores and college grades are correlated, those students from the weaker end of the SAT distribution tend not to have gone to college, and hence, only the students from the upper end of the distribution influence the correlation. In this group, the correlation is lower than it would be if all who took the SAT went on to college and were thus included in the correlation. If the true range of scores in the population is known, one can compare the score range of the sample with that of the population.

The opposite kind of sampling bias is to fail to sample scores in the middle of the distribution of scores, and the correlation would tend to be artificially inflated to some unknown extent. This kind of extreme-group analysis is the greater sin of the type 1 error, in that it frequently can conclude that a relationship exists between two variables when indeed none does.

Yet another source of spuriously inflated values of correlation is in the part-whole correlation. In this instance, the correlation between the two variables is at least in part based on an identical element common to both variables; for example, the correlation between total IQ and verbal IQ.

Another sampling bias that results in reduced correlation arises from the skewed nonsymmetric distribution of scores being correlated. Even if one can establish that the true or real distribution of variables is skewed in the population, unless both variables are skewed in the same way, the fact remains that the maximum possible correlation is something less than 1. To the extent that the underlying populations are nonnormal (or at least nonsymmetrical), Fisher Z-tests are less accurate. We might want to find the relationship between severity of hallucinations prior to treatment and overall response to treatment. Although hallucinations are a hallmark of schizophrenia, more than half of schizophrenic patients may not hallucinate. Those who do hallucinate do so according to some reasonably symmetric distribution. However, the total distribution now shows a pileup of scores at the zero point. Under the circumstances, it can be demonstrated that the maximum possible correlation with any other variable is less than 1. An example of this point with a categorical variable is one where we are obtaining a point biserial correlation between sex and improvement. To the extent that there is a grossly uneven split between the number of males and females, the maximum obtainable correlation and, from that, the percent variance accounted for would be accordingly reduced more than if we had an even split of the sexes.

Correlations within subgroups may differ in size and direction from the correlation on the groups as a whole. An illustration is given in the accompanying Table 2, showing the relationship between improvement and drug dose in paranoid and hebephrenic schizophrenics separately. In each subgroup, the higher the dose, the more the improvement. However, if we disregarded subgroup, the opposite conclusion would be drawn. The subgroup analysis is intuitively more credible. How could this situation come about? Paranoids have a better prognosis than hebephrenics without drug treatment, and while both benefit additionally from drug treatment, hebephrenics tend to require higher doses to achieve an effect.

Table 2

Positive correlation between dose and improvement within subdiagnosis and negative correlation disregarding diagnosis

	Dose	Improvement
Paranoid patients:		
A	1	10
B	2	20
C	3	30
D	4	40
E	5	50
Hebephrenic patients:		
F	10	0
G	11	1
H	12	2
I	13	3
J	14	4

An analogous situation might be obtained in a psychotherapy study which included subtypes who differed in prognosis and who required different durations of psychotherapy. Carroll (1961) contains an interesting discussion of these issues.

CONTROL VARIABLES AND CONTROL GROUPS IN EXPERIMENTAL STUDIES

The definition of an experimental study is one in which at least one of the independent variables is manipulated by the experimenter. A nonexperimental study is one in which no variables are manipulated by the experimenter. An example of a nonexperimental or correlational study would be sex differences in frequency of hallucinations. In this case, the experimenter did not have any control over which subject became male and which female. On the other hand, if a study were done of the difference between psychotherapy and its absence in the reduction of hallucinations, the experimenter does indeed have control over which subject will get the psychotherapy and which will not. He does this by randomly assigning half the patients to one treatment and half to the other.

Principle of random assignment

The idea of random assignment to treatment is a relatively new one. In an earlier day, assignment to treatment would have been made with the attempt to match the patients in each group with regard to some relevant characteristic such as age, sex, or duration of illness. There is a limited number of variables on which one could match even when the matching characteristics are known. Only if a roster of patients and their characteristics are avialable before the study can the matching on a variety of variables be managed. Often we do not know the patient's scores on the characteristics to be matched until after the patient becomes available. Finally, matching is frequently done on variables that are easy to ascertain rather than on variables that might be relevant to the dependent variable. There is no value to be gained by matching or controlling any variable unless that variable can be shown to be related to the dependent variable in question. For that matter, there is a loss in degrees of freedom. Ideally then, one would like to be able to have both treatment groups in the experiment equivalent on any personalistic variable correlated with the criterion. Random assignment to the two treatment groups can be shown to yield equivalent means and standard deviations on any personalistic variable (e.g., age, duration of illness) if the sample size is large enough (Hays, 1963, p. 449). It therefore follows that *any* personalistic variable related to the criterion would also be evenly distributed between the two treatment groups even though we have not yet been able to think of it and may never think of it. This makes random assignment such an enormously powerful means for controlling personalistic variables. Uneven distributions are more likely with small samples, and that is why results based on small samples are far more tentative.

Definition of control

In asking a question such as the effect of a drug versus placebo on improvement in hallucinations, we recognize that there are variables other than the drugs which can also have an effect on the amount of improvement shown. We will want to identify and measure as many of those other determinants of improvement as we can. At the end of the study, if there is a difference between drug and placebo with regard to improvement, we will want to discredit or rule out as many as we can of the other possible determinants of improvement as being plausible reasons for the apparent difference between drug and placebo. This process of discrediting the other possible determinants of improvement is called *controlling* these other variables. If the interviewer knew which patient was getting the active drug, his judgment of improvement could very well be biased by that knowledge. In order to control for knowledge of who was getting active medication, we can disguise the identity of the medication so that both the active and the inactive medications appear identical to the interviewer. In so doing, we have discredited knowledge of who is getting the medication as a determinant of the difference between the two treatment groups. Further, if it were known from other studies that females tend to improve more than males and there was a disproportionate number of females in the drug group, obviously both being female and getting active drugs would be equally plausible explanations for the greater amount of improvement in the drug group. Equal numbers of both sexes in each treatment would obviate this difficulty. Concealing the identity of the medication is controlling a variable which is not a personal characteristic of the patient. Not only does it control the effect of knowing who is getting the medication on the judgment of improvement by the interviewer, but it also controls the effects of the patient's knowledge that he or she is getting some kind of pill. It would have been possible for half the patients to get a placebo pill and the other half to get no pill at all, in which case those getting the pill might improve because getting a pill implies presence of active medication. In using the disguised medication, we have employed a so-called double-blind procedure, the first blind being that of the interviewer with regard to which is active and which is inactive medication, while the second blind is the effect on improvement as felt by the patient due to getting the pill. Control of these variables is not accomplished by random assignment but by concealing the identity of the treatment to the recipients and to those who judge effect. If the active medication produced a side

effect such as dry mouth, it would become apparent to the rater of improvement which patients were on active medication and thereby bias
the judgment of improvement. It would be necessary to administer an
active placebo capable of producing dry mouth and nothing more to
both groups.

Control as a means for sensitizing treatment comparisons

When making a treatment comparison, we make a bet that the treatment
accounts for a greater amount of the total variability among patients than
the amount of variability among patients we are unable to account for
by any other means. This latter unaccounted for variability is frequently
entitled *error variability*. If we can demonstrate within our own data a
relationship between outcome and a variety of variables (such as age,
sex, marital status, or premorbid competence), then the variability due
to those variables is excludable from the error variability. The exact same
drug-placebo difference could have very different significance levels,
depending on the number of extraneous variables one was able to control.
Control, in this case, means measuring and determining the relationship
between these variables and criterion, which then allows a reduction in
the error variability by the amount accounted for. Using sex as an example, if it was known that females improve more than males, the variability
due to sex can then be set aside from the unaccounted for variability
or error variability, and a *reduced error* term is now used for comparison
with the variability due to drug treatment. All of this must sensitize the
drug-placebo comparison. Ideally, one should do this with as many control
variables as can be thought of, if the sample size is large. Again, however,
a control variable is not a control variable unless it is related to the criterion.
Otherwise, controlling it is a meaningless exercise. There is no limit to
the variables that should be controlled to the extent that our sample
size is very large: for every variable that is controlled, we lose one degree
of freedom. The principle is simply that the more questions we want to
ask of the data, the greater sample size we need. What should we do
if our sample size is small and we are certain that there are sex differences
in improvement? In this case, we might decide not to include sex as a
variable at all and do the study exclusively on males or exclusively on
females, in which case sex is a constant. Smaller sample size means there
are fewer variables that we should allow to vary. Naturally, we get less
information but the necessary price for more information is greater sample
size.

Summary

In summary, control has meant to rule out a possible explanation of
results. This is done by (*a*) equating two treatment groups with regard
to personal characteristics of their subjects, (*b*) matching the identity of

the treatments, and (c) reducing unaccounted for variability by measuring and accounting for variables other than the treatments related to outcome. Huitema (1980) contains an interesting discussion of these issues.

FACTORIAL DESIGNS

Reducing unaccounted for variation

Two investigators, one studying psychotherapy and one studying drug effects have decided to join forces in a single study to compare their treatments. They submit their first design to a statistical consultant as follows:

Drug versus Psychotherapy versus Waiting list

Instead of a one-way analysis of variance, the consultant suggests a more efficient two-by-two factorial, with one factor being drug versus placebo and the other being psychotherapy versus waiting list. It is more efficient because it studies the treatments in combination, in which case it is possible to detect the separate effect of each treatment and whether they interact, and also because the same number of subjects can serve to examine more hypotheses. Moreover, one reason they joined forces is that each recognized in the other a source of variation he wished to account for (or control) in order to get a more sensitive test of his own treatment.

In his earlier study on psychotherapy, the first investigator was not able to control the receipt of drug treatment, and although there were as many drug patients in his psychotherapy group as in the waiting list, his treatment differences only leaned in the right direction and were not significant. The improvement scores (high is better) looked something like the following:

Psychotherapy	Waiting list
10	5
50	45
12	7
55	50
15	10
52	47

Their consultant suggested a factorial design with results that might have yielded the following arrangement of the above data:

	Psychotherapy	Waiting list
Drug	50	45
	55	50
	52	47
Placebo	10	5
	12	7
	15	10

In the new design, the variability between drug and placebo patients is no longer included in the error term. The considerably reduced error-term results in a more sensitive test of treatment effects.

Discovering interactions

The second investigator studying drug effects was able to find significance even without controlling psychotherapy because the treatment difference was so large. However, he realized the possibility that the strength of the drug effect might differ depending on whether or not the patient was getting psychotherapy. In other words, the drug-placebo difference for patients treated with psychotherapy should be smaller than the drug-placebo difference for patients on the waiting list. If the investigator's theory is correct, a significant interaction should be found between the two treatments, and the group means in another experiment might look like this:

	Mean improvement		
	Psychotherapy	Waiting list	Marginal mean
Drug	50	50	50
Placebo	50	10	30
Marginal mean	50	30	

Note that this interaction also says that the effect of psychotherapy is larger for placebo treated patients than for drug treated patients. It can be put in either way.

One advantage of a factorial design, in addition to reducing unaccounted for variance, is that an interaction may be detected (Winer, 1971). Interactions may be troublesome embarrassments in agricultural research, but in clinical behavioral data, they represent complex realities which challenge the ingenuity of the investigator to rephrase his hypothesis in more general terms. In the example given above, there is no simple answer to the question of whether drugs or psychotherapy are effective. In each case, the answer depends on what else the patient is getting. The practical significance of this result is that we can obtain the same improvement with either drugs or psychotherapy, and giving both together produces no additional benefit to either one alone. With a one-way analysis of variance we would not know what the combined therapies did. From now on, patients can be given one or the other treatment depending on other considerations such as tolerance for drugs or time available for psychotherapy. The theoretical significance of this result is in its implication about the process of improvement in schizophrenia, especially if there is more than one way to accomplish the same things.

Hopefully, now the investigator will generate a post hoc theory to explain the interaction and then put it to test in another experiment or another analysis of the same data.

Interpretation of interactions

In the preceding example, there were certain conditions when drugs showed no effect (when only the psychotherapy patients were considered). Our colleague could have obtained an interaction with somewhat different specific results and conclusions, such as the following:

Mean improvement

	Psychotherapy	*Waiting list*	*Marginal mean*
Drug	50	45	47.5
Placebo	35	10	22.5
Marginal mean	42.5	27.5	

The analysis (assuming sufficiently low-error variance), as in the prior example, shows main effects for both drug and psychotherapy plus an interaction, because the size of the drug-placebo difference differs for the psychotherapy group from the waiting list group. Although the statistical results are similar, the practical results are somewhat different. In the latter example, the patient is better off getting both drugs and psychotherapy, while in the former example, he would do as well getting either treatment alone. The nature of interactions has to be examined and, hopefully, interpreted. We should not refrain from testing for interactions just because they might be difficult to interpret. Maybe we can interpret them and maybe we cannot.

In another hypothetical study, still another kind of interaction might present itself:

Mean improvement

	Schizophrenics	*Neurotics*	*Marginal mean*
Drug	50	10	30
Psychotherapy	10	50	30
Marginal mean	30	30	30

This is an example in which one factor, diagnosis, is a randomized block. Patients are not randomly assigned to being schizophrenics or neurotics, as they are to drug or psychotherapy. Diagnosis is an organismic or personalistic variable or, in statistical terms, a *block within which* patients are randomly assigned to treatment. In this illustration (assuming sufficiently low-error variance), there are no main effects at all but there is an interaction; an examination of the cell means indicates drugs to be more effective for schizophrenics than for neurotics, with the reverse being true for psychotherapy. The practical lesson of what treatment we give for each diagnosis is obvious. The theoretical lesson is that this is evidence against the contention of neurosis and psychosis being on the same continuum. Rather, the result would indicate a qualitatively different process underlying these diagnoses because they behave differently in response to treatment.

This study example could have arisen from a prior study with these results:

Mean improvement

	Psychotherapy	Waiting list	Marginal mean
Drug	10	50	30
Placebo	50	10	30
Marginal mean	30	30	30

Here both factors are treatments. There are no main effects but only a seemingly uninterpretable interaction. The treatments seem to cancel each other out. In the attempt to understand what may have produced this interaction, the investigator examined the diagnoses of his cases and found there were mostly schizophrenics in the drug waiting list cell, mostly neurotics in the psychotherapy-placebo cell, and an even split of both diagnoses in the other two cells. On seeing diagnosis as a possible explanation, he re-analyzed his data to test the notion that drugs work with schizophrenics, and not neurotics, with the reverse being true for psychotherapy. This is a more sophisticated and powerful kind of hypothesis because it recognizes that there are conditions under which a treatment is effective and when it is not, and it specifies what those conditions are. The hypothesis is a step forward departure from the more simplistic question of just whether or not a treatment is effective in general.

Interaction as a test of treatment generality

Frequently, randomized blocks are employed to test the generalizability of a treatment effect. For example, many studies have gotten data from two or more hospitals in order to see if the same treatment effects are obtained in all locations. If so, confidence in the treatment is increased more than if the same treatment effect were obtained with the same size sample but in only one hospital. An illustration from real data is the study by Hogarty, Goldberg, Schooler, and Ulrich (1974) testing the effects of maintenance drug treatment and social casework on relapse over a 12-month period in recently discharged schizophrenics. The same protocol was followed in three different clinics, each of which studied 120 cases. If a significant interaction were obtained between treatment and hospital, that would be taken as evidence of failure to generalize the treatment result to different locations, and there would be lessened confidence in the effectiveness of the treatment. Their results of no interaction show that the effect of drug versus placebo and the effect of social casework versus its absence are relatively constant across three clinics. It is reasonable to criticize this procedure for drawing a positive conclusion (generalizability of results) from a failure to reject the null hypothesis. While true of a statistical hypothesis, in asking a scientific or practical question of substance, it must be possible to conclude no difference, providing the lack of significance cannot be accounted for by unreliability of measurement, biased sampling, or small sample size (not so here). If there had been a significant interaction between the treatments and clinic, one might or might not speculate on what produced it. Perhaps it would be because of different kinds of patients at the three clinics, but to find out would require further data analyses. The practical implications, however, would be clear regarding nongeneralizability.

Replicating the findings of others may often not be possible because the small available sample sizes would never yield statistical significance, considering the number of cases that were necessary to detect significance in the findings one is attempting to replicate. If the replication uses *identical* measures and procedures, one could test whether the replication results are significantly different from those already published, in which case the N for this test is the total of the original and the replication samples. For instance, the published results, significant at the .05 level, might show the following mean improvement with 20 cases per treatment:

Psychotherapy	*Waiting list*
10	5

In your replication study with five cases per treatment, you obtain the same treatment means but you cannot detect significance. However, a test of whether your replication treatment-difference differs from the original findings can now be done with 50 cases, and you will conclude that the replication sample does not differ from the original. If your replication showed improvement results opposite the original findings, 5 for psychotherapy and 10 for waiting list (but nonsignificant with only 10 cases), with 50 cases you could find a significant interaction between treatment and study, drawing the conclusion of failure to replicate. However, both experiments must be identical.

Blocks as differential predictors of response

In comparing two drugs in schizophrenia, the patient's subdiagnosis (simple, paranoid, or hebephrenic, etc.) was also examined for its relationship to the results. This would be done in a treatment-by-diagnosis design and, if these two factors interacted, there would be evidence that one subtype responded more on one drug while another subtype responded more on the other drug. Such a result was found in a landmark study by Overall, Hollister, Honigfeld, Kimball, Meyer, Bennett, and Caffey (1963). Patients were classified according to an empirical typology based on the Brief Psychiatric Rating Scale (BPRS). Their results show that core schizophrenic patients respond more than paranoids do on perphenazine, while the reverse is true on acetophenazine. The practical lesson is to give each patient type the drug on which he will respond most. In this way, treatment can be made more efficient.

In the foregoing example, patient typology may be regarded as a variable in which each level is meaningfully characterized. Note, however, how different our interpretation might be if patients were a random effects variable. Suppose the same two drugs were being compared on two randomly selected groups. By *randomly selected,* we mean we could have randomly divided our single sample into two groups; or we could have gotten the patients from two clinics; or we could have done two studies in succession. If the drug effects were opposite in the two samples of patients, most of us would rightfully conclude that we had chance drug effects. As soon as we characterize the nature of the two samples, we have a theoretically meaningful result, as in the Overall et al. (1963) example.

Nonorthogonal designs and disproportionate cell frequencies

The original intention of analysis of variance was for the comparison of treatments to which cases had been randomly assigned. If, in a one-way analysis of variance, the number of cases in each treatment differs, one can still perform the usual analysis, although with some loss of power. It is only in factorial designs that unequal frequencies in cells have appeared to be a problem for analysis. Unequal cell frequencies are not a problem if they are proportional, because most design texts have formulas for the proportional case.

In the following two-by-two factorial of drug by psychotherapy, there are twice as many drug cases as there are placebo cases and twice as many psychotherapy cases as there are in the waiting list. The cell frequencies are unequal but proportional:

	Drug	Placebo
Psychotherapy	$n = 60$	$n = 30$
Waiting list	$n = 30$	$n = 15$

In the results of this analysis of variance (all the sums of squares for each factor), the interaction and within-treatment sums of squares will add up to the total sum of squares as independently computed. Suppose, however, that a naive student designed the study with the following cell frequencies:

	Drug	Placebo
Psychotherapy	$n = 60$	$n = 15$
Waiting list	$n = 30$	$n = 30$

In this case, the cell frequencies are not only unequal, they are disproportionate: the ratio of drug cases to placebo cases for those getting psychotherapy (60 to 15) is not the same as the ratio of drug cases to placebo cases on the waiting list (30 to 30). Why does disproportionality make a difference? With disproportionality, there is a relationship between the drug factor and the psychotherapy factor: a case that receives drug is also more likely to get psychotherapy than to be in the waiting list, and a case that gets placebo is more likely to be in the waiting list than to get psychotherapy. Thus, if one of our findings was that drug was more effective than placebo, how could we tell that this was not because drug cases were also likely to have gotten psychotherapy? A design with disproportionate cell frequencies is also referred to as a *nonorthogonal design:* that is, the factors are not uncorrelated. If we computed a chi-square between the drug and psychotherapy variables in the last design, using the cell frequencies as the dependent variable, we would find a nonzero relationship. The factors are not independent. A further ramification of this situation is that the total sum of squares on the dependent variable will not equal the sum of the component sums of squares. The substantive penalty is that it might be impossible to separate the effects of the factors because of this relationship.

One way out of this difficulty is never to design nonorthogonal treatment studies. Always make certain that the cell frequencies are proportional. But even here one may suffer some losses because of patients who drop out of the study in an uneven way. For instance, a design of 2 factors with 10 cases intended for each cell might be somewhat disproportionate because of unavoidable dropouts:

	Drug	Placebo
Psychotherapy	9	8
Waiting list	7	9

Before there were high-speed computers, it was impractical to analyze nonorthogonal designs properly because the calculations were too complex to be done by hand. Consequently, most design textbooks contain only the formulas for the orthogonal case. (In addition, since the calculations are too complex for hand, and most texts are directed to students who will be doing the calculations by hand as exercises, the nonorthogonal formulas have been omitted.)

The proper way to handle nonorthogonal ANOVA is to use the full least-squares formulas rather than the special-case least-squares formulas found in most texts. Most of the popular computer programs (SAS, MANOVA, and MULTIVARIANCE) use these formulas and thus are capable of analyzing nonorthogonal designs correctly.

One reason orthogonality is useful is because it allows the researcher to estimate effects and test hypotheses about effects independently. In such a case, the total variation in the experiment can be uniquely decomposed into a set of mutually exclusive and exhaustive subsets, wherein each subset contains the variation due to each effect (main or interaction). For nonorthogonal designs, such a unique decomposition is impossible because there are many possible decompositions, some neither mutually exclusive nor exhaustive.

Another reason orthogonality is useful is that for a given number of subjects, allocating these subjects in equal numbers to all cells provides more powerful tests of hypotheses than any other allocation of these subjects.

A third reason why equal cell sizes are often useful is because these allow the cell parameters (cell population means and variances) to be estimated with equal precision. When cell sizes are unequal, the parameters of cells with larger sizes are estimated with greater precision.

This brings us to some rare, but conceivable, circumstances under which unequal cell sizes may be desirable. It might be desirable to estimate cell population parameters more precisely for one cell in the design. Such a circumstance might occur if the cell is one which corresponds to a new treatment or treatment combination, and while the treatments or treatment combinations corresponding to other cells have been investigated in detail before, this one has not been. It might also be desirable to allocate subjects differentially to cells based upon the expenses involved in the treatments. It might be, for example, that the treatment combination in one cell is 100 times more expensive than other cells. Thus, giving up one subject in the expensive cell allows the researcher to gain 100 additional subjects at no greater expense.

The last circumstance under which it might be desirable to have unequal sample sizes is if the populations are unequally sized and you wish to reflect the population sizes via the samples. This will often be true when the factors are naturalistic variables rather than treatment variables.

Disproportionality with intact groups

A greater problem arises when intact groups or naturalistic variables rather than treatment variables are used in a factorial design (i.e., where a factor is really a block factor). In an example given earlier, we showed a factorial design between sex and marital status with the following cell frequencies when cases were taken consecutively.

	Married	*Single*
Male	$n = 30$	$n = 70$
Female	$n = 70$	$n = 30$

It is important to note that this relationship between the two factors occurs naturally. No amount of additional sampling is likely to even things out. Unlike a factorial of treatments, this disproportionately is no accident.

Our problem is how to find the effects of marital status which are independent of the effects of sex. One solution used in the past but virtually abandoned is to discard at random 40 of the cases from the cells that have 70, so that our revised design had 30 cases in each cell. Obviously, this reduces our sample size considerably. Moreover, there is more than one way to select the 40 discards, and the different samplings could yield different results. In addition, data are often expensive, and it is a waste to discard them.

A second solution, similar to the one above, is to stratify on both factors if possible. In short, select into the study an equal number for each cell. A moment's thought will reveal that stratifying is equivalent to the procedure of discarding cases except that the discarding occurs before the study begins. If the married male cell is already filled, a married male who appears at the project office will not be accepted into the study. Both methods have the effect of destroying the relationship between sex and marital status. Are we justified in destroying the relationship? A good argument can be made that to the extent that our sampling differs from the universe, the results based on the sample will also differ from the universe.

In the case of our reference example, let us suppose that we found the following results:

	Married	*Single*	*Both*
Male	$n = 30$ $\bar{X} = 20$	$n = 70$ $\bar{X} = 10$	$\bar{X} = 13$
Female	$n = 70$ $\bar{X} = 40$	$n = 30$ $\bar{X} = 30$	$\bar{X} = 37$
Both	$\bar{X} = 34$	$\bar{X} = 16$	

Also assume for simplicity that within any cell, all cases have the same score. Without taking into account disproportionality, main effects for both marital status and sex are significant. If we follow the procedure of Winer (1971), we want to find the effect of sex after removing the effect of marital status with which sex overlaps. This is done by subtracting the variation due to interaction and the variation due to marital status from the total variation among cells. The remainder, if any, should be the variation due to sex, which is not shared by any other variation. The same question could be asked for the other variable, marital status; how much of the total variation among the cells remains after removing the interaction and the unadjusted variation due to sex? Perhaps there is so much overlap between sex and marital status that little is left from each when the effect of the other is removed. In this case, no variation is left for marital status after removing the effects of sex. However, a little variation remains for sex after removing the effects of marital status.

The procedure is remarkably analagous to that of determining the contribution of correlated predictors in a multiple regression equation. These data could indeed be analyzed by multiple regression; the relevant correlations would be (a) a point biserial between sex and outcome, (b) a point biserial between marital status and outcome, and (c) a phi coefficient between sex and marital status. From these, the least-squares regression coefficients would correspond, in conclusions, to the least-squares method of analyzing a factorial design with nonorthogonal factors. Similar problems in interpretation would also exist. That is, just because sex accounts for all the predictive power of marital status does not in itself deny a valid effect for marital status.

Difference between weighted and unweighted marginal means

When marginal means are obtained using the cell frequencies as weights, the frequencies represented in each cell are assumed to be the way things really are. Therefore, in obtaining the mean for one level in a factor (for example married subjects), we include every married subject into the calculation. That is, 30 Ss have a score of 20, and 70 have a score of 40, giving us a mean of 34. However, if we felt it is only a chance accident that there were 30 married males and 70 married females and the *true* state of affairs was really 50-50, then we should weight the married male cell no differently than the married female cell. In this case, the mean for married subjects would be the mean of the means for married males and married females (30 instead of 34). The unweighted marginal means look as follows:

	Married	Single	Both
Male	$n = 30$ $\bar{X} = 20$	$n = 70$ $\bar{X} = 10$	M $\bar{X} = 15$
Female	$n = 70$ $\bar{X} = 40$	$n = 30$ $\bar{X} = 30$	M $\bar{X} = 35$
Both	$\bar{X} = 30$	$\bar{X} = 20$	M

The two methods can yield different results. It is not a matter, however, of choosing the more powerful method but rather of choosing the one more appropriate to our assumptions of what the truth is. (This is not the analysis commonly called an *unweighted means analysis.*)

ANALYSIS OF COVARIANCE

Correcting false positive results

Suppose we are comparing a drug with placebo and we know that the patient's age is also related to improvement. If we were to find a significant difference between drug and placebo, we would want to be certain that it was not artificially due to an uneven distribution of age across the two treatments. If age does vary and is unevenly spread across the treatments, we could think of comparing the treatments for each level of age separately, providing there were some cases at each level. Such an instance is illustrated in the following table where the mean for drug is 2.5 and the mean for placebo is 1.5:

		Drug		Placebo		Total	
Age		n	Mean	n	Mean	n	Mean
10		3	0	8	0	11	0
20		4	1	7	1	11	1
30		3	2	3	2	6	2
40		7	3	4	3	11	3
50		8	4	3	4	11	4
	Total	25	2.5	25	1.5	50	2.0

The data are also constructed so that there is a relationship with age, wherein the mean for age 10 is 0 and the mean for age 50 is 4. Looking at the drug-placebo difference at each age level, we can easily see that there aren't any. Yet, had we done a simple one-way analysis of variance between drug and placebo, we would incorrectly conclude there was a drug effect that we know now was really due to age even though we randomly assigned to treatment. How, with this unfortunate distribution, can we remove the effect of age to see if there is a real drug effect? Using the same data as in the sample on the table, we would plot improvement against age regardless of which treatment each case received. The total columns would be used for this. From the regression line of improvement on age, we can get an estimate of the amount of improvement associated with being a certain age. So, for example, the best estimate for age 30 is 2, and the best estimate for age 50 is 4. If we then subtract the improvement due to age from observed improvement under treatment, we get the patient's improvement due to whatever treatment received. This subtraction removes the effect of age from the table: we see that the amount of improvement due to being 50 years old is 4, while the improvement due to being 20 years old is 1. In both ages, the observed improvement under treatment is no different than the improvement due to age. Thus, all cases have an improvement-due-to-treatment score of zero even though there are wide individual differences in total improvement. This process is what the analysis of covariance does (Huitema, 1980, p. 15).

Correcting false negative results

Two treatments which appear not to differ in improvement may, in fact, be different if the effects of the covariate are removed. This can be illustrated in the following table wherein the treatments differ on mean age but not on mean improvement:

		Drug		Placebo		Total	
Age		n	Mean	n	Mean	n	Mean
10		5	1	0	—	5	1
20		5	2	0	—	5	2
30		5	3	5	1	10	2
40		5	4	5	2	10	3
50		5	5	5	3	10	4
60		0	—	5	4	5	4
70		0	—	5	5	5	5
	Total	25	3	25	3	50	3

Note that all levels of age cannot be compared because there are no cases of some levels in each treatment. We cannot compare drug and placebo at ages 60 and 70 because these ages were not in the drug group. However, we can see that at each age level that can be compared, drug exceeds placebo by two points. From the regression of improvement on age, if we obtain for each case an improvement-due-to-treatment score by subtracting the improvement-due-to-age score from the observed improvement under treatment, we find that all drug-treated cases improved +1, while all placebo-treated patients improved −1. Now a treatment difference exists when it originally appeared there was none.

Reduction of within-treatment variability

Suppose there is random assignment to drug and placebo, and we discover that age is equally distributed to both treatments. Now any observed difference between treatments cannot be accounted for by age, and the more naive investigator might rest easy because he has stereotyped covariance analysis as a means to adjust for unequal distributions. His comparison of treatments may show a difference which leans in the expected direction but does not quite reach significance. He can sensitize his treatment comparison by using age as a covariate (Huitema, 1980, p. 24). We illustrate this in the following table in which we may note that some placebo patients (age 50) improve more than some drug patients (ages 10 and 20):

	Drug		Placebo		Total	
Age	n	Mean	n	Mean	n	Mean
10	5	2	5	0	10	1
20	5	3	5	1	10	2
30	5	4	5	2	10	3
40	5	5	5	3	10	4
50	5	6	5	4	10	5

Now, if we determine for each case the amount of improvement due to treatment by subtracting the amount of improvement due to age from improvement under treatment, then every drug-treated patient improved 1 point, and every placebo-treated patient improved -1 point. Within each treatment, the variability in improvement due to treatment has been reduced to zero; formerly scores within treatments had a range of 5 scale points. One often hears of lack of interest in treatment effects that cannot shine through other variations without benefit of covariance. This is a superficial toughmindedness which allows interest only in the most powerful variables which may, in fact, rarely exist in clinical psychopathology.

Multiple covariates

Suppose an investigator finds correlations between improvement and (a) age, (b) number of prior hospitalizations, and (c) age at onset. He can covary all three simultaneously. From the multiple regression equation between improvement and the three covariates, he obtains for each patient the amount of improvement due to all three covariates together and subtracts that from the patient's observed improvement under treatment in order to obtain the improvement due to treatment. This is the same principle and procedure as with the single covariate. What we have just described is what analysis of covariance conceptually does. This is not, however, how analysis of covariance is actually computed. Not only must the cell means be adjusted for the covariate, but so must the degrees of freedom. Huitema (1980) describes the process in detail.

Heterogeneous regressions

Suppose our investigator obtained data as in the following table, wherein improvement on drug and placebo are equivalent but the relationship between age and improvement under drug is in the opposite direction as the same relationship under placebo.

		Drug		Placebo		Total	
Age		n	Mean	n	Mean	n	Mean
10		5	1	5	5	10	3
20		5	2	5	4	10	3
30		5	3	5	3	10	3
40		5	4	5	2	10	3
50		5	5	5	1	10	3
	Total	25	3	25	3	50	3

If analysis of covariance were done on these data, we would find no treatment difference. The overall relationship between improvement and age as shown by the marginal means is zero. That is, by disregarding treatment, mean improvement is a constant of 3 at all age levels. In most discussions of covariance analysis, we are cautioned that the regression of improvement on age would have to be the same in both treatments before we can believe the results of a covariance analysis. However, finding different regressions of improvement on age between treatments is de facto an indication of treatment differences. The results are more complicated than originally envisioned, but they are bona fide results in that they indicate an interaction between age and treatment. When there are different regressions in each group, and we fit a model which allows for this, we are no longer doing what is called *analysis of covariance,* we are doing a more complicated linear models analysis. Inspection of the results shows that for patients age 10, placebos improved 5 points, and drug patients improved only 1 point. At the same time, at age 50, drug patients improved 5 points and placebos only 1 point. Obviously, we should give drug treatment to older patients and definitely not to younger ones. There are large treatment differences, but their size and direction depend on age. We should not hesitate to use these results.

Large treatment differences on covariate

Some treatises on covariance analysis caution that the results should not be accepted when the treatment difference on the covariate is large or significant, even when such differences emerged despite random assignment to treatment. If assignment has been truly random, by definition, any treatment difference on the covariate, regardless of size, is a chance difference. Extreme examples would be where there was little or no overlap of the distributions on the covariate between treatments, as when the age range for drug patients was from 10 to 25, while for placebo patients it was from 26 to 40. In such an instance, covariance analysis would not be possible because the treatments could not be compared at *any* given age level except by projection. In the accompanying table, we assume that *if* there were drug cases at age 60, they would have a mean score of 6:

		Drug		Placebo	
Age		n	Mean	n	Mean
10		5	1	0	—
20		5	2	0	—
30		5	3	0	—
40		5	4	0	—
50		5	5	0	—
60		0	—	5	1
70		0	—	5	2
80		0	—	5	3
90		0	—	5	4
100		0	—	5	5
	Total	25	3	25	3

Using projected data and an analysis of covariance on the data in the table would show drug to be superior to placebo, the untested implication being that this is true at all age levels. Because the treatments cannot be compared at every given level of age, the results of this significant covariance analysis should be regarded as highly tentative, pending a replication without these difficulties of age distribution. With less extreme examples of treatment differences on the covariate, one could be conservative by performing the analysis only on those ages represented in both treatment groups. A large group difference on the covariate should encourage the experimenter to examine the randomization process to see if the group assignment was truly random.

Comparison of change in intact groups

In all of the preceding examples, we compared change in groups to which there had been random assignment of cases. Other research may not compare treatments but might compare diagnostic subgroups of schizophrenia in their course of illness. There has not been random assignment to subgroups; rather, they are intact, and they may really differ

on many variables we would consider covariates. Recall that in the treatment groups, all the differences on the covariate, regardless of how large,
are by definition *chance* as there was random assignment. In intact
groups, they are real and adjusting them as if they did not exist defies
reality. Does this mean that we cannot compare, for example, paranoid
and hebephrenic schizophrenics on response to treatment if they differed
markedly as they do on an important covariate such as age and rapidity
of onset? With full recognition of the current controversy on the appropriateness of covariance analysis for intact groups, we suggest a limited
use of covariance to be applied only to those levels of the covariate
where there are real cases in both groups.

Suppose we were comparing weight gain in the adolescents of Swedes
and Pygmies while covarying height. In the accompanying table, there
were no cases of Swedes four feet tall nor cases of pygmies seven feet
tall.

	Pygmies		Swedes	
Height (feet)	n	Mean	n	Mean
4.0	5	10	0	—
4.5	8	20	0	—
5.0	10	30	5	30
5.5	6	40	7	40
6.0	0	—	15	50
6.5	0	—	8	60
7.0	0	—	2	70

It is unrealistic to compare the weight gain of a Swede and a Pygmy
both of whom are seven feet tall, because such a Pygmy will never exist.
However, if we were comparing diet A with diet B on weight gain and
found cases seven feet tall only in diet A, we might be willing to make
a projection of the amount of weight gain a seven-foot case would show
in diet B because it is chance only that such a case did not fall into
diet B. Returning to the accompanying table, it is eminently possible to
compare, by means of covariance analysis, their weight gain on the levels
of height where both groups have cases.

Designs which use intact groups are termed *quasi-experimental.* Cook
and Campbell (1979), and Campbell and Stanley (1963) devote entire
books to the analysis of quasi-experiments.

Measurement of change

Treatment implies change, and we have just considered covariance
analysis as a means for controlling determinants of change other than

the treatments we are comparing. If change is measured as the simple difference pre- and post-treatment, then a frequently observed correlate of the amount of change is the pre-treatment level. This relationship has been described as the *law of initial value*. People with more extreme initial values are more likely to move toward the mean on a second measurement than are those with less extreme scores. One way of controlling for initial value is analysis of covariance. Every reason for using a variable as a covariate also applies to the use of initial level as a covariate; that is, adjustment for treatment differences on the covariate and reduction of within-treatment variability on the dependent variable.

In earlier days, some investigators analyzed their data in two ways: a treatment comparison of raw change scores with and without covarying initial levels. If one method showed significance and the other did not, they retained the method showing significance. Suppose this was the case when employing raw change scores without covariance. We have already seen that a treatment difference on a covariate can account for a false positive result. Disregarding a covariate (in this case, initial level) can result in a false positive statement of results.

Using initial level as a covariate in evaluating treatment differences, if we use only the post-treatment score as the dependent variable instead of the change between pre- and post-treatment, we will obtain the same results.

The following two tables, one using pre-post-difference scores and the other using only post-treatment scores, will give identical results in the adjusted post-treatment scores, except for the artifact of sign.

Pre-post-treatment difference scores

		Drug			Placebo		Total or outcome due to pre	
Pre	n	Raw Mean	Adjusted Mean	n	Raw Mean	Adjusted Mean	n	Mean
10	10	5	2.5	10	0	−2.5	20	2.5
20	10	10	2.5	10	5	−2.5	20	7.5
30	10	15	2.5	10	10	−2.5	20	12.5
40	10	20	2.5	10	15	−2.5	20	17.5
50	19	25	2.5	10	20	−2.5	20	22.5
Post-treatment scores								
10	10	5	−2.5	10	10	2.5	20	7.5
20	10	10	−2.5	10	15	2.5	20	12.5
30	10	15	−2.5	10	20	2.5	20	17.5
40	10	20	−2.5	10	25	2.5	20	22.5
50	10	25	−2.5	10	30	2.5	20	27.5

A pre score is higher (has more pathology) than a post score and therefore, the greater the reduction in pathology, the higher the score. When regarding post-treatment scores as change measures, the lower the score, the greater the change; hence the opposite signs. Both tables now read for adjusted means (at every level of pre-treatment), a reduction of 2.5 scale points under drug, and an increase of 2.5 scale points under placebo.

CROSS-OVER DESIGNS

If two patients, perfectly matched in all respects, are given different treatments, any observed difference between treatments could not possibly be due to differences between patients on personal characteristics because there are none. Aside from the rare use of monozygotic twins for matching, the perfect match for a patient is himself, even for those characteristics we do not know about. An experiment might be done comparing a tranquilizer and alcohol on reaction time in normals in which cases are randomly assigned, treatment effects are noted, and then (after enough time to allow the effects of each drug to wash out), each subject undergoes the second treatment not yet received. For each subject, we calculate a treatment difference and then test significance of the differences by a single-sample t-test. If there is an effect of the order the treatments were received, this is evenly distributed, because half the subjects received the tranquilizer first and half the subjects received alcohol first. Compared to an independent groups design (in which a separate group receives each treatment), the cross-over repeated-measure design (in which each subject is his own control) can be far more sensitive, providing certain conditions are satisfied. In the example, after the first treatment was washed out, it is likely that subjects returned to their original baseline of reaction time before starting the second treatment, in which case there probably would be no effect of order. In other studies, there might be an effect of order for a variety of reasons. Some outside event (such as extraneous noise) might have occurred during the first treatment so that it raised reaction time. There might have been a practice effect so that performance is better on the second treatment. Some maturational process may have occurred over time so that the second treatment has better performance than the first. This could certainly occur if we were dealing with patients whose clinical state improved spontaneously over time. If there is an effect from order, instead of simply counterbalancing the order, the study would be more sensitive if order were controlled as a block. The design would now be tranquilizer versus alcohol by first versus second order.

Mean reaction time

	Tranquilizer	Alcohol
1st Order	10	5
2d Order	5	5

This design would have the further advantage of determining whether treatment interacted with order which, if true, would create grave doubts about the efficiency of the design. In the results in the table above, a treatment difference occurs only in the first order so no advantage is gained from the second order. The interaction with order is one of the major disadvantages to the cross-over design and thus should always be tested. If there is an interaction with order, we can use the results of the first order, but now we no longer have a cross-over design.

There are other disadvantages to the cross-over that make it inappropriate in certain situations. The time necessary to wash out the first treatment may not be known and if too short, there would be carry-over effects from the first to the second treatment. The washout of the first treatment may take so long that the subjects may no longer be available for the second. After washing out the first treatment, the subject may not return to the original state obtained before the first treatment, and if treatment efficacy depends on initial level (as it often can), one would get different treatment differences in the second order than in the first, which would dilute the overall effect.

It is of some value to consider various cases which would or would not be appropriate or feasible for a cross-over design. The first is the effect of insulin versus a new drug on diabetic coma. Suppose that those who got insulin got better and that those on the new drug did not. After washing out the insulin, the patients are likely to return to their state of coma. Treatment differences in the second order are likely to be the same as in the first.

Now consider testing the effects of aspirin versus placebo on headache. After the first order, we probably note that aspirin is effective. However, on washing out the aspirin before beginning the second treatment, many patients would not have a return of headache. Some of the patients who received placebo first would also have a spontaneous remission. The headache level on beginning the second treatment is less than the headache level on beginning the first treatment. Consequently, the second order may show no drug effect at all and, if added into the total results, would tend to dilute the results found in the first order. Instead of a more sensitive design, in this case the cross-over would be less sensitive.

Turning now to psychiatric examples, it is more likely that schizophrenia is analogous to the insulin-and-diabetes example because it seems to be a disorder that can be turned off by drugs. Depression and mania are more self-limiting disorders and would be more analogous to the aspirin-with-headache example in which a cross-over was less feasible.

There is a further difficulty with some treatments (like psychotherapy or shock) in knowing whether or not they have been washed out. One can measure the presence of drugs in body fluids or tissue. It is suggested that a behavioral definition of washout i.e., return to initial state be adopted. With this criterion, few cross-overs would be done because they would be too difficult to monitor.

Feasibility of a cross-over design in uncharted areas of research might be pretested in a pilot study before committment to the final design. Even when judged feasible, the interaction between treatment and order must be tested and if significant, only the results of the first order may be accepted.

ANALYSIS OF DROPOUTS

In a six-week study of drug and placebo on schizophrenic symptoms, a number of patients have to discontinue study medication and procedures before completing the study.

1. Two drug patients and 10 placebo patients had to be dropped after three weeks because of worsening clinical condition.
2. Ten drug patients and two placebo patients discontinued after four weeks and had to be discharged because of marked early remission.
3. Five drug patients and one placebo patient were dropped after two weeks because of uncontrollable side effects.
4. Two drug patients and three placebo patients were found to be non-schizophrenic after all but were amphetamine and LSD abusers.
5. Two drug patients and one placebo patient were dropped early because they moved out of town.

Should these early terminators be replaced with other cases? What should be done with all of the data collected on those who terminated early? Should we include them or leave them out? How can they be included?

If there are enough cases that completed the study to analyze, suppose a comparison of drug and placebo shows no significant differences? This result is puzzling because a crude analysis of the dropouts due to treatment failure (2 drug and 10 placebo) and early remission (10 drug and 2 placebo) indicates a marked effect favoring the drug. Why should the cruder analysis of dropouts show a treatment difference and the more sensitive analysis using parametric statistics on the much larger number of remaining cases not do so? The following reasons become apparent.

Treatment failure is associated with low improvement scores, and removing these from the group has the effect of raising the mean improvement of the group which did not fail. As most of the treatment failures are in the placebo group, the mean improvement of placebo patients who survive the study will be higher.

Because early remission is associated with high improvement scores and there are more early remissions in the drug group, those who remain for the full six weeks would have a lower mean improvement than all the drug cases. Obviously, if we analyze only those cases who survived the full study, we are comparing a placebo group biased toward higher improvement with a drug group biased toward lower improvement, and the chances for finding a difference between treatments is correspondingly reduced.

Depending on the proportion of such dropouts, an investigator may be tempted to replace each dropout with a new patient until he has satisfied the full number of study patients committed for. If one of the replacements is subsequently dropped, it will be replaced with still another case. It is obvious that, sooner or later, treatment failures on placebo will be replaced with cases who, for some reason, can survive the full study period. At the same time, treatment remissions on drug treatment will eventually be replaced by patients who do not remit early. Replacement of early failures and early remissions will yield results biased against finding a treatment difference. The only alternative here is to include the data of the early terminators in the full analysis. If a comparison was to be done on improvement after six weeks, a patient's scores at termination are often used as the estimate of what the scores would have been if the patient had been able to complete the full six weeks. This is not a perfect solution to the problem but it is the least evil of the available alternatives.

A common practice among many investigators is to examine whether the dropouts are differential by treatment; if dropouts are not unevenly distributed across both treatments, they will be less concerned about any possible biasing effects on the results. This may or may not be so. The effect of leaving out any particular case depends on the termination score of that case. Leaving out a case with a high improvement score will have the effect of lowering the mean and reducing the variability of the remaining cases. Leaving out a case with a low score will raise the mean and lower the variability of the remaining group. Leaving out a case with a mid-level improvement will have no effect on the mean of the remaining group but will enlarge its variability. Suppose we are comparing a new drug with a standard and we know that each treatment had an equal number of early remissions and treatment failures. The tendency in prior research is to analyze the remaining cases without concern for bias from the dropouts because they are equally distributed in both treatments. It may be demonstrated, however, that leaving out these extreme scores will artificially reduce the variability of the remaining cases, although there will be no effect on the means. This artificial reduction of within-treatment variability (error term) in turn leads to an inflated statement of the significance of the difference between treatments. In short, one could incorrectly conclude that a treatment difference existed when it really did not.

Suppose, on the other hand, that there were an equal number of dropouts because of administrative reasons in both groups and that those dropouts had mid-level improvement scores. The effect of leaving out these scores is to artificially increase variability within treatments, leading in turn to greater difficulty in detecting a treatment difference (if one really exists). The point is that leaving out dropouts will have some effect on the nature of the results based only on the remaining cases regardless of the reasons for the drop and regardless of whether the drops are differential by treatment. The nature of the effect depends entirely on the termination score of the dropped case. Only if the distribution of scores of the dropped cases is identical to the distribution of the remaining cases will there be no biasing effect on the analysis of the remaining cases.

Naturally, if the number of dropped cases is small, the effects of excluding them will be correspondingly small. However, it is difficult to say by inspection whether the effect will be crucial. Consequently, it is prudent not to exclude the data of dropout cases. The only justification for replacement is if the dropped case was inappropriate to the study (that is, misdiagnosis) or if the patient was terminated so early as to not be given any trial of the assigned treatment.

The illustration given earlier was of a six-week study in which estimates of six-week scores had to be made for patients terminated at some time earlier. The easiest (and therefore, most popular) procedure is to use the score at early termination as the best estimate as to what the patient would have looked like by going through the full study period. This has come to be known as *endpoint analysis.* If treatment failures were continued to the end, it is likely they would become even worse than they were at early termination. Their level of illness is being underestimated to some extent. Early remissions, if continued for the full study, might get even better, so their level of health is being understated. The problem is in saying exactly how much over- and underestimating is going on to make the appropriate corrections; so out of ignorance, no correction is made. There will be little bias if a 3-week score is taken as an estimate of a 6-week score, but we are more reluctant to estimate a 26-week score from a 3-week score.

Other methods of estimation have been proposed to accommodate such an instance, each with its own attractions and difficulties. The first proposal is to use the mean of those who complete the full study. This has the fault of giving the same score to all dropouts, regardless of whether they were early successes or failures; moreover, the range of survivors may be different from the range of dropouts, thus artificially decreasing variation. A second proposal is to correlate among study completers the scores at some early point in time with final scores. Using this correlation and regression, or other statistical procedures, an estimate of final score is made for a dropout from the early termination score. This procedure has advantages if its correlation is relatively high; otherwise, the estimate becomes the mean final score of the study completers and is not different from using the mean of the study completers. The final proposal is that a projection be made on a clinical basis according to the course the patient has followed thus far. Although this procedure is not as objective as other methods, it has some merits of appearing to do what ought to be done. It has disadvantages in that whoever is making the projection can bias the results unless he is blind to treatment assignment. If safeguards can be taken against personal bias, the clinical procedure can have considerable merit.

MULTIPLE REGRESSION AND CORRELATION

A number of investigators are often astonished to discover that their strongest independent variable accounts for relatively little of the variance in the criterion. The more experienced investigator discovers over time that, in the behavioral sciences, he lives in a world of correlations between single variables usually in the .20s and .30s and often at most in the .40s. Rather than being discouraging, it follows that in order to account for more of the variance in the criterion, he will need more than one independent variable. Thus, for example, in the study by Hogarty et al. (1974) the criterion of months until relapse was associated not only with whether or not the patient received drug or placebo but also with a measure of premorbid competence. The correlation of these two independent variables, drug and premorbid competence combined, against the criterion of months until relapse, is larger than either one alone. Theoretically, it would be possible to develop, for example, five independent variables, each of which correlated only .30 with outcome, but which as a composite correlated .71 with outcome. The statistical procedures underlying this process are multiple regression and correlation, which allow us to say how much of the outcome variance is accounted for by each of the independent variables individually and cumulatively. Multiple regression tells us how to weight the independent variables optimally to attain the highest possible correlation with the criterion. In principle, independent variables more strongly associated with the criterion are weighted more strongly.

Multiple correlation/regression (Hays, 1963, pp. 566–573) is a technique for assessing the relationship between one variable and a number of other variables. When all variables are measured concurrently, correlation/regression is a technique for measuring association (the degree to which changes in one group of variables are associated with changes in another). When the group of variables is measured before the dependent variable, correlation/regression is a tool for prediction. When the independent variables are actually manipulated (as with a treatment variable) and not just measured, regression is a tool for discovering causation. We tend to speak of correlation as the index of association and of regression as a means for estimating a score on one variable from the score on another variable with which it is correlated.

Which schizophrenic patients should be given drug treatment? The study by Goldberg, Schooler, Hogarty, and Roper (1977) on maintenance drug treatment found large individual differences in response to drug, even though drug-treated patients on the average were noticeably better than placebo-treated patients. Some few drug patients did poorly and some placebo patients did well. Patients who receive drug without therapeutic benefit will only suffer side effects—all cost and no benefit. If we can identify these prior to treatment assignment, we can exercise more informed treatment. A variety of demographic and historical variables were obtained and correlated with the criterion of months until relapse. Poor drug response was found to be associated with (a) being male, (b) coming from disrupted nuclear families, (c) living alone currently, and (d) irregularity in taking medication. A patient closely approximating this pattern is a poor bet for drug treatment. Note that some of these independent variables refer to historical events (such as family disruption) while others are concurrent (such as regularity of medication taking). Interpretation depends on the nature of the variable rather than on the statistic employed.

In another analysis of this study, outcome among all patients was inspected regarding its correlates, one of which was whether the patient received drug or placebo. This was the single most powerful predictor and since it was experimentally manipulated, it could be interpreted as causative. From multiple regression a formula is obtained for estimating one score as a linear function of the other score. This is done by adding up all of an S's predictor scores (in standard score form), after having multiplied each by its strength of relationship (regression coefficient) with the criterion, correcting for (partialing) correlation with other predictors. This procedure yields a score in the same scale range as the criterion, and it is an estimated criterion score whose correlation with the real criterion score *is* multiple R. The size of R indicates how well we were able to estimate with this battery of predictors, while the regressions indicate the predictive (estimating) efficiency of each predictor.

Regardless of the purpose for which we perform multiple regression, (whether estimation, prediction, or causation), the general index of predictive efficiency is the square of the multiple correlation, R^2, which can vary between 0 and 1, with 0 indicating no prediction and 1 indicating perfect prediction. R^2 is the proportion of variation in the dependent variable which the independent variables are able to predict jointly in that sample. Unfortunately, this R^2 is usually an overestimate if applied to other samples, because chance associations in that particular sample also helped the prediction in that sample. A correction is necessary.

Pitfalls in using multiple correlation and regression

Some users of multiple regression are unaware of the cautions that should be observed and, because of the strange results they obtain, tend to abandon the technique as unreliable. There are some characteristics of multiple correlation which differ from the simple bivariate correlation.

Multiple correlation is only positive. If some of the predictors are positively and some negatively correlated with criteria, the multiple correlation is always expressed as positive and hence says nothing about the direction of relationship.

The addition of a predictor to the battery may raise but will never diminish the multiple R. Thus, it is theoretically possible to raise the multiple correlation to 1 by the addition of a sufficient number of negligible predictors. It follows from this that the face value of the multiple correlation must be evaluated in terms of the number of predictors required to achieve that value. The multiple correlation is never lower than the best single predictor in the battery.

Multiple correlation based on a particular sample of subjects is always spuriously higher, never lower, than the multiple correlation in the population from which the sample was drawn. Consequently, one must never take the sample value of the multiple correlation as the indication of real population size of the relationship without further exploration. All one can say, if the multiple correlation is significant, is that the strength of the relationship is different from zero. Estimates of the population value of the multiple correlation are made by cross-validation methods. There are two main reasons for the spuriously inflated sample values of multiple correlation. The first, discussed earlier, could be the sheer number of predictors employed. The second is the fact that each member of the sample participated in the determination of least-squares regression coefficients, from which each member's predicted criterion score was obtained—a bias which must inflate the correlation.

It is possible to raise the multiple correlation by the addition of a predictor variable which is not at all correlated with the criterion of outcome, but which is correlated with one or more of the other predictors. This is known as a *suppressor variable,* and subtle suppressor effects are often responsible for seemingly significant but uninterpretable results.

The statistical significance of the bivariate correlation depends only on the size of the correlation and the number of cases. The significance of multiple correlation is an inverse function of the number of predictors employed, in addition to the size of the multiple correlation of the number of cases.

Unlike the bivariate correlation whose square is directly translatable into percent variance accounted for, the multiple correlation, even when legitimately significant, is an inflated value. Before one can answer the question of percent variance accounted for by the collective predictors, a determination of the uninflated value of multiple correlation would have to be made by means of cross-validation.

Cross-validation instead of significance

The major problem in multiple correlation is that investigators frequently underestimate the true number of predictors with which they are really dealing. This then results in an inflated statement of significance and size of the multiple correlation, which then fails to be replicated in a future study. One solution to these problems is to abandon the test of significance for multiple R and to rely on cross-validation, which is what the significance test attempts to estimate. Consider what is being said by the result of a significant multiple R. It says, if we go to a new sample of subjects and multiply their predictor scores by the regression weights obtained in the first sample and add them up, we will get a predicted criterion score for each case in the new sample; the correlation between the real criterion scores in the second sample and the ones we predicted can be taken as a more realistic value of the relationship between that set of predictors and the criterion.

Another way of doing exactly the same thing is to compare the regression weights from the two samples directly. Just as we tend to compare a simple regression between two variables in two separate samples, we can also compare an entire set of regressions between two samples. The samples may be from two successive studies, or from two separate clinics, or both. The strategy is to do a comprehensive search in one sample for every conceivable predictor. Regression weights from the small resulting battery are then obtained separately in each sample and compared for homogeneity. If the regression weights are not different, we have cross-validated successfully.

The requirement for two samples is a difficulty. If only one sample is at hand, all is not lost. We can split our sample into two, using one for the search for predictors and the other for cross-validation. If there is successful cross-validation between random portions of a sample, there is no guarantee that there would be cross-validation to a sample from a second clinic; however, if there is no cross-validity between two random halves of a sample, there is little likelihood of being able to cross-validate to a second location. Thus, with a single sample, cross-validation on random portions may be used to decide whether to repeat the entire study elsewhere.

An interesting extension of cross-validation on a single sample is the so-called Jack-knifelike procedure (Mosteller and Tukey, 1968) which became possible only since the advent of high-speed computers. This procedure requires generating as many separate multiple regression equations as there are subjects in the sample. With 100 subjects, one obtains a multiple regression equation based on each subject in the sample except case 1. That regression equation is used to obtain the predicted criterion score for case 1, who did not participate in generating that equation. We then go on to case 2, where we obtain an analogous multiple-regression equation based on every subject in the sample except for case 2 and obtain his predicted criterion score in the same way. This is done for every case in the sample, which results in a set of predicted criterion scores for each case based on multiple regression equations which each case did not participate in generating. The correlation between the predicted and the actual criterion scores would be the cross-validity.

Interaction terms as predictors

In the study of schizophrenic outcome, both sex and marital status have been found repeatedly to be significant predictors. Yet being married means something psychologically different for males than it does for females. Translated into statistical terms, one would posit a statistical interaction between sex and marital status with regard to outcome. Although interactions are usually thought of in ANOVA terms, it is quite possible to test for the significance of interaction within a multiple regression context (Cohen and Cohen, 1975). To do so in our example, it is necessary to generate a cross-product term of the two variables in question (simply the product of marital status and sex score). This cross-product score can then be correlated with the criterion. To test for the significance of the interaction, there must be a significant correlation between the cross product and the criterion after partialling out the simple correlations between each of the predictors and the criterion. The interpretation would then have to be made by inspecting the criterion means for each possible combination of sex and marital status.

The art of predictor selection

Given two samples, the problem is to select the small battery of predictors most likely to cross-validate. A first principle is that predictors are more likely to cross-validate if they are uncorrelated with each other. This is so because the regression weight for each predictor depends on its correlation with the criterion and on its correlation with the other predictors. In the special case of uncorrelated predictors, the regression depends on one less consideration. Thus, a set of rating predictors which intercorrelate with each other because of halo effect can lead to some very unstable results. A small change in the correlation with the criterion and/or the correlation with other predictors can make a large change in regression weights. Since we never achieve absolutely uncorrelated predictors, a rule of thumb is that correlations with the criterion should exceed correlations among predictors.

The second principle is that suppressor variables rarely cross-validate and should therefore be excluded from the battery. Those suppressors having zero correlation with the criterion and having a higher correlation with another valid predictor can be detected by inspection. There are other less obvious suppressors which do show simple predictions of the criterion but, because of their higher correlation with the set of other predictors, they have a suppressor effect.

A third principle is to keep the batteries small. Enlarging the battery will at best include some nonvalid predictors, but at worst could include some redundant predictors which can only confuse the regression equation (through suppressor effects) and weaken the cross-validity.

Applying these principles to our data would require the following procedures. First, obtain the simple validities of each predictor with the criterion and the intercorrelation among predictors. Second, eliminate all nonsignificant predictors because they are either nonvalid in a simple way or because they are suppressors and probably will not cross-validate. Third, identify predictors which are predicting on the same basis and combine them. This will make the remaining predictors less correlated. This reduced battery will be cross-validated in a second sample. If the cross-validity is significant, it means the entire battery (as it is weighted) is significant. We have replicated a pattern of weights. The significance of the cross-validity is evaluated as a bivariate correlation. Its size is a more credible estimate than multiple R of the correlation in the universe between the criterion and the battery of predictors.

This procedure does not say as much about the relative value of each predictor. Ordinarily, this is done by inspecting the regression weights in the equation, but our procedure gave us as many regression equations as there were patients. What we can do is look at the distribution of regression weights for a particular predictor in all the equations that were generated. Those with greater variability are suspected of being less stable to small changes in the sample of the patients.

FACTOR ANALYSIS

Suppose an investigator has accumulated 300 items of behavior on a large sample of schizophrenic patients which he or she intends to observe over time to detect changes in response to various treatments. The psychologist feels it unlikely that there are really 300 unique aspects of schizophrenia and, in addition, notices that certain of the items tend to be correlated very highly with certain other items. A reasonable hypothesis is that items which are highly correlated are measuring the same thing (whatever it is), and those items which are uncorrelated are either measuring nothing or are measuring different things. The psychologist would like to acquire more insight into these relationships because, if by somehow reducing the number of items measured without loss of information, the monitoring of the patients will become easier and take less time, while still gathering just as much information. Factor analysis (FA) and principal components analysis (PCA) are techniques which allow us to discover which items hang together (and thus may have a common cause) and which do not (Muliak, 1972). There are many kinds of factor analysis, and often but not always, the results using one type are similar to the results using another type. Both FA and PCA operate on the matrix of correlations between the variables, and it is assumed that the group is homogenous with respect to these variables. This is not to say that all subjects in the group are assumed to respond in the same way to the variables, but rather that there are not any subgroups which might systematically respond differently. For example, it might be wrong to collect the same 300 behavioral items on normals as we collected on schizophrenics and then perform a factor analysis of everyone together, because it is unreasonable to suppose that the relationships between the variables is the same for the schizophrenics as it is for the normals.

In addition, we can only factor analyze the items we measure. While it seems simple to state, the implication is that if we fail to include items which reflect some underlying process, all the factor analyses in the world will not uncover the underlying process.

Factor analysis has a number of advantages over groupings of items based upon either clinical judgment or rationality (face grouping). In factor analysis, the manner in which items are grouped together depends on how they intercorrelate. An item in a factor should correlate higher with its factormates than with items in another factor. An equation for putting the items in each group together to make a factor score which represents the hypothesized underlying dimension is similar to a multiple regression equation.

In factor analysis, the initial results are usually rotated in such a way as to render them more useful or interpretable. That is because factor analysis in reality produces an infinite number of equally good mathematical solutions in terms of explaining variation in the data, and we choose the solution that is most easily interpretable. Thus, factor results depend to a great extent on the interpreter.

Another issue in factor analysis is how many factors to extract. In general, the more factors extracted, the more that variance will be explained, but with diminished parsimony. There are various rules for attempting to discover if the returns have diminished sufficiently to stop. However nice the mathematical rules for deciding when to stop, there is a place for rational thinking. If the next factor appears to be useful and interpretable, it might be worthwhile to use, even if it explains a small percentage of the variance. In principle, we try to obtain greatest variance accounted for with greatest parsimony in number of factors consistent with interpretability. Factors which are formed by one or perhaps two items (called *singlet* or *doublet* items) which do not bear a relationship to any factors are often discarded as unimportant, unless there is an independent reason to retain them. Remembering what we said earlier about the factors depending on the item content, it is sometimes useful to attempt to discover what behavior such items measure and include more items in a subsequent study to see if there is indeed an underlying process.

There are many reasons why a factor may or may not emerge from a factor analysis. The items and subjects used can determine, to a large extent, the results. Items may be unreliable. Subjects may introduce a halo effect. Items sampling a particular domain may not be included. Subjects high on a particular factor may not be included in the sample.

All the various things which can influence correlations (such as restriction in range) may thus influence factor analysis.

Thus, when one thinks one has discovered a factor structure, replicating it is important because much of the results are interpretive. By a cross-validation process similar to that used for multiple regression, one can confirm or disconfirm prior factor results. Beyond confirmation, the utility of any factor is in its relationship to other variables (such as treatment, diagnosis, outcome, etc.).

MULTIDIMENSIONAL SCALING

When a psychiatrist or a psychologist initially sees a patient, the chief complaint or complaints may or may not be obviously correlated with the diagnosis, problem, or treatment. Thus, it behooves us to understand as fully as possible the manner in which lay persons characterize problems which turn out to be psychological or psychiatric.

Rosenberg and Cohen (1977) asked 25 college students to list "reasons someone might need to be examined by a professional person in the

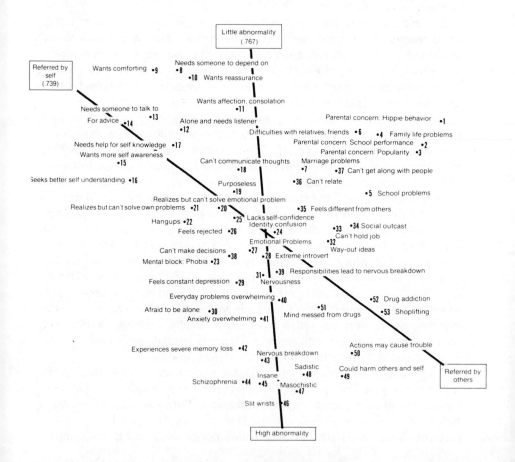

field of mental health" (p. 179). They then used 22 new subjects and a sorting procedure to get measures of "psychological distance" among 89 common reasons. In addition, they obtained ratings of the 89 reasons on 4 scales (abnormality, referral source, feelings, and inner discomfort).

Among other analyses, they used a technique called *multidimensional scaling* (MDS) to derive a two-dimensional spatial representation of the 89 problems and drew in lines representing the two ratings which were significantly related to the configuration (Young et al., in press). The figure contains the plot from Rosenberg and Cohen (1977).

It is interesting to note that items close to each other seem to be similar, and items far from each other appear to be dissimilar. It is also interesting to note the two directions going through the space, those of degree of abnormality and referring source. The problems of high abnormality and referral by others, for example, (the lower right-hand corner of the figure) are actions, violent or destructive, while those in the opposite corner are internal problems.

Using MDS, as well as a cluster analysis, Rosenberg and Cohen (1977) were able to comment upon the meaning of and importance of referral source in characterizing psychopathology. They stated, "The students' implicit beliefs here seem to be that as the psychopathology of an individual becomes severely deviant, the complaint source cannot remain exclusively intrapersonal—his problems become a source of concern to others (p. 191).

SINGLE-CASE ANALYSIS

Suppose, in order to avoid being shocked, a rat has been trained to run to the other end of the cage whenever he hears a tone. Suppose further that, in the first several trials, the rat actually received the shock and ran to the other end of the cage to escape it. With a certain number of trials in which the rat actually suffered the shock, he soon learned to run to the other end whenever he heard the tone. The experimenter was able to demonstrate that the rat would respond to the tone almost invariably, for a very large number of trials. After this, he gave the rat a drug, and on the succeeding series of trials, the rat began to show signs of extinguishing the avoidance response on hearing the tone. It is the contention of the experimenter (Sidman, 1960) that he does not need formal statistics to conclude that the drug had an effect on the rat's behavior: he could tell by looking at it. However, by looking at it, the experimenter does make the judgment that the change in behavior after the drug was beyond chance expectations. He, therefore, makes a judgmental significance test. It would be difficult to do a classical significance test (comparing behavior on the trials prior to treatment with those after the treatment) because the trials are not independent observations. Other experimenters attempting to replicate this result may find that not all rats are as astute and are not capable of showing such regular behavior over numerous trials. The question of whether the results on the original rat can be generalized to other rats is very much in controversy. Our contention is that it is a matter of empirical test.

Behavior modification in clinical psychology is a direct outgrowth of the kind of experimentation conducted in operant conditioning with its tradition of single-case analysis to derive general principles. One argument in favor of single-case analysis is that we eventually would like to make clinical statements concerning the individual case; results based on group data may not apply to any individual case.

Individual-case analysis is primarily employed as a test of the effect of certain interventions on behavior. One of its virtues is that the subject serves as his own control in experiencing two or more interventions. The illustration given of the rat avoiding shock is known as an AB design, in which the rat is observed first under condition A for a number of trials and then under condition B. If the experiment were extended to a point where the drug is discontinued and the rat then resumes his pre-drug behavior, the results are even more convincing that the change in behavior from A to B was not possibly due to a chance variable rather than condition B. This would obviously be called an ABA design. If we were now able to demonstrate the same drug effect of ABA in a female as well as a male rat, our confidence in the results (now generalizing across sex) would be accordingly enhanced. Or, if the same drug effect were demonstrable under different reinforcement schedules or with somewhat different behaviors, the confidence in the results would increase further.

Demonstration of essentially the same effect on different subjects, on different behaviors, and in different settings, is referred to as a *multiple baseline* or *multiple phase analysis* (Hayes, 1981) and is valuable in that it allows a test of the robustness (generalizability) of the result to different conditions. Interaction terms can be tested by comparing, for example, the effect of receiving treatments A + B with only receiving treatment B. Multiple observations are required over time under each treatment; the greater the variability over time, the greater number of trials required. Since there is the possible effect of treatment order or of maturation over time, a treatment should be phased in more than once. The treatments are compared with regard to the level, variability, and slope of their trend within treatments. Thus, if a disorder is self-remitting (such as some depressions), one would look for a change in the slope of the remission trend before and after the intervention. A change in the level of psychopathology might not mean as much since there was a natural tendency to remit.

Single-case analysis has seen considerable use in the study of anorexia nervosa, partly because this is a rare disorder without a sufficient number of cases for the classical parallel group design. The variables in the disorder (eating and body weight) easily lend themselves to the multiple observations required. For example, one could use daily body weight, or daily caloric intake, or the number of mouthfuls ingested, or the time taken to consume the meal. Some of the interventions tested are desensitization of anxiety with regard to food, rewarding the patient with social privileges for gaining weight, feedback on the amount ingested, and the size of the meal presented (Agras et al., 1975). Since one is comparing slopes over time before and after an intervention, numerous observations over time are a distinct advantage. This requirement is far easier in the behaviors of anorexia nervosa than it would be, for example, in schizophrenia, phobic anxiety, or depression, in which the behavior to be modified is most usually obtainable only through interview and is not as frequently observed.

The same shortcomings and disadvantages as in cross-over designs apply to single-case analysis. The principal shortcoming is in the carryover effect of the first treatment on the second. The effect of the first treatment may not wash out over time, and what appears to be an effect of the second treatment is really an effect of the combination of the two. Second, while order effects can be counterbalanced, doing so does not eliminate the possibility that the effect of the treatment depends on the state of the patient at that time. Hence, the effect of the second treatment might have been different had it been first only because the patient was more severely ill at the earlier point in time. Third, with only a single case, there is no way of knowing whether this applies to any other case. Replication of the analysis to other cases automatically transforms the analysis into a group data design.

One of the greatest shortcomings of the design is the requirement of a large series of observations before and after the intervention because of the intrinsic variability of the behavior being observed. This is a shortcoming because a sufficiently large series of observations are usually not available in most clinical situations. In some published research, three or four timepoints have been used to represent one condition. Although, generally, no formal significance tests are made, a judgment is made of a significant difference before and after the intervention with regard to the level, variability, or slope of the timepoints. We would contend that with only three or four observations, stable estimates of level, variability, and slope are not possible.

Notwithstanding these criticisms, single-case analysis does have a role to play in clinical research in conjunction with the analysis of group data. One is not a substitute for the other. If one finds a significant result in the group data; he would like to know whether he can generalize that result to any specific case. Can he do so?

Single-case analysis should be used in conjunction with parallel group designs. In the treatment of anorexia nervosa, the single-case literature shows that desensitization as a technique has not been effective, while social reinforcement and feedback have seemed to be. Accordingly, one would be more justified in mounting a large and expensive parallel group design testing the effects of feedback and social reinforcement rather than using desensitization therapy. The single-case analysis provides the opportunity to explore the experimental manipulation from patient-to-patient before settling on a standardized procedure that would be applied to the parallel group design. Because even the best treatments will not be effective on some subjects, the single-case analysis provides a preliminary opportunity to identify the characteristics of those subjects for whom the treatment does or does not work. This can lead to a more sophisticated case selection for the subsequent parallel group design.

SUMMARY

The premise of this chapter is that the task of research in clinical psychopathology is the establishment of lawful relationships among clinically relevant variables. The particular index of any relationship depends on whether the variables are categorical (e.g., psychiatric diagnosis) or quantitative (e.g., number of days spent in the hospital). The expression of any relationship should include not only its statistical significance but also its size. To what extent is the relationship obtained in the sample representative of the universe from which it was drawn? Sampling and measurement artifacts (e.g., restriction or expansion of range, halo, unreliability) may either inflate or deflate the relationship obtained in the sample.

Posing the research question is possibly the most difficult conceptual problem faced by the researcher. In clinical psychopathology, research questions may be grouped in terms of etiology, clinical course and outcome, and, finally, the effect of certain interventions.

Experimental studies are those in which at least one independent variable is under the control of the experimenter. This is accomplished by means of the random assignment of consecutive subjects to the various levels of the independent variable. The prime advantage of an experimental study is that it may attribute causation to one of the variables.

In declaring that a relationship exists between two variables, one needs to control (rule out) the possibility that another variable was, in reality, responsible for the relationship. Such control is achieved by means of factorial designs, analysis of covariance, and partial correlation.

Dropouts from treatment studies can seriously bias the results if the dropout is replaced or simply not included in the analysis. The particular bias depends on the termination score of the dropped case. Dropouts must be included in the analysis by use of the best estimate of what their scores would have been had they completed.

In multiple correlation and regression, most investigators underestimate the true number of predictors they are dealing with and, consequently, overestimate the significance and size of the multiple correlation obtained, which then fails to cross-validate in a subsequent study. A solution is to abandon the test of significance for multiple correlation and to substitute cross-validation instead.

Single-subject analysis, which requires multiple observations before and after an intervention, can be valuable in the initial explorations prior to mounting an extensive group design. The test is made whether the level, variability, and slope of the data prior to treatment is different than the post-treatment trends. Generalizability to other subjects is always an open question.

REFERENCES

Agras, W. S., Barlow, D. H., Chapin, H. N., Obel, G. C., & Leitenberg, H. Behavior modification of anorexia nervosa. *Archives of General Psychiatry,* 1975, *30,* 279–286.

Appelbaum, M. I., & Cramer, E. M. Some problems in the nonorthogonal analysis of variance. *Psychological Bulletin,* 1974, *81,* 335–343.

Bateson, G., Jackson, D., Haley, J., & Weakland, J. Toward a theory of schizophrenia. *Behavioral Science,* 1956, *1,* 241–264.

Bleuler, E. [*Dementia praecox or the group of schizophrenias*] (J. Zinkin, trans.). New York: International Universities Press, 1950. (Originally published, 1911.)

Campbell, D. T., & Stanley, J. C. *Experimental and quasi-experimental designs for research.* Skokie, Ill.: Rand McNally, 1963.

Carroll, J. B. The nature of data, or how to choose a correlation coefficient. *Psychometrika,* 1961, *26,* 347–372.

Chassan, J. B. *Research design in clinical psychology and psychiatry* (2nd ed.). New York: Irvington Publishers, 1979.

Cohen, J. A coefficient of agreement for nominal scales. *Educational and Psychological Measurement,* 1960, *20,* 37–46.

Cohen, J. Weighted kappa: Nominal scale agreement with provision for scaled disagreement or partial credit. *Psychological Bulletin,* 1968, *70,* 213–220.

Cohen, J., Cohen, P. *Applied multiple regression correlation analysis for the behavioral & sciences.* Hillsdale, N.J.: Lawrence Erlbaum Associates, 1975.

Cook, T. D., & Campbell, D. T. *Quasi-experimentation: Design and analysis issues for field settings.* Skokie, Ill.: Rand McNally, 1979.

Draper, N. R., & Smith, H. *Applied regression analysis.* New York: John Wiley & Sons, 1966.

Fleiss, J. Estimating the magnitude of experimental effects. *Psychological Bulletin,* 1969, *72,* 273–276.

Fromm-Reichmann, F. Some aspects of psychoanalytic psychiatry with schizophrenics. In E. B. Brody, & F. C. Redlich (Eds.), *Psychotherapy with schizophrenics.* New York: International Universities Press, 1952.

Goldberg, S. C., Schooler, N. R., Hogarty, G. E., & Roper, M. Prediction of relapse in schizophrenic outpatients treated by drug and sociotherapy. *Archives of General Psychiatry,* 1977, *34,* 171–184.

Hamer, R. M., & Hosking, J. T. The nonorthognoal analysis of variance. *Representative Research in Social Psychology,* 1977, *8,* 71–87.

Hayes, S. C. Single-case experimental design and empirical clinical practice. *Journal of Consulting and Clinical Psychology,* 1981, *49,* 193–211.

Hays, W. L. *Statistics.* New York: Holt, Rinehart & Winston, 1963, 1968.

Hersen, M., & Barlow, D. H. *Single case experimental designs: Strategies for studying behavioral change.* New York: Pergamon Press, 1976.

Hogarty, G. E., Goldberg, S. C., Schooler, N. R., & Ulrich, R. F. Drug and sociotherapy in the aftercare of schizophrenic patients: II Two-year relapse rates. *Archives of General Psychiatry,* 1974, *31,* 603–608.

Huitema, B. E. *Analysis of covariance and alternatives.* New York: John Wiley & Sons, 1980.

Kallmann, F. J. *The Genetics of Schizophrenia.* New York: J. J. Augustin Publishers, 1938.

Kety, S. S., Rosenthal, D., Wender, P. H., & Schulsinger, F. The types and prevalence of mental illness in biological and adoptive families of adopted schizophrenics. In D. Rosenthal & S. S. Kety (Eds.), *The transmission of schizophrenia.* New York: Pergamon Press, 1968.

Kim, J., & Muller, C. W. *Factor analysis.* Beverly Hills, Calif.: Sage Publications, 1978.

Kraepelin, E. [*Dementia praecox*] (R. M. Barclay, trans.). Edinburgh: E. S. Livinstone, 1919.

Kruskal, J. B., & Wish, M. *Multidimensional scaling.* Beverly Hills, Calif.: Sage Publications, 1978.

Lidz, T., Fleck, S., & Cornelison, A. *Schizophrenia and the family.* New York: International Universities Press, 1965.

May, P. R. A. *Treatment of schizophrenia: A comparative study of five treatment methods.* New York: Science House, 1968.

Mosteller, F., & Tukey, J. W. Data analysis, including statistics. In G. Lindsey & E. Aronson (Eds.), *The handbook of social psychology.* Reading, Mass.: Addison-Wesley Publishing, 1968.

Muliak, S. A. *The foundations of factor analysis.* New York: McGraw-Hill, 1972.

Overall, J. E., Hollister, L. E., Honigfeld, G., Kimball, I. H., Meyer, F., Bennett, J. L., & Caffey, E. M. Comparison of acetophenazine with perphenazine in schizophrenics: Demonstration of differential effects based on computer-derived diagnostic models. *Clinical Pharmacology and Therapeutics,* 1963, *4,* 200–208.

Overall, J. E., & Spiegel, D. K. Concerning the least-squares analysis of experimental data. *Psychological Bulletin,* 1969, *72,* 311–322.

Philips, L. Case history data and prognosis in schizophrenia. *Journal of Nervous and Mental Disease,* 1953, *117,* 515–525.

Rosenberg, S., & Cohen, B. D. A method for the study of lay conceptions of psychopathology: A response-free approach. *American Journal of Community Psychiatry,* 1977, *5,* 177–193.

Sidman, N. *Tactics of scientific research.* New York: Basic Books, 1960.

Urquhart, N. S., Weeks, D. L., & Henderson, C. R. Estimation associated with linear models: A revisitation. *Communications in Statistics,* 1973, *1,* 303–330.

Wender, P. H., Rosenthal, D., Kety, S. S., Schulsinger, F., & Welner, J. Cross-fostering: A research strategy for clarifying the role of genetic and experiential factors in the etiology of schizophrenia. *Archives of General Psychiatry,* 1974, *30,* 121–128.

Williams, E. J. *Regression analysis.* New York: John Wiley & Sons, 1959.

Winer, B. J. *Statistical principles in experimental design* (2nd ed.). New York: McGraw-Hill, 1971.

Young, F. W., & Hamer, R. M., *Multidimensional scaling: Theory and method.* Hillsdale, N.J.: Lawrence Erlbaum Associates, in preparation.

5

Evaluations of social programs ▬

Lee Sechrest, Ph.D.*
David Ametrano, M.S.†
and
Irene Mass Ametrano, Ed.D.‡

The task of any researcher, but certainly that of a program evaluator, is to plan and carry out the research in such a way that whatever conclusions the researcher thinks warranted will be persuasive. The first questions, then, that need to be asked and answered are who must be persuaded and what kind of evidence would be required to be persuasive? The first of these questions is often discussed in terms of the audience for the evaluation report, although only infrequently is the issue of persuasability mentioned (but see Hutchison, 1981). Problems immediately arise because, for most program evaluations, there are multiple audiences, for example, those who pay for the program, those who are supposed to benefit from it, those who administer it, and so on (Krause and Howard, 1976). The various audiences are likely to differ substantially in the ease with which they will be persuaded to any conclusions; and they may be more difficult to persuade to some conclusions, (e.g., that a program is worthless) than others (e.g., that a program is wonderful). The fact of the matter is, however, that many researchers have tough but distant and uninvolved audiences in mind when they conduct evaluations, and those audiences may provoke researchers to plan and carry out the research in ways beyond the ken and desires of more immediately concerned audiences. Specifically, researchers frequently must carry out program evaluations with the views and special requirements of their academic colleagues, journal reviewers, and editors in mind. Those pro-

* Center for Research on the Utilization of Scientific Knowledge, Institute for Social Research, University of Michigan, Ann Arbor.
† Department of Psychology, University of Michigan, Ann Arbor.
‡ Department of Counseling, Eastern Michigan University, Ypsilanti.

fessional peers may care much more about randomization, reliability of measures, and multivariate statistical tests than do the audiences toward whom the evaluation is more immediately directed. In truth, however, we know very little about what it takes to persuade any audience (other than journal editors), so that planning research with a favorable cost-effectiveness index for persuasiveness is not easy. Still, a good first step for an investigator beginning the planning of an evaluation study is to talk to members of the diverse audiences for the report about what evidence they would consider persuasive for what conclusions. The research ought, at the very least, to have reasonable capability of being persuasive to its most immediate audiences. Even so, researchers should keep in mind that it is very difficult to foresee the uses to which a research report might be put. Current interest in meta-evaluation and data synthesis (Glass, McGaw, and Smith, 1981) suggests that researchers should not underestimate the sophistication of potential users of their data and reports. The review by Lipton, Martinson, and Wilks (1975) of research on criminal-offender rehabilitation employed a methodological screen that resulted in a large proportion of available studies being regarded as uninterpretable. They may have seemed persuasive studies to those who originally planned them, but they failed more stringent tests by ultimate audiences.

If an investigator can make some reasonably well-informed judgements, it ought to be possible to plan a program evaluation that has the capability of producing persuasive evidence on conclusions that the investigator regards as likely alternatives. In order to develop the best plan, however, it is necessary for the program evaluator to be involved from the beginning in the planning for the program and its evaluation. The ways in which some program activities are carried out may have a good bit to do with whether evidence concerning their effectiveness will be persuasive. For example, it is often necessary for evaluation purposes to keep more and better records than may be required purely for program purposes. Program activities may need to be documented and verified more carefully and more often. Screening of applicants may have to be more extensive and more formal. Nothing is more frustrating for a program evaluator than to be brought in to evaluate an ongoing program and find that simple but important records were not kept or were kept too haphazardly to be useful.

Planning research to be persuasive means (1) the devising of a research design that will produce plausible results, (2) the selection of measures that will be considered relevant and otherswise satisfactory, and (3) the development of an administrative plan for the study that will guarantee sufficient quality in the enterprise. The term *devise* is used in relation to the research design because it seems so rarely the case that a program evaluator can simply take a design off the shelf (or out of the book) and apply it directly. Adaptations are usually required, extra data series must be collected, and allowances must be made. A wise evaluator will often try to devise a research plan that includes a "fall-back" research design, in case the original, favored design fails for some reason. Care must be taken in selecting (devising would be a useful term in this context also) measures that potential audiences will consider realistic and meaningful. A researcher may have great faith in a paper-and-pencil measure of problem solving, for example, or in the scores from a driving simulator, but if decision makers or other audiences are disdainful of such indirect measures, the program evaluator would be ill-advised to rely on them.

In program evaluation (as in all else in life), there is many a slip. Consequently, an administrative plan is required to see to it that the research actually gets carried out as planned and that the carrying out is adequately documented. If persons are to be assigned randomly to program conditions, there must be a mechanism for doing so, and there must be a way of verifying that the mechanism was not bypassed. If follow-up telephone interviews are to be obtained, then someone should be in charge of obtaining phone numbers and of ensuring that the calls get made at the time stated in the plan. If data forms are to come in from diverse sources, then there should be a plan for receiving them, coding them properly, scoring them, and so on. The aim of all this activity is not some sort of pointless tidiness, but to produce data of sufficiently high quality to persuade whoever must be persuaded. It may be that a particular evaluator expects to be held to standards which are lower than those implied here, but it is nearly always better to overshoot by a good bit. A fundamental rule in program evaluation is that nothing ever goes better than expected; once a project starts, things are as good as they are ever going to be.

How much should an evaluation cost?

One of the writers once knew a stable owner whose stock reply to how much a good horse was worth was "Any horse is worth $100 plus however much you want to own him." Any program can be evaluated for $100 plus however much more it will take to be persuasive. Hutchinson (1981) noted that persons with different involvements in programs will have quite different ideas about how much ought to be spent on evaluation. Those responsible for service delivery, for example, may be already persuaded of the value of the program and may regard any money spent on evaluation as diverted from service delivery and wasted. Those funding programs may regard any money well spent if it produces program improvements that can be demonstrated to be worth more than they cost. And academic scientists may regard program-evaluation money as well spent as long as the research continues to produce quality information and publications. Whatever one's view, however, it should be considered that money spent on evaluations that do not produce persuasive results for whatever reasons—poor design, careless execution, or inadequate measures—is truly money wasted (Sechrest, 1977). For example, the hundreds of studies of offender rehabilitation ruled unacceptable by Lipton et al. (1975) could be regarded as wasted effort and money if they ended up having no impact on the field.

Actually the amount of money that ought to be spent on an evaluation depends also on the nature of the program and the larger purposes, if any, of the evaluation. Thus, the evaluation of a small, group-therapy program for mothers of victims of child molestations should not absorb resources in such an amount as to threaten the quality of the program. On the other hand, if the particular implementation of a program being evaluated is but one of a larger number, or if the program is a prototype of one with potentially widespread emulation, an evaluation that costs more than the program might well be justified (Sechrest, 1977). Sex therapy, biofeedback, psychoanalytic therapy, and encounter groups are all instances of types of interventions whose early and careful (even if expensive) evaluations would have been justified in light of the extent to which they have spread and persisted.

Who should pay for such evaluations is another matter, of course. Money for evaluations may not be available if there is no constituency with a clear, financial interest in the program. It may help the potential program evaluator (in negotiating for funds to do the evaluation) to have a clear picture of the financial interest of the prospective source of funds and to determine the level at which that source is interested in the outcome (i.e., as a local program, as a typical program, as a prototype, and so on).

DESIGN ISSUES IN EVALUATION

Perhaps the simplest question one can ask about a program is, "At what level are its participants functioning when they leave?" Such a question is often answered by a single observation, such as "ninety percent of the children completing this swimming course know how to swim." Evaluation, however, must go beyond such simple observation to allow causal inferences as unambiguous as possible about the program under consideration and its effects. This task is rarely straightforward but is of crucial importance in determining the fate of an evaluation. To the extent that the design of an evaluation allows one to rule out alternative explanations of the causal relationship (e.g., that children in swimming classes get more instruction at home), it produces clear-cut, useful information. To the extent that it allows alternative explanations of the results (i.e., that observed effects may be attributed to factors other than the program), the evaluation is problematic and has failed to fulfill one of its primary objectives.

Validity

Before entering into a discussion of the strengths and weaknesses of various evaluation designs, it may be helpful to review briefly the concept of validity as it applies to interpretations of evaluation findings. Of concern is that the evaluation generate a product that is, in a general sense, valid. It is useful to break down this overall quality of validity into manageable subtypes. Various authors conceptualize validity as consisting of subtypes varying in number and specificity, which are reflected in the various conclusions growing out of a study.

Potential problems with the validity of interpretations will, obviously, depend on the nature of the statement whose validity is at issue. For example, consider the following statements that might be made following an evaluation of a program involving efforts to improve the social skills of retarded children:

1. At the end of the study, the children in the experimental group were significantly better than the children in the comparison group in amount of smiling, polite requests, and eye contact.
2. The experimental intervention resulted in better performance by the experimental children than by the comparison children.
3. Systematically rewarding retarded children for prosocial responses improved their performance on social-skills tasks.
4. Programs centering upon positive reinforcements for prosocial responses will improve the social skills of retarded children.

Each of these statements implies that the experiment was a valid test of some proposition, but the validity implications are somewhat different for each statement.

Cook and Campbell (1979) have described four validity concepts that we wish to illustrate with the above statements: Statistical-conclusion validity, internal validity, construct validity, and external validity.

Statistical conclusion validity. The assurance one is able to place in the conclusions of an evaluation depends initially on the adequacy of the statistical justification for the conclusions. For example, a conclusion would lack statistical validity if it were the result of an arithmetic error. Similarly, it would lack validity if important statistical assumptions were not met, if inappropriate statistical tests were employed, if the wrong units of observation were the focus of the analysis, and so on. Statement 1 might be invalid for all of the reasons just mentioned as well as for others (e.g., selection of a few significant values from a larger number of nonsignificant findings). A frequent, potential source of invalid statistical conclusions of no treatment effect is the use of a number of observations too small to make likely the detection of effects of the size expected. This problem has to do with statistical power analysis (Cohen, 1977) and requires prior determination of the likelihood of being able to detect effects or relationships. Another frequent, potential source of invalid statistical conclusions (usually resulting in the same erroneous conclusion of no effect) is the use of unreliable outcome measures.

Obviously the best protection one can have against threats to statistical-conclusion validity is to plan a study carefully, so as to have dependent measures of adequate reliability and a sufficient sample size to provide for the statistical power that is desired, and then to do the statistical analysis with high accuracy and wisdom in the choice of statistical tests. One should also be cautious about overanalyzing data in a search for something significant and be forthright in reporting all the analyses actually done. Adjustment of significance levels or some other maneuver to compensate for multiple statistical tests may also be desirable. Unlike some other validity problems, those involving the validity of statistical conclusions are usually easily spotted, and most are under the control of the investigator.

Internal validity.   Statement 2 asserts that the observed difference between experimental and comparison children was the result of the experimental treatment and not the result of some extraneous variable. In general, the aim of what is usually referred to as *experimental design* is to increase confidence in the internal validity of the experiment. To the extent that some alternative explanation, a plausible, rival hypothesis (Campbell & Stanley, 1966) remains possible, the experiment lacks internal validity. For example, if the study mentioned previously consisted of experimental children, volunteered for the study by their parents, and comparison children, whose parents would not or could not permit them to participate, the difference at the end of the experiment might have been attributable to some initial difference between the children. Problems with internal validity will be discussed in later sections of this chapter.

Construct validity.   Conclusions about experiments usually assume that the nature of the experimental intervention is known and described accurately. That may not always be the case for a variety of reasons. For example, statement 3 suggests that the systematic rewarding of prosocial responses constituted the effective treatment. If that treatment involved more interaction between children and teachers, however, then it might be plausible that the increased interaction produced the effect. Or, if parents knew the general nature of the experiment, and that knowledge led to increased parental coaching of the children in the experimental group, then the inference about systematic rewards would be incorrect. In traditional experimental design, problems of construct validity are referred to as *confounding* (Underwood & Shaughnessy, 1975). Often treatments will be multifaceted and complex, so that one could not be certain what the critical element(s) might be. In fact, for most interventions designed to ameliorate social and personal ills, interventions are likely to be multifaceted and complex. In such instances, problems of construct validity can easily arise.

Our confidence in our understanding of treatments and their construct validity is proportional to the adequacy with which interventions are described, the strength of the rationale underlying them, and the extent of documentation of their implementation. That is not to say there cannot be subtle problems arising out of "nonspecific treatment effects" (Kazdin & Wilcoxin, 1976), or other failures of understanding; but, generally speaking, construct validity problems can be avoided and are largely under control of the investigator if the project has been well conceived and adequately funded so as to provide for the documentation needed.

External validity. Rarely are we interested in the specific outcome of a single experiment or study. Rather, we are interested in the likelihood that the results obtained would hold with other samples, in other places, with other arrangements, and so on. This is the problem of external validity. In the last statement of outcomes mentioned above, it was implied that the findings would pertain generally to retarded children, that a wide range of positive reinforcements would be effective, and that a broad range of social skills (e.g., rather than simply smiling and having eye contact) would be improved. There are many reasons why the results of a single study might not be very widely generalizable. If a sample is narrowly constructed (e.g., only Down's syndrome cases were included), the results might not be generalizable to a larger population. Results obtained with one type of reinforcement might not be generalizable to other types of reinforcements. And results obtainable with such specific-response measures as eye contact and smiling might not be generalizable to what we would more generally refer to as social skills.

Frequently, a troublesome limitation on external validity is the *reactive arrangements* involved in many experiments. By that is meant that experiments—and quasi-experiments—are often carried out under such special arrangements that the findings are not generalizable to situations not characterized by those arrangements. A common belief, which may not be invariably true (e.g., see Cook, 1967), is that experiments are highly subject to the *Hawthorne effect*, which refers to a presumed tendency of research subjects to respond differently when they believe they are part of an experiment than they would respond ordinarily. Certainly there are experimental arrangements likely to produce responses not characteristic of those occurring in other situations. Under experimental conditions, everyone involved in a program may try harder and work harder. Often, the conditions of an experiment produce a pressure for certain types of responses, a phenomenon known in social psychology as *demand characteristics* (Orne, 1969). The example par excellence of reactive arrangements and demand characteristics is the formal, military inspection. The television commercial testimonial is an example of a common arrangement with obvious demand characteristics. Not only is it clear that an enthusiastic endorsement is expected, but the interviewer frequently provides the subject with subtle (and sometimes not so subtle) cues to which product is to be preferred. Subsequent interviews have found that some subjects actually disliked the products they endorsed. There are counterparts in experiments, including those involving program evaluation.

True experiments

In most respects, the issue of internal validity may be considered prior to all others. If one cannot with confidence assert that a particular intervention caused or produced a particular effect, then other issues are moot. The external validity of a questionable effect is not of much interest. Similarly, it does not much matter whether we can define an intervention or statistically analyze for it, if we cannot connect it to an outcome in any case.

The strength of the true experimental design (Campbell & Stanley, 1966) is that it allows one, under most circumstances, to rule out alternative explanations of the results. This assurance of internal validity is based on two aspects of the true experiment. One of these is the random assignment of cases (which may be individuals, families, wards, etc.) to treatment conditions, and the other is the inclusion of a control group assumed equivalent to the experimental group(s) in all ways except for the treatment(s). When numbers are reasonably large, assigning cases randomly to treatment conditions minimizes the possibility that the groups will differ substantially from each other on any unknown variables. Consequently, any final, post-treatment differences between the control subjects and the experimental subjects can be attributed with a high level of confidence to the treatment or program. Designs other than true experiments too often allow one or more rival hypotheses to remain plausible, thus failing to assure internal validity.

Threats to internal validity

A threat to internal validity is a factor that, because of the research design, yields or supports a hypothesis that is a plausible alternative (or rival) to the one of interest. Campbell (1969) has provided a description of nine threats to internal validity that a true experiment rules out: history, maturation, instability, testing, instrumentation, regression artifacts, selection, experimental mortality, and selection maturation interaction. Detailed presentations of these are available elsewhere (Campbell, 1969; Campbell & Stanley, 1966; Cook and Campbell, 1979; Neale & Liebert, 1973), so all will not be reviewed here. Deserving of mention, however, are several of these threats that are especially common in program evaluation.

History. This refers to events, other than the program, that may occur between pre-test and post-test measures and, in the absence of a strong design, provide alternative explanations of the results. As an example, an evaluation of the effect of increasing the legal drinking age on auto fatalities might be rendered inconclusive if some extraneous but possibly relevant event (such as the introduction of mandatory, passive restraints) occurred during the evaluation period.

Regression artifact. Social programs are often initiated at a time when a problem appears to be rapidly worsening. If the problem then returns to its previous level, that change may be attributed to the program. Because, statistically, such a return to baseline would usually be expected to occur as a *regression artifact* (but see Nesselroade, Stigler, Baltes, 1980), attributions of effectiveness to the program would be unjustified. Statistical regression is not always easy to understand, and some of its manifestations are subtle, but it is a possibility that always remains plausible when the initiation of an intervention occurs because a problem has reached some extreme point of intolerability. Any program evaluator even suspecting such a state of affairs should consult a detailed discussion of statistical regression problems in research design, such as is found in Cook and Campbell (1979).

Selection. Perhaps the most frequent shortcoming of nonexperimental evaluation is the differential *selection* of subjects into treatment and nonequivalent control conditions. Without random assignment to conditions, selection itself could be responsible for any differences obtained. For example, in an evaluation of an alcohol-treatment program, if a number of subjects were admitted into treatment because an admissions director judged them to be especially appropriate for the program, any findings favorable to the treatments group might be attributable to the more favorable prospects of these specially admitted persons. Similarly, the exclusion of patients from insight therapy on the basis of inadequate ego strength to undergo the treatment would make interpretation of findings of comparisons between therapies quite hazardous.

Instrumentation. Changes in *instrumentation* during an evaluation can also result in problems of interpretation. The evaluator should take care not to institute major changes in reporting or recording procedures during an evaluation that could account for apparent changes in the dependent variables. An investigator some years hence doing an archival study could be misled by not knowing that a treatment facility shifted from DSM II to DSM III in the middle of a series of cases being studied.

Small effects. The greater efficiency of a true experimental design enables measurement of smaller, subtler effects that might be washed out in a looser, quasi-experimental design. Thus, when documentation of what are expected to be small effects is needed (Gilbert, McPeek, & Mosteller, 1977), the evaluator should be aware that a true experimental design may offer the only reasonable expectation of detecting those effects. In general, quasi-experiments seem to require larger, more consistent outcomes to be persuasively interpretable.

The often highly persuasive nature of the findings of true experiments means that, all other things being equal, those findings are more likely to be utilized than similar findings arrived at through quasi-experimental or nonexperimental approaches.

Ideally, virtually every program might be subjected to the rigors of a true experiment. Unfortunately, true experiments are usually difficult, often very difficult, and in many instances simply impossible. Planning for evaluations of programs often begins after the program is well underway and operating under circumstances that make random assignments to intervention conditions impossible. Once programs are operational, many factors can stand in the way of the implementation of a true experiment. Service providers may be resistant to changes in modes of operation required for experimental design purposes. A program evaluator ought not accept without objection the protests of service providers or others who would frustrate the implementation of a strong evaluation design, but the evaluator has to be realistic. Part of the task of the evaluator is to provide the ingenuity necessary to develop the strongest design possible in the face of any obstacles that exist.

Ethics and design of program evaluations. Objections are often raised to randomization of interventions on the grounds that valuable, or at least potentially valuable, treatments are being withheld from some persons. Obviously, it would be unethical to withhold an effective treatment from someone who could benefit from it in an important way. On the other hand, it can be argued that an untested intervention, especially one thought to require justification through a research demonstration of its effectiveness, is not, in fact, a treatment. Evaluations are generally conducted specifically because there is good reason to doubt the effectiveness of the intervention. Problems arise, however, because the doubt may be shared in unequal degrees by different persons involved in the process of delivering the intervention. Clinicians may not be as doubtful as those who provide funds for the intervention and so may be opposed to withholding the intervention in order to facilitate a test they regard as superfluous. The program evaluator can often be caught in a dilemma and can only respond by pressing for the best solution possible. Borgatta (1955) has argued that a service not actually useful is wasteful and may prevent the client from receiving an effective service in its place. The possibility that interventions might be harmful should also be considered. Failure to provide for a conclusive evaluation of an intervention could also be regarded as an ethical problem.

It is not invariably the case that ethical concerns and good research design are incompatible. A delayed-treatment design, similar to the familiar wait list control design in psychotherapy studies, may be both feasible and ethical (Weiss, 1972). Feasibility would depend, in part, on whether it would be realistic to think that people would not seek alternative sources of care comparable to the experimental treatment rather than endure delay. Ethicality would depend largely on the extent of distress that would have to be endured during the delay period. The delayed-treatment design is especially well justified if the capacity to handle all the cases available is lacking so that some, perforce, must be delayed. In that situation, a random process to determine who receives the intervention first seems eminently fair and is advantageous from a design standpoint.

Other possibly ethical adaptations have been suggested. Some alternative treatment (one perhaps useful but weaker than the experimental treatment) might be offered in lieu of a placebo (Scriven, 1967). Another possibility might be to break a treatment down into components, if doing so does not altogether destroy the integrity of the treatment. The components might then be given separately to different groups at different times.

In planning any comparison of treatments, whether of an experimental treatment with a no-treatment or a placebo, or of an experimental treatment with an alternative, a paradox arises that can have important consequences for the conclusions reached. Specifically, as the condition against which the experimental treatment is to be compared is made stronger or better, the probability of finding any advantage for the experimental treatment decreases (Baum, Anish, Chalmers, Sacks, Smith, & Fagerstrom, 1981). Decisions based on ethical concerns ought to take into account the full range of ethical issues, including the possibility that a poorly planned experiment will have proved both risky to those involved as subjects and inconclusive with respect to findings. It could be regarded as quite unethical to involve people in research with no prospects for good quality data coming from it. Moreover, it is often enough the case that innovative interventions prove worse than more standard treatments (no matter how attractive they might have seemed), that great thought should be given to the presumption that putting persons in other than the experimental group is somehow or other placing them at a disadvantage (e.g., see Gilbert, Light, & Mosteller, 1975; Sechrest, West, Phillips, Redner, & Yeaton, 1979).

The null hypothesis.   Not infrequently, the aim of a researcher is to render the null hypothesis plausible (i.e., the researcher really wants to demonstrate that there is no difference between experimental and control conditions). That might be the case, for example, when the innovation is the use of paraprofessionals to manage cases ordinarily seen by more expensive professionals or when a program for outpatient care of alcoholics is being compared to an inpatient program. In such cases, it is not expected that the innovative treatment will be better than the standard, only that it will be as good as the standard (i.e., that there will be no difference between them). As even neophytes in research know, however, proving the null hypothesis is impossible. Even though that is the case, we do end up accepting the null hypothesis with great frequency. However, since the null hypothesis is, strictly speaking, never true (e.g., Bakan, 1966), and there are so many ways of doing research badly so that differences are not likely to be significant, doing research in support of the null hypothesis is especially demanding of the most careful attention to considerations of design and implementation. Remembering that the purpose of research is to persuade, support of the null hypothesis against those who would persist in believing that differences must exist requires the strongest designs, substantial statistical power, precision in conduct of the experiment, and the best of outcome measures. Only under such circumstances is the null hypothesis likely to be defensible.

Murphy's law and experimentation.   Even if a true experiment is planned and mounted, it is to be expected that things will go wrong, and none of the unexpected happenings will improve the experiment. People in different conditions may become "contaminated" by talking to each other or may seek treatment from other sources. In a study of treatment of diabetics by multiple injections of insulin (Job, Eschwege, & Guyot-Argenton, 1976), 21 patients were randomly assigned to the experimental treatment conditions, but only 4 of them actually received the treatment for the full period of time because the others asked to have their treatments changed. Spillover effects must often be regarded as a possibility when there is a chance that clinicians or patients are aware of treatment conditions other than their own. For example, a study of the effects of different types of information provided about cases may be frustrated by tendencies of clinicians to seek out the information not provided to them on some of their cases or that they know is being provided to other clinicians in the study. Finally, but without exhausting the list of things that might go wrong, randomization itself might fail if some of those involved in the study believe that one treatment is superior to the others and have the capability of altering the method of assignment so that some favored cases get into the right condition. Randomization processes must be closely and continuously monitored.

Quasi-experimental designs

There are strong arguments in favor of true experiments when they are at all possible, but when they are not, other research methods are available. Under the best of circumstances, one or more of the alternatives may provide information that is of a quality approaching that of an experiment, thus permitting reasonably definitive conclusions (Campbell & Stanley 1966; Cook & Campbell, 1979). What is important is that the design alternatives be carefully considered and that the strongest possible design consistent with circumstances be chosen. Choice of the best design will require a careful analysis of the threats to validity (likely to be the most plausible rival hypotheses) and of the immediate circumstances that rule out a randomized experiment.

The nonequivalent control group designs (NCGD). Probably the most often used quasi-experimental design is the NCGD, recognizable by the twin facts that there is a comparison group and that cases get into the comparison condition by other than random assignment. Because the comparison group is not chosen randomly, it is assumed to be nonequivalent to the experimental treatment group, but researchers should make every attempt to choose or develop a comparison group as much like the experimental group as possible. Thus, for example, a comparison group for disturbed children being treated in a special school environment should be other disturbed children with highly similar problems and from similar circumstances. A great part of the challenge in doing quasi-experimental work comes from the need to develop the best possible comparison groups. If the special school is taking a large proportion of the disturbed children in the community, then the best comparison group might be disturbed children from another community lacking the intervention, rather than less disturbed children in the same community. The goal is to decrease (or eliminate) plausible rival explanations for any conclusion favoring the exerimental intervention. The task of the researcher is to anticipate those plausible alternative explanations (implausible explanations may be ignorable) and to devise the NCGD study in such a way that plausible rival explanations are weakened as much as possible. Very often, a good bit of leverage can be gained by employing multiple comparison groups, each of which helps to weaken one or more alternatives and which, in sum, leave the preferred hypothesis as the best explanation. As long as additional comparison groups do not make the study too expensive to undertake, they can be of value. A study of treatment of disturbed children, for example, might include as comparison groups disturbed children in other programs, disturbed children whose parents refused to enter them into the program, disturbed children in another community lacking any program, and children not in the program because of a criterion of insufficient severity of the problem.

Matching often seems to be a way of decreasing initial dissimilarity between groups, but there are serious problems with matching that almost always make it an undesirable tactic. One can probably never match on all relevant variables and would have no way of knowing it, anyway. Matching on some variables will often create a compensating mismatch on other variables; and matching often increases the potential for regression effects, sometimes resulting in the addition of a rival hypothesis that did not initially exist in a NCGD. Studies employing matching to try to compensate for initial differences between groups have a great potential for being positively misleading and should always be looked upon with great suspicion (Campbell & Stanley, 1966; Cook and Campbell, 1979; Neale and Liebert, 1973).

Time series designs. A type of research design that often yields high-quality data and defensible conclusions is the interrupted time series design (Judd & Kenny, 1981). The time series design utilizes a series of measures taken before an intervention starts (usually called a *baseline period*) and then a series of measures taken after the intervention starts. Such designs are common in the evaluation of behavioral interventions with individual subjects, but in that context, they usually lack a statistical analysis and depend for their interpretation on such tactics as removal of treatment with subsequent observation of return to baseline. The time-series research design has been developed in relation to formal statistical tests, albeit often of considerable complexity (Gottman and Glass, 1978) to ensure that any change associated with the onset of treatment is not simply a reflection of a general trend that was occurring anyway or of some artifact. A time series analysis may be undertaken to show that the mean levels of some phenomenon are different before and after treatment, that the slope of change over time is different, or that there is a change at the time of treatment that is of an abrupt nature. For example, records might be examined of arrests for drunkenness in a community over a period of two years prior to the opening of a new detoxification and treatment center and for two years afterwards. A time series analysis might show that arrests dropped after the center opened and that they stayed lower. Or, it might show that arrests were gradually dropping anyway but that the rate of change was faster after the intervention. Or, it might show an initial drop followed by gradual recovery to former levels.

A time series design can often be made stronger and more persuasive (in some instances, matching the convincingness of an experiment) by the development of several different time series representing different observations of the effect of onset of an intervention. Such an elaborated design is known as a *multiple time series* design. An example might be observations, as above, on perhaps three alcohol treatment centers in different communities, with services beginning at different times. Even fairly subtle effects might be persuasive if it were shown, for example, that arrest rates dropped in each community just after the treatment centers opened. The multiple time series design could actually be implemented as a true experiment, with random assignment, but it is usually a combination of a time series and NCGD. The design may be especially powerful against the threats of history and any interaction of selection with other variables (such as maturation) because if there were any of the latter effects, they should be evident during the series of pretreatment measures. The multiple time series may also consist of comparisons between two or more series of observations, some of which should have been suscepti- ble to the intervention and some not. For example, a time series for arrests for drunkeness might be accompanied by a similar time series for other misdemeanor arrests and for calls for other than alcohol problems to a psychiatric crisis service. The comparison with misdemeanor arrests might rule out the possibility that police were reducing minor arrests generally, and the comparison with psychiatric crisis calls might rule out the possibil- ity that, for whatever reasons, psychiatric and behavior problems were decreased generally in the community.

Time series designs can often be implemented with existing records, and they may be relatively inexpensive if adequate records exist. Often no new data will have to be collected. On the other hand, time series designs tend to require a fairly large number of data points both before and after the intervention. The requirement for a long series of observa- tions after an intervention begins may be especially bothersome if it means that conclusions about the effect of an intervention must be long delayed. The time series analysis tends to be more appropriate for determining the effects of interventions whose outcomes should already be evident.

Separate sample pre-test–post-test designs. This design is used in an attempt to exercise some degree of experimental control when random assignment of subjects is not possible. Instead, subjects are ran- domly selected into a condition at the time of assessment, either before or after the entire population receives the treatment. Thus, the resulting groups of before-treatment and after-treatment can be compared as no treatment versus treatment. This is not a particularly strong design, and it fails to rule out several threats to internal validity, especially history. If well done, however, it can provide useful information and is certainly superior to a pre- or nonexperimental design.

Patching-up designs. Institutional cycle designs or patched-up de- signs (Campbell & Stanley, 1966) often involve ongoing modifications to the design as the evaluation progresses. As threats to validity become apparent, the evaluator modifies the design, usually by additional compar- ison groups or series, so as to decrease or eliminate likely threats. Only those viewed as most likely are dealt with, with the philosophy that ruling out as many of these as possible is better than ruling out none of them. These designs are, by their nature, difficult to generalize about, because the changes made depend upon the unique characteristics of each evalua- tion.

Case studies. Case studies, whether with or without a pre-test, are not recommended for most evaluations. Causal inferences drawn from these studies are almost always open to many sources of internal invalidity and thus to many alternative explanations of purported effects. They are sometimes useful in formative evaluations and may help convince decision makers of the need for further investigation. They can sometimes, though rarely, provide valuable information by revealing a startling, completely unexpected phenomenon. But, in general, these designs will not provide conclusive information, and a reader will be reminded of many alternative explanations of any findings.

We have written the present chapter as an introduction to the area of program evaluation for those psychologists who may find themselves having to evaluate programs in diverse settings, from community agencies to schools to government. With the growth and emergence of program evaluation as a discipline over the past several years, psychologists are finding increasing employment opportunities where program evaluation is the primary task. Furthermore, the growing emphasis on accountability in all areas has made evaluation a component of most programs in which psychologists find themselves involved. Thus, a broad knowledge of this area is important even for those who do not plan to conduct evaluations themselves.

By the term *program evaluation,* we are referring to the process of gathering information (data) about a program, in order to make judgments regarding the program's effectiveness. Some view evaluation as an assessment occurring at one point in time during a program, after which decisions are made regarding continuation or termination of the program. Actually, program evaluation has come to represent much more than this.

Rossi, Freeman, and Wright (1979) see a comprehensive program evaluation as including phases of program planning research, the monitoring of program operations, the assessment of program effects (outcome), and the assessment of program efficiency (cost-benefit, etc.). In this view, the evaluation process begins, whenever possible, before the start of the program itself. Others have stressed the need for program evaluation to be geared toward program improvement: toward learning how program components and procedures contribute to positive or negative effects and working on how to change these to make the program more effective (see Cronbach, Ambron, Dornbusch, Hess, Hornik, Phillips, Walker, & Weiner, 1980; Parlett & Hamilton, 1979).

Because program evaluations are conducted to answer a large variety of questions regarding programs, the exact focus of the evaluation has to be determined by the information being requested. We would suggest, however, that efforts to answer questions about program processes and operations, as well as questions about ultimate program effects, can all be considered forms of program evaluation, or parts of the program evaluation process. Furthermore, methods of obtaining information about the program, in order to answer these questions, can range from true experiments to more qualitative ways of knowing (Campbell, 1974). All are rightly a part of program evaluation.

ROLE OF THE EVALUATOR

In the same way that it is difficult to get complete agreement on just what activities constitute program evaluation, it is difficult to describe the role of the program evaluator in simple terms. The program evaluator's role varies, depending on issues such as the relationship of the evaluator to the program organization (i.e., the evaluator's position within the organizational structure). In order to conduct a succesful evaluation, it is of utmost importance that the evaluator understand these relationships from the beginning.

Program evaluators are either internal (in-house) people who are part of the regular staff of the program or external—brought in from the outside for the sole purpose of conducting an evaluation. Which relationship is preferable depends on a particular evaluation's need for factors such as evaluation objectivity, program familiarity/understanding, administrative confidence in the evaluator, and so on (Weiss, 1972). Thus, for example, if program familiarity were a critical factor in conducting a certain evaluation, an internal person might be preferable; objectivity might necessitate an external person.

Many agree that the goal of the evaluation makes a difference in terms of which evaluation program relationship is more effective. When the goal is one of program improvement—*formative* evaluation in Scriven's (1967) terms—an internal person who is more responsive to program needs and who has a better understanding of program operations may be preferable (Caro, 1971; Glaser, 1973; Posavac & Carey, 1980). On the other hand, when the evaluation is to provide an assessment of outcome—*summative* evaluation (Scriven, 1967)—an external person may be more objective and more likely to question organizational premises (Caro, 1971; Posavac & Carey, 1980; Weiss, 1972).

Anderson and Ball (1978) make a finer distinction than internal-external when describing the evaluator's relationship to the program. Their evaluator is either dependent or independent in relation to the program director in the areas of administrative and financial concerns. Thus, where the evaluator may report to the program director in administrative matters, the director may have no voice when it comes to money matters. Furthermore, they add the dimension of relatedness for cases where the evaluator and the program director report to the same person or have funds coming from the same source. Anderson and Ball assert that where the evaluation goal is one of program improvement, dependent relationships may pro-

mote more responsivity to program needs; whereas in the case of summative evaluation, independent relationships are preferable.

Anderson and Ball's (1978) description of the possible relationships
between the program evaluator and the program director begins to address the issue of the evaluator's location in the organizational hierarchy,
regardless of whether the relationship to the organization is internal or
external. Whether it is preferable for the evaluator to report to a policy
maker or a program manager may again be dependent on the purpose
of the evaluation. In the case of policy-level questions (such as, how
good the program is overall), it is probably better for the evaluator to
report to levels above the program manager: that is, to policy makers
(Lumsdaine & Bennett, 1975; Weiss, 1972). On the other hand, in the
case of questions about specific program features (staff patterns, techniques, etc.), it may be preferable to report directly to the program manager
who is more involved in the daily operations of the program (Weiss,
1972).

A different (but related) question concerns the role of the evaluator
in regard to decision making about the program. It may be more likely
for the in-house evaluator to be involved in this process, especially if
this person is also involved in the program; external evaluators, on the
other hand, often see their task as finished once the results are presented.
However, as Weiss (1972) points out, utilization of the results is more
likely to occur when the evaluator is involved in the decision-making
process, at least so that results can be explained and/or clarified. Attkisson, McIntyre, Hargreaves, Harris, and Ochberg (1974) describe a range
of possible evaluation roles, from clerical and data collection to active
involvement in decision making and education. Their assertion is that
the evaluation process (including planning and subsequent decision mak-
ing/utilization) is most effective when the evaluator is involved throughout.

It is of utmost importance for those involved in conducting program
evaluations to be aware of the range of possible evaluator roles in and
relationships to the organization. Proceeding with an evaluation before
these issues are clarified can doom the evaluative effort to failure before
it is even begun.

Another issue with which the evaluator should be familiar before proceeding is the potential interpersonal conflicts which may arise between
evaluation staff, program staff, and administrators. Caro (1971) discusses
differences in orientation that may lead to conflict between evaluators
and administrators. Evaluators, being more research-oriented than administrators and perhaps more interested in the acquisition of broad-based
knowledge, may be willing to try out courses of action that more service-
oriented staff are reluctant to introduce for fear of harming clients; evaluators tend to focus on more long-range solutions, whereas administrators
are more concerned with the solution to immediate problems; evaluators
want to identify inefficiencies and encourage change, while administrators

are more likely to want to keep the status quo; evaluators usually want more explicit statements of objectives and strategies; and in explaining program failures, evaluators are likely to point to a lack of understanding of the initial problem and suggest program changes, while administrators are more likely to focus on individuals.

In addition to conflicts arising out of the differences just delineated, formal evaluation is often resisted by both administrators and service providers who do not want evidence that their objectives have not been reached or that their efforts have not been measurably effective (Caro, 1971; Weiss, 1972). Furthermore, fears that a program may be terminated if it is not assessed as effective enter the picture. (Campbell & Boruch, 1975; Gilbert et al., 1975). Campbell (1969) speaks of "trapped administrators," who resist evaluations because they are already committed to the program as it is, and "experimental administrators," who are more interested in addressing a problem than in remaining attached to one program as the solution to the problem. The experimental administrator remains open to trying out different program variations and thus is not threatened by evaluation or by the failure of a program. Unfortunately, evaluators are likely to find trapped administrators more the norm than their experimental counterparts.

An awareness on the part of the evaluator of these potential conflict areas is the first step toward preventing them from interfering with the evaluation. A willingness to address these issues must follow. Administrative support can be gaind by involving administrators whenever possible in the planning stages of the evaluation, so that a common understanding and definition of the problem can be gained (Sechrest, 1977; Weiss, 1972). Involving service delivery personnel from the onset can also minimize the threat to them, as can an emphasis that theoretical and programmatic issues (not individual performance) will be the focus of the evaluative effort (Caro, 1971).

Changing programs

Since most program evaluation occurs in action settings, the evaluator does not often have the luxury of being able to hold conditions constant, as would be possible in a laboratory or even on an applied-research project where the primary purpose is research. In an action setting, the provision of services is the program's primary function, and any program-evaluation research is likely to take second place. The nature of programs (for example, in community mental health centers) is such that changes occur gradually and informally, altering the program from the way they were originally conceived. Clinicians make small changes in the way they deliver services; staffing patterns change; budgets are changed, etc. (Weiss, 1972). As Glaser (1973) points out, programs unofficially take on functions other than those for which they were originally created, and they become guided by these acquired (latent) objectives. Glaser notes that staff are often reinforced for activities other than their primary task (i.e., report writing is emphasized instead of counseling/client care). However, they are then evaluated in terms of what their primary role is supposed to be.

Evaluators must be prepared to deal with changing programs by designing evaluations that are continuous and that provide ongoing feedback to the program (Edwards & Guttentag, 1975; Glaser, 1973). Glaser (1973) argues for routinizing evaluation—making research a built-in endeavor that routinely guides both practice and policy. Instead of trying to hold programs constant, it may be more effective to carefully describe changes, clarify them when they occur, and assess the effects of different program phases (Weiss, 1972). Suchman (1970) describes the development and evaluation of a program through four successive stages—from a trial-and-error pilot phase, to a controlled experimental stage, to a stage when actual operating conditions are introduced, to a final stage in which the program is operating on an ongoing basis as part of a larger organization. Changes in program operations are welcome during any phase other than the controlled experimental stage.

Tharp and Gallimore (1979) propose what they acknowldge to be an idealistic (but possible) model for evaluating a program as it develops and changes. In their description of a complete research-and-development process, program *components* are developed, tested, modified, and evaluated in association with other program components. Determinations of a program component's benefits are made via a variety of ways of knowing, from true experiments to qualitative, personal knowing (Campbell, 1974).

For Tharp and Gallimore, the final program condition cannot be designed completely in advance; any operating program is the result of a developmental process during which ongoing evaluation is taking place.

Although the unique conditions under which Tharp and Gallimore (1979) were able to implement their research-and-develoment model are not available to most evaluators, their view that evaluation should be geared toward program developments and improvement is becoming more widespread (see Cronbach, et al., 1980; Parlett & Hamilton, 1976). It is in this context of developing and changing programs that we will discuss the elements of the evaluation endeavor.

Planning

Some of the issues discussed up to this point (i.e., questions about the role of the evaluator, interpersonal conflicts, changing programs) should have begun to point to the fact that program evaluation has the best chance of succeeding and being utilized when it is built in and planned for from the beginning of the program's inception. Although many have argued for this (Lumsdaine & Bennett, 1975; Posavac & Carey, 1980; Riecken, 1977; Rossi, et al., 1979; Sechrest, 1977), one more commonly finds situations in which evaluation is requested after a program has been operating for some time. Although we recognize this less ideal state of affairs as reality, we will recommend that, whenever possible, plans for evaluation should be made during the program planning process. As Sechrest (1977) has pointed out, once programs have been operating, they develop their own momentum and internal logic, people become identified with them, and thus it becomes increasingly difficult to come on the scene and try to assess the program's effectiveness. The evaluator (and the notion of evaluation) will be accepted more readily and will be viewed as part of the program's operation if they are present from the onset.

The first point at which the evaluator can have an impact is in helping assess need for the program. Since programs (or interventions) are designed to address an existing problem (or to improve a given condition), verification of the existence and extent of the problem is a critical first step (Rossi et al., 1979; Siegel, Attkisson, & Cohn, 1977). Part of the needs assessment process should also involve clear identification of who makes up the target group, in other words, those members of the population expected to benefit from and utilize the program (Boruch, 1980; Posavac & Carey, 1980; Rossi et al., 1979). As Iscoe (1977) has pointed out, one of the difficulties involved in evaluating community mental health center effectiveness has been a lack of clarity in defining the target population. If a mental health center has been set up to serve a community's indigent population, but instead its programs have been primarily serving upper-middle-class clients with insurance, the center's effectiveness would be questionable. However, without a clear statement of just who the programs were intended for, there would be no way of knowing that the wrong population was being served.

Once the target population has been identified, their perspective of their needs is critical (see Rossi et al., 1979, for a good discussion of needs assessment methods). Obviously, if the target group does not see the need for a program, they are probably not going to utilize it once it is operating. In addition, the perspectives of other constituents who have an interest in the program (i.e., the larger community, staff, decision makers, funding sources, etc.) should be obtained. For example, Sechrest (1977) has stressed the importance of evaluator's and administrator's agreement on a definition of the problem to be addressed early in the process. Others have similarly called for the early identification and involvement of the various audiences involved in or affected by the program and its evaluation (Anderson & Ball, 1978; Joint Committee on Standards, 1981). Involving these different constituents in the planning phases will not only help to clarify what the problem is from several perspectives, but will serve to increase their commitment to evaluation as part of the program's development. Granted, all perspectives cannot be taken into account equally; some will take priority over others.

One other area in which the evaluator can offer valuable assistance at this beginning stage is in regard to questions of what can be evaluated, what kind of information can be obtained, etc. (Posavac & Carey, 1980).

Program implementation

An aspect of program evaluation that is often overlooked, but that must be planned as part of any thorough evaluation, is some assessment of program implementation—those inputs or program operations that are expected to cause the desired effects. Unless the important elements in an operating program are identified, clearly described, and monitored, there is no way of knowing what actually contributed to the outcomes; there is only knowledge of what might have contributed or what was supposed to have contributed. As we pointed out earlier, programs frequently do not operate exactly as planned. Thus, the need to monitor programs as they actually operate is of utmost importance if we are to understand what it is about a program that worked.

Many writers have stressed the importance of addressing implementation in the evaluation of programs (Patton, 1978; Quay, 1977; Rossi, 1978; Rossi et al., 1979; Weiss & Rein, 1972). Sechrest and his associates (Sechrest & Redner, 1979; Sechrest, West, Phillips, Redner, & Yeaton, 1979; Yeaton & Sechrest, 1981) have noted that the clear identification and operational definition of effective treatment components contributing to outcomes (construct validity issues) have been given little attention in the literature in comparison to the attention given internal validity issues (the confidence with which outcome can be attributed to treatment). They have identified two issues in construct validity—integrity of treatments and strength of treatments—which evaluators need to consider in assessing programs if their results are to have any meaning.

Integrity of treatment. The degree to which an intervention (or program) has been delivered as planned determines its integrity of treatment. The failure of a program to produce a desirable outcome may be due to the fact that the intervention was not delivered as planned, and we have seen that random program changes are not uncommon. A study by Kassebaum, Ward, and Wilner (1971) concluded that a group counseling program for prison inmates was ineffective; however in a later analysis of this study, Quay (1977) noted that the treatment as it was actually delivered was given little attention. Sechrest and Redner (1979) point out that data concerning participation in the group counseling program were not presented and that the actual delivery of the treatment (counseling) may not have occured in many cases. In evaluating programs in which counseling/psychotherapy is the main intervention, the issue of treatment integrity should be given high priority. In such programs, a client's failure to attend three out of six counseling sessions may render the treatment nonexistent; failure to note such absences means that critical information is lost. It is important to note here that departures from program plans may also be advantageous, as in a case where clients who dropped out of treatment early experienced more positive gains than those who stayed for the prescribed length of time. Again, this is important information that needs to be monitored.

The evaluator can help insure high treatment integrity by addressing several issues during the planning stages including: the clarity of description of the intervention; the degree of staff commitment and supervision; the complexity of the intervention; and the population receiving the treatment.

The more clearly and specifically an intervention is described, the greater the likelihood it will be delivered as intended. Vagueness of the plan leaves room for individual interpretations by those implementing it, and thus much variation in the actual intervention results. Since counseling interventions (no matter now clearly described) leave room for individual interpretation, these interventions in particular need to be described as clearly as possible. A program to reduce recidivism in recently hospitalized patients may call for outpatient counseling as one of the program interventions. A plan that prescribes "counseling using behavior modification techniques, twice a week, for 50 minutes per session" is more specific and less likely to vary across situations than is a plan calling for "counseling several times a week."

Levels of staff commitment and supervision can also affect integrity of treatment delivery. Lack of commitment to a program can certainly affect a staff member's delivery of services, and although it is difficult to accurately gauge the staff's feelings about a job before they begin, this issue is one with which the evaluator should be concerned. In addition, planning for close supervision of staff is one better way to insure that the intervention is delivered as intended.

Consideration of just how complex and difficult an intervention is to deliver becomes important in terms of planning for monitoring efforts to ensure proper implementation. A very complex program is more likely to be changed during delivery. In such a case, it is important to set up systems, not only to monitor the delivery of services, but also to support staff in the delivery of difficult interventions.

Lastly, delivering an intervention to a population for which it was not originally intended can certainly affect outcome. A program designed for women alcoholics may not be at all appropriate for male alcoholics; however, it is certainly conceivable that such an extension could be attempted with little consideration of the possible effects on the outcome. The evaluator is the person who must keep such considerations in mind.

Strength of treatment. This issue concerns the a priori likelihood that a treatment could have the intended outcome (Yeaton & Sechrest, 1981). Unlike medical treatments (were a specific dosage of medication is prescribed), social interventions have been lax in quantifying interventions in terms of strength. Questions of how much counseling is required for one type of client versus another are not addressed. As was the case for treatment integrity, assessment of a program's effectiveness must take into consideration the strength of the interventions contributing to outcomes.

The a posteriori assumption that if program effects are large, the intervention was strong, and vice versa, is not an adequate method of assessing treatment strength. A weak or nonexistent effect may have a variety of meanings: that the treatment was inappropriate to the problem, that the treatment was administered in too weak a form, or that the treatment itself was inherently weak (Yeaton & Sechrest, 1981). An evaluator who at least attempts to assess an intervention's strength before it is implemented has a better chance of accurately assessing that intervention's effects. Potentially effective interventions and· programs have most likely been abandoned because they were tested at inappropriately low strengths.

We recognize that the a priori assessment of the strength of social interventions is not an easy or clear-cut task. However, Sechrest and Redner (1979) and Sechrest et al. (1979) have suggested some approaches that we will briefly delineate here. The adequacy of an intervention's theoretical basis has a lot to do with the strength of that intervention. If the mechanisms that are expected to cause the desired outcome are clearly delineated and supported by prior research, the intervention is strong in this dimension (see Quay, 1977). An intervention with questionable causal mechanisms may be inappropriate to the problem and thus, as we pointed out earlier, the effect may be weak.

Strength might also be assessed by having experts rate the intervention in terms of how much change they would expect to occur; by developing norms for a standard treatment with which to compare the intervention being evaluated (for example, what would be a typical treatment plan for post-hospital patients in terms of counseling, medication, frequency of visits, training level of the counselors, etc.); or by developing an ideal intervention with which to compare the present one.

Whatever method for assessment of strength is chosen, there should be a standardized set of parameters on which to compare interventions. Sechrest and his associates (1979) have suggested several parameters; however, this list is certainly not exhaustive. Possible dimensions on which to compare interventions include: intervention intensity (i.e., the number of contacts with the client per week); length of the intervention; clarity of the plan; qualifications/training of staff; specificity of the focus of the intervention (is the target a specific problem, such as alcoholism, or is it less clear, such as neurosis?); and differential assignment of candidates (are candidates assigned to the intervention based on their suitability?).

Program monitoring

We have discussed ways of increasing integrity of treatment delivery during the program planning stage and ways of assessing strength of treatment before the intervention is implemented. However, additional questions about the strength and integrity of the intervention can only be answered during the operation of the program and afterwards. In terms of treatment integrity, it is critical for the evaluator to determine not only whether the treatment was delivered as described in the program plans (Sechrest et al., 1979), but whether the treatment was delivered at all (Patton, 1978; Rossi, 1978). As Patton has noted, a determination should be made before the intervention gets underway, regarding how far from the plans the intervention can deviate and still be concluded as having been implemented. Regarding treatment strength, one must assess whether mediating processes expected to lead to the desired outcome actually did occur. If a reduction in drinking behavior is expected as a result of a program designed to change attitudes about alcohol, some assessment of attitudes is necessary in addition to a measure of alcohol consumption.

Methods of monitoring program implementation in order to address some of these concerns have been discussed at length (Posavac & Carey, 1980; Rossi et al., 1979). For the purposes of the present chapter, we will only mention some of these methods and stress that monitoring program implementation must be addressed in any thorough evaluation.

One consideration is the extent of participation of the target population. Are those persons for whom the program is intended utilizing the services? Are there certain subgroups who utilize the program more than others? (e.g., more women than men). Program records and surveys of participants and members of the larger community can begin to answer these questions.

Next, as much information concerning program operations as possible must be gathered so the program as implemented can be described. If possible, ways of observing service delivery should be devised; service providers should be described; records should be inspected; persons receiving services should be tapped for information about the program. A useful way of obtaining data on program implementation would be to devise some nonreactive measures (see Webb, Campbell, Schwartz, Sechrest, & Grove, 1981). In essence, the evaluator's goal here becomes one of developing strategies for gaining a clear and accurate picture of the day-to-day realities of the program. Again, we point out that knowing what actually occurred (as opposed to what was supposed to occur), is the only way the evaluator will know what really contributed to the outcome.

Outcome assessment

Monitoring program operations is of great importance to the evaluation endeavor, but assessing program effects is most likely the reason the evaluation was called for. As we have already noted, outcome assesment does not necessarily mean assessment at one final endpoint. Program effects can and should be measured in an ongoing fashion as the program operates, develops, and changes. The formulation of program objectives, development of outcome criteria, and identification of measurement techniques are all part of the outcome assessment task. Although it is often not the case that the evaluator is called in early enough to help develop objectives, a clear understanding and statement of objectives is necessary before the evaluation can proceed.

Program objectives can be developed to answer intermediate- and long-range questions regarding program effects and to address the concerns of a variety of constituents who have an interest in the program. The evaluator's first job is to help identify and delineate the causal gains or linkages in the intervention that are expected to lead to the ultimate outcome (Suchman, 1970; Rossi et al., 1979; Weiss, 1972). Any intervention designed to deal with a problem has, behind it, hypotheses regarding just how the intervention is expected to lead to the desired end result. For example, a program designed to decrease acting-out behavior among third- through sixth-grade boys might involve one intervention of teaching parents and teachers behavior modification techniques. Before acting-out behaviors can be expected to decrease, a number of other effects must occur: parents and teachers must learn the skills (knowledge and perhaps attitude change); they must be able to use or apply these techniques; and they must actually use these techniques consistently at home and at school. Unless each step occurs, we could not expect childrens' behaviors to change (see Hilton & Lumsdaine, 1975). Thus, the occurrence of each step in the chain can be seen as an interim objective that must be assessed before the ultimate goal is assessed. In the event that an interim effect is not obtained, the evaluator can suggest program modifications aimed at correcting the situation. It should be fairly obvious that failure to develop and assess interim objectives can mean not only failure to reach ultimate program goals but also a tremendous waste of time, money, and effort which could have been redirected in more effective ways. Rossi et al. (1979) describe an intervention model in which a causal hypothesis, an intervention hypothesis, and an action hypothesis are developed from theory and research.

Program objectives can also be developed to address the differential interests of multiple audiences. In evaluating community mental health center programs, for example, the different values and concerns of consumers, program staff, administration, federal funding sources, etc. must be given consideration (Edwards & Guttentag, 1975; Schulberg, 1977). Service deliverers have different questions than do those at high administrative levels regarding a program's effectiveness. Administrators want to know whether a program has been successful, for example, at reducing the number of psychiatric hospitalizations over the past year. Service-delivery staff, on the other hand, want more practical information concerning better techniques for working with clients (Weiss, 1972). And, clients may simply want to feel better. These three perspectives do not necessarily lead to one and the same goal.

We have already suggested involving various constituents in the planning stages of the program so that their values can be addressed. Since these varied concerns will point toward different outcome issues (Bennett & Lumsdaine, 1975), the evaluator must be prepared to prioritize and differentially incorporate these interests (see Edwards & Guttentag, 1975, for a discussion of multi-attribute utility measurement).

Another consideration in developing program objectives is the importance of trying to anitcipate unintended program effects (Caro, 1971; Riecken, 1972; Rossi et al., 1979; Weiss, 1972; Sechrest & Olbrisch, 1977). There is always the possibility that desired, expected outcomes will be affected by unintended, perhaps undesirable, effects that could have been anticipated before the program began.

If such unintended consequences are anticipated by the evaluator, plans should be made to assess them; If unintended consequences are not foreseen, the evaluator must at least remain open to the possibility of such occurrences and watch for them. Scriven (1967) discusses *goal-free evaluation* as a way of learning about all program effects, not just those delineated in specific objectives.

Once program objectives have been identified, the evaluator's task becomes one of choosing appropriate outcome criteria (operational indicators). Selection of indicators of outcome is an extremely important part of the evaluation process; since a range of indicators can answer questions about the same program objective, the evaluator must try to determine which indicators would be the most meaningful to the particular situation. In assessing the effectiveness of an inpatient psychiatric treatment program, outcome indicators which could be used include patients' self-reports of feelings and behaviors; actual patient behaviors as reported by others; subsequent job performance; recidivism and so on. Conclusions drawn from recidivism rates might be very different from those based on patient self-reports. As Glaser (1975) points out in his discussion of evaluation of crime and delinquency programs, questionnaire responses

are frequently very misleading as predictors of actual behavior; unfortunately, however, agencies rely more on self-reports than on actual behavior in assessing program effectiveness.

In order to address this problem of choosing meaningful indicators
of outcome, many have called for the use of multiple measures, from
multiple sources, reflecting different biases (Posavac & Carey, 1980; Rossi
et al., 1979; Weiss, 1972). Utilizing different sources of data (patient,
significant other, or staff); different types of measures (behavioral or attitudinal); and measures of constructs related to, but not necessarily the same
as, the construct of central concern (for example, measuring not only
depression but anxiety, confusion, fatigue, etc. as well) can all reduce
the bias inherent in only one of these indicators. The work of Strupp
and Hadley (1977) is important in this area for their discussion of the
differences between the patient, the family/society, and the staff in regard
to assessment of treatment effectiveness. One perspective certainly cannot
tell the whole story. Similarly, Ellsworth (1975) has noted the lack of
agreement between these three groups regarding program effectiveness
and adds that perhaps the most meaningful indicator (post-treatment community adjustment as rated by significant others) is often not used.

The choice of outcome indicators must be based on judgments of
what best reflects the particular program objectives. If a crisis intervention
program is set up with decreasing psychiatric hospitalizations as the most
important objective, then client feelings about their well-being, client behaviors in the community, or significant others' perceptions about the
client would not be indicators of choice, even though they may be related
to hospitalization; number of hospitalizations would be the most-direct
indicator. However, these other indicators would be meaningful in terms
of another program objective—increasing clients' ability to handle personal crises. Obviously, enabling persons to better handle crises may
affect hospitalization rates, and one might argue that number of hospitalizations could be used as an indicator of ability to handle crises. However,
it is possible that clients could learn how to handle crises while still seeking
hospitalization. As Rappaport, Seidman, and Davidson (1979) found in
a program to divert adolescents from the legal system, arrest rates decreased while no changes were found in self-reports of behavior or school
performance.

Kelling (1977) provides a good discussion of issues in the selection
of effectiveness indicators. He points to the importance of researchers
working closely with those involved in service delivery, in order to get
an understanding of the context in which indicators are found. Going
back to our example above, those working in community settings are
well aware of factors affecting psychiatric hospitalization, some of which
may not be related to client level of functioning (i.e., funding, beds available etc.). The evaluator is well advised to spend some time doing as
Kelling has suggested.

Data collection and management

Every evaluation plan should have a detailed and explicit protocol for collection and management of data. Program evaluation tends to involve extensive data collection, resulting in data sets of large (often huge), size. Things can easily get out of hand, even with the best of intentions, and they are almost certain to get out of hand with anything less. Data-collection protocols should be definite with respect to what data are to be collected, when, from whom, where, by whom, by what method, and, perhaps, even why. Without such specification, respondents tend to get overlooked, different staff tend to believe that someone else must be collecting the data, data are collected in highly unstandard ways, and so on. The result is that the quality of the evaluation effort falls, and the legitimacy of the interpretations can be jeopardized. Missing data are always a problem in an analysis, and in any large-scale project, missing data seem inevitable. The quantity of missing data can be minimized, however, by a rigorous data collection plan.

The instruments to be employed in data collection should, of course, be carefully devised. The old rule, a place for everything and everything in its place, is a good one to keep in mind. The program evaluator should make sure that every desired bit of information is provided for on the set of data forms. It is probably also a good idea to determine that every item on the data form is actually needed for the study. Collection of unneeded data is wasteful, but it may be more wasteful than would appear initially. The unneeded data (often so easy to add to a form) will increase coding and data entry costs, will increase computer costs for file management, may prove too tempting to resist when the time for analysis comes, and will increase the conceptual burden (thereby adding to the complexity of results).

There should be a detailed and explicit plan for data management. Researchers should number and keep track of data forms, so that unused ones can be accounted for; and they should log in all completed data forms, so that it will become evident when problems begin to arise. The data management plan should be explicit about who is to receive completed data forms, what is to be done with them immediately, who will do coding and data entry, and so on. Provision for a systematic way of storing data forms so that they can be easily retrieved should also be made.

The data management plan should also include quality control measures. As data forms come in, they should be checked for completeness, legibility, and so on. Any deficiencies should immediately be noted to the field staff, so that corrective steps can be taken. As data are entered into the computer, there should be regular checking of the values for their reasonableness and consistency. If there are a number of data collectors involved in the study, a simple computer routine can be used to compare them and determine whether they are producing results consistent with each other and with expectations. In that way, potential difficulties can often be detected early and steps taken to deal with them.

A wise evaluator will also formulate a data analysis plan well in advance of data collection and then ensure that the data will conform to the plan. In addition, the evaluator should ensure that data are entered into the computer in a way compatible with the ultimate analyses to be completed. Although it is true that once data are in the computer, they can be manipulated and moved around in almost any imaginable way, it is not true that such manipulations are always either easy or inexpensive. File manipulation can be very expensive in terms of programing time and in terms of computer charges when data sets become large. Planning ahead and monitoring will save grief and money in the long run.

Measuring change

The aim of intervention programs is, of course, to bring about change (in a desirable direction) or to reduce or prevent change (in an undesirable direction). It therefore seems only natural to evaluate programs in terms of the changes they produce or prevent. In either case, one compares what happens in an experimental group with what happens in one or more comparison groups. If there is a systematic difference in the amount of change observed, the difference can be attributed to the intervention.

In fact, however, change is difficult to measure dependably and to analyze legitimately. Change scores result from subtracting a pre-test score from a post-test score and are, thus, difference scores. When thinking about change scores and considering their dependability, it is often difficult to keep in mind just what they represent. When one asks about the reliability of a change score, one is asking whether there are dependable *differences between persons in the amount by which they change*. Only if people change to varying degrees, and only if those changes are systematic, will change scores be reliable. One could, as an example, assess the split-half reliability of change scores on an aggression measure by correlating the estimated change on odd-numbered items with the estimated change on even-numbered items. In fact, change scores suffer from being an index based on two scores because the change scores then accumulate the unreliability in both measures. One way of seeing that point is to realize that the variance in change scores is almost certain to be less than the variance in the original components. Hence, an error of one or a few points in either component score represents a relatively large error when attached to the change score.

Change scores may also be insensitive because of either floor or ceiling effects (Reichardt, 1979). A floor effect usually occurs when a pre-test measure is so difficult that few respondents pass it (i.e., the pre-test is insensitive at the low end to initial differences among respondents). If everyone scores at a chance level on a pre-test, for example, it may be difficult to demonstrate subsequent differential change. A ceiling effect is typically found when the post-test does not discriminate at the upper end, so that everyone passes (or scores) within a narrow range. A delinquency intervention program evaluation, for example, that did not provide for a sufficiently long follow-up period, might result in the conclusion that experimental and comparison groups did not differ when, in fact, had the test been made more difficult by extending the follow-up period, differences between groups might have been evident. Ceiling effects may be evident for some persons and not others. If one uses a self-ideal Q-sort measure, as an instance, a person with an initially high self-ideal correlation cannot change much. A youth with only infrequent pre-intervention delinquencies cannot improve much. A ratio of change observed to change theoretically possible may be useful in some cases, but only if the ceiling effects are not severe.

Change scores also present the possibility of regression artifacts (Judd and Kenny, 1981). Since in any approximately normal distribution extreme scores can be expected to have larger error components than scores near the mean, extreme scores are likely to regress more toward the mean. However, since low scores will tend to regress upward and high scores downward, with any intervention to improve scores, low scores should generally show more change than high scores.

Some years back, Cronbach and Furby (1970) considered the difficulties in measuring change and concluded that, generally, the measurement of change should be avoided. That paper elicited great concern (and even some anguish) because the logic of measuring change was so compelling. Since the Cronbach and Furby article, there have been many suggestions about how to assess the outcomes of interventions, and no perfectly satisfactory solution has emerged. Generally speaking, in true experiments the problem can be finessed, because one can simply assess group differences on the post-test measure, it being assumed that randomization would have produced initial equivalence. The change measurement problem becomes difficult only when the groups demonstrably were not, or cannot be assumed to have been, equivalent at the beginning of the intervention. It is by now well established that analysis of covariance is not a satisfactory way of equating for initial differences (Judd and Kenny, 1981; Reichardt, 1979), and that analysis should not be used. If reliability measures for the variables involved are available, it appears that the best recommendation at present is to use a transformation that equates pre- and post-test scores for *true score variance* and that permits estimation of true (i.e., error-free) scores (Judd and Kenny, 1981). In the meantime, the forewarned evaluator will know that great caution will be required in interpreting results.

Perhaps this is a good place to make the point that careful implementation of a strong intervention is one of the best types of insurance against equivocal findings. Large effects, as long as they are credible, tend to be difficult to write off as artifacts (i.e., relatively few alternative explanations are plausible), and weak effects with strong interventions may not be of great interest, equivocal or not.

Benefits and costs of interventions

In recent years, there has been increasing concern for assessing the benefits of social interventions in relation to the costs of producing them. This is not the place for a technical discussion of what is certainly a difficult enterprise. Nonetheless, program evaluators are likely to have to pay increasing attention to issues concerning the costs of interventions and the size of the benefits that may be produced. Probably nearly any intervention tested from now on should involve at least some attempt to assess costs.

Assessment of program costs is by no means simple, and most evaluators are likely to require at least some specialized help in estimating and allocating costs. Direct program costs are often no problem, but indirect costs (e.g., overhead) can be troublesome. Other costs that economists call *opportunity costs*—the foregone gains of having used resources in some other way—are usually very difficult to estimate. Economists also prefer to discount both costs and gains that are deferred (i.e., a dollar spent today is worth more than a dollar that does not have to be spent until next year). The rates at which costs and benefits should be discounted involve highly technical judgments. A particularly useful reference for program evaluators is Gramlich (1981).

The concept of the *benefit-cost ratio* is frequently encountered. Obviously, it is the ratio of the benefits achieved by a program to the costs of producing them. A positive ratio means that benefits exceed costs. The problem is that relatively few benefits of social programs can be *monetized* (i.e., expressed in terms of dollars of value). Benefits may, of course, be expressed in nonmonetary terms (e.g., lives saved, mental distress averted), and judgments can then be made as to whether the costs seem justified in light of obtained outcomes, but that is only a weak substitute for a benefit/cost study.

Even if benefits (or outcomes) cannot be monetized, if they can be quantified, it may be possible to determine the *cost effectiveness* of an intervention. An intervention is cost effective to the extent that it produces outcomes at a lower unit (whatever the unit may be) cost than alternative ways of producing the same outcomes. For example, if a secondary prevention program using volunteers reduces re-arrests of delinquent youngsters at a lower cost per averted re-arrest than a program using trained professionals, the volunteer program may be said to be cost effective. The volunteer program might actually avert fewer arrests (and thus be less effective at an absolute level) but it would still be cost effective.

Cost effectiveness analyses may be useful in many settings and should certainly be considered in an evaluation. They do not, however, provide any basis for deciding whether the outcome produced is worth the cost. A volunteer prevention program might avert arrests at a cost that would still be considered prohibitive, even if less than the cost associated with a professional program.

Despite the problems with assessing and analyzing costs of interventions, the effort seems worthwhile. The effort may become inescapable with growing demands for accountability of all sorts.

CODA

The problems of program evaluation are far more complicated than the presentation in this chapter might imply. Space and other limitations have prevented us from presenting more than an overview, an introduction to the field. Certainly this chapter cannot serve as a manual by which to plan and carry out evaluations. There are by now many useful books devoted to program evaluation and to specialized topics within the field. The quantity of articles certainly numbers in the thousands. Our hope is that this chapter may have increased the awareness of the reader to the complexities (but also to the challenges and excitement) of program evaluation. The reader will need to seek more specific, focused technical guidance elsewhere.

SUMMARY

A successful evaluation is one whose findings are persuasive. From the outset, an investigator should be aware of who is to be persuaded and what evidence will be persuasive to that audience. The evidence provided by a thoughtfully planned evaluation will be persuasive, in part, because it rules out alternative explanations. The product of an evaluation should be, in a general sense, valid. A design that ensures reasonably high levels of internal validity, construct validity, external validity, and statistical-conclusion validity will go far toward producing a generally valid product. Designs employing true experimental designs are the strongest and should be used whenever possible. In social program evaluations, ethical concerns, lack of funds, unwillingness to alter ongoing interventions, and other factors may preclude the use of true experimental designs. In these cases, quasi-experimental designs such as time series, nonequivalent control group, or separate sample pre-test–post-test designs may be utilized. Each has its own strengths and vulnerabilities, and choices will depend on the goals of the evaluation project.

The role of the program evaluator varies, depending on the relationship of the evaluator to the organizational structure of the program. He or she may be in-house (part of the regular staff of the program) or external, may be dependent or independent in relation to administrative decisions of the program director, and may be dependent or independent with regard to financial decisions of the director. To avoid serious conflict, it is of the utmost importance that the evaluator understand from the outset his or her position in the organizational hierarchy. Ideally, the evaluator should be involved in the planning of the intervention and should remain involved through the phases of implementation, monitoring to assure delivery as planned, data collection, and outcome assessment.

The goal of most social programs is to produce change in a postitive direction or, less frequently, to prevent change in an undesirable direction. The evaluator may be tempted to use change scores or difference scores to assess outcome. However, owing to problems of unreliabiltiy, regression, and floor and ceiling effects, the use of change scores is highly problematic. True experimental designs circumvent such problems by utilizing randomization with its assumption of initial equivalence.

Many evaluations will involve some consideration of costs and benefits. In business and economics, benefit-cost ratios can be constructed easily. But it is usually impossible to assign a monetary value to the benefits of a social program, thus preventing the construction of such ratios. It is, however, often possible to assess cost effectiveness; if one intervention produces the same social benefit or level of effectiveness as another but at a lower cost per unit, it is more cost effective. The cost of conducting a poor evaluation probably can never be justitfied, but the cost of a good evaluation is probably money well spent.

REFERENCES

Anderson, S. B., & Ball, S. *The profession and practice of program evaluation*. San Francisco: Jossey-Bass, 1978.

Attkisson, C. C., McIntyre, M. H., Hargreaves, W. A., Harris, M. R., & Ochberg, F. M. A working model for mental health program evaluation. *American Journal of Orthopsychiatry*, 1974, *44*, 741–753.

Bakan, D. *On method: Toward a reconstruction of psychological investigation*. San Francisco: Jossey-Bass, 1966.

Baum, M. L., Anish, D. S., Chalmers, T. C., Sacks, H. S., Smith, H., & Fagerstrom, R. M. A survey of clinical trials of antibiotic prophylaxis in colon surgery: Evidence against further use of no-treatment controls. *New England Journal of Medicine*, 1981, *305*, 795–799.

Bennett, C. A., & Lumsdaine, A. A. Social program evaluation: Definitions and issues. In C. A. Bennett & A. A. Lumsdaine (Eds.) *Evaluation and experiment: Some critical issues in assessing social programs*. New York: Academic Press, 1975.

Borgatta. E. Research: Pure and applied. *Group Phychotherapy*, 1955, *8*, 263–277.

Boruch, R. F. Case studies of high-quality outcome evaluations. In E. S. Solomon (Ed.), *Evaluating social action: Principles, methodological aspects, and selected examples*. Paris: UNESCO, 1980.

Campbell, D. T. Reforms as experiments. *American Psychologist,* 1969, *24,* 409–429.

Campbell, D. T. On qualitative knowing in action research. Kurt Lewin Memorial Address, Society for the Psychological Study of Social Issues, meeting with the American Psychological Association Annual Convention, Washington, D.C., September 1974.

Campbell, D. T., & Boruch, R. F. Making the case for randomized assignment to treatments by considering the alternatives: Six ways in which quasi-experimental evaluations in compensatory education tend to underestimate effects. In C. A. Bennett & A. A. Lumsdaine (Eds.), *Evaluation and experiment: Some critical issues in assessing social programs.* New York: Academic Press, 1975.

Campbell, D. T., & Stanley, J. C. *Experimental and quasi-experimental designs for research.* Skokie, Ill.: Rand McNally, 1966.

Caro, F. G. Issues in the evaluation of social programs. *Review of Educational Research,* 1971, *41,* 87–114.

Cohen, J. *Statistical power analysis for the behavioral sciences.* New York: Academic Press, 1977.

Cook, T. D. *The impact of the Hawthorne effect in experimental designs in educational research* (U.S. Office of Education, No. 0726, June 1967). Washington, D.C.: U.S. Government Printing Office, 1967.

Cook, T. D., & Campbell, D. T. (Eds.). *Quasi-experimentation: Design and analysis issues for field settings.* Skokie, Ill.: Rand McNally, 1979.

Cronbach, L. J., Ambron, S. R., Dornbusch, S. M., Hess, R. D., Hornik, R. C., Phillips, D. C., Walker, D. F., & Weiner, S. S. *Toward reform of program evaluation.* San Francisco: Jossey-Bass, 1980.

Cronbach, L. J., & Furby, L. How should we measure "change"—or should we? *Psychological Bulletin,* 1970, *74,* 68–80.

Edwards, W., & Guttentag, M. Experiments and evaluations: A reexamination. In C. A. Bennett & A. A. Lumsdaine (Eds.), *Evaluation and experiment: Some critical issues in assessing social programs.* New York: Academic Press, 1975.

Ellsworth, R. B. Consumer feedback in measuring the effectiveness of mental health programs. In M. Guttentag & E. L. Struening (Eds.), *Handbook of Evaluation Research.* Beverly Hills, Calif.: Sage Publications, 1975.

Gilbert, J. P., Light, R. J., & Mosteller, F. Assessing social innovations: An empirical base for policy. In C. A. Bennett & A. A. Lumsdaine (Eds.), *Evaluation and experiment: Some critical issues in assessing social programs.* New York: Academic Press, 1975.

Gilbert, J. P., McPeek, B., & Mosteller, F. Progress in surgery and anesthesia: Benefits and risks of innovative therapy. In J. P. Bunker, B. A. Barnes, & F. Mosteller (Eds.), *Costs, risks, and benefits of surgery.* New York: Oxford University Press, 1977.

Glaser, D. *Routinizing evaluation: Getting feedback on effectiveness of crime and delinquency programs.* (DHEW Publication No. [HSM] 73–9123). Rockville, M.: National Institute of Mental Health, 1973.

Glaser, D. Achieving better questions: A half-century's progress in correctional research. *Federal Probation,* 1975, *39,* 3–9.

Glass, G. V., McGaw, B., & Smith, M. L. *Meta-analysis in social research.* Beverly Hills, Calif.: Sage Publications, 1981.

Gottman, J. M., & Glass, G. V. Analysis of interrupted time series experiments. In T. R. Kratochwill (Ed.), *Single-subject research: Strategies for evaluating change.* New York: Academic Press, 1978.

Gramlich, E. *Cost-benefit analysis of government programs.* Englewood Cliffs, N.J.: Prentice-Hall, 1981.

Hilton, E. T., & Lumsdaine, A. A. Field trial designs in gauging the impact of fertility planning programs. In C. A. Bennett & A. A. Lumsdaine (Eds.), *Evaluation and experiment: Some critical issues in assessing social programs.* New York: Academic Press, 1975.

Hutchinson, W. R. Fitting evaluation form to its function. In A. J. McSweeney, W. J. Fremouw, & R. D. Hawkins (Eds.), *Practical program evaluation in youth treatment.* Springfield, Ill.: Charles C Thomas, 1981.

Iscoe, I. Community and hopital mental health and mental-retardation facilities. *Professional Psychology,* 1977, *8,* 573–582.

Joint Committee on Standards for Educational Evaluation. *Standards for evaluation of educational programs, projects, and materials.* New York: McGraw-Hill, 1981.

Job, D., Eschwege, E., & Guyot-Argenton, C. The effect of multiple daily insulin injections on the course of diabetic retinopathy. *Diabetes,* 1976, *25,* 463–469.

Judd, C. M., & Kenny, D. A. *Estimating the effects of social interventions.* New York: Cambridge University Press, 1981.

Kassebaum, G., Ward, D., & Wilner, D. *Prison treatment and parole survival: An empirical assessment.* New York: John Wiley & Sons, 1971.

Kazdin, A. E., & Wilcoxin, L. A. Systematic desensitization and nonspecific treatment effects: A methodological evaluation. *Psychological Bulletin,* 1976, *83,* 729–758.

Kelling, G. L. Developing indicators of program effectiveness: A process. *Emergency medical services: Research methodology.* (DHEW Publication No. [PHS] 78–3195). Hyattsville, M.: National Center for Health Services Research, 1977.

Krause, M. S., & Howard, K. I. Program evaluation in the public interest: A new research methodology. *Community Mental Health Journal,* 1976, *12,* 291–300.

Lipton, D., Martinson, R., & Wilks, J. *The effectiveness of correctional treatment.* New York: Praeger Publishers, 1975.

Lumsdaine, A. A., & Bennett, C. A. Assessing alternative conceptions of evaluation. In C. A. Bennett & A. A. Lumsdaine (Eds.), *Evaluation and experiment: Some critical issues in assessing social programs.* New York: Academic Press, 1975.

Neale, J. M., & Liebert, R. M. *Science and behavior: An introduction to methods of research.* Englewood Cliffs. N.J.: Prentice-Hall, 1973.

Nesselroade, J. R., Stigler, S. M., & Baltes, P. B. Regression toward the mean and the study of change. *Psychological Bulletin,* 1980, *88,* 622–637.

Orne, M. T. Demand characteristics and the concept of quasi-controls. In R. Rosenthal & R. L. Rosnow (Eds.), *Artifact in behavioral research.* New York: Academic Press, 1969.

Parlett, M., & Hamilton, D. Evaluation as illumination: A new approach to the study of innovatory programs. In G. V. Glass (Ed.), *Evaluation Studies Review Annual,* (Vol.) Beverly Hills, Calif.: Sage Publications, 1976.

Patton, M. Q. Evaluation of program implementation. In M. Q. Patton (Ed.), *Utilization-focused evaluation.* Beverly Hills, Calif.: Sage Publications, 1978.

Posavac, E. J., & Carey, R. G. *Program evaluation: Methods and case studies.* Englewood Cliffs, N.J.: Prentice-Hall, 1980.

Quay, H. C. The three faces of evaluation: What can be expected to work. *Criminal Justice and Behavior,* 1977 *4,* 341–354.

Rappaport, J., Seidman, E., and Davidson, W. S., II. Demonstration research and manifest versus true adoption: The natural history of a research project to divert adolescents from the legal system. In R. F. Munoz, L. R. Snowden, & J. G. Kelly and Associates (Eds.), *Social and psychological research in community settings.* San Francisco: Jossey-Bass, 1979.

Reichardt, C. S. The statistical analysis of data from nonequivalent group designs. In T. D. Cook & D. T. Campell (Eds.), *Quasi-experimentation: Design and analysis issues for field settings.* Skokie, Ill.: Rand McNally, 1979.

Riecken, H. W. Memorandum on program evaluation. In C. H. Weiss (Ed.), *Evaluating action programs: Readings in social action and education.* Boston: Allyn & Bacon, 1972.

Riecken, H. W. Principal components of the evaluation process. *Professional Psychology,* 1977, *8,* 392–410.

Rossi, P. H. Issues in the evaluation of human services delivery. *Evaluation Quarterly,* 1978, *2,* 573–599.

Rossi, P. H., Freeman, H. E., & Wright, S. R. *Evaluation: A systematic approach.* Beverly Hills, Calif.: Sage Publications, 1979.

Schulberg, H. C. Issues in the evaluation of community mental health programs. *Professional Psycholgy,* 1977, *8,* 560–572.

Scriven, M. The methodology of evaluation. In R. W. Tyler, R. M. Gagne, & M. Scriven (Eds.), *Perspectives of curiculum evaluation.* AERA Monograph Series on Curriculum Evaluation (No. 1). Skokie, Ill.: Rand McNally, 1967, pp. 39–83.

Sechrest, L. Evaluation results and decision making: The need for program evaluation. In L. Sechrest (Ed.), *Emergency medical services research methodology.* (DHEW Publication No. [PHS] 78–3195). Hyattsville, Md.: 1977.

Sechrest, L., & Olbrisch, M. E. Special considerations in conducting evaluations of encounter groups. *Professional Psychology,* 1977, *8,* 516–525.

Sechrest, L., & Redner, R. *Strength and integrity of treatments in evaluation studies.* Washington, D.C.: National Criminal Justice Reference Service, National Institute of Law Enforcement and Criminal Justice, Law Enforcement Assistance Administration, U.S. Department of Justice, June 1979.

Sechrest, L., West, S. G., Phillips, M. A., Redner, R., & Yeaton, W. some neglected problems in evaluation research: Strength and integrity of treatments. In L. Sechrest, S. G. West, M. A. Phillips, R. Redner, & W. Yeaton (Eds.), *Evaluation studies review annual.* (Vol. 4). Beverly Hills, Calif.: Sage Publications, 1979.

Siegel, L. M., Attkisson, C. C., & Cohn, A. H. Mental health needs assessment: Strategies and techniques. In W. A. Hargreaves, C. C. Attkisson, & J. E. Sorenson (Eds.), *Resource materials for community mental health program evaluation.* (DHEW Publication No. [ADM] 77–328). Rockville, M.: National Institute of Mental Health, 1977.

Suchman, E. A. Action for what? A critique of evaluative research. In R. O'Toole (Ed.), *The organization, management, and tactics of social reserach.* Cambridge, Mass.: Schenkman, 1970.

Tharp, R. G., & Gallimore, R. The ecology of program research and evaluation: A model of evaluation succession. In L. Sechrest, S. G. West, M. A. Phillips, R. Redner, & W. Yeaton, (Eds.), *Evaluation studies review annual.* (Vol. 4). Beverly Hills, Calif.: Sage Publications, 1979.

Underwood, B. J., & Shaughnessy, J. J. *Experimentation in psychology.* New York: John Wiley & Sons, 1975.

Webb, E. J., Campbell, D. T., Schwartz, R. D., Sechrest, L., & Grove, J. B. *Nonreactive measures in the social sciences* (2nd ed.). Boston: Houghton Mifflin, 1981.

Weiss, C. H. *Evaluation reasearch: Methods of assessing program effectiveness.* Englewood Cliffs, N.J.: Prentice-Hall, 1972.

Weiss, R. S., & Rein, M. The evaluation of broad aim programs: Difficulties in experimental design and an alternative. In C. H. Weiss (Ed.), *Evaluating action programs: Readings in the social action and education.* Boston: Allyn & Bacon, 1972.

Yeaton, W. H., & Sechrest, L. Critical dimensions in the choice and maintenance of successful treatments: Strength, integrity, and effectiveness. *Journal of Consulting and Clinical Psychology,* 1981, *49,* 156–167.

PART II

Psychotherapy research

6

Psychotherapy process research

Leslie S. Greenberg, Associate Professor*

A VIEW OF THE FIELD

A reinspection of psychotherapy research efforts over the last decade has shifted the beam of interest away from the differential-treatment question (what therapy for whom?) back onto process research in psychotherapy. Over the last 40 years, there has been a pendulum-type swing between the two extremes of outcome and process research, and it has become increasingly apparent that process and outcome researchers must synthesize their approaches to produce research which relates psychotherapeutic process to outcome. Cronbach (1975), an early proponent of the interactional design underlying the differential treatment question, has recently shown that aptitude/treatment interaction designs have provided less yield in psychological research than initially promised. He has, consequently, called for a return in psychological research to *intensive observation* of performance in specific situations. He points out that the scientific observation of human behavior has often been neglected in favor of hypothesis testing and that this bias needs to be redressed.

The importance of intensive observation and measurement of performance as an approach to psychological investigation is therefore again coming to the fore in clinical research. The effect of this renewed interest in observation of psychotherapy research has been to emphasize the need for the observation, description, and measurement of specific therapist/client acts and effects in the context in which they occur (Fiske, 1977). *Psychotherapy process research* is defined here as any investigation in

*Department of Counseling Psychology, University of British Columbia, Vancouver, B.C., Canada.

Thanks to Sue Johnson for her untiring help with the review and to Meta Murphy for her patience in helping prepare the manuscript.

which the conduct of therapists and/or clients or their interactions are observed and measured directly or indirectly in psychotherapy or counseling sessions. *Conduct* is used here to refer to both observable behavior and internal perceptions and experiences.

Process research based on the rigorous observation and measurement of in-therapy conduct is an essential requirement for the growth of psychotherapy research as a science. There is considerable working agreement that the three general aims of science are description, explanation, and prediction (Nagel, 1961). The basic step in any comprehensive science is the description of phenomena, and this empirical component must precede the other steps if the science is to be well grounded. Although it is difficult to determine how theory-free any observation is (Nagel, 1961), it is clear that the first endeavor of any infant science is an attempt to describe or classify that portion of nature with which it is concerned. Explanation then brings meaning to the description, and answers, by various forms of argument, the questions "why?" or "how?" what was observed occurred (Hempel, 1965). Prediction is the final step of an orthodox scientific enterprise and has been referred to as "the most desirable fruit of scientific labours" (Feigl, 1953). Although description must precede explanation or prediction, it is important to note that explanation does not necessarily precede prediction. It is possible to predict without explanation, but this type of prediction is most often a limited prediction—and a poorer prediction than it would be if the explanation was available. One might, for example, be able to predict that sucking the bark of a particular tree cures malaria, but this prediction, although helpful, has many undesirable features, the least of which is being accused of shamanism. This type of prediction is not nearly as useful as predicting the effect of specific doses of quinine, the curative element. Similarly, some intra-uterine devices provide effective birth control, but whether they are prophylactic or abortive is not known. Lack of explanation, in this instance, has highly significant moral and ethical implications. Description and explanation are, therefore, highly significant aspects of science. Description is the basic empirical step of scientific investigation, while explanation provides significance and meaning to the descriptions.

Psychotherapy research, although it has provided some general, predictive statements of efficacy (Frank, 1979), has lacked descriptive and explanatory power. Research, to date, on the process of psychotherapy has yielded some interesting and useful findings but has not led to the kind of understanding for which the field had hoped (Orlinsky & Howard, 1978). The research on the variables derived from client-centered theory, particularly therapist empathy, seemed at one time to hold considerable promise for understanding and improving psychotherapy. However, recent reviews show that the relationship between the Rogerian variables and client change is not as strong as concluded earlier and is far more complex (Lambert, de Julio, & Stein, 1978; Mitchell, Bozarth, & Krauft, 1977). According to current research perspectives, psychotherapy appears to be somewhat beneficial (Bergin & Lambert, 1978; Frank, 1979), but there is little or no data to show what effective psychotherapy really is, what the effective components are, and no data-based explanations of how and why it works.

Recent developments in psychotherapy process research hold some promise of remedying the lack of rigorous description and explanation of effective therapy. New process instruments have been developed, and the construction of others is being encouraged in order to enhance the description of the process of psychotherapy (Greenberg & Pinsof, in press). New questions are being asked, and new research methods are being devised, in which process measurement is used to aid in the task of explanation and prediction (Horowitz, 1979; Rice & Greenberg, 1982). The importance of using process instruments in the service of *pattern identification* as an aspect of process research has been stressed as a means of making process research contribute to the explanation of how therapy works (Gottman & Markman, 1978; Horowitz, 1979; Greenberg, 1980b; Luborsky, 1978; Rice & Greenberg, 1982). In addition, the necessity of *relating process to outcome* in psychotherapy has been reiterated and has become a new hope for improving prediction in psychotherapy (Bordin, 1974; Gottman & Markman, 1978; Greenberg, 1980a; Keisler, 1971; Orlinsky & Howard, 1978; Parloff, Waskow, & Wolfe, 1978).

Progress in the possible explanatory and predictive uses of process measures has resulted from a number of developments. The first (and most local) development was the recognition by process researchers that process research appears to have been operating under an unidentified "uniformity myth"—that all psychotherapy process within the session and across sessions is the same. Operating under this myth of uniform process, investigators had overlooked the significance of different phases, events, and moments in therapy (Luborsky, 1968; Rice & Greenberg, 1974; Greenberg, 1975). This uniformity assumption led to a random sampling of process segments within and across sessions as means of measuring what was occurring in therapy. The ratings were then averaged, and this score was used to characterize what had occurred in therapy. Even an assumed "core condition" of therapy—therapist level of communicated empathy—was shown to vary considerably over the hour and across sessions (Beutler, Johnson, Neville, & Workman, 1972; Gurman, 1973). Given the nature of client-centered practice, there was some reason to believe that some uniformity of this process might be found, but even this variable was found to fluctuate over time. The error of the assumption that all process is uniform and can be sampled randomly has been clearly demonstrated. It is, therefore, essential to study therapeutic performance in the context in which it occurs. Clearly, process varies over time, and particular processes have different meanings in different contexts. All process in psychotherapy is not the same, just as all clients, all treatments, and all therapists are not the same.

With the recognition of the significance of immediate context for understanding process, a move toward the description of patterns and sequences of client performance and descriptions of the structure of therapist interventions has begun (Greenberg, 1979, 1982(a); Gottman, Markman, & Notarius, 1977; Horowitz, Sampson, Siegelman, Weiss, & Goodfriend, 1978; Rice, 1974). Gottman and Markman (1978) make the important point that it is clearly not rates but patterns that we should be studying in process research, and it is unreasonable to simply presume that the more frequently a client does something (such as self-disclose) the better. The need in process research for more description of client performance, rather than a continued focus on therapist performance, has also been stressed (Gottman & Markman, 1978; Rice & Greenberg, 1982). It is the client who is changing, and it is this change process that needs to be understood. In addition to studying client change, the need for a taxonomy of in-therapy intervention contexts has been stressed—a process diagnosis of client "moments," is made in which client markers (or states) which indicate the use of particular therapist interventions are identified (Greenberg, 1975, 1979; Horowitz, 1979; Rice, 1974).

A second general development in the field of psychotherapy research which has served to renew interest in the explanatory and predictive uses of process measurement was the call for greater specificity of description in differential treatment studies. This move toward specificity of description started with specification of treatments, clients, and outcomes (Bergin, 1971; Kiesler, 1971) and led logically to realization of the need for specifying therapeutic process more clearly. For example, Sloane, Staples, Cristol, Yorkstan, and Whipple (1975), in their differential-treatment study, surprisingly found that behavior therapists were rated as communicating more empathically than insight-oriented therapists, and both groups made equal and frequent use of causal interpretations. This study demonstrated the need for specification of in-session therapist behavior. In order to clearly specify what is occurring in therapy, it is additionally necessary to observe and describe client performance and change in therapy and to link these performances to changes made beyond therapy. Relating specific in-therapy process to specific outcomes has therefore emerged as a natural consequence of the move toward greater specification in psychotherapy research.

As Kiesler (1971) has noted, "Process research begins with the in-the-interview behavior of the patient; outcome investigation begins with his outside-the-interview improvement. The crucial point is that for either to be maximally useful, the other focus or perspective must be considered" (p. 46). It is necessary for investigators to combine these perspectives and to relate in-therapy variables to extra-therapy variables. This synthesis of descriptive and predictive aspects of psychotherapy research in studies which relate process to outcome represents an important direction for process research.

The above-mentioned developments in psychotherapy research—studying process in context and relating specific processes to outcome—hold promise of providing improved explanation and prediction in psychotherapy, based on the reliable description of therapeutic process. The literature on process research will be reviewed below under the following three headings related to this view of the field: (1) Prediction—relating process to outcome, (2) Explanation—identifying patterns, and (3) Description—development of new process systems.

PREDICTION—RELATING PROCESS TO OUTCOME

In a major review of the literature relating process to outcome, Orlinsky and Howard (1978) developed an empirically grounded picture of the beneficial process ingredients of effective psychotherapy. To do this, they discriminated four domains of therapy process and, within the domains, made a number of minor distinctions. The major domains were: (1) *Therapy as activity*, which emphasizes the behavioral, interactional aspects of therapy or what people actually do in therapy, such as technique used, communicative activity, etc., (2) *Therapy as experience*, which denotes the phenomenological perceptual dimensions of what occurs, such as a patient's perceptions of the therapist, etc., (3) *Dramatic interpretation*, which indicates the meaning formulated and communicated by the participants in the relationship, such as patient depth of experiencing, expressed hostility, etc., and (4) *Regular association*, which refers to the normative patterns in the relationship, such as length and frequency of meetings, size of collectivity, etc. This framework—which allows for some organization of the findings relating process to outcome—will be used below to summarize the literature.

Activity

In the therapy as activity domain, findings suggest that, in cases with better therapeutic outcome, therapists exhibit active and positive instrumental task behavior and are warm and respectful to their clients in their interpersonal behavior. Thus, "leading" behavior (Ashby, Ford, Guerny, & Guerny, 1957), confrontation (Johnson, 1971; Truax & Wittner, 1973), and direct approval (Sloane et al., 1975) were all associated with positive outcome. Abramowitz, Abramowitz, Robach, and Jackson (1974), in a more differentiated study of group therapy, showed that subjects assigned to an external-locus-of-control category did relatively better in directive rather than nondirective groups, and internal subjects did relatively better in nondirective groups.

A great deal of research on therapist warmth and empathy has been done to test Rogers' theory of facilitative conditions. Orlinsky and Howard (1978) state that two thirds of the twenty-three studies on warmth and a similar percentage of the studies on empathy show a significant positive association between the externally rated aspects of these behaviors and outcome. There have, however, arisen major methodological concerns with the research and the measurement of empathy (Kurtz & Grummon, 1972); and so, although it still appears that warmth and empathy are important, they are possibly only of major significance in client-centered therapy (Bergin & Suinn, 1975), they interact with other therapist variables such as directiveness (Mintz, Luborsky, & Auerbach, 1971), and they are possibly facilitative only at particular, precise times in therapy (Lambert et al., 1978; Mitchell et al., 1977).

In relation to patient activity, it appears that in successful cases of psychotherapy, patients relate to their therapists in a likeable, support-seeking way (Crowder, 1971; Stoler, 1966) yet are able to express negative feelings (Mintz et al., 1971; Truax, 1971), while patients' use of speech (communicative activity) is relatively sustained and vocally expressive. Sloane et al. (1975) reported a positive association between outcome and the total time the patient spoke during the fifth interview. The successful patients did not speak more often but rather in longer blocks. Cook (1964) found that successful patients tended to be silent for longer periods. Rice and co-workers (Rice & Wagstaff, 1967; Butler, Rice, & Wagstaff, 1962) showed that patients successful in client-centered therapy spoke with more vocal expressiveness than did less successful patients. Nichols (1974) showed that successful outcome in brief cathartic therapy was correlated with patient expressiveness as defined in terms of degree of emotional discharge.

In an attempt to relate strategic performances in therapy to outcome, Greenberg & Webster (1982) studied a brief treatment focused on resolving decisional conflict. They found that those clients in a Gestalt two-chair dialogue who engaged in a process sequence of self-criticism, followed by an expression of feeling and wants, followed by a softening in attitude of the previously harsh critic, were significantly more resolved than those clients who did not manifest the three process components of criticism, felt wants, and softening. This is one of the few studies found in the literature relating direct observation of strategic interactions between client and therapist to outcome.

Gomes-Schwartz (1978), in a study of brief therapy with 35 college males exhibiting symptoms of depression, anxiety, and social introversion, showed that therapy outcome was most consistently predicted by the patient's willingness and ability to become actively involved in the therapy interaction, as measured by the Vanderbilt Psychotherapy Process Scale.

This prediction held across theoretical orientation (analytic or client-centered) and professional/nonprofessional status of the therapists (professional therapist or helpful college professors). Patients who were not hostile or mistrustful and who actively contributed to the therapy interaction achieved greater changes than those who were withdrawn, defensive, or otherwise unwilling to engage with the therapist in a therapeutic process. Patient involvement was found to be a better predictor of outcome than either measures of exploratory processes or therapist-offered relationship. The results of analyses of two individual cases from this study suggest that therapy outcomes are importantly determined by the patient's ability to take advantage of the particular relationship the therapist has to offer (Strupp, 1980).

Experience

Patients who experience a sense of participation early in therapy (around the third session) seem to be more successful than those who are less involved. In a study of clients at a university counseling center, Saltzman, Luetgert, Roth, Creaser, and Howard (1976) found that clients who, by the third session, felt a sense of movement or progress, a sense of responsibility for solving their own problems, and perceived themselves as open and understanding of what their therapist was trying to communicate, did better than clients who felt less progress and responsibility and were less open and less comprehending of their therapists.

In a recent study (Horvath & Greenberg, in press; Horvath, 1981) of the predictive efficacy of a measure of Bordin's working alliance (Bordin, 1979), patient-perceived relevance of the tasks in therapy (after the third session) was found to be the most effective predictor of outcome. In this study, those patients engaged in brief therapy at various outpatient facilities who reported forming a working alliance by the third session (as measured by a combined score of attained bond, mutuality of goals, and perceived task relevance) did better than those who did not achieve an alliance. It was found that the measure of the alliance was a better predictor of outcome than either a measure of therapist social influence—the Counselor Rating Form (CRF) (Barak & Lacrosse, 1975)—or client-perceived empathy (Barrett-Lennard, 1962). Lacrosse (1980), in a study of the validity of the CRF, found a positive relationship between clients' pre- and post-counseling perceptions of the counselor and outcome. Therapist-perceived expertness accounted for most of the variance in predicting outcome. With regard to Barrett-Lennard's (1962) measure—although different measures of empathy are not highly correlated (Kurtz & Grummon, 1972), and empathy has been shown to possess theoretically distinct elements (Barrett-Lennard, 1981)—perceived empathy shows promise as a predictive indicator of therapeutic outcome (Gurman, 1977); but more research is still needed (Parloff et al., 1978).

Tovian (1977), analyzing 118 female outpatients in individual therapy, found that early "experienced benefit," attainment of catharsis, encouragement, and a sense of mastery and insight experienced by patients in their sessions were predictive of outcome. In more successful cases, patients view their therapists as competent and confident rather than unsure (Ryan & Gizynski, 1971; Beutler, Johnson, Neville, Elkins, & Jobe, 1975; Tovian, 1977), as involved (Bent, Putnam, & Kiesler, 1976; Strupp, Wallach, Jenkins, & Wogan, 1963), as genuine or likeable (McClanahan, 1974; Bent et al., 1976), as affirming and empathic (Barrett-Lennard, 1962; Bent et al., 1976; Gurman, 1977; Parloff et al., 1978; Cain, 1973; Kurtz & Grummon, 1972), and as understanding, accepting, and encouraging independence (Cooley & Lajoy, 1980, Lorr, 1965; Martin & Sterne, 1976).

Findings on the relationship between therapist perception of patient participation and outcome are in conflict regarding both therapist perception of patient's "understanding" of what the therapist is saying (Saltzmann et al., 1976; Sloane et al., 1975) and therapist perception of early motivation or movement (Saltzmann et al., 1976; Malan, 1976; Prager, 1971). One of the few findings on therapists' perceptions of themselves is that therapists view themselves (both early on and retrospectively) as more accepting and warm with successful cases (Strupp et al., 1963; Saltzman et al., 1976). In an interesting study of the summary notes of brief analytic treatment, Malan (1976) found that undirected interpretations were negatively correlated with outcome, while transference interpretations linking the therapist and the parent were positively related to outcome. The interpretation ratings were made from therapist summaries of the therapy. They consisted, therefore, of therapist perceptions of having given a linking interpretation, rather than rating actual interpretations. Marziali and Sullivan (1980), using Malan's original data, replicated his findings but were unable to show that any interpretative linkages between defense, anxiety, and impulse were related to outcome.

Dramatic interpretation

Turning to the construing and communicating of meaning by the participants in therapy (what Orlinsky and Howard, 1978, referred to as *dramatic interpretation*), it appears that patients who talk about themselves in a concrete way with feeling are more successful than those who focus on external situations and are objective in manner. The dominant findings came from studies focused on client-centered process using the experiencing scale (Klein, Mathieu, Keisler, & Gendlin, 1969). Luborsky, Chandler, Auerbach, Bachrach, and Cohen (1971), in their review of the literature, concluded that experiencing (rated in early sessions) was found in a number of studies to relate to psychotherapeutic outcome. Orlinsky and Howard (1978) noted that 9 out of the 10 studies using the experiencing variable found significant positive correlations with good outcome. The most recently published study was Kiesler's (1971) demonstration of experiencing levels in psychoneurotics and schizophrenics. The causal nature of the relationship between depth of experiencing and outcome, however, remains to be demonstrated.

Process-outcome studies dealing with cognition have shown that too-great intellectual self-control is not predictive of good outcome (Wargo, Millis, & Hendricks, 1971), while higher and increasing levels of cognitive differentiation of feelings and problems (Schauble & Pierce, 1974) and an expressive stance which achieved a balance between objective analysis and subjective reaction were correlated with outcome (Butler et al., 1962). In a recent surge of research in cognitive behavior modification, some attention is being paid to cognitive processes in therapy, particularly with depressives (Phillips & Bierman, 1981), although the emphasis is on assessment of these processes. Teasdale and Rezin (1978), in an interesting experimental study of depressed patients, presented external information at a high rate to reduce the frequency of negative thoughts and examined the subsequent effect on depressed mood. Significant reduction in negative thoughts and depressed mood was achieved in two cases. In a second study, the same procedure produced reduction in negative thoughts in 7 out of 13 depressed patients; however, this did not lead to improvement in depressed mood. This appeared to be due to the small extent of thought reduction achieved. There is some promise of more process research on the cognitive treatment of depression emerging from the collaborative depression study (Waskow, 1979).

In relation to meaning of therapist messages, successful cases are likely to be those in which therapists direct their comments to clients' inner experience (Rice, 1965; Nagy, 1973) and psychological processes (Truax & Wittmer, 1971, 1973). Outcome has been negatively correlated, in predominantly client-centered cases, with a therapist observing orientation, i.e., analyzing patient's self as an object (Rice, 1965) and with the rationality of therapist messages, i.e., emphasis on logic (Wargo et al., 1971).

The stylistic aspect of therapist messages which relate to their meaning that has been most intensively studied is the client-centered notion of genuineness. As Orlinsky and Howard (1978) conclude on reviewing the 20 studies on this variable, "cumulatively, these studies seem to warrant the conclusion that therapist genuineness is at least innocuous, is generally predictive of good outcome, and at most may indeed be a causal element in promoting client improvement" (p. 307).

Association

Summarizing process-outcome studies bearing on therapy as association, there is some evidence that educating patients for effective role performance is worthwhile (Hoehn-Saric, Frank, Imber, Nash, Stone, & Battle, 1964; Latorre, 1979; Sloane, Cristol, Peperrik, & Staples, 1970; Truax & Carkhuff, 1965; Strupp & Bloxom, 1973), although results on the negative effects of disconfirmed client role expectations are far from conclusive (Duckro, Beal, & George, 1979). There is no consistent evidence that size or composition of therapy meetings is a major factor in outcome (Luborsky, Singer, & Luborsky, 1975). Research to date suggests, according to Orlinsky and Howard (1978, p. 314), that "time-limited contracts and session schedules of moderate frequency are on balance more beneficial than unlimited and infrequent sessions."

In summary of the process-outcome literature, it appears that the positive quality of the relationship that develops *between* the participants in therapy, plus an active *sense of participation* by the client in therapy, is what seems to be most consistently related to outcome. A number of authors—Bordin (1975, 1979), Luborsky (1976), and Strupp (1977)—have suggested that measurement of the working alliance may help capture the sought-after general psychotherapeutic factor. A *helping alliance* can be characterized by a client perceiving that he or she is being helped or that the client and therapist are working together on the client's problems. This formulation emphasizes the general relationship factors where a bond is formed through good personal contact and mutual affirmation. Technical factors are, however, an aspect of alliance formation, in that the client must perceive what is being done in therapy as relevant and helpful and must actively participate in the activities.

The above interpretive synthesis of the literature of the empirical relationship between actually measured process and actually measured outcome in actual cases of psychotherapy is unfortunately indicative of the lack of *standard definitions* of therapeutic process and the lack of research specificity. Reviewing authors are forced to rely on general language to convey their results, because there are no accepted measures used across studies which allow comparisons, nor are there sufficient studies of specific therapeutic tasks or strategic interactions between therapist and client to show any clear effects of particular technical factors.

In the measurement of process, there has been extraordinary diversity in what researchers attempt to measure. Concern has been shown about the most appropriate size of unit (Mintz et al., 1971), which has stretched from momentary client pauses (Matarazzo, 1965), to depth of experiencing in segments of a number of minutes (Klein et al., 1969), to general ratings of the therapist or client as empathic or dependent over the hour. In addition to the diversity of measurement systems and unit size, there are so many different general processes identified by different therapeutic approaches (such as catharsis, cognitive restructuring, and graduated exposure or awareness) that any attempts at comparison across therapies are most difficult, and it is only possible to achieve comparability at the most general level of therapy process.

The development and study of a number of major general measures regarded as significant to therapy independent of school, such as the exemplary work done in constructing the Depth of Experiencing Scale (Klein et al., 1969), is needed to enable a comparison of the relationship between process and outcome across approaches. Kiesler (1973) provided coverage of the different process systems to that time, but it is apparent that these process systems were developed and studied in relative isolation from one another without an adequate structure to integrate the diverse process research enterprises. Various measures have failed to be consistently applied to a common data base. Klein (1978) suggests that a first order of business for process research is to identify a meaningful data base for collaborative study, in which discrepancies and overlap of different measurement schemes would be explored to provide an estimate of the relationship among the diverse variables and to derive guidelines for choosing those for more concerted study. This type of endeavor would lead to a pan-theoretical process research (with a group of standard measures) as opposed to a therapy school process research (with idiosyncratic measures). Orlinsky and Howard's (1978) conceptual scheme (which transcends any one school of therapy) could provide a framework for integrating process variables as measuring either activity, experience, or meaning.

EXPLANATION—PATTERN IDENTIFICATION

In order to increase understanding of what is occurring in psychotherapy, it is essential to investigate specific phenomena at specific times in therapy and to relate this to both immediate effects and long-term outcome (Rice & Greenberg, 1982). A study of recurring events in psychotherapy has been suggested (Rice & Greenberg,1974; Greenberg, 1975), in which the specific effects of specific interventions applied at specific client moments are investigated. To do this, investigators will need to construct process measures designed for specific recurring in-therapy situations such as transference, interpretations, resolution of a conflict, and insight events. The study of process in context is a method of overcoming the uniformity myth that all process is the same and that random sampling will capture therapeutic phenomena. Kiesler (1980) suggests that this type of episode-oriented process research must also take the individual difference variable into account, resulting in measures of specific process for specific personality types (e.g., specific resistances of obsessive clients or the specific behaviors by which a hysteric client leaks anxiety, rather than a measure of any resistance or anxiety in general). The literature on process research which has sought for associations between variables in the therapeutic situation will be reviewed below. The initial attempts in this area generally studied single variables in isolation, while more-advanced methods have attempted to study organized patterns of phenomena.

Intervention effects

An area in which some attention has been paid to context has been the study of specific intervention effects. One type of study examines the effects of interventions on ensuing client process, while another relates this to session outcomes—providing a session-based process-outcome study.

Speisman (1959), in a classic study of the effects of depth of interpretation measured by an adaptation of the scale developed by Harway, Dittman, Raush, Bordin, and Rigler (1955), found that interpretations of medium depth were most productive, as measured by client resistance in terms of ensuing opposition and exploration. Dittman (1952), in an earlier study, found some support for this effect, showing that deeper (rather than superficial) responses tended to be associated with progressive (rather than regressive) movement in psychotherapy. Auld and White (1956) also found that therapist interpretations were not followed by patient-resistant remarks. Kanfer, Philips, Matarazzo, and Saslow (1960), however, have shown that interview interpretation appeared to function as an inhibitor of speech duration. More recently, working in a social-psychological framework, Strong, Wambach, Lopez, and Cooper (1979), in a single-session study, showed that interpretations increase client's motivation to change and that interpretations identifying causal factors under the client's control lead to greater client change than do interpretations identifying causes that clients cannot directly control. Hill and Gormally (1977), in another single-session study of the effects of counselor interventions, showed that counselor probes resulted in more discussion of feelings than did either restatements or reflections.

In a series of studies on the effects of Gestalt dialogue, Greenberg and co-workers have shown that the application of Gestalt two-chair dialogue at an in-therapy statement of a split (Greenberg, 1979) leads to greater depth of experiencing than empathic reflection of feeling (Greenberg & Clarke, 1979; Greenberg & Dompierre, 1981; Greenberg & Rice, 1981) or focusing (Greenberg & Higgins, 1980). These studies were characterized by specifying not only the therapist intervention but also the client state at which they are effective. In the Greenberg and Dompierre (1981) study, the Gestalt intervention was also shown to lead to better session outcomes and progress after a week than emphatic reflection.

In-therapy behavior

A large body of research has been generated on general therapist and client in-therapy behavior. These variables have, however, usually been studied as isolated variables in relation to single (or isolated) situations reflecting the very early stages of development of this area of study. Pope (1977, 1979) has recently reviewed the research on interview studies. Dividing therapist behavior into stylistic and expressive behaviors, he highlights that the important aspects of style that have received attention in the literature have been the directive/nondirective dimension, therapist activity level, and therapist ambiguity and specificity. He observes that, after years of research on the relative merits of the directive/nondirective approach, there is little that can be said conclusively. This would seem to result from the lack of attention paid to individual difference and context variables. In several investigations of therapist verbal activity level as defined by gross productivity level, interviewees have expressed a preference for interviews in which the therapist was relatively active (Heller, Davis, & Myers, 1966; Lennard & Bernstein, 1960; Pope, Nudler, Vonkorff, & McGee, 1974). It appears that active therapists are more reinforcing (Pope, 1979), and there is some evidence that active therapists are regarded as warmer (Pope et al., 1974) and more empathic (Truax, 1970) than their more passive counterparts. Evidence on the relationship between therapist and client activity level is conflicting, with both reciprocal (Lennard & Bernstein, 1960) and inverse relationships (Matarazzo, Wiens, Matarazzo, & Saslow, 1968) having been shown. The research findings on the ambiguity-specificity dimension are quite uniform in pointing to a positive relationship between message ambiguity and interviewee productivity (Pope & Siegman, 1965, 1968; Siegman & Pope, 1965).

In the expressive domain, a number of process studies of affect in therapy and speech as an indicator of emotional states have been completed. Isaacs and Haggard (1966) investigated the relationship between therapist interventions containing affective words and the meaningfulness of patient response, and they found that affective interventions were more evocative of meaningful patient responses than non-affective interventions. Duncan, Rice, & Butler (1968) found that a group of paralinguistic variables taken together distinguished between therapist behavior in peak and poor hours of psychotherapy. The peak interviews were characterized by paralinguistic attributes such as oversoft intensity or pitch, unfilled hesitation, pauses, repeats, etc. In this type of interview, the therapist would sound serious, warm, and relaxed. Wexler and Butler (1976) showed in a single case that therapist spontaneity and use of vivid, evocative expression produced an increase in client expressiveness.

Eldred and Price (1958) found discernible, paralinguistic differences between anxiety, anger, and depression in the patient's speech. Gottschalk, Springer, and Gleser (1961) showed that emotional congruence develops between therapist and patient-communication content over the therapy session; while Lennard and Bernstein (1960) showed increasing synchrony in the percentage of propositions dealing with affect over four months of therapy. Anxiety has been shown to increase speech disruptions both in and out of therapy (Mahl, 1956; Mahl & Schulze, 1964; Siegman

& Pope, 1965), and produce greater productivity (number of words uttered), higher speech rate, and shorter reaction time (Siegman & Pope, 1972; Pope, Blass, Siegman, & Raher, 1970). Research generally supports the thesis that speech disturbance reflects the waxing and waning of anxiety (Kasl & Mahl, 1958, 1965). Recently, Horowitz and co-workers, using a measure referred to as a *discomfort quotient,* have observed in a single case significantly more speech disruption as the client began to talk about thoughts and feelings he had previously avoided, that discomfort drops when the therapist is neutral (Horowitz, Sampson, Siegelman, Wolfson, & Weiss, 1975), and that subjects describing four anger experiences showed increasingly more speech disruption in the more sensitive episodes (Horowitz, Weckler, Saxon, Livaudais, & Boutacoff, 1977).

Hostile client behavior has been shown to evoke greater counselor anxiety than friendly client behavior (Russel & Snyder, 1963), while therapists who expressed hostility directly in their social lives and therapists low in need for approval were more likely to respond to patient expression of hostility with approval reactions than therapists who were indirect in anger expression or had a high need for approval (Bandura, Lipsher, & Miller, 1960). Therapists' avoidance of hostile topics led patients in this study to terminate discussion of these topics.

In a study of therapist warmth, Strupp, Fox, and Lessler (1969) found that therapist warmth was an important factor in patients' descriptions of psychotherapy, while a number of studies have shown that interviewer warmth facilitates interviewee communication in the forms of productivity and verbal fluency (Pope & Siegman, 1972; Pope et al., 1974), although not necessarily meaningful communication (Heller et al., 1966; Sarason & Winkel, 1966). Factors influencing free association have been studied (Bordin, 1966; Strupp, 1968; Colby, 1961), suggesting that interpretations resulted in significantly greater amounts of free association. Frank and co-workers (Frank, Hoehn-Saric, Imber, Liberman, & Stone, 1978) have studied the effect of emotional arousal on focal attitude change and showed that client "focal concepts" changed in the direction of therapist suggestion while they were in an emotionally aroused state produced by ether or adrenalin. In a study by Hoehn-Saric, Liberman, Imber, Stone, Pande, and Frank, (1972) focal concepts demonstrated more liability and shifted more in the high-arousal group of patients than the low-arousal group, although the changes were more transient than in the first experiment.

In investigations of nonverbal communication (an area of increasing significance), Hill, Siegelman, Gronsky, Sturniolo, and Fretz (1981) studied the relationship of nonverbal abilities, nonverbal behaviors, and verbal/nonverbal congruence to the judgment of counseling outcome by counselors and clients. Results indicated that only verbal/nonverbal congruence was significantly related to outcome. Stockwell and Dye (1980) examined the effects of counselor touch on client evaluation of counseling and level of self-exploration in a single individualized vocational counseling session. Counselor touch was not found to have a significant effect. Contrary to these results, Pattison (1973) found that touch positively influenced subject exploration. Alagna, Whitcher, Fisher, and Wicas (1979) provided some evidence that touched subjects evaluated counseling more positively than control subjects. In addition to these studies of effects of nonverbal communication, a number of studies on the effect of nonverbal behaviors on perceptions of counselors can be found. Haase and Tepper (1972) found that nonverbal channels accounted for more than twice as much variance in perceived counselor-empathy level than did the verbal channel. However, in a study of inconsistent verbal/nonverbal communication on rated counselor regard and effectiveness, nonverbal channels were not found to be dominant (Reade & Smouse, 1980). In general, results in this area are complex due to the number of different nonverbal behaviors possible and the complex interactions between nonverbal behaviors which are often uninterpretable and even contradictory (Graves & Robinson, 1976; Strahan & Zytowski, 1976; Smith-Hanen, 1977; Tepper & Haase, 1978; Young, 1980).

Experience

In investigations of client and therapist perceptions of therapy, clients have been shown—in both behavior therapy and psychotherapy (Llewelyn & Hume, 1979)—to report that relationship (nonspecific) factors were more useful in treatment than behavioral or psychotherapeutic activities; and there was no difference between patients in behavior therapy or psychotherapy with respect to the rated importance of relationship factors.

Lohman and Mittag (1979) clustered therapists' behaviors in therapy from a questionnaire (FEPT) which tapped client perceptions of therapist behavior. Clustering therapists according to their actual behavior was found to be far more descriptive than classification based on theoretical orientation. The three clusters were: dramatizing behavior and active exploration, inactive or passive, and active reinforcing and opinion giving.

In studies of the characteristics of good therapy hours, Orlinsky and Howard (1967, 1975) examined therapists' and clients' immediate post-session ratings. They found that good therapy hours, as rated by therapists and clients, had much the same character: psychoanalytic in content (e.g., insight-oriented focus on intimate personal relationships, exploration of self) and experiential in manner (warm, collaborative, expressive). By means of factor analysis of responses to the therapy session report, they found patient-experience dimensions logically grouped by basic attitude to patient role, therapy as a helpful experience, therapy as a threatening experience, dependency, and manipulation. Dimensions of therapist experience were grouped into four interpretive categories: helping the patient, coping with patient resistances, responding nontherapeutically, and experiencing distress. Dimensions of conjoint experience were found and classified as normative, therapeutic, or conflictual patterns. They found that therapists' object perceptions of patients were not very accurate as guides to what patients report about themselves; but there was a high degree of sensitivity shown by therapists in empathic induction (i.e., an intuitive feeling one gets in the other's presence). They concluded that both the client and therapist appear to be part of a larger system (or process), which allows the therapist to use what is occurring in herself/ himself in therapy in relational areas as an indication of what is occurring in the client. In their report on therapist experience, Orlinsky and Howard (1977) stress that therapists are not neutral technicians administering techniques without feelings, and an important aspect of method that should not be overlooked is therapist experience while using a method.

In further studies of "good" sessions, Auerbach and Luborsky (1968) had experienced clinicians judge sessions. They found that "good" sessions were defined as being high on the variable of "therapist responds effectively to patient's main communication." Hoyt (1980) showed that experienced clinicians judged sessions to be especially "good" when the actions of the therapist and patient (rated on the Therapist and Patient Action Scales) emphasized the patient's expression of thoughts, feelings, and the collaborative exploration of the meanings of these expressions in terms of the patient's own concept, reactions to the therapist, and links between past and present. "Poor" sessions were characterized by emotional suppression, introduction of unrelated topics and advice, and information seeking. Stiles (1980) factor analyzed 113 session ratings of client and therapist responses to the Session Evaluation Questionnaire and found that two factors (depth/value and smoothness/ease) emerged in both client and therapist data, and clients and therapists tended to agree on their session's position on these two dimensions. He found that client post-session feelings were more positive following smooth, easy sessions, while therapist post-session feelings were more positive following deep, valuable sessions.

Organized patterns

Some research approaches, which overcame the uniformity assumption found in much process research by intensively studying process patterns in specific contexts, are reviewed below. Luborsky (1967) developed the symptom context method in which the in-session context of recurring behaviors or symptoms are examined to test theoretical propositions. Critical segments in which a recurrent symptom appears, such as momentary forgetting, a headache, or stomach pain (Luborsky & Auerbach, 1969), are matched with segments of therapy from the same patient in which the critical event did not occur. The two sets of events are then rated to see on what variables the context of the symptom differ. In a study of stomach pain, Luborsky (1978) reports that three categories (concern over loss of supplies, anxiety, and helplessness) discriminated between critical and control segments, with the critical segments all being higher on the three variables.

In work on momentary forgetting, 37 pairs of critical and control segments were rated on 12 categories. Luborsky (1978) found that some categories that discriminated critical from control segments were: new attitude or behavior, guilt, and feeling of lack of control. Another comparison was tried on a symptom that did not require a self-report as did those above. Petit-mal epileptic attacks signaled by an EEG wave was used as the symptom. For a single patient in psychotherapy, significant differences were found for critical and control segments—especially on helplessness and related variables. Five intensive single-case analyses of different symptoms have shown that patient helplessness (considered central by Freud in his theory of symptom formation) was discriminating (Luborsky, 1978). A factor of crucial importance in this work is the selection of categories for rating contexts, for it is these categories which will ultimately determine the findings (although this comment is true of all process research). This method, which has been used primarily for understanding conditions leading to symptom formation, can be applied to any recurrent behavior of therapists or clients in therapy in order to understand the conditions leading to this behavior.

Another approach to the study of recurrent events in psychotherapy has been proposed in which recurring statements of client problems (such as conflicts or problematic reactions) mark the beginning of the event, and resolution of the problem measured by suitable process indicators marks the end of the event (Rice & Greenberg, 1974; Greenberg, 1975). In this approach, the effects of specific interventions on the marker and the process of resolution is studied by means of a task analysis of the event (Greenberg, 1975, 1982). In this task-analytic approach to the study of therapeutic events, a hypothetical, *idealized* client performance—which represents the clinician's best understanding of how resolution takes place—is compared with descriptions of *actual* client resolution performance in a series of intensive single cases. This is done in a cyclical manner, moving back and forth between idealized and actual performances, until a refined proposed model of a resolution performance is built. The post-dictive, discovery-oriented, aspect of the approach involves looping around the clinical/theoretical expectations to observation and back again, until the investigator is satisfied that the phenomena at hand have been described. The model constructed by this method is then subjected to appropriate verification procedures (such as relating these performances to outcome). This cyclical procedure of comparing actual and possible performances represents a rigorous form of inductive clinical theorizing, which results in the construction of a model in terms which can be tested by process measurement (Rice & Greenberg, 1982).

Using this task-analytic approach to the study of therapeutic events, a model of the steps in intrapsychic conflict resolution have been constructed (Greenberg, 1982(a); Johnson, 1980), as well as a model of the resolution of problematic reactions (Rice, 1982). This type of approach leads to the description and testing of performance patterns associated with productive in-therapy events. In a task analysis of nine conflict resolution events from three clients using two-chair dialogue, Greenberg [1975, 1980(a)] found a characteristic pattern of voice quality and depth of experiencing associated with resolution for each side of the conflict. It appeared that a critical aspect of resolution was the change in a previously externally focused, harsh critic, to a more internally focused stance, as measured by higher levels of experiencing and a use of focused voice. In an extension of this study, Greenberg (in press) showed that a sample of 14 resolvers (selected on the basis of client and therapist report) could be clearly distinguished from 14 nonresolvers on the basis of in-session performance patterns, this time using Benjamin's (1974) structural analysis of social behavior—which measured affiliation and dominance as well as voice and experiencing. He found that, in the initial phase, the dialogue between the parts of the self in conflict in the two groups was indistinguishable on the three measures; but, as the dialogue progressed, the harsh critic in the resolution group became more affiliative, and this process of becoming more accepting of the self clearly distinguished resolvers from nonresolvers. The nonverbal index of change of voice quality in the critic was also an important indicator which distinguished the groups, and this (plus the increase in depth of experiencing of the critic) suggests that softening one's attitude to oneself occurs by a process in which attention is turned inwards to generate new meanings (Greenberg & Rice, 1981).

Gottman et al. (1977), using a related approach based on their Program Development Model (Gottman & Markman, 1978), studied patterns of client performance in an innovative study of couples' communication. Using a form of task analysis (in which they delineated components of competent performances), they showed that nonclinic couples differed from clinic couples in the pattern of their communication on problem-solving tasks. Analyses of sequential interaction patterns revealed that clinic couples entered into a "cross-complaining" loop at the beginning of a discussion and were subsequently likely to enter into a negative exchange. A negative exchange involved mind reading, with negative affect, by one partner, which was taken as a blaming criticism by the other partner, which was then refuted with negative affect. On the other hand, nonclinic couples were likely to begin the discussion with a validation sequence (characterized by agreement with neutral affect), they

avoided negative exchanges, and they ended the discussion with a contract sequence (characterized by agreement interspersed with problem-
solving proposals). Gottman et al. (1977, p. 476) stress that the two groups
differ in pattern: "they do not simply differ in response frequencies, but
they traverse essentially different terrains in their interaction."

The behaviors in this study were categorized on message content,
nonverbal delivery of message by the speaker (referred to as affect),
and the nonverbal behavior of the listener (context). On the basis of
this coding scheme, nonverbal behaviors discriminated distressed from
nondistressed couples better than did verbal behaviors. In addition, distressed couples were more likely to deliver statements summarizing their
own feelings and position (rather than summarizing their partner's statements) and to deliver their mind-reading statements with negative affect.
The evidence gathered did not support a simple behavioral reciprocity
model, in which specific behaviors are seen as being under the control
of specific "mate" antecedent behaviors.

This study (with its emphasis on precise description of couples' verbal
and nonverbal behaviors and their analysis of the data in a sequential
rather than a summative fashion using sequential-lag analysis) revealed
patterns of performance which helped explain dysfunctional communication in couples. This is a process study which demonstrates the advances
in process research as far as procedure and analysis; and although the
findings have limited generalizability, the methodology is exemplary and
points the way for future research.

Gottman (1979) has subsequently reported on further studies of couples' communication. In a re-analysis of data from the Raush, Barry, Hertel,
and Swain (1974) study, Gottman found support for the fact that agree-
ment/disagreement and negative-affect codes discriminated between
more and less distressed couples and that the cross complaining loop
cycle characterized the couples in the Raush, et al. study—which all qualified as distressed according to Gottman's criteria. A valuable feature of
Gottman's approach is that his sequential analysis is suited for both description of single cases and also for later generalization based on the
group data.

Horowitz and co-workers (Horowitz, 1979; Horowitz, Marmar, & Wilner,
1979), using a method called *configurational analysis,* have been studying patient states and state transitions. In this method, the problem states
of a person are carefully described in terms of behavior and reported
subjective experiences and are distinguished from other states before,
during, and after therapy. In addition to identification of states, a full
configurational analysis involves the description of these three points in
time, from two other points of view (labeled *relationship* and *information*).
Relationship refers to an analysis of the key images of self and other
that underlie and relate to states. Here, self and object role attributes
and role relationships that characterize each state are listed. Information

refers to how data on self, other, and environment are processed by the person, and it involves describing defenses and style of information processing. States and state transitions can then be related to in-therapy events. For example, Horowitz (1979) shows that marked change in the pattern of states, relationship, and information processing occurs over time in a brief therapy of a single client, and he relates the change to developments in the therapeutic alliance. Reliability of state descriptions has been shown (Marmar, Wilner, & Horowitz, 1982); and although this approach is in the developmental phase, it holds great promise of tackling the true complexities of studying psychotherapeutic change.

In another intensive analysis of performance patterns in therapy, the first 100 hours of a psychoanalytic treatment of a woman whose presenting complaint was sexual frigidity were studied (Horowitz et al., 1978). The sequence of change in two classes of behavior concerning cohesive (closeness) and dispersal (fighting) behaviors were tracked. It was shown that both these classes of behavior decreased over the therapy, but progress in dispersal-type behaviors preceded progress in cohesive-type behaviors. It was also shown that complaints in the form of "I can't do something" or "I have to do something" declined in frequency during treatment.

These studies of intrapsychic processes relied on precise descriptions of verbal and nonverbal behaviors and analyzed them with regard to the context in which they occurred, not by aggregate analyses but by a rigorous, intensive structural analysis (Greenberg, 1982; Piaget, 1970), in which elements were identified and the rules governing the relationship of these elements were statistically demonstrated. Process research of this type (which identifies the patterned characteristics of successful in-therapy performances) holds promise for increasing our understanding of mechanisms of client change in psycotherapy. More studies of the type described above—which observe the performance of people engaged in an ecologically valid task and compare them to the performance of others who are less successful in the task under study—will greatly enhance the explanatory power of research findings. This type of study of the characteristics of competent performance will, by providing descriptions of "how things are" in successful performances, also be providing clinicians with evidence of "how things ought to be" with their clients. This provision of normative standards based on the empirical description of patterns of effective functioning will provide a factual base to guide the action of practitioners.

There has been a large gap between research and practice (Luborsky, 1972), and researchers have tended to study what they know how to study (or can study relatively easily) rather than what is of importance to the conduct of psychotherapy. Researchers have studied self-references or pauses because they can be counted and are amenable; but what makes some self-references or pauses highly significant, while others are inconsequential, has not been studied. Thus, until recently, process research has had little impact on the practice of psychotherapy. Practitioners will begin to take greater guidance from research findings as studies illuminate the practice of therapy by discovering patterns of performance which explain how clients change in therapy.

DESCRIPTION—DEVELOPMENT OF PROCESS SYSTEMS

Without good instruments (such as telescopes, microscopes, and accelerators), astronomers, biologists, and physicists could not have progressed. Similarly, progress in psychotherapy research is dependent on available measurement instruments. Kiesler (1973) collected the existing process-measurement systems in his volume, which serves as reference of systems to that date. Instruments which have been developed since that time are covered in a new handbook of process systems (Greenberg & Pinsof, in press), and some of these are discussed briefly below.

Interactional

Benjamin (1974, 1979, 1977) has developed an instrument (the Structural Analyses of social behavior) for classifying interpersonal interactions in terms of focus (other, self or introjection), the degree of interdependence and affiliation, and on nine topics (such as approach/avoidance, need fulfillment, intimacy, and identity). This scale represents progress in the measurement of interaction content, in that it is set up for sophisticated ratings of interaction on a number of dimensions and, in addition, lends itself to sequential analysis of interaction (Benjamin, 1979). The most recent version of the scale has been shown to possess good reliabilities, and results of a number of analyses have provided strong support for the construct validity of the model (Benjamin, 1977).

The Impact Message Inventory (Perkins, Kiesler, Anchin, Chirico, Kyle, & Federman, 1979) assesses momentary emotional engagements of one person by another during ongoing therapeutic transactions. The measure was derived from the literature on interpersonal behavior and from the Interpersonal Behavior Inventory of Lorr and McNair (1965). The scale consists of 82 items, which yield 15 interpersonal subscales. The data collected consists of *subjects recording their impacts to paragraph descriptions of pure, interpersonal styles* and suggests a circumplex ordering of these categories (but on only three factors—dominance, affiliation, and submission). Additional development and testing of this instrument could provide a useful addition to assessing therapeutic-interaction effects. The inventory has been shown to reliably discriminate groups of assertive versus nonassertive subjects and obsessive versus hysteric behavior.

A number of instruments have recently been constructed by different therapeutic or working groups working on the measurement of the alliance. Luborsky (1976) developed a list of "signs" used to categorize the helping alliance into one of two types. Type I was defined as a therapeutic alliance based on the patient experiencing the therapist as supportive and helpful, and Type II was defined as an alliance based on a sense of working together in a joint struggle against what is impeding the patient. Marziali, Marmar, and Krupnick (1981) report on the development of patient and therapist alliance scales, which focus on the attitudinal/affective climate of the therapy. They found that the patient's contribution to the therapeutic alliance was predictive of outcome. A client and therapist perceived-alliance scale, based on Bordin's conceptualization of components of the alliance scale, has also been developed (Horvath, 1981; Horvath & Greenberg, 1982). The measurement of the alliance has generated a lot of interest, and there is hope that these measures will capture the "general relationship factor" regarded by many as the active ingredient of therapy.

Therapist behavior

Hill's Counselor Verbal Response system is an integrative taxonomy of counselor skills obtained from a factor analysis of 11 different taxonomies which she found could be reduced to 17 categories (Hill, 1978). Further analysis reduced the taxonomy to 14 counselor response categories. This system requires that counselor statements be unitized according to the rules of Auld and White (1956) and that each unitized response be placed on 1 of the 14 categories of the system. These categories are: minimal encourager, approval, reassurance, information, direct guidance, open question, closed question, restatement, reflection, nonverbal referent, interpretation, confrontation, self-disclosure, silence, and others. A recent study (Hill, Thames, & Rardin, 1979) suggests that this system represents a reliable taxonomy of counselor verbal behavior. Using this system, Hill et al. (1979) compared Rogers, Perls, and Ellis in their sessions with Gloria in the film, *Three Approaches to Psychotherapy.* The system was able to distinguish the three according to their differential use of categories such as reflection, confrontation, direct guidance, open question, and nonverbal referents.

Stiles (1979), in an elaboration and evolution of a framework proposed by Goodman and Dooley (1976), presents a taxonomy of verbal-response modes, which identifies eight basic modes of interaction in which the form and intent of utterances are coded separately. In addition, three principles (classification, source of experience, and frame of reference and focus) serve to relate the modes.

The eight basic modes are: disclosure, question, edification, acknowledgment, advisement, interpretation, confirmation, and reflection. Each mode is defined by the intersection of three principles and not by examples of the meanings of the modes. Disclosure, for example, concerns the speaker's experience, in the speaker's frame of reference, focused on the speaker, whereas advisement concerns the speaker's experience, in the speaker's frame of reference, focused on the other. The scoring unit is the utterance. The system showed good reliability and was shown to distinguish client-centered gestalt and psychoanalytic therapists by their use of reflection, advisement, and interpretation, respectively. In addition, it was found that gestalt and analytic therapists used a wider variety of modes than the client-centered therapist, who predominantly used the pure modes of reflection and acknowledgment. For the client-centered sample, the form and intent of the majority of all utterances were in the client's frame of reference, while for the gestalt therapists, the majority were in the therapist's frame of reference. For the psychoanalytic sample, the form and intent of the majority of utterance concerned the patient's experience.

Pinsof (1981) has developed the Family Therapist Coding System (FTCS) to identify and differentiate the verbal behaviors of family therapists from a variety of theoretical orientations. It consists of nine nominal scales (topic, intervention, emporal, to whom, interpersonal, membership, route, grammatical form, and event relationship), each one containing a number of distinct categories. A therapist intervention is coded on each of the scales. The FTCS is the most complex coding system of therapist behavior in the field of psychotherapy research, and it allows a clinically meaningful reconstruction of most therapist interventions from the nine codes. Reliability of an earlier version of this system has been shown to be adequate, and the system has been shown to discriminate between novice and experienced family therapists.

Client behavior

An instrument measuring therapist's perception of therapeutic process has recently been reported (Baer, Dunbar, Hamilton, & Beutler, 1980), in which 74 items were rated over 99 patients by 26 psychotherapists. These ratings were factor analyzed to yield four meaningful psychotherapeutic-process factors: (1) therapeutic participation, in which the therapist perceived the patient as participating effectively in therapy, (2) resistance, especially in the form of interpersonal hostility, (3) directive support, in which the therapist was seen as giving directions, homework, setting goals, and (4) dysphoric concerns, in which the patient verbalized negative feelings—such as guilt or insecurity—and was self-derogatory. Factor scores were found to be highly reliable, and they were related to other variables in a conceptually consistent manner. For example, patient participation in the therapeutic process was strongly related to the therapist's judgments of outcome, while patients demonstrating less pathology on MMPI pre-therapy scores were rated as being the best therapeutic participants.

The above instrument is comparable in some ways to the Vanderbilt Psychotherapy Inventory, described by Gomes-Schwartz (1978), which possessed four parallel factors: patient participation, therapist directiveness, patient hostility, and patient psychic distress. Four additional factor scales were reported by Gomes-Schwartz: therapist warmth and friendliness, therapist negative attitudes, patient exploration, and therapist exploration. Another instrument of interest constructed by the Vanderbilt groups is the negative-indicators scale (Strupp, Hadley, & Gomes-Schwartz, 1977), which is designed to measure factors involved in the negative effects of psychotherapy.

Rice, Koke, Greenberg, and Wagstaff (1979) have recently produced a manual on client vocal quality, which now makes the system available for more general use. In this system, client statements are classified into one of four categories (focused, emotional, external, or limited), each identified in terms of six features: (1) energy, (2) primary stresses, (3) regularity of stresses, (4) face, (5) timbre, and (6) contours. The clinical impression of a focused voice is one in which there is a turning inward of attentional energy deployed toward tracking inner experience and symbolizing it in words. Focused voice has a pondering quality of generating new facets of experience. External voice seems to involve a deployment of attentional energy outward in an effort to produce some effect on the outside world. Content is being recounted, rather than being newly experienced and symbolized. Limited voice seems to involve holding back or withdrawal of energy, while the distinguishing characteristic of emotional voice is a disruption of the speech pattern (Rice & Koke, 1981).

Development in process research is further evidenced by the attempts to go beyond individual therapy into the study of process in group and family therapy. Beck and her associates have been using process variables to analyze group development and tackling important issues of identifying phase boundaries (Beck, Eng, Dugo, & Lewis, 1980). They have used speech-interaction measures, depth of experiencing, and pronoun contents to study phases of group development, as well as tracking emergent leadership and concerns with normative/organizational and personal issues.

Pinsof (1981), in his comprehensive review of process research in family therapy, indicates the existence of eight coding systems that have been used to directly observe family therapist behavior, a few self-report studies on the process of family therapy, and eight direct observation measures of family (patient) behavior. Process research can therefore be seen to be developing in family therapy, and although there is great scope for further exploration in the field of group and family therapy process research, a start has been made.

The development of new systems will increase the need for some sort of organizing frameworks which will allow the systems to be coordinated in a rational fashion. Russel and Stiles (1979) have, for example, in a recent review of language-analysis systems employed in psychotherapy research, suggested a three-category typology for these measures (content, intersubjective, and extralinguistic) with two coding strategies (classical and pragmatic). In addition, more-sophisticated analyses of process data are being attempted and beginning to show some promise. Increased computer availability and advances in the fields of artificial intelligence and information processing suggest the possibility of computer simulation models to help explain the process of change, while methods of sequential analysis appear to be highly appropriate for improving rigor in process research. Stochastic methods of analysis—such as Markov chain analysis of interaction and uncertainty analysis (Hertel, 1972; Lichtenberg & Hummel, 1974; Church, 1981)—allow for probabalistic relationships between process variables—such as therapist statement and client response—to be captured. Gottman (1979) reports on the potential of spectral analysis of time series for detecting cyclical patterns in dyadic relationships and has demonstrated the use in therapy research of the lag-sequential analysis devised by Sackett (1974).

Process research is, in the final analysis, an attempt to study the process of change in psychotherapy. Therapeutic change (or its cause) clearly occurs in the transactions between therapist and client, and process research is an attempt to catch, by various measuring devices, the crucial aspects of the transaction. Measurement is the core issue in process research and any research is only as good as the measurement system used. Observation of difference in performance and the rigorous categorization of these differences must serve as the basis for good process measurement. Without the ability to see (i.e., measure) these differences, the researcher is as blind to the phenomena of significance as is the astronomer without a telescope or a microbiologist without a microscope. The development of new systems for recognizing differences in psychotherapeutic process is an important task for the new generation of process researchers.

SUMMARY AND CONCLUSIONS

In this chapter, the importance of process research for the development of psychotherapy research (both as a science and as an endeavor which can aid clinical practice) was stressed. Psychotherapy process-research studies were reviewed in terms of whether their fundamental purpose was predictive, explanatory, or descriptive. From the review of the studies in the predictive domain, it appears that a positive relationship quality which develops between the participants in therapy is related to outcome. No clear, unitary measure of this quality has emerged; however, it does appear that an active sense of participation by the client in the therapeutic tasks that appear relevant to the client is related to outcome. In the domain of explanation of therapeutic process, advances in method have occurred, in which researchers are moving beyond the study of single variables in isolation from their context, toward the study of the relationship of meaningful patterns of variables. Using this approach, client feelings of helplessness have been shown to be related to the occurrence of various types of symptoms in psychotherapy sessions, while changing from a self-critical to a more self-supportive attitude in a therapy session has been related to measures of intrapsychic conflict resolution. In studying couples' communication patterns, the behaviors of clinic and nonclinic couples in resolving interpersonal conflict has been shown to differ by the *sequence* of expression of agreement, complaining, negative affect, and validation. The approaches used to generate these findings hold promise of transforming process research from its infant strivings into a predictive enterprise which will help explain what actually occurs in the therapeutic process and influence clinical practice. Finally, the development of new descriptive systems were reviewed, and the importance of measurement as the cornerstone of process research was emphasized. The importance of developing nonverbal coding systems was stressed. In addition, the development of a process research in family and group therapy and the development of methods of sequential analyses for describing interaction were noted as encouraging trends.

This overview of psychotherapy process research leaves an impression of a resurgence of interest in an area which came to life in the 1950s and then quietly faded from the scene, only to force itself back into view in the late 1970s. Process research demanding time, patience, effort, and commitment, and not promising a quick study, has been neglected by many researchers governed by pressures of granting agencies and university evaluation. In addition to these factors, there also were not clear perspectives on the potential yields of all the effort involved in process research. New perspectives have, however, begun to emerge, and the potential of process research for aiding in the prediction and explanation of what occurs in psychotherapy seems promising.

REFERENCES

Abramowitz, C. V., Abramowitz, S. I., Robach, H. B., & Jackson, C. Differential effectiveness of directive and nondirective group internal-external control. *Journal of Consulting and Clinical Psychology,* 1974, *42,* 849–853.

Alagna, F., Whitcher, S., Fisher, J., & Wicas, E. Evaluative reaction to interpersonal touch in a counseling interview. *Journal of Counseling Psychology,* 1979, *26,* 465–472.

Ashby, J. D., Ford, D. H., Guerny, B. C., & Guerny, L. F. Effects on clients of a reflective and a leading type of therapy. *Psychological Monographs,* 1957, *71,* 24.

Auerbach, H. H., & Luborsky, L. Accuracy of judgments of psychotherapy and the nature of the "good hour." In J. Shlien, H. F. Hunt, J. P. Matarazzo, & C. Savage (Eds.), *Research in psychotherapy* (Vol. 3). Washington, D.C.: American Psychological Association, 1968.

Auld, F., & White, A. Rules for dividing interviews into sentences. *Journal of Psychology,* 1956, *42,* 273–281.

Baer, P., Dunbar, P., Hamilton, J., & Beutler, L. Therapists perceptions of the psychotherapeutic process: Development of a psychotherapy process inventory. *Psychological Reports,* 1980, *46,* 563–570.

Bandura, A., Lipsher, D., & Miller, P. E. Psychotherapists' approach-avoidance reactions to patients' expressions of hostility. *Journal of Consulting Psychology,* 1960, *24,* 1–8.

Barak, A., & Lacrosse, M. B. Multidimensional perception of counselor behavior. *Journal of Counseling Psychology,* 1975, *22,* 471–476.

Barrett-Lennard, G. T. Dimensions of therapist response as causal factors in therapeutic change. *Psychological Monographs,* 1962, *76* (43, Whole No. 562).

Barrett-Lennard, G. T. The empathy cycle: Refinement of a nuclear concept. *Journal of Counseling Psychology,* 1981, *28,* 91–100.

Beck, A., Eng, A., Dugo, J., & Lewis, C. *Measures for the analysis of group development.* Paper presented at the Society for Psychotherapy Research, Asilomar, Calif., 1980.

Benjamin, L. S. Structural analysis of social behavior. *Psychological Review,* 1974, *81,* 392–425.

Benjamin, L. S. Structural analysis of family in therapy. *Journal of Consulting and Clinical Psychology,* 1977, *45,* 391–406.

Benjamin, L. S. Use of structural analysis of social behavior (sasb) and Markov chains to study dyadic interactions. *Journal of Abnormal Psychology,* 1979, *88,* 303–319.

Bent, R. J., Putnam, D. A., & Kiesler, O. J. Correlates of successful and unsuccessful psychotherapy. *Journal of Consulting and Clinical Psychology,* 1976, *44,* 149.

Bergin, A. E. The evaluation of therapeutic outcomes. In A. E. Bergin & S. L. Garfield (Eds.), *Handbook of psychotherapy and behavior change.* New York: John Wiley & Sons, 1971.

Bergin, A. E., & Lambert, M. B. The evaluation of therapeutic outcomes. In S. L. Garfield & A. E. Bergin (Eds.), *Handbook of psychotherapy and behavior change.* New York: John Wiley & Sons, 1978.

Bergin, A. E., & Suinn, R. M. Individual psychotherapy and behavior therapy. *Annual Review of Psychology,* 1975, *26,* 509–556.

Beutler, L. E., Johnson, P. T., Neville, C. W., Elkins, D., & Jobe, A. M. Attitude similarity and therapist credability as predictors of attitude change and improvement in psychotherapy. *Journal of Consulting and Clinical Psychology,* 1975, *43,* 90–91.

Beutler, L. E., Johnson, D. T., Neville, C. W., & Workman, S. W. Accurate empathy and the ab dichotomy. *Journal of Consulting and Clinical Psychology,* 1972, *38,* 372–375.

Bordin, E. S. Free association: An experimental analogue of the psychoanalytic situation. In L. A. Gottschalk & A. H. Auerbach (Eds.), *Methods of research in psychotherapy.* New York: Appleton-Century-Crofts, 1966.

Bordin, E. S. *Research strategies in psychotherapy.* New York: John Wiley & Sons, 1974.

Bordin, E. S. *The generalizability of the psychoanalytic concept of the working alliance.*

Paper presented at the annual meeting of the Society for Psychotherapy Research, Boston, June 1975.

Bordin, E. S. The generalizability of the psychoanalytic concept of the working alliance. *Psychotherapy: Theory, Research and Practice,* 1979, *16,* 252–259.

Butler, J. M., Rice, L. N., & Wagstaff, A. K. On the naturalistic definition of variables: An analogue of clinical analysis. In H. H. Strupp & L. L. Luborsky (Eds.), *Research in psychotherapy* (Vol. 2). Washington, D.C.: American Psychological Association, 1962.

Cain, D. J. The therapists' and clients' perceptions of therapeutic conditions in relation to perceived interview outcome. *Dissertation Abstracts International,* 1973, *33,* 6071.

Church, M. *Sequential analyses of moment-by-moment psychotherapeutic interactions.* Unpublished doctoral dissertation, York University, 1981.

Cook, J. J. Silence in psychotherapy. *Journal of Counseling Psychology,* 1964, *11,* 42–46.

Cooley, E. J., & Lajoy, R. Therapeutic relationship and improvement as perceived by clients and therapists. *Journal of Clinical Psychology,* 1980, *36,* 562–70.

Cronbach, L. J. Beyond the two disciplines of scientific psychology. *American Psychologist,* 1975, *30,* 116–127.

Crowder, J. E. Transference, transference dissipation, and identification in successful versus unsuccessful psychotherapy. *Dissertation Abstracts International,* 1971, *31,* 6894B.

Dittman, A. T. The interpersonal process in psychotherapy: Development of a research method. *Journal of Abnormal and Social Psychology,* 1952, *47,* 236–244.

Duckro, P., Beal, D., & George, C. Research on the effects of disconfirmed client role expectations in psychotherapy: A critical review. *Psychological Bulletin,* 1979, *86,* 260–275.

Duncan, S., Rice, L. N., & Butler, J. M. Therapist's paralanguage in peak and poor psychotherapy interviews. *Journal of Abnormal Psychology,* 1968, *73,* 566–570.

Eldred, S. H., & Price, D. B. A linguistic evaluation of feeling states in psychotherapy. *Psychiatry,* 1958, *21,* 115–121.

Feigl, H. Notes on causality. In H. Feigl & M. Brodbeck (Eds.), *Readings in the philosophy of science.* New York: Appleton-Century-Crofts, 1953.

Fiske, D. W. Methodological issues in research on the psychotherapist. In A. S. Curman & A. M. Razin (Eds.), *Effective psychotherapy.* Elmsford, N.Y.: Pergamon Press, 1977.

Frank, J. The present status of outcome studies. *Journal of Consulting and Clinical Psychology,* 1979, *47,* 310–317.

Frank, J. D., Hoehn-Saric, R., Imber, S. D., Liberman, B. L., & Stone, A. R. *Effective ingredients of successful psychotherapy.* New York: Brunner/Mazel, 1978.

Gomes-Schwartz, B. Effective ingredients in psychotherapy: Prediction of outcome from process variables. *Journal of Consulting and Clinical Psychology,* 1978, *46,* 1023–2035.

Goodman, G., & Dooley, D. A framework for help-intended interpersonal communication. *Psychotherapy: Theory Research and Practice,* 1976, *13,* 106–117.

Gottman, J. M. *Marital interaction.* New York: Academic Press, 1979.

Gottman, J. M., & Markman, H. J. Experimental designs in psychotherapy research. In S. L. Garfield & A. E. Bergin (Eds.), *Handbook of psychotherapy and behavior change.* New York: John Wiley & Sons, 1978.

Gottman, J., Markman, H., & Notarius, C. The topography of marital conflict: A sequential analysis of verbal and nonverbal behavior. *Journal of Marriage and the Family,* August 1977, 461–477.

Gottschalk, J. A., Springer, M. J., & Gleser, G. Experiments with a method of assessing the variations in intensity of certain psychological states occurring during two psychotherapeutic interviews. In L. A. Gottschalk (Ed.), *Comparative psycholinguistic analysis of two psychotherapeutic interviews.* New York: International Universities Press, 1961.

Graves, J. R., & Robinson, J. D. Proxemic behavior as a function of inconsistent verbal and nonverbal messages. *Journal of Counseling Psychology,* 1976, *23,* 333–338.

Greenberg, L. S. *Task analysis of psychotherapeutic events.* Unpublished doctoral dissertation, York University, 1975.

Greenberg, L. S. Resolving splits: Use of the two-chair technique. *Psychotherapy: Theory Research and Practice,* 1979, *16,* 310–318.

Greenberg, L. S. Advances in clinical intervention research: A decade review. *Canadian Psychology,* 1980, *22,* 25–34. (a)

Greenberg, L. S. The intensive analysis of recurring events from the practice of Gestalt therapy. *Psychotherapy: Theory Research and Practice,* 1980, *17,* 143–152. (b)

Greenberg, L. S. A task analysis of interpersonal conflict resolution. In L. Rice & L. S. Greenberg (Eds.), *Patterns of change: An intensive analysis of psychotherapeutic process.* New York: Guildford Press, 1982(a).

Greenberg, L. S., & Clarke, K. The differential effects of the two-chair experiment and empathic reflections at a conflict marker. *Journal of Counseling Psychology,* 1979, *26,* 1–8.

Greenberg, L. S., & Dompierre, L. The specific effects of Gestalt two-chair dialogue on intrapsychic conflict in counseling. *Journal of Counseling Psychology,* 1981, *28,* 288–294.

Greenberg, L. S., & Higgins, H. The differential effects of two-chair dialogue and focusing on conflict resolution. *Journal of Counseling Psychology,* 1980, *27,* 221–225.

Greenberg, L. S., & Pinsof, W. *Psychotherapeutic process: A research handbook.* New York: Guilford Press, in press.

Greenberg, L. S., & Rice, L. The specific effects of a Gestalt intervention. *Psychotherapy: Theory Research and Practice,* 1981, *18,* 210–216.

Greenberg, L. S., & Webster, M. Resolving decisional conflict: Relating process to outcome. *Journal of Counseling Psychology, 1982, 29,* 468–477.

Gurman, A. S. Instability of therapeutic conditions in psychotherapy. *Journal of Counseling Psychology,* 1973, *20,* 16–24.

Gurman, A. S. The patient's perception of the therapeutic relationship. In A. S. Gurman & A. M. Razin (Eds.), *Effective psychotherapy.* Elmsford, N.Y.: Pergamon Press, 1977.

Haase, R. F., & Tepper, D. T. Nonverbal components of empathic communication. *Journal of Counseling Psychology,* 1972, *19,* 417–424.

Harway, N. I., Dittman, A. T., Raush, H. L., Bordin, E. S., & Rigler, O. The measurement of depth of interpretation. *Journal of Consulting Psychology,* 1955, *19,* 247–253.

Heller, K., Davis, T. D., & Myers, R. A. The effects of interviewer style in a standardized interview. *Journal of Consulting Psychology,* 1966, *30,* 501–508.

Hempel, C. G. *Aspects of scientific explanation.* New York: Free Press, 1965.

Hertel, R. K. Application of stochastic process analyses to the study of psychotherapeutic processes. *Psychological Bulletin,* 1972, *77,* 421–430.

Hill, C. Development of a counselor verbal-response category system. *Journal of Counseling Psychology,* 1978, *25,* 461–468.

Hill, C. E., & Gormally, J. Effects of reflection, restatement, probe, and nonverbal behavior on client affect. *Journal of Counseling Psychology,* 1977, *24,* 92–97.

Hill, C. E., Siegelman, L., Gronsky, B. R., Sturniolo, F., & Fretz, B. R. Nonverbal communication and counseling outcome. *Journal of Counseling Psychology,* 1981, *28,* 203–212.

Hill, C., Thames, T., & Rardin, D. Comparison of Rogers, Perls, and Ellis on the Hill counselor verbal-response category system. *Journal of Counseling Psychology,* 1979, *26,* 198–203.

Hoehn-Saric, R., Frank, J. D., Imber, S. D., Nash, H. E., Stone, A. R., & Battle, G. C. Systematic preparation of patients for psychotherapy: Effects on therapy behavior and outcome. *Journal of Psychiatric Research,* 1964, *2,* 267–281.

Hoehn-Saric, R., Liberman, R., Imber, S. D., Stone, A. R., Pande, S. K., & Frank, J. D. Arousal and attitude change in neurotic patients. *Archives of General Psychiatry,* 1972, *26,* 51–56.

Horowitz, L. M., Sampson, H., Siegelman, E. Y., Weiss, J., & Goodfriend, S. Cohesive and dispersal behaviors: Two classes of concommitant change in psychotherapy. *Journal of Consulting and Clinical Psychology,* 1978, *46,* 556–564.

Horowitz, L. M., Sampson, H., Siegelman, E. Y., Wolfson, A. W., & Weiss, J. On the identification of warded-off mental contents. *Journal of Abnormal Psychology,* 1975, *84,* 545–558.

Horowitz, L. M., Weckler, D., Saxon, A., Livaudais, J. D., & Boutacoff, L. I. Discomforting talk and speech disruptions. *Journal of Consulting and Clinical Psychology,* 1977, *215,* 1036–1042.

Horowitz, M. J. *States of mind.* New York: Plenum Press, 1979.

Horowitz, M. J., Marmar, C., & Wilner, N. Analysis of patient states and state transitions. *Journal of Nervous and Mental Disease,* 1979, *167,* 91–99.

Horvath, A. *An exploratory study of the working alliance: Its measurement and relationship to therapy outcome.* Unpublished doctoral dissertation, University of British Columbia, 1981.

Horvath, A., & Greenberg, L. S. The working-alliance inventory. In L. Greenberg & W. Pinsof (Eds.), *Psychotherapeutic process: A research handbook.* New York: Guilford Press, in press.

Hoyt, M. F. Therapist and patient actions in "good" psychotherapy sessions. *Archives of General Psychiatry,* 1980, *37,* 159–170.

Isaacs, K. S., & Haggard, E. A. Some methods used in the study of affect in psychotherapy. In L. Gottschalk & A. Auerbach (Eds.), *Methods of research in psychotherapy.* New York: Appleton-Century-Crofts, 1966.

Johnson, D. J. The effect of confrontation in counseling. *Dissertation Abstracts International,* 1971, *32,* 180A.

Johnson, N. E. *Model building of Gestalt events.* unpublished master's paper, University of British Columbia, 1980.

Kanfer, F. H., Philips, J. S., Matarazzo, J. D., & Saslow, G. Experimental modification of interviewer content in standardized interviews. *Journal of Consulting Psychology,* 1960, *24,* 528–536.

Kasl, W. V., & Mahl, G. F. Experimentally induced anxiety and speech disturbance. *American Psychologist,* 1958, *13,* 349.

Kasl, W. V., & Mahl, G. F. Disturbance and hesitation in speech. *Journal of Personality and Social Psychology,* 1965, *1,* 425–433.

Kiesler, D. J. Experimental designs in psychotherapy research. In A. E. Bergin & S. L. Garfield (Eds.), *Handbook of psychotherapy and behavior change.* New York: John Wiley & Sons, 1971.

Kiesler, D. J. *The process of psychotherapy: Empirical foundations and systems of analysis.* Hawthorne, N.Y.: Aldine Publishing, 1973.

Kiesler, D. J. *Psychotherapy process research: Empirical foundations and systems of analysis.* Hawthorne, N.Y.: Aldine Publishing, 1973.

Klein, M. *Psychotherapy process research: Has it made a difference?* Paper presented at the Society for Psychotherapy Research, Toronto, 1978.

Klein, M., Mathieu, P., Keisler, O., & Gendlin, E. *The experiencing scale.* Madison, Wis.: Wiseman Psychiatric Institute, 1969.

Kurtz, R. R., & Grummon, D. L. Different approaches to the measurement of therapist empathy and their relationship to therapy outcomes. *Journal of Consulting and Clinical Psychology,* 1972, *39,* 106–115.

Lacrosse, M. B. Perceived counselor social influence and counseling outcomes. *Journal of Counseling Psychology,* 1980, *27,* 320–327.

Lambert, M. J., de Julio, S. S., & Stein, D. M. Therapist interpersonal skills: Process, outcome methodological considerations, and recommendations for future research. *Psychological Bulletin,* 1978, *85,* 467–89.

Latorre, R. Pre-therapy role-induction procedures. *Canadian Psychologist,* 1979, *18,* 4.

Lennard, H. L., & Bernstein, A. *The anatomy of psychotherapy.* New York: Columbia University Press, 1960.

Lichtenberg, J. W., & Hummel, T. J. Counseling as stochastic process: Fitting a Markov chain model to initial counseling interviews. *Journal of Counseling Psychology,* 1976, *23,* 310–315.

Llewelyn, S. P., & Hume, W. I. The patient's view of therapy. *British Journal of Medical Psychology,* 1979, *52,* 29–35.

Lohman, J., & Mittag, O. The assessment of therapist actual in-therapy behaviour as perceived by the patient. Paper presented at the Society for Psychotherapy Research, Oxford, 1979.

Lorr, M. Clients' perceptions of therapists: A study of therapeutic relation. *Journal of Consulting Psychology,* 1965, *29,* 146–149.

Lorr, M., & McNair, D. Expansion of the interpersonal behavior circle. *Journal of Personality and Social Psychology,* 1965, *2,* 823–830.

Luborsky, L. Momentary forgetting during psychotherapy and psychoanalysis: A theory and research method. In R. Holt (Ed.), *Motives and thought: Psychoanalytic essays in honor of David Rappaport. Psychological Issues,* 1967, *5,* 177–217.

Luborsky, L. Research cannot yet influence clinical practice. In A. Bergin & H. Strupp (Eds.), *Changing frontiers in the science of psychotherapy.* Hawthorne, N.Y.: Aldine Publishing, 1972.

Luborsky, L. Helping alliance in psychotherapy. In J. C. Claghorn (Ed.), *Successful Psychotherapy.* New York: Brunner/Mazel, 1976.

Luborsky, L. Quantitative research on psychoanalytic therapy. In S. L. Garfield & A. E. Bergin (Eds.), *Handbook of psychotherapy and behavior change.* New York: John Wiley & Sons, 1978.

Luborsky, L. Chandler, M., Auerbach, A. H., Cohen, J., & Bachrach, H. M. Factors influencing the outcome of psychotherapy: A review of quantitative research. *Psychological Bulletin,* 1971, *75,* 145–185.

Luborsky, L., Singer, B., & Luborsky, L. Comparative studies of psychotherapies. *Archives of General Psychiatry,* 1975, *32,* 995–1008.

Mahl, A. F. Disturbances and silences in patients' speech in psychotherapy. *Journal of Abnormal and Social Psychology,* 1956, *53,* 1–15.

Mahl, G. F., & Schulze, A. Psychological research in the extralinguistic area. In T. A. Sebeok (Ed.), *Approaches to Semiotics.* The Hague: Mouton, 1964.

Malan, O. *Toward the validation of a dynamic psychotherapy.* New York: Plenum Press, 1976.

Marmar, C., Wilner, N., & Horowitz, M. Recurrent patient states in psychotherapy: Segmentation and quantification. In L. Rice & L. S. Greenberg (Eds.), *Patterns of change: An intensive analysis of psychotherapeutic process.* New York: Guilford Press, 1982.

Martin, P. J., & Sterne, A. L. Post-hospital adjustment as related to therapist's in-therapy behaviour. *Psychotherapy: Theory Research and Practice,* 1976, *13,* 267–273.

Marziali, E., Marmar, C., & Krupnick, J. Therapeutic alliance scales: Development and relationship to psychotherapy outcome. *American Journal of Psychiatry,* 1981, *138,* 361–364.

Marziali, E. A., & Sullivan, J. M. Methodological issues in the content analysis of brief psychotherapy. *British Journal of Medical Psychology,* 1980, 53, 19–27.

Matarazzo, J. D. The interview. In B. B. Wolman (Ed.), *Handbook of clinical psychology.* New York: McGraw-Hill, 1965.

Matarazzo, J. O., Weins, A. N., Matarazzo, R. A., & Saslow, G. Speech and silence behavior in clinical psychotherapy and its laboratory correlates. In J. M. Shlien (Ed.), *Research in psychotherapy.* Washington, D.C.: *American Psychological Association,* 1968.

McClanahan, L. D. Comparison of counseling techniques and attitudes with client evaluations of the counseling relationship. *Dissertation Abstracts International,* 1974, *34,* 5637.

Mintz, J., Luborsky, L., & Auerbach, A. Dimensions of psychotherapy: A factor-analytic study of ratings of psychotherapy sessions. *Journal of Consulting and Clinical Psychology,* 1971, *36,* 106–120.

Mitchell, K. M., Bozarth, J. D., & Krauft, C. C. Reappraisal of the therapeutic effectiveness of accurate empathy, nonpossessive warmth, and genuineness. In A. S. Gurman & A. M. Razin (Eds.), *Effective psychotherapy.* Elmsford, N.Y.: Pergamon Press, 1977.

Nagel, E. *The structure of science.* New York: Harcourt Brace Jovanovich, 1961.

Nagy, T. F. Therapist level of functioning and change in clients' quantifiable anxiety level and verbal behaviour. *Dissertation Abstracts International,* 1973, *34,* 878B–879B.

Orlinsky, D. E., & Howard, K. I. The good therapy hour. *Archives of General Psychiatry,* 1967, *16,* 621–632.

Orlinsky, D. E., & Howard, K. I. *Varieties of psychotherapeutic experience.* New York: Teacher's College Press, 1975.

Orlinsky, D. E., & Howard, K. I. The relation of process to outcome in psychotherapy. In S. L. Garfield & A. E. Bergin (Eds.), *Handbook of psychotherapy and behavior change.* New York: John Wiley & Sons, 1978.

Orlinsky, D. and Howard, K. The therapist's experience of psychotherapy. In A. Gurman and A. Razin (Eds.), *Effective psychotherapy.* New York: Pergamon Press, 1977.

Parloff, M. B., Waskow, I. E., & Wolfe, B. E. Research on therapist variables in relation to process and outcome. In S. L. Garfield & A. E. Bergin (Eds.), *Handbook of psychotherapy and behavior change.* New York: John Wiley & Sons, 1978.

Pattison, J. Effects of touch on self-exploration and the therapeutic relationship. *Journal of Consulting and Clinical Psychology,* 1973, *40,* 170–175.

Perkins, M., Kiesler, D., Anchin, J., Chirico, B., Kyle, E., & Federman, E. The impact-message inventory: A new measure of relationship in counseling/psychotherapy and other dyads. *Journal of Counseling Psychology,* 1979, *26,* 363–367.

Phillips, J. S., & Bierman, K. L. Clinical psychology: Individual methods. *Annual Review of Psychology,* 1981, *32,* 405–438.

Piaget, J. *Structuralism,* New York: Harper & Row, 1970.

Pinsof, W. Family therapy process research. In A. Gurman & D. Kniskern (Eds.), *Handbook of family therapy.* New York: Brunner/Mazel, 1981.

Pope, B. Research on therapeutic style. In A. S. Gurman & A. M. Razin (Eds.), *Effective psychotherapy.* Elmsford, N.Y.: Pergamon Press, 1977.

Pope, B. *The mental health interview.* Elmsford, N.Y.: Pergamon Press, 1979.

Pope, B., Blass, T., Siegman, A. W., & Raher, J. Anxiety and depression in speech. *Journal of Consulting and Clinical Psychology,* 1970, *35,* 128–133.

Pope, B., Nudler, S., Vonkoroff, M. R., & McGee, J. P. The experienced professional interviewer versus the complete novice. *Journal of Consulting and Clinical Psychology,* 1974, *42,* 680–690.

Pope, B., & Siegman, A. W. Interviewer specificity and topical focus in relation to interviewer productivity. *Journal of Verbal Learning and Verbal Behaviour,* 1965, *4,* 188–192.

Pope, B., & Siegman, A. W. Interviewer warmth in relation to interviewee verbal behavior. *Journal of Consulting and Clinical Psychology,* 1968, *32,* 588–595.

Pope, B., & Siegman, A. W. Relationship and verbal behavior in the initial interview. In A. W. Siegman & B. Pope (Eds.), *Studies in dyadic communication.* Elmsford, N.Y.: Pergamon Press, 1972.

Prager, R. A. The relationship of certain client characteristics to therapist-offered conditions and therapeutic outcome. *Dissertation Abstracts International,* 1971, *31,* 5634B–5635B.

Raush, H. L., Barry, W. A., Hertel, R. K., & Swain, M. A. *Communication, conflict, and marriage.* San Francisco: Jossey-Bass, 1974.

Reade, M. N., & Smouse, A. D. Effects of inconsistent verbal/nonverbal communication and counselor response mode on client estimate of counselor regard and effectiveness. *Journal of Counseling Psychology,* 1980, *27,* 546–553.

Rice, L. N. Therapist's style of participation and case outcomes. *Journal of Consulting Psychology,* 1965, *29,* 155–160.

Rice, L. N. The evocative function of the therapist. In D. Wexler & L. N. Rice (Eds.), *Innovations in client-centered therapy.* New York: Wiley Interscience, 1974.

Rice, L. N., & Greenberg, L. S. *A method for studying the active ingredients in psychotherapy: Application to client-centered and Gestalt therapy.* Paper presented to the Society for Psychotherapy Research, Denver, 1974.

Rice, L. N., & Greenberg, L. S. *Patterns of change: An intensive analysis of psychotherapeutic process.* New York: Guilford Press, 1982.

Rice, L. N., & Koke, C. Vocal style and the process of psychotherapy. In J. Darby (Ed.), *Speech evaluation in psychiatry.* New York: Grune & Stratton, 1981.

Rice, L., Koke, C., Greenberg, L., & Wagstaff, A. *Manual for client vocal quality.* Toronto: York University, 1979.

Rice, L. N., & Wagstaff, A. Client voice quality and expressive style as indexes of productive psychotherapy. *Journal of Consulting Psychology,* 1967, *31,* 557–563.

Russel, P. D., & Snyder, W. U. Counselor anxiety in relation to amount of direct experience and quality of affect demonstrated by clients. *Journal of Consulting Psychology,* 1963, *27,* 358–363.

Russel, R., & Stiles, W. Categories for classifying language in psychotherapy. *Psychological Bulletin,* 1979, *86,* 404–419.

Ryan, V. L., & Gizynski, M. N. Behavior therapy in retrospect: Patients feelings about their behavior therapies. *Journal of Consulting and Clinical Psychology,* 1971, *37,* 1–9.

Sackett, G. P. *A nonparametric lag-sequential analysis for studying dependency among responses in observational scoring systems.* Unpublished manuscript, University of Washington, 1974.

Saltzman, C., Luetgert, M. J., Roth, C. H., Creaser, J., & Howard, L. Formation of a therapeutic relationship: Experiences during the initial phase of psychotherapy as predictors of treatment duration and outcome. *Journal of Consulting and Clinical Psychology,* 1976, *44,* 546–555.

Sarason, I. G., & Winkel, G. H. Individual differences among subjects and experimenters and subject's self-descriptions. *Journal of Personality and Social Psychology,* 1966, *3,* 448–457.

Schauble, P. G., & Pierce, R. M. Client in-therapy behavior: A therapist guide to progress. *Psychotherapy: Theory Research and Practice,* 1974, *11,* 229–234.

Siegman, A. W., & Pope, B. Effects of question specificity and anxiety-arousing messages on verbal fluency in the initial interview. *Journal of Personality and Social Psychology,* 1965, *4,* 188–192.

Siegman, A. W., & Pope, B. The effects of ambiguity and anxiety on interviewee verbal behavior. In A. W. Siegman & B. Pope (Eds.), *Studies in dyadic communication.* Elmsford, N.Y.: Pergamon Press, 1972.

Sloane, R. B., Cristol, A. H., Peperrik, L., & Staples, F. R. Role preparation and expectation of improvement in psychotherapy. *Journal of Nervous and Mental Disease,* 1970, *150,* 18–26.

Sloane, R. B., Staples, F. R., Cristol, A. H., Yorkstan, N. J., & Whipple, K. *Psychotherapy versus behavior therapy.* Cambridge, Mass.: Harvard University Press, 1975.

Smith-Hanen, S. Effects of nonverbal behaviors on judged levels of counselor warmth and empathy. *Journal of Counseling Psychology,* 1977, *24,* 87–91.

Speisman, J. C. Depth of interpretation and verbal resistance in psychotherapy. *Journal of Consulting Psychology,* 1959, *23,* 93–99.

Stiles, W. Verbal response modes and psychotherapeutic technique. *Psychiatry,* 1979, *42,* 49–62.

Stiles, W. B. Measurement of the impact of psychotherapy sessions. *Journal of Consulting and Clinical Psychology,* 1980, *2,* 48.

Stockwell, S. R., & Dye, A. Effects of counselor touch on counseling outcome. *Journal of Counseling Psychology.* 1980, *27,* 443–446.

Stoler, N. *The relationship of patient likeability and the A-B psychiatric resident types.* Doctoral dissertation, University of Michigan, 1966. (Unicweairy Microfilms)

Strahan, C., & Zytowski, D. A. Impact of visual, vocal, and lexical cues on judgments of counselor qualities. *Journal of Counseling Psychology,* 1976, *23,* 387–393.

Strong, S. R., Wambach, C. A., Lopez, F. G., & Cooper, R. K. Motivational and equipping functions of interpretation in counseling. *Journal of Counseling Psychology,* 1979, *26,* 98–107.

Strupp, H. H. Psychoanalytic therapy of the individual. In J. Marmon (Ed.), *Modern psychoanalysis: New direction and perspectives.* New York: Basic Books, 1968.

Strupp, H. H. Reformulation of the dynamics of therapists' contributions. In A. S. Gurman & A. M. Razin (Eds.), *Effective psychotherapy.* Elmsford, N.Y.: Pergamon Press, 1977.

Strupp, H. H. Success and failure in time-limited psychotherapy. *Archives of General Psychiatry,* 1980, *37,* 595–603.

Strupp, H. H., & Bloxom, A. Preparation of lower-class patients for group psychotherapy. *Journal of Consulting and Clinical Psychology,* 1973, *41,* 373–384.

Strupp, H. H., Fox, R. E., & Lessler, K. *Patients view their psychotherapy.* Baltimore: Johns Hopkins Press, 1969.

Strupp, H. H., Hadley, D., & Gomes-Schwartz, B. *Psychotherapy for better or worse: An analysis of the problem of negative effects.* New York: Jason Aronson, 1977.

Strupp, H. H., Wallach, M. S., Wogan, M., & Jenkins, J. W. Psychotherapists' assessments of former patients. *Journal of Nervous and Mental Disease,* 1963, *137,* 222–230.

Teasdale, J. D., & Rezin, V. The effects of reducing frequency of negative thoughts on the mood of depressed patients—tests of a cognitive model of depression. *British Journal of Social and Clinical Psychology,* 1978, *17,* 65–74.

Tepper, D. T., & Haase, R. F. Verbal and nonverbal communication of facilitative conditions. *Journal of Counseling Psychology,* 1978, *25,* 35–44.

Tovian, S. M. *Patient experiences and psychotherapy outcome.* Unpublished doctoral dissertation, Northwestern University, 1977.

Truax, C. B. Length of therapist response, accurate empathy, and patient improvement. *Journal of Clinical Psychology,* 1970, *26,* 539–541.

Truax, C. B. Degree of negative transference occurring in group psychotherapy and client outcome in juvenile delinquents. *Journal of Clinical Psychology,* 1971, *27,* 132–136.

Truax, C. B., & Carkhuff, R. R. The experimental manipulation of therapeutic conditions. *Journal of Consulting Psychology,* 1965, *29,* 119–124.

Truax, C. B., & Wittmer, J. Patient nonpersonal reference during psychotherapy and therapeutic outcome. *Journal of Clinical Psychology,* 1971, *27,* 300–302.

Truax, C. B., & Wittmer, J. The degree of therapist's focus on defense mechanisms and the effect on therapeutic outcome with institutionalized juvenile delinquents. *Journal of Community Psychology,* 1973, *1,* 201–203.

Wargo, O. G., Millis, W. E., Hendricks, N. G. Patient rational verbal behavior as an antecedent to outcome in psychotherapy. *Psychotherapy: Theory Research and Practice,* 1971, *8,* 199–201.

Waskow, I. E. *Presidential address.* Presented at the Society for Psychotherapy Research, Oxford, England, 1979.

Wexler, D. A., & Butler, J. M. Therapist modification of client expressiveness in client-centered therapy. *Journal of Consulting and Clinical Psychology,* 1976, *44,* 261–265.

Young, D. W. Meanings of counselor nonverbal gestures: Fixed or interpretative? *Journal of Counseling Psychology,* 1980, *27,* 447–452.

7

Therapist characteristics and their contribution to psychotherapy outcome

Michael J. Lambert*
and
Allen E. Bergin*

In initial studies of the effects of psychotherapy, researchers soon discovered that the unique contribution of relational style and personality characteristics of particular therapists were often more powerful than the presumed treatment technique under investigation. When studying a particular form of therapy or contrasting various forms of treatment, researchers recognized that research designs must control for the effects of these therapist traits on psychotherapy outcome. Researchers not only controlled for the inadvertent personal effect of therapists but, recognizing the size of their contribution to outcome, began exploring therapist characteristics as a possible primary independent variable in outcome studies. Subsequently, there has developed a large body of literature on the therapist's contribution to psychotherapy outcome. This chapter provides an overview of research on the therapist's contribution to effective psychotherapy. In addition to this overview, the chapter will focus upon those therapist variables that appear to be most important in influencing patient improvement in clinical practice. Specifically, the focus of this section will be on the implications of research relating to therapist variables for clinical practice.

TOWARD A TAXONOMY OF THERAPIST INFLUENCE

Several therapist characteristics, qualities, and especially, activities have been suggested as contributors to positive and negative psychother-

---

* Brigham Young University, Provo, Utah.

apeutic outcome. In fact, many clinicians believe these qualities (in contrast to techniques) to be the most important determinants of patient improvement. Therapist variables (such as warmth, experience, self-disclosure, empathic communication, specific personality characteristics, and personal adjustment) are among those that have received the greatest attention in empirical studies. The identification of therapist variables that influence outcome has led to greater specification of salient skills in training programs and has been the catalyst for attempts by training institutions to select candidates for training on the basis of these variables (Matarazzo, 1978).

There are many ways of classifying therapist variables. The organizational method employed here calls for the division of variables on the basis of how data on them is usually produced. In psychotherapy research, investigators may measure the ongoing psychotherapeutic process (interaction) by studying such variables as therapist empathy and patient experiencing, or they may study static traits such as therapist personality (e.g., dominance). These two research strategies have various advantages and disadvantages, both practical and scientific. Research in psychotherapy can be easily classified into one or the other of these procedures. Such a classification is presented in Figure 1.

A major advantage of static traits (such as gender, race, and experience level) is the ease with which they can be collected and tabulated. Demographic data, personality traits, level of personal adjustment, and the like can all be easily collected at the inception of a study. They lend themselves to ready classification. In addition, they can be used for practical decision making, matching (patients and therapists), and selecting therapists. On the other hand, their static nature is rather uninformative. For example, when race is used as a variable, many unknown or unidentified variables of a less superficial nature may be affecting results (e.g., values associated with social class, perception of patient, interactions of the therapist and patient). Static traits are not ideal for the study of causality. For example, experience level is a commonly studied therapist trait. Although a correlation between experience and patient outcome may allow patients to maximize treatment success by choosing an experienced therapist, it does little to inform us of the mechanisms of influence. Do experienced therapists tend to have better outcomes because they are perceived as more confident and less anxious? Is it their sense of timing in using interpretation or reflection? To leave analysis of interpersonal or psychotherapeutic influence at the level of variables such as race, gender, and personality, is to close the door to a significant understanding of causality. However, research on static traits is still important because it allows for testing of gross hypotheses (e.g., black patients have better outcomes when seen by black therapists). It also can be used in making valuable, practical treatment decisions which can reduce dropout rates and increase patient satisfaction and positive outcomes.

Figure 1

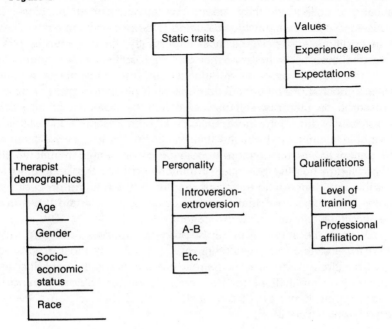

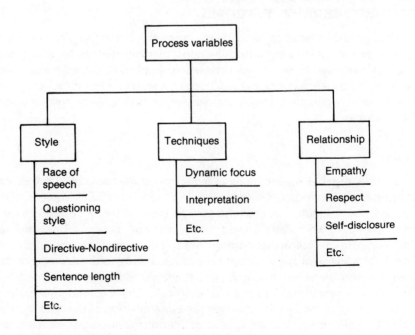

Process variables, on the other hand, are difficult, expensive, and time-consuming to collect; yet they seem to be tapping something closer to the cause-and-effect relationships assumed to be operative in psychotherapy. In addition, and perhaps most importantly, these variables often involve qualities of the therapist that can be modified with training. As a result, research on process variables is, perhaps, more important and potentially much more influential than research on static traits. For example, research on therapist self-disclosure has the potential of directing therapist activity during the therapeutic encounter. Research on this therapist variable illuminates both the immediate (in-therapy) consequences on the patient as well as the more remote effects on patient mental health. This knowledge has the potential of influencing both the beginning as well as the experienced therapist and shaping future training procedures, because it can be shown that therapist disclosure of certain types and at specific times can influence the patient.

In our view, the study of therapist process variables holds the most promise for a science of psychotherapy. It is not only most promising, but past research in this area has already produced significant findings that have clear implications for professional practice. Before turning to this research, an overview of the most important research on so-called static variables is provided.

STATIC THERAPIST TRAITS AND PSYCHOTHERAPY OUTCOME

Several recent studies have been undertaken, and they provide evidence for the value of exploring the effect of some static traits on psychotherapy outcome. Here we will review research related to therapist race, gender, experience, personal adjustment, expectancies, socioeconomic status, and personality. Major conclusions and illustrative research will be presented.

Race

A large number of studies have investigated the topic of racial effects on psychotherapy outcomes (Harrison, 1975; Sattler, 1977). There is some evidence that blacks have a tendency to leave therapy at higher ratios than expected when they have a white therapist. Typical of research in this area are the following studies: Jones (1978) explored the effects of therapist and client race on the process and short-term outcome of dynamic insight-oriented therapy. No significant differences were found among four racial matchings when therapist outcome ratings of patient improvement served as the criterion. In a continuation of this study, Jones (1978) again examined the effects of therapist and client race on the process and outcome of psychotherapy. One hundred and sixty-four black and white patients, evenly divided by race, were seen in individual psychotherapy. Half of the patients were assigned to racially similar therapist-patient matches and half to racially dissimilar pairings. The results indicated that white therapists generally rated their clients, and especially their black clients, as psychologically more impaired than did black therapists. In conjunction with previous research, however, no differences were found in psychotherapy outcome as a function of matching patients and therapists racially. Finally, Costello, Baillargeon, Biever, and Bennett (1979) reported on a two-year follow-up of Anglo- and Mexican-American patients treated for alcoholism with a multifaceted inpatient/outpatient program. Patients were classified into three groups on the basis of the Social Adjustment Inventory. Outcomes were reported via this classification as well as by racial groupings. The overall success of the program was estimated to be 39 percent. In general, the Mexican-American patients ($n = 26$) fared as well or better than the Anglo-American patients ($n = 44$), all of whom were treated by a group of predominately Anglo therapists.

Current research has failed to provide new information supporting the effect of therapist race on therapy outcome. Moreover, support for the notion that there are no differences in psychotherapy outcome as a function of client-therapist racial matching continues (Lambert, 1982).

Gender

Past research has not indicated that patients fare better under male or female therapists (Geer & Hurst, 1976; Grantham, 1973; Sullivan, Miller, & Smelser, 1958; Pardes, Papernik, & Winston, 1974; Scher, 1975). Despite discussions about male bias against females in therapy, there is little support for this position in empirical research. Two studies have suggested that female therapists seeing female clients had a poorer outcome (Mintz, O'Brien, & Luborsky, 1976; Meyer & Freeman, 1976), and one showed the opposite trend (Hill, 1975). Norkus (1976) showed that outcome and satisfactory termination were better when female clients were placed with the counselor of whichever sex they preferred.

One of the more interesting recent studies on gender effects considered both the biological gender of therapists and their sexual-social role orientation (androdgyny). Feldstein (1979) studied the effects of client and counselor sex and sex role on the counseling relationship. He found that: male subjects were more satisfied with the counseling process than female subjects; male subjects indicated greater satisfaction and a higher level of counselor regard with "feminine" counselors than with "masculine" counselors, regardless of counselor sex; female subjects indicated greater satisfaction and a higher level of regard for "masculine" counselors than "feminine" counselors, regardless of counselor sex; male subjects talked most about themselves with feminine female counselors and least about themselves with masculine female counselors; and, female subjects talked most about themselves with feminine male counselors and least about themselves with masculine male counselors.

At this point in time, assignment of patients to therapist on the basis of therapist gender is not supported by research literature. Future research may yet discover patient attitudes or other variables that interact with therapist gender and make assignment on this dimension worthwhile.

Qualifications and experience

Qualifications of the therapist (as determined by type of training, the inclusion of personal therapy as a part of training, and professional affiliation) have received attention in the research literature. There is no evidence to suggest that a person from one professional discipline is more effective in employing psychotherapy than another. Like professional discipline, the personal therapy of the therapist, as well as the type of training received, have not demonstrated differential effects on patient outcome.

The experience of the therapist is perhaps the most interesting and important of the variables concerned with qualifications. It is generally accepted that experience increases the ability of the therapist to treat patients. It seems likely that this rather gross variable is tapping numerous qualities that may be assumed to increase with age, training, and practice. These variables might include confidence, security, integration, flexibility, knowledge, etc. One would assume that experience would show a strong relationship to outcome, as a variety of skills are fostered by practice.

In fact, previous reviews of the research in this area have found experience to be one of the few therapist static factors that has a reliable relationship to outcome. Recent findings in this area, however, are not as strongly supportive of this belief as expected. Auerbach and Johnson (1977) have provided the most recent review of literature pertaining to the relationship of experience and therapeutic outcome. Their review was not supportive of the belief that experience is *highly* related to outcome. They did, nevertheless, find experienced therapists more likely to have positive outcomes. Further, 6 of the 11 studies investigating this topic found no difference or favored experienced therapists as contributing to positive outcome. After reviewing the literature, Parloff, Waskow, and Wolfe (1978) reached a similar conclusion and stated that the data available, pertaining to the therapists' level of experience on outcome, were not sound enough to permit any firm conclusions.

Previous research has identified several methodological problems in studying the therapist-experience variable. One difficulty is that few studies have sought to examine therapist experience as a major independent variable. Thus, random assignment to either experienced or inexperienced therapists has rarely been accomplished, and frequently, assignment to one or the other group has been biased. Hence, therapist experience needs to be studied while systematically manipulating client varibles such as symptom complexity. This type of study would help in making systematic assignment of client types to more and less experienced therapists.

An example of a relatively tightly controlled study on therapist experience that showed some difference between persons of various experience levels illustrates research in this area. Haccoun and Lavigueur (1979) utilized an interaction design to study the effects of clinical experience and client emotion on therapist's responses during therapy. Actresses (portraying the role of clients expressing standardized problems in angry or sad ways) interacted with therapists varying in prior therapy experience (e.g., high—had seen over 100 cases, medium—had seen 6 cases, low—had no experience). Results indicated that therapists judged angry clients less favorably than sad clients. Therapist experience and client emotion interacted and suggested that more experienced therapists showed a greater tolerance of anger. Moreover, therapists' behavior during the therapy session was consistent with their evaluation of the clients. Experienced therapists intervened less with angry clients, provided less support and less direction, and asked fewer questions. Presumably this more-appropriate behavior on the part of more-experienced therapists would have tangible benefits to the patients treated.

Personal adjustment

On an intuitive basis, the more healthy, integrated therapist is expected to have better results than the less healthy therapist who may even cause deterioration in a portion of patients. And, indeed, the research evidence does suggest that the more indications of psychological disturbance in the therapist, the poorer the treatment outcome. For example, Donner and Schonfield (1975) found that student therapists who were more conflicted about ideal and real behavior were more likely to respond with depression to clients' expressions of depression and anxiety. Student therapists seen as better adjusted were also seen as more facilitative to their patients.

Bugen (1979) studied the moderating effect of high and low anxiety on counselor perception of stages of dying. Thirty-one counselor trainees were rated as either high- or low-anxiety subjects (according to the A-State Anxiety Scale) and then asked to rate a dying person on denial, anger, depression, acceptance, and hope. It was found that high-anxiety subjects were more likely to project their own aversive feelings onto the dying person. This study suggests that counselors tend to perceive clients according to their own anxiety levels. However, no outcome data were gathered to clarify the effects this might have on patients.

Evidence has also indicated that a "pathogenic" therapist may manipulate dependent individuals to meet his or her own needs. Ricks (1974), for example, identified behavioral and attitudinal differences between two therapists who saw 28 disturbed boys. Clear differences in outcome were evident in the patients treated by these two therapists. Those boys treated by the therapist who was undergoing serious psychological problems were unsuccessful in later life adjustments. These results were dramatic when contrasted with the results achieved by an especially effective therapist. Work has also been conducted investigating the relationship between therapist personality integration and successful termination of psychotherapy. Those dyads that were most successful included a therapist and client high in personality integration (Anchor, 1977). Studies examining countertransference indicate that difficulties in this area result in a less effective therapist and poorer patient outcome (Singer & Luborsky, 1977). The evidence, although mainly anecdotal, continues to suggest that therapist's personality integration and adjustment have a positive impact on patients. Adjustment of the therapist has not been adequately explored in controlled outcome studies and ought to be more thoroughly investigated.

Expectancies

While client expectations for *therapist role performance* and *improvement* have received considerable attention in the research literature, therapist expectancies have received relatively little attention. In addition, most studies of therapist expectancies have not correlated these with patient outcome. Instead, past research has focused on the effects of pre-therapy expectancy manipulations on subsequent therapist behavior with clients. These manipulations have usually involved providing therapists with information about client traits (e.g., friendly versus hostile), diagnosis, or prognosis, followed by observations of the therapists' behavior or attitudes.

Many controversial issues surround research on therapist expectancies. Of interest here is whether therapist expectancies for positive or negative outcome accurately predict outcome or cause it. Unfortunately, the majority of studies in this area have been either correlational (thus precluding cause-effect conclusions) or laboratory designs (making generalization to actual therapy difficult). At this point, it is probably safe to say that there is little empirical support for the position that therapist expectancies play a direct role in causing patient change. Actual behavior has a more powerful effect on therapist behavior than pre-set therapist expectancies that have resulted from intentional manipulations of therapist views in laboratory research.

Despite these findings, there is some evidence that therapist diagnostic and prognostic expectancies have an indirect effect on outcome by determining the type and quantity of treatment made available to patients (Heitler, 1976). Those patients seen by therapists as being poor candidates for psychotherapy are frequently excluded from verbal psychotherapies and referred for treatments assumed to be more helpful (e.g., medication). They, of course, cannot profit from psychosocial interventions they never receive.

SES

While patient socioeconomic status has received widespread attention in outcome research, this demographic, as a therapist trait, has not received much attention. This is probably due to the fact that most therapists are from upper- or middle-class backgrounds, making controlled research on this topic difficult. Certainly, therapist SES has been indirectly implicated as a variable of importance in studies of patient SES. The general trend of evidence has suggested that patients from lower socioeconomic strata do not profit from the traditional psychotherapies to the extent that middle- and upper-class patients do (Heitler, 1976; Lorion and Cowen, 1976). Even more clear is the finding that they drop out of treatment in disproportionate ratios when compared with high-SES patients. While this trend could be solely a function of this patient characteristic, it has been suggested that it may be the result of matching these patients with the traditionally middle-class therapists who are providing treatment. The typical middle-class therapist frequently shows a lack of common experiences and values with the low-SES patient. This plausible hypothesis lacks clear empirical verification, although it has some support in current research (Lambert, 1982).

Personality variables

The personality of the therapist undoubtedly interacts with the personality of the client and results in positive or negative effects for the client. Much has been said about the personality traits of the ideal therapist. As frequently described, they seem very close to a picture of an ideal person (insightful, flexible, wise, mature, warm, etc.). Still, there are some therapist characteristics that have a less obvious and less value-laden connotation (such as introversion/extroversion, dominance, psychological mindedness, and nurturance). These personality traits may interact with various patient traits and facilitate positive outcomes. The possibility of matching individual therapists and patients on these personality traits is attractive.

The most frequently studied characteristics of the therapist have been those traits associated with the so-called *A-B* dichotomy. This research originated with a report by Whitehorn and Betz (1954), who used the Strong Vocational Interest Blank to identify two groups of therapists (as *A* group and a *B* group) who appeared to be differentially effective with schizophrenic patients. The more effective *A* therapists seemed to become more actively involved than the more passive, permissive, and didactic B therapists. The results of this study became widely quoted and achieved widespread acceptance. Since this study, however, numerous replications and refinements have *not* confirmed the notion that subgroups of differentially effective therapists can be identified through the use of the A-B personality dimension, nor have specific therapist behaviors been shown to be consistently related to these scales. Recent reviews (Razin, 1977; Gomes-Schwartz, Hadley, & Strupp, 1978) are now calling for a moratorium on A-B research.

Razin (1977), in the most thorough review of this dimension published thus far, summarized his interpretation of the literature with several points: (1) the A-B variable does reliably correlate with and predict a consistent constellation of therapist personality differences; (2) however, the A-B variable is not a powerful predictor of any significant outcome or process variable; and (3) there has never been a successful replication of the Whitehorn-Betz study.

Dent (1978) published an interesting report on the personality characteristics of effective therapists and the interaction of therapist personality with patient diagnosis. The author reanalyzed the A-B data from several past studies and controlled for variables he felt were important. In addition, Dent studied therapist personality as measured by the Personal Tendencies Questionnaire. He is much more optimistic about the possibilities of discovering effective matching strategies based upon therapist personality than are most current researchers and reviewers. The interested reader will want to read in detail Dent's monograph on this subject.

Among the conclusions drawn were:

> (a) the effective therapist, in the general sense, does not exist; (b) specific personal tendencies and interests define effectiveness with particular types of mental or behavioral problems; (c) neurotics are not well served by active directive therapists who have a need to solve problems; while (d) schizophrenics are best served by a therapist who is active and personally involved with the patient. In addition to these findings, conclusions are drawn about the traits that make therapists effective with different types of delinquents, depressives, etc.

We find the results of Dent's reanalysis interesting, but not nearly as convincing nor as authoritative as the author would have us believe. Nevertheless, the analysis provides many suggestions and procedures for future research on therapist and patient personality, including the use of appropriate matching strategies. It also provides a plausible explanation for the consistent failure to replicate the original Whitehorn-Betz data.

No other therapist personality trait has generated as much research nor been any more successful than the A-B personality factor at developing prescriptive therapy and devising therapist selection criteria. In the recent past, however, several personality traits have been studied in isolation and also matched with a variety of patient traits: MMPI scales, FIRO-*B* scales, Leary's Interpersonal Circle, Myers-Briggs Type Indicator, Role Construct Repertory Test, etc. Despite the frequent failure to successfully match patients and therapists, the search for critical personality variables continues.

One of the most practical attempts to implement the belief that ideal matches can be identified and employed in clinical settings was the Indiana Matching Project reported by Berzins (1974, 1977). This project used sophisticated statistical techniques in a four-year study of brief crisis-oriented psychotherapy. Each of the 10 therapists in the study saw an average of 75 patients. Clients were evaluated on several role dimensions: avoidance of others, turning against the self, dependency on others, and turning toward others and self. Eight patient-predictor scores tapping these four roles were derived from questionnaire responses. Therapist-predictor scores were based on the Personality Research Form (Jackson, 1967). Analytical factor-derived scores on impulse expression, ambition, acceptance, dominance, caution, and abasement were calculated for each project therapist.

Patients were assigned to therapists randomly and were then seen for about three weeks. Post-therapy ratings involved 13 scales factored into three variables: client improvement, therapist self-appraisal, and client-experienced rapport. The first of these variables was the outcome measure used as a criterion for evaluating matches. It was made up of both client and therapist perceptions that had shown modest agreement.

Favorable pairings usually involved complementarity of participants on the same personality tests. Generally, submissive, inhibited, passive patients did better with dominant, expressive, active structure-emitting therapists and vice versa. Some differences were found between male and female clients in terms of the most viable matches.

To replicate the findings, patients in a second study were assigned to therapists on the basis of therapist personality scores and patient personality pre-test scores. The assignments were based on the therapist/patient interactions identified in the earlier study. The results indicated that optimally paired dyads did show higher improvement scores. The full results of this study have not yet been reported and so preclude an adequate understanding of the limits of the study. However, this project has demonstrated the feasibility of empirical therapy assignment procedures, a step toward more professional services.

THERAPIST PROCESS VARIABLES AND PSYCHOTHERAPY OUTCOME

Among the factors considered most important in understanding the therapist's contribution to effective psychotherapy are the ways in which the therapist exerts influence during the therapy session. The direct study of the ways therapists behave with patients and the immediate and remote consequences of these behaviors is a most hopeful area of investigation. Having the potential of being a dynamic and somewhat less-abstract and general arena, process research offers the possibility of very practical findings, and it has clear implications for training and practice.

Process research can be conceptualized in many different ways. For the purpose of our discussion, we will focus on three types of process variables: therapist *style*, *intervention*, and *relationship*, as these variables assume a central role in the research literature. Although the discussion will focus on process research, at times the discussion may drift away from studies that are strictly concerned with therapist in-therapy behavior. This is necessary because research strategies have included methods other than process studies on topics that are important to the presentation of clinical results. For example, some of the discussion dealing with the therapist-offered relationship is based on client ratings of therapist behavior obtained well after therapy was terminated. For the most part, however, the study of the effects of therapist behaviors will be emphasized.

Therapist style and related in-therapy behavior

Style refers to the unique ways in which the therapist communicates with the client, especially with regard to the nonlexical, rather than content, aspects of interacting. Aspects of speech that have been studied include such variables as rate of speech, duration of utterances, disruptions, pitch, and inflections. These aspects of therapist speech imply something of the uncontrolled expression of affect by the therapist. The therapist's expressiveness may be considered instrumental, though perhaps not intended, and it can be opened to study when specifically defined.

For example, Hurndon, Pepinsky, and Meara (1979), and Meara, Pepinsky, Shannon, and Murray (1981) used the Paragraph Completion Method to identify conceptual level and a Computer-Assisted Language Analysis System (CALAS) to identify structural features of client's and counselor's language. Using CALAS information, differences were found among therapist's number of sentences, average sentence length, average block length, and average clause depth. Their results seem to provide a basis for inferring that there may be a number of significant relationships between the natural language of therapists and patients and the dynamics and effectiveness of counseling.

Kleinke and Tully (1979) found that graduate counseling students (as well as undergraduate students) preferred counselors who engaged in low (i.e., small amount of time) rather than medium or high levels of talking. Additionally, they suggested that counselors engaging in low levels of talking should not allow long periods of silence, as this may imply they are not doing enough to encourage client participation. In a similar study, Natale (1978) examined the relationship between crisis-line telephone interviewers' timing of speech and interviewers' empathy, warmth, and genuineness as perceived by the interviewee. It was found that on all three dimensions, the interviewer was rated higher when there were fewer pauses between interviewer statements.

Studies of this type of therapist stylistic behavior show change as a function of experience and training (Matarazzo, 1978) but rarely closely associated with outcome (e.g., utterance length and latency prior to speaking decrease with experience or training).

Characteristic of more recent studies in this area was a study conducted by Ehrlich, D'Augelli, and Danish (1979) investigating the effects of counselor verbal responses on client's verbal behavior and on their perceptions of these counselors. The verbal responses were affect, content, influencing, advice, open question, and closed question. The results indicate that affect responses (e.g., feeling reflections) were found to be the most effective in eliciting desirable client behavior, and the counselor using more affective responses was considered more attractive, expert, and trustworthy. Just the opposite result was found with counselors emitting closed-question responses. Further, while content responses and open questions were effective in eliciting desirable client behavior, advice responses (even though liked by the clients) were not effective at eliciting desired behaviors.

In addition to these somewhat atheoretical and formal stylistic properties of therapist behavior, considerable research has focused on more conceptually based and theoretically significant characteristics. These include directive/nondirective therapist style, therapist initiative, authoritarianism, and degree of ambiguity-specificity, as well as a host of other variables.

Research on the nondirective/directive dichotomy is illustrative of investigations in this area. The study of this variable has a long tradition as a focal point of study and is also of contemporary concern. This dimension of therapist style clearly distinguishes between therapists who take a leading, structuring, initiating, directing role in therapy and those who choose to respond to patients with open-ended invitations to talk. Operationally, this dichotomy has been defined differently, depending upon the investigators undertaking the study.

An interesting study of this style with psychoneurotics who underwent at least four sessions of treatment was reported by Ashby, Ford, Guerney, and Guerney (1957). Six clinical psychology students were trained in either a reflective style or a leading style. Most interesting among the results was the finding that those clients who were more defensive before treatment behaved more defensively in treatment with a leading (directive) therapist but not with a reflective therapist. In addition, more aggressive clients (pre-therapy) acted more aggressively with the directive style. At the same time, clients who had manifested a greater autonomy need reported feeling less defensive in directive therapy. Clearly, the two styles had different effects on different patient types.

More recent research has focused upon therapy/therapist directiveness and patient locus of control (the degree to which patients generally attribute consequences in their lives to events external to themselves, rather than to their own efforts). The locus-of-control construct has been measured by the *I-E* scale (Rotter, 1966). The basic hypothesis which has emerged is that clients who see themselves as being in control of and responsible for their fate are likely to prefer and have better outcomes in treatments that are minimally directive. On the other hand, patients who see themselves as the victims of fate, as being determined by forces outside of themselves, will prefer and gain the most from controlling therapies or those with the greatest structure.

The following study is illustrative of contemporary research related to the effects of directive counseling with patients who varied on the *I-E* continuum. Schwartz and Higgins (1979) studied the effects of a highly structured assertiveness training treatment on the behavior of a low-assertive college student population. Improvement in this group ($n = 24$) was contrasted with improvement in expectancy ($n = 24$) and nontreatment ($n = 24$) control groups. Utilizing Rotter's Locus of Control Scale, they studied the interaction between this patient personality variable and the treatments. Patients in the treatment group were clearly more improved than controls at termination. Consistent with previous research, locus of control interacted with the treatment. Those who had an internal locus of control profited less in the treatment group and less relative to externals, but they improved more in the control groups. Internal patients also felt treatment took away too much of their control of the environment. They felt more uncomfortable in treatment than those with an external locus of control.

The studies involving locus of control and directive therapist style have included as criterion preference for therapist or therapy as well as actual therapy outcome. The current status of this research (e.g., Rozensky & Bellack, 1976; Wallston, Wallston, Kaplan, & Maides, 1976; Best, 1975; Abramowitz, Abramowitz, Roback, & Jackson, 1974; Friedman & Dies, 1974; Best & Steffy, 1971) can be summarized briefly. Externals show a preference for treatments which are more directive (such as many behavioral techniques and rational-emotive psychotherapy), while internals prefer less externally controlled and less directed procedures. As yet, however, there is little evidence that differential outcomes result from suitable and unsuitable matches of client types and therapist styles, although some evidence does point in this direction.

To summarize: the directive/nondirective dimension of therapist behavior has frequently been shown to relate to patient in-therapy behavior. Its relationship to preference, comfort, and initial perceptions of the attractiveness of therapy is more complex. But it appears that therapist directiveness interacts with a variety of patient variables (especially locus of control) to predict these early positive and negative reactions to therapy. The link between directive style and outcome is less clear. It would seem that this therapist/therapy variable may be modestly predictive of outcome when patient characteristics are taken into account. Nevertheless, additional studies are needed to supplement the data already collected.

Therapist intervention or operation

This category refers to the intentional behavior of therapists that is guided by a specific theory of behavior change. The boundary between interventions of the therapist and the behaviors described and explored under the heading of style (e.g., directive/nondirective) is not at all clear. Likewise, it is difficult to distinguish between the manner in which therapists relate to clients (e.g., therapist warmth) from therapeutic operations, because many theories posit warmth and the like as central therapist activities. Nevertheless, we can identify several verbal techniques or therapeutic operations that are especially important in effective psychotherapy.

One therapist intervention that has drawn considerable attention both in theoretical work and in research is the use of interpretation. Interpretations by the therapist are purported to provide the patient with (or aid the patient in developing) an intellectual understanding of the relationship between feelings and behavior, feelings and thought patterns, or behavior patterns and early life experiences. In the ideal form, the patient experiences not only an intellectual grasp of life patterns, but has a significant emotional reaction that implies greater personal integration.

Interpretations are used for a variety of purposes: to reduce anxiety, provide support, overcome resistance, facilitate communication, and inhibit the likelihood of acting out. Not only is interpretation an important therapist activity for the psychosocial therapies, but it is also used in one form or another in many behavioral therapies. For example, in the comparative study by Sloane, Stapes, Cristol, Yorkston, and Wipple (1975) comparing behavior and psychodynamically oriented therapists, it was found that behavior therapists actually made more interpretations than the insight-oriented therapists.

Kiesler (1973) has suggested that interpretation might be operationalized as a causal inference made by the therapist about the client based on an evaluation of the case material. The usefulness of therapeutic interpretation is seen differently depending upon the theoretical orientation of the therapist. In the client-centered framework, Rogers (1942) felt that interpreting unexpressed feelings was "definitely dangerous," whereas those adhering to a psychoanalytic philosophy see the interpretive process as an instrumental factor facilitating therapeutic change.

It is natural to ask: is there evidence that interpretation leads to the desired or predicted behavior? While there are numerous studies that bear on this issue, we will highlight a few of the more interesting ones. First, it should be noted that interpretation, as operationally defined, usually involves the application of rating scales that measure depth or plausibility of interpretation. The usual hypothesis in a study of depth of interpretation would suggest a relationship between depth (or plausibility) and patient self-exploration, acceptance of therapist statement, or resistance to interpretation and therapy in general. Speisman (1959), for example, is typical of research in this area. He reported a positive relationship between interpretations rated as superficial or moderate in depth and patient behaviors typed as positive and nonrestrictive. At the same time, deep interpretations seemed to be associated with patient opposition, doubt, and negativism.

Another area of research on interpretation has examined the consequences of particular types of interpretations. Malan (1976a, 1976b) summarized the pioneering series of studies he and his colleagues conducted at the Tavistock Clinic in London. In these naturalistic studies, series of 21 and 39 patients were treated with brief (10 to 40 sessions) psychoanalytically oriented psychotherapy. Among other purposes, the studies sought to discover whether brief treatment, which applied the same types of interpretations as full-scale analysis, could be as effective as traditional analysis with patients who varied considerably in degree of disturbance. Follow-up data were collected five to six years after treatment termination to determine whether changes induced by brief therapy would be enduring.

Although the results of these studies may be limited because of the research design employed, it appears that brief analytic treatment can be effective with some patients. The characteristics of those who were helped most by this treatment could not be clearly specified, but factors most highly related to positive outcome in both series of studies were (1) *interpretive focusing on the transference/parent link*, and (2) *patient's motivation for change*. In more general terms, positive outcome correlated with the process factor called *successful dynamic interaction*, defined as a patient who wanted insight and accepted the interpretations of the therapist, especially with regard to the importance of early life relationships on current behavior patterns.

In a broader sense, it is possible to identify certain therapist technical operations and rate the degree to which they illustrate effective psychotherapy. Sandell (1981) conducted one of the few empirical investigations specifically aimed at illuminating the process that leads to negative effects. Using data from the Vanderbilt study (Strupp & Hadley, 1979) she applied the Vanderbilt Negative Indicators Scale (VNIS) to therapist/patient interactions drawn from the first three therapy sessions. This instrument, revised for this study, contained 42 items which were rated by two trained judges. The total scale was made up of five subscales: Patient Qualities, Therapist Personal Qualities, Errors in Technique, Patient-Therapist Interaction, and

Global Factors, which presumably measured different aspects of the ongoing therapy. The scale items were developed through an analysis of past literature on patient deterioration (c.f. Lambert, Bergin, & Collins, 1977; Strupp, Hadley, & Gomes-Schwartz, 1977) and from an earlier version of the scale applied in this same project (Gomes-Schwartz, 1978).

The VNIS items and subscales were successfully used to predict outcome, which was assessed with six different dependent measures (drawn from different perspectives). Negative factors in the therapeutic relationship, as measured by the VNIS, were shown to be highly associated with therapeutic outcome. Of even greater interest was the identification of the best predictors of outcome. Past research on deterioration (Lambert et al., 1977) would have led one to expect that therapist personal qualities (e.g., empathy) perhaps followed by patient personal qualities (e.g., degree of impairment) and patient-therapist interaction would be most predictive of outcome. Most dramatic in identifying success and failure in psychotherapy, however, was the Errors in Technique subscale. This finding suggests the possibility that it is not so much the relationship qualities of the therapist (although relationship did predict outcome), but rather his competence and skill in applying verbal techniques that led to positive or negative change. Thus, in this particular study, errors in technique were found to be quite important in predicting outcome. One error that could be reliably rated and proved all too frequently involved the failure to *structure* or *focus* the session, as operationalized by the following rating-scale definition:

> The session seems aimless or lacks coherence. The therapist fails to make interventions that would help to organize the content or process of the therapy session. Evidence for this item includes:
> a.   Therapist fails to identify focal therapeutic issues in material presented by the patient.
> b.   Therapist fails to integrate the material presented by the patient. The therapist does not identify themes or patterns in the patient's communications, reported behaviors, or manner of interaction with the therapist.
> c.   Therapist lets the patient flounder, ramble and/or repeatedly pursue tangents.

Additionally, several other errors seemed important, including the failure of the therapist to address the patient's negative attitudes toward either the therapist or the therapy; the passive acceptance of problematic aspects of the patient's behavior (such as resistance or evasiveness); and the use of harmful interventions (such as poorly timed or inappropriate interpretations). The relative contribution of these therapist errors to negative change has not as yet been identified.

One thing that makes the importance of therapist errors in predicting outcome particularly interesting is the fact that the therapists studied in this research were all experienced clinicians. Thus, one cannot attribute the strength of the errors in technique findings to a lack of experience on the part of therapists. Naturally, these results have implications for training therapists, supervision of student therapists, and the practice of experienced clinicians.

It should be noted, however, that the results of this study are limited by several factors. First, the VNIS was developed as well as applied on the same patients and is in need of cross-validation. Second, ratings on all of the VNIS items were done by the same raters. The different factors studied were not rated by independent raters, raising questions about the validity of the factors. Third, and perhaps most important, the Errors in Techniques subscale was difficult for therapists with different theoretical orientations to use. The scale definitions are not sufficiently precise to allow for ratings that require a minimum of inference and clinical judgment. This raises questions about the applicability of the scale in other settings with other raters and different therapies. The therapy conducted was brief psychotherapy, either psychodynamic or experiential. For the most part, the patients were not seriously disturbed. These as well as a host of other variables could limit the generalizability of the results.

Therapist school. Differences in the styles of therapists of different schools and levels of experience have been discovered in various experiments. For example, in an extensive study of the verbal therapeutic behavior of expert psychoanalytically oriented Gestalt and behavior therapists, Brunink and Schroeder (1979) found that these expert therapists were similar in their communication of empathy, but that theoretical orientation differentially influenced use of direct guidance and facilitative techniques. Further, Gestalt therapists were found to be the most dissimilar to the other therapists.

Similar findings have been reported in studies of therapists from different theoretical orientations. Gustavson, Cundick, and Lambert (1981), for example, studied the verbal behavior of three well-known therapists all seeing the same filmed client (Gloria). Analysis of the behavior of these client-centered, cognitive, and Gestalt therapists showed markedly different behavior in an initial interview. These differences seem to be consistent with theoretical orientation. Rogers (client-centered) used reflection extensively (74 percent of his responses). Ellis (cognitive), on the other hand, used predominantly interpretations (41 percent) and advisements (34 percent). Perls (Gestalt) tended to use a variety of responses: reflections (17 percent), personal disclosures (15 percent), personal questions (15 percent), interpretations (13 percent), simple disclosures (13 percent), and advisement (10 percent).

While some research is able to show that different behavior is associated with therapists of different orientations, other research has not always supported this claim. For example, Yalom and Lieberman (1971) found that the behavior of leaders who were identified with different schools of therapy (e.g., psychoanalytic, Gestalt, etc.) were more similar to each other than they were to members of their same school. Each group leader in their study was rated both by participant questionnaires and by observer schedules. The participant and observer ratings were reduced to four basic dimensions of leader behavior: emotional stimulation, caring, meaning attribution, and executive functions. The leaders were then grouped into seven types: Aggressive Stimulators, Love Leaders, Social Engineers, Laissez-Faire, Cool and Aggressive Stimulators, High Structure, and Tape Leaders.

Although the data showed that characteristics of some participants made them more vulnerable to negative changes than others, the main finding was that the style of the group leader was the major cause of casualties. The most damaging style, Aggressive Stimulator, was characterized by an intrusive, aggressive approach that involved considerable challenging and confronting of the group members. These leaders were impatient and authoritarian in approach, and they insisted on immediate self-disclosure, emotional expression, and attitude change. There were five leaders of this type, and all produced casualties except one (a total of nearly one-half of the most severe casualties). The one exception stated that he realized there were fragile persons in his group, so he deviated from his usual style and "pulled his punches."

Another leader, whose group had three casualties, commented: ". . . it was a stubborn group, full of people 'too infantile to take responsibility for themselves and to form an adult contract . . .' I saw that most of the group didn't want to do anything so what I did was just go ahead and have a good time for myself" (Yalom & Lieberman, 1971, p. 28).

An example of a casualty resulting from one of the aggressive, confronting groups where the leader holds center stage in a charismatic manner was described by Yalom and Lieberman (1971):

> This subject was unequivocal in her evaluation of her group as a destructive experience. Her group, following the model and suggestions of the leader, was an intensely aggressive one which undertook to help this subject, a passive, gentle individual, to "get in touch with" her anger. Although the group attacked her in many ways, including a physical assault by one of the female members, she most of all remembers the leader's attack on her. At one point he cryptically remarked that she "was on the verge of schizophrenia." He would not elaborate on this statement, and it echoed ominously within her for many months. For several months she remained extremely uncomfortable. She withdrew markedly from her family and friends, was depressed and insomniac; she was so obsessed with her leader's remark about schizophrenia that she dreaded going to bed because she knew her mind would focus on this point of terror. Often she lapsed into daydreams in which she relived, with a more satisfying ending, some event in the group. The only benefit of the experience, she said, was to help her appreciate how lonely she was; her discomfort has been so great,

however, that she has been unable to make use of this knowledge. We consider this subject a severe and long-term casualty; at the interview eight months after the end of the group, she felt that she was gradually reintegrating herself but was not yet back to the point she was before the group began. Her negative experience was a function of aggressive, intrusive leadership style which attempted to change her according to the leader's own values by battering down her characterological defenses. (p. 24)

Although numerous variables influenced outcome, participants identified as gaining the most from their group encounters emphasized the importance of being accepted, liked, and cared for by group members and the leader. Of importance here is the finding that outcome was associated more highly with actual leader behavior than with the leader's theoretical orientation.

The above example illustrates the importance of conducting further process research to identify potential sources of help as well as harm. It also illustrates the difficulty of studying the school of the therapist independently of ratings of actual in-therapy behavior. Clearly, future research should not use school or theoretical orientation with the expectation that it adequately reflects therapist interventions.

There are, of course, many other topics that could be covered under the heading of therapist intervention strategies. These include other verbal techniques such as self-disclosure, and the use of role playing, role rehearsal, and the like. In addition, it might also include the use of imagery techniques and behavioral and cognitive methods. However, a review of the contribution of these techniques to patient improvement is beyond the scope of this chapter. The interested reader may consult Garfield and Bergin (1978) for a review of this sort. We turn our attention now to a well-researched aspect of the therapists' contribution to psychotherapy: the therapist-patient relationship.

Relationship variables

The importance of such therapist variables as confidence, hope, liking of patient, and active involvement of the therapist in treatment have been stressed recently by Frank (1979) in his review of psychotherapy research. An interesting interchange resulted that emphasizes several current issues in the empirical study of psychotherapy outcome (Telch, 1981; Frank, 1981). Telch (1981) exemplifies the position of those who believe the major determiners of psychotherapy outcome are technique variables. In fact, he argued that the degree of influence exerted by client and therapist variables is inversely related to the potency of the therapeutic intervention. One implication of this stance is that future research would focus on the further development of specific intervention procedures, rather than the identification of relevant client and therapist attributes and their interaction. Telch (1981) also recommends greater use of laboratory research, single-case studies, and fewer comparative studies, in the hope of identifying specific, potent therapeutic techniques that work with a variety of patients.

In contrast, Frank (1981), in response to Telch, suggests that specific treatments have been found to be effective with specific problems with only a very small percentage of the clinical population. In summarizing his position, he wrote:

> In short, I remain persuaded that the technique that would be most effective for a particular patient-therapist combination would be the one that best mobilizes the patient's hopes, enhances his or her self-efficacy, and so on. This depends, I believe, less on the patient's specific symptoms or difficulties or on the technique in itself than on attributes of the particular patient and therapist in interaction and the appropriateness of the technique to these. (p. 477)

Our impression is that the weight of evidence favors the position taken by Frank. We cannot disagree with the idea that patient and therapist variables will be less important as technique variables become more important. This statement is almost tautological: if outcome is constant and an additive factor that leads to that constant increases in value, then at least one of the other additive factors leading to the constant must decrease. The question really is: shall we invest our scientific attention in the investigation of specific procedures, or in understanding the meaning of influential relationship qualities that are at least partially dependent on the therapist's manner, or perhaps in both? We do not feel that laboratory research that ignores therapist and patient factors should hold primacy for future study in psychotherapy outcome. It has its place. But a more promising strategy for future research will be to study the interaction between the therapist-patient relationship and the technical procedures or techniques of therapy.

The most extensively studied therapist relationship variables have been those identified by the client-centered school as "necessary and sufficient conditions" for patient personality change: accurate empathy, positive regard, nonpossessive warmth, and congruence or genuineness. Rogers provided a somewhat philosophical discussion of the therapist's contribution in the following quote, where he emphasizes the place of therapist attitudes (versus techniques) in treatment outcome and elaborates on the highly personal nature of the therapeutic interaction:

> I feel that when I'm being effective as a therapist, I enter the relationship as a subjective person, not as a scrutinizer, not as a scientist. I feel, too, that when I am most effective, then somehow I am relatively whole in that relationship, or the word that has meaning to me is "transparent." Then I think, too, that in such a relationship I feel a real willingness for this other person to *be what he is*. I call this *acceptance*. And then another aspect of it which is important to me is that I think in those moments I am able

to sense with a good deal of clarity, the way his experience seems to him
. . . Then, in addition to those things on my part, my client or the person
with whom I'm working is able to sense something of those *attitudes* in
me, then it seems to me that there is a real, experiential meeting of persons,
in which each of us is changed. (Buber & Friedman, 1965, pp. 169–170)

Virtually all schools of therapy accept the notion that therapist-relationship variables are important for significant progress in psychotherapy
and, in fact, fundamental in the formation of a working alliance. Rogers
(1959) made his formulation of these therapist attitudes and their relation
to outcome explicit and stated their hypothesized relationship to this constructive personality change with near mathematical precision. Since this
formulation, a large number of studies have investigated therapist interpersonal skills or facilitative attitudes and their relationship to psychotherapy
outcome. A good example of research conducted in this area was published by Truax, Wargo, Frank, Imber, Battle, Hoehn-Saric, Nash, and
Stone (1966), who studied the treatment of 40 outpatients seen in individual psychotherapy. The patients who were seen by therapists judged
as offering high levels of accurate empathy, nonpossessive warmth, and
genuineness showed significantly more improvement on overall indices
of change than did patients whose therapists were judged as low in
the combined conditions.

Additional studies showing both positive and equivocal support for
the hypothesized relationship have been reviewed elsewhere (c.f. Gurman, 1977; Lambert, DeJulio, & Stein, 1978; Mitchell, Bozarth, & Krauft,
1977; Parloff et al., 1978). These reviewers are unanimous in their opinion
that the therapist-patient relationship is critical; however, they point out
that research support for this position is not as clearly positive as was
once thought. An example of this more tentative position on relationship
variables is illustrated in the following recent report.

Strupp (1980) reported a case study of two patients seen by the same
therapist. One of the patients was seen as having had a successful outcome, while the contrasting patient was classified as a treatment failure.
This report was part of a larger study (to be discussed later) that used
extensive outcome measures and an analysis of patient/therapist interactions during the process of therapy. Of interest for our discussion is the
notion that although therapy was offered by a therapist who was seen
as having good interpersonal skills, a different relationship developed
with the two patients. Patient 1, who had a successful outcome, appeared
to be more able and willing to relate than patient 2, who remained at
a superficial level before prematurely terminating therapy after 12 sessions.

In the opinion of Strupp, the offerings of the therapist remained relatively constant throughout therapy, and the differences in outcome could
be attributed to patient factors such as the nature of the patient's personal-

ity make-up, including ego organization, maturity, motivation, and ability to become productively involved in therapy. He adds:

> While these findings are congruent with clinical lore, they run counter to the view that "therapist-provided conditions" are the necessary and suffi- cient conditions for therapeutic change. Instead, psychotherapy of the vari- ety under discussion can be beneficial provided the patient is ready and able to avail himself of its essential ingredients. If these pre-conditions are not met, the experience is bound to be disappointing to the patient as well as the therapist. The fault for such outcomes may lie not with psychother- apy as such, but rather with human failure to use it appropriately (p. 602).

Several general conclusions can be reached regarding this literature. The first well-accepted and experimentally substantiated finding is that the quality of the relationship, as defined by these therapist-offered condi- tions and as experienced by the patient, correlates with (and perhaps produces) positive outcomes. A corollary finding is that low levels of these relationship variables have been found to be associated with patient deterioration. Empathy, warmth, and genuineness have been shown to correlate moderately with outcome, as measured by a wide variety of measures collected from diverse patient types. Systematic training and selection on these dimensions is advised, although little research supports the efficacy of current training procedures when actual in-therapy behav- ior is the outcome desired. It has also been found that client-perception measures of the relationship correlate more highly with outcome than objective judge's ratings.

Research has also examined the place of client-centered relationship variables on the process, rather than the outcome, of therapy. Studies investigating self-disclosure have found a significant relationship between group leader self-disclosure, member experiencing, and member self- disclosure (Davis & Sloane, 1974). Research has also shown that client self-disclosure can be predicted from pre-therapy self-disclosing behav- iors, and client self-disclosure is related to therapist empathy, warmth, and self-disclosure, but not genuineness (Curtis, 1981). Other studies have found that therapist nonverbal behavior has a significant effect on client ratings of warmth. In general, studies of therapy process indicate the client-centered variables achieve, with some reliability, the predicted relationship with the in-therapy behavior of patients. They show statistically significant positive correlations with self-disclosure, self-exploration, expe- riencing, and the like.

Numerous methodological problems have been encountered in re- search on the client-centered variables. It is not yet clear, for example, how independent therapist-offered relationship variables are from patient characteristics and behaviors. Several lines of evidence are emerging to suggest that the patient, not the therapist, is most responsible for the quality of the therapeutic relationship. Marziali, Marmor, and Krupnick

(1981), for example, studied the relative contributions of the therapist and the patient to the development of a therapeutic alliance and to psychotherapy outcome. These authors reported that the therapists' contributions to the alliance (as measured by ratings on such items as: "The therapist is hopeful and encouraging, conveying the belief that the patient has made, is making, or can make progress") did not discriminate between successful and unsuccessful patients.

On the other hand, the ratings of the patients' participations (based on such items as: "The patient indicates that he or she experiences the therapist as understanding or accepting" or "The patient acts in a hostile, attacking and critical manner toward the therapist") in therapy discriminated very well between the patients who profited from therapy and those who did not. The raters did not judge the therapists of poor outcome patients to be unempathic, critical, or confused about focus. Rather, it appeared that poor outcome patients brought a negative disposition with them that persisted in therapy despite seemingly appropriate therapist behavior.

This finding is in agreement with the results of the Vanderbilt psychotherapy project (Gomes-Schwartz, 1978), where essentially identical findings on a different patient population were found. Both studies raise important questions about the types of actions, techniques, or timing of therapeutic interventions that might reduce patient behaviors that prevent the development of a cooperative patient-therapist relationship. It is clear that better success could be achieved by an understanding of therapist actions that could modify negative patient reactions. These in turn could be used in training therapists. In the absence of such knowledge, monitoring early patient reactions to treatment could result in referral for other types of intervention procedures before valuable energy and time are expended by patient and agency.

The exact contribution of relationship variables, their interaction with client characteristics, and their relative importance in contrast to specific techniques remain an area of continuing debate. Thus, although it was once felt that the client-centered hypothesis had been clearly confirmed, it appears that the relationship between these therapist-relationship variables and outcome is more ambiguous than previously believed. Despite the ambiguity and debates, past research has confirmed their peripheral (if not central) place in facilitating patient improvement.

In addition to research that specifically tested the Rogerian hypotheses, a variety of related studies have been carried out in recent years. These studies examined the Rogerian position without testing it in the traditional manner. Perhaps the best-designed of these was undertaken at Vanderbilt University and published by Strupp and Hadley (1979). The Vanderbilt study contrasted the relative contribution of therapist technical skills with the contribution of so-called nonspecific relationship factors to outcome.

Strupp and his colleagues contrasted the effectiveness of professionally trained expert therapists and a select group of college professors. They examined the process and outcome in therapy offered to 15 college students (with high MMPI scores on scales 2, 7, and 0) by five analytically or experientially oriented psychotherapists. These results were compared with "therapy" offered by seven nonprofessional college professors to 15 clients with similar disturbances. Outcomes for the two treatment groups were also contrasted with those attained by students assigned to either a minimal-contact wait-list control group or a so-called silent group of students from the college population who achieved similar MMPI profiles as the treatment subjects who had not sought help for their problems.

Change was measured by: the MMPI; patients', therapists', and clinicians' ratings of changes in target complaints; self-rated overall change; and experts' ratings on clinical scales of disturbance. Process analysis was done via the Vanderbilt Process Scale, a scale that taps therapist dimensions such as warmth and empathy.

Comparisons of amount of change among groups revealed that: (1) there were no significant differences between groups on any of the six measures based on the patient's own perspective, (2) therapist measures, which apply to the two treated groups only, showed no significant differences between these two groups, (3) with respect to ratings made by the independent clinician, there were no significant differences between the two treatment groups, and (4) post hoc pair comparisons showed that both treated groups were significantly more improved than the control groups on four of these six variables. On the remaining two variables, only the professional therapist group was significantly more improved than the controls.

Analyses of process indicated that:

1. Professional therapists (dichotomized into analytic and experientially oriented groups) and alternate therapists behaved quite differently in therapy. Therapists with an analytic orientation tended to maintain distance between themselves and their patients. Experiential therapists offered friendlier, more personal relationships. Alternate therapists were generally warm, supportive listeners who offered their patients specific suggestions about how they might change their lives.

2. Therapist activities positively related to good outcome on all measures were *facilitation of communication*, maintaining a current time focus, and *talking about the patient's own experiences and feelings*.

Not only can one find support for the importance of relationship factors in the Vanderbilt study, but even some literature on behavior therapy suggests the importance of these variables. Morris and Suckerman

(1974a, 1974b, 1975) and Wolowitz (1975), for example, discussed the place of therapist warmth in behavioral desensitization. This therapist-relationship variable was shown to be necessary for effecting positive change with desensitization. These studies demonstrated that even with a simple phobia and the application of a technical behavioral procedure, a therapist variable (such as warmth) may play a significant role in mediating change. More recent research on this topic, however, was more equivocal.

Morris and Magrath (1979) studied the effect of therapist warmth on the contact (in vivo) desensitization treatment of acrophobia. Height-fearful subjects were assigned to either a warm-therapist group, a cold-therapist group, or a waiting-control group. While both treatment groups showed significant improvement when compared to the waiting-list group, no consistent differences were found between the warm- and cold-therapist groups. Unlike the Morris and Suckerman (1974a) study, which found that a warm, friendly therapist using systematic-desensitization treatment was more effective in reducing fear of snakes than a cold, impersonal therapist, these results suggest that therapist warmth is not a critical factor in effecting positive behavior change when using contact (in vivo) desensitization.

Miller, Taylor, and West (1980) investigated the comparative effectiveness of various behavioral approaches aimed at helping problem drinkers control their alcohol consumption. While the focus of the study was upon the comparative effects of focused versus broad-spectrum behavior therapy, the authors collected data on the contribution of therapist empathy to patient outcome.

Ratings of therapist interpersonal skills were made by three independent raters after eight months of contact with the therapists. The therapists ($n = 9$) were paraprofessionals or graduate students in clinical psychology who had received training in both the behavior methods employed and in the Rogerian conditions. Several of them were quite experienced in offering these treatments. The raters had been involved in the supervision of the therapists. Using the Bergin-Soloman revision of the Truax Accurate Empathy Scale (Truax & Carkhuff, 1967), the raters simply rank-ordered therapists on their overall empathic ability. Statistical comparisons were based on the average rank of the three independent raters.

One finding—surprising to the authors and important for our discussion—was the discovery of a strong relationship between empathy and patient outcome obtained from the six- to eight-month follow-up interviews dealing with drinking behavior. Therapist rankings correlated at $r = .82$ with patient outcomes, thus accounting for 67 percent of the variance in therapist successfulness. In addition, it was found that, by and large, those therapists who were rated highest in empathy exceeded the 60 percent improvement rate for the minimal-contact self-help control, while the rank orders (on empathy) of those therapists who did not surpass the self-help group were fifth, seventh, eighth and ninth for the nine therapists.

These results argue persuasively for the importance of therapist communicative skills even with behavioral interventions. They were also presented in a context where variations in specific techniques did not prove to have a similar powerful effect on outcome. While these results can be used to show the real importance of the therapists' general attitude and skills, the reader should be aware that methodological shortcomings limit the importance of this data. Unfortunately, one major drawback in the Miller et al. (1980) investigation was lack of sophistication in the data collection procedure. Because of the way the data were collected, one cannot be sure that the rank orderings were actually based on therapist empathy. The ratings were not of the actual therapy process and were not confirmed by patient ratings of empathy. In addition, we cannot be sure that rankings were not partially based on assessments of patient outcome. This study was not primarily intended to study the place of therapist interpersonal skills on outcome and therefore did not pay careful attention to methodology in this area.

Another approach to understanding the contribution of the therapist to effective outcome has involved the use of behavioral or adjective checklists filled out by clients following their therapeutic contacts. Lorr (1965), for example, had 523 psychotherapy patients describe their therapist on 65 different statements. A subsequent factor analysis identified five factors—understanding, accepting, authoritarian (directive), independence-encouraging, and critical-hostile. Scores on these descriptive factors were correlated with improvement ratings, with the result that client ratings of understanding and accepting correlated most highly with client- and therapist-rated improvement.

In a more recent study, Cooley and Lajoy (1980) attempted to replicate the Lorr study. In addition, they studied the relationship between therapist ratings of themselves and outcome, as well as the relationship of discrepancies between patient and therapist and outcome ratings. The patients were 56 adult community mental health outpatients who had been treated by one of eight therapists at the clinic.

As with the Lorr study, ratings by patients of therapist understanding and acceptance correlated most highly with outcome when it was rated by the client. On the other hand, when ratings of therapist attributes were compared to therapist-rated patient outcome, the correlations were insignificant, suggesting that therapists did not perceive their personal attributes as a factor influencing therapeutic outcome. At the same time, the expected relationship was found between discrepancies in client-therapist perception of therapist qualities and outcome: the greater the similarity, the more improved the patient.

Overall, the data from this study suggest the importance of relationship dimensions emphasized by the client-centered school. Still, it should be noted that the data are correlational in nature, and there are other plausible explanations for the relationship rather than the notion that therapist understanding or acceptance causes improvement. For example, it may be that an improving client is more likely to be understood and accepted by the therapist or, perhaps more plausible, an improved client rewards the therapist with high ratings on understanding and acceptance.

Regardless of these explanations, it should be emphasized that patients frequently attribute their success in treatment to the personal qualities of the therapists. That these personal qualities bear a striking resemblance to each other, across studies and methodologies, is evidence that they are highly important in psychotherapy outcome. This notion was also emphasized by Lazarus (1971) in an uncontrolled follow-up study of 112 patients who he had seen in therapy. These patients were asked to provide information about the effects of their treatment, the durability of improvement, and their perceptions of the therapeutic process and characteristics of the therapist. With regard to therapist characteristics, those adjectives used to describe Lazarus most often were *sensitive*, *gentle*, and *honest*. These adjectives bear a striking resemblance to the therapeutic conditions advocated by Rogers and his associates. Patients clearly felt the personal qualities of the therapist were more important than specific technical factors about which there was little agreement.

In a more recent study comparing behavioral and more traditional insight-oriented therapy, Sloane et al. (1975) reported a similar finding and elaborated upon the place of therapist variables in positive outcome. Although they failed to find a relationship between judges' ratings of therapists' behavior during the third therapy session (on empathy) and later outcome, they did find that patients tended to emphasize the personal qualities of their therapists as causing personality changes. These authors administered a 32-item questionnaire four months following treatment. These items included statements descriptive of both behavior therapy techniques (e.g., training in muscle relaxation) as well as dynamic therapy techniques (e.g., explaining the relationship of your problem to early life events). In addition, some characteristics thought to be common in all forms of therapy were included. Each item was rated on a five-point scale.

Surprisingly, perhaps, the successful patients in both therapies placed primary importance on more or less the same items. In fact, 70 percent or more of these successful patients listed the following items as "extremely important" or "very important" in causing their improvement:

1. The personality of your doctor.
2. His helping you to understand problems.
3. Encouraging you to gradually practice facing the things that bother you.
4. Being able to talk to an understanding person.
5. Helping you to understand yourself.

None of the items regarded as very important by the majority of either patient group described techniques specific to one therapy (although item 3 is, in general, approached more systematically in behavior therapies). These results suggest that, at least from the patient's point of view, effective treatment was due to factors associated with relationship variables such as empathy and active involvement. Although this type of data is limited by serious methodological problems (e.g., patients may not know how they are being helped), its repeated occurrence suggests (cf. Ryan & Gizynski, 1971) that it should not be ignored.

FUTURE DIRECTIONS FOR RESEARCH ON THE THERAPIST'S CONTRIBUTION

Despite the relatively long history of empirical investigations into the therapist's personal contribution to psychotherapy outcome, investigations in this area are still in need of new strategies and procedures. The following recommendations reflect what we consider to be the most hopeful directions for future research on the therapist's contribution to outcome.

1. The study of process variables (those derived from the in-therapy behavior of therapists) should be emphasized over personality and other static traits.

2. The therapist's contribution to effective psychotherapy might best be studied through the simultaneous examination of multiple therapist variables.

Orlinsky and Howard (1978) have suggested that therapist behavior may not show a strong relationship with outcome, because only a single aspect of the therapist is studied at once. Thus, the Rogerians have studied empathy regardless of the intent of a therapist intervention and have studied it without attending to contextual variables, timing, etc. Likewise, analytical research has focused upon such therapist activities as interpretation, while neglecting empathy or other dimensions of the patient-therapist relationship. This sort of narrow research is encouraged both by practical considerations and the biasing influence of limited theoretical orientation.

One study that provided support for the idea that single therapist variables may be most predictive when combined with other therapist (or patient) variables was published by Mintz, Luborsky, and Auerbach (1971). These authors studied whole hours of psychotherapy and rated them on over 100 ordinal scales of therapist and patient behavior. These scales were factor analyzed, which produced four underlying factors that could be correlated with patient outcome. A factor they labeled *optimal empathic understanding*, which was made up of items describing therapist manner (secure, reassuring and warm, empathic, accepts patients,

and likeable) or skill (skillful, perceptive), accounted for 24 percent of
the variance in items. The second largest factor, which explained 19
percent of the variance of the items, was labeled *directive mode*. Directiveness was independent of optimal empathic understanding, and neither
was significantly related to outcome. However, when combined they
correlated .50 with therapist-rated patient satisfaction and patient improvement. The successful therapists were high on directiveness and low on
empathy or high on empathy and low on directiveness.

Recently, Schaffer (1981) emphasized the importance of separating
therapist variables into three separate dimensions. These dimensions
(which are to be studied simultaneously) include therapist tactic, skill,
and manner. He suggested a productive strategy for future research that
would involve clearly specifying and measuring each of these dimensions.
First, the tactic or type of intervention would be identified. Next, the
researcher would estimate both the level of competence illustrated in
carrying out this tactic and the manner in which the therapist related to
the patient during this interchange. He posits that, if future research on
the therapist were to involve the simultaneous study of these three dimensions, a more accurate picture of the therapeutic process and a higher
level of predictive ability may result. Before this can be accomplished,
theorists and researchers will need to clarify both the valued and intended
interventions of therapists and develop proper scales to measure the
level of competence (or skill) demonstrated by therapists.

Partial application of this procedure has shown promising results. In
a recent comparative study of cognitive behavioral therapy and interpersonal therapy for the treatment of depression, four factors that seem to
account for positive outcomes were identified (DeRubeis, Hollon, Evans,
& Bemis, in press). These factors and the percentage of variance they
accounted for were as follows: cognitive behavioral therapy (43 percent);
therapist interpersonal skills (13 percent); therapist directiveness (7 percent); and interpersonal therapy (6 percent). The interrelationship of these
variables demonstrated a high degree of relationship between cognitive
behavioral therapy and therapist interpersonal skills ($r = .61$), suggesting
that therapists employing this therapy and having success were characterized by high levels of therapist interpersonal skill as well as competence
in cognitive techniques. While only a pilot study, the above research is
part of an overall research program that attempts to identify specific therapy tasks, quantify the degree to which they have been carried out effectively, and rate the manner in which they were carried out (in terms of
patient-therapist relationship).

The procedure of studying multiple therapist behaviors presents challenging methodological problems for future research. The difficulties of
separating competence or skill from therapist interpersonal behaviors in
a reliable and valid fashion should occupy researchers for a long time.

3. The therapist's contribution must be studied in interaction with patient and contextual variables.

As has been pointed out, therapists do not make their responses independently of patient behavior. Thus, future research should study therapist behavior in response to specific patient behavior. This type of research can be based on theory (e.g., transference interpretations) or on the study of critical incidents in therapy. Before meaningful study based on theory can proceed, theories will need to make more specific predictions about the in-therapy behavior of patients and therapists. A way of proceeding independently of theory would be to closely examine effective moments in the process of therapy. These effective moments could be identified after the fact. For example, the patient, raters, or the therapist could identify incidents in therapy where the patient seemed open to influence or especially in need of an appropriate intervention.

Another method of taking the patient's contribution more fully into account involves the use of pattern analysis. In studying the pattern of therapy, the researcher focuses upon the sequence of events in psychotherapy. Thus, the events that routinely either proceed or follow either patient or therapist behavior can be identified and studied. *Chains* of behavior that lead to positive outcomes can then be identified. Such a procedure (using Markovian Chain Analysis in studying effective teaching) has been applied successfully by Wadham, Young, and Preston (1974). Methods of analyzing the consequences of single-therapist behavior or longer sequences of therapist-patient behaviors have been rarely applied in psychotherapy research.

4. The importance of therapist variables in the behavior therapist needs to be more carefully explored.

It is possible (and many hope) that the therapist has, or will come to have, an unimportant role in patient improvement. To many, the science of psychotherapy and behavior change involves strengthening the technical aspects of treatment. As technical advances are made and more powerful treatments are identified, the treatments (independent of practitioners) will cause psychotherapy outcome. Although we favor a psychotherapy that rests on a firm scientific foundation, we doubt that psychological problems are so analogous to physical disease that such a predictable and controllable result will be forthcoming. Nevertheless, it would be desirable to maximize our scientific knowledge and take full advantage of the causal bonds that control personal growth and behavior change.

Studying the role of therapists who are applying technical behavioral procedures may at the very least, point out the limitations of these procedures. In addition, study of these therapies may provide the ideal situation

for process studies that also measure competence and relationship variables. Hopefully, studies of this type will be carried out by experienced
therapists with actual patients.

Until technical procedures can be demonstrated to be effective independent of therapist characteristics, budding therapists and clinical training programs should direct considerable energy and resources into the
development of the clinician as a person. Preferably, a person who values
others and who is willing and able to enter into a helping relationship—
a wholly human process.

SUMMARY

This chapter deals with the contribution of the therapist to the outcome
of psychotherapy. The focus is upon salient findings that have been discovered through the use of quantitative research methods. An attempt
is made to ascertain the contribution of the therapist apart from contributions that can be attributed to specific techniques.

The therapist's contribution is discussed with regard to either static
traits of the therapist, such as demographic variables (gender, race), personality, values, and expectations; or as process variables, such as direc-
tive-nondirective style, specific verbal procedures (dynamic focus), and
relationship skills. The emphasis is placed upon process variables rather
than static traits, because they are more appealing theoretically and, although difficult to study, more likely to lead to conclusions about cause/
effect relationships and to be effected by training.

In general, it was found that therapist-relationship skills (the therapist's
ability to form a meaningful relationship with the patient) have been consistently related to positive outcomes with a variety of patients. Several recommendations for future research were made. These include the importance of studying process variables and simultaneous study of multiple
therapist variables (including therapy technique) along with patient and
contextual variables. At this point in time, it must be concluded that until
technical procedures can be demonstrated to be more powerful and
possibly independent of therapist characteristics, budding therapists and
clinical training programs should continue to direct much of their energy
toward the development of the trainee as a person.

REFERENCES

Abramowitz, C. V., Abramowitz, S. I., Roback, H. B., & Jackson, C. Differential effectiveness
of directive and nondirective group therapies as a function of client internal-external
control. *Journal of Consulting and Clinical Psychology*, 1974, *42*, 849–853.

Anchor, K. N. Personality integration and successful outcome in individual psychotherapy.
Journal of Clinical Psychology, 1977, *33*, 245–246.

Ashby, J. D., Ford, D. H., Guerney, B. B., & Guerney, L. F. Effects on clients of a reflective and a leading type of therapy. *Psychological Monographs*, 1957, *71*, 24.

Auerbach, A. H., & Johnson, M. Research on the therapist's level of experience. In A. S. Gurman & A. M. Razin (Eds.), *Effective psychotherapy: A handbook of research*. New York: Pergamon Press, 1977.

Berzins, J. I. *Matching patients with therapists: Conceptual, empirical, and pragmatic perspectives*. Paper presented at fifth annual meeting of the Society of Psychotherapy Research, Denver, June 1974.

Berzins, J. I. Therapist-patient matching. In A. S. Gurman & A. M. Razin (Eds.), *Effective psychotherapy: A handbook of research*. New York: Pergamon Press, 1977.

Best, J. A. Tailoring smoking withdrawal procedures to personality and motivational differences. *Journal of Consulting and Clinical Psychology*, 1975, *43*, 1–8.

Best, J. A., Owen, L. E., & Trentadue, L. Comparison of satiation and rapid smoking in self-managed smoking cessation. *Addictive Behavior*, 1978, *3*, 71–78.

Best, J. A., & Steffy, R. A. Smoking modification procedures tailored to subject characteristics. *Behavior Therapy*, 1971, *2*, 177–191.

Brunink, S. A., & Schroeder, H. E. Verbal therapeutic behavior of expert psychoanalytically oriented, Gestalt, and behavior therapists. *Journal of Consulting and Clinical Psychology*, 1979, *47*, 567–574.

Buber, M., & Friedman, M. *The knowledge of man*. New York: Harper & Row, 1965.

Bugen, L. State anxiety effects on counselor perceptions of dying stages. *Journal of Consulting Psychology*, 1979, *26*, 89–91.

Claiborn, C. D., Ward, S. R., & Strong, S. R. Effects of congruence between counselor interpretations and client beliefs. *Journal of Counseling Psychology*, 1981, *28*, 101–109.

Cooley, E. J., & Lajoy, R. Therapeutic relationship and improvement as perceived by clients and therapists. *Journal of Clinical Psychology*, 1980, *36*, 562–570.

Costello, R. M., Baillargeon, J. G., Biever, P., & Bennett, R. Second-year alcoholism treatment outcome evaluation with a focus on Mexican-American patients. *American Journal of Drug and Alcohol Abuse*, 1979, *6*, 97–108.

Curtis, J. M. Effects of therapist's self-disclosure on patients' impressions of empathy, competence, and trust in an analogue of a psychotherapeutic interaction. *Psychological Reports*, 1981, *48*, 127–136.

Davis, J. D., & Sloane, M. L. The basis of interviewer matching of interviewer self-disclosure. *British Journal of Social and Clinical Psychology*, 1974, *13*, 359–367.

Dent, J. K. Exploring the psycho-social therapies through the personalities of effective therapists. *DHEW*, 1978, *77*, 527.

DeRubeis, R. J., Hollon, S. D., Evans, M. D., & Bemis, K. M. Can psychotherapies for depression be discriminated? A systematic investigation of cognitive therapy and interpersonal therapy. *Journal of Consulting and Clinical Psychology*, 1982, *50*, 744–756.

Donner, L., & Schonfield, J. Affect contagion in beginning psychotherapists. *Journal of Clinical Psychology*, 1975, *31*, 332–339.

Ehrlich, R. P., D'Augelli, A. R., & Danish, S. J. Comparative effectiveness of six counselor-verbal responses. *Journal of Counseling Psychology*, 1979, *26*, 390–398.

Feldstein, J. C. Effects of counselor sex and sex rate and client sex on clients' counseling analogue study. *Journal of Counseling Psychology*, 1979, *26*, 437–443.

Frank, J. D. The present status of outcome studies. *Journal of Consulting and Clinical Psychology,* 1979, *47,* 310–316.

Frank, J. D. Reply to Telch. *Journal of Consulting and Clinical Psychology,* 1981, *49,* 476–477.

Friedman, M. L., & Dies, R. R. Reactions of internal and external test-anxious students to counseling and behavior therapies. *Journal of Consulting and Clinical Psychology,* 1974, *42,* 921.

Garfield, S. L., & Bergin, A. E. *Handbook of psychotherapy and behavior change.* New York: John Wiley & Sons, 1978.

Geer, C. A., & Hurst, J. C. Counselor-subject sex variables in systematic desensitization. *Journal of Counseling Psychology,* 1976, *23,* 296–301.

Gomes-Schwartz, B. Effect ingredients in psychotherapy: Prediction of outcome from process variables. *Journal of Consulting and Clinical Psychology,* 1978, *46,* 1023–1035.

Gomes-Schwartz, B., Hadley, S., & Strupp, H. Individual psychotherapy and behavior therapy. *Annual Review of Psychology,* 1978, *29,* 435–471.

Grantham, R. J. Effects of counselor sex, race, and language style on black students in initial interviews. *Journal of Counseling Psychology,* 1973, *20,* 553–559.

Gurman, A. S. The patient's perception of the therapeutic relationship. In A. S. Gurman & A. M. Razin (Eds.), *Effective psychotherapy: A handbook of research.* New York: Pergamon Press, 1977.

Gustavson, J. L., Cundick, B. P., & Lambert, M. J. An analysis of observer responses to the Rogers, Perls, and Ellis films. *Perceptual and Motor Skills,* 1981, *53,* 759–764.

Haccoun, D. M., & Lavigueur, H. Effects of clinical experience and client emotion on therapists' responses. *Journal of Consulting and Clinical Psychology,* 1979, *47,* 416–418.

Harrison, I. K. Race as a counselor-client variable in counseling and psychotherapy: A review of the research. *Journal of Counseling Psychology,* 1975, *2,* 124–133.

Heitler, J. B. Preparatory techniques in initiating expressive psychotherapy with lower-class, unsophisticated patients. *Psychological Bulletin,* 1976, *83,* 339–352.

Hill, C. E. Sex of client and sex and experience level of counselor. *Journal of Counseling Psychology,* 1975, *22,* 6–11.

Hurndon, C. J., Pepinsky, H. B., & Meara, N. M. Conceptual level and structural complexity in language. *Journal of Counseling Psychology,* 1979, *26,* 190–197.

Jackson, D. N. *Personality research form manual.* New York: Research Psychologist's Press, 1967.

Jones, E. E. Effects of race on psychotherapy process and outcome: An exploratory investigation. *Psychotherapy: Theory Research and Practice,* 1978, *15,* 226–236.

Kiesler, D. S. *The process of psychotherapy.* Hawthorne, N.Y.: Aldine Publishing, 1973.

Kleinke, C. L., & Tully, T. B. Influence of talking level on perceptions of counselors. *Journal of Counseling Psychology,* 1979, *26,* 23–29.

Lambert, M. J. *The effects of psychotherapy* (Vol. 2). New York: Human Sciences Press, 1982.

Lambert, M. J., Bergin, A. E., & Collins, J. L. Therapist-induced deterioration in psychotherapy. In A. S. Gurman & A. M. Razin (Eds.), *Effective psychotherapy: A handbook of research.* New York: Pergamon Press, 1977.

Lambert, M. J., DeJulio, S. S., & Stein, D. M. Therapist interpersonal skills: Process, outcome, methodological considerations, and recommendations for future research. *Psychological Bulletin,* 1978, *85,* 467–489.

Lazarus, A. A. *Behavior therapy and beyond.* New York: McGraw-Hill, 1971.

Lorion, R. P., & Cowen, E. L. Comparison of two outcome groups in a school-based mental health project. *American Journal of Community Psychology,* 1976, *4,* 65–73.

Lorr, M. Client perceptions of therapists. *Journal of Consulting Psychology,* 1965, *29,* 146–149.

Malan, D. H. *The frontier of brief psychotherapy.* New York: Plenum Press, 1976. (a)

Malan, D. H. *Toward the validation of dynamic psychotherapy: A replication.* New York: Plenum Press, 1976. (b)

Marziali, E., Marmor, C., & Krupnick, J. Therapeutic alliance scales: Development and relationship to psychotherapy outcome. *American Journal of Psychiatry,* 1981, *138,* 361–364.

Matarazzo, Ruth G. Research on the teaching and learning of psychotherapeutic skills. In S. L. Garfield & A. E. Bergin (Eds.), *Handbook of psychotherapy and behavior change: An empirical analysis* (2d ed.). New York: John Wiley & Sons, 1978.

Meara, N. M., Pepinsky, H. B., Shannon, J. W., & Murray, W. A. Semantic communication and expectations for counseling across three theoretical orientations. *Journal of Counseling Psychology,* 1981, *28,* 110–118.

Meyer, R. G., & Freeman, W. M. A social episode model of human sexual behavior. *Homosexuality,* 1976, *2,* 15–20.

Miller, W. R., Taylor, C. A., & West, J. C. Focused versus broad-spectrum behavior therapy for problem drinkers. *Journal of Consulting and Clinical Psychology,* 1980, *48,* 590–601.

Mintz, J., Luborsky, L., & Auerbach, A. H. Dimensions of psychotherapy: A factor analytic study of ratings of psychotherapy sessions. *Journal of Consulting and Clinical Psychology,* 1971, *36,* 106–120.

Mintz, J., O'Brien, C. P., & Luborsky, L. Predicting the outcome of psychotherapy for schizophrenics. *Archives of General Psychiatry,* 1976, *33,* 1183–1186.

Mitchell, K. M., Bozarth, J. D., & Krauft, C. C. A reappraisal of the therapeutic effectiveness of accurate empathy, nonpossessive warmth, and genuineness. In A. S. Gurman & A. M. Razin (Eds.), *Effective psychotherapy: A handbook of research.* New York: Pergamon Press, 1977.

Morris, R. J., & Magrath, K. H. Contribution of therapist warmth to the contact desensitization treatment of acrophobia. *Journal of Consulting and Clinical Psychology,* 1979, *47,* 786–788.

Morris, R. J., & Suckerman, K. R. The importance of the therapeutic relationship in systematic desensitization. *Journal of Consulting and Clinical Psychology,* 1974, *42,* 147. (a)

Morris, R. J., & Suckerman, K. R. Therapist warmth as a factor in automated systematic desensitization. *Journal of Consulting and Clinical Psychology,* 1974, *42,* 244–250. (b)

Morris, R. J., & Suckerman, K. R. Morris and Suckerman reply. *Journal of Consulting and Clinical Psychology,* 1975, *43,* 585–586.

Natale, M. Perceived empathy, warmth, and genuineness as affected by interviewer timing of speech in a telephone interview. *Psychotherapy: Theory Research and Practice,* 1978, *15,* 145–152.

Norkus, A. G. Sex of therapist as a variable in short-term therapy with female college students. *Dissertation Abstracts International,* 1976, *36,* 6361.

Orlinsky, D. E. & Howard, K. I. The relation of process and outcome in psychotherapy. In S. L. Garfield & A. E. Bergin (Eds.), *Handbook of psychotherapy and behavior change* (2nd ed.). New York: John Wiley & Sons, 1978.

Pardes, H., Papernik, D. S., & Winston, A. Field differentiation in inpatient psychotherapy. *Archives of General Psychiatry,* 1974, *31,* 311–315.

Parloff, M. B., Waskow, I. E., & Wolfe, B. E. Research on therapist variables in relation to process and outcome. In S. L. Garfield & A. E. Bergin (Eds.), *Handbook of psychotherapy and behavior change* (2nd ed.). New York: John Wiley & Sons, 1978.

Razin, A. M. The *A-B* variable: Still promising after twenty years? In A. S. Gurman & A. M. Razin (Eds.), *Effective psychotherapy: A handbook of research.* New York: Pergamon Press, 1977.

Ricks, D. F. Supershrink: Methods for a therapist judged successful on the basis of adult outcomes of adolescent patients. In D. F. Ricks & M. Roff (Eds.), *Life history research in psychopathology.* Minneapolis: University of Minnesota, 1974.

Rogers, C. R. *Counseling and psychotherapy.* Boston: Houghton Mifflin, 1942.

Rogers, C. R. A theory of therapy, personality, and interpersonal relationships as developed in the client-centered framework in psychology: A study of science. In S. Koch (Ed.), *Formulations of the person and the social context.* New York: McGraw-Hill, 1959.

Rotter, J. B. Generalized expectancies for internal versus external control or reinforcement. *Psychological Monographs,* 1966, *80.*

Rozensky, R. H., & Bellack, A. S. Individual difference in self-reinforcement style and performance in self- and therapist-controlled weight reduction programs. *Behavior Research and Therapy,* 1976, *14,* 357–365.

Ryan, V., & Gizynski, M. Behavior therapy in retrospect: Patient's feelings about their behavior therapists. *Journal of Consulting and Clinical Psychology,* 1971, *37,* 1–9.

Sandell, J. A. *An empirical study of negative factors in brief psychotherapy.* Nashville: Vanderbilt University, 1981.

Sattler, J. M. The effects of therapist-client racial similarity. In A. S. Gurman & A. M. Razin (Eds.), *Effective psychotherapy: A handbook of research.* New York: Pergamon Press, 1977.

Schaffer, N. D. *Neglected aspects of process in research on therapist's behavior: Methodological implication.* Paper presented to the Society for Psychotherapy Research, Aspen, Colo. June 1981.

Scher, M. Verbal activity, sex, counselor experience, and success in counseling. *Journal of Counseling Psychology,* 1975, *22,* 97–101.

Schwartz, R. D. & Higgins, R. L. Differential outcome from automated assertion training as a function of locus of control. *Journal of Consulting and Clinical Psychology,* 1979, *47,* 686–694.

Singer, B. A., & Luborsky, L. B. Countertransference: The status of clinical versus quantitative research. In A. S. Gurman & A. M. Razin (Eds.), *Effective Psychotherapy: A handbook of research.* New York: Pergamon Press, 1977.

Sloane, R. B., Staples, F. R., Cristol, A. H., Yorkston, N. J., & Whipple, *Psychotherapy versus behavior therapy.* Cambridge, Mass.: Harvard University Press, 1975.

Speisman, J. C. Depth of interpretation and verbal resistance in psychotherapy. *Journal of Consulting Psychology,* 1959, *23,* 93–99.

Strupp, H. H. Success and failure in time-limited psychotherapy: A systematic comparison of two cases (comparison 1). *Archives of General Psychiatry,* 1980, *37,* 595–603.

Strupp, H. H., & Hadley, S. W. Specific versus nonspecific factors in psychotherapy: A controlled study of outcome. *Archives of General Psychiatry,* 1979, *36,* 1125–1136.

Strupp, H. H., Hadley, S. W., & Gomes-Schwartz, B. *Psychotherapy for better or worse: An analysis of the problems of negative effects.* New York: Jason Aronson, 1977.

Sullivan, P. L., Miller, C., & Smelser, W. Factors in length of stay and progress in psychother-apy. *Journal of Consulting Psychology,* 1958, *1,* 1–9.

Telch, M. J. The present status of outcome studies: A reply to Frank. *Journal of Consulting and Clinical Psychology,* 1981, *49,* 472–475.

Truax, C. B., & Carkhuff, R. R. *Toward effective counseling and psychotherapy: Training and practice.* Hawthorne, N.Y.: Aldine Publishing, 1967.

Truax, C. B., Wargo, D. G., Frank, J. D., Imber, S. D., Battle, C. C., Hoehn-Saric, R., Nash, E. H., & Stone, A. R. Therapist's contribution to accurate empathy, nonpossessive warmth and genuineness in psychotherapy. *Journal of Clinical Psychology,* 1966, *22,* 331–334.

Wadham, R. A., Young, J. R., & Preston, R. E. *TICOR: A micro-computer for research on operant interaction in the classroom and group settings.* Unpublished manuscript, Brig-ham Young University, 1974.

Wallston, B. S., Wallston, K. H., Kaplan, G. D. & Maides, S. A. Development and validation of the health locus of control scale (HLC). *Journal of Consulting and Clinical Psychology,* 1976, *44,* 580–585.

Whitehorn, J. C., & Betz, B. J. A study of psychotherapeutic relationships between physicians and schizophrenic patients. *American Journal of Psychiatry,* 1954, *111,* 321–331.

Wolowitz, H. M. Therapist warmth: Necessary or sufficient conditions in behavioral desensiti-zation? *Journal of Consulting and Clinical Psychology,* 1975, *42,* 584.

Yalom, I. D., & Lieberman, M. A. A study of encounter group casualties. *Archives of General Psychiatry,* 1971, *25,* 16–30.

8

Outcome studies in psychotherapy

Stanley D. Imber, Ph.D.*
and
Paul A. Pilkonis, Ph.D.*
and
Lawrence Glanz, Ph.D.*

A remarkable feature of psychotherapy research in recent years has been the prodigious number of outcome studies reported in the literature. The authors of this chapter recently conducted a computer search for which the data base was books as well as articles published in the major psychological and psychiatric journals over the past 10 years. The count came to more than 2,000 separate items dealing with outcome, and these did not include chapters in edited books or special reports, such as those prepared specifically for governmental agencies. Moreover, a reading of these publications indicates that, relative to investigations in previous years, there has been a marked increase in the sophistication and scientific adequacy of the work. Unfortunately, many of these publications have only tangential relevance for practitioners, because the investigations focus principally on specialized theoretical issues or on types of therapists, treatment techniques, and patient populations that are limited in their applicability to standard clinical practice. This paradox presents a special problem in organizing a review of the literature that has pertinence for both researchers and clinicians, and it accounts for the unconventional selection of topics in the chapter.

Two criteria were used in the choice of topics. First, material was chosen that would speak to the overlapping interests of the researcher and clinician and have bearing on good clinical practice. Second, an attempt was made to identify current research developments, particularly those likely to receive increased future attention. There are seven separate sec-

---

* Department of Psychiatry, University of Pittsburgh School of Medicine.

tions in the chapter. The first one summarizes work in the growing movement toward the integration of therapy techniques and of outcome indices. The second section reviews the most recent methods for evaluating the efficacy of treatment for purposes of accountability. Next, there is a section that presents work on the durability of change in the context of follow-up studies and then one that summarizes outcome findings where psychotherapy and medication are combined in treatment. Another section considers the effects of psychotherapy on physical health, followed by one that deals with recent work in the critical area of noxious or deterioration effects in psychotherapy. The final section briefly reviews the current status of process studies, as these relate to outcome.

For the most part, the treatment techniques that receive attention in the chapter involve individual, short-term therapy of adults, as it is practiced in outpatient settings, partly because this remains the most prevalent form of treatment today, and partly because the most extensive and competent research has been done in that area. With respect to theoretical orientation, psychodynamic and behavioral-cognitive work representing the more standard mainstream of practice are included. The many exotic brands of treatment (despite considerable publicity in the popular press) are mainly off-shoots of the major approaches, seem likely to be short-lived in spite of promotional efforts, and remain almost entirely unevaluated. In addition, clinical or case-report studies are not included in the literature surveyed.

A number of other aspects of psychotherapy outcome research are not touched upon here but do receive attention in other chapters within this volume. Thus, we do not include group, family or marital therapy; the treatment of children, the psychotherapy of addictive and sexual disorders; and specialized techniques, such as hypnotherapy, biofeedback and stress management.

RAPPROCHEMENT

Few phenomena of the past decade have so confused patients, practitioners, and researchers alike as the mounting proliferation of psychotherapies. By some counts, there may be as many as 250 different brands listing themselves under the banner of psychotherapy (Herink, 1980). Even if this number represents an exaggeration by more restricted professional standards, no one can doubt there is an enormous variety of therapy practices in the marketplace. Moreover, those treatments that have been subjected to comparative evaluations have been demonstrated, repeatedly and with only minor exceptions, to show few important differences in effectiveness. This fact has forced clinicians and researchers to give serious consideration to the possibility that therapeutic potency does not lie in elements specific to any one method or theory of treatment but in factors shared by all successful procedures. However, the notion of common features is hardly new. It was promulgated almost 50 years ago by Rosenzweig (1936) and, more recently, represented the major theme in the series of psychotherapy studies conducted by the Johns Hopkins Psychotherapy Research Unit over a 25-year period (Frank, Hoehn-Saric, Imber, Liberman, & Stone, 1978). In the past few years, the concerted attention given to this topic has become the core of a movement that may be termed *rapprochement*, attracting both researchers and practitioners. In this section, we summarize only limited aspects of the broader area of common features, as these relate to the rapprochement movement. An extensive review may be found in Korchin and Sands' chapter in the present volume, Principles Common to All Psychotherapies.

A confluence of recent events has intensified the movement toward rapprochement. Many therapists of widely disparate theoretical orientations have openly recognized the shared techniques (if not underlying theories) through which they conduct their clinical work and the fact of common outcome objectives (Wachtel, 1977). Behavioral therapists have notably expanded their techiques, applying them to an extended assortment of patient populations. In the process of this expansion, they have found the need to broaden their repertoire, which now includes overtly cognitive methods (e.g., imagery and the use of thoughts), techniques that in the not-distant past would have been viewed as anathema to behavioral work. Behaviorists have also found it necessary to include more comprehensive outcome measures to evaluate the effects of their procedures. On the other hand, psychodynamic and interpersonally oriented therapists are finding advantages in incorporating frankly behavioral and cognitive methods into their procedures and in examining extratherapeutic contingencies and behavior. For the most part, this somewhat free exchange of techniques has long been present in the work of all therapists and signifies the primacy of patient needs in the determination of treatment strategies and appropriate outcomes. It represents not so much an amorphous eclecticism as a flexible application of available procedures to particular treatment problems. It has perhaps always been true that the theoretical base of therapists is far less descriptive of their actual practices than one might suppose. What may be different at this point is an open recognition of the shared techniques and the value of integration.

Teachers and supervisors, faced with multiple theories and procedures as well as diverse objectives, are seeking more general principles and limited outcome measures to transmit to their charges. With respect to the latter, Mintz (1981) for example, carefully reassessed data derived from psychoanalytically oriented psychotherapy and demonstrated that simple symptom improvement per se is a significant component of outcome even in methods based on complex psychodynamic hypotheses.

Researchers have become wary of comparative contests without a clear decision among the many competing forms of treatment and have come to appreciate the importance of common factors and the need for far more careful evaluation of their contribution to treatment efficacy. Kazdin (1979) notes the relative lack of work in this area and points out the basic error in designs that treat common factors (frequently called *nonspecific* factors) as artifacts to be controlled in order to evaluate the presumed active factors specific to a particular treatment. He stresses the futility of such efforts as no treatment can be administered free of nonspecific (common) features, which deserve research scrutiny as possible active ingredients in their own right. He suggests further that work on these features will be more productive to the extent that they are conceptualized in theoretical frameworks allowing for prediction.

One other major set of events has a direct influence on the movement to rapprochement. There is increasing pressure from groups outside the psychotherapy field that no longer can be discounted. Third-party insurance payers, agencies of the federal government, and consumer organizations are now demanding firm evidence on the efficacy, safety, and cost-effectiveness of the psychotherapies (see the section below on Efficacy and Accountability). Parloff (1980) observes that these insistent pressures are bound to destroy the long-time "misalliance" between therapists and researchers—a kind of silent agreement not to interact or deal with each other's activities. Researchers have typically overlooked much of psychotherapy as it is actually practiced, because it is too difficult to study; whereas psychotherapists tend to pay little attention to research findings, presumably because many of them appear irrelevant to the real clinical setting. Requirements for accountability will now force an active interdependence between the two, because therapists must turn to investigators to conduct the studies currently demanded, which will have to be done principally in those settings where therapists actually engage their patients. This turn of events (essentially forced from the outside) is likely to provide a positive impetus toward integration and rapprochement (Goldfried, 1980b).

One of the more visible figures in the movement is Goldfried (1980a, 1980b). He notes that surveys of psychologists show that most describe their work as a kind of admixture drawn from a variety of theoretical sources. Nonetheless, there tends to be an adherence to specific theoretical schools that provide a basis for professional identification, a tendency that has discouraged attempts in the past to define commonalities. He suggests that consensus might be reached by an examination of "clinical strategies" used in dealing with specific patient problems (Goldfried, 1980b). He recently solicited the comments of a group of highly reputable psychotherapists, representing differing theoretical positions, on the underlying principles and clinical strategies associated with change (Goldfried, 1980a). The comments indicated a number of shared strategies, including the utilization of new experiences, feedback to patients, attention to patient-therapist interaction, use of cognitive awareness, and emphasis on patient self-mastery. This exercise demonstrated that commonalities are much more likely to be discovered by inspecting what therapists do in their work than by an exposition of their theoretical positions.

Goldfried has actively pursued the task of rapprochement by convening a small working conference of researchers and therapists to jointly design empirical tests of clinical strategies and methods for determining efficacy (Goldfried, 1981). Interestingly, the initial mission on which the group agreed to work was the development of a "common language" based on nontechnical words and devoid of attachments to particular theories. The adoption of a common language has also been urged by other writers (e.g., Ryle, 1978). This continuing work group is but one promising model that could provide the kind of data needed in the field.

Doubts, of course, continue to be expressed concerning the eventual success of rapprochement. For example, Messer and Winokur (1980) point out limitations to the integration of psychoanalytic and behavior therapy, as these schools seem to embody contrasting visions of human existence. Behavioral approaches emphasize "nonambiguous happy endings . . . through direct action and removal of situation obstacles" (Messer & Winokur, 1980, p. 818), while an analytic orientation leads to an acceptance of the inevitability of internal conflicts and the limits set by an individual's history. However, rapprochement does not seek a complete merging of theoretical positions but rather identification of those existing (but rarely acknowledged) commonalities in clinical techniques or strategies and in outcome objectives. A complete blending of procedures and outcomes is not the goal of the movement, nor would it be a desirable consequence given the heuristic value of competing positions.

The ongoing task of designating and testing common ingredients is facilitated by some work already reported. The experimental studies of the Hopkins Psychotherapy Unit have supplied some important leads (Frank et al., 1978). A summary of these findings by Frank (1979) makes reference to positive expectations of patient and therapist, cognitive and experiential learning, and the enhancement of the patient's sense of mastery—factors that are prominent in the statements of therapists in the Goldfried paper noted above. Additional common ingredients have been cited (Parloff, 1980), many relating to therapist qualities, including the ability to establish a therapeutic alliance; clinical intuition, judgment, and sensitivity; and provision of plausible explanations of the causes of distress and the rationale of treatment. It should be noted that many of these factors refer to procedures in treatment itself rather than to common goals or outcomes. Yet, here as well, there is evidence of a consensus leading to the adoption of a common set of measures.

A number of recently developed procedures to evaluate outcome have come into use by researchers and practitioners representing diverse theoretical schools and treatment techniques. Goal Attainment Scaling (Kiersuk & Sherman, 1968), the Problem-Oriented System (Weed, 1968), and target complaint techniques (Battle, Imber, Hoehn-Saric, Stone, Nash, &

Frank, 1966) are examples of these procedures. The most ambitious effort to move the field toward a shared set of outcome measures has been made by Waskow and Parloff (1975). They present a selected core battery relevant to a wide range of theoretical interests, developed from the recommendations of a group of competent investigators and reviewed by a panel of experts. At this date, the full anticipated impact of this comprehensive effort has not been felt, in part because of the size of the battery and the time required for its completion, and in part because researchers continue to devise measures tailored to their own unique theoretical interests. Moreover, the core battery only indirectly taps intrapsychic dimensions, which together with affective variables, are the most elusive to measure but are clearly important as they are manifested so prominently in psychopathology (Imber, 1978). Nevertheless, the project has exerted a significant impact on researchers and has potential utility for practitioners who consult it.

Studies of long-term outcome have generally received scant attention and, in fact, have rarely been done. However, this situation is likely to change, because durability has come to be recognized as a significant aspect of treatment outcome. (See the section below on Durability of Psychotherapy Effects). There is reason to believe that the processes responsible for immediate change are different than those that account for its persistence (Imber, 1978). These persistence or maintenance processes seem likely to involve factors shared by different treatment forms; and therefore, measures of long-term outcome are likely to be similar regardless of the type of treatment administered.

A final area that has received relatively little attention in the field of psychotherapy is that of environmental events. The influence of events external to treatment on the psychotherapeutic process has begun to recieve careful study only recently (Imber, Pilkonis, Harway, Klein, & Rubinsky, 1982), but the impact of such events on change and its persistence may be considerable in all forms of treatment. The rapprochement movement can usefully address this problem by arriving at some consensus regarding significant events, designing studies of their effects on treatment, and identifying measures of outcome sensitive to the influence of life circumstances.

EFFICACY AND ACCOUNTABILITY: SECONDARY AND AGGREGATED TECHNIQUES OF ANALYSIS

There has been a rising chorus of demands that the efficacy of the psychotherapies be more convincingly demonstrated, these demands coming mainly from consumers, third-party payers, and government policymakers. As Parloff (1979) points out, government policy decisions already are underway, but the serious deficiencies in available research reports may lead to improper decisions or force decision makers to disregard the findings. Demands for adequate evidence are especially difficult to meet, because they tend to be stated in global terms paying little heed to the limited conditions under which particular treatments are evaluated. Most effectiveness research has assessed outcome differences among specific techniques and the complex interplay of treatments, therapists, patients, and settings. Outcome criteria tend to be multiple, varied, and noncomparable across studies. However, a number of integrated methods of analysis are now available (some developed very recently) which seek to synthesize the large number of efficacy studies accumulated over the years and provide simplified indices for interpretation. The most comprehensive and sophisticated current account of these methods has been provided by Yates and Newman (1980a, 1980b, 1980c), and we lean heavily on their summations in this section.

Program evaluation techniques have received considerable attention in recent years (Perloff, E. & Perloff, R., 1977). These approaches assess outcome by evaluating a complex of treatment variables organized as a program (for example, in a community mental health center where patients may receive a number of therapies conjointly and be treated by multiple therapists). While this design is consistent with treatment as actually practiced, it makes it difficult to separate the specific effects of different components. Moreover, there is no simple answer to the problem, because controlled studies with random assignment have been especially difficult to implement in these settings. For a comprehensive discussion of program evaluation the reader is refered to Chapter 5 by Lee Sechrest, David Ametrano, and Irene Mass Ametrano.

The methodology of program evaluation represents a relatively new technique in the history of psychotherapy research, however. The preponderance of efficacy studies reported in the literature have been executed in individual investigations. These studies typically make use of classical experimental designs, which in application are often seriously flawed or compromised. No single study, moreover, can be expected to provide definitive findings on treatment outcome because of limits on sample size, diversity of populations, the variety of criteria against which such research must be evaluated, limitations in the measures used, and the idiosyncrasies of different theoretical approaches. Recognition of these issues has generated a number of procedures to integrate findings across numerous individual studies. Because these procedures do not produce original experimental data per se, they may be termed *secondary analyses*.

Traditionally, these methods have taken the form of literature reviews published in scholarly journals. A number of reviews of this kind have appeared in the psychotherapy literature, many of outstandingly high quality. Undoubtedly, the most provocative was that of Eysenck (1952) published nearly 30 years ago and updated on several occasions (1960,

1965) in response to criticism. Meltzoff and Kornreich (1970), Bergin (1971), and Bergin and Lambert (1978) have also contributed influential reviews, a good portion of these devoted to a refutation of Eysenck, whose work has generally been viewed as an indictment of the effectiveness of psychotherapy. Another important overall summary of research was done by Luborsky, Singer, and Luborsky (1975), who included only controlled studies of actual patients and excluded analog studies of questionable validity that had comprised a large portion of earlier reviews. Luborsky et al. concluded that patients who undergo a course of formal psychotherapeutic treatment do, in fact, show significantly more improvement than members of control groups. The most recent reviews have been compiled by Lambert (1979), VandenBos (1980), and Parloff (1979). Parloff also interpreted the outcome evidence as indicating that patients treated by psychotherapy show significantly more improvement than comparable samples of untreated patients, although this conclusion was strongest for certain specific disorders, such as anxiety states, fears, and phobias.

The most significant problem in the soundness of literature reviews is the selective nature of data included. Usually, it is not possible to include all relevant research. In the course of making choices concerning what will be covered, an author inevitably selects or emphasizes work that supports a particular viewpoint. Moreover, authors do not often establish clear criteria regarding the methodological adequacy of the variety of studies reviewed. There have been two outstanding procedures developed to deal with this issue, and they are intended to make the review process more systematic. These procedures are *box-score analyses* and *meta-analyses*.

In the box-score analysis, a limited set of studies is selected for inclusion according to some well-defined standard. This approach is similar to that of the usual literature review, except that here the criteria are more sharply defined and explicitly described. Each study is evaluated in terms of the pre-defined inclusion criteria, and then outcome scores are tallied for particular categories of comparison (e.g., disorder, technique, theoretical orientation). The Luborsky et al. report (1975) is an example of this approach. The method has been criticized because it still allows for bias in selection by the author, may use overly simple measures of outcome, and may disregard differences in the strength of findings across studies. It does have the merit of imposing greater systemization on the literature-review process.

Meta-analysis is a technique drawn from educational research and only recently applied to psychotherapy studies. It is exemplified by the work of Smith, Glass, and Miller (1980), who pioneered the adaptation to psychotherapy. The technique uses statistical methods for aggregating data and determining relationships between causal and outcome variables. Studies are selected according to particular criteria and then coded on variables considered to be related to outcome (for example, therapist experience, patient symptoms, treatment setting, and quality of research design). Such measures are correlated with study outcomes, and these relationships form the basis for organizing the results in terms of varying design aspects of the studies. In the Smith et al. work, only controlled investigations were included. A special feature of the work was the use of a "size of the effect" (of outcome), computed as a standard score, which could then be applied across all 475 studies in the sample. Because the studies reviewed frequently included more than one outcome measure, Smith et al. treated each outcome variable as a separate case, finally producing a total of 1,766 effect-size measures. Their main finding was that, on the average, the difference between treated and untreated groups was 0.85 standard-deviation units. This result indicates that the average person receiving therapy is better off than 80 percent of those who do not receive therapy.

The meta-analysis technique has been criticized because it includes an enormous number of variables (some of which appear to be of only minor relevance) and because some evaluated studies had design flaws. However, the Smith et al. work was done with special attention to methodological criteria, excluding in particular poorly designed studies.

The meta-analysis technique does show considerable potential and allows for a more systematic approach than most other available methods. It has not yet been applied, however, by enough workers to provide a reliable assessment. Its most obvious limitation—a reliance on the variable quality of existing literature—is of course a problem inherent in all types of secondary analyses.

The most recently adapted method of secondary analysis is that set of techniques called *cost-effectiveness* and *cost-benefit analyses* (CEA/CBA). These techniques have been explicated most prominently by Yates and Newman (1980a, 1980b, 1980c). At this point, they are the least developed and probably most controversial of all the areas of psychotherapy research.

For CEA/CBA purposes, the costs, as well as the benefits, of psychotherapy must be valued; and decisions regarding what to include and what to exclude are bound to reflect the subjective judgments of different interest groups and their goals. As these analyses can be expected to be used to determine quite directly the type and extent of treatment that will be offered and reimbursed, it is apparent that how the procedures are developed and who makes use of them will be matters of considerable dispute. With respect to cost assessment, the following are a few of the variables that can be included: salary and time of professionals, paraprofessionals, and support staff; expenses of operating facilities; monetary costs of therapy and of patients' time; psychological cost of the suffering of patients as a result of negative effects of therapy; and cost to employers for released time for patient treatment. Benefit assessment can include reduction in symptoms, changes in patients' earnings, change in the quality of life of patients and their relatives, drop in absenteeism and accidents at the place of employment, reduction of criminal and drug activities, and maintenance of employment levels in society generally.

The technical procedures involved in CEA/CBA cannot be presented here, but it is important to note that in CEA, the effects usually are not valued in monetary units but can be expressed in any convenient units that are relevant (e.g., reduction in anxiety). CBA requires that costs and outcomes be valued in monetary terms. In CBA, benefits are summed using a particular unit (e.g., dollars), and costs are summed in the same unit. A ratio is then derived by dividing total benefits by total costs. The ratio is larger than 1 if benefits exceed costs.

It is clear that considerable refinement in methodology must be made in CEA/CBA in order for it to be applied with validity to psychotherapy. These techniques are as much dependent on the quality of available outcome data as are other methods of secondary analysis. Moreover, there is certain to be an ethical objection to the notion of evaluating therapy in monetary terms. Yet this is the ultimate criterion used by funding sources, which already look with skepticism at the provision of psychotherapy and are aware of precedents for the use of these techniques in the health industry. The dilemma for psychologists is that if they do not readily engage in this kind of research, the techniques will be applied by others with much less direct investment in, and understanding of, the field.

DURABILITY OF PSYCHOTHERAPY EFFECTS

Although the importance of evaluating maintenance of psychotherapy outcomes has been acknowledged, research in the area has been relatively neglected. Methodological problems have retarded research progress, but there also has been a certain degree of reluctance on the part of investigators and therapists to engage in the needed studies. The rationale of some treatment formats seems to promote the assumption that permanence of positive effects is ensured by a course of treatment that produces measurable changes at termination. However, the research findings that are available cast doubt on this assumption.

Empirical evidence for the long-term effectiveness of therapy is equivocal. Longitudinal follow-up studies are inherently time-consuming and costly and tend, therefore, not to be pursued except over quite limited periods of time. Moreover, methodological problems (such as difficulty in retaining a representative sample for the follow-up) may confound the results of long-term projects. Furthermore, the occurrence of environmental events may obscure the results of treatment, and findings may be confounded when patients participate in additional treatments subsequent to the original psychotherapy. Despite these problems, there have been some important studies that bear on the issue of durability.

Liberman (1978) reported on the results of separate cohorts of patients in a series of experiments conducted by researchers at Johns Hopkins over a 25-year period. Patients were followed over time intervals of 5, 10, and 20 years. Liberman reported that patients receiving group, individual, or minimal therapy (1/2 hour biweekly) all improved over the initial six-month treatment period and continued to improve at each evaluation interval. Only about 50 percent of the observed improvement had been achieved during treatment, however, suggesting that factors accounting for maintenance may be different from those that produce changes at treatment termination.

In another major psychotherapy research project, Sloane, Staples, Cristol, Yorkston, & Whipple (1975) reported on a comparison of behavioral and psychodynamic psychotherapies. Initial improvements were more pronounced than those found at one-year and two-year follow-ups. Although sample attrition mitigated the conclusions, the authors contended that the effects obtained during treatment did persist in a sizable percentage of patients.

Lieberman, Yalom, and Miles (1973) interviewed former participants who had benefited from encounter groups. They found that participants who maintained their gains engaged in a continuing process of interpersonal "experimenting" (e.g., relating to others in new ways) and seemed better able to cope with significant life events than nonmaintainers who reported perceiving their environment as overwhelming. The evidence suggested that maintenance of change is an active process engaged in by the individual, and treatment results do not persist spontaneously.

However, surveys of existing work on long-term effects indicate that relatively few studies demonstrate persisting results following treatment. For example, Goldstein, Lopez, and Greenleaf (1979) reviewed 192 controlled psychotherapy studies conducted from a variety of theoretical perspectives. The sample was selected on the basis of soundness of methodology. The authors reported that the rate of positive outcomes, though high at the conclusion of therapy, was much lower at follow-up. Although 85 percent of studies surveyed reported positive results at termination, only 14 percent reported transfer or maintenance effects. It was concluded that maintenance is more often the exception than the rule and that, when it does occur, it is not an automatic process but rather a function of identifiable elements operating during and after therapy.

There have been a number of efforts to specify the components contributing to the persistence of change, particularly in the behavioral literature. Stokes and Baer (1977) described 9 paradigms (culled from some 270 behavioral studies) of generalization-enhancement procedures. Strategies ranged from "train and hope" to teaching generalization as a skill in itself. Marholin and Touchette (1979) maintained that the persistence of therapeutic gain can be explained in terms of stimulus control and response consequences. From this operant viewpoint, the authors suggest numerous techniques based on learning theory, including rehearsal in the natural environment, peer control, and reinforcement of behaviors incompatible with dysfunctional behavior. Another major behavioral effort has been the work of Kanfer (1971, 1977), whose ideas bridge, to some extent, the gap between behavioral and psychodynamically oriented theorists. In his cognitive mediational model, Kanfer described self-regulatory mechanisms involving the interaction of person and environment. Specific self-management strategies included methods to train individuals in altering self-regulatory processes and cognitions.

A somewhat different component that may produce maintenance has been examined in a study of cigarette smokers by Relinger, Bornstein, Bugge, Carmody, and Zohn (1977). Patients in their control group, untreated during follow-up, were led to believe that their personality profiles suggested they could remain abstinent without additional therapeutic support. Only this group showed no relapse at follow-up. The results indicate the important role of self-attribution, which may be of greater influence in maintaining change than the technology designed to promote it. Imber et al. (1982), in a recent paper describing a set of alternate maintenance procedures, also stress the significance of self-attribution. They cite a study reported by Frank (1976), in which patients who understood improvement to be a direct result of their own efforts maintained their gains in contrast to a group of patients who attributed improvement to medication (which was actually a placebo). The patient's sense of mastery or control in acting on the environment is, of course, a related phenomenon. In this connection, Imber et al. also emphasize that maintenance methods should include procedures that prepare patients for specific future life events and for periods of stress which are inevitable for all persons. Precisely how and when particular maintenance interventions may be made most appropriately remains a research question. It is, however, worth noting that the division between formal therapy and follow-up is quite arbitrary (cf. Mash and Terdal, 1977), and research on durability of change is contributing to its dissolution.

Finally, adequate evaluation of the persistence of treatment effects would be facilitated by data from studies of the natural history of different psychiatric disorders. However, the inordinate difficulties in conducting such studies, especially since treatment interventions must be partialled out or excluded, are considerable. Ethical issues alone make it unlikely that reliable studies of this kind will be forthcoming shortly.

COMPARATIVE OUTCOMES WITH DRUG THERAPY AND PSYCHOTHERAPY

It has become increasingly common in clinical practice to combine the use of medication and psychotherapy in the treatment of major cognitive and affective disorders. The use of combined treatments is often justified on the assumption that medication and psychotherapy may exert their effects in different areas (e.g., symptom reduction versus improvement in social functioning) and at different times (e.g., the effects of drugs may appear quickly, while the effects of psychotherapy may develop more gradually). Therefore, good clinical judgment would suggest the use of both modalities in order to provide the best possible care. Such reasoning is intuitively appealing, but it is helpful to evaluate it against the available research evidence. Two questions are of particular importance: first, what are the effects of drugs alone when compared to psychotherapy alone; and second, what are the effects of combined treatments when compared to either modality alone? In attempting to answer these questions, we have not been exhaustive in reviewing the drug versus psychotherapy literature, but rather have relied heavily on what we regard as the best recent reviews of the area. The reader is also referred to Chapter 16 in the present volume for more detail on the current status of psychopharmacology and organic treatments.

Drug studies and comparative drug-psychotherapy studies (as opposed to outcome studies of the psychotherapies alone) have tended to involve older and more chronic patients, often bearing psychotic diagnoses and a history of institutionalization. Among such patients with severe psychiatric disorders, there is general agreement that the effects of drugs alone are superior to outcome with psychotherapy alone. Luborsky et al. (1975) cited eight such comparisons, seven of which favored the use of medication. Hollon and Beck (1978) were reluctant to make broad statements about findings from the comparative drug and psychotherapy literature because of the methodological inadequacies they discovered there, but they drew their strongest conclusions in stating:

1.   The efficacy of drugs appears most firmly established in the schizophrenias and the affective disorders.
2.   The relative ineffectiveness of psychotherapies (of the types used) seems most apparent in the schizophrenias. . . .
3.   The impact of psychotherapy on the affective disorders appears to depend on the type of psychotherapy utilized. (p. 486)

For the treatment of major unipolar depressive disorders, Weissman (1979) described the evidence as "equivocal" in direct comparisons of drugs versus psychotherapy. She cited five studies: one in which psychotherapy was superior to medication in symptom reduction, a second in which the two modalities were equivalent, and three others in which drugs were more effective than psychotherapy in both symptom reduction and prevention of relapse, but psychotherapy was more beneficial in the area of social functioning.

In contrast to most earlier reviewers, Smith et al. (1980) were impressed by similarities, rather than differences, in outcome studies of drugs versus psychotherapy. They contended, "Psychotherapy is scarcely any less effective than drug therapy in the treatment of serious psychological disorders" (p. 188). In their meta-analysis of drug-only and drug and psychotherapy studies, they did find that the mean effect size attributable to drugs alone (approximately .40 standard-deviation units) was greater than the average effect size accounted for by psychotherapy separately (approximately .30 standard-deviation units). However, they pointed out that the difference was small and emphasized the similarity in magnitude of the treatment effects of the two modalities.

Although their position with regard to drug versus psychotherapy effects is a minority one, Smith et al. agreed with several other reviewers that combined treatments are more effective than either drug therapy or psychotherapy alone. Their results indicated that the effect size of combined treatments was slightly smaller than the sum of the separate effects of medication and psychotherapy, but that the overall effect size (.60 standard-deviation units) was still considerably larger than that for either treatment separately. In this same vein, Luborsky et al. described the advantage of combined treatment as "striking." Weissman (1979) was also persuaded of the value of combined approaches, pointing out that in all the relevant comparisons she examined, there was unanimity in the "superiority of combined treatment over a control group or either treatment alone" (p. 1266).

In summary, there is considerable evidence for the superiority of drugs alone when compared with psychotherapy alone in the treatment of the most serious psychiatric disorders, especially schizophrenia. However, the two modalities may well exert their influence in different areas of functioning, and the available data are most consistent in supporting the use of combined treatments for major affective and cognitive disorders.

PSYCHOTHERAPY AND OUTCOMES IN PHYSICAL HEALTH

Evidence for the "intimate relations of mental states to bodily illnesses" (Frank, 1975, p. 192) suggests that psychological variables play a role in the etiology of (or vulnerability to) various physical illnesses, and psychological interventions may be helpful in both the acute treatment and long-term management of such conditions. As always, the quality of research evidence to support such a conclusion varies, depending on the treatment method and physical condition considered and the methodological adequacy of the empirical work itself. However, regardless of the present state of the art, interest among psychologists in this area is likely to remain strong for at least two reasons: (1) it is estimated that the majority of persons seeking general medical care are suffering from problems which are primarily psychological in nature, a fact that creates enormous burdens for the physical health care system (Kiesler, 1980); and (2) follow-

ing impressive 19th- and 20th-century triumphs over many acute, infectious diseases, the field of medicine is still left with even more difficult
problems in managing chronic conditions (e.g., cardiovascular disease,
cancer, diabetes). Such illnesses not only require acute treatment but
also demand long-term changes in lifestyle, coping patterns, and physical
and social environments (Engel, 1977; Mechanic, 1977). Promoting such
changes is a task for which psychologists have particular expertise.

Psychotherapy for psychosomatic disorders

Kellner (1975), Olbrisch (1977), and Ramsay, Wittkower, and Warnes
(1976) have provided the most complete reviews of the evidence on
the effectiveness of psychotherapy for psychosomatic conditions such
as asthma, skin disorders, gastrointestinal disorders, and chronic pain
syndromes. Kellner defines such conditions as:

> organic disease in which emotions appear to act as precipitating or aggra-
> vating factors, and psychophysiologic reactions in which the patient is dis-
> tressed by somatic symptoms in the absence of physical disease. (p. 1021)

These reviews tend not to consider behavioral treatments (see below)
for habit disorders and vascular problems (e.g., headache, hypertension),
but rather focus on more traditional modes of support and therapy. Their
conclusions tend to be conservative—with Olbrisch describing the research evidence as "uneven," and Kellner suggesting that the "experimental evaluation of the effects of psychotherapies in physical illness is
at an early stage" (p. 1028). By contrast, Luborsky et al. (1975) are
enthusiastic in their evaluation of the empirical data. In a review of comparative outcome studies of various kinds, Luborsky et al. describe 11 studies
where the major concern was treatment of a "psychosomatic symptom."
In their judgment, nine of these studies support the contention that psychotherapy plus a medical regimen (or psychotherapy alone, in two cases)
was superior to a medical regimen alone. They argue that the treatment
of psychosomatic conditions is one of the very few areas in which it is
possible to match a specific form of treatment (psychotherapy plus medical
care) to specific kinds of patients (those with psychosomatic complaints).
By contrast, Kellner prefers a more conservative, "stepped" approach
in making treatment recommendations, suggesting not an immediate trial
of psychotherapy but rather the addition of therapy to the treatment of
those persons who do not respond adequately to routine medical care.

Behavioral medicine

A large literature (e.g., Ferguson & Taylor, 1980) has developed in
the recent past describing the use of behavioral techniques and psycho-

logical interventions with habit disorders (obesity, smoking, lack of physical exercise, substance abuse, insomnia), various medical conditions responsive to treatment with relaxation and biofeedback (headache, hypertension, chronic pain, Raynaud's disease), and lifestyles and personality characteristics which appear to enhance vulnerability to physical illness (type A personality, inadequate self-control and coping skills). There is considerable evidence for short-term treatment efficacy in many of these areas (see the related chapters in this volume), but less consistent evidence regarding the comparative efficacy of different approaches or the most potent components of different multimodal treatment programs. Since many behavioral treatments are designed to be limited in time and specific to targeted areas of change, there is also increasing concern with issues of generalization of treatment effects across settings and maintenance of effects over time.

Preparation for surgery

Since Janis' (1958) investigation of stress associated with surgery and the "work of worry" attendant to it, several studies (e.g., Aiken & Henrichs, 1971; Egbert, Battit, Welch, & Bartlett, 1964; Lazarus & Hagens, 1968) have documented the beneficial effects of psychological preparation for surgery. Preparatory techniques have varied, from the simple giving of information to the teaching of specific skills for coping with pain or the effects of invasive procedures. Outcome measures used in such studies have included both patient self-reports of affect, adaptation, and pain and less reactive indices such as judgments of pain and recovery done by medical personnel blind to the preparatory manipulation or data regarding requests for pain killing medication, length of hospitalization, and length of follow-up care. The evidence in this area consistently supports the effectiveness of psychological techniques in preparing patients for drastic medical procedures, with the one qualification that we know little about the longer-term effects of such interventions, if any. However, regardless of longer-term consequences (assuming that they are not likely to be negative), such interventions can, in general, be valuable, as their costs are minimal (treatments are typically brief) and their short-term benefits have been well documented and are of considerable clinical significance.

Psychological interventions in chronic disease and with geriatric patients

Demoralization, hopelessness, and a sense of powerlessness are frequently associated with chronic disease at any age and with the particular problems of the elderly. Various investigators have attempted to combat such attitudes with psychological treatments and to illustrate the beneficial effects of these treatments on both psychological and physical outcome measures. For example, Schulz (1976) has demonstrated the positive effects of increasing a sense of perceived control and predictability among older persons living in group settings, and such manipulations do appear to influence both psychological and physical outcomes.

Chronic diseases or catastrophic illnesses with long-term consequences are obviously not restricted to elderly patients. Some research has been done with younger chronic disease patients, which also illustrates the beneficial effects of alleviating a sense of helplessness, deindividuation, and isolation in these groups. For example, Frank (1975) cites the results of a Veterans Administration project aimed at aggressively rehabilitating chronic neurological patients regarded as "hopeless," in which 40 percent of such patients became self-supporting outside the hospital after initially being consigned to indefinite institutionalization. Seligman's (1975) work on "learned helplessness" and depression is similar to these other studies in emphasizing the role of mastery and perceived control in psychological well-being.

More controversial are psychological treatments for conditions which have traditionally been thought of as organic in origin. Simonton's (Simonton, Matthews-Simonton, & Creighton, 1978) work with meditation and imagery techniques in cancer patients, and Cousins' (1979) popular account of his recovery from severe collagen disease provide examples of remissions in physical diseases which appear to have important psychological components. Frank (1961, 1975) attributes such "cures" (and those associated with various forms of religious healing) to attitudes of "expectant faith," and he regards the healer's task as being, in part, the mobilization of such attitudes in patients.

The effects of psychological care on medical utilization

In addition to her discussion of psychosomatic complaints, Olbrisch (1977) reviews the evidence on the influence of psychotherapy on medical overutilization, both in general practice and in prepaid health insurance programs. The data across several studies (e.g., Cummings & Follette, 1968; Follette & Cummings, 1967; Goldberg, Krantz, & Locke, 1970) suggest that short-term psychotherapy can significantly decrease the use of medical and laboratory services in groups of overutilizers with significant levels of psychological distress. However, such studies do not typically involve random assignment to psychotherapy, and it may be that persons prepared to define their problems in psychological terms and to participate in therapy are different in important and uncontrolled ways from members of the comparison groups usually included in such research (i.e., control subjects matched on the basis of demographic and medical characteristics).

From a scientific viewpoint, methodological limitations create difficulties in interpreting the effects of psychotherapy per se on medical overutilization, but as Kiesler (1980) points out, the data still allow us to draw important policy conclusions. "The effectiveness of psychotherapy taken in isolation is not the principal policy issue; rather, the primary issue is the marginal utility of psychotherapy when added to an existing system" (p. 1068), a system where health care costs are seriously inflated by inappropriate or unnecessary medical care. The currently available data from prepaid health plans make it clear that psychotherapy "reduces significantly the cost of medical care and . . . has been shown to reduce absenteeism [from work] as well" (Kiesler, 1980, p. 1068).

NEGATIVE EFFECTS OF PSYCHOTHERAPY

There are few beneficial medical treatments or surgical procedures which do not also carry the threat of noxious side effects or unexpected, negative outcomes. This state of affairs has long been accepted as an inevitable part of medicine, but only recently have psychotherapy researchers given attention to the potential negative effects of therapeutic interventions.

Bergin (1966, 1971) made the first systematic case for the existence of "deterioration" effects, pointing to the results of several studies which indicated specific, negative changes for certain patients and a general tendency for treated groups to display greater variance in outcome than untreated groups. He attributed this greater variability in outcome to the potency of psychotherapy, which was capable of making patients worse as well as better. The argument that deterioration effects provide evidence of the power of therapy is a rather ironic one, promoted in response to earlier critics who denied any effects at all for therapy. The need to defend psychotherapy per se has lessened, as a consensus has grown among both researchers and clinicians regarding its effectiveness when compared to the absence of treatment. As a result, more recent discussions of negative effects have become more substantive, pointing to the need to identify them more carefully and to appreciate their implications for the practice of therapy.

Lambert, Bergin, and Collins (1977) have provided a comprehensive review of "therapist-induced deterioration in psychotherapy." They summarized the history of research on negative effects and expanded the definition of such effects to include "not only worsening symptoms but also lack of significant improvement when it is expected and even the acceleration of ongoing deterioration" (p. 454). They described the evidence which does exist for negative effects in individual, group, and marital therapy and the patient variables (diagnosis, prior history, limited ego strength) and therapist characteristics (exploitativeness, lack of experience, pathological personality) which appear to contribute to the occurrence of negative outcomes. Because the research evidence is especially sparse in this area, they did not offer definitive conclusions, but instead emphasized the importance of examining routinely in future outcome research the kind and degree of negative change which may emerge.

Hadley and Strupp (1976) relied not on previous empirical evidence, but rather on a survey of 70 experts, to point out that negative effects are seen as a serious problem by psychotherapists of many different theoretical orientations. In summarizing the results of their survey, they described five general categories of negative effects identified by their respondents:

1. Exacerbation of presenting symptoms.
2. Appearance of new symptoms.
3. Patients' misuse of therapy (e.g., therapy becomes an end in itself and promotes the avoidance of action in other areas of patients' lives).
4. Patients' undertaking of unrealistic tasks or the setting of inappropriate life goals which promotes personal failure.
5. Patients' disillusionment with the therapist or therapy in general, which may lead to a general loss of confidence in close, interpersonal relationships.

Hadley and Strupp attribute such effects to deficient initial assessment, certain therapist qualities (deficits in training or skills, pathological personality characteristics), various patient qualities (little or no motivation, poor ego strength), specific misapplications or deficiencies in technique, and more general problems in the patient-therapist relationship (inadequate or too intense involvement, including sexual involvement in the latter case; transference and countertransference problems).

They emphasize an additional point in a second paper (Strupp & Hadley, 1977): the need for assessment from multiple perspectives in defining negative (and positive) outcome. They suggest the use of information from at least three points of view: those of society (particularly the significant others in patients' lives), patients themselves, and trained clinicians, as each of these parties is likely to use different criteria in judging outcome. In general, adequate assessment of both positive and negative effects is enhanced to the extent that:

1. Multiple perspectives are used to assess outcome across several indices of change (symptomatology; changes in interpersonal functioning at home and at work; changes in subjective well-being; cognitive and personality restructuring).
2. Long-term, follow-up data are collected.
3. Information about the natural history of untreated disorders is available.

RELATIONSHIP BETWEEN PROCESS AND OUTCOME

Although the focus of the present chapter is on outcome studies rather than process research (see the chapter by Greenberg in this volume), it is important to note that certain findings from the outcome literature have stimulated continued interest in examining the process of therapy.

Difficulty of predicting outcome from pretreatment measures

A recent report by Luborsky and his colleagues (Luborsky, Mintz, Auerbach, Christoph, Bachrach, Todd, Johnson, Cohen, & O'Brien, 1980) of findings from the Penn Psychotherapy Project and the Chicago Counseling Center Study documents the difficulty of predicting therapy outcomes from pretreatment measures. Neither direct predictions by patients, therapists, and independent clinicians nor indices derived from other data provided by these informants were very accurate in predicting outcome status at termination. Correlations between the predictors and measures of outcome were generally smaller than .30; therefore, the predictors accounted for less than 10 percent of the outcome variance. Although general prediction success was low from all perspectives, patient characteristics tended to be better predictors than therapist measures, patient-therapist match measures, or certain treatment characteristics (e.g., length of treatment, use of psychotropic drugs in combination with psychotherapy). In interpreting their results, Luborsky et al. suggest that "predictive factors may not be sufficiently apparent until the patient and therapist have had a chance to interact" (p. 480), and they describe their own process research designed to examine intensively initial therapy sessions among patients who benefited most versus patients who benefited least from psychotherapy. They contend that, for patients helped most, "a working alliance developed as well as a sense of mastery over the main conflictual relationship themes that were identifiable initially" (p. 480).

Lack of comparative outcome effects

We have commented earlier in this chapter on the relative lack of distinctive treatment effects across psychotherapies using ostensibly different techniques, a fact which has led some investigators to argue for the larger impact of variables shared by all therapies. As described in the rapprochement section, all credible treatments provide a rationale for change, arouse positive expectations and other strong affect, and involve a supportive, socially sanctioned helping relationship. In order to characterize more carefully the quality of the relationship which develops between patient and therapist, some researchers have designed measures for examining the "therapeutic alliance" directly (Gomes-Schwartz, 1978; Luborsky, 1976). Although such measures include some items assessing differences in technique and therapist activity, they are, in large part, devoted to determining the "attitudinal affective climate of the therapy" (Marziali, Marmar, & Krupnick, 1981). Interestingly, and consistent with results from work on pretreatment prediction, patient measures of alliance seem to be more closely related to outcome than therapist measures. For example, in a study of outcome in brief, psychodynamic therapy, Marziali et al. reported that "Only the patient's contribution to the therapeutic alliance was predictive of outcome. Patients who developed and maintained positive attitudes toward the therapist and the work of therapy achieved the greatest gains" (p. 361).

Similarities and differences between naturally occurring, helpful relationships and formal psychotherapy

Strupp and his colleagues in the Vanderbilt Psychotherapy Project (Strupp & Hadley, 1979) have recently completed a study comparing outcome of brief treatment with experienced therapists versus counseling and support provided by members of the Vanderbilt faculty noted for their interpersonal skill, warmth, and interest in students. In general, there were few group differences when comparing results with lay counselors and trained professionals. However, Strupp (1980a, 1980b, 1980c, 1980d) has done a more intensive investigation of four pairs of patients treated by four different therapists in the study; one member of each pair did well in therapy, while the second member did poorly. The purpose of Strupp's analysis was to identify those factors in the course of therapy which distinguished between the members of each pair. His conclusion is that:

> the therapeutic outcome was a function of the patient's ability to become involved in a therapeutic relationship and to work productively within the framework proffered by the therapist. Equally important were countertransference reactions that seriously interfered with successful confrontation and resolution of the patient's negative transference. (Strupp, 1980d, p. 947)

Again, the emphasis is on what the patient brings to the working relationship. With patients who are capable of and motivated to engage productively in therapy, outcomes tend to be good. The therapist's particular skills are more thoroughly tested by those patients who are wary, hostile, or otherwise negativistic and by those moments in treatment when the therapeutic relationship is jeopardized by negative feelings (either on the part of therapist or patient) which must be acknowledged and resolved.

SUMMARY

This chapter presents a selective review of the extensive literature on outcome studies in psychotherapy, focusing on the most promising recent work considered relevant to the interests of both researchers and practicing therapists. The review centers principally on individual, short-term treatments within the psychodynamic and behavioral-cognitive orientations, partly because these tend to be the most prevalent current forms, and partly because they appear to have been subjected to the most competent research scrutiny.

The cumulative evidence seems to sustain the conclusion that, while the psychotherapies in general do yield positive outcomes for patients, there are at best only minimal differences in effectiveness for treating most disorders among the variety of competing formats and theoretical positions. These findings provide considerable support for the continuing search for common factors of therapeutic potency presumed to be present in all successful procedures and indicate that such factors may be far more significant than features specific to any one method or theory. One interesting reaction to this situation has been the emergence of an active rapprochement movement among both investigators and therapists of disparate theoretical positions. This movement presently is working toward the identification of clinical strategies and treatment objectives that are shared by different therapy approaches. It is possible that this work may lead eventually to the design of an integrated or unified theory of psychotherapy, although that is not a declared current goal of the movement. Regardless of how this movement fares, it would seem advisable for therapists to acquaint themselves with the most prevalent clinical strategies and outcome objectives and for researchers to recognize the value of investigations which deal with issues that reach beyond their own, favored theoretical position and have implications for contending viewpoints as well.

One unfortunate characteristic of the outcome research literature has been a proclivity for studies that only tangentially deal with the standard working conditions of clinical practice and the pragmatic demands of patient care. Important advances in psychotherapy research as reported in scholarly publications often go unnoticed by clinicians, who view the work as irrelevant to their interests. There have been some recent attempts by Barlow (1981) and Kazdin (1981) to correct this failure of communication. Both advocate a wider use of case studies by researchers, pointing out that when these are done systematically, using careful clinical description and valid change measures, they can have considerable scientific value. Such studies, it is anticipated, would have the special advantage of bringing together researchers and clinicians, promoting the interests of both.

There have been insistent demands that psychotherapy research meet requirements for accountability by providing better and more systematic evidence than the outcome studies now typical of the field. In response to these demands, certain new, integrated methods of analysis have been developed, which provide simplified outcome indices by synthesizing findings from otherwise noncomparable studies independently executed. The most prominent of these integrated methods are meta-analysis techniques and cost-effectiveness and cost-benefit analysis. Although these methods have only recently been applied to psychotherapy data, and their ultimate value is still uncertain, it can be anticipated that they (and probably other similar procedures) will be used increasingly in the near future. The developments in the area of accountability are bound to affect quite directly the clinical work of therapists, and thus it would seem prudent for them to become informed in this field. Researchers should be prepared to engage far more actively in these types of investigations, especially to help refine the newly adopted techniques and even develop others that will reduce the possibility of crude or inappropriate applications.

The question of durability of positive changes following treatment has received more attention in recent years. Some findings suggest that therapists should more deliberately incorporate directly in their treatment techniques certain procedures specifically designed to ensure long-term maintenance. What procedures may be the most effective for this purpose is not certain at this point, and much research remains to be done. In the meantime, it is clear that therapists should attend far more carefully to assessments of their patients over the long term, since persistence of change is a questionable assumption.

In the treatment of the major cognitive and affective disorders, the combined use of psychotherapy and medication has become more common practice. Some research findings suggest that the two modalities may complement each other, by exerting influence on separate areas of psychological functioning. Most psychotherapists today deem it important that they become knowledgeable regarding psychopharmacology, in order to make appropriate referrals and to adequately monitor patients during the course of a combined treatment regimen.

The application of psychological interventions, including psychotherapy, to physical health problems has stimulated increasing research activity. It is now acknowledged that the majority of persons seeking medical care are suffering from problems primarily psychological in nature, and chronic medical conditions can be ameliorated through psychological methods (in addition to medical management). Outstanding examples of the many studies done on physical health problems include the use of psychotherapeutic techniques in the preparation of patients for surgery, in the relief of a number of psychosomatic conditions, and in the treatment of certain chronic diseases. Also there is convincing evidence of decreases in medical overutilization for patients who receive short-term psychotherapy.

Although there no longer is doubt that psychotherapy can yield noxious (as well as positive) effects, there has been little empirical work done on this important topic, which would seem especially ripe for investigation as issues of accountability become more prominent. Until reliable and tested methods for detecting negative effects become available, therapists would be well advised to attempt the development of some clinical indices for determining the existence of such effects in their ongoing work.

Finally, process research in psychotherapy seems to be undergoing a kind of revival in recent years. Current efforts are mainly centered on the nature and quality of the relationship between patient and therapist and its influence on outcome. Work on the "therapeutic alliance" is a major current concern of researchers that has clear and pragmatic implications for the practicing therapist.

REFERENCES

Aiken, L. H., & Henrichs, T. F. Systematic relaxation as a nursing intervention technique with open-heart surgery patients. *Nursing Research,* 1971, *20,* 212–217.

Barlow, D. H. On the relation of clinical research to clinical practice: Current issues, new directions. *Journal of Consulting and Clinical Psychology,* 1981, *49,* 147–155.

Battle, C. C., Imber, S. D., Hoehn-Saric, R., Stone, A. R., Nash, E. R., & Frank, J. D. Target complaints as criteria of improvement. *American Journal of Psychotherapy,* 1966, *20,* 184–192.

Bergin, A. E. Some implications of psychotherapy for therapeutic practice. *Journal of Abnormal Psychology,* 1966, *71,* 235–246.

Bergin, A. E. The evaluation of therapeutic outcomes. In A. E. Bergin & S. L. Garfield (Eds.), *Handbook of psychotherapy and behavior change.* New York: John Wiley & Sons, 1971.

Bergin, A. E., & Lambert, M. J. The evaluation of therapeutic outcomes. In S. L. Garfield & A. E. Bergin (Eds.), *Handbook of psychotherapy and behavior change: An empirical analysis.* New York: John Wiley & Sons, 1978.

Cousins, N. *Anatomy of an illness as perceived by the patient: Reflections on healing and regeneration.* New York: W. W. Norton, 1979.

Cummings, N. A., & Follette, W. T. Brief psychotherapy and medical utilization in a prepaid health plan setting: Part II. *Medical Care,* 1968, *6,* 31–41.

Egbert, L. D., Battit, G. E., Welch, C. E., & Bartlett, M. K. Reduction of post-operative pain by encouragement and instruction of patients: A study of doctor-patient rapport. *New England Journal of Medicine,* 1964, *270,* 825–827.

Engel, G. L. The need for a new medical model: A challenge for biomedicine. *Science,* 1977, *196,* 129–136.

Eysenck, H. The effects of psychotherapy: An evaluation. *Journal of Consulting Psychology,* 1952, *16,* 319–324.

Eysenck, H. The effects of psychotherapy. In H. Eysenck (Ed.), *The handbook of abnormal psychology*. New York: Basic Books, 1960.

Eysenck, H. The effects of psychotherapy. *International Journal of Psychiatry*, 1965, *1*, 97–178.

Ferguson, J. M., & Taylor, C. B. (Eds.). *Comprehensive handbook of behavioral medicine* (Vols. 1–3). New York: SP Medical and Scientific Books, 1980.

Follette, W. T., & Cummings, N. A. Psychiatric services and medical utilization in a pre-paid health plan setting: Part I. *Medical Care*, 1967, *5*, 25–35.

Frank, J. D. *Persuasion and healing*. Baltimore: Johns Hopkins University Press, 1961.

Frank, J. D. Psychotherapy of bodily disease: An overview. *Psychotherapy and psychosomatics*, 1975, *26*, 192–202.

Frank, J. D. Psychotherapy and the sense of mastery. In R. L. Spitzer & D. L. Klein (Eds.), *Evaluation of Psychotherapies: Behavioral therapies, drug therapies, and their interactions*. Baltimore: Johns Hopkins University Press, 1976.

Frank, J. D. The present status of outcome studies. *Journal of Consulting and Clinical Psychology*, 1979, *47*(2), 310–316.

Frank, J. D., Hoehn-Saric, R., Imber, S. D., Liberman, B. L., & Stone, A. R. (Eds.). *Effective ingredients of successful psychotherapy*. New York: Brunner/Mazel, 1978.

Goldberg, I. D., Krantz, G., & Locke, B. Z. Effects of a short-term outpatient psychiatric-therapy benefit on the utilization of medical services in a pre-paid group-practice medical program. *Medical Care*, 1970, *8*, 419–428.

Goldfried, M. Some views on effective principles of psychotherapy. *Cognitive Therapy and Research*, 1980, *4*(3), 271–306. (a)

Goldfried, M. Toward the delineation of therapeutic change principles. *American Psychologist*, 1980, *35*(11), 991–999. (b)

Goldfried, M. Personal communication, April 12, 1981.

Goldstein, A. P., Lopez, M., & Greenleaf, D. O. Introduction. In A. P. Goldstein & F. H. Kanfer (Eds.), *Maximizing treatment gains: Transfer enhancement in psychotherapy*. New York: Academic Press, 1979.

Gomes-Schwartz, B. Effective ingredients in psychotherapy: Prediction of outcome from process variables. *Journal of Consulting and Clinical Psychology*, 1978, *46*, 1023–1035.

Hadley, S. W., & Strupp, H. H. Contemporary views of negative effects in psychotherapy: An integrated account. *Archives of General Psychiatry*, 1976, *33*, 1291–1302.

Herink, R. (Ed.). *The psychotherapy handbook: The A to Z guide to more than 250 different therapies in use today*. New York: Meridan, 1980.

Hollon, S., & Beck, A. T. Psychotherapy and drug therapy: Comparisons and combinations. In S. L. Garfield & A. E. Bergin (Eds.), *Handbook of psychotherapy and behavior change: An empirical analysis* (2nd Ed.). New York: John Wiley & Sons, 1978.

Imber, S. D. Some research issues in psychotherapy. In J. D. Frank, R. Hoehn-Saric, S. D. Imber, B. L. Liberman, & A. R. Stone (Eds.), *Effective ingredients of successful psychotherapy*. New York: Brunner/Mazel, 1978.

Imber, S. D., Pilkonis, P. A., Harway, N. I., Klein, R. H., & Rubinsky, P. A. Maintenance of change in the psychotherapies. *Journal of Psychiatric Treatment and Evaluation*, 1982, *4*, 1–5.

Janis, I. L. *Psychological stress: Psychoanalytic and behavioral studies of surgical patients.* New York: John Wiley & Sons, 1958.

Kanfer, F. H. The maintenance of behavior by self-generated stimuli and reinforcement. In A. Jacobs & L. B. Sachs (Eds.), *The psychology of private events.* New York: Academic Press, 1971.

Kanfer, F. H. The many faces of self-control, or behavior modification changes its focus. In R. B. Stuart (Ed.), *Behavioral self-management.* New York: Brunner/Mazel, 1977.

Kazdin, A. E. Nonspecific treatment factors in psychotherapy outcome research. *Journal of Consulting and Clinical Psychology,* 1979, *47,* 846–851.

Kazdin, A. E. Drawing valid inferences from case studies. *Journal of Consulting and Clinical Psychology,* 1981, *49,* 183–192.

Kellner, R. Psychotherapy in psychosomatic disorders: A survey of controlled studies. *Archives of General Psychiatry,* 1975, *32,* 1021–1028.

Kiersuk, T. J., & Sherman, R. E. Goal-attainment scaling: A general method for evaluating comprehensive community mental health programs. *Community Mental Health Journal,* 1968, *4,* 443–453.

Kiesler, C. A. Mental health policy as a field of inquiry for psychology. *American Psychologist,* 1980, *35,* 1066–1080.

Lambert, M. J. *The effects of psychotherapy.* St. Albans, Vt.: Eden Press, 1979.

Lambert, M. J., Bergin, A. E., & Collins, J. L. Therapist-induced deterioration in psychotherapy. In A. S. Gurman & A. M. Razin (Eds.), *Effective psychotherapy: A handbook of research.* New York: Pergamon Press, 1977.

Lazarus, H. R., & Hagens, J. H. Prevention of psychosis following open-heart surgery. *American Journal of Psychiatry,* 1968, *124,* 1190–1195.

Liberman, B. L. The maintenance and persistence of change: Long-term follow-up investigations of psychotherapy. In J. D. Frank, R. Hoehn-Saric, S. D. Imber, B. L. Liberman, & A. R. Stone (Eds.), *Effective ingredients of successful psychotherapy.* New York: Brunner & Mazel, 1978.

Lieberman, M. A., Yalom, I. D., & Miles, M. B. *Encounter groups: First facts.* New York: Basic Books, 1973.

Luborsky, L. Helping alliances in psychotherapy. In J. L. Claghorn (Ed.), *Successful psychotherapy.* New York: Brunner/Mazel, 1976.

Luborsky, L., Mintz, J., Auerbach, A., Christoph, P., Bachrach, H., Todd, T., Johnson, M., Cohen, M., & O'Brien, C. P. Predicting the outcome of psychotherapy: Findings of the Penn psychotherapy project. *Archives of General Psychiatry,* 1980, *37,* 471–481.

Luborsky, L., Singer, B., & Luborsky, L. Comparative studies of psychotherapies: Is it true that "everybody has won and all must have prizes"? *Archives of General Psychiatry,* 1975, *32,* 995–1008.

Marholin, D., & Touchette, P. E. The role of stimulus control and response consequences. In A. P. Goldstein & F. H. Kanfer (Eds.), *Maximizing treatment gains: Transfer enhancement in psychotherapy.* New York: Academic Press, 1979.

Marziali, E., Marmar, C., & Krupnick, J. Therapeutic alliance scales: Development and relationship to psychotherapy outcome. *American Journal of Psychiatry,* 1981, *138,* 361–364.

Mash, E. J., & Terdal, L. G. After the dance is over: Some issues and suggestions for follow-up assessment in behavior therapy. *Psychological Reports*, 1977, *41*, 1287–1308.

Mechanic, D. Illness behavior, social adaptation, and the management of illness: A comparison of educational and medical models. *Journal of Nervous and Mental Disease*, 1977, *165*, 79–87.

Meltzoff, J., & Kornreich, M. *Research in psychotherapy.* New York: Atherton, 1970.

Messer, S. B., & Winokur, M. Some limits to the integration of psychoanalytic and behavior therapy. *American Psychologist*, 1980, *35*(9), 818–827.

Mintz, J. Measuring outcome in psychodynamic psychotherapy. *Archives of General Psychiatry*, 1981, *38*, 503–506.

Olbrisch, M. E. Psychotherapeutic interventions in physical health: Effectiveness and economic efficiency. *American Psychologist*, 1977, *32*, 761–777.

Parloff, M. B. Can psychotherapy research guide the policymaker? *American Psychologist*, 1979, *34*(4), 296–306.

Parloff, M. B. Psychotherapy and research: An anaclitic depression. *Psychiatry*, 1980, *43*, 279–293.

Perloff, E., & Perloff, R. Selected processes for evaluating service delivery programs: Overview. *Professional Psychology*, 1977, *8*, 389.

Ramsay, R. A., Wittkower, E. D., & Warnes, H. Treatment of psychosomatic disorders. In B. B. Wolman (Ed.), *The therapist's handbook: Treatment of mental disorders.* New York: Van Nostrand Reinhold, 1976.

Relinger, H., Bornstein, P. H., Bugge, I. D., Carmody, T. P., & Zohn, C. J. Utilization of adverse rapid smoking in groups: Efficacy of treatment and maintenance procedures. *Journal of Consulting and Clinical Psychology*, 1977, *45*, 245–249.

Rosenzweig, S. Some implicit common factors in diverse methods of psychotherapy. *American Journal of Orthopsychiatry*, 1936, *6*, 412–415.

Ryle, A. A common language for the psychotherapies? *British Journal of Psychiatry*, 1978, *132*, 589–594.

Schulz, R. Effects of control and predictability on the physical and psychological well being of the institutionalized aged. *Journal of Personality and Social Psychology*, 1976, *33*, 563–573.

Seligman, M. E. P. *Helplessness: On depression, development, and death.* San Francisco: W. H. Freeman, 1975.

Simonton, O. C., Matthews-Simonton, S., & Creighton, J. *Getting well again.* New York: J. P. Tarcher, 1978.

Sloane, R. B., Staples, F. R., Cristol, A. H., Yorkston, N. J., & Whipple, K. *Psychotherapy versus behavior therapy.* Cambridge, Mass.: Harvard University Press, 1975.

Smith, M. L., Glass, G. V., & Miller, T. I. *The benefits of psychotherapy.* Baltimore: Johns Hopkins University Press, 1980.

Stokes, T. E., & Baer, D. M. An implicit technology of generalization. *Journal of Applied Behavior Analysis*, 1977, *10*, 349–367.

Strupp, H. H. Success and failure in time-limited psychotherapy: A systematic comparison of two cases: Comparison 1. *Archives of General Psychiatry*, 1980, *37*, 595–603. (a)

Strupp, H. H. Success and failure in time-limited psychotherapy: A systematic comparison of two cases: Comparison 2. *Archives of General Psychiatry*, 1980, *37*, 708–716. (b)

Strupp, H. H. Success and failure in time-limited psychotherapy: With special reference to the performance of a lay counselor: *Archives of General Psychiatry,* 1980, *37,* 831–841. (c)

Strupp, H. H. Success and failure in time-limited psychotherapy: Further evidence: Comparison 4. *Archives of General Psychiatry,* 1980, *37,* 947–954. (d)

Strupp, H. H., & Hadley, S. W. A tripartite model of mental health and therapeutic outcomes with special reference to negative effects in psychotherapy. *American Psychologist,* 1977, *32,* 187–196.

Strupp, H. H., & Hadley, S. W. Specific vs. nonspecific factors in psychotherapy: A controlled study of outcome. *Archives of General Psychiatry,* 1979, *36,* 1125–1136.

VandenBos, G. R. (Ed.). *Psychotherapy: Practice, research, policy.* Beverly Hills, Calif.: Sage Publications, 1980.

Wachtel, P. L. *Psychoanalysis and behavior therapy.* New York: Basic Books, 1977.

Waskow, I. E., & Parloff, M. B. (Eds.). *Psychotherapy change measures.* DHEW Publication No. (ADM) 74–120, 1975.

Weed, L. I. Medical records that guide and teach. *New England Journal of Medicine,* 1968, *278,* 593–657.

Weissman, M. M. The psychological treatment of depression: Evidence for the efficacy of psychotherapy alone, in comparison with, and in combination with pharmacotherapy. *Archives of General Psychiatry,* 1979, *36,* 1261–1269.

Yates, B. T., & Newman, F. L. Approaches to cost-effectiveness analysis and cost-benefit analysis of psychotherapy. In G. R. VandenBos (Ed.), *Psychotherapy: Practice, research, policy.* Beverly Hills, Calif.: Sage Publications, 1980. (a)

Yates, B. T., & Newman, F. L. The efficacy and cost-effectiveness of psychotherapy. *The implications of cost-effectiveness analysis of medical technology* (Background Paper #3, Office of Technology Assessment). Washington, D.C.: U.S. Government Printing Office, 1980. (b)

Yates, B. T., & Newman, F. L. Findings of cost-effectiveness and cost-benefit analyses of psychotherapy. In G. R. VandenBos (Ed.), *Psychotherapy: Practice, research, policy.* Beverly Hills, Calif.: Sage Publications, 1980. (c)

9

Principles common to all psychotherapies*

Sheldon J. Korchin†
and
Susan H. Sands†

Barely a century ago, psychotherapy emerged in the western world as an organized and rational effort to relieve psychological suffering. Its roots, however, lie deep in human history. Even today, it has been argued persuasively (e.g., Frank, 1973; Torrey, 1972a, 1972b), that the essential ingredients of all approaches to psychological healing have much in common, whether practiced by faith healers, or by the shamans and witchdoctors of primitive societies, or by professional psychotherapists. For that matter, the same processes are to be found in the naturally occurring support networks which have always existed among ordinary people, as well as in the many forms of self-help and support systems that have been consciously developed in recent years. In this chapter, we will consider some of the processes intrinsic to all psychotherapies, despite their manifest differences. Recognition of such common properties has grown apace with a decided movement toward rapprochement among contending theories and methods of psychotherapy (e.g., Goldfried, 1980, 1982; Marmor & Woods, 1980; Wachtel, 1977).

Psychotherapy of one or another sort has become the treatment of choice—for some a panacea—for problems ranging from the traditionally psychiatric to a wide variety of problems of living, some of which have been suffered in silence in earlier times or brought only to the attention of family, community, or priest. With few exceptions, those seeking psychotherapeutic help are deeply troubled by anxieties, depression, self-doubts, and other negative affects; they are discontented with their lot

* An earlier version of this chapter was presented by the senior author at the First European Conference on Psychotherapy Research, University of Trier (West Germany), on September 18, 1981.
† University of California, Berkeley.

and feel helpless to change it; overall, in Frank's (1973) term, they are *demoralized.* This seems to be virtually as true for those seeking self-improvement and growth as for those electing psychological treatment.

The number of distinguishable psychotherapies has grown at a remarkable rate. Recently, Herink (1980) estimates that one can choose from at least 250 different psychotherapies. Each of these is endorsed enthusiastically by at least its founder, a loyal band of acolytes, and a number of satisfied customers, all of whom are prepared to argue stoutly the virtues of their system over all contenders (although often enough there is little evidence to support their contentions). Parloff (1968) also notes:

> No form of therapy has ever been initiated without a claim that it had unique therapeutic advantages. And no form of therapy has ever been abandoned because of its failure to live up to these claims. (p. 493)

That each of the many competing psychological treatments operates in different ways and is differentially effective is, on the face of it, highly improbable. Rosenzweig (1936) was perhaps the first to express the suspicion that all therapeutic systems might relieve psychological suffering precisely because of factors they share in common, rather than because of those features which distinguish them. In particular, he pointed to three factors, which have reemerged in varying forms in later analyses: (1) the therapist's personality which, if stimulating and inspiring, could itself catalyze change, (2) the value of interpretations which, if not literally true, might still produce change by giving the patient plausible alternate views of his dilemmas, and (3) the fact that personality is so multifaceted and complex that change in any area, instigated by any particular therapeutic approach, might ramify out into other areas of functioning.

In more recent years, a growing and increasingly more sophisticated body of empirical reasearch on psychotherapy outcome solidly supports the premise that no one form of psychological treatment is uniformly more effective than any other (Frank, 1979; Meltzoff & Kornreich, 1970; Luborsky, Singer, & Luborsky, 1975; Bergin & Lambert, 1978; Sloane, Staples, Cristol, Yorkstron, & Whipple, 1975). Surely, a particular approach may be better for one or another sort of patient, when used by one or another sort of therapist, under particular conditions, and the like; but careful analyses of the overall effects of different therapeutic systems leads to the conclusion, as in *Alice in Wonderland,* that "All have won and all must have prizes" (Luborsky et al., 1975). At the same time, this fact in no way supports the conclusion, argued on much less sufficient data, that psychotherapy is no better than no therapy at all (e.g. Eysenck, 1966). Instead, a careful meta-analysis of numerous outcome studies of many forms of therapy shows that the average person who has undertaken psychotherapy is better off than 75 percent of those who had no treatment (Smith & Glass, 1977; Smith, Glass, & Miller, 1980). However, recognizing that all therapies help and that none are demonstrably superior should spur the search for those ingredients that they have in common which might account for their therapeutic value. Greater knowledge of such common principles might allow us to use them more systematically in practice and training, thus contributing to an overall improvement of psychotherapeutic methods and hence to greater human well-being.

Much of the clinical and research literature on psychotherapy has focused on detailed analyses of different techniques or on the differential effectiveness of their outcomes. Attention has centered, in both cases, on those qualities which distinguish one therapy from another. This in understandable, for as Frank (1971) observed: "Features which all therapies share have been relatively neglected, since little glory derives from showing that the particular method which one has mastered with so much effort may be indistinguishable from other methods in its effects" (p. 350). However, if we can isolate and understand those features which are common, then we should be in better position to discover the differential effects of particular techniques for the particular problems of different patients.

The need to improve all forms of psychological intervention is made more urgent by the social realities of these times. There are great unmet mental health needs, and we are being challenged by society, as well as by our professional consciences, to make our methods more effective (Kiesler, 1980; Parloff, 1979; Strupp, 1978). Over 20 years ago, Albee (1959) warned that there were not enough trained professionals to treat all of the people needing mental health care, and that with the predicatable increase in the number of potential patients compared to the rates at which professional were being trained, the gap was bound to widen. Kiesler's (1980) recent analysis of the relation between need and helping resources shows that, by the most optimistic estimate of need, there are only 3 hours of professional time for each person needing help; with more pessimistic estimates, this ranges downward to 40 minutes per person per year! This has obvious policy implications, Kiesler notes. He argues for greater attention to prevention, greater utilization of paraprofessionals, indigenous support systems, self-help, more mental health training for related professionals, as well as increasing the number of trained mental health professionals. But these same data also argue persuasively for sharpening therapeutic techniques.

Pressure toward this same end results from increased insistence on accountability and cost-effectiveness. Particularly as government and insurance companies are becoming increasingly involved in making third-party payments for psychotherapy, they want assurance that their money is being spent wisely on treatments that maximize effectiveness while minimizing cost (Parloff, 1979). Psychotherapy is no longer simply a voluntary contract between a patient and a therapist. Third-party agencies, paying the bills for greater numbers of people each year, can have great impact on the future direction of the field, for good or for bad.

WHAT IS PSYCHOTHERAPY?

Anna O.—whose treatment launched psychoanalysis—called it "the talking cure" (Breuer & Freud, 1895), which may well be the briefest and hardly the least satisfying definition on record. Surely, cure is not always the result, and often things other than talking go on; but Anna captured what most people have in mind when they visualize psychotherapy.

> At its core is a unique relationship between the clinician and the patient within which there is communication which can relieve distress and set conditions for relearning and personal growth. More broadly, and closer to the literal meaning of "psychological treatment," psychotherapy describes any intentional application of psychological techniques by a clinician to the end of effecting sought-after personality or behavioral changes. (Korchin, 1976, p. 281).

Psychotherapies can be described and distinguished in numerous ways, in terms of their goals, procedures, practitioners, formal arrangement, and above all, the guiding theory as to the nature of human functioning and malfunctioning and the conditions for producing change. Systems of therapy can be grouped as psychodynamic, behavioral, or humanistic-existential, but these are overly broad groupings resulting in some strange bedfellows. Therapies have been distinguished as explorative versus supportive, insight-oriented versus action, long-term versus short-term, or in terms of such diverse goals as effecting personality reorganization through gaining insight into core unconscious conflicts, changing behaviors through systematic learning procedures, facilitating personal growth through encounter, correcting erroneous cognitions of the self and world, and relieving tension through emotional release, among others; but as we will see shortly, in some respects, all of these processes occur in all therapies. In the final analysis, as Reisman (1971) notes, the essential definition of psychotherapy must rest not on what therapists *intend* nor on what they *accomplish* but on what they *do*, which most centrally includes " . . . the communication of person-related understanding, respect, and a wish to be of help" (p. 66).

ESSENTIAL INGREDIENTS OF PSYCHOTHERAPY

In looking more closely at the elements common to all or most forms of psychological intervention which might account for their therapeutic effectiveness, two broad classes of factors are distinguishable. Most basic are those that define what might be called a *therapeutic climate* (a set of basal conditions which in and of themselves may produce change) but, in any case, provide the foundation from which more specific *therapeutic processes* (strategies or events) can have their effects. The therapeutic climate is the product of qualities of the patient (motivation, expectations, faith), of the therapist (status, warmth, respect), of the relationship between them (compatibility, alliance, etc.), and of the larger culture which they share. With these as background, we can look at processes that occur, in greater or lesser degree, in all therapies. Such therapeutic processes (or "common therapeutic strategies," in Goldfried's (1980) phrase) include learning (whether in cognitive, emotional, or operant terms), emotional arousal, self-exploration and understanding, feedback and reality-testing, and practice and mastery. In this analysis, we will draw heavily on the thinking of Frank (1971, 1973, 1974, 1979, 1981), Frank et al. (1978), Garfield (1980), Goldfried and Padawer (1982), Marmor (1976), Marmor and Woods (1980), Rosenzweig (1936), and Strupp (1973, 1976), who have all explored the possibility that the curative effects of psychotherapy might rest more on features they share than on those that distinguish them.

The therapeutic climate

Cultural beliefs.   The very existence of psychotherapy in our society rests on the widely shared belief in the modifiability of human nature and behavior through human actions. Laity and professionals alike see behavior as determined by earlier experiences and alterable by new experiences. Change is viewed both as possible and desirable. By contrast, a society that conceives human actions as dependent on predestination, divine will, or a vagrant fate could hardly conceive psychotherapy as we know it, although psychological healing might still go on through incantation and magic.

Coupled to the belief in modifiability is faith in knowledge and technical expertness. As there are people who know more than we do and can be trusted to repair our cars, fix the TV, or heal our bodies, so there are those who are expert in the workings of the mind to whom we can take our emotional problems. They have trained expertness, witnessed by diplomas and professional credentials, and their procedures, even if they seem arcane, can be expected to be of help. As society becomes more technologically and socially complex, and as people more readily accept the premise of psychological determinism, greater numbers are turning to psychotherapists for aid with human problems they see as psychological in nature and amenable to professional change efforts. Indeed, in the minds of some social critics (e.g. Gross, 1979; Lasch,

1979), the process is running out-of-hand, as psychological healers are taking over greater responsibility for spiritual, moral, and social problems formerly outside of their ken. As traditional sources of social support, guidance, and morality have weakened, psychotherapy has filled the void.

Not only does psychotherapy rest on supportive cultural beliefs, but the particular forms it takes reflect changes in cultural values in different eras (Frank, 1971). Freud's therapy, consistent with the values of his day, was a highly private and professional interaction that took place in a parent/child-type relation; his concepts of psychological development and pathology as well as of therapeutic change also derived from the family dynamics of his time. Patients could discover and work through unacceptable impulses toward powerful parental figures under the guidance of a more benevolent—if still somewhat distant—father. In contrast, current therapies, including psychoanalysis, reflect the more open, less-inhibited, and more egalitarian culture of present-day America. Today, the therapeutic encounter is likely to be more of an interaction between peers, with much of the therapeutic dialogue focusing on problems of work, social relations, and personal values, as well as unresolved familial conflicts. An increasing number of people are being treated in groups or even in public, outside of the sacred privacy of the consultation room. Individual therapies have been supplanted by group therapies, therapies with nuclear families or even with their entire social network, and at the extreme there are EST seminars with several hundred people in attendance. But—now as then—the entire enterprise of psychotherapy rests on the underlying faith in human modifiability through expert intervention.

The patient's faith, expectations, and motivation for change. Patients predicatably approach psychotherapy both frightened and hopeful. They know time and money are involved, and there are likely to be painful revelations. Even among the sophisticated, some stigma may be attached to going to a "shrink," who may indeed find them even sicker than they feared. To others and themselves, seeking therapy is a painful admission that they have not been able to manage their own lives.

Still, patients entering therapy are filled with hope. In the first instance, seeking help is a postive act, for it reveals conscious recognition that there is a psychological problem with which they cannot cope unaided. No longer denying life realities, they have made a decisive step out of demoralization toward psychological health.

Moreover, prospective patients are seeking the help of a psychological expert. Others may have offered sympathy, advice, encouragement, urged or threatened them to get hold of themselves, but this person will understand and respect their pain and undo their problems, although patients are not sure exactly how. Patients entering therapy have faith in the therapist's scientific knowledge and technical skills and may indeed invest the therapist with undeserved power and magic. But they know they can confide in this authority and their confidences will be treated with respect. They can reveal weaknesses and share ugly needs and wishes, without risking condemnation and rejection. Although told that they must work hard in the collaborative venture of therapy, and that much of the outcome will depend on their own sincerity and effort, still patients can readily believe that it is the therapist's actions—rather than their own—which really count. Many patients start with the assumption, rarely consciously encouraged by the therapist, that if only they do what is expected of them, they will quickly improve. In fact, many do. It is a commonplace observation, supported by empirical research (e.g., Friedman, 1963), that there is often a great sense of relief and some functional improvement early in psychotherapy.

Many students of psychotherapy have viewed the patient's faith and trust in the therapist as a major, if not primary, determinant of therapeutic change. Because of this belief in the therapist, patients develop and sustain hope and an expectancy that they will be benefited by the treatment. This is a common denominator of all or most forms of psychological healing, including faith healing and shamanism, as well as professional psychotherapy (Frank, 1973).

Faith is important in different ways at different points in therapy. At the outset, patients would not enter therapy without belief in its curative powers nor, once in, would they continue. But even if they start enthusiastically, patients are typically unprepared for the plodding session-to-session work of therapy, which requires them to confront old anxieties and substitute new behaviors for accustomed (hence safe, even if inadequate) ones. In part, patients' motivation is sustained by their need to please the therapist; but as time goes by, it is no longer based on blind faith, but increasingly on evidences of understanding and respect communicated in earlier encounters. To the extent that patients feel therapists are making efforts to understand them, value them personally, and sincerely trying to help, they in turn are sustained in their faith in the process, despite the effort, pain, and—at times—simple boredom involved. Motivation is thus maintained by the evolving therapeutic relation, though anchored originally in a vague "expectancy of benefit."

Concern with expectancy effects in psychotherapy is related to a long-standing interest in placebo effects in medicine. It is well established that response to a drug may depend on belief in the drug's action, faith in the physician, and other psychological effects unrelated to the specific physiological drug effects. In medical research, to distinguish nonspecific and attitudinal effects from specific drug effects, a placebo control is used. A *placebo* is an inert substance which resembles the drug in appearance, color, and taste and which is given in exactly the same way as the experimental drug. Patients given placebos under these conditions have shown considerable amelioration of their physical symptoms. Indeed, it has been argued by some that many of the substances used by physicians have had positive effects mainly because of the faith invested in them by physicians and by their patients, rather than because of any intrinsic physiological actions. "The history of medical treatment until relatively recently is the history of the placebo effect" (Shapiro, 1959, p. 303).

The considerable literature on placebo and expectancy effects in psychotherapy has been well surveyed in recent years (Frank, 1973; Goldstein, 1962, 1981; Shapiro & Morris, 1978; Wilkins, 1973). There seems hardly any doubt that generalized expectancy effects can profoundly influence patients to stay in and gain from psychotherapy (Goldstein, 1981). However, a closer look at this literature suggests greater complexities. For one thing, patients hold expectancies of different sorts. There are expectancies related to desired outcomes, which we have just been discussing, but also expectancies as to what is necessary to reach these goals, what the therapist is and does, and what behaviors are required of the patient. These have been distinguished as *prognostic expectancies* and *role expectancies* by Goldstein (1981). Early literature suggested that, where role expectancies of therapist and patient converged, therapy went smoother and led to better outcome than when they differed; but more recent research shows more-equivocal results (Garfield, 1978). Moreover, the empirical study of expectancy effects has been beset by methodological problems (Garfield, 1978; Wilkins, 1973). It is beyond the scope of this chapter to consider these issues or the particular ways in which the interaction of patient and therapist role expectancies affect the course of psychotherapy. It seems fair, however, to conclude that where prognostic expectancies are positive, where the patient and therapist enter therapy hopeful of a successful outcome, it is, in fact, more likely to occur.

Qualities of the therapist. Regardless of differences in training, orientation, and therapeutic method, all therapists have qualities in common which contribute to the therapeutic climate. These include their status as sanctioned healers, their adherence to a therapeutic rationale or theory, and personality qualities (as well as role behaviors), all of which encourage the patient's faith and provide a power base for further and more particular therapeutic interventions.

Status. Psychotherapists are respected members of learned professions and share with their colleagues the public's admiration of the knowledgeable and skilled expert. Perhaps, as some have argued, it is essentially their personalities and human-relations skills which make therapists effective; but higher degrees, licenses, and diplomas visibly evident (perhaps along with Freud's portrait) on the consulting room wall cannot fail to impress and influence clients. For example, studies show that there is greater client-attitude change (Bergin, 1962) and more acceptance of therapeutic interpretations (Browning, 1966) with "high-prestige" therapists than with "low-prestige" therapists. So too, the therapeutic setting (particularly if in a majestic clinical center) further adds to belief in the power of therapy. Patients respond therapeutically, someone once quipped, because of an "edifice complex." The more prestigious the setting, the more the therapist can be seen as competent to help with one's problems. Thus, in our own clinic at the University of California at Berkeley, home of many Nobel laureates (mainly in the physical sciences, of course), the status of the institution rubs off on psychological interns in training, who have yet to prove their personal competence.

Theoretical framework.   Every therapist operates within a theoretical system. Although widely differing from one another, such systems provide a rationale for the patient's troubles, goals which might be attained, and a set of technical operations for reaching them. Whether in some ultimate sense correct or not, the theoretical system makes the actions of both therapist and patient meaningful. Thus, Frank (1971) tells of the young therapist who said: "Even if it doesn't help the patient, it's good to know that I'm doing the right thing." In Strupp and Hadley's (1979) study, which contrasted professional therapists with kindly professors who met with comparable distressed student-patients, there was little difference in the degree to which they helped their "clients;" but it is notable that the professors (unlike the therapists) confessed to greater uncertainty and more often ran out of things to say! From the patient's vantage, the shared system reduces the mystery and anxiety of having a frighteningly unknown problem and no knowledge of how to change it. Simply naming a problem is a step toward mastering it; Torrey (1972a) describes this as the "Principle of Rumplestiltskin." We are not arguing, of course, that any concept or technique, in principle or in fact, is as good as any other, but rather that, regardless of their nature, these "myths and rituals" (Frank, 1981) serve therapeutic ends by providing comfort and meaning to both participants in the therapeutic encounter.

Personal qualities of the therapist.   For therapy to proceed, the therapist must be able to inspire trust and confidence, communicate respect while holding the patient's respect, provide a secure atmosphere within which the patient can do the work of therapy, and in other ways, gain the whole-hearted cooperation of the patient. The importance of the therapeutic relationship has been perhaps more emphasized by humanistic-existential psychotherapists than by dynamic or behavioral therapists; but therapists of all persuasions note the fundamental importance of a good therapeutic relationship, some seeing it as the essential base for therapeutic change, while others view it as the necessary pre-condition for further therapeutic interventions (Brady, Davison, Dewald, Egan, Fadiman, Frank, Gill, Hoffman, Kemple, Lazarus, Raimy, Rotter & Strupp, 1980). A survey of psychotherapists of a number of distinct schools showed that they differed widely in expressing their views on many aspects of the therapy process but hardly at all when responding to items describing the necessary patient-therapist relationship (Larson, 1980).

However, Rogers (1957), in his famous paper, went beyond general agreement on the importance of relationship to assert that there were six conditions which were "necessary and sufficient" for "constructive personality change." The first three of these were attitudinal characteristics of the therapist—genuineness, unconditional positive regard, and empathy—and the fourth condition required that the patient perceive these qualities. The remaining two conditions stated that the therapist and client must be in psychological contact and that the client must be in a state of incongruence (being vulnerable and anxious). These latter three principles are apparently so self-evident that they were dropped in later discussions of the necessary and sufficient conditions, while considerable interest focused on the three primary therapist qualities.

Genuineness, to Rogers (1957), meant that the therapist should be a "congruent, genuine, integrated person" who within the relationship "is freely and deeply himself" (p. 97). *Unconditional positive regard* for the client exists when "the therapist finds himself experiencing a warm acceptance of each aspect of the client's experience as being a part of that client" (p. 98). *Empathy* was defined in these terms: "the therapist is experiencing an accurate, empathic understanding of the client's awareness of his own experience. To sense the client's private world as if it were your own, but without ever losing the 'as if' quality . . . this is empathy . . ." (p. 98). Over the years, these three factors came to be more commonly described as genuineness, nonpossessive warmth, and accurate empathy.

Unless these factors are experienced by the client, therapy cannot take place. Nor, according to Rogers' hypothesis, are they limited to any particular type of therapist (school, experience, training, etc.) or any particular client or problem. By clear implication, Rogers dismissed the view that the techniques used by any therapy system had any specific value, except as they contributed to his hypothesized conditions. These and only these were not only necessary, but sufficient for therapeutic change. Indeed, he went a step further and stated: "If one or more of these conditions is not present, constructive change will not occur" (Rogers, 1957, p. 100). In this paper, Rogers courageously laid down a hypothesis of great specificity, which he hoped would challenge the field to do research testing this hypothesis, which might ultimately identify the critical elements in the therapy process.

A great deal of research followed, most of it undertaken, understandably, by workers of a client-centered therapy orientation. In reviewing the large literature which cumulated through 1970, Truax and Mitchell (1971) felt that there was solid support for the altered hypothesis that therapists who are genuine, accurately empathic, and warm, rather than just being perceived by their clients as having these qualities, do provide necessary and sufficient conditions for positive outcome, regardless of therapist orientation or patient problem. Indeed, they suggested further that low levels of these facilitative conditions might account for deterioration. Their view of the field has been challenged as being overly favorable to the Rogerian hypothesis by subsequent reviewers (cf. Parloff, Waskow, & Wolfe, 1978, for a fine analysis of the research literature, the views of other reviewers, and their own position). As in much therapy research, this field is beset with many methodological issues, which we cannot treat in this brief space.

By now, it seems clear enough that the precise hypothesis framed by Rogers in 1957 has not been supported by subsquent research (Parloff, Waskow, & Wolfe, 1978). But it is also clear that therapist warmth, genuineness, and empathy—whether rated by judges from therapist behaviors in therapy sessions or by clients themselves—do matter, even if they are not the "necessary and sufficient" conditions of therapeutic change that Rogers boldly claimed. Thus, Mitchell, Bozarth, and Krauft (1977) conclude: "The recent evidence, although equivocal, does seem to suggest that empathy, warmth, and genuineness are related in some way to client change but that their potency and generalizability are not as great as once thought" (p. 481).

What this sizeable body of research also reveals is that any simple hypothesis, however appealing and challenging, about particular factors in a particular realm—in this case, the empathy, warmth, and genuineness of the therapist—must necessarily be incomplete. Therapeutic gain must rest on a much more complex set of factors—including qualities of the culture, the patient, the therapist, their interaction, and particular facets of therapeutic strategies—which reflects principles common to all therapies.

The therapeutic alliance

Central to psychotherapy, as already noted, is a particular relationship which gives patients sufficient security to reveal and work on their problems. It is marked by trust, mutual respect, and faith in the outcome. The patient is assured of privacy, confidentiality, and moral neutrality and convinced that the therapist—putting aside personal concerns—will work toward the singular goal of advancing the well-being, autonomy, and personality competence of the patient. Above all, therapists do not manipulate patients to serve their own needs (whether financial, sexual, ideological, or power-oriented).

Within this context, the essential task of the therapist is to listen with unswerving attention, sympathetic concern, and a continuous effort to understand the patient's personal meanings. Being able to listen without responding in terms of one's own needs and feelings or the demands

of social convention is, according to Fromm-Reichmann (1950), the fundamental requisite of effective psychotherapy. At appropriate points, the
therapist communicates understanding to the patient or otherwise acts
to relieve the patient's suffering. The clinician values the patient's integrity
and striving for self-betterment but does not fault the patient for his inadequacies. At the same time, the clinician maintains necessary objectivity
and detachment. The therapist is simultaneously compassionate and dis-
passionate (Korchin, 1976).

It is the blending of these characteristics which gives the psychotherapeutic relationship its special character as a setting within which emotional
learning can take place. Though in some regards similar, psychotherapy
differs importantly from other relationships. In some ways, it is like that
between any expert and client; in other respects, it more resembles the
interplay between friends and intimates. While like and unlike each, it
is ultimately distinctive.

Relatively early in the history of psychoanalysis, Freud (1910) called
attention to the particular importance of a "working alliance" between
patient and therapist. Although the development and analysis of transference was (and still is) seen by psychoanalysts as the cornerstone of therapeutic change, Freud (1910) early on distinguished transference from
the working alliance. More recently, this distinction has received increased
emphasis in the writings of psychoanalytic theorists (e.g., Greenson,
1967). The working alliance is based on the patient's realization that
the therapist is understanding him, well-disposed toward him, and working
on his behalf. Therefore, he can join the therapist in the discovery and
resolution of his problems. One way of viewing the situation is to conceive
of the patient as if he were two people. One is compulsively driven by
neurotic needs, distrustful of proferred help, demoralized, and self-defeat-
ing, quite unable to see problems with any detachment. But within the
same skin, as it were, is another person who knows himself to be in
pain, driven, and irrational and by that very token is rational. This person
has hope and a vision, however vague, of a better future. While the
irrational self might desire to stay that way, the rational health-seeking,
self-critical self strives for growth. This facet of the self allies with the
therapist in the common cause of therapeutic change (Greenson, 1967).

Ideally, the therapeutic alliance should be fully collaborative. But, as
Luborsky (1976) notes, two types of therapeutic alliances can be distinguished, the first a less-complete partnership than the second. Thus, his
type 1 alliance is "based on the patient's experiencing the therapist as
supportive and helpful with himself as the recipient" (p. 94). By contrast,
type 2 is a "therapeutic alliance based on a sense of working together
against what is impeding the patient. The emphasis here is on shared
responsibility for working out the treatment goals. When this is present,
the alliance qualities of the relationship are evident in a sense of 'we-
ness' " (p. 94). Therapy may start with type 1 and move toward type 2

in later phases. Luborsky (1977) hypothesized that people who improve in therapy are more likely to have type 2 than type 1 alliances, though obviously each should fare better than those incapable of forming any sort of therapeutic alliance. In fact, he found that those patients who improved most (compared to nonimprovers) were more likely to form positive relationships and to develop them earlier, although they were more usually of the type 1 than the type 2 sort.

The therapeutic climate: A brief overview

In this analysis of the elements common to all forms of psychological treatment, we have looked first at those which define what might be called the *therapeutic climate*. At the first level, there is the profound cultural belief in the modifiabilty of human nature and behavior through intentional interventions, shared by therapists and patients, without which psychotherapy could not exist. The effectiveness of therapy then rests on the patient's faith in the therapist and expectation of positive benefit which, in turn, reflect qualities of the therapist, his status, the explanatory value of his concepts, and, of greatest importance, aspects of his personality (such as empathy, warmth, and genuineness) which, if not the "necessary and sufficient" conditions once thought, are still powerful determinants of therapeutic change. Though patient and therapist qualities are discussed separately, of ultimate importance is the nature of the therapeutic relationship—particularly the therapeutic alliance reflecting the interaction of patient and therapist. Taken together, these aspects of the therapeutic climate may account, in fair part, for the power of psychotherapy to effect change, or at least, they give a substantial base for the operation of more specific therapeutic maneuvers.

Specific therapeutic processes

The line between what we have called therapeutic climate and the more specific therapeutic processes is necessarily arbitrary, for both sets of factors are found in most if not all therapeutic efforts. We believe, however, that the distinction is valuable for distinguishing those qualities which *inhere* in the person of the therapist and patient, the relationship and situation (climate) from those therapeutic events which *take place* during the course of therapy (processes). It can also be argued that the climatic dimensions are more *basic* in two senses: first, they empower, or provide the conditions for, the therapeutic events; second, therapeutic schools vary less along the climatic dimensions than along the process dimensions. Thus, while affective arousal may be a necessary part of all therapies, as we would hold, it is clearly more central to cathartic therapies than to, for example, behavioral or client-centered methods.

In the present section, we will consider briefly each of a number of processes which are important to all therapies, though to greater or lesser degree and whether intended or not by their proponents.

Suggestion and persuasion. Although suggestion played a central role in early therapies, the intentional use of direct suggestions has fallen from favor in modern psychotherapies. But, however nondirective therapists intend to be, they often communicate their desires to patients and, to some degree, coerce patients to act in ways they favor. Thus, when Klein and her colleagues (Klein, Dittman, Parloff, & Gill, 1969) observed Lazarus and Wolpe in the work of systematic desensitization, they were struck by the degree in which suggestion was taking place, although this was denied by Lazarus and Wolpe as reflecting either their concept of therapy or their actions with these specific patients.

Emotional arousal. Psychotherapy, whatever its form, is not a cold encounter. In our judgment, therapeutic change could not occur if it were. Expressing and ventilating feelings—whether related to outside persons or to the therapist—is central to many therapies, and conscious efforts are made to have the patient relive (rather than simple describe) important affective relationships. The long-term goal may be to reduce affect—particularly negative affects, such as anxiety, depression or anger—but the route toward its attainment necessarily involves the arousal of such affects in the process of therapy. Frank (1974) provides evidence from three studies showing that emotional arousal by inhalation of ether or adrenalin increases attitude change in response to therapists' suggestions.

Nonetheless, at the outset, it may be necessary to reduce affects to manageable levels, but this is done to make it possible for patients to confront them later on. Thus, the first stage of systematic desensitization involves progressive relaxation, intended to reduce the patient's general anxiety, but this technique is used so that the patient is in better position to approach and master specific phobic objects (e.g., Wolpe, 1973).

It is interesting to note a pendulum effect in conceptualization of the role of affect arousal over the years. In the earliest days of psychoanalysis, central importance was given to the necessity of the cathartic expression of repressed memories and their associated affects, but then emphasis shifted toward self-understanding and insight, rather than catharsis. Beginning in the 1960s, there was a renewed interest in catharsis, reflected not in psychoanalysis but in such diverse treatments as primal scream therapy, implosive therapy, and Gestalt therapy. Even more recently, there has been a shift to the other direction: cognitive-behavior therapies are now de-emphasizing the role of emotional arousal by asking patients to very rationally recognize and change their "maladaptive cognitions" (e.g., Beck, 1976). Perhaps these swings in therapy recapitulate the eternal opposition between the Apollonian and Dionysian in art and philosophy.

Learning and relearning.   All systems of psychotherapy, we have seen, rest on the fundmental assumption that human behavior can be changed. Personality and coping capacities, whether adaptive or maladaptive, are the residuals of a lifetime of learning. The attitudes, values, skills, habits, competencies, and inadequacies, as well as one's feelings toward the self, and ways of relating to others were learned in earlier interplay with others. As human problems develop through learning, so we believe that they can be undone through unlearning and relearning. That psychotherapy provides the conditions for such learning is the faith on which therapists operate; a faith which patients must share—along with discontent and a desire for change—if therapy is to proceed.

In this sense, psychotherapy can be essentially equated with learning; many psychologists, indeed, define psychotherapy as learning, albeit of a particular sort. However, equating psychotherapy and learning defines the field too broadly. Learning occurs in many forms, some (but not all) of which are exemplified in psychotherapy. There is little doubt, however, that a number of learning processes are involved in therapeutic change. Among these are the following:

Operant conditioning.   Direct use of operant principles is central to a number of forms of psychological intervention, including token economies and aversion therapies. In such cases, reinforcers (positive or negative) are given by the therapist as the patient acts (in wanted or unwanted ways) in order to shape the patient's future behavior. However, operant conditioning likely occurs in more subtle ways in all therapeutic encounters. Years ago, Greenspoon (1955) showed experimentally that saying "uh-huh" when a person brought up a particular topic in an interview led to increasing emphasis on that topic later on. Studying the transcript of one of Carl Rogers' therapy sessions, Truax (1966) found the same mechanism at work, even though unintended by Rogers. It seems likely therefore, that in all forms of therapy, subtle nonverbal actions as well as comments serve as reinforcers to guide the flow of therapeutic conversations, separate the important from the unimportant, and convey the therapist's approval or disapproval.

Cognitive learning.   Similarly, patients learn facts of potential importance to their adaptive efforts. Whether or not the therapist intends to teach, information is conveyed. Some things (such as the best route home) are trivial; other bits of information (such as the fact that the patient's problem is shared by many other people) can be of considerable consequence. Within the security of the therapeutic relation, the patient can raise questions, clarify beliefs, and gain knowledge around issues which cannot be discussed even with intimates. Most therapists do not see the information-giving role as central to their therapeutic efforts, and some avoid it as much as possible, yet all therapists instruct their patients to some degree.

The cognitions of the patient are the special focus of therapists of the cognitive-behavioral orientation (e.g., Beck, 1976; Meichenbaum, 1977). The patient's maladaptive cognitions are systematically isolated and explored, in the belief that these faulty cognitions are at the base of the patient's emotional problems. The patient is then encouraged to substitute more adaptive beliefs for the maladaptive ones.

Decision-making strategies.   Related is the fact that patients learn how to think about and solve problems in the course of therapy. Although therapists are reluctant to advise or suggest solutions, their responses to patients' concerns often encourage patients to consider alternate possible meanings, available choices, gains and losses of one or another course of action; in general, the processes of rational analysis and decision making. In good part, this is learned through the example of the therapist. Although the therapist intends only to guide the patient's problem-solving effort, at the same time, through the questions raised, a model of rational decision making is conveyed. Out of neurotic fears and compulsive drives, many patients act without first considering options and alternatives; in the therapeutic session, they can learn the advantages of vicarious trial and error.

Emotional learning.   What most clearly distinguishes psychotherapy from other forms of human encounter and learning situations, in the minds of most therapists, is that it provides a unique sort of emotional learning. The relearning that takes place in therapy is only in a limited sense intellectual, as when we acquire new knowledge in areas where we were formerly ignorant. For therapeutic change to occur, the process must also include new, personally meaningful and emotionally important experiencing in the therapy relationship itself. What Alexander and French (1946) once called "corrective emotional experiences" must take place. Patients have to reexperience emotions with which they have been unable to cope in the past. Coming to know one's problems better, including knowledge of their origin, is secondary. (We will have more to say about the role of insight in a later section.)

Therapeutic change occurs as the patient learns—through repetitive and controlled emotional experiences in therapy—how not to be afraid, rather than of what and why he is afraid. In behavior therapy, for example, a phobic person may literally be put into contact with the feared object, through moving in graded doses from fantasy visualization to actual confrontation, which allows him to discover that his fears are now groundless whatever their origin. Similarly, in dynamic psychotherapy, the neurotic is led to reexamine painful impulses, rigid defenses, and maladaptive behaviors. Doing so, the patient suffers the pain of self-confrontation, feeling again anxiety, guilt, and other negative effects, some now directed toward the therapist himself.

Identification and modeling. In therapy, as in life, change occurs through identification with more powerful and respected persons. At the first level, identification with the therapist can facilitate any of the learning processes we have been discussing by intensifying their emotional meaning. More directly, however, identification can lead to modeling on the therapist, (whether consciously or unconsciously), taking on values, behaviors, and attitudes of this stronger and more competent person. Modeling has been identified as a primary vehicle of change by some therapists (e.g., Bandura, 1977b). As a trivial (though not uncommon) example, some patients end a course of therapy wearing tweed jackets, smoking a pipe, and saying "Ah, so?" in a slightly Viennese accent. But those who have internalized ways of remaining calm amid angry emotions, ways of delaying implusive actions, and an ability to sort out confusing alternatives, have obviously gained something of real value.

Identification, we would guess, is more likely to occur with charismatic therapists. Most therapists do not encourage patients to mimic them; in principle, they wish to foster autonomy and the capacity of the patient to cope in his own way. Still, identificational learning occurs—often to the patient's advantage—which gives an additional reason why therapists should have their own emotional houses in order.

Self-exploration and understanding. Traditional psychoanalysis gave central importance to the attainment of insight. Early on, Freud believed that recapturing repressed memories and bringing them to the light of consciousness was the essence of the analytic cure. But it is by now widely recognized by psychoanalysts (as well as by therapists of other persuasions) that insight—in its narrow meaning—is insufficient (e.g., Levenson, 1972). Thus, psychoanalysts often distinguish between intellectual insight and emotional insight. The same distinction is implied in "I *know* there's nothing to be afraid of, but I'm still afraid." Therapeutic change occurs—we have already noted—as the patient learns how not to be afraid, rather than of what he is afraid and why; and this is gained through corrective emotional experiences in psychotherapy. This does not mean, however, that insight always precedes behavior change. Often change in how one *does* something sparks change in how one *thinks* about that something, the self, and others; or sometimes the two seem to arise simultaneously. Indeed, the change process can probably best be described as following a sort of zigzagging course between insight and behavior change.

Still, self-awareness and self-knowledge are important bases for self-regulation, mastery and more-effective functioning generally. While simply knowing is not sufficient, it is an important step toward therapeutic change. It is also true that the correctness of an interpretation aimed at explaining some facet of the patient's character or behavior may be less-critical than its plausibility—as was demonstrated in one experimental study by Mendel (1964)—for engendering a sense of understanding and therapeutic progress. Indeed, as mentioned earlier, the process of simply naming a problem can make it more understandable and manageable (the "Principle of Rumpelstiltskin"). This concept has been given central importance by Watzlawick (1974), among others. He uses the technique of "reframing" to help the patient see his seemingly insurmountable problems in a new, more hopeful light.

Feedback and reality-testing. In this quest for understanding, therapists of all schools help their patients become more aware of what they are doing, thinking, and feeling in various situations, although the particular techniques used may differ. Whether involving Rogerian reflection of feelings, or psychoanalytic interpretation, or role-playing, or whatever, the common process involved is that the therapist provides feedback which—in the context of the therapeutic climate—the patient is better able to accept. In fact, as Goldfried (1980) notes, behavior therapists using self-monitoring as an assessment device have noted that their clients changed merely as a result of observing their own behavior. And in studies of group therapy, feedback has emerged as one of the central therapeutic variables (Bednar and Kaul, 1978). In all these cases, the patient is seeing himself from as external perspective provided by the therapist, and self-knowledge increases.

Feedback is, of course, common to all social transactions; but in daily life, its impact is attenuated, because the source is either unimpressive or threatening, the information conveyed is only tangentially relevant, or defensive manuevers blunt its reception or acceptance. Acceptance is far more likely to occur in therapy where feedback comes in the context of help from a trusted expert. Under these circumstances, therapeutic feedback facilitates the patient's objectifying and examining his own acts and feelings, with the therapist serving not only as a guide but also as a secure base for reality testing. While ultimately it is a case of one opinion confronting another, the therapist's perception is (at least one hopes) less-clouded by neurotic needs and defenses, and his view of the patient more closely approximates "reality."

Practice and rehearsal. All of the various processes we have been discussing occur not once but many times over, as they must if change is truly to take place. People come into therapy with problems developed over a lifetime; and, as in any learning situation, repeated experiences are required for their undoing. All therapies (whether shorter- or longer-term) involve a process in time, within which the lessons learned in one session are practiced and consolidated in subsequent ones, with progress occurring in small, sometimes miniscule, steps. The importance of practice occurring over time is explicitly recognized in the psychoanalytic concept of "working through" (e.g., Greenson, 1967). The full meaning and implications of a new insight cannot truly be realized without many reexaminations in varying contexts.

In a related though somewhat different sense, therapy provides an opportunity for rehearsing new ways of behaving before trying them in the arena of the outside world. In the more protected environment of therapy, behaviors can be tried out tentatively, with encouragement of the therapist and feedback aimed at their further perfection, before exposing them before an audience which is more (or less) critical.

Mastery and success experiences. Ultimately, as the old saying goes, "nothing succeeds like success." As failure builds on failure, continuously weakening and demoralizing the patient, so too experiencing sucess leads to confidence in one's ability to succeed, and thence to further efforts and new successes. In every form of therapy, opportunity is built-in to encourage the experience of success and, with it, the sense of mastery of one's world and one's self.

Success experiences, in the first instance, occur wholly within the therapeutic process. Being able to reveal hidden secrets and shameful memories, without meeting disgust or disapproval from the therapist, is a positive experience. Discovering more about oneself, in the quest for understanding or attaining a sense of insight, is a true success experience. Even more palpably, being able to carry through an action previously blocked by phobic fears—as in the exercises of behavior therapy—cannot help but lead to a sense of mastery.

Alexander and French (1946) early on pointed out the importance of carrying over such success experiences to the world beyond the consulting room walls. In a time when psychotherapy focused largely on the patient's inner conflicts and feelings, they noted the real value of encouraging patients to try out new behaviors or confront inhibitions in their lives outside of therapy which could lead to experiences of success; in turn, strengthening the resolve to change and thus feed back into and facilitate therapy itself. The importance of experiencing the self as competent, effective, and capable of mastery has received more specific attention from White (e.g., 1959) and Bandura (1977a).

In more recent years, it has become not uncommon for therapists to suggest "homework," actions for patients to try in their life situations, which can then be examined in the therapeutic context; such prescriptions are much more regularly used in behavioral, cognitive, and rational-emotive therapies. That patients will sometimes meet rebuffs and suffer setbacks is predictable, and reparative measures will be necessary; but if suggestions are skillfully chosen and well timed, the likelihood of their leading to success is increased. In any case, the patient stands to learn the essential truth of another old saying—"nothing ventured, nothing gained."

A brief recapitulation

Central to psychotherapy, we have suggested, is an essential therapeutic climate. In addition, however, there are a number of processes shared by all therapies, although differently emphasized by competing schools. Among these are (a) suggestion and persuasion, (b) affective arousal, (c) various forms of learning, including direct conditioning, cognitive learning, acquiring decision-making skills, emotional learning and identificational learning, (d) self-exploration and understanding, (e) receiving feedback, (f) practice and rehearsal, and (g) experiencing success, both within and outside of therapy.

Such a listing is intended to call attention to what we believe to be important processes that exist to some degree in all therapies—whether the particular therapeutic theory admits it or not. Obviously the processes overlap, and more detailed analysis might suggest other principles of comparable importance or ways of organizing these into a coherent scheme. In a broad way, we are trying to map out a territory. It is premature to suggest the relative importance of each of these factors or even to suggest that all are necessary for therapeutic change. What is necessary, although perhaps not sufficient, is a therapeutic climate, marked by a therapeutic alliance and relationship based on faith and trust. With this as base, the various processes or therapeutic events we have just discussed can facilitate therapeutic change; without the essential therapeutic climate, no therapy can occur.

Does this mean that the conjunction of these conditions will necessarily lead to positive outcomes? Although these conditions are conceived as necessary or facilitative, outcome can obviously depend on factors outside of our present analysis. The success or failure of any therapeutic effort depends largely on the patient's capacity to use these conditions, above all to relate in a trusting way to others. Strupp (1973, 1976). for example, has suggested that those who enter psychotherapy having experienced in their own childhood a better parent-child relation are better able to accept and gain from the therapeutic relationship. The patient's capacity for integration (ego strength, in a broad sense) predicts a better outcome. One of the most durable findings in the psychotherapy-research literature is that those who fare better in psychotherapy are those who are initially healthier (e.g., Luborsky et al., 1975; Bergin & Lambert, 1978). It is also true, of course, that specific interventions in a particular therapeutic relation may or may not be appropriate to a particular patient's emotional state or character. Thus far, we have been considering patients and therapeutic conditions only in very broad and general ways; success or failure in the specific case depends on, for example, the appropriateness and timing of interpretations, the degree to which the patient can manage the affect aroused, and the particular matching of patient and therapist qualities, among many others. Not least, a continuingly pathogenic environment or unpredictable traumatic events can override the efforts of any therapist. Any or all of these considerations can limit the degree to which the general conditions we have discussed relate to the outcome of psychotherapy, certainly in the individual case. Still, we would propose that these factors are central and important to all therapies, however conceived.

THE MOVEMENT TOWARD RAPPROCHEMENT AMONG THEORIES OF PSYCHOTHERAPY

Recognition of the importance of common factors in all psychotherapies has grown apace with an emerging realization that no approach to psychotherapy can lay claim to having all the answers (Goldfried, 1980; Goldfried & Padawer, 1982). The long history of psychotherapy is the story of contending schools and theoretical systems, differing not only in their concepts of intervention but—more profoundly—in their theories of human personality and pathology. Allegiances to one or another school have been durable and strong; they determine not only how one thinks and works, but also what literature one exposes oneself to, what meetings one attends, and whose ideas one respects. Still, within each of the therapeutic orientations, voices are emerging wondering whether things of importance cannot be learned from therapists of other orientations and proposing that methods originating in other conceptual settings may be of value outside of their original contexts. Many suspect that therapists may, in actuality, practice more similarly than they preach (Grinker, 1976; Klein et al., 1969 Strupp, 1978), and what therapists say they do need not accurately reflect what they actually do. Years ago, Fiedler (1950) showed that more experienced therapists of different schools were more similar than neophytes of the same schools.

Partly because of the growing body of research showing that no mode of therapy is consistently superior and that all could stand much improvement, and partly because of the growing pressure for accountability and cost-effectiveness, clinicians seem more inclined to question the limitations and insularity of their schools. One expression of this is found in survey data in which over half of the clinical psychologists questioned described themselves as "eclectic" (Garfield & Kurtz, 1976; Kelly, Goldberg, Fiske, & Kilkowski, 1978), rather than holding to any one school. Eclecticism here seems to reflect a pragmatic concern with doing the best clinical job possible, rather than any intellectual confusion or indecision (as the term might have suggested in an earlier era). While it is unlikely, as

Goldfried suggests, that convergence at the broadest theoretical and philosophical levels can readily come about—reflecting as they do profound differences among schools in the conceptualization of human nature—pragmatic concerns can lead to greater utilization of intermediate-level concepts and methods: what he calls "common clinical strategies" or what we have described as "common therapeutic principles".

However, along with the pragmatic reasons for bringing concepts and methods of different schools into closer harmony, the trend toward rapprochement does also reflect important changes in theoretical orientations. Thus, psychoanalytic theory has—over the years—moved from an exclusive concern with drives and unconscious processes to a greater recognition of the role of ego processes involved in healthy adaptations (as well as in pathology). From an ego-psychological perspective, psychoanalysts were better prepared to deal with cognitive processes and contemporary behavior in their conceptualization of human functioning and psychological intervention. Thus, 50 years ago, French (1933) pointed to continuities between psychoanalytic and learning theory, as did Dollard and Miller (1950) in their classic book, and Alexander (1963) in one of his last papers. More recently, Wachtel (1977), in a fine, scholarly analysis of both clinical and theoretical issues, argues persuasively for the integration of psychoanalytic and behavioral approaches to intervention.

Meanwhile, behavior therapists have moved from a more extreme to a more moderate position, giving greater credence to conscious experience and even dynamic processes. A major trend has been the emergence of cognitive behavior modification (e.g., Beck, 1976; Goldfried & Davison, 1976; Lazarus, 1971; Mahoney, 1974; Meichenbaum, 1977). Concern with behavior per se has been extended to include the patient's concepts of the world and himself, his beliefs and fantasies, wishes and desires. The language used to describe these cognitive facets of human functioning may be more consonant with the behavioral tradition, but the connotations are clear. Therapists of every persuasion, as Wachtel (1977) notes, are hesitant to use the "x-rated concepts" of theoretical enemies; though often, substitute words carry much the same meaning, just as actual therapeutic acts may be more alike than different across theoretical boundaries. Early leaders of the behavioral therapeutic movement are arguing that it is time now to move beyond ideology, since the traditional conceptualization of the field is too limited to make understandable all that happens in clinical practice, and to consider what other approaches may have to offer (Lazarus, 1977; London, 1972). In another context, while considering the limitations of the dynamic and behavioral approaches, London (1964) noted:

> There is a quiet blending of techniques by artful therapists of either school;
> a blending that takes account of the fact that people are considerably simpler

than the Insight schools give them credit for, but that they are also more complicated than the Action therapists would like to believe (p. 39).

As both psychoanalytic and behavioral clinicians are giving greater concern to phenomenal experience, bridges are being built between these orientations and humanistic psychotherapy (which was originally launched as a "third force" in American psychology, opposed conceptually and methodologically to both psychoanalysis and behaviorism). Thus, Thoresen (1973) sees the possibility of synthesizing humanistic and behavioral therapeutic approaches into a "behavioral humanism," a phrase which would have been a contradiction in terms to both behaviorists and humanists only a few years earlier, and probably still is to many.

We should not exaggerate, of course, the magnitude of this movement toward rapprochement. There are many in every camp adamantly opposed to "alloying the pure gold of (my school) with the base metal of (yours)." But there is growing and, we believe, substantial agreement with the sentiment expressed by Marmor and Woods (1980, p. xi) in the preface to their book: "no one theory or discipline is likely, in the foreseeable future, to explain, much less predict, all of the complexities of human behavior." Already underway are conscious efforts to combine strategies derived from differing schools in the treatment of particular types of patients, apparently with some success (e.g., Birk & Brinkley-Birk, 1974; Rhoads & Feather, 1972), although in a less formal sense, eclectic therapeutic efforts are surely commonplace.

There is great need in these times to discover what therapeutic interventions, done by what kind of therapists, to what kind of people, with what kinds of problems, under what kind of circumstances, are likely to be of greatest help; this proposition has been stated repeatedly by many thoughtful students of the therapeutic scene. Unyielding adherence to a theoretical position—within which one's own model is conceived as a panacea—can only limit inquiry. What is needed is an open-minded examination of what people do that seems to make a difference (starting more from clinical experience than from theory as such), in order to distinguish the essential from the ephemeral in therapeutic practice. The need is for dialogue among clinicians of differing persuasions, for as Goldfried (1980) notes:

> To the extent that clinicians of varying orientations are able to arrive at a common set of strategies, it is likely that what emerges will consist of robust phenomena, as they have managed to survive the distortions imposed by the therapists' varying theoretical biases. (p. 996, italics in original)

TO AVERT SOME MISUNDERSTANDING

In any analysis of the common principles in psychotherapy and the need for rapprochement among different schools, certain misconceptions are possible. To avoid some misunderstandings, we would like in conclusion to respond to some hypothetical (but predictable) questions from the audience.

So you think psychotherapy is one big placebo effect?

By pointing to the central importance of the patient's faith and trust in the therapist, we certainly do not mean to imply a "nothing-but" effect. Such faith empowers the therapist as it motivates the patient, and it cannot be neglected; but in and of itself, this is of only limited curative power. Indeed, if the therapist mishandles power by inept interventions, positive harm can be done.

By emphasizing nonspecific factors in the therapeutic climate, are you suggesting that the therapist's knowledge and training are irrelevant?

The assumption is often made that what is essential for successful therapy is an encounter with a person who is warm, accepting, and genuine, and that these are personality characteristics a person has or does not have but which cannot be taught. Indeed, in simplest form, Rogers' (1957) characterization of the "necessary and sufficient" conditions of therapy did support this view; but as we have shown, there is no simple relation between such personal qualities and positive outcome. Without at all minimizing the importance of personal qualities such as these, we believe that they are not sufficient for therapeutic change. Knowledge of how and why people behave as they do, self-knowledge to understand one's own impact on people, and training to sharpen one's native "psychological helping skills," as it is coming to be called in a growing literature, are of great importance. It is true that warm and sensitive people, without explicit psychological training, have contributed notably as nonprofessional workers in mental health; but they cannot substitute for the well-trained clinician, who also must be warm and sensitive but understand how to modulate these and other conditions on the patient's behalf.

But you are suggesting that theory is not essential and even dangerous?

We have argued that blind adherence to a theoretical orientation can block progress in the field (and, possibly, the treatment of particular patients) while noting with Jerome Frank that a theoretical position, right or wrong, can provide meaning and comfort to both the therapist and patient. However, what we are pointing to here is theory at the broadest level. We agree with the essential wisdom in Kurt Lewin's famous saying, "There is nothing so practical as a good theory." The problem with theory in the field of psychotherapy is that many concepts are phrased at too broad and abstract a level and do not make effective contact with basic clinical phenomena; what is urgently needed is "good theory" that would allow the discovery and utilization of critical factors, now camouflaged by the overly grand conceptualizations of contending systems. To argue in favor of pragmatic and eclectic analysis of psychotherapy is not to favor an atheoretical view.

Does it really help to translate constructs of one system into those of another?

No, nor have we suggested that translation is needed. Indeed, translation of concepts has been attempted in the past, and little has been added to our understanding of psychotherapy. What is really needed is a new conceptual language, one that stays close to the phenomena of psychotherapy, within which workers from different orientations can communicate in the quest for common principles. At a later stage, perhaps, these notions can be aligned with those of major theoretical systems to see whether they fit and make sense, but doing this too early can create more confusion than clarification.

How would this emphasis on common principles affect clinical training?

Training based on a common-principles approach would encourage therapists-in-training to cultivate the personal and professional qualities discussed earlier as essential to a therapeutic climate, and to use these personal and professional qualities to full advantage to build patient faith and trust. The training would focus relatively more on the quality of the therapeutic relationship and the ongoing therapist-patient interaction than on the content of the patient's utterances and on underlying psychodynamics.

Do you really think that psychotherapy is important enough to be worth all this effort?

Yes.

SUMMARY

The recognition that all psychotherapies have properties in common reflects (1) an increasingly sophisticated body of empirical research showing that no one form of psychotherapy is uniformly more effective than any other, (2) growing societal pressure on the helping professions for accountability and cost-effectiveness, and (3) a decided movement toward rapprochement among contending psychotherapeutic theories and methods.

Two broad classes of factors can be distinguished which are common to all or most forms of psychological intervention and which might account for their therapeutic effectiveness. Most basic are those that define what might be called a *therapeutic climate,* a set of basal conditions which in and of themselves may produce change and which empower or provide the foundation for more specific *therapeutic processes* (strategies or events) which take place during the course of therapy. The therapeutic climate is the product of qualities of the patient (motivation, expectations, faith), of the therapist (status, warmth, respect), of the relationships between them (compatibility, alliance), and of the larger culture which they share (the belief in the modifiability of human behavior). The more specific therapeutic processes shared by all therapies, though differently emphasized by competing schools, include (a) suggestion and persuasion, (b) affective arousal, (c) various forms of learning, including direct conditioning, cognitive learning, acquiring decision-making skills, emotional learning and identificational learning, (d) self-exploration and understanding, (e) receiving feedback, (f) practice and rehearsal, and (g) experiencing success, both within and outside therapy.

REFERENCES

Albee, G. W. *Mental health manpower trends.* New York: Basic Books, 1959.

Alexander, F. The dynamics of psychotherapy in light of learning theory. *American Journal of Psychiatry,* 1963, *120,* 440–448.

Alexander, F., & French, T. M. (Eds.). *Psychoanalytic therapy.* New York: Ronald Press, 1946.

Bandura, A. Self-efficacy: Toward a unifying theory of behavioral change. *Psychological Review,* 1977, *84,* 191–215. (a)

Bandura, A. *Social learning theory.* Englewood Cliffs, N.J.: Prentice-Hall, 1977. (b)

Beck, A. T. *Cognitive therapy and the emotional disorders.* New York: International Universities Press, 1976.

Bednar, R. L., & Kaul, T. J. Experiential group research: Current perspectives. In S. L. Garfield & A. E. Bergin (Eds.), *Handbook of psychotherapy and behavior change: An empirical analysis.* New York: John Wiley & Sons, 1978.

Bergin, A. E. The effect of dissonant persuasive communications upon changes in a self-referring attitude. *Journal of Personality,* 1962, *30,* 423–438.

Bergin, A. E., & Lambert, M. J. The evaluation of therapeutic outcomes. In S. L. Garfield & A. E. Bergin (Eds.), *Handbook of psychotherapy and behavior change: An empirical analysis.* New York: John Wiley & Sons, 1978.

Birk, L., & Brinkley–Birk, A. Psychoanalysis and behavior therapy. *American Journal of Psychiatry,* 1974, *131,* 499–510.

Brady, J. P., Davison, G. C., Dewald, P. A., Egan, G., Fadiman, J., Frank, J. D., Gill, M. M., Hoffman, I., Kempler, W., Lazarus, A. A., Raimy, V., Rotter, J. B., & Strupp, H. H. Some views on effective principles of psychotherapy. *Cognitive Therapy and Research,* 1980, *4,* 271–306.

Breuer, J., & Freud, S. *Studies on hysteria.* New York: Basic Books, 1957. (Originally published, 1895.)

Browning, G. J. An analysis of the effects of therapist prestige and levels of interpretation on client response in the initial phase of psychotherapy (Doctoral dissertation, University of Houston, 1966). *Dissertation Abstracts International,* 1966, *26,* 4803.

Dollard, J., & Miller, N. E. *Personality and psychotherapy.* New York: McGraw-Hill, 1950.

Eysenck, H. J. *The effects of psychotherapy.* New York: International Science Press, 1966.

Fiedler, F. E. A comparison of therapeutic relationships in psychoanalytic, nondirective, and Alderian therapy. *Journal of Consulting Psychology,* 1950, *14,* 436–445.

Frank, J. D. Therapeutic factors in psychotherapy. *American Journal of Psychotherapy,* 1971, *25,* 350–361.

Frank, J. D. *Persuasion and healing* (Rev. ed.). Baltimore: Johns Hopkins Press, 1973.

Frank, J. D. Therapeutic components of psychotherapy. *Journal of Nervous and Mental Disease,* 1974, *159,* 325–342.

Frank, J. D. The present status of outcome studies. *Journal of Consulting and Clinical Psychology,* 1979, *47,* 310–316.

Frank, J. D. Therapeutic components shared by all psychotherapies. Master lecture, American Psychological Association, Los Angeles, August 24, 1981.

Frank, J. D., Hoehn-Saric, R., Imber, S. D., Liberman, B. L., Stone, A. R. *Effective ingredients of successful psychotherapy.* New York: Brunner/Mazel, 1978.

French, T. M. Interrelations between psychoanalysis and the experimental work of Pavlov. *American Journal of Psychiatry,* 1933, *89,* 1165–1203.

Freud, S. The future prospects of psycho-analytic therapy. London: Hogarth Press, 1957. (Originally published, 1910.)

Friedman, H. J. Patient expectancy and symptom reduction. *Archives of General Psychiatry,* 1963, *8,* 61–67.

Fromm-Reichmann, F. *Principles of intensive psychotherapy.* Chicago: University of Chicago Press, 1950.

Garfield, S. L. Research on client variables in psychotherapy. In S. L. Garfield & A. E. Bergin (Eds.), *Handbook of psychotherapy and behavior change: An empirical analysis.* New York: John Wiley & Sons, 1978.

Garfield, S. L. *Psychotherapies: An eclectic approach.* New York: Wiley Interscience, 1980.

Garfield, S. L., & Kurtz, R. Clinical psychologists in the 1970s. *American Psychologist,* 1976, *31,* 1–9.

Goldfried, M. R. Toward the delineation of therapeutic change principles. *American Psycologist,* 1980, *35,* 991–999.

Goldfried, M. R. (Ed.). *Converging themes in the practice of psychotherapy.* New York: Springer, 1982.

Goldfried, M. R., & Davison, G. C. *Clinical behavior therapy.* New York: Holt, Rinehart & Winston, 1976.

Goldfried, M. R., & Padawer, W. Current status and future directions in psychotherapy. In M. R. Goldfried (Ed.), *Converging themes in the practice of psychotherapy.* New York: Springer, 1982.

Goldstein, A. P. *Therapist-patient expectancies in psychotherapy.* Elmsford, N.Y.: Pergamon Press, 1962.

Goldstein, A. P. Evaluating expectancy effects in cross-cultural counseling and psychotherapy. In A. J. Marsella & P. B. Pedersen (Eds.), *Cross-cultural counseling and psychotherapy.* Elmsford, N.Y.: Pergamon Press, 1981.

Greenson, R. R. *The technique and practice of psychoanalysis* (Vol. 1). New York: International Universities Press, 1967.

Greenspoon, J. The reinforcing effect of two spoken sounds on the frequency of two responses. *American Journal of Psychology,* 1955, *68,* 409–416.

Grinker, R. R. Discussion of Strupp's "Some critical comments on the future of psychoanalytic therapy." *Bulletin of the Menninger Clinic,* 1976, *40,* 247–254.

Gross, M. L. *The psychological society.* New York: Simon & Shuster, 1979.

Herink, R. (Ed.). *The psychotherapy handbook: The A to Z guide to more than 250 different therapies in use today.* New York: New American Library, 1980.

Kelly, E. L., Goldberg, L. R., Fiske, D. W., & Kilkowski, J. M. Twenty-five years later: A follow-up study of the graduate students in clinical psychology assessed in the V.A. selection research project. *American Psychologist,* 1978, *33,* 746–755.

Kiesler, C. A. Mental health policy as a field of inquiry for psychology. *American Psychologist,* 1980, *35,* 1066–1080.

Klein, M., Dittman, A. T., Parloff, M. B., & Gill, M. M. Behavior therapy: Observations and reflections. *Journal of Consulting and Clinical Psychology,* 1969, *33,* 259–266.

Korchin, S. J. *Modern clinical psychology: Principles of intervention in the clinic and community.* New York: Basic Books, 1976.

Larson, D. Therapeutic schools, styles, and schoolism: A national survey. *Journal of Humanistic Psychology,* 1980, *20,* 3–20.

Lasch, C. *Haven in a heartless world: The family beseiged.* New York: Basic Books, 1979.

Lazarus, A. A. *Behavior therapy and beyond.* New York: McGraw-Hill, 1971.

Lazarus, A. A. Has behavior therapy outlived its usefulness? *American Psychologist,* 1977, *32,* 550–554.

Levenson, E. A. *The fallacy of understanding.* New York: Basic Books, 1972.

London, P. *The modes and morals of psychotherapy.* New York: Holt, Rinehart & Winston, 1964.

London, P. The end of ideology in behavior modification. *American Psychologist,* 1972, *27,* 913–920.

Luborsky, L. Helping alliances in psychotherapy. In J. L. Claghorn (Ed.), *Successful psychotherapy.* New York: Brunner/Mazel, 1976.

Luborsky, L. Curative factors in psychoanalytic and psychodynamic therapies. In J. P. Brady, J. Mendels, M. Orne, & W. Rieger (Eds.), *Psychiatry: Areas of promise and advancement.* New York: Spectrum, 1977.

Luborsky, L., Singer, B., & Luborsky, L. Comparative studies of psychotherapies: Is it true that "Everyone has won and all must have prizes?" *Archives of General Psychiatry,* 1975, *32,* 995–1008.

Mahoney, M. J. *Cognition and behavior modification.* Cambridge, Mass.: Ballinger, 1974.

Marmor, J. Common operational factors in diverse approaches to behavior change. In A. Burton (Ed.), *What makes behavior change possible?* New York: Brunner/Mazel, 1976.

Marmor, J., & Woods, S. M. (Eds.). *The interface between psychodynamic and behavioral therapies.* New York: Plenum Press, 1980.

Meichenbaum, D. H. *Cognitive behavior modification.* New York: Plenum Press, 1977.

Meltzoff, J., & Kornreich, M. *Research in psychotherapy.* New York: Atherton Press, 1970.

Mendel, W. H. The phenomenon of interpretation. *American Journal of Psychoanalysis,* 1964, *24,* 184–190.

Mitchell, K. M., Bozarth, J. D., & Krauft, C. C. A reappraisal of the therapeutic effectiveness of accurate empathy, nonpossessive warmth, and genuineness. In. A. S. Gurman & A. M. Razin (Eds.), *Effective psychotherapy: A handbook of research.* Elmsford, N.Y.: Pergamon Press, 1977.

Parloff, M. Analytic group psychotherapy. In J. Marmor (Ed.), *Modern psychoanalysis.* New York: Basic Books, 1968.

Parloff, M. B. Can psychotherapy research guide the policy-maker? A little knowledge may be a dangerous thing. *American Psychologist,* 1979, *34,* 296–306.

Parloff, M. B., Waskow, I. E., & Wolfe, B. E. Research on therapist variables in relation to process and outcome. In S. L. Garfield & A. E. Bergin (Eds.), *Handbook of psychotherapy and behavior change: An empirical analysis.* New York: John Wiley & Sons, 1978.

Reisman, J. M. *Toward the integration of psychotherapy.* New York: Wiley Interscience, 1971.

Rhoads, J. M., & Feather, B. W. Transference and resistance observed in behavior therapy. *British Journal of Medical Psychology,* 1972, *45,* 99–103.

Rogers, C. R. The necessary and sufficient conditions of therapeutic personality change. *Journal of Consulting Psychology,* 1957, *21,* 95–103.

Rosenzweig, S. Some implicit common factors in diverse methods in psychotherapy. *American Journal of Orthopsychiatry,* 1936, *6,* 412–415.

Shapiro, A. K. The placebo effect in the history of medical treatment—implications for psychiatry. *American Journal of Psychiatry,* 1959, *116,* 298–304.

Shapiro, A. K., & Morris, L. A. Placebo effects in medical and psychological therapies. In S. L. Garfield & A. E. Bergin (Eds.), *Handbook of psychotherapy and behavior change: An empirical analysis.* New York: John Wiley & Sons, 1978.

Sloane, R. B., Staples, F. R., Cristol, A. H., Yorkston, N. J., & Whipple, K. *Psychotherapy versus behavior therapy.* Cambridge, Mass.: Harvard University Press, 1975.

Smith, M. L., & Glass, G. V. Meta-analysis of psychotherapy outcome studies. *American Psychologist,* 1977, *32,* 752–760.

Smith, M. L., Glass, G. V., & Miller, T. I. *The benefits of psychotherapy.* Baltimore: Johns Hopkins Press, 1980.

Strupp, H. H. On the basic ingredients of psychotherapy. *Journal of Consulting and Clinical Psychology,* 1973, *41,* 1–8.

Strupp, H. H. The nature of the therapeutic influence and its basic ingredients. In A. Burton (Ed.), *What makes behavior change possible?* New York: Brunner/Mazel, 1976.

Strupp, H. H. Psychotherapy research and practice: An overview. In S. L. Garfield & A. E. Bergin (Eds.), *Handbook of psychotherapy and behavior change: An empirical analysis* (2d ed.). New York: John Wiley & Sons, 1978.

Strupp, H. H. & Hadley, S. W. Specific versus nonspecific factors in psychotherapy: A controlled study of outcome. *Archives of General Psychiatry,* 1979, *36,* 1125–1136.

Thoresen, C. E. Behavioral humanism. In C. E. Thoresen (Ed.), *Behavior modification in education.* Chicago: University of Chicago Press, 1973.

Torrey, E. F. *The mind game: Witch doctors and psychiatrists.* New York: Emerson Hall, 1972. (a)

Torrey, E. F. What western psychotherapists can learn from witch doctors. *American Journal of Orthopsychiatry,* 1972, *42,* 69–76. (b)

Truax, C. B. Reinforcement and nonreinforcement in Rogerian psychotherapy. *Journal of Abnormal Psychology,* 1966, *71,* 1–9.

Truax, C. B., & Mitchell, K. M. Research on certain therapist-interpersonal skills in relation to process and outcome. In A. E. Bergin & S. L. Garfield (Eds.), *Handbook of psychotherapy and behavior change: An empirical analysis.* New York: John Wiley & Sons, 1971.

Wachtel, P. L. *Psychoanalysis and behavior therapy. New York: Basic Books, 1977.*

Watzlawick, P., Weakland, J. H., & Fisch, R. *Change.* New York: W. W. Norton, 1974.

White, R. W. Motivation reconsidered: The concept of competence. *Psychological Review,* 1959, *66,* 297–333.

Wilkins, W. Expectancy of therapeutic gain: An empirical and conceptual critique. *Journal of Consulting and Clinical Psychology,* 1973, 40, 69–77.

Wolpe, J. *The practice of behavior therapy* (2nd ed.). Elmsford, N.Y.: Pergamon Press, 1973.

PART III

Diagnosis and assessment

══ 10 ══

══ The diagnostic and statistical manual of mental disorders: History, comparative analysis, current status, and appraisal

Peter E. Nathan*
and
Sandra L. Harris*

Clinical psychology and the three editions of The *Diagnostic and Statistical Manual of Mental Disorders*—*DSM-I* (1952), *DSM-II* (1968), and *DSM-III* (1980)—have shared an uneasy but productive relationship for more than three decades. On the one hand, the *DSM* is the standard American nomenclature which psychologists must use, both as mental-health team members and as independent practitioners who complete third-party reimbursement forms. On the other hand, as independent professionals, psychologists have found it difficult to adapt easily to a nomenclature developed by and for psychiatry, with that profession's unique needs, methods, and goals foremost. Happily, the three successive revisions of the *Manual* (culminating in *DSM-III*, the edition of the instrument which will be detailed here) have been successively less self-serving, more descriptive and empirical and, hence, more useful to psychology.

This chapter includes a brief history of psychiatric nomenclature as well as a comparative analysis of the three editions of *The Diagnostic and Statistical Manual*. The major portion of the chapter is given over to a critical appraisal of adult and childhood syndromes as detailed in

---

* Graduate School of Applied and Professional Psychology, Rutgers, The State University.

DSM-III, their distinguishing differential-diagnostic criteria, and syndromal changes through the three editions of the *Manual* (which reflect
concomitant changes in societal and professional conceptions of psychopathology).

HISTORY

So far as anyone knows, humankind has always been fascinated by
the abnormal, the bizarre, and the unusual—and desired to name them
in their infinite complexity. Nonetheless, it was not until asylums for the
insane were established, in the late 18th century, that enough patients
could be assembled in one place at one time to permit systematic observation and subsequent categorization. It was Phillippe Pinel—known best
for his earlier efforts to humanize the new asylums and to convert them
from custodial to therapeutic institutions—who first developed a comprehensive classification system, a distinct step forward for his time.

Most historians of classification accord responsibility to Emil Kraepelin—a German psychiatrist whose major work was done in the latter part
of the 19th century—for developing the first modern psychiatric nomenclature. His most notable contributions came from seeing commonalities
among disorders that other German taxonomists had seen as separate;
these commonalities ultimately brought together the schizophrenias—
Kraepelin called the syndrome *dementia praecox*—and the manic-depressive disorders. Kraepelin's work was distinguished by extraordinarily
detailed systematic observation, a distinct organic "tilt," and diagnoses
based on prognosis and history as well as on signs and symptoms. Kraepelin did not accord nonpsychotic conditions attention or importance in
his classification system. It remained for Freud and the dynamic psychologists and psychiatrists of the 20th century to recognize the significance
of these disorders and to evolve diagnostic criteria for them.

The situation confronting American physicians from the turn of the
century to the middle of the century's third decade was a system of nomenclature (for both physical disease and mental disorder) developed
and maintained by each large teaching institution as a function of the
kinds of patients the institution served. In late 1927, however, the New
York Academy of Medicine began the process which led to a National
Conference on Nomenclature of Disease, held in March 1928. The ultimate product of this effort was the first edition of the *Standard Classified
Nomenclature of Disease,* published in 1933. One section of this *Nomenclature,* Diseases of the Psychobiologic Unit, was drawn largely from a
standardized psychiatric nomenclature begun in 1917 by a group which
ultimately called itself the American Psychiatric Association.

The psychiatric nomenclature in the *Standard Nomenclature* and its
revisions (including the 1942 revision) proved inadequate to the psychiatric demands of World War II. Based on the categories of disorder seen

most often at public mental hospitals, where most of the persons who developed the nomenclature worked, the standard nomenclature made scant mention of the anxiety, stress, personality, and psychophysiologic disorders which impaired ability to function effectively under the stress of combat. Instead, the standard taxonomy focused on the organic and functional psychoses which filled the public mental hospitals but not the ranks of the Armed Forces.

Accordingly, the Armed Forces revised the *Standard Nomenclature* toward the end of the war to conform to its needs; the Veterans Administration did likewise, for similar purposes, in 1946. This meant that three classification systems for psychiatric disorders were being used shortly after the end of World War II. In recognition of this fact, the Committee on Nomenclature and Statistics of the American Psychiatric Association undertook to develop a new, more comprehensive system in 1948. The first edition of *The Diagnostic and Statistical Manual of Mental Disorders*, published in 1952, was the result. A second edition of the Manual, *DSM-II*, appeared in 1968. *DSM-III* was published in 1980.

THE MANUALS: *DSM-III* AND ITS PREDECESSORS

DSM-III is both larger and more comprehensive than *DSM-II*, itself more substantial than *DSM-I*. Figure 1 provides tangible evidence of the successively greater diagnostic breadth of the *Manuals*. The quantitative and qualitative leap in diagnostic range represented by *DSM-III* reflects the decision by the Task Force on Nomenclature and Statistics which developed it to be inclusive rather than exclusive: to include clinical conditions whenever they can be described with clarity and relative distinctness. This phenomenological approach to an empirically based classification is reflected throughout the instrument, specifically in its eschewal of theory and unsubstantiated opinion in favor of descriptive diagnoses and data on etiology and treatment validated by empirical-research findings. While the goal of a phenomenological, data-based taxonomy is not always met in the instrument (Garmezy, 1978; McReynolds, 1979; Schacht & Nathan, 1977; Zubin, 1978), the goal remains a desirable one—and *DSM-III* is clearly more than a single step in this direction.

The most important overall distinctions to be drawn between *DSM-III* and its influential predecessor, *DSM-II*, include: (1) a modification of major diagnostic groupings to include, for the first time, separate diagnostic attention to the Substance Use Disorders, the Gender Identity Disorders, the Psychosexual Disorders, the Disorders of Impulse Control, and what were unified in *DSM-I* and *DSM-II* as the Neurotic Disorders and are now separated; and (2) dramatic expansion in the depth and breadth of Childhood and Substance Use Disorders. Both these groups of changes are detailed in the following section of the chapter, The Syndromes.

Figure 1

DSM-I, DSM-II, DSM-III: A comparison of diagnostic depth and breadth

DSM-I	*DSM-II*	*DSM-III*
Acute Brain Disorders (13 diagnoses)	I. Mental Retardation (6 diagnoses)	Childhood Disorders (45 diagnoses)
Chronic Brain Disorders (25 diagnoses)	II. Organic Brain Syndrome (40 diagnoses)	Organic Mental Disorders (58 diagnoses)
Mental Deficiency (6 diagnoses)	III. Psychoses Not Attributed to Physical Conditions Listed Previously (24 diagnoses)	Substance Use Disorders (19 diagnoses)
Psychotic Disorders (17 diagnoses)	IV. Neuroses (11 diagnoses)	Schizophrenic Disorders (5 diagnoses)
Psychophysiologic Autonomic and Visceral Disorders (10 diagnoses)	V. Personality Disorders and Certain Other Nonpsychotic Mental Disorders (33 diagnoses)	Paranoid Disorders (4 diagnoses)
Psychoneurotic Disorders (7 diagnoses)	VI. Psychophysiologic Disorders (10 diagnoses)	Psychotic Disorders Not Elsewhere Classified (4 diagnoses)
Personality Disorders (18 diagnoses)	VII. Special Symptoms (10 diagnoses)	Affective Disorders (9 diagnoses)
Transient Situational Personality Disorders (8 diagnoses)	VIII. Transient Situational Disturbances (5 diagnoses)	Anxiety Disorders (10 diagnoses)
Total diagnoses: 104	IX. Behavior Disorders of Childhood and Adolescence (7 diagnoses)	Somatoform Disorders (5 diagnoses)
	Total diagnoses: 146	Dissociative Disorders (5 diagnoses)
		Psychosexual Disorders (22 diagnoses)
		Factitious Disorders (3 diagnoses)
		Disorders of Impulse Control (6 diagnoses)
		Adjustment Disorder (8 diagnoses)
		Psychological Factors Affecting Physical Condition (1 diagnosis)
		Personality Disorders (12 diagnoses)
		Total diagnoses: 216

Other changes in *DSM-III*, more general in character, include: (3) Multiaxial Diagnoses designed to link diagnostic judgments to their environmental determinants, as an aid to treatment planning and prediction of course; (4) diagnostic decision making from empirically derived Operational Criteria, in order to enhance the reliability of *DSM-III* diagnoses; (5) extensive pre-publication testing of the instrument's assumptions, underlying concepts, and major and minor diagnostic groupings, to ensure that acceptable levels of reliability could be attained, professional support for the instrument was gathered, and necessary changes in the instrument from this process were incorporated; and (6) extended discussion, in the *Manual,* of each syndrome's differential diagnosis, etiology, treatment, prognosis, and management.

Multiaxial diagnosis

Diagnoses in *DSM-III* take a multiaxial form. Each diagnosis is to provide information on five predetermined dimensions—axes—designed to help plan treatment and predict outcome as well as categorize and classify. Figure 2 summarizes the multiaxial system introduced in *DSM-III:*

Figure 2

The multiaxial system

Axis 1   Clinical Syndromes and Conditions Not Attributable to a Mental Disorder That Are a Focus of Attention or Treatment

Axis 2   Personality Disorders and Specific Developmental Disorders

Axis 3   Physical Disorders and Conditions

Axis 4   Severity of Psychosocial Stressors

Axis 5   Highest Level of Adaptive Functioning Past Year

The multiaxial system was designed to meet one of the most common criticisms of *DSM-II,* that its diagnoses were of little or no help in treatment planning or management. While *DSM-II* makes no mention of any other purposes for the diagnostic process than categorization, a substantial section in *DSM-I* was given over to "General and Special Requirements for the Recording of Psychiatric Conditions." "General Requirements" specified the order and form in which diagnoses were to be given. The same information on "General Requirements" is included in the *DSM-II.* What is not included are the "Special Requirements" outlined in *DSM-I,* which observe that "the mere stating of the diagnosis is not sufficient for certain conditions, since it does not furnish enough information to describe the clinical picture. . . . Therefore, for most conditions a complementary evaluation must be entered in the clinical records" (page 4, DSM-I). This additional evaluation is to include information on External Precipitating Stress, Premorbid Personality and Predisposition, and Degree of Psychiatric Impairment. In other words, the same elements required for axes 4 and 5 of the "new and innovative" Multiaxial System have actually come down through the 28 years that separate *DSM-I* and *DSM-III!*

The multiaxial system, then, formalizes an intent to aid treatment and prognosis first expressed in *DSM-I*. It also confronts problems of multiple diagnosis that burdened the drafters of both *DSM-I* and *DSM-II*. The multiaxial format requires frank psychiatric conditions to be listed and described first, in axis 1. When more than one such diagnosis is to be listed, that condition responsible for the most recent or current diagnosis is to be listed first. Characterological problems and transient disorders of childhood, less often a diagnostic or treatment focus, are listed next, in axis 2; followed by axis 3, physical disorders and conditions which relate directly or indirectly to the conditions listed in axes 1 and 2.

Despite the laudable intent of this system, problems with it remain. The first has to do with the apparent simplicity of the multiple diagnosis system, a simplicity which belies the enormous complexity of the task. In fact, the categories for which judgments are called for by the multiaxial system almost certainly exist at different levels of abstraction and possess diverse meaning structures. Accordingly, the judgments made for multiaxial purposes may reflect but a portion of the universe of important judgments to be made about a patient, and, in their simplicity, may disguise the range of more important judgments that ought to be made of a patient.

A related concern, that of the reliability of judgments on Severity of Psychosocial Stressors in the Year Preceding Diagnosis (axis 4) and Highest Level of Adaptive Functioning in the Past Year (axis 5), has been lessened to some extent by promising early data suggesting that the reliability of these judgments will be acceptably high both for adults (Spitzer & Forman, 1979) and children (Russell, Cantwell, Mattison, & Will, 1979). These promising data may reflect the decision—made during the latter stages of preparation of *DSM-III* for publication—to include guides to the seven-point axis 4 scale and the seven-point axis 5 scale. Nonetheless, difficult unresolved conceptual problems remain. One of the most important is how to rate the severity of axis 4 stressors. The *Manual* states that the judgment is to be made based on "the clinician's assessment of the stress an 'average' person in similar circumstances and with similar sociocultural values would experience." Yet, the clinician must also take into account the patient's unique set of experiences with the stressor and what its special meaning to him or her may be. Such stressors as hallucinations and delusions are particularly difficult to rate; it is impossible to know how an "average" person would respond to such unusual phenomena.

One must also ask whether the five axes which comprise the multiaxial system are the most useful dimensions along which psychopathology might be rated. For example, Schacht and Nathan (1977) suggested that an axis coding response to treatment might be very helpful; other axes can also be conceived of.

Another concern with the multiaxial system raised by some nonmedical mental health practitioners relates to the system's potential to be used to exclude nonphysicians from the diagnostic enterprise. To this end, some have suggested that the separation of the Personality Disorders and the Specific Developmental Disorders of Childhood from all other syndromes on axes 1 and 2 and the provision for axis 3 (where physical disorders affecting axis 1 and axis 2 syndromes are to be identified) present an opportunity to deny nonmedical mental health workers recognition for reimbursement for diagnosis and treatment of axis 1 and axis 3 disorders. Although Robert Spitzer has explicitly denied this intent, and proof of such a plan does not now exist, suspicion persists among some psychologists. Ultimate proof, presumably, may come later, if physicians and psychiatrists are given the chance to circumscribe the activities of psychologists and others in this way.

Operational criteria

The diagnostic cues and rules which comprise operational criteria for many *DSM-III* syndromes were adapted from research diagnostic criteria generated and tested by Feighner and his colleagues (1972), and Spitzer, Endicott, and Robins (1975). The strengths of operational criteria, an illustration of which is given in Figure 3, include that: (1) they make explicit the signs and symptoms required for the diagnosis; (2) they are, for the most part, based on cues and decision rules which have been empirically validated; and (3) they are descriptive, phenomenological, and behavioral.

By no means were all of *DSM-III*'s operational criteria derived from empirically validated research diagnostic criteria, however. Criteria for many of the "softer" diagnoses (including the Personality Disorders, some of the Somatoform, Dissociative, and Psychosexual Disorders, and the Childhood Disorders) were not included in the program of research reported by the St. Louis and New York groups; drafters of these sections of *DSM-III*, accordingly, had to rely on more traditional "armchair" operationalizing. Although pilot and field testing did provide subsequent opportunity for empirical testing of all criteria, empirically derived or not, some operational criteria are not buttressed by empirical confirmation to the extent that others are.

The import of an explicit set of diagnostic criteria is, above all, the boon it gives to reliable diagnosis. When all clinicians operate from a common, consensually and empirically validated set of diagnostic criteria,

Figure 3

Operational (diagnostic) criteria for paranoid personality disorder

The following are characteristic of the individual's current and long-term functioning, are not limited to episodes of illness, and cause either significant impairment in social or occupational functioning or subjective distress.

A. Pervasive, unwarranted suspiciousness and mistrust of people as indicated by at least three of the following:
  1. Expectation of trickery or harm.
  2. Hypervigilance, manifested by continual scanning of the environment for signs of threat, or taking unneeded precautions.
  3. Guardedness or secretiveness.
  4. Avoidance of accepting blame when warranted.
  5. Questioning the loyalty of others.
  6. Intense, narrowly focused searching for confirmation of bias, with loss of appreciation of total context.
  7. Overconcern with hidden motives and special meanings.
  8. Pathological jealousy.

B. Hypersensitivity as indicated by at least two of the following:
  1. Tendency to be easily slighted and quick to take offense.
  2. Exaggeration of difficulties, e.g., "making mountains out of molehills."
  3. Readiness to counterattack when any threat is perceived.
  4. Inability to relax.

C. Restricted affectivity as indicated by at least two of the following:
  1. Appearance of being "cold" and unemotional.
  2. Pride taken in always being objective, rational, and unemotional.
  3. Lack of a true sense of humor.
  4. Absence of passive, soft, tender, and sentimental feelings.

D. Not due to another mental disorder such as Schizophrenia or a Paranoid Disorder.

---

they are much more apt to agree on resultant diagnoses. In fact, initial data on the reliability of *DSM-III* diagnoses of adults (Spitzer, Forman, & Nee, 1979) and children (Cantwell, Mattison, Russell, & Will, 1979; Cantwell, Russell, Mattison, & Will, 1979) are encouraging. While heightened reliability does not guarantee diagnostic utility, it is certainly prerequisite to it.

The importance of empirically validated diagnostic criteria is that they offer the likelihood that most patients a clinician is called upon to diagnose can be diagnosed according to the criteria provided. That is, unlike their predecessors, *DSM-III* diagnoses are not ideal collections of modal diagnostic cases; instead, they represent a considerable approximation to real life psychopathology, with its skewedness, idiosyncrasies, and exceptions, as well as its commonalities and predictabilities.

A descriptive, phenomenological system—the *DSM-III* operational criteria—makes it possible to observe and record psychopathology, then subject it to the decision-rules specified, without having to temper or qualify observations by theoretical assumptions or unfounded clinical expectation. Descriptive diagnoses demand no further interpretation, definition, or translation than enumeration of behaviors observed.

Neither *DSM-I* nor *DSM-II* specified operational criteria; the scanty diagnostic information these instruments provided was not empirically derived; it was sometimes descriptive and phenomenological; at other times, theory-based, second-order, and obscure. Hence, diagnoses based on these instruments were often unreliable, and their ultimate utility, accordingly, was uncertain at best (Greenberg, 1977; McGuire, 1973; Winokur, 1977).

Consultation/liaison and field trials

Because the consultation/liaison and field-testing processes that were an important part of the development of *DSM-III* were very extensive, the instrument took five years to develop (two more than had originally been planned). The result, however, is an instrument that reflects a multitude of worthwhile official and unofficial inputs. By contrast, there appears to have been little sharing in the developmental process that led to *DSM-I* or *DSM-II*, either within psychiatry or between that profession and the other mental-health professions.

The process of development of *DSM-I* contrasts most sharply with that of *DSM-III*. As the Foreword to *DSM-I* recalls, once the need for standardization of the several nomenclatures in use in the U.S. in 1948 was recognized by the Committee on Nomenclature and Statistics of the American Psychiatric Association, "the sentiments of the membership (of the American Psychiatric Association) regarding the need for a change in the then-current *Standard*" were ascertained. "A high percentage" of psychiatrists contacted felt that changes were needed. Those working in clinics or private practice and with patients suffering from personality disorders or transient reactions to stress were especially convinced of the need for the new instrument. The committee, a group of seven, then drafted a proposed revision, drawing as well on the experience of Armed Forces and Veterans Administration psychiatrists and a consultant from the biometrics branch of the National Institute of Mental Health. In 1950, mimeographed copies of the proposed nomenclature and a 9-page questionnaire asking for opinions and suggestions were sent to a stratified 10 percent sample of the membership of the American Psychiatric Association. Forty-six percent of those who were sent this material returned comments and/or suggestions. A second revision was then prepared by the Committee on Nomenclature and presented to the governing council of the American Psychiatric Association. Once approved, this second revision became *DSM-I*.

The second edition of *The Diagnostic and Statistical Manual* benefited even less from consultation and collaboration. A draft of the revision, prepared by the Committee on Nomenclature and Statistics, now numbering eight with two consultants (including Robert Spitzer), was circulated to 120 members of the American Psychiatric Association in February 1967, "with a request for specific suggestions to eliminate errors and to improve the quality of the statements indicating the proper usage of terms which the *Manual* describes." The Committee considered this input prior to a meeting in May 1967, at which time it completed the revision and submitted it to the Executive Committee of the APA. In December 1967, the APA governing council approved *DSM-II,* and it was published early in 1968.

Contrasting with these efforts are the five years and hundreds of psychiatrists, psychologists, social workers, and others involved either formally or informally in consultation on or pilot testing of successive versions of *DSM-III.* Initial drafts of sections corresponding to the 14 major syndromes categorized in *DSM-III* were produced by advisory committees numbering from 4 to 18 persons each, then transmitted to the Task Force on Nomenclature and Statistics, now composed of 19 persons. As well, various liaison committees from units of the American Psychiatric Association, other mental health disciplines (e.g., the American Psychological Association, the American College Health Association, the American Orthopsychiatric Association) and special interest groups (e.g., the American Group Therapy Association, the American Psychoanalytic Association, the Association for Advancement of Behavior Therapy) made comments on drafts and had the opportunity to provide direct input to the chair of the task force. These inputs—sometimes heated—resulted in significant modifications in the draft. Particularly important to psychologists were the successful efforts of the liaison committee from the American Psychological Association (Maurice Lorr, chair, Leonard Krasner, and Peter E. Nathan) to delete from *DSM-III* Prefacatory material a statement to the effect that "Mental disorders are a subset of medical disorders." This statement, which would have caused all sorts of problems for organized psychology, would as well almost certainly have been litigated on publication of *DSM-III* (see Schacht & Nathan, 1977, and Spitzer, Williams, & Skodol, 1980, for a more extended discussion of this matter). Wiser heads on both sides prevailed, however, and the offending statement was removed.

Drafts of *DSM-III* were also reviewed and criticized by many individual mental-health professionals, because they were available to anyone who asked (and paid) for them. Spitzer, chair of the task force, has written (Spitzer et al., 1980), "Every critique of *DSM-III* (which numbered in the hundreds) was considered and personally responded to with a letter from either the senior (Spitzer) or second (Williams) author."

Beyond this successful effort to involve many mental health professionals in drafting and criticizing revisions of the instrument, over 800 clinicians participated in a series of field trials, which began in December 1976. By contrast, no formal pilot testing of either *DSM-I* or *DSM-II* was reported prior to their publication. Pilot field trials and then a large-scale, 2-year field trial of *DSM-III* (sponsored by NIMH, which used several versions of the completed draft of the instrument and involved over 400 clinicians in more than 120 mental health facilities and 80 clinicians in private practice) were undertaken. The final draft of *DSM-III*, then, is the product of a series of revisions based on the results of the field trials, which focused on the reliability and concurrent validity of both major and minor diagnostic groupings. Although the final product continues to be hotly debated and does not please every mental-health professional, it is nonetheless the product of far wider consultation and cooperation than either *DSM-I* and *DSM-II*; psychologists, moreover, played important roles in this process.

The *Diagnostic Manual*

One of the most obvious differences among the three *Manuals* is sheer size. Both of the earlier manuals were 132 pages and had a modest trim-size. By contrast, the 1980 *Manual* is almost 500 pages, in a format that is significantly larger. Moreover, the marked increase in material in the new *Manual* includes more than detailed operational criteria for each diagnostic syndrome, details on multiaxial diagnosis, and discussion of underlying philosophy of categorization. Most interesting and useful to many of those who use the *Manual* will be material on each syndrome's associated features: age at onset, course, impairment, complications, predisposing factors, prevalence, sex ratio, and differential diagnosis. In keeping with the overall concern of the system's creators that it be both descriptive and empirical, discussion of these matters is drawn from existing empirical literature, not from undocumented clinical lore.

One of the major goals of the drafters of *DSM-III* was to produce a definition of mental disorder that would meet with widespread acceptance and have consequent utility. A major criticism of conventional diagnostic systems by those unconvinced of the utility of diagnosis has been the absence of such a definition. Hence, the drafters of *DSM-III* worked hard to develop this statement. An initial effort to develop the statement resulted in a bitter exchange with the liaison committee from the American Psychological Association, when the statement concluded that mental disorders are to be viewed as a subset of medical disorders. After prolonged and heated exchange, the task force withdrew this offending statement, in favor of the following more even-handed position:

> In *DSM-III*, a mental disorder is conceptualized as a clinically significant behavioral or psychologic syndrome or pattern that occurs in an individual and that is typically associated with either a painful symptom (distress) or impairment in one or more important areas of functioning (disability). In

addition, there is an inference that there is a behavioral, psychologic, or biologic dysfunction and that the disturbance is not only in the relationship between the individual and society. When the disturbance is limited to a conflict between an individual and society, this may represent social deviance, which may or may not be commendable, but is not by itself a mental disorder. (page 6, DSM-III)

While this statement treads a middle line among theoretical persuasions on etiology and among disciplines on intervention in its effort to serve a variety of masters, it does focus on distress and disability rather than, simply, on signs and symptoms as key stigmata, on clinical significance rather than illness, and on the fact that problems involving the individual in conflict with society need not be seen as psychopathologic. For psychologists, simply the admission that psychopathology need not involve biologic dysfunction (however broadly conceived) is a welcome one.

THE SYNDROMES

Disorders usually first evident in infancy, childhood, or adolescence

Historically, there has been a tendency to view children as miniature adults. Indeed, prior to the 19th century, there were no written discussions of children's psychological disorders. In the 20th century, we have suddenly become aware that children, as part of the developmental process gone wrong, may suffer from a variety of difficulties which have no direct adult counterpart. Thus, we have moved from a society in which childhood was a direct, downward extension of adult consciousness to a society in which childhood is viewed as a distinctive developmental experience with perceptions and realities far different from those of the adult. A child and an adult, even when using the same word (such as "divorce," "sex," "adoption," or "death") may be talking about very different phenomena. Likewise, children of different ages will have different world views as a reflection of their level of development. The clinician who ignores such developmental substance will have little success in gaining access to the inner world of childhood.

Before reviewing specific categories of child psychopathology, it is important to note some of the issues which must be considered by the clinician attempting to identify a childhood disorder. Change and variation is a natural part of childhood. This variability makes it more difficult to diagnose the problems of children than those of adults. What is more typical of childhood than the trying on of various roles? Over the course of a day, a child may shift from being "mommy" to "daddy" to an astronaut and a fire fighter; she may be both mommy's good little girl and a small ruffian. Today's social butterfly may hide timidly behind his parents the next day. We welcome signs of fertility of imagination, experimentation, and variation in mood among the young. However, these changing roles also mean that the diagnostician must be careful to separate fleeting difficulties and problems of normal development from more enduring and troublesome behaviors. Rutter (1975) offers a series of guidelines for those who seek to determine whether a child's behavior is statistically abnormal in terms of age, sex, social context, frequency, severity, and persistence. In addition, one wishes to know whether the behavior creates suffering for the child, restricts his or her social interactions, interferes with development, or has an adverse impact upon other people.

A historical look. As a consequence of our increased recognition of the special experiences of childhood, there have emerged various attempts to categorize child psychopathology. Although we focus here mainly upon *DSM-III*, it is useful to examine some of its historical antecedents. The past 30 years have witnessed several increasingly more sophisticated attempts to develop descriptive systems of child psychopathology. One of the first of these was *DSM-I*. This initial attempt to categorize the behavior disorders of childhood was severely restricted. More than a decade after its initial publication, Rosen, Bahn, and Kramer (1964) examined the diagnostic records of children seen at 1,200 clinics and reported that 30 percent of the youngsters had been given no diagnosis, while an additional 40 percent had received a diagnosis of "adjustment reaction." In a similar study in Florida, Dreger and his colleagues (1964) likewise found that clinicians were reluctant to use any but the most nondescript terms in diagnosing children. They write, "Looked at realistically, what this means is that after the elaborate procedures used in most clinics are completed, the child is placed in a category which says exactly what we knew about him in the first place, that he has a problem."

Publication of *DSM-II* brought with it somewhat more extensive coverage of children. In spite of this apparent improvement, Cerreto and Tuma (1977), in a study of the clinical utility of *DSM-II* for children, noted that, for nearly 38 percent of the children studied, a diagnosis of "adjustment reaction" had been applied.

Shortly after the publication of *DSM-II*, the Group for the Advancement of Psychiatry (GAP) introduced an alternative classification system for children. The length and detail of their approach exceeded anything done to that date. But the GAP system was criticized for being so complex that it could not be used reliably in most clinical settings. It was also highly psychodynamic in orientation. The GAP system has never been put to widespread use.

An overview of *DSM-I, DSM-II,* and the GAP system reveals that all three suffer some common faults. One is the failure to adhere to any consistent classification principle. For example, they use such diverse bases as behavior (Runaway Reaction, *DSM-II*); age (Developmental Deviations, GAP; Adjustment Reaction of Childhood, *DSM-II*); severity (Psychotic Disorder, GAP); and etiology (Brain Syndrome, GAP). It is also apparent that, given the alternatives possible with these systems, most clinicians would rather use a vague term like "adjustment reaction" to describe a child. There are at least two reasons why this may be so. One is the understandable reluctance of clinicians to stick a child with a label that will remain long after the child leaves the clinic. A second reason may be that, to date, there has not been a diagnostic system for children of sufficient demonstrated utility that it seemed worthwhile to attempt a more precise classification than "adjustment reaction."

The entry of *DSM-III*. The introduction of *DSM-III* offers clinicians the most extensive and potentially useful nomenclature for child psychopathology to date. Although it is still too soon to know whether its expanded coverage will, in fact, provide more utility than its predecessors, the potential does appear to be present. Perhaps the most conspicuous difference between *DSM-II* and *DSM-III* is the sheer number of categories for children (roughly twice as great) in the new system as in the old. These categories are also more explicitly behavior-based and carefully described than they were in *DSM-II*.

The disorders

Mental retardation. Mental Retardation has been subsumed under Childhood and Adolescent Disorders in *DSM-III* because, by definition, retardation occurs before the age of 18 years. If such a behavior were to begin after age 18, it would be labeled as *dementia*. *DSM-III* specifies four levels of retardation (mild, moderate, severe, and profound); the concept of Borderline Retardation (IQ 68 to 83), used in *DSM-II*, has been dropped. A specific biological condition (such as PKU or Down's syndrome) is noted on axis 3, not as part of the primary diagnosis. In general, the diagnosis of mental retardation in *DSM-III* conforms to the practices of the American Association on Mental Deficiency.

Attention deficit disorder. What *DSM-II* called Hyperkinetic Reaction of Childhood is called Attention Deficit Disorder with Hyperactivity in *DSM-III*. Under the broad category of Attention Disorder, there is also the concept of Attention Deficit Disorder without Hyperactivity. Although both of these conditions fall within the same broad heading, no assumption is made that they reflect the same etiology. Rather, the new labels suggest that it is the child's failure to attend (rather than sheer activity level) which forms the core problem. The term Attention Deficit Disorder also drops the biological implications of such terms as Minimal Brain Dysfunction.

Conduct disorder. *DSM-II* had several diverse categories to describe the conduct disorder child: these included Unsocialized Aggressive Reaction of Childhood, Group Delinquent Reaction, and Runaway Reaction. In *DSM-III,* there are four categories of conduct disorder: Undersocialized, Aggressive; Undersocialized, Nonaggressive; Socialized, Aggressive; and Socialized, Nonaggressive. Although these form a tidy quartet, it remains to be demonstrated whether they can be reliably distinguished from one another and whether implications for treatment vary with the category.

Figure 4

Disorders usually first evident in infancy, childhood, or adolescence

Mental Retardation
Mild Mental Retardation
Moderate Mental Retardation
Severe Mental Retardation
Profound Mental Retardation
Unspecified Mental Retardation

Attention Deficit Disorder
with hyperactivity
without hyperactivity
residual type

Conduct Disorder
Undersocialized, Aggressive
Undersocialized, Nonaggressive
Socialized, Aggressive
Socialized, Nonaggressive
Atypical

Anxiety Disorders of Childhood or Adolescence
Separation Anxiety Disorder
Avoidant Disorder of Childhood or Adolescence
Overanxious Disorder

Other Disorders of Infancy, Childhood or Adolescence
Reactive Attachment Disorder of Infancy
Schizoid Disorder of Childhood or Adolescence
Elective Mutism
Oppositional Disorder
Identity Disorder

Eating Disorders
Anorexia Nervosa
Bulimia
Pica
Rumination Disorder of Infancy
Atypical Eating Disorder

Stereotyped Movement Disorders
Transient Tic Disorder
Chronic Motor Tic Disorder
Tourette's Disorder
Atypical Tic Disorder
Atypical Stereotyped Movement Disorder

Other Disorders with Physical Manifestations
Stuttering
Functional Enuresis
Functional Encopresis
Sleepwalking Disorder
Sleep Terror Disorder

Pervasive Developmental Disorders
Infantile Autism
Childhood Onset Pervasive Developmental Disorder
Atypical

Specific Developmental Disorders
Developmental Reading, Arithmetic, Language, or Articulation Disorder
Mixed Specific Development Disorder
Atypical Specific Developmental Disorder

Anxiety disorders.   There are three categories of Anxiety Disorder in *DSM-III:* Separation Anxiety Disorder, Avoidant Disorder of Childhood, and Overanxious Disorder. The child with Separation Anxiety Disorder is fearful of leaving home or parents, while the Avoidant Disorder child suffers from marked social avoidance. By contrast, the child with Overanxious Disorder is broadly fearful and worried.

It is unfortunate that the authors of *DSM-III* made no provision for the specification of other childhood fears. Because anxious behavior can often be traced to specific events, it might have been useful to allow the clinician to make a more precise diagnosis. For example, if one encounters a phobic child, one must turn to the adult category of Phobic Disorder for a diagnosis, even though we do not know to what extent an adult diagnosis of Phobic Disorder is actually appropriate for a child.

Other disorders.   Several seemingly unrelated problems are included in *DSM-III*'s heading of Other Disorders of Infancy, Childhood, or Adolescence. These include Reactive Attachment Disorder of Infancy (failure to thrive), Schizoid Disorder (defective social relationships), Elective Mutism (refusal to speak), Oppositional Disorder (disobedient behavior), and Identity Disorder (difficulty forming a coherent sense of self).

Eating disorders.   *DSM-III* offers far more detail concerning the Eating Disorders than did *DSM-II* under the old heading of Special Symptom of Feeding Disturbance. Rumination Disorder of Infancy and Pica are problems of early onset, while Anorexia Nervosa and Bulimia are more likely to begin in adolescence.

Stereotyped movement disorders.   The Stereotyped Movement Disorders include various forms of Tics and Atypical Stereotyped Movement Disorder. The latter refers to behaviors sometimes called *self-stimulation,* problems which are not uncommon among the retarded or Pervasively Developmentally Delayed. It is, however, unfortunate that *DSM-III* made no provision for a more precise description of the motor movement, since head banging, body rocking, and finger posturing are rather diverse behaviors which may or may not share the same etiology.

Other disorders with physical manifestations.   Within this category, the framers of *DSM-III* included Stuttering, Functional Enuresis, Functional Encopresis, Sleep Walking Disorder, and Sleep Terror Disorder. Many clinicians will dispute the extent to which stuttering or bed wetting belong within a psychiatric diagnostic system. *DSM-III* acknowledges that while tradition dictates their inclusion in the system, nonetheless, most children with these disorders do not suffer from a mental disorder.

Pervasive developmental disorders. One observes important changes in diagnostic strategy within the Pervasive Developmental Disorders. The category of Schizophrenia, Childhood Type (which was used in *DSM-II*), has been dropped in the new edition. In those rare instances when a child suffers from a true instance of schizophrenia, he or she should be classified according to the adult categories of that disorder.

For the first time since the American Psychiatric Association began to publish its diagnostic manual, a category of Infantile Autism has been included, as well as Childhood Onset Developmental Disorder. This change is consistent with general clinical practice and reflects the widespread view that these disorders are not likely to be a downward extension of adult schizophrenia but are different disorders, with different prognostic implications. Childhood Onset Developmental Disorder differs from Infantile Autism in that the former begins at a later age and does not show the full syndrome of autism.

DSM-III offers the best categorization of Pervasive Developmental Disorder to date. Nonetheless, it is likely that, as the state of the diagnostic art improves, there will evolve an even more sophisticated categorization of these problems.

Specific developmental disorders. The Specific Developmental Disorders (including Developmental Reading Disorder, Arithmetic Disorder, Language Disorder, and Articulation Disorder) are coded on axis 2 of the multiaxial system. Like Stuttering and Functional Enuresis, clinicians may question whether these problems ought to be included in *DSM-III*, since they are not typically a reflection of mental disorder. Although noting that concern, the authors of *DSM-III* nonetheless believed that these behaviors fall within their purview, as they are appropriate to professional attention or treatment.

Overall

There is no doubt that *DSM-III* offers a far broader and more inclusive description of childhood psychopathology than any of its predecessors. The categories of child psychopathology (like the adult categories) offer a far greater potential for reliable use than in the past. Nonetheless, many child clinicians have serious reservations about the use of some aspects of this new system. One major issue has to do with whether Developmental Reading Disorder, Arithmetic Disorder, Enuresis, or Stuttering belong within this diagnostic domain. One need not question whether or not such difficulties pose problems for children and their parents—but is it appropriate to label them behavioral disorders? And as for any predictive or prognostic import, we have relatively little reason to believe that most cases of bed wetting or stuttering carry implications for adult development.

Indeed, many childhood problems have little predictive value for adult adjustment.

Where do we draw the line between those disorders that belong within *DSM-III* and those that do not? Reading and arithmetic merit special attention in *DSM-III*. Why not spelling or writing? Will adolescents in personal rebellion against what they view as an unjust social system now be labeled as suffering from Identity Disorder? Will that justify society turning a deaf ear to their call for social concern and assigning them to psychiatrists or psychologists for treatment? Will the next generation of social protestors be seen as subjects for psychotherapy or worse? That was not likely the intent of the authors of *DSM-III*, but have they ventured too far in the expansion of their domain?

In spite of these reservations, one notes with respect that *DSM-III* has impressive technical strengths in its discussion of children. Compared to the previous systems for the categorization of childhood disorders, it is broader, more explicit, and consistent with current research.

Organic Mental Disorders

Implicit in the treatment of the organic brain disorders in *DSM-I* and *DSM-II* were the assumptions that: (1) these disorders represent variations of a single syndrome, due to diffuse impairment of brain-tissue functioning; (2) it is possible to separate these disorders into those which are psychotic and those which are not, and it is important to do so because it corresponds to degree of functional impairment and capacity to meet life's ordinary demands; and (3) it is meaningful to distinguish between organic disorders which are acute (and reversible) and those which are chronic (and irreversible). In fact, current thinking and empirical data reflect that all three organizing beliefs are not well founded and that, accordingly, they ought not to be the bases on which categorization of these disorders is made (Lipowski, 1978; Wells, 1978).

As a product of its descriptive bent, *DSM-III* describes nine organic brain syndromes which differ phenomenologically—Delirium, Dementia, Amnestic Syndrome, Organic Delusional Syndrome, Hallucinosis, Organic Affective Syndrome, Organic Personality Syndrome, Intoxication, and Withdrawal. Each has its own characteristic clinical features, course, and complications. When a dementia is due to neurological disease arising during the years of the senium or pre-senium (the 50s and 60s) or when an organic mental disorder is associated with the direct effects of a substance on the nervous system, these disorders are located in section 1 of the Organic Mental Disorders. When some other organic agent is responsible for etiology or when etiology is not known, section 2 is the locus of diagnosis.

Beyond the marked change in diagnostic bases that characterizes the Organic Mental Disorders in *DSM-III*, an equally marked expansion in

Figure 5

Organic mental disorders

Section 1. Organic mental disorders whose etiology or pathophysiological process is listed below.

Dementias arising in the senium and pre-senium
Primary degenerative dementia, senile onset
  With delirium
  With delusions
  With depression
  Uncomplicated
Primary degenerative dementia, pre-senile onset
Multi-infarct dementia

Substance-Induced
Alcohol
  Intoxication
  Idiosyncratic intoxication
  Withdrawal
  Withdrawal delirium
  Hallucinosis
  Amnestic disorder
  Dementia associated with alcohol-
    ism
Barbiturate or similarly acting seda-
  tive or hypnotic
  Intoxication
  Withdrawal
  Withdrawal delirium
  Amnestic disorder
Opioid
  Intoxication
  Withdrawal
Cocaine
  Intoxication
Amphetamine or similarly acting sym-
  pathomimetic
  Intoxication
  Delirium
  Delusional disorder
  Withdrawal
Phencyclidine (PCP) or similarly act-
  ing arylcyclohexylamine
  Intoxication
  Delirium
  Mixed organic mental disorder

Hallucinogen
  Hallucinosis
  Delusional disorder
  Affective disorder
Cannabis
  Intoxication
  Delusional disorder
Tobacco
  Withdrawal
Caffeine
  Intoxication
Other or unspecified substance
  Intoxication
  Withdrawal
  Delirium
  Dementia
  Amnestic Disorder
  Delusional Disorder
  Hallucinosis
  Affective Disorder
  Personality Disorder
  Atypical or Mixed Organic Mental Dis-
    order

Section 2. Organic brain syndromes whose etiology or pathophysiological process is either noted as an additional diagnosis from outside the mental disorders section of ICD-9-CM (The International Classification of Diseases, Revision 9, Clinical Modification) or is unknown.

Delirium
Dementia
Amnestic Syndrome
Organic Delusional Syndrome
Organic Hallucinosis

Organic Affective Syndrome
Organic Personality Syndrome
Atypical or Mixed Organic Brain Syn-
  drome

diagnoses for the acute effects of drugs on the brain has taken place. Though *DSM-II* did label the same seven acute effects of alcohol that *DSM-III* covers, diagnostic notice of the acute effects of the other drugs of abuse was possible with but one *DSM-II* diagnosis, Non-Psychotic Organic Brain Syndrome with Other Drug, Poison, or Systemic Intoxication. By contrast, *DSM-III* provides 38 diagnoses for 9 specific substances and other unspecified substances. Notable in this expansion are: (1) provision for behaviors associated with caffeine and tobacco, substances not previously considered drugs of abuse—their inclusion in a psychiatric nomenclature has aroused considerable opposition; and (2) differentiation of the behaviors associated with Intoxication with and Withdrawal from an abused substance, along with other related behaviors. Those drugs which are not addicting (cocaine, the hallucinogens, and *cannabis*) are listed only in terms of their intoxicating effects, a distinction that recognizes current research on differences in the dependency-inducing actions of the drugs of abuse (e.g., Jones, Benowitz, & Bachman, 1976; Peterson, 1977).

This dramatic increase in the labels for acute drug reactions recognizes the marked increase in use of these drugs that now requires much more diagnostic attention to them. In this way, the drafters of *DSM-III* have again been responsive to an important societal trend affecting incidence and prevalence of a group of disorders.

Although retaining concern for the varieties of acute syndromes associated with alcohol intoxication and withdrawal, *DSM-III* renames some of these conditions and drops one (Alcohol Paranoid State) for want of empirical justification for continued inclusion. Most notable among the name changes are the change of Delirium Tremens to Alcohol Withdrawal Delirium and the change of Korsakoff's Psychosis to Alcohol Amnestic Disorders. Both reflect the effort to maximize phenomenologic description as an aid to the diagnosing clinician.

Substance Use Disorders

Along with phenomenologic, organic, and empirical biases, and bias for compromise—all of which they acknowledge—the drafters of *DSM-III* made consistent efforts to de-stigmatize diagnostic labels and psychiatric and psychological conditions when and where they could. The Substance Use Disorders category, which records the behavioral (rather than organic) accompaniments of alcohol and drug dependence, represents such an effort at de-stigmatization. By contrast, *DSM-I* included the Addictions (Alcoholism and Drug Addiction), along with Sexual Deviation, Dyssocial Reaction, and Antisocial Reaction, as one of the Sociopathic Personality Disturbances. Persons given these labels were considered "ill primarily in terms of society and of conformity with the prevailing cultural milieu . . . sociopathic reactions are very often symptomatic of severe underlying personality disorder, neurosis, or psychosis. . . ." *DSM-II* draws fewer conclusions about discord with society or failure to obey societal norms in its placement of Alcoholism and Drug Dependence (along with the Sexual Deviations and the Personality Disorders) in a general category of Personality Disorders and Certain Other Non-Psychotic Mental Disorders. The contiguity of these diverse disorders itself, of course, still represents unspoken "guilt by association."

In according the Substance Use Disorders separate status, *DSM-III* removes these disorders from linkage with disorders and conditions (like sexual deviation and sociopathy) which society has traditionally condemned as morally unacceptable. Placement of these disorders in a separate category also recognizes an emerging body of empirical data (Secretary of Health and Human Services, 1981) to the effect that alcohol or drug dependence can occur in individuals who are otherwise free from psychiatric disorder.

Figure 6

Substance use disorders

Alcohol Abuse

Alcohol Dependence

Barbiturate or Similarly Acting Sedative or Hypnotic Abuse

Barbiturate or Similarly Acting Sedative or Hypnotic Dependence

Opioid Abuse

Opioid Dependence

Cocaine Abuse

Amphetamine or Similarly Acting Sympathomimetic Abuse

Amphetamine or Similarly Acting Sympathomimetic Dependence

Phencyclidine (PCP) or Similarly Acting Arylcyclohexylamine Abuse

Hallucinogen Abuse

Cannabis Abuse

Cannabis Dependence

Tobacco Dependence

Other Mixed or Unspecified Substance Abuse

Other Specified Substance Dependence

Unspecified Substance Dependence

Dependence on Combination of Opioid and Other Nonalcoholic Substance

Dependence on Combination of Substances, Excluding Opioids and Alcohol

---

DSM-III has also confronted another long-standing problem—how to distinguish between problem drinkers and recreational drug users, on the one hand, and alcoholics and drug addicts, on the other—by differentiating between drug abuse and drug dependence. Abuse involves substantial use of a drug over an extended period of time which results in significant impairment in social or occupational functioning. Dependence requires the stigmata of abuse (when *cannabis* or alcohol are involved), as well as physiological dependence (withdrawal phenomena) and tolerance. This distinction between conditions about which clinicians and researchers have debated for years is both a brave departure and a constructive step. For the first time, a distinction which many have assumed exists, but few have been able to specify, is made clearly and directly. Whether the distinction is one that can easily be made in the clinical setting, of course, is another question, as is the question of whether the distinction between abuse and dependence extends to parallel differences in treatment and course.

Development of the Substance Use Disorder grouping (like that of the Substance-Induced Organic Mental Disorders) required that decisions be made on the dependence-inducing potential of each of the drugs specified. To this end, phencyclidine, the hallucinogens, and cocaine are said to be subject to abuse but not dependence; while tobacco, which induces dependence, cannot be abused because it does not cause a clinically significant intoxication syndrome.

Schizophrenic Disorders

Some historian of psychiatric nomenclature, writing 100 years from now and (for that reason) still unborn, will doubtless speculate on whether a miracle drug was discovered during the early years of the decade of the 1980s that caused the dramatic drop in the incidence of schizophrenia in this country that has already begun. The same person might also notice, to his or her surprise, that similar reductions in the incidence of the disorder did not take place in other countries, many of which had long reported lower rates of schizophrenia than the United States.

Of course, no miracle drug for schizophrenia has been developed to augment the phenothiazines, first used to treat the disorder in the mid-1950s. Instead, *DSM-III* has introduced a series of changes in nomenclature that will narrow the concept of schizophrenia and, accordingly, reduce the frequency of the diagnosis. These changes include the following: (1) reduction in the number of schizophrenic labels from 12 in *DSM-II* to 5 in *DSM-III;* (2) imposition of a requirement that a schizophrenic disorder last for six or more months to qualify for the label; (3) removal of the diagnostic label of Schizoaffective Psychosis from the schizophrenic spectrum; (4) shift of Borderline Schizophrenia to the Personality Disorder grouping; (5) narrowing of the basic criteria for diagnosis of Schizophrenia. These changes will induce a reduction in the frequency of the diagnosis to its approximate frequency in England and Europe more generally, where the diagnosis of Schizophrenia has always been less and the diagnosis of Affective Disorder greater per capita than these diagnoses in this country.

The more narrowly defined concept of schizophrenia now requires a period of active psychotic symptomatology (including delusions, hallucinations, or formal thought disorder) and a deterioration in functioning; these disturbances must last at least six months. Persons whose psychoses last for less than six months but share the stigmata of schizophrenia will now be given the label of Schizophreniform Disorder, a less malignant diagnosis that does not carry the ominous prognosis of Schizophrenia. The new label also permits diagnosis of an acute psychotic condition that may resolve itself within a few weeks or months, without the need to assign a label that will follow the patient his or her entire life. Persons who have lifelong eccentricities or mild thought disorder but have never been psychotic, moreover, will no longer have to carry the stigmatizing schizophrenic label, as in *DSM-II*. Now they will likely be given one of two Personality Disorder labels—Schizotypal or Borderline Personality— which capture oddities of thought and instability of behavior without necessarily implying invariable progression to frank psychosis.

Persons who demonstrate symptoms both of Schizophrenia and Affective Disorder must now be examined very carefully to determine which set of symptoms predominates. Only when the clinician cannot make this judgment ought the diagnosis of Schizoaffective Disorder (which has been placed outside the schizophrenic spectrum) be given. Because the importance of resolution of these conflicting diagnoses is emphasized so strongly in *DSM-III*, moreover, most clinicians who cannot make a decision between them will feel the Schizoaffective label implies a failure of diagnosis.

The five remaining labels for schizophrenia, shown in Figure 7, harken back to the original subtypes of Dementia Praecox, first identified in Kraepelin's classic text on the disorder (1896). Hebephrenic (Disorganized), Catatonic, and Paranoid were the labels he assigned to these subtypes, along with a residual category not unlike the Undifferentiated subtype of *DSM-III*. While the labels were not original with Kraepelin (others had developed them to name unitary functional psychotic syndromes), Kraepelin was the first to bring these disorders together as the single complex we now call Schizophrenia. How unexpected that a careful effort to restore descriptive, phenomenological identity to the Schizophrenic Disorders has yielded this strength of evidence that Kraepelin's original nomenclature remains most adequate, despite the years of research and clinical work with schizophrenics that separate *DSM-III* from Kraepelin's effort. The drafters of *DSM-III*, like Kraepelin, have chosen to restrict the diagnosis to a homogeneous group of psychotic persons whose disorder is most likely to have begun during early adulthood and who suffer from recurrent psychotic episodes, are likely to share the disorder with family members, are often impaired severely, and respond best to somatic, rather than psychological, treatment.

Figure 7

Schizophrenic disorders
Schizophrenia, Disorganized
Schizophrenia, Catatonic
Schizophrenia, Paranoid
Schizophrenia, Undifferentiated
Schizophrenia, Residual

Paranoid Disorders

The rare disorders in this diagnostic grouping were included, with Schizophrenia and the Manic-Depressive psychoses, among the functional psychoses in *DSM-I* and *DSM-II. DSM-III* accords them independent status, not so much because new data suggests them to be more widespread than was thought (they are not), but because their predominant symptomatology is different from that of either the Schizophrenic Disorders or the Bipolar Affective Disorders. As a consequence, *DSM-III*'s adherence to a descriptive classification system demands a separate status for these disorders. The only change that *DSM-III* has introduced is deletion of the Involutional Paranoid State label, because recent clinical data confirm that there are no differences between the paranoid syndrome that occurs during the involutional period and the one that occurs at other times (Retterstol, 1966).

Psychotic disorders not elsewhere classified

Both of *DSM-III*'s predecessors included a group of labels designed to identify functional psychotic conditions that did not fit easily into the three major groups of functional psychosis, the Schizophrenic Disorders, the Manic-Depressive Disorders, and the Paranoid Disorders. This group of other psychotic disorders (restricted in *DSM-I* and *DSM-II* because of the latitude permitted clinicians especially to diagnose Schizophrenia) will be much more important in *DSM-III* because of the narrowing of the concept of Schizophrenia and uncertainty surrounding the boundaries of the Affective and Schizophrenic Disorders.

Symptoms of Schizophreniform Disorder are identical to those of Schizophrenia, except that six months must pass before the latter diagnosis

Figure 8

**Paranoid disorders and psychotic
disorders not elsewhere classified**

Paranoid Disorders
   Paranoia
   Shared Paranoid Disorder
   Acute Paranoid Disorder
   Atypical Paranoid Disorder

Psychotic Disorders Not Elsewhere Classified
   Schizophreniform Disorder
   Brief Reactive Psychosis
   Schizoaffective Disorder
   Atypical Psychosis

can replace the former. Accordingly, virtually all patients who would have been given a label of Acute Schizophrenic Episode in *DSM-II* will be diagnosed Schizophreniform Disorder in *DSM-III*. There is some evidence (Sartorius, Jablensky, & Shapiro, 1978) that Schizophreniform Disorder is more often accompanied by emotional turmoil and confusion, a tendency toward acute onset and resolution, and a better prognosis than the Schizophrenic Disorders; these are good reasons to distinguish the two diagnoses.

Brief Reactive Psychosis, a relatively rare disorder, is always associated with a demonstrable environmental stressor and never lasts more than two weeks. If it does last beyond that time, Schizophreniform Disorder is the appropriate label. These disorders were labeled Acute Schizophrenic Episode or Schizoaffective Schizophrenia in *DSM-II*; in both instances, a stigmatizing label was applied to an isolated behavior pattern that was almost always atypical of the individual through the rest of his or her life span.

Schizoaffective Disorder is the only *DSM-III* diagnosis which has not been provided with differential diagnostic criteria. The diagnosis is given only when the clinician cannot differentiate between Schizophrenic Disorder (or Schizophreniform Disorder) and Affective Disorder. A relatively common diagnosis in *DSM-II*, it is expressly reserved in *DSM-III* for psychotic individuals whose pattern of behavior makes it impossible to assign primacy either to schizophrenic or affective symptoms. Removing this disorder from the schizophrenic spectrum helps narrow the concept of schizophrenia. The change also reflects emerging data (Pope & Lipinski, 1978) which suggest that the Schizophrenic and Affective Disorders differ from each other and from the Schizoaffective Disorders in terms of etiology and treatment.

Affective Disorders

DSM-I and *DSM-II* distributed the affective syndromes—mild, moderate, and severe—among the functional psychoses, the neuroses, and the personality disorders. *DSM-III* brings these conditions together in a single grouping to enable the clinician to diagnose the full range of affective disorder from a consistent framework for the first time. These disorders, although they differ in etiology and in treatment, have been brought together because they share a common phenomenology: that of mood disorder.

The Affective Disorders are separated into three subgroupings: Major Affective Disorders, Other Specific Affective Disorders, and Atypical Affective Disorders. The first of these subgroupings, Major Affective Disorders, include conditions called the Manic-Depressive Illnesses in *DSM-II* and the Manic Depressive Reactions in *DSM-I*. Renaming these disorders in *DSM-III* was largely a function of empirical research which distinguished between bipolar and unipolar forms of Affective Disorder. Bipolar disorders are disorders of affect which involve a manic episode; they are bipolar because virtually every person who experiences a manic episode also experiences a clinically significant period of depression sometime in his or her life. Unipolar disorders are disorders of affect characterized only by depression. Considerable data strongly suggest that (in terms both of etiology and of treatment) these two sets of disorders differ significantly (Winokur, Clayton, & Reich, 1969).

Figure 9

Affective disorders

Major Affective Disorders
  Bipolar Disorder, Mixed
  Bipolar Disorder, Manic
  Bipolar Disorder, Depressed
  Major Depression, Single Episode
  Major Depression, Recurrent

Other Specific Affective Disorders
  Cyclothymic Disorder
  Dysthymic Disorder

Atypical Affective Disorders
  Atypical Bipolar Disorder
  Atypical Depression

Within the Other Specific Affective Disorders category are the affective disorder which was formerly included in the Personality Disorder grouping—Cyclothymic Disorder—and the disorder which was included as a Neurosis—Dysthymic Disorder. The Cyclothymia label refers to persons who are characteristically labile in emotion and show periods of depression and hypomania which, though pronounced, are nonetheless not of sufficient intensity to be included within the Bipolar Affective Disorder spectrum. The Dysthymia category is reserved for persons whose chronic disturbance of mood involves depressed mood, loss of interest in usual activities, or both that are not, however, intense or disabling enough to justify the diagnosis of Major Depression.

The advantage of including the full spectrum of affective disorders—from most benign to most severe and disabling—is the focus that is put on the signs and symptoms which distinguish between disorders that have always been difficult to differentiate. Though some of these differential diagnoses are still difficult (e.g., bipolar versus unipolar affective disorder), the drafters of this section of *DSM-III* have paid particular attention to the problems of diagnostic differentiation, in part because new and more promising treatments are now associated with some of the disorders within this diagnostic spectrum.

Anxiety Disorders

That future historian of psychiatric nomenclature to whom we have already referred might well conclude that something even more dramatic than a marked decrease in diagnoses of schizophrenia had happened in the early 1980s that led to the nearly total elimination of the neuroses.

Except for a brief note in the nomenclature to the effect that the Neuroses are now "included in Affective, Anxiety, Somatoform, Dissociative, and Psychosexual Disorders," the familiar subtypes of the Neuroses (in *DSM-II*) and the Psychoneurotic Disorders (*in DSM-I*) have been renamed, reordered, and much more thoroughly described and differentiated in *DSM-III*. Both the principal reason for this radical restructuring of a familiar nomenclature and the principal bases for the reorganization stem from the intent of the drafters of *DSM-III* to base their system on description and phenomenology rather than on theoretical assumptions about underlying mechanisms.

It is in the Anxiety Disorders grouping that one sees the most-direct impact of the attention behavior therapists have given to the neurotic disorders. One of the disorders responding most often to behavior therapy is phobic behavior (Hersen & Bellack, 1978); behavior therapists have also reported more success with some kinds of phobic behavior than with others (Kazdin & Wilson, 1978). As a consequence, from single labels in both *DSM-I* and *DSM-II* (Phobic Reaction and Phobic Neuroses, respectively), the disorder is now accorded four separate labels in *DSM-*

III, labels which call upon differential behavioral treatment for most-efficacious outcomes.

The increased attention by behavioral clinicians to *DSM-II's* Anxiety Neurosis has also been responsible, in part, for its broadening, in *DSM-III,* to include sudden attacks of fear, apprehension, or terror, and associated physical symptoms (Panic Disorder), and generalized persistent motor tension, autonomic hyperactivity, apprehension, and vigilance in the absence of recurrent panic attacks (Generalized Anxiety Disorder). The two disorders appear to require different approaches to treatment (Hersen & Bellack, 1978).

The Post-Traumatic Stress Disorders, the third component of the Anxiety Disorder grouping, represent the markedly enhanced elaboration of a condition judged to be relatively rare at the time of publication of both *DSM-I* and *II. DSM-III's* enhanced attention to these disorders reflects society's concern over what has come to be called the Post-Vietnam Syndrome. The frequency with which Vietnam veterans have entered Veterans Administration and other hospitals with symptoms of this disorder played an important role in prompting the increase in attention to these disorders in *DSM-III.*

Somatoform Disorders

This group of disorders involves physical symptoms that suggest physical disorders—in the absence of demonstrable physical findings or accepted physiological mechanisms to explain the bodily dysfunction. Psychological factors generally bulk largely in these disorders.

Figure 10

Anxiety, somatoform, and dissociative disorders

Anxiety Disorders
Phobic Disorders
  Agoraphobia with Panic Attacks
  Agoraphobia without Panic Attacks
  Social Phobia
  Simple Phobia
Anxiety States
  Panic Disorder
  Generalized Anxiety Disorder
  Obsessive Compulsive Disorder
Post-Traumatic Stress Disorder
  Acute
  Chronic or Delayed
  Atypical Anxiety Disorder

Somatoform Disorders
  Somatization Disorder
  Conversion Disorder
  Psychogenic Pain Disorder
  Hypochondriasis
  Atypical Somatoform Disorder

Dissociative Disorders
  Psychogenic Amnesia
  Psychogenic Fugue
  Multiple Personality
  Depersonalization Disorder
  Atypical Dissociative Disorder

The first three syndromes in this grouping—Somatization Disorder, Conversion Disorder, and Psychogenic Pain Disorder—are all variants of *DSM-II's* Hysterical Neurosis, Conversion Type, one of the most venerable and yet, least understood diagnoses in the nomenclature. Dating from the time of the Greeks, who attributed physical dysfunction without known-organic pathology to the emotional consequences of a "wandering uterus" (Hysteron), the term *hysteria* at one time referred to most of what came later to be termed the *Neuroses*. In *DSM-II*, the label described psychologically caused alterations in physical functioning (Hysterical Neurosis, Conversion Type) or levels of consciousness (Hysterical Neurosis, Dissociative Type). *DSM-III* has withdrawn these widely misunderstood labels. Instead of the single label Hysterical Neurosis, Conversion Type, there are now three more-descriptive labels for separate disorders: Conversion Disorder (a loss or alteration in physical functioning), Psychogenic Pain Disorder (complaints of pain out of proportion to the physical findings, with a positive history of the role of psychological factors in etiology), and Somatization Disorder (recurrent, multiple somatic complaints not due to any physical disorders for which physical attention is, nonetheless, sought). Included in this grouping, as well, is Hypochondriasis—Hypochondriacal Neurosis in *DSM-II*—which describes preoccupation with the belief that one has a serious disease in the absence of medical data to support that belief.

Dissociative Disorders

Three of the disorders in this grouping—Psychogenic Amnesia, Psychogenic Fugue, and Multiple Personality—circumscribe elements of the Dissociative Type of *DSM-II's* Hysterical Neurosis. These syndromes have to do with abrupt (but temporary) changes in levels of consciousness or psychomotor functioning. Depersonalization Disorder, comparable to *DSM-II's* Depersonalization Neurosis, is included in this diagnostic grouping because it shares with the other disorders a loss of the sense of one's own reality.

Psychosexual Disorders

The unknown historian of psychiatric nomenclature to whom we have referred twice before, writing 100 years from now about the reduction in Schizophrenia and the elimination of Neurosis in this country at the start of the last quintile of the 20th century, may also observe, to the satisfaction of all, that sexual deviation was apparently wiped from American society at about the same time. He or she will also notice a concomitant decrease in diagnoses of homosexuality signifying, presumably, an enhanced heterosexual bias among late 20th-century American men and women. The same observer might also reflect, perhaps with sorrow this time, that disorders relating to sexual *performance,* as against *preference,* had suddenly assumed imposing dimensions at the same time that sexual deviation and homosexuality had come under firm environmental control.

The Psychosexual Disorders, as this fanciful introduction suggests, have been the object of striking changes and reconceptualizations in *DSM-III.* Unlike changes in many other *DSM-III* categories reflecting accretions in knowledge or the interest to recast the instrument as a descriptive system, some of the changes introduced into this diagnostic grouping appear to have been a function more of political pragmatism and consensus than anything else.

As interesting as what has happened to these disorders in *DSM-III* is how they were conceptualized in its predecessor documents. Sexual Deviation was considered a form of Sociopathic Personality Disturbance in *DSM-I,* along with Antisocial Reaction, Dyssocial Reaction, and the Addictions. By implication, these disorders involved voluntary rejection of societal mores, weak will, moral degeneracy, or the equivalent. It was also described in the briefest of terms. The six-line description of these disorders follows:

> This diagnosis is reserved for deviant sexuality which is not symptomatic of more extensive syndromes, such as schizophrenic and obsessional reactions. The term includes most of the cases formerly classed as "psychopathic personality with pathologic sexuality." The diagnosis will specify the type of the pathologic behavior, such as homosexuality, transvestism, pedophilia, fetishism, and sexual sadism (including rape, sexual assault, mutilation). (page 62, DSM-III)

The Psychosexual Dysfunctions, disorders of sexual performance, received even less descriptive space in *DSM-I.* Classified as Psychophysiologic Autonomic and Visceral Disorders, these disorders were part of the Psychophysiologic genito-urinary reaction syndrome, which "includes some types of menstrual disturbances, dysuria, and so forth, in which emotional factors play a causative role."

DSM-II adopted the same classificatory system for these disorders, although it did give over a bit more space to the Sexual Deviations, and it was a bit more comprehensive in noting the kinds of Sexual Dysfunctions that may be observed ("dyspareunia and impotence"). Listing eight Sexual Deviations (Homosexuality, Fetishism, Pedophilia, Transvestism, Exhibitionism, Voyeurism, Sadism, and Masochism), the six lines of *DSM-I* were expanded to nine in *DSM-II:*

> This category is for individuals whose sexual interests are directed primarily toward objects other than people of the opposite sex, toward sexual acts not usually associated with coitus, or toward coitus performed under bizarre circumstances as in necrophilia, pedophilia, sexual sadism, and fetishism. Even though many find their practices distasteful, they remain unable to substitute normal sexual behavior for them. This diagnosis is not appropriate

for individuals who perform deviate sexual acts because normal sexual objects are not available to them. (page 44, DSM-II)

The moral disapprobation explicit in these words is obvious, as is the implication that individuals deserving these diagnoses are both different from and inferior to those given other diagnoses in *DSM-II*.

Figure 11

Psychosexual disorders

Gender Identity Disorders
  Transsexualism
  Gender Identity Disorder of Childhood
  Atypical Gender Identity Disorder
Paraphilias
  Fetishism
  Transvestism
  Zoophilia
  Pedophilia
  Exhibitionism
  Voyeurism
  Sexual Masochism
  Sexual Sadism
  Atypical Paraphilia

Psychosexual Dysfunctions
  Inhibited Sexual Desire
  Inhibited Sexual Excitement
  Inhibited Female Orgasm
  Inhibited Male Orgasm
  Premature Ejaculation
  Functional Dyspareunia
  Functional Vaginismus
  Atypical Psychosexual Dysfunction
Other Psychosexual Disorders
  Ego-Dystonic Homosexuality
  Psychosexual Disorder Not Elsewhere
    Classified

Although some of the key changes in the nomenclature of the Psychosexual Disorders were not motivated only by empirical findings or descriptive intent, the net result is a system which is clearly less stigmatizing and judgmental, more coherent, and better integrated into the overall nomenclature than before. Four subgroupings are specified: Gender Identity Disorders, Paraphilias, Sexual Dysfunctions, and Other Psychosexual Disorders.

The two syndromes included as Gender Identity Disorders are Transsexualism and Gender Identity Disorder of Childhood. Both are characterized by strong, persistent feelings of unhappiness at one's anatomic sex and equally strong and persistent behavior patterns characteristic of the other sex. In removing these disorders from the Sexual Deviations, where they had been located, the drafters of this section of *DSM-III* recognize that these individuals do not direct sexual interests toward objects or people other than the opposite sex but, rather, feel themselves to be *of* the opposite sex.

In choosing to rename the Sexual Deviations the Paraphilias, the drafters of *DSM-III* have both made another effort at de-stigmatization and reinforced their commitment to descriptive classification (the term emphasizes that the sexual deviation—*para*—is in the objects of the individual's attractions—*philia*). Seven of the conditions listed in *DSM-III* were also listed as Sexual Deviations in *DSM-II.* Zoophilia has been added. Most notable is the removal of Homosexuality from this group of disorders; Homosexuality in *DSM-III* is not a Paraphilia.

Instead, Homosexuality has been altered conceptually, renamed, and removed to a separate category euphemistically named Other Psychosexual Disorders. The new term, Ego-Dystonic Homosexuality, refers to persons who experience impaired heterosexual arousal and express dissatisfaction with and distress from their homosexual-arousal pattern. Homosexual individuals who are not distressed by their failure to experience heterosexual arousal and who are satisfied with their pattern of homosexual arousal are not categorized, because they are not considered to suffer from psychological, psychiatric, ·or behavioral disorder. This change, clearly a compromise, reflects the controversy that has surrounded traditional societal (and psychiatric) views of homosexuality as a psychiatric disorder by definition. Although important segments of the mental-health community remain unconvinced that only those troubled by their homosexuality merit a diagnosis, the political realities of the role of mental health workers in contemporary society, a worthwhile desire to de-stigmatize behavior which is both voluntary and generally benign to society, and simple fairness to the persons themselves, make this decision a reasonable one.

The attention given the disorders of sexual performance by Masters and Johnson and other sex therapists during the 1970s called a great deal of attention to a group of disorders that had remained relatively unknown, undiscussed, and untreated. But the success of the "new sex therapists" and the general openness of contemporary society to behaviors and problems which had remained obscure previously has resulted in a new diagnostic grouping, the Psychosexual Dysfunctions. These conditions involve inhibition in the appetitive or psychophysiological changes that characterize the complete sexual-response cycle. Notable in the development of this diagnostic grouping is attention not only to recognized problems of performance (impotence and frigidity, renamed Inhibited Sexual Excitement) but to problems that have only recently been recognized (Inhibited Sexual Desire).

Factitious Disorders

These disorders were not a part either of *DSM-I* or *DSM-II.* They refer to individuals who feign psychological or physical symptoms effectively enough to avoid discovery. As a result, these persons are successful at voluntarily producing disease, either psychological, physical, or both. This behavior is considered psychopathological because, though it is compulsive and voluntary, and hence, deliberate and purposeful, it is beyond the control of the patient. By contrast, malingering, which is not a part of the *Standard Nomenclature,* is within the patient's control.

Disorders of impulse control not elsewhere classified

This residual grouping includes impulse-control disorders not classified elsewhere in the nomenclature. Distinguishing features include: (1) inability or unwillingness to resist the impulse to carry through an act that may harm oneself or others; (2) the experience of an increase in tension/anxiety before commission of the act; and (3) a feeling of relief on completing the act.

Figure 12

Factitious disorders and disorders of impulse control not elsewhere classified

Factitious Disorders
    Factitious Disorder with Psychological Symptoms
    Chronic Factitious Disorder with Physical Symptoms
    Atypical Factitious Disorder with Physical Symptoms
Disorders of Impulse Control Not Elsewhere Classified
    Pathological Gambling
    Kleptomania
    Pyromania
    Intermittent Explosive Disorder
    Isolated Explosive Disorder
    Atypical Impulse Control Disorder

The only one of these disorders previously included in the *Standard Nomenclature* is Intermittent Explosive Disorder, roughly comparable to *DSM-II's* Explosive Personality.

Adjustment Disorder

This group of generally self-limiting disorders replaces the Transient Situational Personality Disorders category in *DSM-I* and Transient Situational Disturbances in *DSM-II*. The classification basis for both earlier groupings was age of onset. Adjustment Reactions of Infancy, Childhood, Adolescence, and Later Life could be diagnosed, as could Adult Situational Reaction in *DSM-I* and Adjustment Reaction of Adult Life in *DSM-II*.

By contrast, *DSM-III's* Adjustment Disorders are grouped according to predominant symptomatology in order both to aid in treatment planning

and to carry through the instrument's commitment to a descriptive nomenclature.

Figure 13

> **Adjustment disorder and psychological factors**
> **affecting physical condition**
>
> *Adjustment Disorder*
>   With Depressed Mood
>   With Anxious Mood
>   With Mixed Emotional Features
>   With Disturbance of Conduct
>   With Mixed Disturbance of Emotions and Conduct
>   With Work (or Academic) Inhibition
>   With Withdrawal
>   With Atypical Features
> *Psychological Factors Affecting Physical Condition*
>   Specify physical condition on Axis 3
>   Psychological Factors Affecting Physical Condition

Other differences between the concept of Adjustment Disorder in *DSM-III* and that of Transient Situational Reaction include the new grouping's exclusion of psychotic reactions which can be classified adequately else-where (although the diagnosis can be given to persons who suffer from other mental disorders). For example, some individuals suffering from Personality Disorders are particularly vulnerable to the effects of stress.

Adjustment Disorders involve a dysfunctional reaction to environmental or psychosocial stress that appears within three months of the onset of the stressor. It is a residual category, in that stress reactions that can be diagnosed elsewhere in the nomenclature negate need for this diagnosis.

These labels (which are relatively benign because they refer to mild, self-limiting conditions) are often given when a diagnosis is required by a third-party reimburser or governmental agency and a more ominous diagnosis is considered undesirable.

Psychological factors affecting physical condition

That unknown historian to whom we have already made frequent refer-ence will likely conclude—unless he or she is unusually knowledgeable about the ins and outs of this nomenclature—that psychosomatic disorders virtually disappeared from the United States early in the 1980s. In fact, this conclusion is unwarranted: these disorders continue to be codable, although the manner in which the coding must now be done represents an important change in form, if not in substance.

The psychosomatic disorders (termed the Psychophysiologic Autonomic and Visceral Disorders in *DSM-I* and, more simply, the Psychophysiologic Disorders in *DSM-II*) were identified by the organ system (nine were listed) of which the physical disorder caused or influenced by emotional factors was a part. This diagnostic approach had important limitations, including that some of the nine categories were rarely diagnosed and, more important, that the decision that a physical disorder was influenced or caused by psychological factors had to be made idiosyncratically and without direction.

The *DSM-III* response to this problem separates identification of the physical disorder in question and the affirmation that psychological factors contributed to its etiology or exacerbation. Clinicians diagnose the physical disorder (e.g., gastric ulcer, eczema, asthma) on axis 3 of the multiaxial system and include, in axis 1, the diagnosis Psychological Factors Affecting Physical Condition. The linkage of the axis 1 and axis 3 judgments, then, constitutes the diagnosis of psychosomatic disorder.

Personality Disorders

The Personality Disorders are coded on axis 2 of the multiaxial system in order to recognize that they are typical of the individual's long-term functioning and not simply expressions of a circumscribed disease process.

Figure 14

Personality disorders	
Paranoid	Avoidant
Schizoid	Dependent
Schizotypal	Compulsive
Histrionic	Passive-Aggressive
Narcissistic	Atypical, Mixed, or Other
Antisocial	Personality Disorder
Borderline	

The Personality Disorders have undergone an interesting evolution from *DSM-I* that constitutes a revealing microcosm of the pressures that have influenced the three editions of the diagnostic manual. The Personality Disorders were separated into four distinct groups in *DSM-I*. Personality Pattern Disturbances included Inadequate, Schizoid, Cyclothymic, and Paranoid personalities; Personality Trait Disturbances included Emotionally Unstable, Passive-Aggressive, and Compulsive Personalities; Sociopathic Personality Disturbances included Antisocial and Dyssocial Reactions, Sexual Deviation, and the Addictions; Special Symptom Reactions included Learning and Speech Disturbances, Enuresis, and Somnambulism. While disorders in the first group, the Personality Pattern Disturbances, have all come down to *DSM-III* intact, the concepts of Personality Trait Disturbance and Sociopathic Personality Disturbance have been markedly altered, both because they were stigmatizing and because they were not descriptive; the Special Symptom Reactions have been incorporated in the broader major category of childhood disorders.

Although *DSM-II* included the Personality Disorders and the Sexual Deviations, Alcoholism, and Drug Dependence in a catch-all grouping (Personality Disorders and Certain Other Nonpsychotic Mental Disorders), in that way maintaining *DSM-I's* association of the Personality Disorders with disorders which have received society's disapprobrium, it did distance the two groups of disorders from one another. *DSM-III* completes this separation—a decision which makes sense since the Personality Disorders share few distinguishing characteristics with the disorders with which they were previously linked.

Several *DSM-III* Personality Disorders also appear in *DSM-II*, others have been slightly modified or expanded, two have been eliminated, and several new categories have been added. Paranoid, Obsessive-Compulsive (without the Obsessive), Antisocial, and Passive-Aggressive Personalities are all personality disorders in *DSM-III*, as they were in *DSM-II*. The former diagnosis of Passive-Aggressive Personality, Dependent Type, has been renamed Dependent Personality, while the former Cyclothymic Personality is included (as Cyclothymic Disorder) as an Affective Disorder. Explosive Personality has been shifted from the Personality Disorders to Disorders of Impulse Control Not Elsewhere Classified because, unlike the other Personality Disorders, it is not ego-syntonic. Hysterical Personality Disorder has been renamed Histrionic Personality Disorder in order to conform to the instrument's descriptive focus. Asthenic Personality was dropped since it could not be differentiated reliably from mild forms of Dysthymic Disorder, while Inadequate Personality was eliminated because a distinctive behavior pattern for the diagnosis could not be described.

The most important additions to the personality disorders reflect the efforts (to which we have referred above repeatedly) to cleanse the concept of schizophrenia by removing all conditions that do not share the cardinal stigmata of the disorder from the Schizophrenic Disorders category. This effort has affected the entire nomenclature, including the Personality Disorders, which now include Borderline or latent schizophrenic conditions which share some (but not all) of the behavioral characteristics of schizophrenia; key among the missing behaviors are the cognitive and affective dysfunctions that are central to the diagnosis of schizophrenia.

DSM-II's Schizoid Personality has been replaced by three labels

(Schizotypal, Schizoid, and Avoidant Personality) which augment the former label by making it possible to be far more precise in identifying the oddities of behavior, thought, and interpersonal interaction that were the hallmarks of the former diagnosis. Closest to *DSM-II's* Borderline Schizophrenia diagnosis is *DSM-III's* Schizotypal Personality: these individuals have been reported to have an elevated incidence of familial chronic schizophrenia (Spitzer, Endicott, & Gibbon, 1979). The new diagnostic label Borderline Personality most resembles the *DSM-II* label Schizophrenia, Latent Type. The two diagnoses share instability of identity, interpersonal interaction, mood, and impulse control.

V codes

DSM-II's Conditions Without Manifest Psychiatric Disorder (Marital, Social, Occupational Maladjustment and Dyssocial Behavior) have been replaced by an expanded list of Conditions Not Attributable to a Mental Disorder That Are a Focus of Attention or Treatment, in recognition of the frequency with which problems or dysfunctions that do not derive from actual psychological or psychiatric disorder, nonetheless, demand treatment or attention.

Figure 15

> **V codes for conditions not attributable to a mental disorder that are a focus of attention or treatment**
>
> Malingering
> Borderline Intellectual Functioning
> Adult Antisocial Behavior
> Childhood or Adolescent Antisocial Behavior
> Academic Problem
> Occupational Problem
> Uncomplicated Bereavement
> Noncompliance with Medical Treatment
> Phase of Life Problem or Other Life Circumstance Problem
> Marital Problem
> Parent-Child Problem
> Other Specified Family Circumstances
> Other Interpersonal Problem

THE PRESENT AND THE FUTURE

Although we are pleased with the process of development of *DSM-III* and with many of its results, and although we acknowledge that the instrument appears to have met the enhanced reliability goals set for it, inevitable questions, problems, and concerns remain. One of the most fundamental of these is whether the instrument will actually be useful now that its reliability has been improved enough to permit assessment of validity and utility. On this issue—perhaps the most important of all— data will not be available for several years. In fact, there are few good ideas on how to gather these data. We believe, for what it's worth, that clinicians' judgments of utility are almost certainly a poor way to assess the instrument's utility.

Another fundamental, unanswered question, one which has been raised often before, is whether syndromal diagnosis (which has served as the basis for all three editions of *DSM*) is as relevant for the diagnosis of psychological, psychiatric, and behavioral dysfunctions as it is for the diagnosis of physical disorders and diseases. Said another way, although *DSM-III* has raised syndromal diagnosis to new heights of precision and reliability, one must still ask whether differentiating troubled persons on the basis of "signs and symptoms," eventuating in a syndrome, is as helpful to an understanding of their behavior and planning for their treatment as would be a separation on some other variable (like pre-morbid functioning, adaptability to change, or antecedants to or consequences of the disordered behavior). On this important issue, too, the data are not in. Psychologists have led others in proposing alternative systems, many of which organize behavior around some functional-analysis model. Yet no such system has evolved enough to represent a viable alternative to *DSM-III.*

During recent years, pioneering behavior therapist Joseph Cautela and a committee of interested psychologists under the sponsorship of the American Psychological Association have attempted to develop comprehensive, behaviorally based diagnostic systems by and for psychology. Neither attempt generated much enthusiasm, even from psychologists. Reasons include the hold syndromal diagnosis has on most of us, the difficulty of evolving a system that captures behavioral regularities and irregularities that does *not* generate syndromes, and the absence of available empirical data to justify discarding syndromal approaches. While many psychologists remain eager to adopt a system that is both their own and distinct from psychiatry's *DSM-III,* prospects do not appear bright that such a system is imminent.

Another unanswered question (one that is a good deal less important in the final analysis because it is discipline-linked and, hence, parochial) is the impact the removal of the statement "mental disorders are a subset of medical disorders" from the Foreword to *DSM-III* will have on relationships among the mental health professions. Even with removal of that offending statement, *DSM-III* remains strong "medical model" in parts— in its insistence that syndromal-based diagnosis is most appropriate, in its use of words like "disorder," "dysfunction," and "condition," in its implication that biophysiological derangements play central etiologic roles in most of the psychotic disorders, and in its suggestion that somatic treatments are often treatments of choice. But what ought one expect from an instrumentality of the American Psychiatric Association?

Our own view is that *DSM-III* marks an important benchmark. On the one hand, it signals psychiatry's earnest effort to view the psychotic disorders as of organic etiology, to be treated by somatic means. On the other hand, it accords the nonpsychotic, nonorganic disorders a strongly behavioral, phenomenologic cast, with an environmental rather than the psychoanalytic etiologic bias that earlier instruments favored. Since this differential treatment of psychosis and nonpsychosis generally accords with our own views, on balance, we are satisfied.

SUMMARY

The history of efforts to classify and categorize human behavior, normal and abnormal, is very long, dating back to the dawn of recorded human history. Systematic efforts to diagnose as well as classify, however, are generally traced to the work of Kraepelin, a German taxonomist working in the latter part of the 19th century. And it was not until the middle of this century's third decade that a standard nomenclature for physical and mental disease was first proposed in this country and not until 1952 that the first edition of the *Diagnostic and Statistical Manual of Mental Disorders* appeared. Successive editions of the *Manual* were published in 1968 and 1980.

DSM-III is both larger and more comprehensive than its predecessors. Other important features differentiating this edition of the *Manual* from its forebears include: (1) a marked modification of major diagnostic groupings to highlight, for the first time, the Substance Use, Gender Identity, and Psychosexual Disorders, the Disorders of Impulse Control, and the component syndromes of what were the Neurotic Disorders in *DSM-II;* (2) a dramatic expansion in the Childhood and Substance Use Disorders; (3) development of multiaxial diagnosis, designed to heighten diagnostic utility; (4) provision for diagnosis from operational criteria—for the most part empirically derived—designed to increase reliability; (5) extensive field testing of the instrument prior to its publication; and (6) expansion of the textual material in the *Manual* to include discussion of issues of differential diagnosis, etiology, treatment, prognosis, and management.

The bulk of the chapter is given over to extended discussion of the 16 major syndromal groupings in *DSM-III* and their evolution through the three editions of the *Manual*. The chapter concludes in an effort to capture the current status and predict the future of syndromal diagnosis and its alternatives.

REFERENCES

American Psychiatric Association. *Diagnostic and Statistical Manual of Mental Disorders.* Washington, D.C.: Author, 1952.

American Psychiatric Association. *Diagnostic and Statistical Manual of Mental Disorders* (2nd ed.). Washington, D.C.: Author, 1968.

American Psychiatric Association. *Diagnostic and Statistical Manual of Mental Disorders* (3rd ed.). Washington, D.C.: Author, 1980.

Cantwell, D. P., Mattison, R., Russell, A. T., & Will, L. A comparison of *DSM-II* and *DSM-III* in the diagnosis of childhood psychiatric disorders, IV: Difficulties in use, global comparison, and conclusions. *Archives of General Psychiatry,* 1979, *36,* 1227–1228.

Cantwell, D. P., Russell, A. T., Mattison, R., & Will, L. A comparison of *DSM-II* and *DSM-III* in the diagnosis of childhood psychiatric disorders, I: Agreement with expected diagnosis. *Archives of General Psychiatry,* 1979, *36,* 1208–1213.

Cerreto, M. C., & Tuma, J. M. Distribution of *DSM-II* diagnoses in a child-psychiatric setting. *Journal of Abnormal Child Psychology,* 1977, *5,* 147–156.

Dreger, R. M., Reed, M., Lewis, P., Overlade, D., Rich, T., Taffel, C., Miller, K., & Flemming, E. Behavioral classification project. *Journal of Consulting Psychology,* 1964, *28,* 1–13.

Feighner, J. P., Robins, E., Guze, S. B., Woodruff, R. A., Winokur, G., & Munoz, R. Diagnostic criteria for use in psychiatric research. *Archives of General Psychiatry,* 1972, *26,* 57–63.

Garmezy, N. *DSM-III:* Never mind the psychologists. Is it good for the children? *The Clinical Psychologist,* 1978, *31,* 1–6.

Greenberg, J. How accurate is psychiatry? *Science News,* 1977, *112,* 28–29.

Hersen, M., & Bellack, A. S. *Behavior therapy in the psychiatric setting.* Baltimore: Williams & Wilkins, 1978.

Jones, R. T., Benowitz, N., & Bachman, J. Clinical studies of *cannabis* tolerance and dependence. *Annals of the New York Academy of Sciences,* 1976, *282,* 221–239.

Kazdin, A. E., & Wilson, G. T. *Evaluation of behavior therapy: Issues, evidence, and research strategies.* Cambridge, Mass.: Ballinger, 1978.

Kraepelin, E. *Dementia praecox and paraphrenia.* Edinburgh: Livingston, 1896.

Lipowski, Z. B. Organic brain syndromes: A reformulation. *Comprehensive Psychiatry,* 1978, *19,* 309–322.

McGuire, R. J. Classification and the problem of diagnosis. In H. J. Eysenck (Ed.), *Handbook of abnormal psychology.* London: Pittman Medical, 1973.

McReynolds, W. T. *DSM-III* and the future of applied social science. *Professional Psychology,* 1979, *10,* 123–132.

Petersen, R. C. *Marihuana research findings.* NIDA Research Monograph 14. Rockville, Md.: U.S. Department of Health, Education, and Welfare, 1977.

Pope, H. G., Jr., & Lipinski, J. Diagnosis in schizophrenia and manic-depressive illness: A reassessment of the specificity of "schizophrenic" symptoms in the light of current research. *Archives of General Psychiatry,* 1978, *35,* 811–828.

Retterstol, N. *Paranoid and paranoiac psychosis.* Springfield, Ill.: Charles C Thomas, 1966.

Rosen, B., Bahn, A., & Kramer, M. Demographic and diagnostic characteristics of psychiatric outpatient clinics in the U.S.A. *American Journal of Orthopsychiatry,* 1964, *34,* 455–468.

Russell, A. T., Cantwell, D. P., Mattison, R., & Will, L. A comparison of *DSM-II* and *DSM-III* in the diagnosis of childhood psychiatric disorders, III: Multiaxial features. *Archives of General Psychiatry,* 1979, *36,* 1223–1226.

Rutter, M. *Helping troubled children.* New York: Plenum Press, 1975.

Sartorius, N., Jablensky, A., & Shapiro, R. Cross-cultural differences in the short-term prognosis of schizophrenic psychoses. *Schizophrenia Bulletin,* 1978, *4,* 102–113.

Schacht, T., & Nathan, P. E. But is it good for the psychologists? Appraisal and status of *DSM-III. American Psychologist,* 1977, *32,* 1017–1025.

Secretary of Health and Human Services. *Fourth Special Report to the U.S. Congress on Alcohol and Health.* Washington, D.C.: National Institute on Alcohol Abuse & Alcoholism, 1981.

Spitzer, R. L., Endicott, J., & Gibbon, M. Crossing the border into borderline personality and borderline schizophrenia: The development of criteria. *Archives of General Psychiatry,* 1979, *36,* 17–24.

Spitzer, R. L., Endicott, J. E., & Robins, E. Clinical criteria for psychiatric diagnosis and *DSM-III. American Journal of Psychiatry,* 1975, *132,* 1187–1192.

Spitzer, R. L., & Forman, J. B. W. *DSM-III* field trials, II: Initial experience with the multiaxial system. *American Journal of Psychiatry,* 1979, *136,* 818–820.

Spitzer, R. L., Forman, J. B. W., & Nee, J. *DSM-III* field trials, I: Initial interrater diagnostic reliability. *American Journal of Psychiatry,* 1979, *136,* 815–817.

Spitzer, R. L., Williams, J. B. W., & Skodol, A. E. *DSM-III:* The major achievements and an overview. *American Journal of Psychiatry,* 1980, *137,* 151–164.

Wells, C. E. Chronic brain disease: An overview. *American Journal of Psychiatry,* 1978, *135,* 22–28.

Winokur, G. Genetic patterns as they affect psychiatric diagnosis. In V. M. Rafoff, H. C. Stancer, & H. B. Kedward (Eds.), *Psychiatric diagnosis.* New York: Brunner & Mazel, 1977.

Winokur, G., Clayton, P., & Reich, T. *Manic-depressive illness.* St. Louis: Mosby, 1969.

Zubin, J. But is it good for science? *The Clinical Psychologist,* 1978, *31,* 1.

11

The initial interview

*Benjamin Pope**

INTRODUCTION

It would be a rare experience indeed to meet a person who has lived in our society, however briefly, during the last half-century without having participated in the kind of dyadic encounter we have come to designate as an interview. Anyone who has sought employment, admission to an educational institution, legal aid, government assistance, medical or psychological treatment, or has negotiated passage from A to B through a socially constructed barrier could hardly have avoided taking part in an interview in order to accomplish any of the above objectives.

The *initial interview* referred to here is usually the diagnostic interview conducted by a psychiatrist, psychologist, social worker, psychiatric nurse, activity therapist, mental health worker, or any other person charged with receiving an individual in need of mental health services at the point of entry into a hospital or outpatient facility. The task of the interviewer is that of eliciting the kind of information needed to assess the problem(s) presented by the client, initiating a relationship that will facilitate communication by the interviewee, and facilitating the client's entrance into and sojourn within the institution or program.

The author is hesitant to refer to this interview solely as a diagnostic event, because diagnosis is only one of its functions. Moreover, it would not be accurate to speak about the diagnostic interview as though it were totally distinct in character from any other type (employment interview, legal interrogation, admission interview, psychotherapy session). Indeed, any discussion of the interview and the research that has illuminated it might emphasize its specialized aspects—for example, those that distinguish the diagnostic interview from the psychotherapeutic one. It

* The Sheppard and Enoch Pratt Hospital, Towson, Maryland.

might also, by contrast, stress the more generic aspects of a dyadic communication event. This author has chosen the latter course. However, a definition of the interview must have reference to both its general and specific functions.

> An interview is a conversational encounter between two individuals encompasssing both verbal and nonverbal interactions. It is not an encounter between equals for it is based on a differentiation of roles between the two participants. The one to whom the major responsibility for the conduct of the interview is assigned is designated the *interviewer;* the other, the *interviewee.* Although the interviewee may request the interview as a consequence of his/her own motivations or needs and thus introduce his/her personal objectives into the exchange, the goals of the interview as a dyadic system are generally determined by the interviewer. The following are frequently occurring objectives: The interviewer elicits information from the interviewee (e.g., a physician obtains a medical history from a patient); s(he) imparts information to the interviewee (e.g., a school counselor conveys college entrance information to a student); s(he) assesses or evaluates the interviewee as in the diagnostic interview; s(he) influences, changes, or modifies the behavior of the interviewee as in the psychotherapeutic interview. (Pope, 1979, p. 3)

The following brief excerpts from three fictional interviews illustrate the contrasts in interviewer style that could occur if three different interviewers were working with the same interviewee. The patient is a young woman, 27 years of age, with an increasingly debilitating phobia about separation from her husband. Anxiety symptoms have grown in severity to the point of threatening her occupational future and that of the marriage of five years' duration. The first of the three brief excerpts is taken from an interview that a behavioral therapist might have conducted in preparation for setting up a desensitization program.

Er: When did you last experience this panic?

Ee: Yesterday.

Er: When?

Ee: When my husband was leaving for work.

Er: What did you say to each other then?

Ee: I asked him to call me as soon as he got to work.

Er: And?

Ee: He would not promise to do it, and left.

Er: What did you do then?

Ee: Nothing. [*Pause.*] Nothing. I cried. I couldn't stand the thought of not knowing when he would reach his office. Of not knowing where he was from the time he left home to the time he got to work.

Er: How did you feel?

Ee: Like always. My heart started beating. I perspired. I thought I would faint.

Er: Tell me about the last time, before yesterday, this kind of thing happened to you.

Ee: [*Silence.*]

Er: How about the day before yesterday? Did anything happen then?

Ee: Yes.

Er: When?

Ee: In the afternoon, about 2 or 3 o'clock.

Er: Exactly what happened?

Ee: I called him at work.

Er: And?

Ee: He wouldn't come to the phone. He got his friend who shares an office with him to say that he was in a meeting.

The interviewer has a specific objective in the interview. Because he needs a sampling of situations in which the patient's phobia occurs, his questions are quite specific. Indeed, his remarks are all interrogative. His focus is on current experiences and is objective in character. His style is that of a benign interrogator. Clearly, he is dominant in the relationship and actively directs its course. It is difficult to tell from this excerpt whether his attitude toward the patient is warm or cold, but the probability is high that in this interrogatory interlude it is neutral.

If the interviewer were pursuing a psychoanalytic approach to the treatment of this patient his style would be quite different, as exemplified in the following interview segment.

Er: Tell me what you can about the problems that have brought you here.

Ee: I can't stand being away from my husband for even short periods of time. I need to know where he is every minute of the day. [*Silence.*]

Er: Go on.

Ee: Well, that's the problem. There's nothing else to tell.

Er: How do you feel when he's away?

Ee: I feel panicked. I cry. [*Pause.*] My heart beats. I'm soak-drenched in . . . by perspiration and I feel as though I mi . . . might faint.

Er: Have you ever fainted when he's away?

Ee: No.

Er: Can you tell me more?

Ee: It's embarrassing. I can't let him go without promising to tell me where he'll be and how I can reach him. And he . . . he gets angry at me now. He feels that I'm interfering with him at work. But I won't-can't stop myself.

Er: Has it always been this way?

Ee: No. When I first met him during my sophomore year in college we had a good time. We were close, but not like this. I really get panicked when I know-think I may be wrecking our marriage.

Er: Have there been other times in your life when you had similar problems?

Ee: Yes.

Er: Tell me about them.

Ee: Well, when I first left home to go to college, I remem-it was touch and go for the first few months. I called home every other day. I cried . . . cried a lot and stayed in my dorm quite a bit. [*Pause.*]

Er: Go on please.

Ee: I kept having crazy thoughts that mother would die and I would not be there. Crazy-well, my mother is a diabetic but she's had everything under control for years now.

Er: So?

Ee: Well, it wasn't only that. My younger sister is just starting high school. I keep-kept thinking about her—just thinking that she might get involved in drugs and I wouldn't be there to help.

Er: Yes?

Ee: And, then I think . . . thought that without me in the house mother might forget me entirely and become completly involved with my sister. Mother has always favored her. She is popular and attractive. Mother enjoys helping her shop for clothes.

Later, the Er explored the patient's school years and elicited an admission from her that her first two years in school were blighted by a serious school phobia; there were long periods when her mother would give in and let her stay at home.

This interview is quite different from the first. The Er's style is less interrogatory. He directs the interview by focusing on certain areas, but his inputs are minimal and assume the form of brief invitations to the Ee to speak about areas of interest in her own way. His purpose is to be as ambiguous as he might within the constraints of the general topical direction he exercises so that the associative course of the patient's narrative might assert itself. The information he wished is contained both in the topical content of the patient's communications and in such nonverbal aspects of speech as silent pauses and speech disturbances. The Er's interpersonal manner is not a dominant one; without surrendering his topical control of the interview, he leaves the Ee considerable initiative. Since expressive tone of voice is muted in a transcript, one cannot make a ready judgment about the affective quality in the interviewer's speech. But its verbal content would suggest a tone of neutral exploration.

Finally, we might conjecture about the course that a client-centered interview might take with the same patient.

Er: You've come here because you feel upset about your phobia?

Ee: Yes, I'm afraid that I may lose my job and that my husband may leave me.

Er: The thought that these things might happen makes you feel really scared inside.

Ee: Yes, whenever I think of these things my heart starts beating, and I perspire all over.

Er: So you expect something terrible might happen.

Ee: Yes. Sometimes I feel I might faint.

Er: And you expect something might happen between you and your husband?

Ee: Yes, I don't know how much longer he will put up with me; with all the things I expect him to do.

Er: Your're afraid that he's getting impatient with the demands you make on him.

Ee: Yes. Wouldn't you? When he leaves for work I say: "Please call me when you get to the office." When I call him at noon I try to get him to tell me exactly when he will be at his desk and when he'll be away so I won't get panicked when I call and he's not there. When I call in the afternoon I might say to him: "Please telephone me before you leave so I'll know how long it will be before you come home."

Er: Yes. You wish I or somebody could reassure you about what your husband might do. You're afraid he might leave you, but you can't keep yourself from calling him anyway.

The third interview diverges from the others in its apparent lack of concern with an informational exploration of the problem. The Er is quite willing to be as active as he needs to be to reflect the patient's feelings. However, there is not a trace of interrogation; instead, there is an empathic reflection of what the patient experiences. There is a similarity between the first and the third interviews in the consistency of interviewer input. But the character of the input in these two interviews is quite different. In the first, all of the Er's remarks are specific questions; in the third, they are reflective statements about the Ee's feelings. The relationship between interviewer and interviewee are also markedly contrasting. In the first, the interviewer is dominant; in the third, both interviewer and interviewee enter into a sort of egalitarian relationship. Finally, one would expect the vocal tone of the third interviewer to be warm, contrasting to that of the first in this respect, too.

Practitioners of the mental health interview are aware of diversity in their styles of interviewing, associated with the schools to which they adhere, their background experiences, the models they have emulated, and their personal attitudes and dynamics. Thus, a client-centered interview is readily distinguishable from a psychoanalytic one; and the former two from a behavioral assessment interview. Just as varied are the modes of communication and relationship of interviewees, and the interactions that occur between the two participants in a dyadic encounter.

What is not as evident, on first glance, is the operation of certain correlations and contingencies which traverse the range and diversity of interview types and idiosyncracies. These represent the system aspects of an interview interaction. In a generic sense, the interview is a dyadic communication system, in which certain variables are primarily related to the communication of information, and others, more directly to relationship. Both communication and relationship are overlapping aspects of an interview interaction, distinguishable but not independent of each other. (Pope, 1979, p. lx)

The remainder of this chapter will deal with the contingencies that occur between selected dimensions of *communication* and *relationship,* both within each category and between the two, and how these govern the interview interaction. Data will be sought primarily in research studies, although the clinical relevance of the data will always be a primary concern. Thus, there will be an effort to bridge the gap between research and clinical application. However, brevity will compel an economic selection of studies for discussion. In many instances, reference will be limited to the findings of the studies, with little or no focus on the research procedures. Some may, therefore, reproach me for omitting studies and areas of investigation that they find particularly significant. Others might wish that there had been a greater emphasis on the critique of research procedures.

COMMUNICATION IN THE INTERVIEW

Verbal content

In the first of the three preceding fictional interviews, the topics covered in the interview and their sequence were determined solely by the interviewer. To construct a desensitization hierarchy, he required certain classes of information and inquired about them directly and specifically. The third interviewer left the initiative to the interviewee and selectively responded to expressions of feeling through reflective comments. It may be assumed that these comments served to reinforce such expressions. Because affective self-disclosure is considered to contribute to the healing process, the interviewer was engaged in treatment from the beginning. The analytic interviewer in the second example took a middle position between the first and the third. He was indeed interested in certain categories of information, such as the current problem and related past history, both recent and remote. But the inquiry was not constrained into channels laid down by specific questions. Instead, it was conducted with the use of ambiguous leads, such as "go on," "tell me about them," and others equally open-ended. This was done to permit the patient to follow her own associational directions in developing her narrative. If the interviewer listened closely, he would have noted the following clustering of words and phrases in the narrative that evolved: panicked-perspiration-faint-embarrassing; husband-know where he is-angry; mother-die-diabetic-sister-drugs-popular-attractive. Clinicians with a psychoanalytic orientation regard the words and phrases in such clusters as associatively linked because of a common connection in each cluster, with an underlying dynamic theme, conflict, or motivational focus. The difficulty in the use of such associational clusters is the subjectivity that governs their interpretation. Thus, the cluster related to mother in the above example might be regarded as an expression of the patient's dependent attachment to mother and fear of losing her, or the patient's anxiety about being displaced in mother's affection by her sister, or a complex expression of both themes. Nevertheless, ". . . clusters of concepts or images provide the interviewer with fertile sources of clinical inference regarding the dynamics of the interviewee" (Pope, 1979, p.89).

Several authors have utilized computer technology to demonstrate the information value of verbal clusters that occur when the interviewee is free to say things without undue interviewer constraint. Harway and Iker (1969) have based a study in this area on five interviews selected from the fully recorded, psychoanalytic treatment of one patient, a 27-year-old divorced salesman. His presenting problems included poorly controlled outbursts of hostility, frequent loss of employment, a brief unsatisfactory marriage, and compulsive stealing.

Briefly, the computerized analysis of the interview content was carried out in the following way: verbatim transcripts of the selected interviews were divided into five-minute segments, and the frequencies of words considered to be clinically important were intercorrelated across the time segments and factor analyzed. All words significantly loaded on a factor were assumed to belong to an associational cluster. The following is an example of a cluster that emerged in the factor analysis: affection, cry, mother, help, wake, show, job, mean, and remember. The authors have labeled this factor as *dependency*. Clearly, the labeling of a factor is not an objective process but is rather one of clinical inference. Whether it is based on clusters separated out by computerized processes based on verbatim transcripts, or on the direct perception of the interviewee's associational flow by the interviewer, interpretation is a subjective matter. However, the verbatim transcripts and the subsequent computerized intercorrelations provide objective evidence of the actual occurrence of frequency-determined verbal clusters (i.e., of an associational structure).

In conclusion, Harway and Iker remark:

> The concept of content . . . is based on an associative model. People, objects, attributes, events, actions, states, affects, which tend to co-occur in a person's speech, define an area of content. In the clinical setting inferences are made as to the patient's perceptions and conflicts, not only as explicitly stated by him, but also from associations in his verbalizations which

may or may not be in the range of the patient's awareness and consciousness. (p. 97)

Verbal content is one of the interviewer's major sources of information
about the interviewee. When it is not communicated directly by the interviewee, it may be inferred from the kind of associative clustering briefly
reviewed above. But it is not enough to identify the thematic content
offered by the interviewee. It must also be evaluated so that its salience
and dynamic significance to the interviewee might be understood. In
this task, the interviewer is helped by the interviewee's psychological
reactions to the verbal content s(he) communicates. One of the major
distinctions that the interviewer must make in an initial interview is that
between high and low anxiety arousing topics. In perceiving this distinction, the interviewer functions as a finely tuned clinical sensor, for the
anxiety arousing potential of a topic may vary from one person to another.
For example, an experienced interviewer may note some acceleration
in the interviewee's speech or some increase in speech disturbance at
the point of transition from one topic to another. These paralinguistic
changes in the interviewee's speech signal an increase in anxiety to the
interviewer. Whatever decision the interviewer may make about his/her
response to this anxiety, the first step will be that of reliably identifying
the anxiety arousing theme.

The correlates in interviewee speech of topically aroused anxiety were
investigated in a series of studies (Pope & Siegman, 1965; Siegman &
Pope, 1965, 1966) with the following results. An anxiety arousing topic,
in contrast to a neutral one, functioned as an activator of speech, i.e., it
elicited higher productivity (Pope & Siegman, 1965), a faster rate of
articulation of words and fewer filled pauses, i.e., expressions of hesitation
such as "ah" (Siegman & Pope, 1965). However, it also disrupted speech
in the following ways: change of topic in the middle of a sentence, incomplete sentence, incomplete word, repetition of word and/or phrase, stuttering, intruding incoherent sound, and tongue slip. Clearly, then, the interviewer is not only an active participant in the interview; s(he) must also
be a perceptive listener. In the above example, a discernible change
in tempo of speech and in its flustering are signals that something important has occurred. It should prompt the interviewer to explore the possibility that a change of topic or the emergence of a new association has
elevated the interviewee's anxiety level.

In all of this, the interviewer is not simply a neutral recorder of interviewee communications. He cannot avoid evaluating them as he receives
them, sometimes with approval, but often with displeasure. The danger
that the interviewer will approve or disapprove on an idiosyncratically
personal basis is mitigated by the fact that certain values and attitudes
about interviewee verbal content are widely shared by mental health
practitioners. There is, for example, a broad concensus among them that
personal self-disclosure is preferable to defensively avoidant speech.

> In the initial interview, self-disclosing communication is used as a source
> of psychological information; in the therapy interview, it is regarded as a
> dynamic of personal change. The belief that both interviewer and inter-
> viewee openness are conducive to a successful outcome of psychotherapy
> is supported by the results of a number of research studies. (Pope, 1979,
> p. 90)

Indeed, in the early 1970s, largely as a consequence of the work of
Jourard (1971a, 1971b), there was a growing advocacy of interviewer
self-disclosure as an effective stimulus for self-disclosure from the interviewee. Proponents of this point of view spoke about the interactional
or dyadic character of self-disclosure. However, mental health practitioners have been divided on this issue. Nearly all would agree that self-
disclosure is commendable in the interviewee, but only some would accept a focus on personal openness as a proper form of communication
for the interviewer. A look at some research studies—pertaining to self-
disclosure both as a form of interviewee verbal communication and as
an attribute of the reciprocal exchange between the two members of a
dyadic-communication situation—is now in order.

Some research attention has been paid to the relative ease with which
interviewees are able to be frankly expressive in different topical areas.
The problem here for the interviewer is that s(he) cannot asssume that
any set of given topics evoke the same psychological responses in different individuals. Thus, in an early study conducted with undergraduate
college students, both male and female, Kanfer (1959) found that his
Ss did not display a concensus about the anxiety arousing effect of the
following five topics: family relationships, the interviewee's degree of
confidence in self, his/her sense of competence and achievement, feelings
of attractiveness to and confidence with the opposite sex, and feelings
of emotional maturity. He concluded that "the assumption of a culturally
determined, universal anxiety arousing effect of the various topics is not
borne out" (Kanfer, 1959, p. 309). It may be assumed that, in most situations, there would be a negative correlation between the anxiety aroused
by a topic and the readiness of a S to speak openly about it.

But Kanfer's finding notwithstanding, one cannot assume that all topics
in all situations are idiosyncratically varied from one person to another.
Some elicit such widely shared perceptions and values as to lead to
similar responses by members of specified population groups. Thus, in
a later study (Jourard & Friedman, 1970) the authors did succeed in
obtaining a signficant level of agreement between male and female college students in their rating of the intimacy level of selected topics. For
example, these Ss agreed that the following question was of a low-intimacy
character: "What are your personal views on politics, the presidency,
foreign and domestic policy?" By contrast, the next question was judged
to be high in intimacy: "What are the actions you have most regretted

doing in your life and why?" In interviews conducted with a second group of Ss, the topics that had been selected in the above study as high in intimacy produced significantly less disclosure (i.e., shorter responses) than those designated as low-intimacy.

Clearly, an interviewer who sets out to conduct a personal exploration of a patient must be attuned to the psychological significance of different topics to the individual. The interviewee may find it easier to speak freely about some topics with little assistance from the interviewer but may need considerable prompting and support to talk openly about other matters.

But the interviewee's capacity to communicate in a freely nondefensive manner depends on other factors as well, not the least of which is the interviewer-interviewee relationship. It is difficult to imagine any degree of openness (on the part of the interviewee) without a feeling of trust in the interviewer; indeed, it may not happen without a sense of personal closeness. The following is a summary statement that Jourard has written of his research in this area: "Researches I have conducted show that a person will permit himself to be known when he believes his audience is a man of goodwill. Self-disclosure follows an attitude of love and trust. If I love someone, not only do I strive to know him; I also display my love by letting him know me." (Jourard, 1971a, p. 5)

The interactional character of self-disclosure was demonstrated explicitly in studies conducted by Jourard (1971b), in which the variable of interviewer self-disclosure was experimentally manipulated. First, female undergraduate Ss (matched for previous histories of self-disclosure and for their current willingness to speak openly about themselves) indicated a greater readiness to communicate about personally intimate topics to the E and to other Ss, after having conversed with an interviewer who was deliberately self-disclosing, than they did after an interview devoid of interviewer openness. In a second experiment, similar to the one above, those Ss who had been interviewed by a self-disclosing (rather than an inexpressive) interviewer were more open about themselves in their actual communications within a subsequent interview.

But the differentiation of interviewer and interviewee roles does shape and limit the reciprocal character of self-disclosure in the interview. Thus, excessive interviewer self-disclosure (Levin & Gergen, 1969) is likely to silence the interviewee because of its inappropriateness. This is particularly true at an early point in the interview (Chaikin & Derlega, 1974), when both participants are still strangers to each other. And finally, there is some research evidence that personal openness is more acceptable from a female interviewer than from a male, regardless of the sex of the interviewee.

The preceding studies notwithstanding, the burden of the evidence on interviewer self-disclosure supports its effectiveness as a means of encouraging a positive relationship and productive communication in the interview.

Control and direction of verbal content

The control and direction of the interviewee's verbal communications present no problems in the first interview quoted above. The interviewer, as interrogator, develops an interview which is very much like a spoken questionnaire. The information needed is usually determined before the interview begins. It is generally objective and factual in character. Sometimes, even the sequence in which specific questions will be asked has been established before the first word is spoken. If this type of interview were universally satisfactory, no further thought or study would need to be given to other procedures for directing and controlling verbal content.

Unfortunately for the mental health interviewer, the simplicity of the interrogation is rarely congruent with his/her interview goals.

> Most clinicians prefer the uncertainties of the relatively unstructured, ambiguous interview to the high predictability of the interview fashioned out of preformulated specific questions. The reason for this choice does not lie in an ingrained perversity . . . in clinicians who would appear to prefer a difficult course, full of uncertainty, rather than a sure and simple one. It pertains rather to the kind of information desired, and the type of interaction that the interviewer wishes to foster. To be sure, some of the information that the interviewer needs is factual and specific. Thus, he/she will need to know the age of the interviewee, the time of onset of the problem, its duration, the patient's marital status, the location and conditions under which he grew up, and many other bits of historical and contextual information. For this type of information, questions that tend to be highly specific are appropriate. But most of the information needed by the clinician is of a more subjective character, obtained largely from self-disclosing messages. These include such verbal-content categories as descriptions of one's problems, self-evaluative remarks, thoughts and memories about self and others, feelings, moods, and many others that are generated by personal introspection. Moreover, the interviewer "reads" the interviewee's style of communication and receives an entire spectrum of nonverbal messages. Self-disclosing and expressive communications are fostered by interview conditions of sufficient ambiguity to permit a communicational interaction to develop.
>
> Whatever the orientation of the interviewer, s(he) must find a balance between enough ambiguity to permit the interviewee to speak freely and expressively and enough structure to conduct the communication into channels that are considered important. . . . To accomplish this balance, s(he) may choose to be more or less active, more or less ambiguous, and to proceed in a more or less interrogatory manner. (Pope, 1979, p. 98)

These are stylistic matters and will be considered later.

At the moment, the following three methods of directing the course of the interview will be considered: orienting instructions to the interviewee (usually at the beginning of the interview), modeling the type of communication desired, and conditioning selected categories of interviewee response. These procedures are congruent with the interactional and expressive type of interview described above. Each procedure will be viewed both in the context of a few selected research studies and—more naturalistically—in its clinical application.

All three of the above methods perform two important functions: they provide the interviewee with information about what is expected of him/her, and they instigate or motivate him/her to communicate in the desired way.

A formal type of initial instruction called the *role-induction interview,* has been demonstrated to be effective with low-socioeconomic patients (Hoehn-Saric, Frank, Imber, Nash, Stone, & Battle, 1964; Orne & Wender, 1968). This interview is conducted by a research clinician, not by the therapist. Scheduled before the beginning.of a psychotherapy sequence, it includes information to the interviewee about topics that will be discussed in the psychotherapy interviews to follow, the style of communication expected of the patient, and a preview of the therapist behavior the client will encounter. Patients who were given the role-induction interview, in contrast to those who were not, were judged by their therapists to show more acceptable in-therapy communication and demonstrated more successful treatment outcomes.

The role-induction interview is an example of a formal pre-interview that has proved effective in making the client's in-therapy communication more appropriate than it might otherwise have been. But it is somewhat awkward in that it is separate and disconnected from the first interview.

The kind of interviewer remark that ordinarily occurs early in the interview, called the *primary-system reference,* is less obtrusive and more integrally a part of the initial, interview, and indeed, of later interviews, too (Lennard & Bernstein, 1960). This is a type of comment made by the interviewer usually at an early point in the interview, pertaining to ". . . reciprocal therapist-patient role relations. . ." (Lennard & Bernstein, 1960, p. 92). Primary system references are means of reducing strain through clarifying role expectations and inducing expectations in the interviewee that are congruent with those possessed by the interviewer. These remarks both direct and motivate the interviewee to assume interview-appropriate roles. They were found to be especially helpful with low-socioeconomic patients, whose knowledge of the interview process was meager. The authors found that those interviews in which there were the most early primary system references were the ones manifesting least strain and most open communication.

> The effectiveness of the interview may also be enhanced through a demonstrative sort of instruction . . . better known as modeling. The interviewee listens to a tape, reads a script, or observes a live interaction between an interviewer and an interviewee (or their surrogates in various experimental designs), demonstrating the content and expected style of communication by the interviewee. (Pope, 1979, p. 123)

One experimental investigation of the efficacy of modeling in overcoming interviewee avoidance or resistance was conducted by Sarason, Ganzer, and Singer (1972). Male undergraduate students were assigned to three experimental groups and to one control group. The members of the four groups were ultimately to participate in 10-minute interviews. But first the Ss in the three experimental groups were differentially exposed to modeling procedures. The members of one group, designated as "defensive," listened to a segment of a taped interview in which the speaker communicated in a defensive manner, speaking about himself in neutral or positive terms only. The members of the second group audited an "ambivalent" tape, in which the speaker communicated with uncertainty, anxiety, and conflict about personal and emotional matters. And the Ss in the third or "expressive" group heard a tape in which the model's speech was direct, open, and self-disclosing in remarks that dealt with both positive and negative self-evaluation. For the control group, there were no modeling tapes. Finally, the members of all four groups were asked to speak for 10 minutes with a focus on what they thought and felt about themselves.

The Ss in the three experimental groups were more productive than those in the control group, but the differences attained only borderline levels of significance. Two of the experimental groups (defensive and ambivalent) were significantly higher than the control group in positive self-references; and the expressive group was significantly more open than the defensive and control groups in frequency of negative self-reference. Thus, modeling facilitated a S's gross verbal output when asked to speak in a personal vein and enhanced the frequency of negative self-disclosure when the taped model demonstrated this form of communication.

A modeling procedure less obtrusive in the interview than the introduction of a tape is the interviewer's self-disclosure as a means of increasing that of the interviewee, i.e., the dyadic effect noted by Jourard (1971a, 1971b).

Perhaps the most effective and least obtrusive procedure for directing the course of an interview is that of reinforcement. This method disrupts the interview exchange less than the other two, because it tends to occur naturalistically in all conversational encounters. Even in informal dyadic exchanges, both participants will attend and respond to certain topics communicated by those with whom they are speaking and tend to ignore others. While this type of selective listening and responding is likely to occur without focal awareness in an informal conversation, its deliberate use in directing the course of an interview has received increasing emphasis as research has illuminated its efficacy.

Given the preference of a mental health interviewer for an unstructured or ambiguous interview, his/her resort to the direction of its verbal content through informal reinforcement procedures is inevitable. Thus, s(he) might encourage psychologically revealing communication from the interviewee with such signals of recognition and attention as "yes," "mm-hm," "go on," "I see," and discourage avoidant interviewee talk through silent response.

In general, the effect of verbal conditioning is most evident in ambiguous interviews (Heller & Marlatt, 1969). When there is little direct guidance from the interviewer, each reinforcing response from him/her has an augmented impact on the interviewee. Thus, the low-active interviewer is in no way lacking in the means of influencing the course of the interview. Indeed, it has been noted that ". . . the less responsive the therapist and the more ambiguous the stimulus field in which the patient must operate, the more likely will the patient be to follow the few orienting cues that the therapist provides" (Heller & Marlatt, 1969, p. 579).

The early studies on verbal conditioning had little to offer the mental-health interviewer because the response classes selected for conditioning were atomistic. For the most part, they were single-word categories such as plural nouns (Greenspoon, 1962) and first-person pronouns (Taffel, 1955). In time, however, the categories became more complex, including affect words and statements (Salzinger & Pisoni, 1958), positive and negative self-references (Rogers, 1960), and expressions of hostility (Bandura, Lipsher, & Miller, 1960), demonstrating the utility of reinforcement in directing the type of verbal content that occurs in a mental health interview.

Indeed, studies dealing with the reinforcing effects of interviewer responses even when not devised primarily as conditioning procedures eventually appeared in the literature. A prominent example is the work done with accurate reflection of feeling as it is practiced by Rogerians. Its primary purpose is communication of the therapist's empathic perception of the patient's feelings, with the objective of developing a positive relationship and a climate conducive to therapeutic change. But clinical observation and research have underscored the verbal conditioning fostered by the use of this form of interviewer communication (Ivey, 1971). Through the use of reflection, the therapist responds selectively to expressions of feeling by the patient. Consider, for example, the following interview excerpt:

> **Client:** So I'm wondering if you can help find a major.
> **Counselor:** [*Silence.*]
> **Client:** I suppose if I did find one, I'd just bungle things again.
> **Counselor:** You feel discouraged. (Ivey, 1971, p. 58)

The counselor focused on the affective side of the client's communication, thus prompting the client into further affective statements.

Finally, the practitioner of the interview must be aware that, in contrast to food pellets for pigeons, verbal reinforcers for humans are variable and dependent on the interview context. Even the word "good" cannot be accepted, a priori, as positively reinforcing to all interviewees. Some may suspect it because of their mental condition. Others may respond to it with varying intensity because they differ in their need for social approval. Clearly, the use of reinforcement as a method of directing and controlling verbal content does not liberate the interviewer from the need to make clinical judgments about specific interview situations. The reinforcers used and the categories of verbal response chosen to reinforce will vary with the interviewee and the goals of the interview. (Pope, 1979, p. 125)

In conclusion, it must be clear that instruction, modeling, and reinforcement are not procedures that have originated in the research laboratory and then were applied to the interview. If anything, the reverse sequence has probably occurred. Introductory, orienting remarks by the interviewer, the tendency of interviewees to emulate in varying degrees the verbal style and content of their interviewers, and the reciprocal reinforcement of verbal content that one finds between dyadic partners (both in interviews and in informal, conversational exchanges) are all naturalistic occurrences. However, research has led to their explicit definition, the illumination of their effects on both members of the dyad, and consequently, their more deliberate deployment in the practice of the interview.

Verbal style in interview communication

Style, as an attribute of communication, has a narrower meaning than that associated with it in its more general application. "Stylistic variables are not decorative embellishments in the process of therapy; they are components of process" (Pope, 1977, p. 391). They designate certain qualities of both interviewer and interviewee communication. Further definition is needed but will be preceded by two illustrations from fictional interviews.

Interviewer A is a male resident admitting his first patient to a private psychiatric hospital. Interviewer B, also male, is a senior member of the psychiatric staff of the same hospital. In these fantasied interview segments, both interviewers will be observed interviewing the same patient. They both know that the patient, a 21-year-old female college student, had experienced an acute anxiety reaction while attending a summer session at a local university. Indeed, anxiety became sufficiently intense to compel her to drop out of the session. Brief excerpts from the two fictional interviews follow.

Interviewer A	*Interviewer B*
Er: When did you come here?	**Er:** When did you come here?
Ee: This morning.	**Ee:** This morning.
E: Why did you have to come?	**Er:** Tell me what you can about the reason for your coming to the hospital.

Ee: I had to drop out of my summer session because I was constantly afraid. I don't know why.

Er: Of what were you afraid?

Ee: Well, I said I didn't know.

Er: How long did you have this anxiety?

Ee: For nearly a year, but it got worse during the summer.

Er: Were you afraid you'd flunk your course?

Ee: No. That wasn't it.

Er: Was there trouble at home?

Ee: No. Things were fine there.

Ee: I was always afraid when I was at school this summer. I don't know why, but it got so bad I had to drop out.

Er: Yes?

Ee: Well, I couldn't control it. It got so bad I was afraid to get out of bed in the morning, afraid to talk to my friends; I could hardly sit still in class.

Er: That must have been really uncomfortable.

Ee: I felt that most of my classmates were avoiding me. I would never get invited to any of the parties. I wasn't even welcome when kids I knew would gather informally in the student union.

The stylistic attributes of the two interviews are quite different. Interviewer A is totally interrogatory. Indeed, his questions are highly specific. In this sense, he was very much like the interviewer at the beginning of this chapter. But he differed from the previous interviewer in some amateurish flaws that may have resulted from his inexperience and, possibly, his anxiety. Thus, the interviewer found it difficult to relinquish his assumption that the patient must know what the cause of her anxiety might be. Again and again he returned to this theme, unable to be content without an instant statement of cause from the patient. If the interview were to continue in the vein in which it began, it would become a sort of interrogation. Small wonder then that the patient replied briefly, not offering any information about which she had not been specifically asked. By contrast, interviewer B was only moderately interrogatory; he was actually much more open-ended in his method of inquiry. Admittedly, the longer interviewee responses might not have occurred instantly, as the example seems to imply, but would have emerged as the inteview progressed. Such a result would have had something to do with the less-extractive style of the interviewer.

Without yet attempting a definition of communication style, one may observe that B was more open-ended than A, and less specifically demanding. Indeed, B varied his modalities of communication from questions to simple reinforcing words ("Yes"), ambiguous requests ("Tell me what you can . . ."), and reflections of feeling ("That must have been really uncomfortable . . .").

Style is contained within linguistic channels of communication, in the above example. Indeed, since the stylistic differences between A and B are found in verbal content, only the lexical component of speech is involved. When this aspect of style is considered, the focus is on ". . . individual differences in the selection of words in various contexts" (Kiesler, 1973, p. 8) and on the communication of verbal content.

However, some researchers have taken the position that the nonlexical aspects of speech are more effective than lexical aspects as vehicles for the expression of style (Mahl, 1963). In Mahl's view, the most significant locus of style is not the verbal content of speech, but rather the manner in which it is spoken. Nonlexical aspects of speech include such attributes as grammatical structure, rate of speech, duration of utterance, and speech disruptions. These channels often betray a person's anxiety, even when it may be carefully filtered out of verbal content. For example, let us assume that interviewer A, flustered with the anxiety of the new situation in which he found himself, was nevertheless able to avoid the type of anxiety control implicit in rigid structure and the use of highly specific questions. In such an event, an anxious interviewer might nevertheless leak his anxiety in certain nonlexical attributes of his speech. His vocal tone might become strident and tremulous, rate of speech might accelerate, and the otherwise smooth flow of communication might be fractured by a higher level of speech disruption than is usually evident. These are instances of nonlexical expressions of style.

To the lexical and nonlexical components of style must be added yet another modality of stylistic expression. Dittman (1963) refers to this when he speaks of expressive movement, demonstrating that movement may discharge internal tensions, such as those generated by mood and affect. Here, Dittman refers to the expressive function of style. For example, an interviewer may note that an interviewee manifests an increase in restless movement and elevations in verbal rate and in flustering of speech. Even if there is no expression of emotion in verbal content, the perceptive interviewer will note the point at which the above changes occurred, for they are instances of expressive style in nonlexical and nonverbal channels of communication.

Both interviewer and interviewee style pertain to the interview *process*, and they are located in all channels of communication—including verbal content, nonlexical aspects of speech, and expressive movement. The earlier studies of interviewer style dealt with the gross comparison of therapy schools, without attempting to separate and refine individual stylistic variables. Some of these investigations will be referred to (very briefly at this point) merely as markers in the progress of interview process research. But these will be passed over quickly, in favor of a closer look at later single-dimension investigations.

Multidimensional studies. Since nondirective counseling was regarded by many psychologists in the 1940s as the wave of the future in psychotherapy, many investigators set out to demonstrate the superiority of the nondirective approach. Most of the studies during this period were limited to linguistic channels and were based on verbal-content analysis. Space will not permit an examination of research methodology. An early, much quoted investigation of this type (Snyder, 1945) had the purpose of assessing the relative efficacy of directive and nondirective therapist styles. Snyder found that the most frequent response to a nondirective lead by a counselor was the client's statement of his problem. By contrast, the client almost never expressed his problems in response to interpretation, persuasion, disapproval, or criticism, all considered to be directive types of counselor remarks. From these findings Snyder (1945) concluded: "The facts of the present study clearly support the theory that it is the nondirective elements of this type of treatment which produce the favorable change in the client's behavior. What directive elements exist are unfavorably received" (p. 203).

This partisan finding did not go unchallenged for long. In 1950, two studies (Fiedler, 1950a, 1950b) questioned the assumption that there are significant stylistic distinctions between proponents of different schools of psychotherapy. However, these studies do not deal with process (as the previous one did) but with relationship. Adherents of the psychoanalytic, Adlerian, and nondirective schools were asked to rate the ideal therapeutic relationship. First, they used a Q-sort assembly of statements to describe their concept of an ideal therapeutic relationship. Then, with the same Q-sort, they rated recordings of actual therapist behavior. The members of the three schools were in essential agreement about the character of the ideal therapeutic relationship in both rating tasks. Indeed, the only significant difference that occurred was between the ratings of experienced and inexperienced therapists, regardless of their school of allegiance.

The next group of studies (Strupp 1958, 1960), utilizing a remarkably complex system of content analysis, dealt with the experienced-inexperienced distinction, among others. Strupp found that experienced—rather than inexperienced psychiatrists—made fewer interrogatory remarks and utilized more interpretation and a higher level of activity. There was no difference between the two groups on empathy, but the experienced psychiatrists manifested a greater degree of warmth. Unlike the psychiatrists (who showed several stylistic differences based on experience) psychologists manifested only two. Like the psychiatrists, psychologists manifested an increase of warmth with experience; but unlike the psychiatrists, psychologists assumed the role of expert or authority with an increase in experience.

One of the difficulties with the multidimensional studies was their failure to adequately define the stylistic variables used. A series of investigations attempted to cope with this problem through the use of factor analysis. In one such study, Sundland and Barker (1962) administered the Therapist Orientation Questionnaire to a large number of members of the American Psychological Association. The questionnaire dealt with therapist attitudes and methods, both closely related to stylistic variables. A second-order factor emerged from the factor analysis of the scales comprising the questionnaire and traced a dimension with an analytic pole at one extreme and an experiential pole at the other. The analytic pole is characterized by ". . . conceptualizing . . . planning of therapy, unconscious process, and a restriction of spontaneity. The experiential pole de-emphasizes conceptualizing and unconscious process, stressing instead the personality of the therapist, an unplanned approach to therapy, and therapist spontaneity" (Sundland & Barker, 1962, p. 205). To test the relationship of these clusters of stylistic variables and the dimension that they defined, representatives of three psychotherapeutic schools were asked to rate their stylistic preferences on the analytic-experiential dimension. Freudian therapists selected the use of interpretation, the conceptualizing of causation, and the therapist's impersonality and lack of spontaneity as preferred stylistic attributes (all close to the analytic pole); while the Rogerians showed a marked preference for spontaneity (at the experiential extreme). The Sullivanians took a middle position, siding with the Freudians in their stress on planning and conceptualization and with the Rogerians in their emphasis on personal expressiveness. And so, Fiedler (1950a, 1950b) notwithstanding, the notion of a connection between theoretical orientation and style has not been totally laid to rest.

A final investigation based on multidemensional ratings of style is included because it deals with the responses of two distinct diagnostic groups to divergent therapist patterns of behavior (Tourney, Bloom, Lowinger, Schorer, Auld, & Grisell, 1966). Two composite therapist stylistic patterns were identified, one designated as errors of commission and the other as errors of omission. The former were consequences of therapist overactivity (interruption of patient, excessive probing, excessive questioning, inaccurate or untimely interpretations); and the latter were consequences of therapist underactivity (failure to provide support and to express empathy, insufficient questioning). Psychoneurotic and schizophrenic patients responded differently to the two stylistic patterns. Psychoneurotic patients became hostile and resistant in response to errors of commission (overactivity), while schizophrenic patients became anxious and withdrawn. In response to therapist errors of omission (underactivity), psychoneurotic patients showed a small but significant increase in verbal activity and anxiety, while schizophrenic patients manifested both increased verbal productivity and thought disorder. In general, neurotic patients were less affected by errors of both types than were schizophrenic patients, who demonstrated a greater sensitivity to the stylistic deviations investigated.

Activity level. The Sundland and Barker (1962) study may serve as a transitional link between multidimensional and unidimensional studies of interview style. The former studies may have been adequate for the gross comparison of schools of interviewing and psychotherapy; but the latter were needed for the experimental investigation of the dyadic interaction. Of the various unidimensional stylistic variables that have been investigated, only two will be considered here: therapist *activity level* and *ambiguity-specificity*. The major activity-level studies have dealt with this dimension, defined as gross productivity or output. Usually this is measured either in temporal terms, such as duration of response, or as verbal units, such as words or clauses spoken.

Activity-level studies have investigated a number of interactional problems that pertain directly to interview process. The following are some examples:

1. Is there an optimum level of therapist productivity, below which the interview process is placed under strain?
2. Is there a naturalistically occurring ratio between interviewer and interviewee productivity? How general is it?
3. How can the interviewer best prompt the interviewee to be more productive? If interviewees are unresponsive, should their interviewers increase or decrease their productivity?

The studies that will now be summarized address these—and other— problems. In part, findings are obtained from a report of a research program conducted by Lennard and Bernstein (1960) in which eight therapies (four therapists with two patients each) were recorded over a period of eight months resulting in more than 500 therapy interview protocols. Two indexes of activity level used were average number of clause units per session and therapist proportion of the total output of a session. Results of this and other studies will be discussed under the three problem headings above.

1. What are the symptoms of interview strain when therapist activity level tends to be low?

In the Lennard and Bernstein (1960) studies, less active therapists sustained more broken appointments than more active therapists. Moreover, the typescripts of the former contained more expressions of patient dissatisfaction than did those of the latter. These two findings were not based on statistical analyses; but the third one was. At a significant level, patients rated interviews in which the therapist was more active as ones in which communication went more easily than those in which the therapist was less-active. Patients preferred interviews in which the therapist spoke more frequently and at greater length. The eight patients of the Lennard and Bernstein (1960) studies therefore found the more-active therapists to be more reinforcing than the more passive ones. Although these results appear to contradict a low therapist activity level ideology, they feel right on an intuitive basis. Two additional studies provide two plausible rationales for these findings. Truax (1970) obtained a positive association between average length of thrapist verbalization and his independently rated accurate empathy. Analogously, Pope, Nudler, VonKorff, and McGee (1974) demonstrated a positive relationship between interviewer productivity (number of words spoken) and his/her independently rated warmth. Clearly then, active therapists tend to be perceived as empathic and warm, and thus, reinforcing.

2.   Is there a stable balance or ratio of productivity between interviewer and interviewee?

The view of the interview as an informational exchange system (Lennard & Bernstein, 1960) would imply a lawful or systematic relationship between the productivity of each participant. Indeed, given enough time, such stable ratios do assert themselves. Thus, with the whole interview as the unit Lennard and Bernstein (1960) found that patients were four times more verbally productive than therapists were. That this ratio of productivity is quite general in the interactional interview is evident in the approximately similar findings obtained in another investigation (Matarazzo, Wiens, Matarazzo, & Saslow, 1968). In this instance, patient-to-therapist duration of utterance ratios ranged from 5-to-1 to 6-to-1.

3.   Granted the above stable balance of productivity between the interviewer and interviewee over a sufficient passage of time, how can the interviewer prompt increases in interviewee productivity at those times when it lapses?

This is a basic process problem that proves frustrating to novice interviewers. It may be expressed in the following question: "How can I get the interviewee to be more productive in the areas that I wish to explore?" The novice's impulse is simply to lay down a barrage of questions until the desired information has been dredged up. But an interviewer very early begins to feel that his approach does not produce the range of information that s(he) wishes.

To avoid the constricting effects of a pressured interrogation, the interviewer will be helped by some familiarity with the research literature dealing with the interview as a communication system. The point at issue now is the response-by-response relationship between the inputs of the two participants in the dyadic exchange.

Two patterns of communication exchange emerge: one designated as a *synchronous* relationship between the communication of the interviewer and interviewee, the other as an *inverse* or *reciprocal* relationship. The task of the interviewer is not simplified by the fact that the two are opposite patterns and that they both occur in different studies. Fortunately, there are some findings that define the conditions under which the two principles may operate. Some guidelines are therefore possible for the utilization of each.

The two studies that follow demonstrate the operation of the synchrony principle. In the first (Heller, Davis, & Myers, 1966), graduate students in speech and theater were trained to act out four different interviewer roles: active-friendly, passive-friendly, active-hostile, and passive-hostile. Only the active-passive dimension concerns us here. The interviewees were introductory psychology students. In the active interviews, the interviewees were indeed significantly more productive than in the passive condition. Thus, there was an interactional pattern of synchrony between the interviewer and interviewee.

A somewhat earlier study by Matarazzo (1965) also demonstrated the operation of synchrony. The interviewers, in this instance, were used to evaluate applicants for positions as policemen and firemen. These were naturalistic interviews into which an experimental manipulation was introduced. In each interview, there were three 15-minute segments. During the first, the interviewer limited each comment to a duration of 5 seconds; during the second, he increased each comment to a duration of 10 seconds; and during the third, he reverted to 5-second comments. The length of interviewee comments rose and fell in synchrony with those of the interviewer, with an average of 24.3, 46.9, and 26.6 seconds successively in the three segments.

But in a later article, Matarazzo et al. (1968) presented data which demonstrated that synchrony did not occur in a sample of naturalistic psychotherapy interviews. Seven uncontrolled psychotherapies were completely tape-recorded and audited. The presence or absence of synchrony was determined by correlating the mean durations of patient and therapist utterances across each of the seven psychotherapy sequences. No significant positive correlations were obtained. Instead, three of the correlations were close to zero, and four were negative. Instead of synchrony, a tendency toward an inverse relationship appeared.

The difference between the types of interviews in the first two studies and in the third provides some explanatory clues about the contradictory findings. In the first two, the interviewer's communication was experimentally manipulated as an independent variable. Under these circumstances, the interviewee was the only responsive member of the dyad. Thus, an increase in interviewer activity prompted an increase in that of the interviewee. The effect was unidirectional—passing from the interviewer to the interviewee. But there were two responders in the interactional interviews in the psychotherapy series. The interviewers' responses were evidently governed by a "therapeutic set" (Matarazzo et al., 1968), prompting them to say as little as possible as long as the interviewee was speaking. In both synchronous and inverse patterns of communication, the interviewer is the major architect of the interaction that results, either because of his/her preprogrammed verbal behavior (first two studies), or because of the therapeutic code that governs his level of activity (third study).

It therefore appears that both models of communication need not be regarded as natural laws that govern all dyadic interactions but rather as interviewer strategies, resulting from past learning and current theoretical preference. This assumption is supported by the findings of a later investigation (Pope et al., 1974) in which the interviewer behavior of professionals and complete novices was compared. Each interviewee (a female freshman) was interviewed twice, once by a seasoned professional (a staff psychiatrist or a senior resident in psychiatry) and once by a student with no previous training in interviewing. Synchrony appeared only in the interviews conducted by the novices, while partial evidence in favor of an inverse pattern was manifested in the interviews conducted by the professionals. These contrasting findings accorded with the view of the nonprofessional interview as a communication system that tends to be nonrole differentiated (as in an informal, conversational exchange); while the professional interview was governed by the predominant operating principles of the psychiatric community. These principles might be paraphrased as follows: the interviewer says little when the interviewee is productive and says relatively more when the interviewee's productivity wanes. Thus, the synchrony of the novice and the reciprocal pattern of the professional are contrasting strategies based on past experience and indoctrination.

Before concluding the section on activity level, an attempt will be made to provide a prescriptive statement about the deliberate (or planned) use of the two strategies. When might each be utilized and for what purpose?

1. There may be times when the interviewer may wish the interview to retain some of the attributes of a conversational exhange and some of the spontaneity of an egalitarian encounter. At such times, the pattern of synchrony may well be utilized. There would then be periods of upsurge in productivity (when both participants increased their activity) and periods when activity for both might lag.

2. Most interviews are begun by the interviewers. At the outset, they do not yet know how the interviewee will respond, and thus, they are under some constraint to prime the pump. Consequently, the opening phase of the interview will be a period of relatively high activity for the inteviewer, maintained as a means of increasing the activity level of the interviewee. This is a period of synchrony.

3. When interviewees have attained relatively stable levels of adequate productivity, interviewers tend to drop theirs and keep it relatively low. Such periods of inverse patterns of communication may tend to be maintained as long as interviewee communication does not lag. When it does, the interviewer may again become more active— invoking once more the strategy of synchrony.

Interviewer ambiguity-specificity. In the preceding section, the position was taken that synchrony and reciprocity of communication are to be regarded as interviewer strategies. This view is particularly relevant to the variable of verbal activity level. The productivity of each participant in the interview occurs at the sensitive interface between two people talking to each other. The duration of an utterance by one of the speakers, or its length in word or clause units, has an immediate impact on the other. All of this happens before the listener has become attuned and responsive to the content spoken. Once the latter occurs, the meaning of the communication intrudes, introducing other factors into the exchange. The role of verbal content has been discussed at an earlier point in this chapter. Some topics are anxiety arousing, and others are neutral. Some are felt to be intrusively intimate, and others are impersonal. Finally, topics vary in their saliency to individuals and groups. These linguistically channeled variables have a range of effects on the interviewees, some of which have already been considered in the section on verbal content. But, content may be evaluated along certain dimensions that are not semantically defined but are considered in general-informational terms. The ambiguity or specificity of the interviewer is such a dimension. When the interviewee is confronted with a question or a comment that is highly specific, s(he) is prompted to respond in a manner that is quite different from that which occurs when the interviewer's input is ambiguous. The law that governs the above relationship is referred to here as that of *informational reciprocity.* The evidence on which it is based is noted in the frequently replicated finding that an ambiguous remark by the interviewer is followed by a relatively long, interviewee response; a specific remark, by a relatively short response. The informational rationale for this finding will be considered later. First, there will be some definitional comments about the ambiguity-specificity dimension.

The positive association of therapist ambiguity and patient productivity is the kind of relationship one would expect in a projective interview. In psychoanalytic terms (Bordin, 1955), this relationship should occur because therapist ambiguity fosters the kind of associational flow in the patient that circumvents ordinary defenses. As in the case of a projective device, the projective interview creates a situation in which a patient may speak about conflicts that he might avoid under other circumstances. "Thus, specific therapist inputs such as narrowly focused questions would provide the patient with the discriminant stimuli needed to activate his defenses. Ambiguous inputs would lack such stimuli and would therefore foster the expression of anxiety arousing communications" (Pope, 1977, p. 375).

In psychoanalytic terms, a specific interviewer question or comment in a sensitive area will arouse the interviewee's defenses and reduce his/her productivity. Interviewer ambiguity is, therefore, a means of letting sleeping defenses maintain their repose and permitting the interviewee to communicate productively in topical areas that s(he) might otherwise avoid.

Lennard and Bernstein (1960) also take the position that interviewer ambiguity elicits interviewee productivity; but their reasons are different. Their model of the interview is that of an informational exchange system, in which both participants provide reciprocal quantities of information, thus maintaining between them a steady level. To be sure, a constant level is obtained only when the communication system in the interview has been activated and stabilized. At such a point, the interviewer's informational input rises when the interviewee's falls; it subsides when that of the interviewee increases. The informational mechanism that regulates and maintains a steady level is understandable only if one utilizes different informational definitions for the interviewer and interviewee. The informational input of interviewers is determined by the ambiguity of their remarks. An ambiguous remark is defined as one which does not restrict the options available to the interviewee for replying. It, therefore, has low informational stimulus value. Since interviewees are left with a large number of alternatives to choose among in formulating their replies, there has been little information communicated. Such an interviewer remark tends to elicit a high level of productivity from the interviewee. By contrast, a specific interviewer remark has high informational-stimulus value, tending to limit the options available to the the interviewee and to reduce the interviewee's productivity in response. If interviewer ambiguity-specificity is the dimension on which his/her informational input is measured, interviewee productivity is the relevant informational dimension for the interviewee.

The Lennard and Bernstein (1960) principle of informational reciprocity requires that ambiguous interviewer remarks be followed by relatively long patient responses and specific interviewer remarks by relatively brief ones. By the same principle, when operating in reverse direction, one would expect that unproductive interviewee responses would be followed by specific interviewer comments and productive patient responses by ambiguous communications. Pope and Siegman (1962) did indeed confirm the therapist-to-patient component of the reciprocal relationship but failed to confirm the patient-to-therapist component.

A basic study of this aspect of interview interaction was conducted by Pope and Siegman (1965) as an experimental analogue of the initial interview. Both interviewer ambiguity-specificity and anxiety arousal were manipulated. The former was accomplished through the use of both highly ambiguous ("Just start by saying anything that occurs to you") and highly specific ("How old is your sister?") remarks; the latter, by focusing on both neutral and anxiety arousing topics. The Ss were junior and senior nursing students in a university-based school of nursing. Ambiguous (rather than specific) interviewer remarks were associated with high interviewee productivity. It was noted, however, that enhanced productivity occurred together with increased hesitation (uncertainty) in the form of filled pauses (such as "Ah") and a slowing down in the rate of speech (Siegman & Pope, 1972). This study was the first in a group in which both interviewee productivity and hesitation were positively associated with interviewer ambiguity (Pope & Siegman, 1968; Pope, Blass, Cheek, Siegman, & Bradford, 1971).

The association between interviewer ambiguity and interviewee productivity has been considered at some length. Unfortunately, space will not permit a similar review of theory and research regarding the analogous finding of a positive correlation between interviewer ambiguity and interviewee hesitation or uncertainty. Suffice it to say that Goldman-Eisler and her colleagues in England (Butterworth & Goldman-Eisler, 1979) have provided extensive and persuasive evidence that hesitations occur in speech at moments of uncertainty when cognitive work is being done. At such times, plans regarding the content and the style of the communication following the moment of hesitation take form. This interpretation of the role of hesitation is readily applicable to the relationship between interviewer ambiguity and interviewee hesitation. When confronted with few guidelines regarding the response desired, the interviewee hesitates, experiences uncertainty, and is prompted by the low informational input of interviewer to work at formulating a plan about how to proceed in the following communication.

Some operational implications of the ambiguity-specificity findings for the work of the interviewer will now be proposed. At the beginning of the interview, the objective is to initiate and prime communication between the two dyadic participants. Specific comments and questions may serve better than ambiguous ones to accomplish these ends. Information from interviewees may come in the form of briefer responses, and they will experience less hesitation and uncertainty and be less reticent about moving toward active participation. The interviewer's task is that of sensitively monitoring the increasing involvement of the interviewee in the exchange and augmenting his/her ambiguity of input as the emerging interaction permits. Thus, an intake interviewer in a psychiatric hospital might begin with very specific questions: such as, "When did you arrive at the hospital?" and "Who brought you here?" A little later s(he) might say: "You appear to be quite sad this morning. Can you tell me about it?" And later, when the communication between the interviewer and interviewee has become stabilized, the interviewer might inquire: "Tell me what you can about your reasons for coming to the hospital."

A progression from high interviewer specificity to high ambiguity may also occur separately for the exploration of each topical area. For example, the interviewer may have spent some time exploring family relations. Aware of the passage of time and the lack of any information about the patient's educational history, the interviewer may make some transitional comment, such as: "I'd like to switch now and talk with you a little about your school experiences." The topic might then be opened with a few specific questions, such as: "How far did you go in school?" and "What schools did you attend?" When the change of topical focus has been accomplished, the interviewer might say: "Tell me what you can about how things went for you in school."

When communication proceeds steadily on the basis of a reciprocal balance between ambiguous interviewer remarks and relatively productive interviewee responses, it is usually maintained by brief prompts from the interviewer such as "yes," "go on," and "mm-mm." If the interviewee's productivity lags, the interviewer may either assume that the area has been adequately explored and move into a new topic, or continue in the same area by increasing the specificity of his/her remarks in an attempt to revive the exchange. Even if there is no lag, the interviewer may change to a higher level of specificity if there is a need for a "mopping-up" operation before terminating the inquiry. For example, the patient has spoken at some length about school experiences but has been vague about some matters. Thus, there was reference to a very positive school adjustment up to a point; then grades dropped, and absenteeism increased. The therapist may then zero in on this change in very specific terms with such questions as: "Exactly when did this change occur?" "Your grades dropped. You hooked school a lot. What other changes occurred in your school behavior at that time?"

The deploying of interviewer activity level and ambiguity follows a unified pattern. At the beginning of the interview, or the initiation of a new topic in the interview, interviewee communication needs to be activated. At such times, the interviewer tends to manifest high activity and specificity, relying on the principle of synchrony between both participants in the dyadic exchange and a strategy that keeps uncertainty and hesitation in the interviewee to a minimum. (Synchrony occurs between interviewer productivity and interviewee productivity. The reduction of uncertainty and hesitation are consequences of interviewer specificity.) Later on, the interviewer switches to low activity and high ambiguity, and these levels are maintained as long as the flow of information from the interviewee continues. At this stage, the principle of an inverse or reciprocal relationship between interviewer and interviewee is applied. (Reciprocity obtains now between the activity level and the informational input of both participants.) If interviewee communication wanes, the interviewer returns to the initial pump-priming operation—characterized by high activity level and high specificity. Through increasing activity level and specificity, the interviewer attempts to reactivate the diminishing informational exchange.

The above comments would appear to imply that the exchange of information is the sum total of that which transpires in the interview. Such an impression would be premature—indeed, erroneous. The section that follows, dealing with the expressive aspects of interview communication, will deal with another facet entirely of the interview exchange.

Expressive aspects of interview communication

In the preceding sections, the instrumental roles of interviewer activity level and ambiguity have been examined. The studies reviewed have dealt with the effects of both on interviewee communication. In the present section, the focus will be on expressive behavior. In a definitional sense, the distinction between instrumental and expressive communication may be sharply drawn.

> Expressive speech or words are said to convey emotion, in contrast to the semantic or syntactic aspects of words and speech which are said to impart meaning. . . . One ends up with the antithesis in sociology between "instrumental" (problem solving) and "expressive" (affective) behavior and in psychology, with the contrast between "cognition" and "emotion." (Spiegel & Machotka, 1974, p. 25)

Actually, the boundary between the two is a permeable one. Thus, a 42-year-old male with a long history of shyness and social anxiety, driven by an exasperated wife to seek help, appears at his third therapy interview with a detailed list of events from the preceding week. Each incident is narrated very much in the style of a pedantic exposition, with its theme being the social anxiety experienced by the patient. But there is no expression of anxiety in the patient's communication. Instead, this schizoid, obsessional person speaks about his anxiety in a dry, expository manner. Thus, what promised to be an affective communication turned out to be a cognitively contained, informational account about affect.

By contrast, consider the following patient who sought help because of hysterical symptomatology, She spoke in a manner that contrasted markedly with that of the shy, middle-aged male described above. At 25 years of age, she had been teaching junior high school for three years. It was evident to the therapist that this young lady was acutely anxious every day she entered the classroom. Yet, she found it impossible to acknowledge her problems in managing a difficult class with many volatile, aggressive students. Indeed, she spent much of her time weaving a rosy verbal tapestry depicting her great enthusiam for the work she was doing. But as she spoke in this vein, her voice would become strident, her verbal tempo accelerated, her speech flustered, while she folded her arms and crossed her legs defensively.

Thus, there is greater plausibility in drawing a distinction between the expressive and the cognitive aspects of communication, rather than in counterposing two separate types. When the two aspects are incongruent with each other, it is well to look and listen for the expressive component, if one is interested in the affect being communicated. Affect may appear in all channels of communication (i.e., linguistic, paralinguistic, and nonverbal). Frequently, however, the interviewer is aware that emotion is expressed with guarded selectivity in the verbal channel and less guardedly in the other two. The usual form of incongruence between the three channels occurs in situations in which negative affect is denied verbally, but leaked paralinguistically and nonverbally. (See the reference to the second patient above.) Occasionally, a reverse type of inconsistency appears, when the speaker gives a totally inexpressive account of experiences that are referred to verbally in emotional terms. (See the reference to the first patient above.)

Because it is important for the interviewer to sense the intrusion of feeling, even when the interviewee may not be speaking about it, a capacity to detect it in paralinguistic (pitch, vocal quality, verbal tempo, speech disturbances) and nonverbal (body language) style is an important training objective. The trainee ". . . should be sensitized to the sounds of expressiveness in the interviewee and rehearsed in the use of such sounds" (Pope, 1979, p. 221).

In this connection, there has long been a belief that sensitivity to subtle signals about the experience of emotion in others is a matter of individual intuition. The implication is that this type of sensitivity is not trainable, and it is highly variable between individuals. The studies summarized below support the individual-difference component of the above belief but not the component or untrainability. Thus, Beldoch (1964) studied the accuracy of untrained, men and women students in recognizing 10 different emotions. These were expressed through vocal tone, abstract graphic representation, and short musical compositions. There was a positive correlation between the accuracy with which the Ss identified the 10 emotions across the three modalities. Individuals, therefore, show a significant level of consistency within themselves in different channels of communication, while simultaneously manifesting a wide range of individual differences. The conclusion is not surprising but worth making explicit: different individuals, all untrained in the art of interviewing, manifest a range of personal assets in sensing and identifying emotion expressed by others.

But the occurrence of individual differences does not in itself negate the efficacy of training. On the basis of an investigation of the efficacy of training in enhancing a person's sensitivity to nonverbal clues of emotion, Davitz (1964) concluded: "We do not know the particular aspects of training which are most effective, and we cannot define the generality of the effect produced. But we do know that practice in expressing and receiving emotional communication results in higher scores on a subsequent test of sensitivity" (p. 474).

One more point relevant to training in this area has been made in a study demonstrating a positive correlation between a person's sensitivity as a receiver of the vocal communication of feeling and his/her accuracy as a sender (Levy, 1964). From this, one may conclude that an interviewer who is attuned to the recognition of expressed emotions is, in all likelihood, sensitive and fluent in their expression. Clearly, such attributes enhance his/her skill as an interviewer.

The implications of the above for the careful selection of persons to be trained as clinical interviewers are clear. Although their susceptibility to the enhancement of their skills as receivers and senders of emotional messages through training has been demonstrated, the methods of such training are not yet sufficiently explicit. But an analogy may be found in the coaching of an actor, in which one utilizes the modeling of the desired behavior and subsequent rehearsal in its performance.

Anxiety. Because of its central role in personality theory and in communication, anxiety is the affect that has received the most-intensive research scrutiny. The studies summarized below deal with the recognition of anxiety in verbal content and paralingustic communication.

The study of the occurrence of anxiety in verbal content is exemplified by the work of Gottschalk and his colleagues (Gottschalk, Springer, & Gleser, 1961; Gottschalk, Winget, Gleser & Springer, 1966; Gottschalk & Gleser, 1969); the study of its occurrence in paralanguage by Mahl (1959) and later by Siegman and Pope (1972). The rationale provided by Gottschalk and others (Gottschalk et al., 1966) for the use of verbal content in assessing transient states (such as anxiety and hostility) rests on the following assumptions:

1. The occurrence of an affect in verbal content is signaled by certain content variables. Thus, the following thematic categories are expressive of anxiety; death, fear, mutilation, separation, guilt, and shame.
2. The strength of the affect (anxiety in this instance) is determined by obtaining the product of the frequency of occurrence of each of the above categories and certain weights determined by attributes of each statement counted. Thus, the more directly a statement expresses an affect and the greater the speaker's personal involvement in the emotion, the greater its weight (i.e., the more intensely the speaker is assumed to experience it).

One of the Gottschalk studies investigated the congruence (or synchrony) between the affect expressed by the interviewer and interviewee (Gottschalk et al., 1961). In a taped psychotherapy interview, the content of the therapist's remarks referred to shame and nonspecific anxiety, with the same two themes dominating the patient's verbalizations. The Gottschalk anxiety scale was used for the content analysis of both interviewee and interviewer verbalizations.

However, the lion's share of the research dealing with anxiety in the interview (usually interviewee anxiety) has been done with paralinguistic variables (i.e., those that relate to how one speaks, rather than what one says). Indeed, one of the early references to the signal value of such variables was made by a clinician, not a researcher (Sullivan, 1954). "The beginning of my definition of the psychiatric interview states that such an interview is a situation of primary vocal communication—not verbal communication alone . . . Much attention may profitably be paid to the telltale aspects of intonation, rate of speech, difficulty in enunciation, and so on—factors which are conspicuous to the student of vocal communication" (Sullivan, 1954, p. 5).

One of the major proponents of this approach to the study of emotion (primarily, anxiety in the interview) is Mahl (1956, 1959, 1963). Six psychotherapy interviews were divided by the therapist into high- and low-anxiety segments. Speech disturbances were scored independently by another person and were found to be significantly more frequent in the high- rather than the low-anxiety segments of the psychotherapy interviews. In a subsequent study (Kasl & Mahl, 1958), male college students were interviewed twice, with the first interview functioning as a control for the second, an experimentally manipulated "anxiety" interview. The rate of speech disturbance rose significantly from the control to the "anxiety" interview.

The methodology followed by Siegman and Pope (1965) in an experimental analogue study of the interview has already been outlined in the section on ambiguity (Pope & Siegman, 1965). In brief, interviewee anxiety was manipulated through the use of two topics—school experiences and family relationships. The Ss were female nursing students. There was an a priori determination that for this population, the former topic was neutral in character, and the latter was anxiety arousing. Thus, within a single interview, there were experimentally controlled periods of low and high anxiety for each S. Anxiety was found to be both an activator and a disruptor of speech. During the high-anxiety segments of the interview rather than the low, productivity and speech rate were higher and reaction time was lower. All three changes are indices of the activation of speech. The last two findings were of borderline significance only; the first was clearly significant. With the activation of speech there was a simultaneous increase in the rate of speech disturbance.

Though these results appear paradoxical, Siegman and Pope (1972) have taken the position that they are congruent with the view that, in many respects, anxiety functions as a drive that tends to have both activating and disrupting effects on speech. Others, in previous studies, had also noted the activating effect of anxiety on speech, particularly in the form of verbal rate acceleration (Kanfer, 1958, 1960). As to the elevation of speech disturbances with anxiety, Siegman and Pope advanced the hypothesis that an increase in its drive effect triggers competing response tendencies (e.g., dynamic conflicts: the motivation to make self-disclosing statements concurrent with the occurrence of defensive resistances to such statements), resulting in speech disruptions.

Later studies by Pope, Siegman, and their colleagues have lent further support to both the above findings. In one study (Pope, Blass, Siegman, & Raher, 1970) dealing with the effects of both anxiety and depression on speech, a series of 10-minute monologues taped by six psychosomatic patients provided the data. These patients resided on a research ward in a medical school-based psychiatric hospital. The daily fluctuations of anxiety and depression in the patients were rated by nurses trained in the use of a scale constructed to measure these two affects (Bunny & Hamburg, 1963). On high-anxiety days rather than low, patient-speech activation was noted in higher speech rates and lower silence quotients, while disruption was noted, as usual, in high speech disturbance ratios.

It has undoubtedly been noted that the preceding studies have dealt with anxiety in the speech of patients and interviewees. This is not surprising, since anxiety is an affect and a symptom of great clinical significance. However, two studies have directed their focus to the interviewer. In one study (Pope, et al., 1974), novice interviewers with no previous training were compared with experienced professionals (third-year psychiatric residents and staff psychiatrist), both interviewing the same female freshman students. As anticipated, the former interviewers manifested higher levels of speech disturbance than the latter.

Finally, an experimental investigation (Russel & Snyder, 1963) manipulated client hostility, by training two male actors to role play a friendly client and a hostile client. The counselors were graduate students in counselor training. A number of significant differences in counselor behavior occurred. The finding most relevant to the current focus was a higher rate of speech disturbance (unfinished sentences, repetition of words and phrases, stuttering, and blocking) in counselors during hostile rather than friendly interviews.

Depression.   If anxiety is a condition that agitates or activates speech, depression must be regarded as one that has a retarding effect. Indeed, this was clearly apparent in the patient monologue study (Pope et al., 1970) referred to above, when patient speech on high-anxiety days was characterized by high verbal rate and low silence quotient and on high-depression days by low verbal rate and high silence quotient. When high-anxiety days were compared directly with high-depression days, the rate of speech was significantly higher in the former. In an earlier investigation (Davitz, 1964), the speech associated with sadness was compared with that associated with joy. If sadness may be equated with depression, the Davitz study (1964) supports the one conducted by Pope et al. (1970), in that the rate of sadness speech was significantly lower than joyous speech. Two other paralinguistic (or vocal) attributes extend the basis for the above contrast. Thus, Davitz found that sadness speech was softer and lower than joyous speech.

The above brief reference to depressive speech completes the present survey of selected dimensions in verbal style that are operative in an interactional interview.

Sequence effects in the interview

"One may learn a good deal about the interview by dividing it into such gross components as communication and relationship; or, further, into the many more narrowly defined variables that are the warp and woof of the larger components. In the end, however, the segments into which the interview has been dissected must be brought together again. In a naturalistic sense, the interview is an indivisible interaction between two people, occurring at a given place, and over a definitive time span" (Pope, 1979, p. 513). In closing this chapter, the clinical and research literature will be scanned for findings about the occurrence of trends and patterns over time.

The beginning.   Sullivan (1954) cautions the interviewer against an excessive display of ritualized hospitality, because even the strained and anxious patient will not have his fears allayed by a show of exaggerated friendliness. Instead, Sullivan (1954) advocates an attitude of "respectful seriousness."

> Thus while I don't try to show a great welcome to the patient, I do try to act as if he were expected—that is, I try to know the name of a person who makes an appointment to see me for the first time, and to greet him with it, relieving him of any morbid anxiety as to whether he came on the wrong day, and so on. (p. 60)

The interview is not effectively underway until rapport has been established between its two participants. The mode of greeting referred to above is the first movement toward such rapport. The initial period when rapport is likely to develop is the time when first impressions are formed. Indeed, these first impressions have much to do with the kind of rapport that evolves. In a book on psychiatric interviewing (MacKinnon & Michels, 1971), the formation of first impressions is discussed: "Important clues to the conduct of the interview can often be obtained during these few moments of introduction. The patient's spontaneity and warmth may be revealed in his handshake or greeting. . . . Suspicious patients might carefully glance around the office searching for 'clues' about the physician" (MacKinnon & Michels, 1971, p. 52). Without giving undue weight to any single type of clue from the interviewee, the interviewer must be alert and open to all channels of communication—in particular, to any behavior that pertains to the evolving relationship.

The experience and learning that leads to the sharpening of one's interpersonal perceptions is a central component of a clinical training program. More difficult, perhaps, than honing one's perceptions of others, is leavening one's perceptions of self. It is not easy to learn how to monitor oneself—to be aware, for example, how a new person may perceive and react to one's behavior and manner of presenting oneself during the first moments of acquaintance. Sullivan (1954) advises the interviewer to "know how he acts." The interviewer ". . . should have learned from experience the *usual* impression obtained of him in the particular circumstances of encouraging the sort of stranger that the interviewee at first glance seems to be" (1954, p. 67).

The early part of the interview is a time for the role induction of interviewees. If they have not previously experienced an interactional interview, they have much to learn about what to expect of the interviewer and what the interviewer may expect of them. The interviewer's use of *primary-system references* (Lennard & Bernstein, 1960) is one way in which this initial orientation is accomplished. These ". . . center around role discussion. The more primary-system references on the part of the patient, the more information the patient is soliciting about his role in treatment. The more primary-system references on the part of the therapist, the more the therapist is teaching the patient his proper role in therapy" (Lennard & Bernstein, 1960, p. 119). In concise, operational terms, Lennard and Bernstein have defined interviewer role in the following terms: "Who shall speak, how much, about what, and when?" (1960, p. 154).

The efficacy of primary-system references, when made early in the interview, has been demonstrated in several studies. In one study (Lennard & Bernstein, 1960), it was demonstrated that the psychotherapy dyads in which therapists make the most frequent primary-system references manifest least strain. In the above study and in a later one (Karl & Abeles, 1969), the naturalistic occurrence of primary-system references decreased rapidly over sequential segments of the interview. Evidently, the crucial time for these references is close to the beginning of the interview.

The body.   The main business of the interview is transacted during the middle segment (i.e., the body of the interview). The preparatory work has been accomplished, mutual role expectations have been clarified, and rapport has developed. Assuming that these tasks have been accomplished satisfactorily, interviewees are now prompted to present and discuss the problems for which they are seeking help and to make any other personal self-disclosures that seem appropriate to them and to their interviewers. If the interview goes well, and the flow of information stabilizes, certain changes in the communication style of each member of the dyad occur. Interviewer specificity decreases, and ambiguity increases (Lennard & Bernstein, 1960), signaling a decrease in informational input by the interviewer and an increase by the interviewee. Two key phrases describing changes in interviewee communication at this transitional point are *increased productivity* and increased *self-disclosure*. Productivity without self-disclosure may be a psychologically avoidant sort of verbosity; with self-disclosure, it signals the interviewee's willingness to speak openly about personal matters. Indeed, a number of studies show that the interviewee becomes personally less avoidant as the transition from the beginning to the middle of the interview is accomplished. Thus, Lennard and Bernstein (1960) found that primary-system references decreased as the psychotherapy interview moved into its middle third, and communication about affect increased. Karl and Abeles (1969) obtained analogous (if not identical) changes. In their study of psychotherapy interviews, they found that comments, between clients and therapists dealing with interpersonal interactions, increased steadily over the first four 10-minute segments. And in another study, experiencing (EXP) level (Gendlin, 1962) in interviewee verbalizations increased steadily over the entire duration of 40-minute psychotherapy interviews. In brief, the predominant pattern—as the mental health interview proceeds from its relatively brief beginning to its middle segment—is one of enhanced psychological communication by the interviewee, reduced avoidance, and increased personal openness.

In addition, two paralinguistic dimensions have been found to change in the above-designated transition from the inception to the body of the interview. "Ah" and allied expressions were found to decrease, and speech rate was found to increase (Lalljee & Cook, 1973). Both of the above changes are indicative of decreased uncertainty. "One may expect the information imparted to the interviewee through primary-system references in the beginning segment to reduce his/her uncertainty about the interview. The middle segment should therefore be characterized by less interviewee hesitation (lower "Ah") and a faster rate of interviewee speech than the beginning segment" (Pope, 1979, p. 518).

However, the meaning of certain temporal fluctuations along another paralinguistic dimension is less clear. Speech disturbances—assumed to be indicative of anxiety—first increased and then decreased. This reversal led Lalljee and Cook (1973) to reject speech disturbance as a variable that relates to temporal changes in the interview.

In a recent study, the above paralinguistic variables and a number of other parameters of speech were investigated further (Pope, Nudler, Norden, & McGee, 1979). The interviewees in the latter study were female, freshman college-student volunteers, while the interviewers were male and female staff psychiatrists and third-year psychiatric residents. The interviews were semistructured, with the designation of two topical areas for exploration and the imposition of a minimum and maximum time limit. There were no further constraints on the behavior of the interviewer. For purposes of sequential analysis, the verbatim transcript of each interview was excerpted by selecting the first four pages as a sample of the opening phase, the median four pages as a sample of the body of the interview, and the last four pages as a sample of the closing phase. The major results—with the following changes noted—pertained to the opening and median segments.

> Primary-system references dropped significantly between the first and second segments. The task of structuring the interview was therefore completed at an early point. Indeed, its completion may be a significant factor in the remaining changes that occurred.
>
> Interviewer specificity dropped significantly over the same timespan, confirming the earlier finding (Lennard & Bernstein, 1960) that informational input by the interviewer decreased after the opening phase of the interview. Indeed, one may conjecture that the interviewer's early specificity was probably contained in his/her primary-system references.
>
> As had been anticipated, interviewee productivity rose significantly between the opening and median phases of the interview. Thus, an initial communication balance between an interviewer speaking in specific terms and an interviewee giving short responses, gave way to a new balance, much more in accord with the major design for a mental-health interview, in which the interviewer spoke in ambiguous terms while the interviewee gave longer responses.
>
> The point has already been made that verbosity is not synonomous with self-disclosure. To an index of productivity must be added some measure of personal openness. Two measures relevant to self-disclosure were used, one designated *superficiality* and the other *resistiveness*. Superficial responses are devoid of psychological content, and are, instead, objective, factual, or psychologically peripheral in other ways. Resistant responses have a stipulatory meaning in this study. They weaken or deny psychologically relevant remarks already made. The rater identifies instances of blocked communication, denial, qualification, and excessive justification of remarks in which interviewees may have disclosed themselves. Thus, the occurrence of resistive phrases and clauses follow or precede self-disclosing ones. One would expect superficiality to decline but resistiveness to mount with an increase in self-disclosure. In the present investigation, superficiality did indeed decline between the opening and the median segments, while resistiveness increased. The initial structuring carried out by the interviewers appeared to have borne fruit, for a productive equilibrium had resulted in the body of the interview, in which the interviewee was both productive and self-disclosing.

In a previous study (Lalljee & Cook, 1973), both high "Ah" and low rate of speech were regarded as indexes of hesitation that signifyed uncertainty. The rate of speech did not change significantly from the opening to the median segment of the interview in the present study. But the "ah" ratio did drop significantly, indicating a decrease in interviewee uncertainty as the interview progressed over time.

The increase in interviewee self-disclosure between the first and the second interview segments did not come without effort and strain, as indicated by the increase in the Resistiveness Scale. Another index of strain is increase of speech disturbance in the median segment, probably a consequence of the higher level of self-disclosure.

At this point, the student interviewer may well wonder how the sequence effects outlined above are to be regarded by the aspiring practitioner. Are the changes in style (from high to low interviewer specificity, for example, or from low to high interviewee self-disclosure) simply learned behaviors that might vary with the theoretical and clinical orientation of the interviewer? Or are these effects a consequence of the interactions that develop in a dyadic communication system, transcending school of allegiance or theoretical bent? The interviewers in the preceding study were all experienced clinicians with a dynamic orientation. But the findings have been replicated with a second group of interviewers who were complete novices, younger than those who provided the data cited, and totally lacking in training and experience. The novice interviewers were quite free of theoretical bias or previously learned interview behavior preferences. This evidence is, to be sure, not conclusive. But the probability is strong that a generic model is operative when two people enter into a communicational system, interacting under role-differentiated conditions. Since the accomplished clinician must be sensitive to both the individual dynamic and the dyadic system aspects of the interview, a balanced emphasis on both would appear to be important in an interview training program.

SUMMARY

Although individual diversity of interviewer style is acknowledged and examined in this chapter, its focus is directed, for the most part, toward the generic-system aspects of an interview interaction. From this vantage point, the interview is regarded as a dyadic communication system, in which variables pertaining to the *communication* of information and to the *relationship* between the *interviewer* and the *interviewee* are operative. The contingencies that occur between selected dimensions of communication and relationship are explored primarily through a review of clinical and research studies. But the dominant consideration is the clinical relevance of what the studies have found. In general, the following sequence is followed within each topic: A clinical problem is posed, frequently through the verbatim quotation of a segment of a fictional interview. Relevent studies are then summarized. Finally, the applied implications of the studies are formulated, with reference to the clinical problem(s) posed, and, when possible, operational specifics for the conduct of an interview are given. Thus, there is an effort to bridge the gap between research and clinical application. With reference to the single interview, there is an attempted response to the type of challenge posed by the question frequently asked today about psychotherapy research: "What difference has research made in my practice of psychotherapy?" Clearly, the same question could be asked about the practice of interviewing.

The following major topics have been dealt with in this chapter:

1. Verbal content in the interview—its definition through the associational structure of the interviewee's communication.
2. The control and direction by the interviewer of interviewee verbal content.
3. Verbal style of the interviewer and the interviewee.
   a. Activity level of both participants (i.e., their productivity).
   b. Interviewer ambiguity-specificity (i.e., the effect on interviewee response of the open-ended versus the specific—interrogatory—interviewer approach).
4. Expressive aspects of interview communication.
   a. Anxiety in interview communication.
   b. Depression.
5. Sequence effects in the interview.
   a. The beginning of the interview.
   b. The body (principal) segment.

Unfortunately, space considerations have not permitted an equal review of both the communication and relationship aspects of the interview. Indeed, the bias has been toward the former. It is therefore proposed to offer the reader who wishes to review the clinical and research literature dealing with relationship some guidance in such an enterprise.

EPILOGUE: A GUIDE TO SELECTED READINGS IN INTERVIEW RELATIONSHIP

Good and poor relationships

Fiedler, F. E. A comparison of therapeutic relationships in psychoanalytic, nondirective, and Adlerian therapy. *Journal of Consulting Psychology*, 1950, *14*, 435–36.

Gardner, G. G. *The psychotherapeutic relationship.* Hawthorne, N.Y.: Aldine Publishing, 1973.

Lorr, M. Client perceptions of therapists: A study of therapeutic relation. *Journal of Consulting Psychology*, 1965, *29*, 140–149

Orlinsky, D. E., & Howard, K. I. The good therapy hour. *Archives of General Psychiatry*, 1967, *16*, 621–632.

Parloff, M. B. Some factors affecting the quality of therapeutic relationships. *Journal of Abnormal and Social Psychology*, 1956, *52*, 5–10.

Parloff, M. B. Therapist-patient relationship and outcome of psychotherapy. *Journal of Consulting Psychology*, 1961, *25*, 29–38.

Reciprocity in relationship

Heller, K., Myers, R. A., & Kline, L. V. Interviewer behavior as a function of standardized client roles. *Journal of Consulting Psyclology*, 1963, *27*, 117–122.

Rosen, A. The treatment relationship: A conceptualization. *Journal of Consulting Psychology*, 1972, *38*, 329–337.

Snyder, W. V., & Snyder, B. J. *The psychotherapy relationship.* New York: Macmillan, 1961.

Truax, C. B., & Mitchell, K. M. Research on certain therapist interpersonal skills in relation to process and outcome. In A. E. Bergin & S. L. Garfield (Eds.), *Handbook of psychotherapy and behavior change: An empirical analysis.* New York: John Wiley & Sons, 1971.

Relationship as attraction

Goldstein, A. P. *Psychotherapeutic attraction.* Elmsford, N.Y.: Pergamon Press, 1971.

Heller, K., & Goldstein, A. P. Client dependency and therapist expectancy as relationship-maintaining variables in psychotherapy. *Journal of Consulting Psychology*, 1961, *25*, 371–375.

Libo, L. M. The projective expression of patient-therapist attraction. *Journal of Clinical Psychology*, 1957, *13*, 33–36.

Libo, L. M. *Manual for the picture impressions test.* Palo Alto, Calif.: Consulting Psychologists Press, 1961.

Pope, B., & Siegman, A. W. Interviewer-interviewee relationship and verbal behavior of interviewee in the initial interview. *Psychotherapy: Theory, Research, and Practice,* 1966, *3*, 149–152.

Dimensions of relationship

Bales, R. F. Communication in small groups. In G. A. Miller (Ed.), *Communication, language, and meaning.* New York: Basic Books, 1973.

Borgatta, E. F. Rankings and self-assessments: Some behavioral-characteristics replication studies. *Journal of Social Psychology*, 1960, *52*, 297–307.

Brown, R. *Social psychology.* New York: Free Press, 1965.

Danziger, K. *Interpersonal communication.* Elmsford, N.Y.: Pergamon Press, 1976.

Leary, T. *Interpersonal diagnosis of personality.* New York: Ronald Press, 1957.

Lorr, M., & McNair, D. M. Methods relating to evaluation of therapeutic outcome. In L. A. Gottschalk & A. H. Auerbach (Eds.), *Methods of research in psychotherapy.* New York: Appleton-Century-Crofts. 1966.

Pope, B., Nudler, S., Norden, J. S., & McGee, J. P. Changes in nonprofessional (novice) interviewers over a 3-year training period. *Journal of Consulting and Clinical Psychology,* 1976, *44*, 819–825.

Pope, B., & Siegman, A. W. Relationship and verbal behavior in the initial interview. In A. W. Siegman & B. Pope (Eds.), *Studies in dyadic communication.* Elmsford, N.Y.: Pergamon Press, 1972.

Rappaport, J., Chinsky, J. M., & Cowen, E. L. *Innovations in helping chronic patients (college students in a mental institution).* New York: Academic Press, 1971.

Schutz, W. C. *The interpersonal underworld.* Palo Alto, Calif.: Science and Bahavior Books, 1966.

Sullivan, H. S. *The interpersonal theory of psychiatry.* New York: W. W. Norton, 1953.

Watzlawick, P., Beavin, J. H., & Jackson, D. D. *Pragmatics of human communication.* New York: W. W. Norton, 1967.

The matching of interviewer and interviewee

Berzins, J. I. Therapist-patient matching. In A. S. Gurman & A. M. Razin (Eds.), *Effective psychotherapy: An empirical assessment.* Elmsford, N.Y.: Pergamon Press, 1977.

Carkhuff, R. R., & Pierce, R. Differential effects of therapist race and social class upon patient's depth of self-exploration in the initial clinical interview. *Journal of Consulting Psychology,* 1967, *31,* 632–634.

Carson, R. C., & Heine, R. W. Similarity and success in therapeutic dyads. *Journal of Consulting Psychology,* 1962, *26,* 38–43.

Meltzoff, J., & Kornreich, M. *Research in psychotherapy..* New York: Atherton Press, 1970.

Mendelsohn, G. A., & Geller, M. H. Structure of client attitudes toward counseling and their relation to client-counselor similarity. *Journal of Consulting Psychology,* 1965, *29,* 63–72.

Sapolsky, A. Relationship between patient-doctor compatibility, mutual perception, and outcome of treatment. *Journal of Abnormal Psychology,* 1965, *70,* 70–76.

Sattler, J. M. The effects of therapist-client racial similarity. In A. S. Gurman & A. S. Razin (Eds.), *Effective psychotherapy: An empirical assessment.* Elmsford, N.Y.: Pergamon Press, 1977.

Sullivan, H. S. *Collected works.* New York: Basic Books, 1965.

Interviewer warmth

Allen, B. V., Wiens, A. N., Whitman, M., & Saslow, G. Effects of warm-cold set on interviewee speech. *Journal of Consulting Psychology,* 1965, *29,* 480–482.

Bordin, E. S. *Psychological counseling.* New York: Appleton-Century-Crofts, 1968.

Greenberg, R. P. Effects of pre-session information on perception of the therapist and receptivity to influence in a psychotherapy analogue. *Journal of Consulting and Clinical Psychology,* 1969, *33,* 425–429.

Greenberg, R. P., Goldstein, A. P., & Parry, M. A. The influence of referral information upon patient perception in a psychotherapy analogue. *Journal of Nervous and Mental Disease,* 1970, *150,* 31–36.

Heller, K., Davis, J. D., & Myers, R. A. The effects of interviewer's style in a standardized interview. *Journal of Consulting Psychology,* 1966, *30,* 501–508.

Heller, K., Silver, R., Bailey, M., & Dudgeon, T. *The interview reactions of patients and students to within-interview changes in interviewer style.* Unpublished research, 1968.

Pope, B., Nudler, S., Vonkorff, M. R., & McGee, J. P. The experienced professional interviewer versus the complete novice. *Journal of Consulting and Clinical Psychology,* 1974, *42,* 680–690.

Pope, B., & Siegman, A. W. Interviewer warmth in relation to interviewee verbal behavior. *Journal of Consulting and Clinical Psychology,* 1968, *32,* 588–595.

Raush, H. L., & Bordin, E. S. Warmth in personality development and in psychotherapy. *Psychiatry,* 1957, *20,* 351–363.

Siegman, A. W. The telltale voice: Nonverbal messages of verbal communication. In A. W. Siegman & S. Feldstein (Eds.), *Nonverbal behavior and communication.* Hillsdale, N.J.: Erlbaum, 1978.

Siegman, A. W. The voice of attraction: Vocal correlates of interpersonal attraction in the interview. In A. W. Siegman & S. Feldstein (Eds.), *Of speech and time.* Hillsdale, N.J.: Erlbaum, 1979.

Strupp, H. H., Wallach, M. S., & Wogan, M. Psychotherapy experience in retrospect: Questionnaire survey of former patients and their therapists. *Psychological Monographs,* 1964, *78* (11, Whole No. 588).

Truax, C. B., & Carkhuff, R. R. *Toward effective counseling and psychotherapy.* Hawthorne, N.Y.: Aldine Publishing, 1967.

Empathy

Cartwright, R. D., & Lerner, B. Empathy, need to change, and improvement in psychotherapy. *Journal of Consulting Psychology,* 1963, *27,* 138–144.

Hargrove, D. S. Verbal-interaction analysis of empathic and nonempathic responses of therapists. *Journal of Consulting and Clinical Psychology.* 1974, *42,* 305.

Mehrabian, A. *Nonverbal communication.* New York: Aldine/Atherton, 1972.

Pierce, W. D., & Mosher, D. L. Perceived empathy, interviewer behavior, and interviewee anxiety. *Journal of Consulting Psychology,* 1967, *31,* 101.

Pope, B., Nudler, S., VonKorff, M. R., & McGee, J. P. The experienced professional interviewer versus the complete novice. *Journal of Consulting and Clinical Psychology,* 1974, *42,* 680–690.

Staples, F. R., & Sloan, R. B. Truax factors, speech characteristics, and therapeutic outcome. *Journal of Nervous and Mental Disease,* 1976, *163,* 135–140.

Strupp, H. H. The psychotherapist's contribution to the treatment process. *Behavioral Science,* 1958, *3,* 34–67.

Strupp, H. H., & Wallach, M. S. A further study of psychiatrists' responses in quasi-therapy situations. *Behavioral Science,* 1965, *10,* 113–134.

Interviewer status

Barrett-Lennard, G. T. Dimensions of therapist response as causal factors in therapeutic change. *Psychological Monographs,* 1962, *76* (43, Whole No. 562).

Exline, R. V. Visual interaction: The glances of power and preference. In S. Weitz (Ed.), *Nonverbal communication.* New York: Oxford University Press, 1974.

Greenberg, R. P. Effects of pre-session information on perception of the therapist and receptivity to influence in a psychotherapy analogue. *Journal of Consulting and Clinical Psychology,* 1969, *33,* 425–429.

Pepitone, A., & Wallace, W. *Experimental studies on the dynamics of hostility.* Paper read at Pennsylvania Psychological Association meeting, 1955.

Pope, B., Nudler, S., Norden, J. S., & McGee, J. P. Changes in nonprofessional (novice) interviewers over a 3-year training period. *Journal of Consulting and Clinical Psychology,* 1976, *44,* 819–825.

Pope, B., & Siegman, A. W. Relationship and verbal behavior in the initial interview. In A. W. Siegman & B. Pope (Eds.), *Studies in dyadic communication.* Elmsford, N.Y.: Pergamon Press, 1972.

Interviewer personality

Bandura, A., Lipsher, D. H., & Miller, P. E. Psychotherapists' approach-avoidance reactions to patients' expressions of hostility. *Journal of Consulting Psychology,* 1960, *24,* 1–8.

Berzins, J. I., Ross, W. F., & Cohen, D. I. Relation of the A-B distinction and trust-distrust sets to addict patients' self-disclosure in brief interviews. *Journal of Consulting and Clinical Psychology*, 1970, *34*, 289–296.

Berzins, J. I., Ross, W. F., & Friedman, W. H. A-B therapist distinction, patient diagnosis, and outcome of brief psychotherapy in a college clinic. *Journal of Consulting and Clinical Psychology*, 1972, *38*, 231–237.

Betz, B. J., & Whitehorn, J. C. The relationship of a therapist to the outcome of therapy in schizophrenia. *Psychiatric Research Reports*, 1956, *5*, 89–140.

Chartier, G. M., & Weiss, L. A-B therapists and clinical perception: Support for a "Super A" hypothesis. *Journal of Consulting and Clinical Psychology*, 1974, *42*, 312.

Feldstein, S., Alberti, L., & Ben Debba, M., Self-attributed personality characteristics and the pacing of conversational interaction. In A. W. Siegman & S. Feldstein (Eds.), *Of speech and time*. Hillsdale, N.J.: Erlbaum, 1979.

Henry, William E. Personal and social identities of psychotherapists. In A. S. Gurman & A. M. Razin (Eds.), *Effective psychotherapy*. Elmsford, N.Y.: Pergamon Press, 1977.

Markel, N. N., Phillis, J. A., Vargas, R., & Howard, K. Personality traits associated with voice types. *Journal of Psycholinguistic Research*, 1972, *1*, 249–255.

McNair, D. M., Callahan, M., & Lorr, M. Therapist "type" and patient response to psychotherapy. *Journal of Consulting Psychology*, 1962, *26*, 425–429.

Razin, A. M. The A-B variable: Still promising after 20 years. In A. S. Gurman & A. M. Razin (Eds.), *Effective psychotherapy*. Elmsford, N.Y.: Pergamon Press, 1977.

Segal, B. A-B distinction and therapeutic interaction. *Journal of Consulting and Clinical Psychology*, 1970, *34*, 442–446.

Seidman, E. A and B subject-therapists' responses to videotaped schizoid and neurotic prototypes. *Journal of Consulting and Clinical Psychology*, 1971, *37*, 201–208.

Singer, B. A., & Luborsky, L. L. Counter-transference: The status of clinical versus quantitative research. In A. S. Gurman & A. M. Razin (Eds.) *Effective psychotherapy*, Elmsford, N.Y.: Pergamon Press, 1977,

Truax, C. B., Silber, L. D., & Wargo, D. G. *Training and change in psychotherapeutic skills*. Unpublished manuscript, University of Arkansas, 1966.

Whitehorn, J. C., & Betz, B. J. Further studies of the doctor as a crucial variable on the outcome of treatment with schizophrenic patients. *American Journal of Psychiatry*, 1960, *117*, 215–223.

Diagnostically defined attributes of the interviewees

Beier, E. G. *The silent language of psychotherapy*. Hawthorne, N.Y.: Aldine Publishing, 1966.

Kaplan, F. Effects of anxiety and defenses in a therapylike situation. *Journal of Abnormal Psychology*, 1966, *71*, 449–458.

Kiesler, D. J. Patient experiencing and successful outcome in individual psychotherapy of schizophrenics and psychoneurotics. *Journal of Consulting and Clinical Psychology*, 1971, *37*, 370–385.

MacKinnon, R. A., & Michels, R. *The psychiatric interview in clinical practice*. Philadelphia: Saunders, 1971.

Markel, N. N. Relationship between voice-quality profiles and MMPI profiles in psychiatric patients. *Journal of Abnormal Psychology*, 1969, *74*, 61–66.

Matarazzo, J. D., & Saslow, G. Differences in interview interaction behavior among normal and deviant groups. In I. A. Berg & B. M. Bass (Eds.), *Conformity and deviation.* New York: Harper & Row, 1961.

Pope, B., Blass, T., Siegman, A. W., & Raher, J. Anxiety and depression in speech. *Journal of Consulting and Clinical Psychology,* 1970, *35,* 128–133.

Pope, B., & Scott, W. H. *Psychological diagnosis in clinical practice.* New York: Oxford University Press, 1967.

Pope, B., & Siegman, A. W. Interviewer specificity and topical focus in relation to interviewee productivity. *Journal of Verbal Learning and Verbal Bahavior, 4,* 1965, 188–192.

Pope, B., Siegman, A. W., & Blass, T. Anxiety and speech in the initial interview. *Journal of Consulting and Clinical Psychology,* 1970, *35,* 233–238.

Siegman, A. W., & Pope, B. Effects of question specificity and anxiety-arousing messages on verbal fluency in the initial interview. *Journal of Personality and Social Psychology,* 1965, *4,* 188–192.

Vetter, H. J. *Language behavior and psychopathology.* Skokie, Il.: Rand McNally, 1969.

Personality attributes of the interviewee

Andrews, J. D. W. Psychotherapy of phobias. *Psychological Bulletin,* 1966, *66,* 455–480.

Bordin, E. S. *Research strategies in psychotherapy.* New York: John Wiley & Sons, 1974.

Heller, K., Myers, R. A., & Kline, L. V. Interviewer behavior as a function of standardized client roles. *Journal of Consulting Psychology,* 1963, *27,* 117–122.

Rayner, E. H., & Hahn, H. Assessment of psychotherapy. *British Journal of Medical Psychology,* 1964, *37,* 331–342.

Snyder, W. U. *The psychotherapy relationship.* New York: Macmillan, 1961.

Weintraub, W., & Aronson, H. The application of verbal behavior analysis to the study of psychological defense mechanisms. II: Speech patterns associated with impulsive behavior. *The Journal of Nervous and Mental Disease,* 1964, *139,* 75–82.

Williams, J. V. *The influence of therapist commitment on progress in psychotherapy.* Unpublished doctoral thesis, University of Michigan, 1959.

Interviewee capacity for success in relationship

Bordin, E. S. *Research strategies in psychotherapy.* New York: John Wiley & Sons, 1974.

Klein, M. H., Mathieu, P. L., Gendlin, E. T., & Kiesler, D. J. *The experiencing scale: A research and training manual* (2 vols.). Madison: Wisconsin Psychiatric Institute, Bureau of Audio-Visual Instruction, 1970.

Liberman, B. L., Frank, J. D., Hoehn-Saric, R., Stone, A. R., Imber, S. D., & Pande, S. K. Patterns of change in treated psychoneurotic patients: A five-year follow-up in the investigation of the systematic preparation of patients for psychotherapy. *Journal of Consulting and Clinical Psychology,* 1972, *38,* 36–41.

Nash, E. H., Hoehn-Saric, R., Battle, C. C., Stone, A. R., Imber, S. D., & Frank, J. D. Systematic preparation of patients for short-term psychotherapy. II: Relation to characteristics of patient, therapist and the psychotherapeutic process. *The Journal of Nervous and Mental Disease,* 1965, *140,* 374–383.

Pope, B., & Nudler, S. Some clinical and sociometric correlates of interviewee verbal behavior. *Proceedings of the 81st Annual Convention of the American Psychological Association,* 1973, *8,* 561–562.

REFERENCES

Bandura, A., Lipsher, D. H., & Miller, P. E. Psychotherapists' approach-avoidance reactions to patients' expressions of hostility. *Journal of Consulting Psychology,* 1960, *24* 1–8.

Beldoch,M. Sensitivity to expression of emotional meaning in three modes of communication. In J. Davitz (Ed.), *The communication of emotional meaning.* New York: McGraw-Hill, 1964.

Bordin, E. S. Ambiguity as a therapeutic variable. *Journal of Consulting Psychology,* 1955, 19, 9–15.

Bunny, W E., & Hamburg, D. A. Methods for reliable longitudinal observation of behavior. *Archives of General Psychiatry,* 1963, *9,* 280–294.

Butterworth, B., & Goldman-Eisler, F. Recent studies on cognitive rhythm. In A. W. Siegman & S. Feldstein (Eds.), *Of speech and time.*Hillsdale, N.J.: Erlbaum, 1979.

Chaiken, A. L., & Derlega, V. J. Variables affecting the appropriateness of self-disclosure. *Journal of Consulting and Clinical Psychology,* 1974, *42,* 588–593.

Davitz, J. P. The communication of emotional meaning. In A. G. Smith (Ed.), *Communication and culture.* New York: Holt, Rinehart & Winston, 1964.

Dittman, A. T. Kinetic research and therapeutic process: Further discussion. In P. H. Knapp (Ed.), *Expression of the emotions in man.* New York: International Universities Press, 1963.

Fiedler, F. E. A comparison of therapeutic relationships in psychoanalytic, nondirective, and Adlerian therapy. *Journal of Consulting Psychology,* 1950, *14,* 435–436. (a)

Fiedler, F. E. The concept of an ideal therapeutic relationship. *Journal of Consulting Psychology,* 1950, *14,* 239–245. (b)

Gendlin, E. T. *Experiencing and the creation of meaning.* New York: Free Press, 1962.

Gottschalk, L. A., & Gleser, G. C. *The measurement of psychological states through the content analysis of verbal behavior.* Berkeley: University of California, 1969.

Gottschalk, L. A., Springer, M. J., & Gleser, G. Experiments with a method of assessing the variations in intensity of certain psychological states occurring during two psychotherapeutic interviews. In L.A. Gottschalk (Ed.), *Comparative psycholinguistic analysis of two psychotherapeutic interviews.* New York: International Universities Press, 1961.

Gottschalk, L. A., Winget, C., Gleser, G., & Springer, K. The measurement of emotional changes during a psychiatric interview: A working model toward quantifying the psychoanalytic concept of affect. In L. A. Gottschalk & A. Auerbach (Eds.), *Methods of research in psychotherapy.* New York: Appleton-Century-Crofts, 1966.

Greenspoon, J. Verbal conditioning and clinical psychology. In A. J. Bachrach (Ed.), *Experimental foundations of clinical psychology.* New York: Basic Books, 1962.

Harway, N. T., & Iker, H. P. Content analysis in psychotherapy. *Psychotherapy: Theory, Research, and Practice,* 1969, *6,* 97–104.

Heller, K., Davis, J. D., & Meyers, R. A. The effects of interviewer style in a standardized interview. *Journal of Consulting Psychology,* 1966, *30,* 501–508.

Heller, K., & Marlatt, G. A. Verbal conditioning, behavior therapy, and behavior change. In C. M. Franks (Ed.), *Behavior therapy, appraisal and status.* New York: McGraw-Hill, 1969.

Hoehn-Saric, R., Frank, J. D., Imber, S. D., Nash, E. H., Stone, A. R., & Battle, C. C.

Systematic preparation of patients for psychotherapy. I: Effects on therapy behavior and outcome. *Journal of Psychiatric Research,* 1964, *2,* 267–281.

Ivey, A. E. *Microcounseling.* Springfield, Ill.: Charles C Thomas, 1971.

Jourard, S. M. *Self-disclosure, an experimental analysis of the transparent self.* New York: Wiley Interscience, 1971. (a)

Jourard, S. M. *The transparent self.* New York: Van Nostrand Reinhold, 1971. (b)

Jourard, S. M., & Friedman, R. Experimenter-subject "distance" and self-disclosure. *Journal of Personality and Social Psychology,* 1970, *15,* 278–282.

Kanfer, F. H. Effect of a warning signal preceding the noxious stimulus on verbal rate and heart rate. *Journal of Experimental Psychology,* 1958, *55,* 73–86.

Kanfer, F. H. Verbal rate, content, and adjustment ratings in experimentally structured interviews. *Journal of Abnormal and Social Psychology,* 1959, *58,* 305–311.

Kanfer, F. H. Verbal rate, eye blinks, and content in structured psychiatric interviews. *Journal of Abnormal and Social Psychology,* 1960, *61,* 341–347.

Karl, N. H., & Abeles, N. Psychotherapy process as a function of time-segment samples. *Journal of Consulting and Clinical Psychology,* 1969, *33,* 207–212.

Kasl, S. V., & Mahl, G. F. Experimentally induced anxiety and speech disturbance. *American Psychologist,* 1958, *13,* 349.

Kiesler, D. J. *The process of psychotherapy.* Hawthorne, N.Y.: Aldine Publishing, 1973.

Kiesler, D. J., Klein, M. H., & Mathieu, P. L. Sampling from the recorded therapy interview: The problem of segment location. *Journal of Consulting Psychology,* 1965, *29,* 337–344.

Lalljee, M., & Cook, M. Uncertainty in first encounters. *Journal of Personality and Social Psychology,* 1973, *26,* 137–141.

Lennard, H. L., & Bernstein, A. *The anatomy of psychotherapy.* New York: Columbia University Press, 1960.

Levin, F. M., & Gergen, K. J. Revealing press, ingratiation, and the disclosure of self. *Proceedings of the 77th annual convention of the American Psychological Association,* 1969, *4,* (Pt. 1), 447–448.

Levy, P. K. The ability to express and perceive vocal communications of feeling. In J. R. Davitz (Ed.), *The communication of emotional meaning.* New York: McGraw-Hill, 1964.

MacKinnon, R. A., & Michels, R. *The psychiatric interview in clinical practice.* Philadelphia: Saunders, 1971.

Mahl, G. F. Disturbances and silences in patient's speech in psychotherapy. *Journal of Abnormal and Social Psychology,* 1956, *53,* 1–15.

Mahl, G. F. Exploring emotional states by content analysis. In I. Pool (Ed.), *Trends in content analysis.* Urbana: University of Illinois Press, 1959.

Mahl, G. F. The lexical and paralinguistic levels in the expression of the emotions. In R. H. Knapp (Ed.), *Expression of the emotions in man.* New York: International Universities Press, 1963.

Matarazzo, J. D. The interview. In B. B. Wolman (Ed.), *Handbook of clinical psychology.* New York: McGraw-Hill, 1965.

Matarazzo, J. D., Wiens, A. N., Matarazzo, R. G., & Saslow, G. Speech and silence behavior in clinical psychotherapy and its laboratory correlates. In J. M. Shlien (Ed.), *Research in psychotherapy.* Washington, D.C.: American Psychological Association, 1968.

Orne, M. T., & Wender, P. H. Anticipatory socialization for psychotherapy: Method and rationale. *The American Journal of Psychiatry,* 1968, *124,* 1202–1212.

Pope, Benjamin. Research on therapeutic style. In A. S. Gurman & A. M. Razin (Eds.), *Effective psychotherapy.* Elmsford, N.Y.: Pergamon Press, 1977.

Pope, Benjamin. *The mental-health interview: Research and application.* Elmsford, N.Y.: Pergamon Press, 1979.

Pope, B., Blass, T., Cheek, J., Siegman, A. W., & Bradford, N. H. Interviewer specificity in seminaturalistic interviews. *Journal of Consulting and Clinical Psychology,* 1971, *36,* 152.

Pope, B., Blass, T., Siegman, A. W., & Raher, J. Anxiety and depression in speech. *Journal of Consulting and Clinical Psychology,* 1970, *35,* 128–133.

Pope, B., Nudler, S., Norden, J., & McGee, J. P. Sequence effects in the initial interview. *Academic Psychology Bulletin,* 1979, *1,* 51–61.

Pope, B., Nudler, S., VonKorff, M. R., & McGee, J. P. The experienced professional interviewer versus the complete novice. *Journal of Consulting and Clinical Psychology,* 1974, *42,* 680–690.

Pope, B., & Siegman, A. W. The effect of therapist verbal-activity level and specificity on patient productivity and speech disturbance in the initial interview. *Journal of Consulting Psychology,* 1962, *26,* 489.

Pope, B., & Siegman, A. W. Interviewer specificity and topical focus in relation to interviewee productivity. *Journal of Verbal Learning and Verbal Behavior,* 1965, *4,* 188–192.

Pope, B., & Siegman, A. W. Interviewer warmth in relation to interviewee verbal behavior. *Journal of Consulting and Clinical Psychology,* 1968, *37,* 588–595.

Rogers, J. M. Operant conditioning in a quasi-therapy setting. *Journal of Abnormal and Social Psychology,* 1960, *60,* 247–252.

Russel, P. D., & Snyder, W. V. Counselor anxiety in relation to amount of clinical experience and quality of affect demonstrated by clients. *Journal of Consulting Psychology,* 1963, *27,* 358–363.

Salzinger, K. & Pisoni, S. Reinforcement of affect responses of schizophrenics during the clinical interview. *Journal of Abnormal and Social Psychology,* 1958, *57,* 84–90.

Sarason, I. G., Ganzer, V. J., & Singer, M. Effects of modeled self-disclosure on the verbal behavior of persons differing in defensiveness. *Journal of Consulting and Clinical Psychology,* 1972, *39,* 483–490.

Siegman, A. W., & Pope, B. Effects of question specificity and anxiety-producing messages on verbal fluency in the initial interview. *Journal of Personality and Social Psychology,* 1965, *2,* 522–530.

Siegman, A. W., & Pope, B. The effect of interviewer ambiguity-specificity and topical focus on interviewee vocabulary diversity. *Language and Speech,* 1966, *9,* 242–249.

Siegman, A. W., & Pope, B. The effects of ambiguity and anxiety on interviewee verbal behavior. In A. W. Siegman & B. Pope (Eds.), *Studies in dyadic communication.* Elmsford, N.Y.: Pergamon Press, 1972.

Snyder, W. V. An investigation of the nature of nondirective psychotherapy. *Journal of General Psychology,* 1945, *33,* 193–223.

Spiegel, J., & Machotka, P. *Messages of the body.* New York: Free Press, 1974.

Strupp, H. H. The psychotherapist's contribution to the treatment process. *Behavioral Science,* 1958, *3,* 34–67.

Strupp, H. H. *Psychotherapists in action.* New York: Grune & Stratton, 1960.

Sullivan, H. S. *The psychiatric interview.* New York: W. W. Norton, 1954.

Sundland, D. M., & Barker, E. N. The orientation of psychotherapists. *Journal of Consulting Psychology,* 1962, *26,* 201–212.

Taffel, C. Anxiety and the conditioning of verbal behavior. *Journal of Abnormal and Social Psychology,* 1955, *51,* 496–501.

Tourney, G., Bloom, V., Lowinger, P. L., Schorer, C., Auld, F., & Grisell, J. A study of psychotherapeutic process variables in psychoneurotic and schizophrenic patients. *American Journal of Psychotherapy,* 1966, *20,* 112–124.

Truax, C. B. Length of therapist response, accurate empathy, and patient improvement. *Journal of Clinical Psychology,* 1970, *26,* 539–541.

12

Behavioral assessment

Ian M. Evans*

The endeavor known as *behavioral assessment* is defined less accurately by reference to specific techniques or measures than by reference to the scientific attitudes, methodological assumptions, and, to some extent, the scholarly sociogram, of its proponents. There is some reason to regret the recent emergence of behavioral assessment as an independent field of study (e.g., Evans & Nelson, 1974), for in its early origins, it simply coexisted with behavior therapy (modification), being that inseparable part of the therapeutic enterprise which involved selecting, defining, and measuring the behaviors of concern. Just as behavior therapy was rooted in the application of behavioral principles—particularly those derived from the experimental study of learning—so the distinguishing feature of assessment was the selection of dependent variables familiar to experimental psychology and naturalistic observation. And in the same way that behavior therapy broadened to become empirical rather than behavioristic in orientation, so behavioral assessment has come to represent a very wide range of procedures, tapping many phenomena other than overt motor behavior and extending to all aspects of clinical inquiry. In this chapter, the author will try to introduce the reader to the fascinating diversity of this approach, illustrating the more significant contributions to clinical research and practice.

Behavioral assessment is alive with controversy. One of the earliest contributions of major importance was Mischel's (1968) carefully reasoned and well-known thesis regarding the inadequacy of trait theory, the situational specificity of behavior, and the lack of utility of traditional testing for the design of treatment. Mischel (1968) wrote, "Behavior assessments *do not* label the individual with generalized trait terms and stereotypes, sort him into diagnostic or type categories, pinpoint his average position on average or modal dimensions, or guess about his private reasons and motives. Instead the focus is on sampling the individual's

* Department of Psychology, State University of New York at Binghamton.

relevant cognitions and behaviors" (p. 190). Although these themes certainly form the behavioral assessment credo, there are surprisingly few true believers. For instance,there is recent indication in some quarters of a swing toward the psychiatric nosology (DMS-III), it being argued (Barlow, 1981) that such classification serves as the springboard for more-detailed assessment of individual functioning. However, the rather furtive plea that DSM-III has to be adopted by clinical psychologists out of practical necessity is clearly belied by trends in children's services, which are becoming increasingly noncategorical and oriented toward functional assessment (Hobbs, 1975).

Mischel (1968) sharply questioned traditional personality and clinical testing assumptions; the various arguments are well presented by Goldfried and Kent (1972) and by Hartmann, Roper, and Bradford (1979). The central point made by these authors is that a personality construct is the abstraction devised to summarize and integrate consistent observations of behavior, not the explanation for the behavior. Traditional assessment interprets test responses as signs of something else; whereas in behavioral assessment, the test response is interpreted as a sample of the way the individual might respond in other, nontesting situations. Thus, as Evans and Nelson (1974) were at pains to point out, behavior assessment is not inherently "anti-testing," but is instead critical of some of the ways in which tests have been used in clinical assessment. There are two keys to any effective clinical assessment: the metric properties of one's instrument or measure, and the use to which the measure is put.

PURPOSES OF BEHAVIORAL ASSESSMENT

Psychological measures—whether formal tests or the informal instruments that tend to be favored in behavioral assessment—are tools and can be evaluated, in the final analysis, only in terms of their uses. The inadequacy of an otherwise valuable can opener for changing a car tire is so obvious because the failure to achieve one's purpose is immediately apparent. In clinical psychology, it is often far less obvious as to whether an assessment has "correctly" identified the client's fundamental problems or laid bare the important variables whose change constitutes therapeutic treatment. Thus, as has been frequently charged, assessment can easily become functionally autonomous, superstitiously reconfirmed by illusory connections between the findings and the treatment plans developed. Recognizing this problem, Nelson and Hayes (1979) have proposed the evaluation criterion "treatment validity," which seeks answers to the question, "Does this assessment enhance treatment outcome?" Without refuting the importance of posing this question, this author would like to propose a more crucial, intermediate criterion, which we can call *interpretive validity*, defined as the degree to which a measure influences the clinician's decisions, independent of other considerations or information that is not formally derived from the assessment. Thus, if the determination of brain damage is going to be made on the basis of clinical signs and medical history, the findings from a neuropsychological test battery might be irrelevant. On the other end of the spectrum, the global description of the patient's cognitive deficits revealed by standardized testing may not be of as much use in developing a specific, rehabilitative treatment plan as more detailed, functional assessment. A great deal of time and effort could be channeled more effectively if clinicians would consistently ask themselves for what purpose any assessment is being conducted and how the results will affect their decisions.

Nelson and Hayes (1979) state that the "goal of behavioral assessment is to identify meaningful response units and their controlling variables for the purpose of understanding and of altering behavior" (p. 13); but there are, in fact, quite a number of very different purposes for assessment which are not always made explicit when different behavioral measures are described. The following categories help identify some of these purposes by considering the different types and levels of decision for which the information is gathered (for a further discussion, see Evans & Wilson, in press).

Screening and needs assessment

The principle behind screening is to measure some feature of the individual and compare the score to a predetermined norm or standard, in order to decide on the need for services or the suitability of offering treatment. The most crucial measurement issues are whether the variable measured or the standard employed adequately represent the phenomenon of interest. For example, deviation from height-weight chart norms is not necessarily a bad sign. As Mahoney, Mahoney, Rogers, and Straw (1979) explain, height-weight chart comparisons are inadequate for the detection of accumulated fat that is unhealthy to the individual, and at the very least, skinfold thickness estimates should be obtained.

Ethical considerations are also very important. Public health programs—geared toward the detection of individuals whose family histories, life styles, or behavioral excesses predispose them to common health problems such as cancer, diabetes, or coronary and vascular disease—are readily accepted features of preventive health care. So too are developmental screening programs designed to identify—as early as possible—children exhibiting developmental delays indicative of future mental retardation or physical handicap. In these cases, the distinction between normal and abnormal and the near universal agreement regarding the undesirability of the latter, make the worth of such programs incontrovertible. This is not the case, however, with early screening programs for behavioral problems, where concern with primary prevention has stimulated interest in the assessment of behavioral excesses or deficits that *may* bode ill for later adjustment and well-being. Consider how the identification of school children supposedly exhibiting social-skill deficits because they are relatively socially isolated is predicated on the unfounded (and rather disquieting) assumption that being unpopular, or having few friends, is a sign of maladjustment. There are dangers in identifying and labeling people as psychologically at risk that cannot be lightly dismissed.

One less controversial use of screening measurement is to reveal the absence of behaviors which are widely assumed to be necessary and present in individuals' repertoires by most other socially responsible people. Poche, Brouwer, and Swearingen (1981), for instance, showed that 90 percent of young children approached by a strange adult (a confederate of the experimenter, of course), readily agreed to leave the preschool with him. These children were then selected for a training program to teach appropriate refusals and other self-protective responses designed to prevent them from becoming the victims of child molestation. Unobtrusive videotaping of young children crossing streets, in another example, revealed that many children's actual safety skills were extremely deficient (Yeaton & Bailey, 1978), suggesting an approach to pedestrian safety instruction that would be rather different from the usual didactic lessons. Such illustrations also reveal that it is not invariably the social norm that sets the standard for treatment goals.

Problem identification and goal definition

Obviously, this is one of the key purposes of assessment, similar in importance to the assignment of a psychiatric diagnosis in traditional assessment, and equally fraught with sources of clinician disagreement (Wilson & Evans, in press). The question the clinician asks at this juncture is: in what specific ways should the client change in order to achieve his or her own personal goals for therapy? Therapeutic goal setting, as many have pointed out, necessitates a contractual arrangement between therapist and client, so that, inevitably, both contribute to the specification of the goals. This is an active, mutual responsibility that should be kept as explicit as possible. Having behaviorally defined, measurable goals is not only good practice for effective therapy, but essential for establishing any degree of professional accountability, which is why behavioral specificity is mandated in the guidelines for such service contracts as the Individualized Educational Plan or pschotherapy provided under CHAMPUS insurance reimbursement.

The specification of a client's problems and needs requires careful adherence to a logical model which contains, at the very minimum, three distinct stages: long-term goals (such as de-institutionalization or successful community adjustment); short-term outcomes oriented toward the referral complaint (such as reduction in tension headaches, elimination of bed wetting, or alleviation of social anxiety); and immediate behavioral changes integral to the therapy. Contrary to popular views, a presenting complaint is never the sole, direct focus of behavior therapy: events which underlie, lead up to, or make possible the complaint are the more common targets for intervention. For a client complaining of depression, the focus of therapy may well be on modifying negative self-statements (Beck, 1976), enhancing the availability of rewards, intrinsically reinforcing activities (Lewinsohn & Lee, 1981), increasing social skills (Carson & Adams, 1981), or some strategic combination (McLean, 1976). Problem drinkers might be taught generalized self-control skills, people with tension headaches might learn relaxation and better ways of coping with or avoiding stress, couples with dysfunctional marriages might be encouraged to adopt problem-solving strategies that emphasize improved communication and enhance exchange of reinforcers. The examples are many.

The consideration given to such strategic targets is based predominantly on theoretical assumptions regarding the characteristic pattern of behavioral difficulties surrounding the most distressing, socially obvious, or most easily labeled feature of the client's repertoire. Increasing the clinician's awareness of these options is one of the major benefits of the published research literature on different disorders. However, every client has unique needs, and the empirical literature—as well as the clinical lore that emerges from it—blended with the clinician's previous experience and personal observations, provides hypotheses to be further pursued in assessment. It is sometimes represented that in assessment, one enumerates all the problems of the client, prioritizes them, and proceeds to treatment. This is rarely possible—or advisable—in practice. Key problems are seldom completely apparent when intervention begins, and the clinician must—throughout the course of treatment—question, rethink, and reexamine. The process is not a random one; like beginning to solve a large jigsaw puzzle, there are good strategies to follow, such as assembling all the pieces that have one straight edge to define the boundaries of the puzzle, or putting together pieces of like color while recognizing that such sections are but parts of the whole picture. These clinical strategies are described in more detail in the next section.

Hypothesis testing and the functional analysis

Strategic decisions regarding the focus of intervention are probably influenced by many subtle variables, including the clinician's previous experience with similar problems, knowledge of current literature regarding certain disorders, and broader philosophical assumptions regarding the general causes of maladaptive behavior—*pre-assessment bias*, as Evans and Nelson (1977) call it. It is clear that these characteristics of the clinician influence the type of assessment information gathered. Whether this information in turn influences the general clinical strategy probably depends on the willingness of the clinician to conceptualize the assessment process as a hypothesis formation-and-testing activity (Hawkins, 1975; Shapiro, 1951; Watts, 1980).

Common problems rarely have common causes. School phobia may be related to separation anxiety, punishing events in school, or the greater reinforcement for staying at home; assessment designed to suggest which is the most probable explanation in a given child will influence the general design of the treatment. One does not initiate parent-child contracts if the child's low school grades are primarily due to a learning disability; enhancing a married couple's communication skills would not be the focus of intervention (at least initially) if one spouse had a serious drinking problem; teaching social skills to a schizophrenic person is not the treatment of choice if the patient is exhibiting severe paranoid delusions. Assessment geared to decide these strategic decisions is not based on specific types of information or tests, but on the formulation of hypotheses about the client (Kanfer & Grimm, 1977) and the testing of these hypotheses by whatever method is available, the most formal being the clinical experiment, or functional analysis.

Perhaps the most interesting aspect of behavioral assessment, the concept of the functional analysis is an extension of the Skinnerian concept of the same name, and it refers to identification of the specific variables which currently control and direct a given behavior. Thus, for example, irrespective of any neurological contribution to hyperactivity, or the history of child rearing received, if we can demonstrate that a child's being frequently out of seat in the classroom is a function both of the interest level of the assigned activity and the degree of social attention received while disruptive, we have identified two significant variables whose alteration should significantly improve the behavior of the hyperkinetic child. The very close relationship between a functional analysis and treatment can be seen especially clearly in this example, because the method whereby the relevance of teacher attention, say, was determined, was the same as the treatment design. The familiar ABAB reversal (or withdrawal) design is not so much a method of evaluating a treatment as it is a means of conducting a functional analysis, concentrating on those variables that the clinician has some ability to control—in this case, the contingencies of the teacher's social rewards and the nature of the classroom activities. It is useful to continue to think of this as a functional analysis (rather than the ioslation and modification of the causes of behavior), because the same strategy can be used for assessing the value of medication (such as Ritalin), the lack of which is clearly not a cause of hyperactivity. A clinical experiment to assess the effects of a drug would involve measuring out-of-seat behavior before medication, while on medication, and while on a placebo, probably following an AB(drug)^C(placebo)^B sequence.

Clearly, this single-subject trial would be the minimum requirement for a careful and ethical use of medication, yet it is not an evaluation of the drug—either for this child or for hyperactive children in general. There is, for instance, no measure of the effects on the child's growth (a serious side effect) nor on his rate of learning (cf., Kauffman & Hallahan, 1979). The same is true of behavioral interventions. If the teacher ignores restless behavior and socially rewards the child for being in seat and thus increases the percentage duration of this behavior, there is no evidence from this alone that other important classroom behaviors have improved, such as attending, accurately completing assigned work, and so on (Ayllon & Rosenbaum, 1977). Thus, single-case designs may be clinically useful in establishing the internal validity of an intervention (the functional relationship between behavior change and a manipulated variable), but are not very useful for evaluating the intervention or its general benefits and consequences.

Network analysis for design or choice of therapy

Once the general strategy and focus of intervention have been determined, a multitude of complex decisions have to be made about the specific details of therapy. A major purpose of assessment is to obtain the information needed to decide issues as: who in the client's environment can be relied upon to help maintain therapeutic gains; what activities might be most reinforcing for the client if initiated; or whether the client has the skills, financial resources, or social opportunities to carry out and maintain a proposed pattern of change. A number of authors have outlined general categories of information that need to be addressed in this aspect of assessment (e.g., Nay, 1979). Kanfer and Saslow (1969) proposed attending to stimulus antecedents, the biological status of the individual, the nature of the response repertoire, the contingency relationships between specific behaviors and their reinforcing consequences, and the general consequences available in the environment. Lazarus (1976), emphasizing the relevance of clinical information rather than the functional analysis, proposed the acronym *BASIC-ID* to remind the clinician that attention must be paid to behavior, affect, sensation, imagery, cognition, interpersonal skill, and drug (or general organic) factors.

Much of this type of information is collected informally in interviews, but empirically oriented clinicians have developed a number of more formal tools for gathering such data. Cautela (1977), for example has published a wide range of simple but useful self-rating forms, checklists, and diary-type records which can indicate preferred reinforcers, types of fattening foods eaten, nature of client's social support systems, whether imagery ability is sufficient for covert techniques, and a host of others. As the successful generalization and maintenance of the best designed intervention seems to hinge on the most-correct and efficient utilization of relevant external variables, the general importance of this analysis of the client's social, vocational, and recreational opportunities is hard to overemphasize. With its heavy emphasis on intrapsychic and historical variables, it is also the facet of behavior most ignored in traditional assessment.

However, where we have some information that, in general, individuals with high scores on specific trait measures will tend to do better with one type of therapy than another, it would seem only sensible to consider such relationships as a helpful guide to treatment selection and design. Examples of this promising area are the relationships between introversion/extroversion and therapy technique (Eysenck, 1976), the importance of locus of control for success in biofeedback (Carlson, 1982), and so on. If anxiety mediates (precipitates) a given problem (such as asthma in children), systematic desensitization might be a useful adjunct treatment; if anger or shyness precipitates asthmatic episodes, assertion training would be preferable (Melamed & Johnson, 1981). The term *trait* is used here rather loosely, as state measures of the same constructs typically show stronger relationships to therapeutic outcome (Zuckerman, 1980). Of course, every practitioner pays close attention to clinicially inferable states, gauging the mood of the client during a therapy session when judging whether treatment plans must be withheld or temporarily modified. In special-education settings, teachers will respond to subtle signs that indicate a handicapped child is too tired, too restless, or in some way not ready for a particular program or lesson plan on a specific day or time.

Monitoring key outcomes

Like all good caricatures, the popular image of the behavior therapist—as someone who encourages the client to go away and record behavior—is accurate—though exaggerated. Gathering systematic data on the critical target behaviors is an important ingredient of empiricially based therapy. Prior to intervention, information regarding the timing, duration, intensity, and general pattern of maladaptive behavior provides the major source of information for a careful functional analysis. Systematic assessment of change in these behaviors provides the critical documentation of the efficacy of the treatment plan. In addition, the action of monitoring behavior—whether by self or by other—seems to have reactive effects which are typically of clinical benefit (Nelson, 1977). However, when discussing systematic data gathering, we should not allow the past emphasis on clinical experimentation (procedural designs for determining whether there was an internally valid relationship between treatment and behavior change) to detract from the primary purpose of systematic monitoring for the clinician, which is to provide objective feedback to guide the conduct of therapy.

The most sophisticated illustration of this principle is povided by data-based instructional techniques, which developed in special education as behavior modification principles were adapted to the needs of classroom practice. The systematic gathering of trial-by-trial data on the correctness of the child's response indicates whether instructional objectives are being met and also whether tasks must be changed, new goals set, or teaching methods altered (White & Haring, 1980). While most clinicians intuitively operate in this fashion—obtaining information from the client or other reliable sources regarding specific progress during the period between sessions—there are few (if any) guidelines regarding when actually to change therapeutic tactics. This is why White and Haring's decision rules are a valuable step forward. In clinical behavior therapy, when clients monitor and report their weight loss, severity of headache pain, frequency of depressed thoughts, number of social contacts, hours of sleep, or whatever, neither they nor their clinicians have proper standards for what constitutes acceptable progress.

In a special series of articles (likely to become classics in the field) edited by Barlow in the *Journal of Consulting and Clinical Psychology*, there is a significant and timely shift in emphasis in behavioral assessment from measurement for scientific documentation of the effects of treatment, to measurement which will empirically guide the routine activities of the clinician. Nelson (1981), for instance, outlines a number of dependent measures for clinical use which are functional and realistic, such as self-monitoring, self-report, card-sorts, and indirect measures (e.g., measuring the size of a bald spot in a client exhibiting compulsive hair-pulling). Yeaton and Sechrest (1981) advocate greater attention to treatment strength ("the a priori likelihood that a treatment could have its intended outcome") and integrity ("the degree to which treatment is delivered as intended"), as well as to plotting the rate and level of expected outcomes, so that the clinician is then in a "position to make mid-stream corrections in the treatment plan or to keep on a pre-charted course" (p. 165).

Evaluating general outcomes

The final major purpose of assessment—and perhaps, after diagnosis, the most traditional—is the general evaluation of therapeutic outcome, which was touched upon in the previous section. Whereas behavior therapy has tended to focus the issue of efficacy on specific improvements in the target behaviors identified, it is usually implicit, as in all schools of psychotherapy, that there are broader scale benefits resulting from— or accompanying—the targeted change. Clients are not just expected to lose weight, no longer avoid feared situations, stop drinking to excess, or have fewer marital conflicts. They are expected to make new relationships, feel more positive about themselves, engage in a wider variety of activities, be more productive at work, enjoy better health, have a more fulfilling lifestyle, and so on. These general benefits are measured objectively far less often than their importance to most people would seem to warrant. Voeltz and Evans (1982), in a review of collateral effects in the child modification literature, show that while many studies report general benefits following specific behavior change, few if any have actually provided detailed documentation of these changes.

It may be obvious that what the present author is discussing here might be better called *evaluation research*. In clinical practice, the global evaluation of therapeutic outcome has often taken the form of changes in personality profiles, changes in self-concept, ratings by the client of general benefits, and consumer satisfaction reports regarding therapeutic outcome. This information, often gathered quite informally, has important influences on clinical decisions regarding termination of treatment and may have significant effects on clinicians' self-appraisals of their role, social value, and efficacy with given cases. From the psychotherapy research point of view, the selection of a generally agreed-upon appropriate measure has been the most controversial issue. A closely related question is whether the change represents a clinically meaningful improvement. This can be judged either on the basis of the degree of the change or on the importance of the change to the general therapeutic goals. Recently, the idea has been promulgated that it might be useful to determine both of these issues on the basis of judgments of individuals significant in the client's social sphere. Examples of this can be seen in such work as having peers, parents, and institutional staff judge the progress in leisure activities of severely and profoundly retarded adolescents who were taught age-appropriate play skills (Voeltz, Wuerch, & Bockhaut, 1981), or having family court judges estimate progress in the social skills of juvenile delinquents (Braukmann & Fixsen, 1975). Although the term *social validity*, often applied to these judgments, is a unitary one, there is a difference between using judges to validate the salience of observable changes and using judges to determine these changes in the first place. Certainly, impressionistic measures, which are very much like traditional ratings, are slipping back into the behavioral literature: Weinrott, Reid, Bauske, and Brummett (1981) showed that the impressions of their observers regarding hostility, disorganization, and child aggression in problem families were moderate predictors of deviant child behavior at discharge.

MEASUREMENT PROCEDURES

Thus far, we have been looking at the purposes of assessment—the use of different measures rather than their nature, which has been the more usual focus in the past. This focus on certain types of measures was not intended to preclude the use of objective clinical instruments (such as the MMPI); rather, these more traditional tests would be administered with a slightly different emphasis or strategy in mind (Nelson, 1980). For any measure to have utility, it must conform to accepted psychometric standards (Cone, 1977); but what is really so exciting about behavioral assessment is the opportunity it affords clinical psychology to use revealing and penetrating measures by introducing the ingenious advances in measurement that characterize the best psychological research. This can be contrasted to projective tests, which, quite apart from the usual criticisms on the grounds of inadequate reliability and validity, are divorced from reality. What has projective testing got to do with real people's aspirations and goals, plans and decision-making strategies, self-esteem and self-doubts, social and interpersonal skills, lifestyles, and relationships with others? These matters are the stuff of life, and they are addressed in a modern psychology which is rich in concepts directly related to the important features of life. Clinical psychology can (and should) draw on this diversity, instead of continuing with procedures that are both technically inadequate and essentially irrelevant.

It is true, of course, that experimentally derived measures may not always be eminently practical for clinical psychologists, particularly those restricted by traditional methods of providing services, like private practice in an office setting. While there is some onus on clinical researchers to adapt or simplify measures so they will have wide-scale applicability, it will also be necessary for clinicians to alter their service networks to accommodate advances in assessment that have clearly demonstrated their unique value for the identification of problems and the design of the most appropriate treatment. Good examples might be: direct behavioral observation in the appropriate setting, such as home, school, or playground; all-night sleep recordings; penile plethysmography at night; and direct behavior-avoidance tests.

Worth remembering is that the *purposes* of assessment in clinical research and clinical practice are rather different. As the present author has written [Evans (1982)]:

> Clinical researchers develop and explore measures for two major purposes: as dependent variables designed to represent veridically the phenomena which are the actual consequences of treatment, and as methods or tools for the discovery of new phenomena. Practicing clinicians, obviously enough, need measures that have utility—that help identify important problems and their controlling variables and that guide both the design and conduct of therapy. (p. 123)

Against the backdrop of these preliminary remarks, let us now look at some of the measures and assessment procedures that have been developed. This is, perforce, a small sampling of the plentiful opportunities that await the ingenious clinician—for good recent reviews, see Barlow (1981) and Mash and Terdal (1981). Various attempts have been made to classify the different types of measures available (e.g. Cone, 1978;

Nay, 1979). Some of the dimensions suggested are trivial (e.g., written versus nonwritten), some more significant (e.g., private versus public events, measures requiring aggregation, inference, or judgment versus those that can be directly quantified). The following categories are heuristic; they are not orthogonal but encompass most popular measures with minimal overlap.

Self-ratings

In behavioral assessment, a variety of paper and pencil self-rating instruments have emerged, usually oriented toward specific clinical constructs such as assertive behavior (Rathus, 1973), depression (Beck, Ward, Mendelsohn, Mock, & Erbaugh, 1961), or anxiety (Watson & Friend, 1969). These instruments usually have high face validity and unsophisticated or nonexistent protection from lying or impression management by the client. Many such questionnaires have inadequately determined psychometric properties, such as reliability, and have not been standardized on clinical populations. Where standardization data do exist, the scales are useful for screening in early intervention and prevention, and they have done yeoman duty in selecting subjects for analog research studies. Self-ratings can be quite helpful in obtaining pre-post measures of a client's perception of change following treatment, and they are possibly useful in monitoring progress; though in both cases, the impact of repeated administration is unknown.

Self-report of information. Scores on self-rating instruments can be validated against other measures of the same construct but rarely verified—in fact, the interest in traditional assessment is in the self-perception, rather than in whether the statement about the individual is true. In behavioral assessment, on the other hand, self-rated information about the individual tends to be taken literally. It may therefore be preferable to simply gather factual information. Of the many ways possible, the simplest maneuver is to ask the client to report information directly—which is what happens in the general interview. Behavioral interviews tend to focus on details of situation behavior interaction that contribute to the functional analysis (e.g., "In what situations are you most likely to feel the craving for a drink?"; "How exactly do you respond when your husband approaches you in the way you describe?"). More general background information regarding social and medical history, previous experiences with therapy, hobbies, friends, social support systems, and so on, can be obtained through written autobiographies and life-history questionnaires (Lazarus, 1971). One can also gather more detailed information on such specialized topics as favorite activities (Cautela & Kastenbaum, 1967), marital relationships (Stuart & Stuart, 1972), and frequency of experiences of pleasant and unpleasant events (Lewinsohn & Amenson, 1978).

All this information could be crucial for planning therapy based on a detailed knowledge of the client's social circumstances, background, vocation, or religious beliefs. Whether the information is gathered according to a structured (following a protocol) or unstructured format, the procedure is not a measure, and can only be evaluated in terms of the accuracy of the information and its relative importance in comparison to the importance of the information one fails to find out.

Self-observation. Because of the difficulty of accurately reporting quantitative details regarding one's own behavior, there has been interest in encouraging clients to record events as and when they happen. Thus, the client is instructed in keeping simple logs, diaries, checklists, etc., of information such as type of fantasy, quantity of food eaten, number of cigarettes smoked, duration of headache. Because self-monitoring tends to be reactive (Nelson, 1977)—increasing desirable behavior and decreasing, at least initially, undesirable behavior—this kind of record keeping is often built into the therapy, seeming to be a major component of successful efforts at self-control (Watson & Tharp, 1972). The reactivity of self-monitoring does not necessarily limit the information from the point of view of veridicality; however, it does complicate research designs which try to use this procedure to obtain pre-intervention baseline information.

Enough studies comparing the accuracy of self-monitoring against externally observed records of the same behavior have now been conducted to indicate that self-monitoring can potentially be very accurate. A good example of the procedure is Maisto, Sobell, and Sobell's (1979) demonstration that external collateral reports corroborated alcoholics' self-reports of drinking. However, it is not possible to generalize about self-monitoring, because accuracy clearly depends on the individual client's motivation, skill, and good faith. Nevertheless, the advantages of being able to obtain records of potentially verifiable but generally private phenomena (such as clients' sexual practices), or of totally private events (such as the frequency of certain kinds of thoughts) are considerable and merit care in instructing clients in the most effective recording methods, emphasizing the importance of accuracy, and reinforcing the effort by examining the results frequently. In some cases, it is worth teaching self-monitoring as a general skill for the self-regulation of behavior—the important concept of the clients being their own "personal scientists" (Mahoney, 1977).

If we ask an individual to report a totally private experience (such as a dream, a thought, or series of thoughts), we obviously have no way of knowing whether these reports are accurate or—even more uncertain—whether they are insightful interpretations of the causes of behavior. Although in interviews we often attempt to have clients explain their behavior and compare the explanations to our own assumptions regarding causes, we might be much better off analyzing these explanations at face value as representative of their thinking styles, rather than accepting them as true explanations. Thus, it might be safest to be interested in the syntax of self-reported cognitions and to determine whether they have components we would tend to consider dysfunctional: limited in their self-directing function (e.g., Meichenbaum, 1977); so illogical as to influence an individual's interpretation of a situation, and hence the affect induced (e.g., Ellis, 1962; Beck, 1976); or contain words or concepts of significant emotional value (Staats, 1975). As Meichenbaum and Butler (1980) have described, reporting cognitions can be concurrent with some other activity, for example, thinking aloud techniques, or in vivo thought sampling when a client notes thoughts at various predetermined points of time (Kendall & Korgeski, 1979), can precede the activity (thus reflecting anticipations regarding the activity), or can be post-performance, retrospective accounts of the dominant cognition. All three methods introduce slightly different sources of error and bias.

Ratings and impressionistic records.   The essence of these methods, which encompass many different instruments in behavioral assessment such as ward behavior checklists and ratings of children's withdrawal or hyperactivity by parents, teachers, or peers (O'Leary & Johnson, 1979) is that they involve impressionistic aggregation of other people's observations of the client. Because of this, the variable being measured includes certain features of the observer's behavior as well as those of the observed. This can be very valuable because, in many clinical situations, it is not sufficient that demonstrable change has taken place, and it is necessary that behavior be seen to be different—and improved—by those individuals most directly concerned with the client. Often, these are the individuals who were responsible for defining the behavior as abnormal or maladaptive in the first place.

Another interesting feature of such ratings is that they provide some attempt at the quantification of molar behaviors which are very difficult to describe in strictly physical terms. For example, whether someone's walk is gender-appropriate—which may be a useful measure for assessing success of programs modifying transvestite and transsexual behavior— can probably only be quantified in terms of social judgment. The panel of judges who decide the winning jump, dive, or display of skating may be able to make finer discriminations than the untrained and amazed spectator—and probably defy quantification.

Direct behavioral observation in contrived settings

Because an important principle of behavioral observation is the assessment of behavior in the situation to which one wishes to generalize, the value of observing behavior in contrived settings might well be questioned. The advantages, however, lie in the convenience and the control that can be exercised. Furthermore, we mostly use contrived settings in assessment when the behavior-in-situation is of interest (such as *test* anxiety, *interview* skills, *sexual* arousal), so that generalization needs occur only to other very similar situations. It is usually assumed that the contrived situation (as well as the context of the observation) is representative of the real-life circumstances, so that, for example, a hard-sell telephone call by a confederate of the experimenter might test assertive skills very realistically. If the measure is being used primarily as a screening procedure or as the dependent variable for evaluating treatment, then the degree to which the individual's response is, in fact, characteristic of similar environments is very important. However, if the measure is being used as one method of monitoring change, then the representativeness is less important. For example, the Direct Behavior Avoidance Test (Bernstein, 1973) for phobic anxiety is very atypical of natural situations (handling a caged snake is different from walking gingerly on a hike), but it is a useful measure of treatment effects.

In contrived observation, the units of measurement may simply be the presence or absence of a particular (adaptive) response or, more commonly, the degree to which the client's response matches some predetermined standard—for instance, the social and vocational self-help skills of schizophrenic individuals can be assessed in such structured situations as simulated job interviews, role-played interactions with sales assistants, and so forth. The most promising use of contrived settings for observation, however, is that they allow the quantification of some particular features of behavior—for example, having subjects participate in a simulated wine tasting test allows for the surreptitious measurement of the amount of alcohol consumed (Marlatt, Demming, & Reid, 1973), or in an eating situation in which amount of food per bite and the time intervals between bites can be measured (cf., Brownell, 1981). Much of the time, these very detailed measures of performance are primarily of research interest, but they could have crucial clinical implications. The behavioral strategy is to examine in much finer detail than is usual the specific features of some behavior loosely subsumed in a diagnostic category. This does not mean that clinicians are supposed to obtain exactly similar measures but simply that, by knowing these features, therapeutic strategies can be more carefully defined. Knowing that alcoholics *tend* to drink in large sips, order second rounds before the first is finished, and drink straight rather than mixed drinks places one in a far better position to design a self-control program for the individual client.

Naturalistic behavioral observation

Information gathered in naturalistic settings usually relates to what is typical rather than what behavior is possible. Naturalistic observation is descriptive rather than analytic because detailed interactions between the behavior and the environment (independent variables) are not readily discernable unless naturally occurring environmental changes are monitored concurrently with the behavior. Direct behavioral observation is probably one of the most obvious hallmarks of behavioral assessment. The introduction of such methods to routine clinical use provided much of the enthusiastic impetus for behavior therapy as a discipline.

There are, broadly, three traditions in observational procedures. First is the ethological, descriptive tradition. The foundation of every science is the careful observation of the phenomena of interest. This type of observation is open-ended (preconceived categories are avoided), sequential, and usually based in real time (i.e., continuous, narrative recordings). Second is observation based on a limited, predetermined set of categories. A coding system of some kind identifies those categories of behavior that appear to be of interest to a given clinical problem. Of those that have had some degree of clinical use and success, the coding systems designed by Patterson and his colleagues (Reid, 1978) for observing family interactions of conduct-disordered children, O'Leary, Romanczyk, Kass, Dietz, and Santogrossi's (1971) code for observing classroom behavior, and Wahler, House, and Stambaugh's (1976) ecological code system, are the best known; although, frankly, there are very few reported instances of these coding systems being used by investigators or clinicians other than their originators. Third, the most commonly reported type of observation is, without doubt, when specific target behaviors have been identified for intervention, and their frequency or duration is monitored on a systematic (usually daily) basis, and the results are graphed for visual inspection of changes in these parameters over time.

There are many advantages to this latter methodology. Individual behaviors can be readily counted by teachers, nurses, parents, or anyone in frequent contact with the client, so that the strategy can be extended in a clinically advantageous way. Frequency and duration estimates of target behavior provide extremely useful information regarding the initial effects of an intervention program. In fact, the procedures are now so well refined that it would be inexcusable for responsible clinicians not to avail themselves of the techniques. Nevertheless, there are some disadvantages which emerge when the observation of a single behavior is relied upon too exclusively. For one thing, the procedure may encourage the identification of problem behaviors according to how easily these behaviors can be observed and recorded. For another, the observation of only one behavior may make it difficult to detect concomitant changes in the client which may be negative side effects or unrecognized positive improvements (Voeltz & Evans, 1982).

A great deal of thought has gone into the psychometric issues surrounding direct observation (Cone & Foster, 1981). A key issue (often referred to as *observer reliability*) is observer agreement. Agreement is measured by the extent to which two observers—recording the same behavior or using the same code—report identical results. Most causes of observer error lie in two sources: ambiguous definition of the behavioral category (such that other responses are coded within the category or examples of the category are not coded) and vigilance issues (which occur when an observer fails to notice a response because of loss of attention, difficulty in properly seeing the client, and so forth). It has been noted that with time and practice, observers' definitions of behavioral categories or their criteria for deciding whether a response belongs in a category alter slightly, a phenomenon known as *observer drift* (Johnson & Bolstad, 1973). Good agreement among equally experienced observers does not, obviously, negate the possibility that both observers are showing comparable drift, or becoming more or less vigilant. Similarly, if agreement between two observers is low, it is difficult to tell which observer is the more correct. The important dimension to establish is observer accuracy, which can be considered by reference to some kind of master (or absolute) standard, by assessment of observer competence, by measuring observer stability over repeated observations of a standard videotape of the subject matter, and by studying the relationship between errors and the complexity of the coded phenomena.

Another major issue is the representativeness of the data, which is a function of the time intervals sampled relative to the duration of the behavior and the duration of the observer/record intervals. This is not such a problem in real-time observation, although both real-time and time-sampling procedures must consider the degree to which the observation period represents the total time period and other situations to which one wishes to generalize the findings. Also of relevance is the effect of the observer on the observed. Being watched is usually a rather reactive process, and behavior under such conditions may be somewhat atypical, although being administered a test is even more intrusive. Clinicians should try to remember that neither type of situation necessarily reveals optimal performance.

Measures of psychological and psychophysiological functioning

The last category that should be mentioned covers an array of measures of psychological functioning and physiological processes that typically require instrumentation in order to obtain a quantifiable variable. Psychophysiological monitoring of heart rate, the electrodermal response, blood pressure, and muscle activity are the classic examples in this category (Ray & Kimmel, 1979). Other similar, useful measures to appear in recent years are genital-response indices such as the reliable mercury-in-rubber strain gauge for measuring penile circumference (Farkas, Evans, Sine, Eifert, Wittlieb, & Vogelmann-Sine, 1979) and photo-plethysmography for measuring vaginal blood flow (see Wincze & Lange, 1981).

In addition to physiological measures, there are psychological measures that have not received much attention in behavioral assessment but which are the backbone of research in psychopathology: for example, critical flicker fusion (measuring the rate at which a flickering light is seen as steady) is an index of cortical arousal; the pursuit-rotor and hand-tremor tests measure important motor skills; dichotic listening techniques have proved valuable in cognitive assessment of schizophrenia. As clinical psychologists seem to have less and less familiarity with the fundamentals of human experimental psychology, we are not likely to see a large increase in the use of these measures, although some have found their way into neuropsychological assessment of brain damage.

Probably the major drawbacks to the clinical use of this category of measures are the daunting cost of the instrumentation and the sophistication required to obtain meaningful, artifact-free measures. One encouraging development is that the commercial production of biofeedback devices has made a number of autonomic indices available for monitoring without the cost and inconvenience of a polygraph. However, clinicians interested in using such measures should ensure that a permanent record of autonomic levels can be provided by their biofeedback instrumentation (for example, a high-speed digital printout device which can keep a summary record of activity levels during an assessment session). Another significant advance is the widening availability of small computers which can be used for the integration of psychophysiological information as well as for a number of other, more general clinical services such as record keeping, client monitoring, and the like (Heise, 1981).

NEW DEVELOPMENTS IN CLINICAL ASSESSMENT

A great deal of the published literature on behavioral assessment is concerned with the elaboration of increasingly complex measures. Although, as already indicated, some of the progress made has little bearing on the use of measures to influence the processes of clinical decision making, it does nevertheless have great importance for the clinician, as it reveals the intricacies of clinical phenomena. It is the essence of scientific progress to examine increasingly specific phenomena and to measure them in increasingly complex ways; new insights then emerge which have broad application. In this section, consideration will be given to some of the most recent and promising areas of research. Only a few, representative examples of developments in behavioral measurement will be presented here, but in the process, an attempt will be made to identify some domains of behavioral analysis that seem especially relevant to clinical practice.

Assessing the physical environment

Psychological assessment has traditionally focused on persons, not the person-environment *interactions* that are so necessary for the prediction of behavior (McReynolds, 1979). Largely due to the growth of public interest in environmentalism, ecological influences on clinically relevant behaviors are becoming more widely recognized (e.g., Moos, 1976). By measuring important environmental features, community psychologists have revealed novel target areas for change: modifying environments known to be deleterious to adaptive behavior might result in large-scale improvements in behavior or, even more important, serve to prevent problems from developing in the first place. High-crime districts, for example, lack certain critical amenities (O'Donnell & Lydgate, 1980), and architectural features of buildings relate to personal adjustment (Kasl, 1977)—a detailed review of some of these influences can be found in O'Donnell (in press).

At the individual level, growing awareness of the impact of the physical environment on behavior suggests important sources of influence to be considered when analyzing clinical problems. Improvement in affect and mood have been frequently observed to follow treatment of allergies in children (Speer, 1963). After an outstanding review of the controversy surrounding Feingold's hypothesis relating hyperkinesis to food additives, Conners (1980) concluded that the behavior of some children is adversely affected by artificial coloring in foods. So many and so varied are the reported effects—caffein producing anxietylike reactions, types of illumination affecting autistic children's behavior, and subtle endocrine influences on mood, sexual arousal, and aggression—that it is well-nigh impossible for the clinician to consider every one. However, there are certain characteristics of behavior which might alert the observer to these sources of influence: sudden changes in behavior, especially when associated with new environments, lifestyle changes, and living conditions; maladaptive behavior which is cyclical or seasonal; behavior which is accompanied by physical symptoms.

In order to investigate environmental influences on behavior, some sort of concurrent measurement of behavior and environment is necessary, so that systematic variations between the two can be observed. This procedure is complicated by the different units of analysis typically employed. However, if the environment is defined in terms of the necessary behavioral characteristics of a person ideally adjusted or adapted to that environment, then we have similar situation/person units, and the environment can be defined according to behavioral templates (e.g., Bem & Funder, 1978). Cone (1980) has demonstrated how one can describe the social skills necessary for young children to interact successfully in a *particular* school or preschool environment and then use these templates as the definitions of the behavioral goals which should be taught to socially isolated children.

Assessing social interactions

Although the great importance of social interaction for understanding behavioral problems has been widely recognized by therapists of all persuasions, opportunities for actually assessing social interactions have been minimal. In the early application of social behavioral principles, the clinical interventions often involved the modification of one aspect of social behavior—the contingency of social reinforcement provided the client by a mediator (ward staff, parent, etc.). The existing social interactions between client and others were rarely studied. Now there is a steadily growing literature, of special clinical significance, on the measurement and appraisal of social interaction. Brazelton (1980) has developed a system for investigating the reciprocal effects of a mother's social responsiveness (smiling, playing, vocalizing, and approaching) and her baby's behavior, which clearly reveals the extreme sensitivity of the handicapped or at-risk premature infant to social intrusion. Lewinsohn (1976) has produced a reliable, observational coding system which identifies—in the verbal realm—social actions and reactions, thereby permitting one to monitor the communications of depressed clients in either therapy or home situations.

Sequential analysis—based on a technique whereby one can determine what follows a social event immediately, after a short time lag, or after a longer time lag—has begun to reveal some very important features of interactions among families of behavior-disordered children. Wahler has introduced a valuable concept into behavior therapy, by arguing that the social support system of family members (especially adults responsible for the routine care of children) is of great importance for the very practical issue of being able to benefit from—and continue to implement—training in effective parenting. The social support system of almost any client seems to be a critical issue in the long-term effectiveness of any therapeutic intervention. Methods for measuring social networks have been developed primarily by social anthropologists, sociologists, and social psychologists, but they can be readily adapted for the purposes of the behavioral assessor. Network analysis allows one to study the structural dimensions of an individual's relationship (e.g., size, density) in certain interactional features (such as the amount of reciprocity among network members), as well as the traditional behavioral measures of frequency and duration of contacts (Mitchell, 1969).

An interesting twist relating to this general issue is that, as noted already, many contemporary treatment programs involve procedures administered by mediators. It is always important to check on the accuracy with which change agents are following the prescribed program—that is to say, treatment integrity. Billingsley, White, and Munson (1980) describe a protocol for assessing the "procedural reliability" of teachers implementing an intervention program. Another important aspect of the study of social interaction is that the successful de-institutionalization and community adjustment of mentally handicapped and severely emotionally disturbed individuals requires careful consideration of the patterns of friendship and acceptance that are available in integrated communities. Social attitudes toward physical and behavioral differences affect the pattern of friendships and supportive networks that are possible (Voeltz, 1982). Finally, it must be recognized that the context and manner of the social interaction with the clinician may well determine the degree to which clients will be able to generalize important principles of problem solving, constructive use of professional services, and independent, active participation in their efforts to effect change and more-adequate personal adjustment.

Assessing behavioral interrelationships

A third area of important technical development in behavioral assessment relates to the interaction among behaviors within individuals. If the previous two categories have considered the ecosystems of physical and social environments in interaction with behavior, this category refers to the ecosystem within behavioral repertoires. In early considerations of this issue, Wahler (1975) suggested that if responses are organized in identifiable clusters within individuals, it seems likely that there may well be specific responses whose change would have widespread beneficial implications for the client. Wahler called these *keystone* behaviors, and suggested, at the molar level, how such behaviors as solitary toy play might be keystones for other appropriate social behaviors. Elaborating on this general theme, Voeltz and Evans (1982) examined both the theoretical aspects of response interrelationships and the evidence presently available indicating that there are collateral or concomitant changes associated with behavioral interventions with specific responses in children. The clear presence of such effects has considerable implication for the evaluation of treatment, the avoidance of iatrogenic effects, and the identification of the most-efficient target behaviors for intervention.

A somewhat related issue can be found in the behavioral literature on different response modes. Lang (1969) suggested some time ago that a concept such as anxiety could be assessed by any or all of three classes of response: physiological change, cognitive/verbal responses (self-report), and overt motor behavior (avoidance, withdrawal, facial change). This notion, known as the *triple-response mode,* has provided a useful impetus to the measurement of concepts in more than one psychological domain, in suggesting the importance of adopting criteria for change that incorporate all three systems, and possibly for tailoring intervention toward the individual pattern of response. However, what is not always made clear in this scheme is the degree to which the different modes interact or can be quite independent and the fact that the three divisions are not conceptually pure—self-report requiring motor behaviors, for instance. The assumption that different measures *should* be intercorrelated reveals an implicit trait concept in which the different modes are all measures of anxiety, the underlying construct. A radical behavioral perspective, on the other hand, assumes that these measures are different features of behavior (sometimes interrelated, sometimes not), from which we infer anxiety as a convenient, descriptive label.

Staats (1975) has proposed a theoretically sophisticated and useful distinction between the emotional-motivational personality system (the various behavioral and environmental stimuli eliciting emotional responses), the sensorimotor personality system (including social, athletic, and vocational skills), and the language-cognitive personality system (including intellectual ability, reasoning, and language). Each of these systems consists of many basic behavioral repertoires which specify the interaction between such significant repertoires as self-labeling and emotion, imagery and language, and so forth. This theory provides a sound behavioral rationale for indirect assessment (Burns, 1980). A great deal of contemporary behavior therapy, as explained in this chapter, involves the indirect manipulation of some other behavior which, it is hypothesized, will positively influence some specific target. For example, attributing behavioral difficulties to irrational beliefs (e.g., Goldfried & Sobocinski, 1975) would require some method of sampling covert language in order to determine that characteristic cognitive processes were irrational. Such a demonstration would then allow one to hypothesize that there was a functional relationship between this cognitive style and the original overt behavior problem (anxiety, depression). This hypothesis could be tested by continuing to monitor these beliefs and seeing whether their frequency (quantitative variable) or rationality (qualitative variable) changed as a result of treatment and that this change altered the original problem. Very few studies in cognitive behavior therapy have begun to follow such a procedure. Neither do we really have well-developed single-subject or group designs which recognize that many interventions involve the modification of one element of a complex behavioral system, thus having multiple, interacting consequences. Response interrelationships pose a formidable challenge to behavioral assessment to develop new methods for the untangling and monitoring of intraindividual interactions.

Differentiation of skill and motivation

Although there are many rather exciting developments in behavioral assessment methods, it is possible to mention just one more feature of this rapidly expanding field, and that is the distinction between skill deficits and motivational problems in the assessment of deficient (or limited) behavioral repertoires. Probably because of the strong psychodynamic influence on clinical psychology (psychodynamic theory being essentially one of motivation), the observation of most forms of deficit has usually been attributed to motivational factors: resistance, underlying fears or guilt, and defense mechanisms of various kinds. Behavior therapy, on the other hand, adopting what is predominantly a learning/educational model of therapy, has always tended to emphasize the importance of teaching new repertoires, and this philosophy is steadily influencing assessment practices. The classic example is the area of assertive behavior, where there has been a careful attempt to separate motivational problems (social anxiety) from performance or skill deficits (knowing and being able to perform the appropriate response).

Conversely, a major criticism of traditional psychological testing in the past has been that it appears to define and fix an individual's capacities, thus, paradoxically, making it harder to achieve what testing was originally created to do—help design remedial programs that confound prediction and allow for change. Behavioral assessment takes an optimistic perspective, as can be seen by the literature on the attempt to raise children's tested-ability scores by the use of reward and enhanced motivation (see Evans & Nelson, 1977, for a review). Another good example is the strong interest in criterion-referenced measures of development and performance that create incentives for achievement rather than standards of failure. Behavior assessment is as interested in assessing a person's strengths and capabilities as it is in assessing deviance and deficit, because it is on these strengths that new response repertoires can be built. Neither is it always necessary to assume that *individuals* must change and adapt. The study of persons in environments reveals much more clearly the way in which social and physical settings might be matched to meet the special needs of clients (Brown, Branston-McClean, Baumgart, Vincent, Falvey, & Schroeder, 1979). It is this author's personal belief that a clinical psychology, oriented toward quality of life rather than sickness, disorder, or deficiency, is more optimistic and less discriminatory than the models of the past.

CONCLUSIONS AND FUTURE DIRECTIONS

In selecting the citations to support or document assertions made in this chapter, an attempt has been made to choose those materials most illustrative of the promising trends in this field, citing review papers or selections from major sources wherever possible, thereby providing the interested reader with a *vade mecum* to behavioral assessment. While trying to emphasize the relevance of new ideas to clinical practice, this author has avoided a detailed presentation of how to *do* assessment, mindful of Meyer and Turkat's (1979) admonition against the technology orientation, which they characterize as the "rapid delineation of the client's complaints in behavioral terms and matching treatment techniques to these complaints" (p. 260). Instead, they recommend a behavior-analytic model which "forces the clinician to embark on a course of continuous hypothesis testing in order to understand the individual's problems and subsequently to innovate appropriate (individually tailored) modification procedures" (p. 261).

Their model is somewhat like the decision-making analysis advocated in this present chapter. Both models attempt to wrestle with the complex issue that without improved measurement, clinical psychology as an applied science cannot possibly move forward; but without demonstration of the usefulness of these measures for enhancing individual treatment—or, more generally, for solving significant social problems—(i.e., having interpretive validity) the measures remain sterile and esoteric.

It is tempting, nevertheless, to end with a few general recommendations regarding practical clinical assessment. Keeping the purposes of one's assessment well to the fore is probably a necessary reminder; before gathering any information—even asking a question in an interview—have a clear idea of what you will do with the information and how it might affect your procedures. Another way of expressing this is to point out that information is always gathered to check on a hypothesis. Keep developing these hypotheses, especially during the progress of the intervention: assessment does not precede treatment, it accompanies, monitors, and evaluates it. If your methods of testing your hypotheses are as sound as possible, your speculations themselves can be as fanciful as your clinical experience and imagination permit. Conversely, having a theoretical model firmly based on empirical documentation (with which one should be very familiar) allows the clinician to more rapidly trim away implausible, unproductive ideas about a client that simply waste precious treatment time. Recognize that the scientific method is not sacrosanct but serves rather well to reduce the biases, distortions, misconceptions, and other sources of error in interpretation to which the individual human observer is so susceptible. The clinician need not always perform clinical experiments to be a scientist-practitioner or publish in research journals to justify one's research training. The scientist-practitioner model is a metaphor for the values of the scientist, respect for rules of evidence, recognition of one's fallability, and a faith that benefit to humanity occurs not in mystery, belief, and superstition, but at the skeptical, questioning edges of public knowledge, however imperfect they may sometimes appear to be.

SUMMARY

The present chapter focuses on behavioral assessment as it accompanies, monitors, and evaluates treatment. Purposes of behavioral assessment are outlined, with attention given to the different types and levels of decisions which these measurements precipitate. Assessment procedures and measuring instruments are categorized with an overview of the more popular ones. Representative examples of recent developments in behavioral measurement are cited, with emphasis on behavioral analysis relevant to clinical practice.

Although a description of *how to do* assessment is avoided in this chapter, the author advocates keeping the purpose of behavioral assessment in mind, with specific guidelines on what to do with the attained information and its effect on treatment procedures.

REFERENCES

Ayllon, T., & Rosenbaum, M. S. The behavioral treatment of disruption and hyperactivity in school settings. In B. B. Lahey & A. E. Kazdin (Eds.), *Advances in clinical child psychology* (Vol. 1). New York: Plenum Press, 1977.

Barlow, D. H. (Ed.), *Behavioral assessment of adult disorders*. New York: Guilford Press, 1981.

Beck, A. T. *Cognitive therapy and the emotional disorders*. New York: International Universities Press, 1976.

Beck, A. T., Ward, C. H., Mendelsohn M., Mock, J., & Erbaugh, J. An inventory for measuring depression. *Archives of General Psychiatry*, 1961, *4*, 561–571.

Bem, D. J., & Funder, D. C. Predicting more of the people more of the time: Assessing the personality of situations. *Psychological Review*, 1978, *85*, 485–501.

Bernstein, D. A. Situational factors in behavioral fear assessment: A progress report, *Behavior Therapy*, 1973, *4*, 41–48.

Billingsley, F., White, O. R., & Munson, R. Procedural reliability: A rationale and an example. *Behavioral Assessment*, 1980, *2*, 229–241.

Braukmann, C. J., & Fixsen, D. L. Behavior modification with delinquents. In M. Hersen, R. M. Eisler, & P. M. Miller (Eds.), *Progress in behavior modification* (Vol. 1). New York: Academic Press, 1975.

Brazelton, T. B. Behavioral competence of the newborn infant. In P. M. Taylor (Ed.), *Parent-infant relationships*. New York: Grune & Stratton, 1980.

Brown, L., Branston-McClean, M. B., Baumgart, D., Vincent, L., Falvey, M., & Schroeder, J. Using the characteristics of current and subsequent least-restrictive environments in the development of curricular content for severely handicapped students. *AAESPH Review*, 1979, *4*, 407–424.

Brownell, K. D. Assessment of eating disorders. In D. H. Barlow (Ed.), *Behavioral assessment of adult disorders*. New York: Guilford Press, 1981.

Burns, G. L. Indirect measurement and behavioral assessment: A case for social behaviorism psychometrics. *Behavioral Assessment*, 1980, *2*, 197–206.

Carlson, J. G. Some concepts of perceived control and their relationship to bodily self-control. *Journal of Biofeedback and Self-Regulation*, in press.

Carson, T. P., & Adams, H. E. Affective disorders: Behavioral perspectives. In S. M. Turner, K. S. Calhoun, & H. E. Adams (Eds.), *Handbook of clinical behavior therapy*. New York: John Wiley & Sons, 1981.

Cautela, J. R. *Behavior-analysis forms for clinical intervention*. Champaign, Ill.: Research Press, 1977.

Cautela, J. R., & Kastenbaum, R. A. Reinforcement Survey Schedule for use in therapy, training, and research. *Psychological Reports*, 1967, *29*, 1115–1130.

Cone, J. D. The relevance of reliability and validity for behavioral assessment. *Behavior Therapy*, 1977, *8*, 411–426.

Cone, J. D. The Behavioral Assessment Grid (BAG): A conceptual framework and a taxonomy. *Behavior Therapy,* 1978, *9,* 882–888.

Cone, J. D. *Template-matching procedures for idiographic behavioral assessment.* Paper presented at annual meeting of Association for Advancement of Behavior Therapy, New York, 1980.

Cone, J. D., & Foster, S. L. Direct observation in clinical psychology. In J. N. Butcher & P. C. Kendall (Eds.), *Handbook of research methods in clinical psychology.* New York: John Wiley & Sons, 1981.

Conners, C. K. *Food additives and hyperactive children.* New York: Plenum Press, 1980.

Ellis, A. *Reason and emotion in psychotherapy.* Secaucus, N.J.: Lyle Stuart, 1962.

Evans, I. M. Review of W. R. Nay's *Multimethod clinical assessment. Behavioral Assessment,* 1982, *4,* 121–124.

Evans, I. M., & Nelson, R. O. A curriculum for the teaching of behavior assessment. *American Psychologist,* 1974, *29,* 598–606.

Evans, I. M., & Nelson, R. O. Assessment of child behavior problems. In A. R. Ciminero, K. S. Calhoun, & H. E. Adams (Eds.), *Handbook of behavioral assessment.* New York: John Wiley & Sons, 1977.

Evans, I. M., & Wilson, F. E. Behavioral assessment as decision making: A theoretical analysis. In M. Rosenbaum, C. M. Franks, & Y. Jaffe (Eds.), *Perspectives on behavior therapy in the Eighties.* New York: Springer, in press.

Eysenck, H. J. Behavior therapy—Dogma or applied science? In M. P. Feldman & A. Broadhurst (Eds.), *Theoretical and experimental bases of the behavior therapies.* New York: John Wiley & Sons, 1976.

Farkas, G. M., Evans, I. M., Sine, L. F., Eifert, G., Wittlieb, E., & Vogelmann-Sine, S. Reliability and validity of the mercury-in-rubber strain gauge measure of penile circumference. *Behavior Therapy,* 1979, *10,* 555–561.

Goldfried, M. R., & Kent, R. N. Traditional versus behavioral assessment: A comparison of methodological and theoretical assumptions. *Psychological Bulletin,* 1972, *77,* 409–420.

Goldfried. M. R., & Sobocinski, D. Effect of irrational beliefs on emotional arousal. *Journal of Consulting and Clinical Psychology,* 1975, *43,* 504–510.

Hartmann, D. P., Roper, B. L., & Bradford, D. C. Some relationships between behavioral and traditional assessment. *Journal of Behavioral Assessment,* 1979, *1,* 3–22.

Hawkins, R. P. Who decided that was the problem? Two stages of responsibility for applied behavior analysts. In W. S. Wood (Ed.), *Issues in evaluating behavior modification.* Champaign, Ill.: Research Press, 1975.

Heise, D. R. Microcomputers in social research. *Sociological Methods & Research,* 1981, *9,* (Whole No. 4).

Hobbs, N. *Issues in the classification of children.* San Francisco: Jossey-Bass, 1975.

Johnson, S. M., & Bolstad, O. D. Methodological issues in naturalistic observation: Some problems and solutions for field research. In L. A. Hamerlynck, L. C. Handy, & E. J. Mash (Eds.), *Behavior change: Methodology, concepts, and practice.* Champaign, Ill.: Research Press, 1973.

Kanfer, F. H., & Grimm, L. G. Behavioral analysis: Selecting target behaviors in the interview. *Behavior Modification,* 1977, *1,* 7–28.

Kanfer, F. H., & Saslow, G. Behavioral diagnosis. In C. M. Franks (Ed.), *Behavior therapy: Appraisal and status.* New York: McGraw-Hill, 1969.

Kasl, S. V. The effects of the residential environment on health and behavior: A review. In L. E. Hinkle & W. C. Loring (Eds.), *The effect of the man-made environment on health and behavior.* Atlanta: U.S. Department of Health, Education, and Welfare, 1977.

Kauffman, J. M., & Hallahan, D. P. Learning disability and hyperactivity (with comments on minimal brain dysfunction). In B. B. Lahey & A. E. Kazdin (Eds.), *Advances in clinical child psychology* (Vol. 2). New York: Plenum Press, 1979.

Kendall, P. C., & Korgeski, G. P. Assessment and cognitive-behavioral interventions. *Cognitive Therapy and Research,* 1979, *3,* 1–21.

Lang, P. J. The mechanisms of desensitization and the laboratory study of fear. In C. M. Franks (Ed.), *Behavior therapy: Appraisal and status.* New York: McGraw-Hill, 1969.

Lazarus, A. A. *Behavior therapy and beyond.* New York: McGraw-Hill, 1971.

Lazarus, A. A. *Multimodal behavior therapy.* New York: Springer, 1976.

Lewinsohn, P. M. Manual of instructions for behavioral ratings used for observation of interpersonal behavior. In E. J. Mash & L. G. Terdal (Eds.), *Behavior therapy assessment.* New York: Springer, 1976.

Lewinsohn, P. M., & Amenson, C. S. Some relationships between pleasant and unpleasant mood-related events and depression. *Journal of Abnormal Psychology,* 1978, *87,* 644–654.

Lewinsohn, P. M., & Lee, W. M. L. Assessment of affective disorders. In D. H. Barlow (Ed.), *Behavioral assessment of adult disorders.* New York: Guilford Press, 1981.

Mahoney, M. J. Some applied issues in self-monitoring. In J. P. Cone & R. P. Hawkins (Eds.), *Behavioral assessment: New directions in clinical psychology.* New York: Brunner/Mazel, 1977.

Mahoney, M. J., Mahoney, B. K., Rogers, T., & Straw, M. K. Assessment of human obesity: The measurement of body composition. *Journal of Behavioral Assessment,* 1979, *1,* 327–349.

Maisto, S. A., Sobell, L. C., & Sobell, M. B. Comparison of alcoholics' self-reports of drinking behavior with reports of collateral informants. *Journal of Consulting and Clinical Psychology,* 1979, *47,* 106–112.

Marlatt, G. A., Demming, G., & Reid, J. B. Loss-of-control drinking in alcoholics: An experimental analogue. *Journal of Abnormal Psychology,* 1973, *81,* 133–241.

Mash, E. J., & Terdal, L. G. *Behavioral assessment of childhood disorders.* New York: Guilford Press, 1981.

McLean, P. Therapeutic decision-making in the behavioral treatment of depression. In P. O. Davidson (Ed.), *The behavioral management of anxiety, depression and pain,* New York: Brunner/Mazel, 1976.

McReynolds, P. The case for interactional assessment. *Behavioral Assessment,* 1979, *1,* 237–247.

Meichenbaum, D. *Cognitive behavior modification: An integrative approach.* New York: Plenum Press, 1977.

Meichenbaum, D., & Butler, L. Cognitive ethology: Assessing the streams of cognition and emotion. In K. R. Blankstein, P. Pliner, & J. Polivy (Eds.), *Assessment and modification of emotional behavior.* New York: Plenum Press, 1980.

Melamed, B. C., & Johnson, S. B. Chronic illness: Asthma and juvenile diabetes. In E. J. Mash & L. G. Terdal (Eds.), *Behavioral assessment of childhood disorders.* New York: Guilford Press, 1981.

Meyer, V., & Turkat, I. D. Behavioral analysis of clinical cases. *Journal of Behavioral Assessment,* 1979, *1,* 259–270.

Mischel, W. *Personality and assessment.* New York: John Wiley & Sons, 1968.

Mitchell, J. C. The concept and use of social networks. In J. C. Mitchell (Ed.), *Social networks in urban situations.* Manchester: Manchester University Press, 1969.

Moos, R. H. *The human context: Environmental determinants of behavior.* New York: John Wiley & Sons, 1976.

Nay, W. R. *Multimethod clinical assessment.* New York: Gardner Press, 1979.

Nelson, R. O. Methodological issues in assessment via self-monitoring. In J. D. Cone & R. P. Hawkins (Eds.), *Behavioral assessment: New directions in clinical psychology,* New York: Brunner/Mazel, 1977.

Nelson, R. O. The use of intelligence tests within.behavioral assessment. *Behavioral Assessment,* 1980, *2,* 417–423.

Nelson, R. O. Realistic dependent measures for clinical use. *Journal of Consulting and Clinical Psychology,* 1981, *49,* 162–182.

Nelson, R. O., & Hayes, S. C. Some current dimensions of behavioral assessment. *Behavioral Assessment,* 1979, *1,* 1–16.

O'Donnell, C. R. Behavioral community psychology and the natural environment. *Clinical Psychology Review,* in press.

O'Donnell, C. R., & Lydgate, T. The relationship to crimes of physical resources. *Environment and Behavior,* 1980, *12,* 207–230.

O'Leary, K. D., & Johnson, S. B. Psychological assessment. In H. C. Quay & J. S. Werry (Eds.), *Psychopathological disorders of childhood* (2d ed.). New York: John Wiley & Sons, 1979.

O'Leary, K. D., Romanczyk, R. G., Kass, R. E., Dietz, A., & Santogrossi, D. *Procedures for classroom observations of teachers and children.* Unpublished manuscript, State University of New York at Stony Brook, 1971.

Poche, C., Brouwer, R., & Swearingen, M. Teaching self-protection to young children. *Journal of Applied Behavior Analysis,* 1981, *14,* 169–176.

Rathus, S. A. A 30-item schedule for assessing assertive behavior. *Behavior Therapy,* 1973, *4,* 298–406.

Ray, R. L., & Kimmel, H. D. Utilization of psychophysiological indices in behavioral assessment: Some methodological issues. *Journal of Behavioral Assessment,* 1979, *1,* 107–122.

Reid, J. B. *A social-learning approach to family intervention: Observation in home settings* (Vol. 2). Eugene, Ore.: Castalia Publishing, 1978.

Shapiro, M. B. An experimental approach to diagnostic psychological testing. *Journal of Mental Science,* 1951, *97,* 748–764.

Speer, F. *The allergic child.* New York: Hoeber, 1963.

Staats, A. W. *Social behaviorism.* Homewood, Ill.: Dorsey Press, 1975.

Stuart, R. B., & Stuart, F. *Marital Precounseling Inventory.* Champaign, Ill.: Research Press, 1972.

Voeltz, L. M. Effects of structured interactions with severely handicapped peers on children's attitudes. *American Journal of Mental Deficiency,* 1982, *86,* 380–390.

Voeltz, L. M., & Evans, I. M. The assessment of behavioral interrelationships in child behavior therapy. *Behavioral Assessment,* 1982, *4,* 131–165.

Voeltz, L. M., Wuerch, B. B., & Bockhaut, C. H. A social validation of leisure-activities training with severely handicapped youth. In L. M. Voeltz, J. A. Apffel, & B. B. Wuerch (Eds.), *Leisure-activities training for severely handicapped students: Instructional and evaluation strategies.* Honolulu: University of Hawaii, 1981.

Wahler, R. G. Some structural aspects of deviant child behavior. *Journal of Applied Behavior Analysis,* 1975, *8,* 27–42.

Wahler, R. G., House, A. E., & Stambaugh, E. E. *Ecological assessment of child problem behavior: A clinical package for home, school, and institutional settings.* Elmsford, N.Y.: Pergamon Press, 1976.

Watson, D., & Friend, R. Measurement of social-evaluative anxiety. *Journal of Consulting and Clinical Psychology,* 1969, *33,* 448–457.

Watson, D. L., & Tharp, R. G. *Self-directed behavior: Self-modification for personal adjustment.* Monterey, Calif.: Brooks/Cole, 1972.

Watts, F. N. Clinical judgement and clinical training. *British Journal of Medical Psychology,* 1980, *53,* 95–108.

Weinrott, M. R., Reid, J. B., Bauske, B. W., & Brummett, B. Supplementing naturalistic observation with observer impressions. *Behavioral Assessment,* 1981, *3,* 151–159.

White, O. R., & Haring, N. G. *Exceptional teaching* (2d ed.). Columbus, Ohio: Charles E. Merrill Publishing, 1980.

Wilson, F. E., & Evans, I. M. The reliability of target-behavior selection in behavioral assessment. *Behavioral Assessment,* in press.

Wincze, J. P., & Lange, J. D. Assessment of sexual behavior. In D. H. Barlow (Ed.), *Behavioral assessment of adult disorders.* New York: Guilford Press, 1981.

Yeaton, W., & Bailey, J. The generalization of pedestrian safety skills from the classroom to the natural environment. *Journal of Applied Behavior Analysis,* 1978, *11,* 121–129.

Yeaton, W. H., & Sechrest, L. Critical dimensions in the choice and maintenance of successful treatments: Strength, integrity, and effectiveness. *Journal of Consulting and Clinical Psychology,* 1981, *49,* 156–167.

Zuckerman, M. To risk or not to risk: Predicting behavior from negative and positive emotional states. In K. R. Blankstein, P. Pliner, & J. Polivy (Eds.), *Assessment and modification of emotional behavior.* New York: Plenum Press, 1980.

Psychological testing

*Anne Anastasi**

Psychological testing covers a wide diversity of assessment techniques that have been developed or adapted for use with virtually all types of clients. Special instruments are available for examining different age levels, from the neonate to the elderly. Some testing programs have been developed with particular reference to cultural minorities. In the construction, selection, and evaluation of instruments, special attention has been given to the assessment requirements of the physically handicapped, the mentally retarded, and persons with emotional and interpersonal difficulties of varying degrees of severity. A burgeoning field is the application of psychometric principles to the development of assessment aids for use in medical practice and public-health programs.

Against this broad background of available testing procedures, the present chapter focuses on certain major theoretical, methodological, and interpretive issues that have come to the fore in the 1970s and early 1980s. Drawn from both cognitive and noncognitive domains, these issues touch on a variety of client types and problems. Because the treatment of each issue in the following sections is necessarily brief, references to fuller published discussons are included throughout.

INTELLIGENCE IN CONTEXT

Population changes in intelligence test performance

What happens to the intelligence test performance of a population over long time periods? This question pertains to what may be called the *longitudinal study of populations.* The usual application of the longitudinal method in psychological research involves the repeated testing of the same persons over time. In the longitudinal study of populations, the comparison is between cohorts of persons born at different times but tested at the same ages. Several large-scale investigations conducted during the first five decades of the 20th century revealed a rising intelli-

* Fordham University

gence in the population as measured by standardized intelligence tests (Anastasi, 1958, pp. 209–211; 1982, chap. 12). With increasing literacy, higher educational levels, and other cultural changes, it was evident that the mean tested intelligence of the general population of all ages showed a steady rise for several decades.

Various procedures were employed in these comparative studies. One procedure is to administer the identical test after a lapse of time, as was done in surveys of 11-year-old Scottish children in 1932 and 1947 (Scottish Council, 1949). Another procedure is to give two tests to a representative sample of persons in order to establish the correspondence between the two sets of scores and thereby "translate" performance from one test to the other. This was done in a comparison of the performance of soldiers in the U.S. Army in World Wars I and II, who had been examined with the Army Alpha in the first instance and with the Army General Classification Test in the second (Tuddenham, 1948). A third and technically sounder approach is based on the establishment of an absolute, sample-free score scale through the use of common anchor items, as is done with the College Board tests (Angoff, 1971). The recent applications of item response theory represent further refinements of this approach.

Population changes in test performance may affect the interpretation of test scores in various ways. For example, in a test such as the Wechsler Adult Intelligence Scale (WAIS), the older members of the normative sample had completed less schooling, on the average, than had the younger members; and accordingly, they scored lower on the test than did the younger. As a result, intelligence seemed to decline with age. A similar phenomenon can be observed with tests standardized at different times. In both the restandardization of the Stanford-Binet (1937 versus 1972)[1] and the revision of the Wechsler Intelligence Scale for Children (WISC-R: 1949 versus 1974), the later normative sample performed substantially better than the earlier sample. The result was that the same children would receive lower IQs if tested with the revised edition than they would on the earlier edition, simply because their performance was evaluated against higher norms. The higher educational level of the parents of children tested in the later sample was one of the conditions mentioned for this rise in tested intelligence. At the adult level, a preliminary comparison of the 1955 WAIS with the 1981 WAIS-R given to 72 cases between the ages of 35 and 44 yielded mean Full Scale IQs of 111.3 on the WAIS and 103.8 on the WAIS-R (Wechsler, 1981). This 7.5-point difference again suggests that the earlier norms were lower than those established more recently.

Whether the intelligence test performance of a given population rises, declines, or remains stable over time depends on many conditions.

---

[1] The intervening 1960 revision of the Stanford-Binet, while introducing marked changes in item selection and placement, followed a norming procedure that related test performance back to the 1937 standardization sample.

Among them are the time period covered, with its concomitant or cultural changes; the age of the persons examined; and changes in the composition, or degree of selection, of the particular population over time. For example, if a larger proportion of the general population attended college in 1970 than in 1950, then the 1950 college students represent a more highly selected sample than do the 1970 college students. The number and complexity of conditions that may account for a population rise or decline in tested intelligence are well illustrated by an analysis of the highly publicized score decline on the College Board's Scholastic Aptitude Test (SAT) between 1963 and 1977. In an effort to understand this steady 14-year score decline, a specially appointed panel commissioned 38 studies by experts in various areas and considered an impressive array of causal hypotheses (Wirtz, 1977).

The results of these studies indicated that, during the first half of this 14-year period, the score decline could be attributed predominantly to a compositional change in the sample taking the SAT. Because of a continuing increase in the proportion of high school graduates going to college over this period, the sampling became progressively less selected in the cognitive skills measured by the SAT. During the second half of this period, however, the college-going population had become largely stabilized, and the explanation for the continuing score decline had to be sought principally in conditions in the home, the school, and society at large. It should also be added that the score decline, while most thoroughly investigated with reference to the SAT, was not limited to this instrument. Not only did it occur in other college admission tests, but there is also evidence of a corresponding decline in test performance at the high school and elementary school levels. The broad educational and societal conditions that underlie such performance changes in the population are beyond the scope of this chapter. From the standpoint of good testing practice, what is relevant is the substantial influence of cultural conditions on the individual's performance on tests of intelligence and scholastic aptitudes. The implications are twofold: (1) test norms require frequent reassessment and updating, and (2) experiential variables should be taken into account in interpreting test scores.

Interpreting present performance against antecedent background

Tests such as the Stanford-Binet and the Wechsler scales are basically individual, clinical instruments. The clinical approach to testing implies an intensive study of the individual, in which tests represent only one of several sources of data. It also implies an examiner who is knowledgeable in psychology and who can draw upon insights from available research and theory (Kaufman, 1979). It should nevertheless be recognized that these instruments, while individually administered by specially trained examiners, are sometimes interpreted in a hasty and routine manner.

Taking IQs at face value in classifying children, for example, may lead to incorrect conclusions in the absence of the needed supplementary observations and background data. This superficial use of tests, often resulting from time pressures and heavy case loads, is likely to be especially misleading when the examinees differ substantially in experiential background.

The question of test fairness in assessing the abilities of cultural minorities has aroused widespread concern and has led to extensive research with both adults and children in various settings (Anastasi, 1982, chaps. 3, 7, 8, 10, 12). A specific effort to bridge the gap between mass testing and individual clinical assessment, with particular reference to the testing of cultural minorities, is illustrated by the work of Mercer (1973, 1978, 1979). Mercer's long-term research project led to the development of the System of Multicultural Pluralistic Assessment: SOMPA (Lewis & Mercer, 1978; Mercer & Lewis, 1978). Mercer was especially concerned about the misclassification of children from culturally and linguistically diverse backgrounds as mentally retarded simply on the basis of intelligence test scores.

SOMPA is a comprehensive assessment program suitable for ages 5 to 11, which includes the WISC (or WPPSI for younger children), together with other standardized measures and supplementary data about the child's health history, present physical condition, and adaptive competence within his or her own environment. Another major feature of SOMPA is the provision of empirically established subgroup norms, thus far available for black, Hispanic, and Anglo (white) samples. The child's intelligence test performance can thus be evaluated within his or her own ethnic group, as well as in terms of the "school culture" to which the child must adapt in order to enjoy the benefits of the core culture. The general norms from the WISC standardization sample are employed as representative of the school or core culture. The test scores are further analyzed with reference to the child's assessed position on four sociocultural scales: family size, family structure, socioeconomic status, and urban acculturation.

In summary, SOMPA provides a prefabricated assessment program of the sort required in a thorough, personalized clinical case study. It is less flexible than the latter, but it offers a powerful corrective for the routine, superficial misuse of test scores in isolation. In addition, it provides empirical norms on the performance of children classified with reference to a number of significant experiential variables.

Predicting competence in specified environments

From another angle, some investigators have focused attention on the specific contexts to which the individual will have to adapt. This approach requires an evaluation of the individual's abilities and personality traits with reference to the demands of particular environments. It requires a joint assessment of both persons and environments. An individual with limited development in academic intelligence or scholastic aptitude, for example, may function successfully in a supportive, noncompetitive context, with appropriate supervision. The assessment of such a person's special aptitudes, physical condition, interpersonal skills, attitudes, and emotional adjustment would be of particular importance in counseling with regard to effective placement.

Procedures for the joint assessment of persons and environments have been most directly discussed with reference to personality characteristics, but the same general approach applies as well to the ability domain. In his book, *Assessment of Persons,* Sundberg (1977) devotes a chapter to "Assessment of Persons in Context" (chap. 9). In it, he emphasizes the need for assessing how individuals respond in different situations; and he cites a few exploratory studies and describes some procedures for gathering the necessary data. Elsewhere, he and his coauthors speak of the "assessment of personal competence and incompetence in life situations," a procedure that focuses on the knowledge, skill, and attitudes the individual can utilize to function effectively in specified environments (Sundberg, Snowden, & Reynolds, 1978).

Under the rubric of "interactional assessment," McReynolds (1979) likewise stresses the need for the joint assessment of the person and the environment in which he or she must function. While noting that the interactional model has been recognized for some time, he observes that little progress has been made toward the development of appropriate assessment procedures. To meet this need, he outlines six possible approaches that have been or can be followed in interactional assessment. These range from the systematic assessment of the person combined with informal observation of relevant environments (as in visiting the foster home to which a child may be assigned) to direct behavior samples of persons-in-situations and simulated behavior samples (as in roleplaying).

COMPREHENSIVE ASSESSMENT OF THE HANDICAPPED

The testing of children with either mental or physical handicaps has undergone a conspicuous spurt of growth in the United States, following the enactment in 1977 of the Education for All Handicapped Children Act (P.L. 94–142). The implementation of this law requires four basic procedures: (1) all handicapped children must be identified through preliminary screening instruments; (2) the children thus identified are to be evaluated by a team of specialists to determine each child's educational needs; (3) the school must develop an individualized educational program to meet these needs; and (4) each child is to be reevaluated periodically in the course of the program (Education, 1977).

Although testing instruments specially adapted for examining the physically handicapped and the mentally retarded have been available over several decades, the late 1970s and early 1980s witnessed an upsurge in their development. New instruments were constructed at an accelerated pace, revisions of earlier instruments appeared, and comprehensive programs incorporating several instruments were designed (Anastasi, 1982, chap. 10). Increasing attention is also being given to adaptations of procedures, materials, and testing environments, to meet the special needs of persons with different physical handicaps (e.g., Ragosta, 1980).

Physical handicaps

With regard to sensory handicaps, adaptations of both individual and group tests of intelligence and educational achievement have been available for some time. Among specially developed tests, the Hiskey-Nebraska Test of Learning Aptitude[2] was developed and standardized on deaf and hard-of-hearing children between the ages of 3 and 16. Being essentially a nonspeeded set of 12 performance subtests, this test samples a wider variety of intellectual functions than those covered by other available performance scales. Research with a tactile form of the Progressive Matrices has shown it to have promise as a nonverbal test for blind children between the ages of 9 and 15 (Rich & Anderson, 1965). The Blind Learning Aptitude Test incorporates some items from the Progressive Matrices, together with other nonverbal items, in a tactile test employing an embossed format. The emphasis in this test is on the learning process rather than on the products of past learning, in which the blind child may have been handicapped.

For the orthopedically handicapped, tests may be presented through visual and auditory modalities; but if the motor disorder is severe, both oral and written responses may be impracticable. Suitable adaptations of several performance and nonverbal tests (including Progressive Matrices and Porteus Mazes) have been developed. In these tests, the examiner manipulates the test materials, while the examinee responds only by appropriate pointing or head movements. Another type of test that permits the utilization of a simple pointing response is the picture vocabulary test. A typical example is the Peabody Picture Vocabulary Test, which was revised and restandardized in 1981 (Dunn & Dunn, 1981). Similar procedures of administration have been incorporated in pictorial classification tests, as illustrated by the Columbia Mental Maturity Scale. This test was originally constructed for use with cerebral palsied children.

---

[2] Information regarding publisher, date, and other particulars about tests cited in this chapter will be found in the *Eighth Mental Measurements Yearbook* (Buros, 1978) and in Anastasi (1982, *Appendix E*).

Mental retardation

In the examination of the mentally retarded, the need for a comprehensive assessment of individual competence has long been recognized, especially for planning appropriate educational and therapeutic programs. The previously discussed SOMPA illustrates this approach. The type of information provided by traditional intelligence tests must be supplemented by measures of motor development and of adaptive behavior in everyday-life situations.

The prototypes of scales designed to assess the development of motor and adaptive behavior, respectively, are the Oseretsky Tests of Motor Proficiency and the Vineland Social Maturity Scale. A recently published adaptation of the former is the Bruininks-Oseretsky Test of Motor Proficiency (Bruininks, 1978). A revision of the Vineland scale is in progress and is scheduled for publication in 1984. Other scales developed for the same general purpose as the Vineland include the more comprehensive Adaptive Behavior Scale prepared by a committee of the American Association on Mental Deficiency (1974) and the Adaptive Behavior Inventory for Children, which is included in SOMPA. In all these social competency or adaptive behavior inventories, the needed information is usually obtained in an interview with a parent or other knowledgeable observer.

Learning disabilities

The 1970s ushered in a wave of crash programs for the diagnosis and remediation of learning disabilities. Educators were becoming increasingly aware of the high frequency of this type of handicap among schoolchildren. Legislative action and government funding helped to focus attention on the problem. Learning disabilities are most frequently characterized by disorders of language, including the abilities to understand or use spoken or written language; less often, the difficulties involve mathematics. The concept of learning disabilities, especially in its legal definitions, typically *excludes* children whose learning problems result primarily from sensory or motor handicaps, mental retardation, emotional disturbance, or environmental disadvantage. The current view is that neurological pathology *may* underlie learning disabilities. Its presence cannot be assumed, but there is evidence of its involvement in at least a sizeable proportion of cases (Golden, 1978; Rourke, 1975).

There is general agreement that the assessment of learning disabilities requires a wide assortment of tests and supplementary observational procedures. Usually, such an assessment process involves the participation of classroom teacher, psychologist, and an educational specialist on learning disabilities. The test batteries may include wide-band screening techniques administered by the classroom teacher (e.g., Slingerland's Screening Test for Identifying Children with Specific Language Disability or Myklebust's Pupil Rating Scale), educational achievement tests (especially wide-range tests such as the Peabody Individual Achievement Test or Jastak's Wide Range Achievement Test), individual intelligence tests, and specially developed tests designed to identify the detailed pattern of disabilities. These special tests focus largely on perceptual and communicative disorders. Two examples are the Illinois Test of Psycholinguistic Abilities (Kirk & Kirk, 1971) and the Porch Index of Communicative Ability in Children (Porch, 1979).

In examining both the mentally retarded and the learning disabled, tests designed to detect cognitive dysfunction or minimal brain damage may also be employed. SOMPA, for example, includes the Bender-Gestalt Test. Such neuropsychological instruments are treated elsewhere in this handbook.

DIAGNOSTIC INTERPRETATIONS OF TEST PERFORMANCE

Intelligence tests

Besides using intelligence tests to assess an individual's general level of intellectual functioning, clinical psychologists customarily explore the pattern of test scores for possible indices of psychopathology. It is likely, for example, that pathological deterioration does not affect all intellectual functions uniformly. Similarly, neurotic anxiety may seriously interfere with performance on certain types of tests which require careful observation and concentration, while leaving performance on others unimpaired. The Wechsler scales lend themselves especially well to such pattern analyses, since all subtest scores are expressed as directly comparable standard scores. From the outset, Wechsler has described a number of diagnostic uses of his scales. Several other clinicians have recommended other techniques and modifications (Guertin et al., 1962, 1966; Kaufman, 1979, Matarazzo, 1972; Rapaport et al., 1968).

Three decades of research on pattern analyses with the Wechsler scales have provided little support for the routine diagnostic application of such analyses. Several methodological requirements must be considered in evaluating this research. First, it is obviously essential to ascertain what is the minimum statistically significant difference between any two test scores. The data required for such evaluation of score differences are now available in the Wechsler scale manuals, as well as in other related publications (e.g., Field, 1960; Zimmerman, Woo-Sam, & Glasser, 1973). A second consideration is the base rate (or frequency of occurrence) of any given difference in the standardization sample (Field, 1960). A third is the cross-validation of empirically obtained group differences in score patterns. A fourth problem arises from the multiplicity of conditions

that may account for atypical variations among subtest scores. Such variations may result not only from pathology but also from differences in
educational, occupational, linguistic, cultural, or other experiential factors.
A fifth point pertains to the nature of the traditional, psychiatric, diagnostic
categories commonly employed as criteria in research on pattern analysis.
In most studies, these categories were too broad, heterogeneous, and
crude to be associated with consistent behavior patterns.

Even if well-designed investigations should conclusively demonstrate
a stable relationship between test response patterns and clearly defined
diagnostic categories, the results would still indicate only group trends
and would not be equally applicable to all individual cases. Such diagnostic signs, therefore, could not be employed routinely by formula. They
would still need to be interpreted in the light of other data about the
individual. At a purely qualitative level, any irregularity of performance
or atypical responses should suggest avenues for further exploration.
Applications of this approach to the Wechsler scales can be found in
Glasser and Zimmerman (1967), Kaufman (1979), Matarazzo (1972, chap.
15), and Zimmerman, Woo-Sam, and Glasser (1973). For each subtest,
these sources provide an interpretive framework, with summaries of relevant data and a discussion of the types of information a clinician may
obtain with regard to both intellectual and personality characteristics.
Similar guidelines have been prepared for the Stanford-Binet (Sattler,
1982, chaps. 8, 18).

An example of the sophisticated clinical use of intelligence tests, com-
bining psychometric data with qualitative observations, is provided by
Kaufman (1979). In a book entitled *Intelligent Testing with the WISC-R,*
Kaufman demonstrates how the clinician can integrate statistical information about test scores (such as significance of differences and the results
of factor analyses) with knowledge about human development, personality
theory, and other areas of psychological research. The test scores, in
combination with background data from other sources, lead to the formulation of hypotheses about the individual; these hypotheses can then be
tested as more information is gathered to round out the picture. The
major feature of this approach is that it calls for individualized interpretations of test performance, in contrast to the uniform application of any
one type of pattern analysis. The same score pattern may lead to quite
different interpretations for different individuals. Similar procedures have
been developed by Kaufman for use with other intelligence tests, such
as the Stanford-Binet (Kaufman & Waterstreet, 1978) and the McCarthy
Scales for Children's Abilities (Kaufman & Kaufman, 1977).

Projective techniques

The distinction between psychometric instrument and clinical tool—
between standardized quantitative analysis and individualized qualitative

interpretation—applies even more cogently to projective techniques than it does to the diagnostic use of intelligence tests. This distinction led one reviewer to remark, "There are still enthusiastic clinicians and doubting statisticians" (Adcock, 1965). Today, the popularity of projective techniques continues unabated, while technical deficiencies remain[3] (Klopfer & Taulbee, 1976; Wade & Baker, 1977).

Nevertheless, signs of progress are appearing, not so much in a narrowing of the gap between psychometric and clinical approaches as in a clarification and explicit recognition of the distinction. We can identify two simultaneous trends in the current development and use of projective techniques. One is a movement toward improving the psychometric properties of projective instruments; the other is a movement toward highly individualized clinical interpretations of projective responses. The two may eventually be integrated, as in some of the procedures described earlier in this section with reference to intelligence tests. Such an integrated approach, however, would be quite different from the intermediate interpretive level typical of projective testing for many decades, which can be characterized as standardized interpretive systems in the absence of standardization data and objective evaluation.

Prior to the 1970s, there were only scattered efforts to strengthen the psychometric quality of projective instruments. One of the earliest examples is the Rosenzweig Picture-Frustration Study (P-F Study). Being more limited in coverage, more highly structured, and relatively objective in its scoring, the P-F Study lent itself better to statistical analysis than did most other projective techniques. Systematic efforts were made from the outset to gather norms and to check the instrument's reliability and validity. Over some 40 years, considerable research has been conducted, by both the test author and other investigators, which bears on the psychometric properties of the P-F Study. Much of this research has been brought together in recent publications by Rosenzweig (1978a, 1978b).

The Holtzman Inkblot Technique represents a major attempt to meet technical psychometric standards in the development of a projective technique (Holtzman, 1968, 1975; Holtzman, Thorpe, Swartz, & Herron, 1961). Modeled after the Rorschach, the Holtzman test was so designed as to eliminate the principal technical deficiencies of the earlier instrument. The changes in stimulus materials and procedures are sufficiently extensive, however, to require that the Holtzman be regarded as a new test and evaluated without reference to either the theoretical or the empirical characteristics of the Rorschach.

With regard to the Rorschach itself, mention should be made of the various collections of norms for children, adolescents, and persons over 70, begun earlier and updated in the 1970s (Ames, Metraux, Rodell,

---

[3] Summaries of the major criticisms of projective techniques can be found in Anastasi (1982, chap. 19) and Klopfer and Taulbee (1976).

& Walker, 1973, 1974; Ames, Metraux, & Walker, 1971; Levitt & Truumaa, 1972). The most ambitious effort to put the Rorschach on a psycho-
metrically sound basis was undertaken by Exner (1974, 1978; Wiener-
Levy & Exner, 1981). First, Exner (1974) developed a comprehensive
Rorschach system which incorporated elements culled from the various
scoring systems employed by different clinicians and researchers. For
this comprehensive system, Exner provides standardized administrative,
scoring, and interpretive procedures. Second, with this uniform system,
Exner (1978) and his associates have already collected a considerable
body of psychometric data, including adult and child norms on many
Rorschach variables, obtained from both patient and nonpatient samples.
Studies of retest reliability over several time intervals indicate considerable
temporal stability for most of the scored variables. Results are also reported
from a number of experiments that contribute to the construct validation
of Rorschach variables. The interpretations are not linked to any one
personality theory, but are predominantly data based. A major contribution of Exner's work is the provision of a uniform Rorschach system that
permits comparability among the research findings of different investigators.

An alternative approach to the Rorschach, more strongly clinical in
its orientation, is described by Aronow and Reznikoff (1976). This approach treats the Rorschach essentially as a semistandardized interview.
The authors recommend a strictly clinical application of the Rorschach
as a means of enhancing the idiographic understanding of the individual
case, and they observe that this is, in fact, how most clinicians use the
Rorschach. The interpretations rely principally on the content of the responses, supplemented by verbal and nonverbal behavior. On the basis
of available research and clinical experience, the authors prepared a
set of guidelines for more effective and dependable idiographic interpretations. For example, responses that depart from the commonplace and
those less closely bound to the stimulus properties of the particular blots
are more likely to be significant in the individual case. The authors rightly
caution against the application of rigid systems of symbol interpretation;
instead, they offer procedures for investigating the meaning of responses
within the individual's own experiential history.

SELF-REPORT PERSONALITY INVENTORIES:
EVOLVING METHODOLOGY

Empirical item selection

The Minnesota Multiphasic Personality Inventory (MMPI) is the classical
example of empirical criterion keying, whereby the selection of individual
items to be retained, their sorting into separate scales, and the assignment
of scoring weights are based on the relation of each item to an external

criterion. In this purely empirical approach to test construction, test items are regarded as verbal stimuli rather than as literal self-descriptions. The responses elicited by these stimuli are scored in terms of their empirically established behavior correlates.

In the construction of the MMPI, items for each scale were selected on the basis of the responses of patients classified according to traditional psychiatric syndromes, in comparison with the responses of a normal control sample. Although this procedure is limited and crude when judged by current test construction standards, the MMPI maintains its clinical popularity largely because of the rich store of interpretive research data that has accumulated over the intervening years. The individual scales are now generally treated as linear measures of personality traits, rather than as indicators of the original diagnostic categories. Through subsequent research, the construct validity of different MMPI profiles, or codes, has gradually been built up. Thus far, over 5,000 references have been published about this test, and the number is mounting steadily (Dahlstrom & Dahlstrom, 1979; Dahlstrom, Welsh, & Dahlstrom, 1972, 1975). There is a growing collection of handbooks, codebooks, atlases, and other user guides. A variety of computerized systems for automated profile interpretation is also available (Buros, 1978, Nos. 617–624).

The early factor-analytic personality inventories also relied principally on empirically established item relationships. Although the scales were given factor names and such factors were often regarded as theoretical constructs, the factors were derived solely from item intercorrelations and were uninfluenced by personality theory. The Guilford-Zimmerman Temperament Survey illustrates this early factor-analytic methodology.

Construct validation

The increasing emphasis on theoretical constructs and the increasing use of construct validation in the development of both ability and personality tests undoubtedly reflect the growing interest in theory in American psychology as a whole. Among the personality theories that have stimulated test development, one of the most prolific has been the manifest need system proposed by Murray and his associates (Murray et al., 1938). One of the first inventories designed to assess the strength of such needs was the Edwards Personal Preference Schedule (EPPS). Using a forced-choice item format, the EPPS yields ipsative scores showing the relative strength of 15 needs for the particular individual.

The more recently developed Comrey Personality Scales foreshadowed current methodology in at least two ways: (1) greater concern for constructs, as illustrated by assigning items to clusters (and item clusters to scales) on the basis of logical—as well as factor-analytic—homogeneity; and (2) the utilization of multiple procedures at different stages in test construction. A noteworthy innovation was the use of a seven-point scale for recording item responses, which increases the amount of information provided by individual items. Empirical validation of the completed scales against external criteria, as well as cross-cultural verification of trait categories, contributed toward the comprehensive evaluation of the instrument.

Current trends in personality inventory construction are well illustrated in two instruments developed by Jackson (1970): the Personality Research Form (PRF) and the Jackson Personality Inventory. The PRF reflects many technical advances in test construction, including some item selection procedures that would have been virtually impossible before the availability of high-speed computers. This inventory exemplifies Jackson's fundamental approach to personality test development, which begins with explicit, detailed descriptions of the constructs to be assessed. These descriptions form the basis for item writing as well as for defining the traits to be rated in validation studies. Like several other personality instruments, the PRF took Murray's personality theory as its starting point. Drawing upon the accumulated research and theoretical literature, Jackson formulated behaviorally oriented and mutually exclusive definitions of 20 personality constructs, 12 having the same names as those covered in the EPPS. A pool of more than 100 items was next generated for each scale. Of these, 20 per scale were finally selected on the basis of high biserial correlation with total scale score, low correlations with other trait scales, and other statistical checks. Subsequent factorial analyses corroborated the grouping of items into the 20 scales. Some data on the empirical validity of the PRF against pooled peer ratings and self-ratings were also obtained. The PRF, however, is primarily a research instrument.

The Jackson Personality Inventory, developed more recently through the same basic procedures as the PRF, has a more practical orientation. The trait scales were chosen partly because of their relevance to the prediction of behavior in a variety of contexts. Among the traits covered by the 16 scales are anxiety, conformity, responsibility, social adroitness, and tolerance. Validity data were gathered not only through correlations with peer ratings and self-ratings but also through studies of particular groups for whom relevant behavioral data in real-life contexts were available.

The theoretically oriented inventories cited thus far in this section were all designed for use with predominantly normal populations. In contrast, the Millon Clinical Multiaxial Inventory (MCMI) was designed chiefly for the same populations for whom the MMPI was developed. Although following the MMPI tradition in several ways, the MCMI introduces significant methodological innovations (Millon, 1977). In fact, its development was deliberately undertaken to meet the criticisms of the older instrument and to utilize intervening advances in psychopathology and test construction. Suitable for either individual or group administration, the MCMI was designed for clinical patients over 17 years of age and with a reading level at or above the eighth grade. The inventory is computer scored; automated interpretive reports are also available. The score profile includes 20 clinical scales, falling into three major categories: basic personality styles, pathological personality syndromes, and symptom disorders.

The MCMI clinical scales were developed to fit syndromes or constructs derived from personality theory. Separate scales were constructed for relatively enduring personality characteristics and for acute clinical states. The scales also distinguish between different levels of severity within parallel personality patterns. To sharpen differential diagnosis, the reference group employed for item analysis was a representative but undifferentiated psychiatric sample, rather than a normal sample. Item development followed the multiple approach characteristic of recent practice in the construction and validation of personality inventories. The procedure included a sequence of three major steps: (1) theoretical-substantive (i.e., writing and selecting items to fit clinically relevant constructs), (2) internal-structural (e.g., item-scale correlations, endorsement frequencies), and (3) external-criterion (e.g., differentiation of diagnostic groups from reference group, cross-validation on new samples).

A sizeable array of data on the reliability and validity of the MCMI has been accumulated in the process of its development and subsequent empirical evaluation. Because of the recency of its publication, however, it is too early to assess its eventual effectiveness as a clinical instrument. The manual calls attention to needed additional research in cross-validation and cross-generalization, among other studies.

Another clinical instrument showing strong family ties to the MMPI is the Personality Inventory for Children (PIC). This inventory was developed through some 20 years of research by a group of investigators at the University of Minnesota, who had been thoroughly exposed to the rationale and clinical use of the MMPI (Lachar & Gdowski, 1979; Wirt & Lachar, 1981; Wirt, Lachar, Klinedinst, & Seat, 1977). The PIC is designed primarily for ages 6 through 16, but can also be used at ages 3 to 5. A major difference between the PIC and the MMPI pertains to the way the information is obtained: the 600 true-false questionnaire items are answered, not by the child, but by a knowledgeable adult, usually the mother. This procedure is consistent with the common practice followed in child clinics of interviewing the mother as the principal source of information about the child's present problem and case history. This inventory, in effect, provides a systematic way of gathering such information and of interpreting it in terms of normative and diagnostic data.

The PIC comprises 16 scales that are regularly reported on the profile sheets. These include three "validity scales," serving the same functions as similar scales on the MMPI, and a screening scale (Adjustment) used to identify children in need of psychological evaluation. The remaining 12 scales are clinical scales designed to assess the child's cognitive development and academic achievement, several well-established types of emotional and interpersonal problems (e.g., Depression, Anxiety, With-drawal, Hyperactivity), and the psychological climate of the home. Some clinical scales were assembled and progressively refined by empirical comparison of response frequencies in criterion and control groups. Others followed essentially construct validation procedures, whereby items were initially chosen on the basis of judges' nominations or ratings for trait relevance. Even in these cases, however, assessment of internal consistency of item responses within scales and factor analyses of items contributed toward the construct validation of the scales. In addition, there is a set of supplementary scales, not regularly included on the profile, but available to clarify diagnosis in individual cases; most of these scales were empirically developed.

A more extensive interpretive guide is provided in a subsequent monograph (Lachar & Gdowski, 1979), which is based on a systematic, comprehensive validation study of 431 inpatients and outpatients at an urban child guidance facility. Although much remains to be done, and plans are evidently under way for continuing research, what has been accomplished in the short period since the publication of the PIC is impressive in extent and quality, and the results are promising.

Traits and situations

A long-standing controversy regarding the generalizability of personality traits versus the situational specificity of behavior reached a peak in the late 1960s and the 1970s. The strongest impetus toward behavioral specificity in personality testing came from social learning theory (Bandura & Walters, 1963; Goldfried & Kent, 1972, Mischel, 1968, 1969, 1973). Both the theoretical discussions and the research stimulated by this controversy enriched our understanding of the many conditions that determine individual behavior; they also contributed to the development of sophisticated research designs.

Concurrently, there was a growing consensus among the adherents of contrasting views. This rapprochement was especially evident in a number of well-balanced and thoughtful discussions of the problem published in the late 1970s (Endler & Magnusson, 1976; Epstein, 1979, 1980; Hogan, DeSoto, & Solano, 1977; Mischel, 1977, 1979). Several noteworthy points emerged from these discussions. Behavior exhibits considerable temporal stability when measured reliably, that is, by summing repeated observations and thereby reducing the error of measurement. When random samples of persons and situations are studied, individual differences contribute more to total behavior variance than do situational differences. Interaction between persons and situations contributes as much as do individual differences, or slightly more. To identify broad personality traits, we need to measure the individual across many situations and aggregate the results.

With regard to testing methodology, the impact of situational specificity was most clearly evident among investigators interested in behavioral assessment, a topic that is treated elsewhere in this handbook. Special instruments have been developed to assess the behavior of individuals in various types of situations (Endler & Hunt, 1966, 1968, 1969; Goldfried & D'Zurilla, 1969; Kjerulff & Wiggins, 1976). These instruments have been used largely in research.

A different application of the concept of traits-within-situations is illustrated by self-report inventories designed to measure test anxiety (Sarason, 1980; Tryon, 1980). A published example of such an inventory is the Test Anxiety Inventory (TAI), developed by Spielberger and his associates (Spielberger, 1980; Spielberger, Gonzalez, Taylor, Algaze, & Anton, 1978). The TAI is essentially a trait scale restricted to a specified class of situations: those centering on tests and examinations. Persons high in test anxiety tend to perceive evaluative situations as personally threatening. The inventory consists of 20 statements describing reactions before, during, and after tests. Respondents indicate how they generally feel by marking how frequently they experience each reaction. The general instructions may be modified to define the anxiety-provoking situations even more specifically, by asking examinees to respond, for example, with reference to mathematics tests or essay tests. The TAI yields a total score on anxiety proneness in test situations, as well as subscores on two major components identified through factor analysis, namely, worry and emotionality. This inventory has proved useful in evaluating the effectiveness of programs for the treatment of test anxiety.

Traits and states

Another way to conceptualize the behavior domain assessed by personality tests involves a differentiation between traits and states. This differentiation is most clearly exemplified in the State-Trait Anxiety Inventory (STAI) developed by Spielberger and his co-workers (Spielberger, Gorsuch, & Lushene, 1970; Spielberger, Vagg, Barker, Donham, & Westberry, 1980). In the construction of this instrument, state anxiety (A-State) was defined as a transitory emotional condition characterized by subjective feelings of tension and apprehension. Such states vary in intensity and fluctuate over time. A-State is measured by 20 short statements which the individual answers in reference to how he or she feels *at the moment* (e.g., I feel calm; I am jittery). The answers are recorded by indicating the intensity of the feeling (not at all, somewhat, moderately so, very much so).

Trait anxiety (A-Trait) refers to relatively stable anxiety proneness, that is, the individual's tendency to respond to situations perceived as threatening with elevated A-State intensity. Respondents indicate how they *generally* feel by marking the frequency with which each of the 20 statements applies to them (almost never, sometimes, often, almost always). Examples of these statements are "I am inclined to take things hard," and "I am a steady person." Only three identical items appear in the two forms of the inventory. The development of the STAI illustrates several innovative methodological features with regard to reliability, validity, and item analysis.

The state-trait differentiation has also been applied by Spielberger and his associates (Spielberger et al., 1980) in two other, recently developed inventories: the State-Trait Anger Scale (STAS) and the State-Trait Personality Inventory (STPI). Like the previously described State-Trait Anxiety Inventory, the STAS includes two subscales, for assessing state and trait anger, respectively. The STPI comprises six subscales, yielding state and trait measures for each of three variables, namely, anger, anxiety, and curiosity.

HEALTH-RELATED INVENTORIES

In the rapidly growing field of health psychology, the diverse contributions of psychologists have included the development of new types of psychometric instruments. These instruments are designed to provide systematic and standardized behavioral information about individuals that can be useful in general medical practice. In their development, some of these instruments have employed psychometric procedures of high technical quality. To illustrate the range of functions served, we shall consider three types of health-related inventories whose purposes vary widely.

Jenkins Activity Survey

Several standardized personality inventories, as well as life-history data, have been used in research on the personality patterns associated with susceptibility to certain diseases, such as cancer, tuberculosis, and coronary disorders, and with recovery from such conditions. More recently, special instruments have been developed for particular diseases. One of the best-known examples concerns the association of Type-A personality with proneness to coronary heart disease. This association was identified and intensively investigated by two cardiologists (Friedman & Rosenman, 1969) through laboratory, clinical, and epidemiological studies. In their major research, these investigators used a structured interview, covering not only the verbal content but also the individual's behavior during the interview. The validation of the Type-A construct was based on both cross-sectional and longitudinal studies of a large sample of employed, middle-aged men (Rosenman, 1978; Rosenman, Friedman, Straus, Jenkins, Zyzanski, & Wurm, 1975).

The Jenkins Activity Survey (JAS) is a 52-item self-report inventory developed as one attempt to approximate the clinical interview and other intensive assessment procedures used in the research on Type-A personality (Jenkins, Zyzanski, & Rosenman, 1979). As defined in this inventory, Type-A behavior is characterized by extreme competitiveness, striving for achievement, aggressiveness, impatience, haste, restlessness, and feelings of being challenged by responsibility and under pressure of time. In contrast, Type-B persons, although they may also be interested in progress and achievement, are characterized by a relaxed, unhurried, mellow style. In its present form, the JAS yields a total Type-A score, as well as scores for three components identified through factor analysis, namely, a Speed and Impatience factor, a Job Involvement factor, and a Hard-Driving and Competitive factor. Although preliminary validity data are promising, more information is needed on the applicability of the JAS to different populations and on the nature of the personality construct under consideration. For instance, there is some evidence suggesting that coronary proneness may be related not so much to achievement drive and upward mobility as to the frustration and anger of motivated strivers whose achievement lags behind their ambition (Hinkle, Whitney, & Lehman, 1968; Spielberger, Crane, & Rosenman, 1981).

Millon Behavioral Health Inventory

The medical practitioner often needs information about the patient's characteristic coping styles, attitudes toward illness and treatment, and other personality tendencies that may significantly influence the patient's reaction to treatment and the course of the illness. Available personality inventories designed for psychiatric patients are usually inappropriate for a nonpsychiatric population. The Millon Health Behavior Inventory (MBHI) represents an attempt to combine in a single instrument a set of variables judged to be particularly relevant to assessment and decision making in general medical settings (Millon, Green, & Meagher, 1979a, 1979b).

Comprising 150 self-descriptive statements to be marked true or false, the MBHI yields scores on 20 scales. The largest number of scales pertain to basic personality styles likely to influence the patient's relation to health-care personnel (e.g., inhibited, cooperative). A second set of scales was designed to identify long-standing attitudes or recent stresses that may interfere with treatment and recovery (e.g., chronic tension, recent upsetting experience, habitual pessimism). The third set of scales assesses the individual's similarity to patients with psychosomatic complications (e.g., allergies, gastro-intestinal susceptibility) and to those showing poor response to either illness or treatment. Test construction procedures followed three major steps: (1) preparation of a theoretically based item pool; (2) item analysis for internal consistency within scales; and (3) criterion-related validation of scale scores. The last step is still in progress, as are studies on the generalizability of validity and norms with diverse populations. The inventory has already been used in several medical settings, such as pain clinics, cancer centers, renal dialysis programs, and health maintenance organizations.

Health status measures

Still another application of psychometric techniques to medical problems is illustrated by the development of health status measures. An example of such a measure is provided by the Sickness Impact Profile (SIP). Developed by an interdisciplinary team, this instrument exemplifies an effective cooperative enterprise of high technical quality (Bergner, Bobbitt, et al., 1981; Bergner & Gilson, 1981). The SIP yields scores in 12 categories: Sleep and Rest, Eating, Work, Home Management, Recreation and Pastimes, Ambulation, Mobility, Body Care and Movement, Social Interaction, Alertness Behavior, Emotional Behavior, and Communication. Items within each category extend over the full range from normal behavior to extreme dysfunction. The form can be filled out by the respondent or by an interviewer. In either case, the patient indicates which statements describe his or her performance *on that day*.

Equal-interval scaling was employed in item selection. As in the Thurstone-type scales, judges rated items on an 11-point scale for degree of dysfunction. Ratings for total patient protocols correlated highly with the total health status score computed from item responses. Various techniques were employed to assess test-retest reliability across forms, occasions, and interviewers, as well as internal consistency of response patterns. Validity for each scale was investigated against assessments of status by the patient, by the clinician, and by another instrument. The resulting correlations were analyzed in a complete multitrait-multimethod matrix. Norms were established on a stratified random sample of the members of a health plan.

A comprehensive approach to the measurement of health is exemplified by a long-term research project conducted by Kaplan and his associates (Kaplan, 1980; Kaplan, Bush, & Berry, 1976). The Index of Well-Being designed in this project also utilizes the respondent's report of actual performance at the time. The scale ranges from complete freedom from dysfunctions that interfere with normal life activities, at one end, to death, at the other. The resulting Index of Well-Being has been subjected to extensive research that demonstrates its content and construct validity. It has proved useful in planning therapy and rehabilitation programs and in evaluating the individual's response to therapy. A further index developed in this project is the Well-Life Expectancy, which adds a temporal dimension to the Index of Well-Being. The time unit employed for this purpose is a "well year." For example, a disease that reduces one's quality of life by one fourth will take away .25 of a well year over the course of a year. Such an index provides a comprehensive health indicator for individuals or groups; it can be used to compare the relative effectiveness of different preventive or treatment programs and can contribute to public-health policy decisions.

SUMMARY

Against the broad and diverse background of testing techniques available for clinical use, this chapter examined a few major theoretical, methodological, and interpretive issues that have come to the fore since the 1970s. Both in the evolving concepts of intelligence and in the interpretation of intelligence test performance, increasing attention is being given to the context in which behavior develops and in which individuals must function. This orientation is reflected in a consideration of population changes in intelligence test performance and of the implications of such changes for the nature and use of test norms. There is also a growing realization that the proper interpretation of the test scores of individuals requires information about their particular experiential backgrounds. From still another angle, the effective assessment of persons calls for a joint evaluation of individuals and of the environments in which they are expected to function. Major societal developments have led to an upsurge of activity in the comprehensive assessment of persons with physical or mental handicaps. The past few years have seen adaptations and revisions of existing instruments, as well as the development of new instruments and of comprehensive assessment programs. Special interest has centered on testing procedures suitable for the intensive evaluation of children with learning disabilities.

Research on the diagnostic interpretation of both intelligence tests and projective techniques has continued with increasing momentum and has led to some notable contributions. Self-report personality inventories have been undergoing evolutionary changes in both test construction methodology and theoretical orientation. Multiple approaches to item selection and greater emphasis on construct validation have been increasingly evident in recently published instruments. The controversy between the extremes of trait theories and situational specificity has gradually led to a more comprehensive orientation that encompasses the contributions of both approaches. The distinction between traits and states has also stimulated productive conceptual analyses and has produced some novel instruments. A notable development has been the application of sophisticated psychometric methodology in new areas, as illustrated by health-related inventories. Designed for a variety of purposes within medical contexts, such inventories illustrate the effective collaboration of psychologists with medical practitioners and specialists in other disciplines.

REFERENCES

Adcock, C. J. Thematic Apperception Test. *Sixth mental measurements yearbook.* Highland Park, N.J.: Gryphon Press, 1965.

Ames, L. B., Metraux, R. W., Rodell, J. L., & Walker, R. N. *Rorschach responses in old age.* New York: Brunner/Mazel, 1973.

Ames, L. B., Metraux, R. W., Rodell, J. L., & Walker, R. N. *Child Rorschach responses: Developmental trends from two to ten years.* New York: Brunner/Mazel, 1974.

Ames, L. B., Metraux, R. W., & Walker, R. N. *Adolescent Rorschach responses: Developmental trends from ten to sixteen years.* New York: Brunner/Mazel, 1971.

Anastasi, A. *Differential psychology* (3rd ed.). New York: Macmillan, 1958.

Anastasi, A. *Psychological testing* (5th ed.). New York: Macmillan, 1982.

Angoff, W. H. (Ed.). *College Board Admissions Testing Program: A technical report on research and development activities relating to the Scholastic Aptitude Test and achievement tests.* New York: College Entrance Examination Board, 1971.

Aronow, E., & Reznikoff, M. *Rorschach content interpretation.* New York: Grune & Stratton, 1976.

Bandura, A., & Walters, R. H. *Social learning and personality development.* New York: Holt, Rinehart & Winston, 1963.

Bergner, M., Bobbitt, R. A., et al. The Sickness Impact Profile: Development and final revision of a health status measure. *Medical Care,* 1981, *19,* 787–805.

Bergner, M., & Gilson, B. S. The Sickness Impact Profile: The relevance of social science to medicine. In L. Eisenberg & A. Kleinman (Eds.), *The relevance of social science to medicine.* Dordrecht, Holland: Reidel, 1981.

Bruininks, R. H. *Bruininks-Oseretsky Test of Motor Proficiency: Examiner's manual.* Circle Pines, Minn.: American Guidance Service, 1978.

Buros, O. K. (Ed.). *The eighth mental measurements yearbook.* Highland Park, N. J.: Gryphon Press, 1978.

Dahlstrom, W. G., & Dahlstrom, L. E. *Basic readings on the MMPI: A new selection on personality measurement.* Minneapolis: University of Minnesota Press, 1979.

Dalhstrom, W. G., Welsh, G. S., & Dahlstrom, L. E. *An MMPI handbook. Vol. I: Clinical interpretation.* Minneapolis: University of Minnesota Press, 1972.

Dahlstrom, W. G., Welsh, G. S., & Dahlstrom, L. E. *An MMPI handbook. Vol. II: Research developments and applications.* Minneapolis: University of Minnesota Press, 1975.

Dunn, Lloyd M., & Dunn, Leota M. *Peabody Picture Vocabulary Test-Revised. Manual for Forms L and M.* Circle Pines, Minn.: American Guidance Service, 1981.

Education for All Handicapped Children Act (P.L. 94–142). *Federal Register, 42*(163), August 23, 1977.

Endler, N. S., & Hunt, J. McV. Sources of behavioral variance as measured by the S-R Inventory of Anxiousness. *Psychological Bulletin,* 1966, *65,* 336–346.

Endler, N. S., & Hunt, J. McV. S-R inventories of hostility and comparisons of the proportions of variance from persons, responses, and situations for hostility and anxiousness. *Journal of Personality and Social Psychology,* 1968, *9,* 309–315.

Endler, N. S., & Hunt, J. McV. Generalizability of contributions from sources of variance in the S-R inventories of anxiousness. *Journal of Personality,* 1969, *37,* 1–24.

Endler, N. S., & Magnusson, D. Toward an interactional psychology of personality. *Psychological Bulletin,* 1976, *83,* 956–974.

Epstein, S. The stability of behavior: I. On predicting most of the people much of the time. *Journal of Personality and Social Psychology,* 1979, *37,* 1097–1121.

Epstein, S. The stability of behavior: II. Implications for psychological research. *American Psychologist,* 1980, *35,* 790–806.

Exner, J. E., Jr. *The Rorschach: A comprehensive system.* New York: John Wiley & Sons, 1974.

Exner, J. E., Jr. *The Rorschach: A comprehensive system, vol. 2: Current research and advanced interpretations.* New York: Wiley Interscience, 1978.

Field, J. G. Two types of tables for use with Wechsler's Intelligence Scales. *Journal of Clinical Psychology,* 1960, *16,* 3–6.

Friedman, M., & Rosenman, R. H. The possible general causes of coronary artery disease. In M. Friedman (Ed.), *Pathogenesis of coronary artery disease.* New York: McGraw-Hill, 1969.

Glasser, A. J., & Zimmerman, I. L. *Clinical interpretation of the Wechsler Intelligence Scale for Children.* New York: Grune & Stratton, 1967.

Golden, C. J. *Learning disabilities and brain dysfunction.* Springfield, Ill.: Charles C Thomas, 1978.

Goldfried, M. R., & D'Zurilla, T. J. A behavioral-analytic model for assessing competence. In C. D. Spielberger (Ed.), *Current topics in clinical psychology* (Vol. 1). New York: Academic Press, 1969.

Goldfried, M. R., & Kent, R. N. Traditional versus behavioral personality assessment: A comparison of methodological and theoretical assumptions. *Psychological Bulletin,* 1972, *77,* 409–420.

Guertin, W. H., et al. Research with the Wechsler Intelligence Scales for Adults: 1955–1960. *Psychological Bulletin,* 1962, *59,* 1–26.

Guertin, W. H., et al. Research with the Wechsler Intelligence Scales for Adults: 1960–1965. *Psychological Bulletin,* 1966, *66,* 385–409.

Hinkle, L. E., Jr., Whitney, L. H., & Lehman, E. W. Occupation, education, and coronary heart disease. *Science,* 1968, *161,* 238–246.

Hogan, R., DeSoto, C. B., & Solano, C. Traits, tests, and personality research. *American Psychologist,* 1977, *32,* 255–264.

Holtzman, W. H. Holtzman Inkblot Technique. In A. I. Rabin (Ed.), *Projective techniques in personality assessment.* New York: Springer-Verlag, 1968.

Holtzman, W. H. New developments in Holtzman Inkblot Technique. In P. McReynolds (Ed.), *Advances in psychological assessment* (Vol. 3). San Francisco: Jossey-Bass, 1975.

Holtzman, W. H., Thorpe, J. S., Swartz, J. D., & Herron, E. W. *Inkblot perception and personality—Holtzman Inkblot Technique.* Austin: University of Texas Press, 1961.

Jackson, D. N. A sequential system for personality scale development. In C. D. Spielberger (Ed.), *Current topics in clinical and community psychology* (Vol. 2). New York: Academic Press, 1970.

Jenkins, C. D., Zyzanski, S. J., & Rosenman, R. H. *Jenkins Activity Survey: Manual.* New York: Psychological Corporation, 1979.

Kaplan, R. M. *Health status measurement for evaluation research and policy analysis.*

Paper presented at the meeting of the American Psychological Association, Montreal, September 1980.

Kaplan, R. M., Bush, J. W., & Berry, C. C. Health status: Types of validity and the index of well-being. *Health Services Research,* 1976, *11,* 478–507.

Kaufman, A. S. *Intelligent testing with the WISC-R.* New York: John Wiley & Sons, 1979.

Kaufman, A. S., & Kaufman, N. L. *Clinical evaluation of young children with the McCarthy scales.* New York: Grune & Stratton, 1977.

Kaufman, A. S., & Waterstreet, M. A. Determining a child's strong and weak areas of functioning on the Stanford-Binet: A simplification of Sattler's *SD* method. *Journal of School Psychology,* 1978, *16,* 72–78.

Kirk, S. A., & Kirk, W. D. *Psycholinguistic learning disabilities: Diagnosis and remediation.* Urbana: University of Illinois Press, 1971.

Kjerulff, K., & Wiggins, N. H. Graduate student styles for coping with stressful situations. *Journal of Educational Psychology,* 1976, *68,* 247–254.

Klopfer, W. G., & Taulbee, E. S. Projective tests. *Annual Review of Psychology,* 1976, *27,* 543–568.

Lachar, D., & Gdowski, C. L. *Actuarial assessment of child and adolescent personality: An interpretive guide for the Personality Inventory for Children profile.* Los Angeles: Western Psychological Services, 1979.

Levitt, E. E., & Truumaa, A. *The Rorschach technique with children and adolescents: Application and norms.* New York: Grune & Stratton, 1972.

Lewis, J. F., & Mercer, J. R. The System of Multicultural Pluralistic Assessment: SOMPA. In W. A. Coulter & H. W. Morrow (Eds.), *Adaptive behavior: Concepts and measurements.* New York: Grune & Stratton, 1978.

Matarazzo, J. D. *Wechsler's measurement and appraisal of adult intelligence* (5th ed.). Baltimore: Williams & Wilkins, 1972.

McReynolds, P. The case for interactional assessment. *Behavioral Assessment,* 1979, *1,* 237–247.

Mercer, J. R. *Labeling the mentally retarded.* Berkeley: University of California Press, 1973.

Mercer, J. R. Theoretical constructs of adaptive behavior: Movement from a medical to a sociological perspective. In W. A. Coulter & H. W. Morrow (Eds.), *Adaptive behavior: Concepts and measurements.* New York: Grune & Stratton, 1978.

Mercer, J. R. *System of Multicultural Pluralistic Assessment (SOMPA): Technical manual.* New York: Psychological Corporation, 1979.

Mercer, J. R., & Lewis, J. F. *System of Multicultural Pluralistic Assessment (SOMPA).* New York: Psychological Corporation, 1978.

Millon, T. *Millon Clinical Multiaxial Inventory: Manual.* Minneapolis: NCS Interpretive Scoring Systems, 1977.

Millon, T., Green, C. J., & Meagher, R. B., Jr. The MBHI: A new inventory for the psychodiagnostician in medical settings. *Professional Psychology,* 1979, *10,* 529–539. (a)

Millon, T., Green, C. J., & Meagher, R. B., Jr. *Millon Behavioral Health Inventory: Manual.* Minneapolis: NCS Interpretive Scoring Systems, 1979. (b)

Mischel, W. *Personality and assessment.* New York: John Wiley & Sons, 1968.

Mischel, W. Continuity and change in personality. *American Psychologist,* 1969, *24,* 1012–1018.

Mischel, W. Toward a cognitive social learning reconceptualization of personality. *Psychological Review*, 1973, *80*, 252–283.

Mischel, W. On the future of personality measurement. *American Psychologist*, 1977, *32*, 246–254.

Mischel, W. On the interface of cognition and personality: Beyond the person-situation debate. *American Psychologist*, 1979, *34*, 740–754.

Murray, H. A., et al. *Explorations in personality*. New York: Oxford University Press, 1938.

Porch, B. E. *Porch Index of Communicative Ability in Children:* Vol. 1. Palo Alto, Calif.: Consulting Psychologists Press, 1979.

Ragosta, M. *Handicapped students and the SAT* (College Board Research and Development Reports, RDR 80–81, No. 1). Princeton, N.J.: Educational Testing Service, 1980.

Rapaport, D., et al. *Diagnostic psychological testing* (Rev. ed., edited by R. R. Holt). New York: International Universities Press, 1968.

Rich, C. C., & Anderson, R. P. A tactual form of the Progressive Matrices for use with blind children. *Personnel and Guidance Journal*, 1965, *43*, 912–919.

Rosenman, R. H. The interview method of assessment of the coronary-prone behavior pattern. In T. M. Dembroski, S. M. Weiss, J. L. Shields, S. G. Haynes, & M. Feinleib (Eds.), *Coronary-prone behavior*. New York: Springer-Verlag, 1978.

Rosenman, R. H., Friedman, M., Straus, R., Jenkins, C. D., Zyzanski, S. J., & Wurm, M. Coronary heart disease in the Western Collaborative Group Study. Final follow-up experience of 8½ years. *Journal of the American Medical Association*, 1975, *233*, 872–879.

Rosenzweig, S. *Aggressive behavior and the Rosenzweig Picture-Frustration Study*. New York: Praeger Publishers, 1978. (a)

Rosenzweig, S. An investigation of the reliability of the Rosenzweig Picture-Frustration (P-F) Study, Children's Form. *Journal of Personality Assessment*, 1978, *42*, 483–488. (b)

Rourke, B. P. Brain-behavior relationships in children with learning disabilities: A research program. *American Psychologist*, 1975, *30*, 911–920.

Sarason, I. G. (Ed.). *Test anxiety: Theory, research, and applications*. Hillsdale, N.J.: Erlbaum, 1980.

Sattler, J. M. *Assessment of children's intelligence and special abilities* (2d ed.). Boston: Allyn & Bacon, 1982.

Scottish Council for Research in Education. *The trend of Scottish intelligence*. London: University of London Press, 1949.

Spielberger, C. D. *Test Anxiety Inventory: Preliminary professional manual*. Palo Alto, Calif.: Consulting Psychologists Press, 1980.

Spielberger, C. D., et al. *Preliminary manual for the State-Trait Anger Scale* (STAS). Tampa: Center for Research in Community Psychology, University of South Florida, August 1980.

Spielberger, C. D., Crane, R. S., & Rosenman, R. H. The role of anger in Type-A behavior and heart disease. In C. D. Spielberger, I. G. Sarason, & P. B. Defares (Eds.), *Stress and anxiety* (Vol. 9). New York: McGraw-Hill/Hemisphere, 1982.

Spielberger, C. D., Gonzalez, H. P., Taylor, C. J., Algaze, B., & Anton, W. D. Examination stress and test anxiety. In C. D. Spielberger & I. G. Sarason (Eds.), *Stress and anxiety* (Vol. 5). New York: McGraw-Hill/Hemisphere, 1978.

Spielberger, C. D., Gorsuch, R. L., & Lushene, R. E. *STAI manual for the State-Trait Anxiety Inventory.* Palo Alto, Calif.: Consulting Psychologists Press, 1970.

Spielberger, C. D., Vagg, P. R., Barker, L. R., Donham, G. W., & Westbury, L. G. The factor structure of the State-Trait Anxiety Inventory. In I. G. Sarason & C. D. Spielberger (Eds.), *Stress and anxiety* (Vol. 7). New York: McGraw-Hill/Hemisphere, 1980.

Sundberg, N. D. *Assessment of persons.* Englewood Cliffs, N.J.: Prentice-Hall, 1977.

Sundberg, N. D., Snowden, L. R., & Reynolds, W. M. Toward assessment of personal competence and incompetence in life situations. *Annual Review of Psychology,* 1978, *29,* 179–221.

Tryon, G. S. The measurement and treatment of test anxiety. *Review of Educational Research,* 1980, *50,* 343–372.

Tuddenham, R. D. Soldier intelligence in World Wars I and II. *American Psychologist,* 1948, *3,* 54–56.

Wade, T. C., & Baker, T. B. Opinions and use of psychological tests: A survey of clinical psychologists. *American Psychologist,* 1977, *32,* 874–882.

Wechsler, D. *Manual for the Wechsler Adult Intelligence Scale—Revised.* New York: Psychological Corporation, 1981.

Wiener-Levy, D., & Exner, J. B. The Rorschach comprehensive system: An overview. In P. McReynolds (Ed.), *Advances in psychological assessment* (Vol. 5). San Francisco: Jossey-Bass, 1981.

Wirt, R. D., & Lachar, D. The Personality Inventory for Children: Development and clinical applications. In P. McReynolds (Ed.), *Advances in psychological assessment* (Vol. 5). San Francisco: Jossey-Bass, 1981.

Wirt, R. D., Lachar, D., Klinedinst, J. K., & Seat, P. D. *Multidimensional description of child personality: A manual for the Personality Inventory for Children.* Los Angeles: Western Psychological Services, 1977.

Wirtz, W. (chair). *On further examination: Report of the Advisory Panel on the Scholastic Aptitude Test Score Decline.* New York: College Entrance Examination Board, 1977.

Zimmerman, I. L., Woo-Sam, J. M., & Glasser, A. J. *The clinical interpretation of the Wechsler Adult Intelligence Scale.* New York: Grune & Stratton, 1973.

14

Clinical psychological practice and principles of neuropsychological assessment

*Aaron Smith**

How much and exactly what should clinical psychologists know about clinical neuropsychology? The wide spectra of specializations in the current practice of clinical psychology are reflected by the 43 other chapters comprising this Handbook of Clinical Psychology. However, despite the diversity of approaches and foci, there are two basic, interrelated concerns in the current practice of clinical psychology: the diagnosis and the treatment of behavioral disorders in children and adults.

DIAGNOSTIC CONSIDERATIONS

Most commonly, patients are referred to or seek the help of the clinical psychologist either because of the sudden or gradual emergence of mental or emotional disturbances, or, more frequently, because of long-standing difficulties with which the patient now finds he or she can no longer cope. In many cases, adults may complain of headaches, difficulty in concentration, loss of memory, depression, irritability, dizziness, and other vague, psychological disturbances. Referrals of children to the clinical psychologist may be prompted by persisting reading or learning disorders, hyperactivity, apathy, delayed development, disorders of speech and/or comprehension, aggressiveness or withdrawal in social situations, difficulties in focusing or sustaining attention, excessive daydreaming, stuttering, clumsiness, or other subtle or apparent motor disorders. Not

* University of Michigan Neuropsychological Laboratory, Ann Arbor.

This research was partially supported by NINCDS Grant 2R01–NS10089. Thanks are due to Margaret Benkert for her special care and effort in preparation of this manuscript.

infrequently, adolescents and young adults with emotional difficulties or physical handicaps are referred for evaluation of vocational potential.

In a small but significant proportion, patients may be referred because of mental, emotional, sensory, and/or motor defects persisting after closed head injuries, strokes, neurosurgical intervention for resectable brain lesions, or other known or suspected pre- , peri- , or post-natal brain insults. The range of treatment techniques (including biofeedback, operant conditioning, and other behavioral methods) has been recently reviewed by Small (1980) and other authors in this volume.

The rationale, validity, economy, and efficacy of techniques used in clinical psychology and psychiatry to treat patients with emotional or mental disorders have been subjects of continuing historical controversies. However, one cannot hope to exorcise a concealed brain tumor, arrest or reverse the insidious processes of progressive mental deterioration in Alzheimer's or Huntington's disease, or curb the bizarre symptoms of Gilles de la Tourette syndrome with even the most efficacious therapeutic techniques. Thus, one of the critical concerns of the clinical psychologist before initiating specific psychotherapeutic techniques is the accurate determination of the etiology of the presenting symptoms by comprehensive and carefully selected diagnostic studies.

In many neurological disorders (such as Huntington's chorea, brain tumors, Parkinson's disease, multiple sclerosis, Alzheimer's or Pick's diseases) and in systemic diseases (such as Cushing's syndrome, diabetes, or endocrine disorders), descriptions of the characteristic symptoms include various references to the appearance of diverse mental or emotional changes at different stages in the course of the underlying disease process. Not infrequently, the earliest presenting symptoms are mental disturbances. In the absence of frank neurological signs, the physician may refer the patient for treatment of these symptoms by psychotherapy. In some diseases, the symptoms may spontaneously remit for varying periods; in others, they may wax and wane in intensity, or change completely in form, reflecting the diverse capacities of the brain in its efforts to reorganize cerebral mechanisms to compensate for the dynamic changes in the underlying progressive neuropathology.

Neurological screening examinations would, therefore, appear to be a reasonable precaution in diagnostic studies of all patients referred for psychotherapy. However, normal findings in neurological examinations are no guarantee of a psychogenic basis for the patient's symptoms, or diagnosis by default. Tissenbaum, Harter, and Friedman (1951) reported the routine use of initial neurological examinations of all patients referred to their Mental Hygiene Clinic before initiating psychotherapy and repeated neurological examinations for those treated for extended periods. Of 395 patients who proved to have underlying neurological disorders, 342 were correctly diagnosed early in the course of illness. The remaining 53 (13.4 percent), however, were incorrectly diagnosed initially and treated psychiatrically *from 1 to 8 years,* the greatest number (17) for 4 years, with a mean of 4.5 years for the total sample.

Parkinson's syndrome, multiple sclerosis, brain tumors, and herniated discs were the most common among those misdiagnosed initially as functional disorders. The authors logically concluded that, prior to acceptance for psychotherapy, all patients should have thorough neurological examinations to rule out or establish the diagnosis of organic disease. The relatively high proportion with long delays and extensive psychiatric treatment before accurate diagnosis is probably exceeded by the number of similarly misdiagnosed cases in similar populations not subject to repeated neurological examinations. Numerous other studies describing psychological disturbances masking or reflecting the presence of brain tumors and other occult intracranial diseases have been cited in previous reviews (Smith, 1975, 1981a).

CAT scans and other advances in neurological diagnostic techniques have contributed to increasing accuracy in earlier diagnosis of such patients. However, in addition to economic considerations, they do not eliminate the "haunting spectre" of false positives or false negatives that vitiates any diagnostic technique (DiChiro, 1962). In the not infrequent cases with equivocal findings in neurological studies, neuropsychological assessments are especially important to the clinical psychologist for other reasons.

The "brain-damaged" patient

First, in cases with suspected organic cerebral involvement and in others with confirmed brain insults, the presence of "brain damage" is obviously an important factor in the clinical psychologist's considerations of treatment or management of the presenting symptoms. How can the therapist evaluate the etiology, evolution, significance, and, especially, the amenability of the various psychological disturbances to psychotherapy in patients with diverse types of brain insults incurred at various intervals—from birth to but a few months—before he or she has been referred to the clinical psychologist? In the present author's experience, in neuropsychological studies of initial and later effects of various brain insults in children and adults over the past three decades, the emotional problems of the brain-damaged patient are often a critical factor, determining the ultimate consequences of the cerebral lesion on the patient's life.

In most cases, it is difficult to accurately differentiate the early presenting psychological or affective disturbances that are a direct reflection of the effects of the destruction of portions of the brain from those that are evoked in reaction to the sensory, motor, cognitive, and memory disorders resulting from such brain insults. In almost all cases, however, the initial and later affective sequelae reflect the patient's feelings—and reactions—to the slight or massive (often life-threatening) assault on her/ his biological integrity and to the variously diminishing or persisting functional deficits. Not surprisingly, such reactions vary from individual to individual. In most cases with recent brain insult, they change with time. Often the severity and duration of these "psychogenic" sequelae are disproportionate to the extent of brain damage and to the presence and severity of any enduring functional deficits.

The various personality and other factors determining the idiosyncratic nature of such affective disturbances cannot be considered in detail here. However, one of the most common and disturbing problems in the patient's attempts to adjust to the initial and later organic deficits is the inconstancy or fluctuation in cerebral efficiency resulting from cortical lesions (Head, 1926; Smith, 1981a). Until recently, the psychological and affective disturbances of brain-damaged patients have received scant attention. However, in the course of neuropsychological studies (including brief sessions of counseling children and adults and their parents or spouses with traumatic and other brain injuries), the present author has referred numerous patients for psychotherapy and observed beneficial results. Thus, as Small (1980) has pointed out, the presence of brain damage in a patient should not be considered as evidence that the patient is unsuitable for psychotherapy. Nor should specific deficits in sensory, motor, and/or cognitive functions manifesting the organic effects of various brain insults be automatically considered as permanent and immutable. As has been described elsewhere (Smith, 1975, 1979, 1981a), earlier psychological studies reflected the concept of brain damage (or organicity) as a unitary disorder with a presumably discrete, characteristic, and permanent defect in a single psychological sphere. This earlier stereotype suggested that "once brain damaged, always brain damaged."

The remarkable capacity of the damaged brain for gradual reorganization of intra- and interhemispheric mechanisms to compensate for the loss of function resulting from lateralized and bilateral cerebral lesions in adults as well as children has been recently illustrated in documented studies (Smith, 1981a,b; Campbell, Bogen, & Smith, 1981). Perhaps the most striking illustration of these capacities is the case reported by Smith and Sugar (1975). Following removal of the left hemisphere for intractable seizures at 5½ years of age, follow-up studies (21 and 26 years later) demonstrated the development of superior adult verbal and nonverbal intelligence. When last examined (in 1981), this 33-year-old man had obtained a college degree and was engaged in post-graduate studies, while working full time as an industrial executive.

Similarly, long-term studies of effects of extensive "resolving" of lateralized lesions in adults as well as in children have demonstrated the subsequent development of normal—and even superior—adult intellectual capacities in other cases (Smith, 1981a,b). Thus, in the role of what Frieda Fromm-Reichmann described as "the ambassador to reality," the psychotherapist treating such patients for the inevitably associated psychic trauma can and should monitor and record the course of recovery in the acute and later stages of brain insults. Often, the patient may note striking improvement in certain functions and be unaware of persisting severe deficits in others. For example, patients with transient hemiplegias or language disturbances after head injuries may recover the ability to walk or talk normally. In many cases, especially children and young adults, the enforced inactivity and social isolation during convalescence is boring, and the patient cannot wait to return to school or work. The striking recovery of the ability to walk and talk normally is often regarded by the patients as evidence that they are fully recovered and able to resume their premorbid school or work activities. At this point, the role of the therapist may be critical. Frequently, despite the apparent recovery of motor and language functions, the patient is unaware of persisting memory and other neuropsychological deficits. Hence, premature resumption of school or work activities is fraught with a risk of failure which may have disastrous consequences for the patient.

Despite strongest advice to the contrary, a young woman who had recovered speech and motor functions after a severe, closed head injury resumed full-time university studies. Six weeks later, the present author received a hysterical phone call: "I've been expelled. My God, my brain is damaged!" Thus, the problems of her long-term rehabilitation from brain trauma had been complicated by the superimposition of the psychological trauma of her academic failure which might have been avoided.

In other cases, the patient may be unaware of gradual but significant recovery and may be reluctant or fearful of attempting to return to work or school. Apart from secondary gains, the patient may have adjusted to the disabilities and limitations resulting from the initial sequelae of brain injuries and become resigned to lower levels of efforts and aspirations. Such patients may be surprised and delighted to learn of the processes of gradual recovery; and the imparting of this information by the clinical psychologist may serve as a warrant to increase their efforts at self-rehabilitation and contribute to more positive perceptions and partially self-fulfilling aspirations.

Thus, conversance with the rationale, limitations, and implications of current techniques of neuropsychological assessment is important for the practice of clinical psychology. Such assessment provides bases for screening patients referred for psychotherapy for various emotional difficulties which may or may not be associated with underlying organic cerebral dysfunction. In others with known brain insults, neuropsychological examinations at fixed periods provide evidence of the nature and severity of initial deficits and of the varying degrees of recovery of the different functions that are obviously important in the course of treatment for associated emotional difficulties.

THE EVOLUTION OF CURRENT
PSYCHOLOGICAL AND
NEUROPSYCHOLOGICAL TESTING
TECHNIQUES

Practical testing came into psychology from medicine (Cronbach, 1960). The recent emergence and rapid development of clinical neuropsychology, however, reflected the convergence of different historical processes that had led to the emergence and separation of neurology and psychology as discrete disciplines in the early 19th century. For example, medical texts by Magendie and other outstanding physicians in the early 19th century included chapters on memory, judgment, will, and other psychological dimensions of behavior (Smith, 1975). The first text describing specific, neurological diagnostic techniques by Romberg (1840–1846)—signaling the emergence of neurology as a specialized field in medicine—included clinical tests of mental (as well as sensory and motor) functions. Shortly thereafter, the establishment of psychological laboratories for studies of interactions of sensory, motor, and mental functions by Wundt, Helmholz, and other physicians and psychologists reflected the growing recognition of the need for another discipline focusing on the scientific study of behavior or psychology (Boring, 1950). However, the establishment of an anthropometric laboratory (by Galton in 1884) and of a biometric laboratory (by Pearson in 1901) similarly reflected the growing recognition of the need for developing objective and standardized methods of measurement and statistical approaches to the problems of defining the significance of and relationships between psychological measurements.

During the same period, the works of eminent neurologists—such as Hughlings Jackson, Fritsch and Hitzig, Munk, Goltz, Meynert, von Monakow and Flechsig (von Bonin, 1960; McHenry, 1969)—reflected increasing efforts to define the relationships between human brain structures and psychological functions. The growing awareness that the problems of defining such relationships overlapped the borders of neurology and psychology was signaled by Flechsig's presentation of his classical paper on brain physiology and theories of mental functions at the Fifth International Psychological Congress in Rome in 1905 (Flechsig, 1905; von Bonin, 1960).

The later emergence of clinical neuropsychology as a discrete discipline focusing on human brain-behavior relationships was presaged by three almost simultaneous developments in the first decade of the 20th century. The first practical intelligence test was constructed in Paris by Binet and Simon (1905) to screen mentally retarded or brain-damaged children who were unable to learn from a normal school curriculum. Two years later, Bekhterev founded the first Psychoneurological Institute in Leningrad (Yakovlev, 1953); and two years later, Burt (1909) reported elaborations and refinements in experimental tests of higher mental processes. These three almost concomitant developments in different parts of the world reflect the same historical processes that are illustrated by the recent emergence and development of clinical neuropsychology throughout the world today.

The continuing development of new intelligence tests to screen millions of soldiers in World War I, the construction and continuing refinements of the Wechsler scales for children and adults, and the introduction of projective-personality and other psychological tests for diagnostic studies of patients with affective disorders have been variously reviewed by Kirsch (Chapter 1) and Anastasi (Chapter 13) in this handbook and others elsewhere (Matarazzo, 1972; Smith, 1975; Korchin & Schuldberg, 1981). Subsequently, intelligence and projective-personality tests were organized into test batteries for routine screening and diagnostic studies of children and adults with suspected or confirmed learning or behavioral disorders in state hospitals, clinics, schools, and mental hygiene centers.

Because neurological diseases produce learning and other behavioral disorders that cannot be readily distinguished from nonorganic affective or psychological disturbances, children with academic difficulties and psychiatric patients with equivocal diagnoses were often referred for psychometric testing to differentiate organic behavioral disturbances from psychogenic disorders. The limitations of the standardized tests used in early psychometric batteries for evaluation of the effects of brain injuries were reflected in a report by Hardwick (1927) of a 14-year-old boy who had been tested for problems of school adjustment and stuttering shortly before suffering a severe brain injury in a truck accident. The left parietal bone had been depressed so far into the brain that brain tissue was forced out of the ear canal, and he remained comatose for several days. Retesting with the same battery—including the Stanford-Binet and other standardized tests—four months after trauma and neurosurgical repair revealed that he was slightly slower—but more accurate—than he had been before brain injury!

Routine psychometric studies of other clinical populations reflected attempts to develop objective criteria for differentiating patients with organic from those with psychogenic disorders. Babcock (1930) reported that certain psychological tests—such as vocabulary—are relatively impervious to brain damage, whereas other tests—memory, learning, and motor speed—were invariably depressed. Thus, in patients with suspected or confirmed brain damage, tests of vocabulary and verbal-reasoning capacities presumably reflected the premorbid intellectual capacities and were described as *hold* tests. Tests of other functions—such as memory, learning, or motor speed—which were highly vulnerable to effects of brain insults were described as *no-hold* tests. The disparities between the levels of performances on hold and no-hold tests were described as evidence of irreversible, organic mental deterioration. The persistence of this early notion and the notion that vocabulary tests reliably indicate premorbid intelligence were reflected by McFie (1960, 1975) and in a recent evaluation by Boyd (1981) of the validity of the Hooper Visual Organization Test as a sensitive indicator of the presence of brain damage.

Because psychiatric patients were often referred to the clinical psychologist for evidence of the presence or absence of organic brain syndrome, this psychiatric diagnostic category suggested another uniform pattern of psychological disturbances as characteristic of brain damage. Hence, numerous other single tests were developed. They were based on the assumption that brain damage resulted in a relatively uniform pattern of deficits in psychological functioning, regardless of the nature, specific site, extent, age, or dynamics of the underlying cerebral lesion, the age or education of the patient, and other factors.

Babcock's concept of the disparity between hold versus no-hold test performances as an index of organicity and mental deterioration and the concept of a relatively uniform pattern of specific deficits in standardized psychological tests were adopted and formalized by Wechsler in the early stages of development of his intelligence scales. However, as described below, with the gradual accumulation of data in studies of diverse clinical populations, Wechsler continued to modify his views. Initially, Wechsler described a pattern of deficits in specific subtests as characteristic of "organic brain diseases" (Wechsler, 1944, pp. 153–162), "ranging all the way from brain tumors to chronic alcoholism" (p. 153). Subsequently, although he cited numerous studies reporting the differential sensitivities of the 11 subtests to the effects of brain insults, he also noted that, "For the most part, correlations between specific localized lesions and performances on particular tests are both limited and inconstant" (Wechsler, 1958, p. 214). In the most recent (fifth) edition of *Wechsler's Measurement and Appraisal of Adult Intelligence*, Matarazzo (1972) noted that the accumulated findings in a vast number of studies comparing subtest performances in brain-damaged populations indicated that, for differential diagnostic purposes, "a correlated index such as a Wechsler profile, no matter how promising, cannot produce anything but fickle, confusing, or otherwise frustrating findings" (1972, p. 430).

Although similarly designed for other purposes, other tests such as the Bender-Gestalt (Bender, 1935) or the Rorschach (Piotrowski, 1937, 1940) included in routine psychometric batteries have also been reported to show specific quantitative or qualitative signs characteristic of brain damage. Pascal and Suttell (1951) developed a scoring system describing 106 scorable characteristics of Bender-Gestalt drawings for identifying patients with "disturbances in cortical function" from normal subjects. Piotrowski (1937) described 10 signs in Rorschach productions (with a minimum of 5 for a diagnosis of brain disease) and specific aberrant characteristics of patients with lesions of the frontal lobes (Piotrowski,

1938). Others reported comparisons of Rorschach responses in patients with right- versus left-hemisphere lesions, tumors, epilepsy, and other brain insults, and described from 7 to 23 different signs as characteristic of organicity (Lezak, 1976).

The diverse and often contradictory findings in such earlier studies spurred efforts to develop specific psychological tests of organicity and brain damage. Because of increasing recognition by clinical psychologists of their importance in diagnostic studies, many were uncritically accepted. For example, Malamud (1946) reported that the Hunt-Minnesota Test for Organic Brain Damage (Hunt, 1943) showed that 6 of 10 members in the psychology department at her hospital were brain damaged. The efficacy of various earlier and newly developed tests and of test batteries (including the Halstead-Reitan) specifically designed for diagnostic studies of children and adults with suspected insults was reviewed by Spreen and Benton (1965).

The validity of earlier psychological tests of brain damage and the continuing ambiguities in concepts and studies of brain damage and organicity have been critically reviewed by Yates (1954) and Smith (1962a, 1962b, 1975, 1979, 1981a). In their comparisons of studies of psychological tests for cerebral damage, Spreen and Benton called attention to the nature of the specific techniques of assessment used: What are the claims of the psychologist for his methods? For the clinical psychologist examining a child or adult referred for differential diagnosis or psychotherapy, Smith (1962a, 1962b, 1981a) has emphasized the importance of a more fundamental question: What is brain damage? Despite the enormous literature following the emergence and rapid development of clinical neuropsychology after World War II, numerous authors continue to report findings based on administrations of different tests and batteries to populations comprised of differing proportions with evolving (or progressive) versus resolving brain insults tested at varying stages in the evolution or resolution of the underlying neuropathological processes (Smith, 1981a,b).

Although they noted the subsequent development of numerous other single tests and of batteries specifically designed for neuropsychological assessments, Korchin and Schuldberg (1981) cited a study reporting that age-appropriate Wechsler scales were the first and the Bender-Gestalt test was the third of the tests most commonly used by neuropsychologists (and probably by clinical psychologists) in such assessments. In their review of the future of clinical psychological assessment, they also observed the resistance of clinicians to substituting new tests and that ". . . psychodiagnosticians cling to their tattered and finger-printed Rorschach and TAT cards as to a security blanket . . . One could [and with respect to the use of the Bender-Gestalt, this author has heard one author of a textbook on clinical neuropsychology] argue, indeed, that the clinical familiarity in the particular psychometric setting may be more important

than psychometric refinement" (Korchin & Schuldberg, 1981, p. 1152).
Thus, before considering some of the more recently developed single
tests or neuropsychological batteries, a brief review may provide criteria
for clinicians using these and other earlier tests (such as the Rorschach,
TAT, and MMPI) for evaluating the rationale and validity of these as
well as more recently developed tests and batteries designed specifically
for neuropsychological assessments.

CURRENT TESTS OF ORGANICITY IN CLINICAL PSYCHOLOGICAL ASSESSMENTS: THE WECHSLER SCALES

Initially, Wechsler (1958, pp. 173–74) described a pattern of deficits
in selected subtests as characteristic of "organic brain diseases . . . ranging all the way from brain tumors to chronic alcoholism . . . irrespective
of type." With the continuing accumulation of findings and periodic reviews of studies of brain-damaged children and adults with the Wechsler
scales and other tests (Klebanoff, 1945; Klebanoff, Singer, & Wilensky,
1954; Guertin, Frank, & Rabin, 1956; Guertin, Rabin, Frank, & Ladd,
1962; Guertin, Frank, Ladd, & Rabin, 1966; Guertin, Ladd, Frank, Rabin,
& Heister, 1971), Wechsler noted the controversial findings reported
for his scales, including growing claims of the ability to localize focal
lesions in either hemisphere according to which specific subtest scores
were depressed.

Wechsler (1958, pp. 18–19) also noted earlier reports by Goldstein,
Halstead, and others claiming that the frontal lobes play a unique role
in intellectual processes. As described below, descriptions of the unique
roles of the frontal lobes in mental functions by Goldstein, Halstead, and
Luria differed, as did the batteries of tests based on those theories that
they and their followers subsequently developed. Wechsler cited numerous studies reporting the differential sensitivity of the 11 subtests to focal
and diffuse brain insults. However, he noted that—in contrast to the claims
of greater intellectual impairment following frontal lobe lesions—the accumulating findings indicated that "lesions of the posterior and intermediate
cortex (post-rolandic) produce more serious intellectual impairment . . ."
(Wechsler, 1958, p. 219). Noting reports of greater intellectual impairment
following left (rather than right) hemisphere lesions, Wechsler also cautioned that interpretation of such findings with the Wechsler scales was
qualified by the frequent association of language difficulties in patients
with left-sided lesions.

Do V-PIQ differences provide reliable lateralizing indices?

In one of the many recent texts of human neuropsychology, Kolb and
Whishaw (1980) referred to earlier, unspecified studies as "having shown

that well-defined left-hemisphere lesions produce a relatively low verbal IQ, whereas well-defined right-hemisphere lesions produce a relatively low performance IQ. Diffuse damage, on the other hand, tends to produce a low performance IQ, leading to the erroneous belief that the verbal-performance IQ difference is not diagnostically useful" (Kolb & Whishaw, 1980, p. 454). The authors were apparently unaware that, although Anderson (1950, 1951) and Reitan (1955) first reported systematically lower V- than PIQs in patients with left-sided lesions and lower P- than VIQs in others with right-sided lesions, this claim was first modified to refer to only "acute" lateralized lesions (Fitzhugh, Fitzhugh, & Reitan, 1963). Subsequently, in describing keys for interpreting Halstead-Reitan test performances for evidence of the presence, lateralization, and localization of brain lesions, Russell, Nueringer, and Goldstein (1970) abandoned the standard V-PIQ ratios and substituted comparisons of three verbal subtests (V, D Sp, and S) versus two performance subtests (BD and OA).

Matarazzo (1972) cited selected studies supporting inferences on the lateralization of acute and chronic focal lesions. However, he called attention to the negative findings in several other studies and to the high incidence of V-PIQ differences of 10 or more points reported in base-rate studies of normals, e.g., ". . . a V-P difference greater than 10 points will be encountered in some 30 cases in 100, a V-P difference of *15 points in 18 cases in 100, a difference of 20 points 4 times in 100,* and so on" (Matarazzo, 1972, p. 389 [italics added]). Inferences on the presence or the lateralization of brain damage based on V-PIQ differences are also qualified by several other factors. For example, the findings in the studies cited by Matarazzo in support of V-PIQ differences for lateralization of brain damage are also qualified by the inclusion of unspecified numbers of aphasics; differences in verbal and performance subtest scores and IQs as a function of education and age; the specific locus, nature, and stage of evolving and resolving lesions in each hemisphere; as well as the confounding effects of the presence or absence of specific impairments of the various modalities involved in perceptions of and/ or responses to the Wechsler verbal and performance subtests (Smith, 1966a,d,e).

The critical roles of the status of the modalities involved in perceptions of and in responses to the Wechsler subtests (as well as to other psychological tests such as the Bender-Gestalt or Rorschach and groups of tests as in the Halstead-Reitan and Luria-Nebraska batteries) have often been overlooked. For example, children and adults with an intact brain but with severe impairment of hearing or of visual acuity may show even greater and more consistent V-PIQ differences than those reported in the studies. In some cases, the presence of covert sensory deficits may escape the attention of the examiner:

> In 1971, the present author administered the Michigan Neuropsychological Test Battery to a 22-year-old man who had been repeatedly examined

by neurologists and variously diagnosed as brain damaged, aphasic, and mentally retarded. Neurological examination was repeated immediately before neuropsychological testing. The neurologist reported that the patient, "was unable to understand very simple requests involving more than 3 to 4 words, could not subtract 7 from 100, and that his speech consisted of only yes or no answers. . . . His hearing, to crude testing, seemed satisfactory, as did his vision." Neurological examination otherwise "revealed no abnormalities whatsoever," and ". . . this is longstanding, most likely congenital, retardation."

On neuropsychological testing, he was only able to repeat 4 digits forward and 2 backward in the WAIS Digit Span subtest. In efforts to administer the 5 other verbal subtests, he shook his head in frustration. Despite the fact that after kindergarten he had been assigned to special education classes for 12 years, his WAIS PIQ was 116, and all performances on nonlanguage tests of cognitive, sensory, and motor functions were eminently normal. Yet, the Peabody Picture Vocabulary Test score (39, mental age 3 years 9 months) indicated severely attenuated development of simple receptive vocabulary skills. As the reader has probably guessed, routine audiologic examination revealed a severe hearing loss.

Curiously, Reitan (Reitan & Davison, 1974), Kolb and Whishaw (1980), and others have continued to cite earlier, selected studies in espousing V-PIQ differences as evidence of the laterality of brain damage. However, the consistently negative findings in later studies of large samples of patients with acute as well as chronic lateralized lesions by Smith (1966a, 1966d, 1981a,b), Todd, Coolidge, and Satz (1977), and others cited by Lezak (1976), Walsh (1978), and Golden (1978), and the high incidence of V-PIQ differences of 10 or more points in normals clearly indicate that such differences are *not* a reliable index of either the presence or laterality of brain lesions.

The continuing controversial findings in studies comparing V-PIQs, individual subtests, and other psychological tests may seem puzzling. However, they reflect the confounding effects of several unwarranted assumptions and methodological errors described by Smith (1962a, 1962b, 1975, 1981b), and Parsons and Prigitano (1978) that are also illustrated in the controversial findings in studies reporting comparisons of organics versus functionals described below.

In describing his "psychologic laboratory tests," specifically designed for studies of patients with confirmed brain lesions, Goldstein observed, "The IQ in patients can be deceptive in either direction; it may lead one to assume too high or too low a grade of activity. Therefore, in cases of frontal-lobe lesion, all conclusions about the mental capacity based on the IQ are of very little value" (Goldstein, 1942, p. 97). Since 1951, findings in thousands of children and adults with diverse focal and diffuse brain insults tested with the Wechsler scales—which are now included in the Michigan Neuropsychological Battery (MNB)—have demonstrated that Goldstein's caution also applies to patients with lesions in other regions of the brain (Smith, 1975, 1981a).

With respect to differences in effects of focal and diffuse brain lesions on specific subtests, Wechsler's eventual discarding of his initial, organic subtest discrepancies (such as the Hewson ratios), disposed of the fond hopes that the Wechsler scales alone could accurately differentiate between organics and functionals (Smith, 1962b). Apparently, as Wechsler (1958) and Matarazzo (1972) have indicated, firm conclusions in such studies based on IQs or subtest discrepancies are unwarranted.

Does this mean that Wechsler's scales are "of very little value" and should be discarded for other, more economic tests in neuropsychological assessments of children and adults with suspected or confirmed brain damage? *Not at all!* When incorporated as part of a battery with other tests carefully selected according to well-defined rationales (Smith, 1975, 1979, 1981a), the Wechsler scales contribute significantly to differential-diagnostic studies of patients with suspected or unsuspected organic cerebral dysfunction, as well as to definition of the nature and severity of neuropsychologic deficits at the time of testing in patients with confirmed brain lesions.

In the past, numerous studies have reflected a primary focus on Wechsler V, P, and FS IQs. However, these aggregate scores often obscure possibly significant differences among the six verbal and five performance subtests that may be especially important in neuropsychological assessments. As noted above, the variabilities in subtest scores and in IQs are not reliable criteria for differential-diagnostic studies and for accurate definitions of the nature and severity of neuropsychological deficits in patients with confirmed insults. However, when supplemented with other, carefully selected tests, the significant contribution of scores in the 11 individual subtests to accurate diagnosis and to definitions of initial and later changes in specific neuropsychological sequelae in children and adults with hemispherectomy, commissurotomy, and diverse focal and diffuse brain insults are illustrated and variously documented in studies by Smith (1962b, 1972, 1975, 1981a,b) and especially in studies of long-term effects of commissurotomy (Campbell et al., 1981). It is therefore not surprising that, despite the considerable time required to administer the original Halstead tests alone, Reitan (1955, 1956) added the Wechsler scales to the Halstead-Reitan battery.

Hierarchy of cerebral functions and the Wechsler subtests

Since 1955, the present author's continuing studies of initial and later effects of hemispherectomy, commissurotomy, tumors, diverse focal (lateralized, bilateral) and diffuse brain lesions have increasingly indicated a consistent hierarchy in the development and preservation or recovery of the various higher (cognitive) functions following evolving and resolving brain insults in early and later life (Smith, 1972, 1978c, 1981a,b). Following early lateralized or diffuse damage to one or both cerebral

hemispheres—including entire removals of the left or right hemisphere—
the development of language and verbal functions generally takes prece-
dence over the development of nonverbal reasoning capacities (Smith,
1972).

Comparisons of cross-sectional samples used in the standardizations
of the Wechsler Adult Intelligence Scale (Wechsler, 1958) indicate normal
declines in each of the 11 subtests with advancing age. However, consistent with the pattern of greater development of language skills with advancing age, the decline of language and verbal reasoning skills (as
measured by Wechsler's verbal subtests, especially Vocabulary) is markedly slower and more limited than the decline in the nonverbal or performance subtests. Unlike the verbal subtests, all five performance subtests
are timed and involve visual-perceptual functions. Wechsler observed
that the earlier and more rapid decline with age of the Digit Symbol
rather than other intelligence tests "suggests that the older person may
be penalized by speed." However, he believed ". . . that the older person
is not only slower but also 'slowed up' mentally" (Wechsler, 1958, p.
81).

Similar analyses of cross-sectional samples used in the standardization
of the Coloured and of the Standard Progressive Matrices (Raven, 1960,
1965)—which are *untimed* tests of nonverbal, visual analogous-reasoning
capacities—reveal similarly normal and even greater declines with age
than those with the Digit Symbol and other Wechsler performance subtests.

It is therefore not surprising that our neuropsychological studies of
younger and older adults with diffuse encephalopathies (such as Alzheimer's and Pick's diseases; closed head injuries; toxic, anoxic, and infectious embarrassments of the brain) show a similar pattern of generally
greater preservation of language and verbal-cognitive rather than nonverbal-cognitive functions.

The Bender-Gestalt test

For clinical psychologists who were initially taught (and uncritically
accepted) repeated reports of the "wondrous efficiency" of the Bender-
Gestalt (BG) test as a sensitive, reliable, and valid test for the presence
or absence of organicity or brain damage, the accumulating findings
documenting its critical limitations for use in neuropsychological diagnostic studies (Benton, 1953; Smith, 1975; Lezak, 1976; Walsh, 1978; Golden, 1979) may be unsettling. All too frequently, the BG is included in
clinical psychological and diagnostic assessments as an infallible test for
the presence or absence of brain damage. In her recent text, *Neuropsychological Assessment,* Lezak also observed, "Unfortunately, it has not
been uncommon for some psychologists to think that a complete neuropsychological examination consists of the WAIS and one or two drawing

tests, usually the Bender-Gestalt and a Draw-A-Person test" (Lezak, 1976, p. 311). In patients subsequently referred to the present author, others have included the Rorschach, Thematic Apperception Test, and/or the Minnesota Multiphasic Personality Inventory (MMPI). Still others occasionally included specific tests that were designed for identifying the presence of brain damage, organicity, or organic brain syndrome, such as the Memory-for-Designs (Graham & Kendall, 1960), Visual Organization (Hooper, 1958), Goldstein-Scheerer (1941), or Weigl Sorting (Weigl, Goldstein, & Scheerer, 1951) tests.

As noted above, Korchin and Schuldberg (1981) have observed that the reluctance of clinical psychologists to relinquish old and familiar instruments—despite increasing evidence of their critical limitations for differential-diagnostic studies in children and adults with suspected brain damage—is understandable. The limitations of these also widely used tests for such purposes have been variously described by Smith (1975), Rathbun and Smith (1982), Lezak (1976), Walsh (1978) and Golden (1978, 1979) and cannot be reviewed here. However, a brief review of the controversial findings in studies using the BG may suffice to provoke considerations or recommendations of the criteria for evaluating the BG and other single tests or neuropsychological batteries—*as well as the rationale underlying the construction and/or selection of such tests or batteries for neuropsychological assessment.*

Reviewing continuing reports illustrating the widespread use of the BG by clinical psychologists and her own extensive personal experiences with this test, Lezak noted that, "Many kinds of brain pathology simply do not affect the specific functions involved in this visuographic exercise" (1976, p. 320). While a recent review by Lacks (1979) commended its usefulness in neuropsychological-diagnostic studies, the critical limitations of the BG for neuropsychodiagnostic purposes were illustrated in a prompt reply by Bigler and Ehrfurth presenting negative findings in five patients with documented, extensive cerebral lesions and severe, associated neurological disorders (which apparently did not encroach on any of the specific functions involved in BG performances). "Regardless of how the BG test is scored or analyzed, as a single measure or as an adjunct screening measure—even when used in conjunction with such tests as the WAIS, WISC, Rorschach or MMPI—its clinical use as a neurodiagnostic technique is specious, at best" (Bigler & Ehrfurth, 1980, p. 88). Perhaps the most striking example of the limitations of the Rorschach (as well as the BG) in neuropsychodiagnostic studies is the case reported by Bruell and Albee (1962) of studies of a 39-year-old man with right hemispherectomy for a malignant tumor. Blind analysis of the BG by an outstanding clinical psychologist with extensive experience (including development of an objective scoring system for the test) described a variety of affective disturbances, such as "mood swings with underlying aggression, distrust, some suspiciousness of the environment and . . .

obsessive-compulsive defenses seem to be no more efficient." Although *the entire right hemisphere* had been excised only four months before, and the patient—with a regrowth of the tumor—died shortly after testing, organicity was included in the blind analysis as only "a remote possibility" (Quoted by Bruell & Albee, 1962, p. 97).

These studies are not cited simply to suggest that the use of the BG as a neurodiagnostic test is, as Bigler and Ehrfurth concluded, "specious, at best." Far more important, these illustrative cases raise critical questions not only about the BG, but about all tests of organicity. What is the rationale underlying the selection of any single test or neuropsychological test battery for differential-diagnostic studies? What specific higher (verbal- and/or nonverbal-cognitive) and/or lower (specific sensory and motor) level cerebral functions are being assayed? What are the critical considerations and tacit or explicit assumptions in selecting a particular test or group of tests in psychological assessments of children and adults with confirmed brain insults and, especially, in diagnostic studies of patients with suspected "organicity?"

Other individual psychological tests and neuropsychological test batteries

The development of psychological tests and their gradual applications in differential-diagnostic studies of patients with suspected brain damage have been variously reviewed by Klebanoff (1945), Klebanoff, Singer and Wilensky (1954), Yates (1954), Burgermeister (1962), Smith, (1962a, 1962b, 1975), Lezak (1976), and Walsh (1978). Gradual recognition of the limitations of such tests for neuropsychological assessments of patients with confirmed (as well as suspected) brain insults prompted the construction of numerous individual tests specifically designed for detection of the presence of organicity or brain damage. As noted above, the introduction of batteries of such tests by Goldstein and Scheerer (1941), Goldstein (1942), and Halstead (1947) reflected continuing efforts to develop new and more effective techniques based on new theories and concepts of human brain functions.

In her book, *Psychological Techniques in Neurological Diagnosis,* Burgermeister (1962) reviewed the assets and limitations of the then-prevailing, diverse "psychological methods in diagnosing neurological disorders," including the controversial theories of brain functions and specific tests introduced by Goldstein (1942, 1948) and Halstead (1947). Since then, a rapidly swelling stream of texts by Luria (1963, 1966a, 1966b, 1973); Russell, Neuringer, and Goldstein (1970); Reitan and Davison (1974); Christensen (1975a, 1975b, 1975c); McFie (1975); Lezak (1976); Brown (1977); Dimond (1978); Golden (1978, 1979); Hecaen and Albert (1978); Walsh (1978); Heilman and Valenstein (1979); Williams (1979); Small (1980); Kolb and Whishaw (1980); and, most recently, a compendium of current testing techniques in the first *Handbook of Clinical Neuropsychology* (Filskov & Boll, 1981), reflected increasing proliferations of neurological and neuropsychological theories of human brain functions, as well as new tests based on the different theories.

Paradoxically, as noted above, in their review of the future of clinical assessment, Korchin and Schuldberg (1981) reported the marked decline of clinical testing by clinical psychologists during the same period.

"APPRAISING THE LITERATURE CORRECTLY": THE RATIONALE IN SELECTION AND CONSTRUCTION OF TESTS AND BATTERIES FOR NEUROPSYCHOLOGICAL ASSESSMENT

Over 2,000 years ago, long before the development of the printing press, Hippocrates (460–370 B.C.) observed, "An important phase of medicine is the ability to appraise the literature correctly." As Smith (1978a) noted, even if we could spend all of our waking hours reading, we still would not have time enough to keep up with the increasing flood of books and articles in the current neuropsychological literature. Clinical psychologists—interested in updating their clinical testing techniques and including the most economic and valid single test or groups of tests— will have special problems in assessing and reconciling the remarkable and controversial findings reported in studies by authors administering the same (or different) neuropsychological test batteries to diverse clinical populations.

The enormous literature cannot be reviewed here. In previous reviews of neuropsychological testing techniques, however, Smith (1975, 1981a) called attention to one criterion that is especially important in the selection of specific tests or batteries. Namely, what is the rationale underlying the construction of the particular test or battery? The critical importance of the rationale (or the tacit or explicit assumptions in selections of current individual tests or batteries used in neuropsychological assessments) was illustrated in the first review comparing the results of clinical neurological versus psychological test findings by Klebanoff (1945). Reflecting the prevailing views at the time, he wrote, "Only a cursory glance at the literature is needed to demonstrate the importance of the anterior regions of the cortex with reference to mental symptoms" (Klebanoff, 1945, p. 597). The special importance attributed to the frontal lobes was illustrated by his inclusion of 2 tables comparing the findings in 20 studies of effects of frontal trauma and in 19 other studies of frontal tumors reported between 1870 and 1939. Although Klebanoff noted the increasing interest by clinical psychologists in psychometric studies of brain-damaged patients, he observed, "Conventional methods are clung to despite repeated demonstrations of their inadequacies" (Klebanoff, 1945, p. 597). However, he also cited studies by Goldstein and by Halstead describing the development of new tests specially designed for definitions of the mental defects resulting from frontal lesions.

The Halstead-Reitan battery (HRB)

Two years later, Halstead (1947) reported a study of 207 patients (with cerebral lobectomies, lobotomies, and head injuries) and 30 controls. Based on extensive factor analyses and correlations of data of 27 "likely" but unstandardized tests, Halstead described four discrete factors which (when combined) comprised a brand new psychological dimension underlying all mental activity: namely, "biological intelligence." Consistent with the prevailing views on "the importance of the anterior regions of the cortex with reference to mental symptoms" (Klebanoff, 1945), Halstead claimed that although biological intelligence was represented throughout the cerebral cortex, its maximal representation and concentration was in the frontal lobes. He therefore selected the 10 tests in his study that were most sensitive (i.e., showed poorest performances) to the presence of lesions in the right, left, or both frontal lobes and weighted them to provide a quantitative measure of the degree of impairment of biological intelligence. He described the sum of the 10 weighted test scores as an "impairment index."

Subsequently, his student—Reitan—added the Wechsler Bellevue I intelligence scales in a comparison of psychometric versus biological intelligence in a validation study of the impairment index and of the biological intelligence as described by Halstead. With respect to the impairment index, Reitan reported, "There is probably no other measure of the psychological effects of brain damage for which such striking evidence of validity could be cited" (Reitan, 1955, p. 34). He also later described his findings as ". . . perfectly compatible with Halstead's factorial structure of biological intelligence" (Reitan, 1956, p. 541).

In a recent review, Boll (1981) cited a subsequent single-blind study of 102 patients with diverse brain insults by Reitan (1964) as an impressive demonstration of the sensitivity "and specific neurological diagnostic validity" of the Halstead-Reitan battery. The 102 patients included 64 with focal lesions, divided into groups of 16, each with lateralized lesions in the right and left frontal and posterior quadrants. The findings reported by Reitan indicated not only remarkable accuracy in identifying patients with diffuse as opposed to occult focal lateralized lesions and correct localizations of such lesions, but even more remarkably, correct identifications of the specific neuropathological processes generating the different types of lesions. Boll also quoted Reitan's conclusion that ". . . the small number of significant differences, however, was almost sufficient to make one who is especially faithful to our conventional statistical models ask if it must not have been extrasensory perception which was responsible . . . for the extraordinarily high, clinical hit rate obtained from these data" (Boll, 1981, p. 603).

Reitan's reported accuracy in diagnosis, localization, and identification of the specific neuropathological processes involved (which Boll attributed to "multiple inferential methods") is indeed remarkable; other aspects of the findings, however, are bemusing. For example, the basis for Halstead's selection of 10 of the 27 tests to comprise the impairment index was because of their greater sensitivity to the mental effects of lesions in the frontal lobes. Reitan reported that only 2 measures (performances with the preferred and nonpreferred hands) showed statistically significant differences between groups with lateralized lesions, while 30 other psychological variables failed to show appreciable differences between frontal and nonfrontal lesions in the right or left hemisphere. Thus, the findings in this study clearly contradicted the conclusions reported by Halstead (1947) as well as his concepts of biological intelligence and the impairment index he reported to be particularly sensitive to frontal-lobe lesions.

Perhaps an even more intriguing finding in this study is the absence of the systematic differences between right versus left-lesion groups in Wechsler V-PIQs, which, as noted above, Reitan continued to report for the past two decades (Reitan, 1954; Reitan and Davison, 1974).

Moreover, in contrast to the results reported by Reitan (1964), in a review of subsequent studies, Lezak reported, "Efforts to use the Halstead-Reitan battery for localizing lesions have had equivocal results" (Lezak, 1976, p. 443). While she cited two studies suggesting that the battery may show differences in test performances with left- and right-hemisphere lesions, she also listed two others indicating ". . . these right-left differences do not occur with sufficient consistency to warrant basing clinical decisions on the Halstead-Reitan test scores alone" (p. 443). Lezak also noted that accuracy in studies differentiating between organic and psychiatric patients with the HRB was actually lower than that reported in similar studies with single tests with the Bender-Gestalt or simply on the basis of WAIS scores alone.

Of special interest to the clinical psychologist is the study by Matthews, Shaw, and Klove (1966) indicating the limitations of the HRB in efforts to differentiate neurologic from pseudoneurologic patients. As these authors had been strongly committed to the HRB, the evidence of their scientific integrity in reporting findings that raise serious questions about the battery is especially noteworthy. They reported that, despite significant differences between the two groups in several individual measures comprising the HRB, "the use of any one of them to classify individuals remains a doubtful procedure" (p. 250) and, "Even the composite measure, the Impairment Index, was relatively inefficient as a 'yes' or 'no' discriminator."

The result of comparisons of MMPI clinical scales of the two groups in this study has conceivably important implications for clinical psychologists engaged in psychotherapy. "Emotional disturbances as reflected by average elevation of MMPI clinical scales, appeared to be as characteristic of the brain-damaged subjects as it was of the 'pseudoneurologic'

group, suggesting that the mere presence of MMPI evidence of psychopathology is not sufficient to distinguish between these broad categories
of disorders" (Matthews et al., 1966, p. 251). While this finding indicates
the limitations of the MMPI scales for differential-diagnostic studies of
such patients, it also adds weight to the earlier point about the need of
brain-damaged patients for psychotherapy. Finally, in contrast to the selected studies cited by Russell, Neuringer, and Goldstein (1970), Reitan
and Davison (1974), and Boll (1981), special studies by Watson, Thomas,
Anderson, and Felling (1968) raised serious questions about the claims
as well as the validity of the HRB in clinical applications. Eight highly
experienced and Reitan-trained examiners reported blind analyses of
HRB protocols of 24 organics and 24 schizophrenics. While 24 correct
classifications could be expected by pure chance, the mean number of
correct classifications of the eight judges was 25.5, range 20 to 28. However, using only the Wechsler subtest scores of the same patients, another
neuropsychologist correctly identified 30 of the 48 diagnoses. Thus, the
authors concluded, "Apparently the Reitan-Halstead tests are of little, if
any, value in separation of NP hospital organics from schizophrenics,
regardless of whether they are applied in actuarial or clinical fashion"
(Watson et al., 1968, p. 683).

While noting the wide use of the HRB, recent texts by Walsh (1978)
and by Kolb and Whishaw (1980) also cited several serious limitations
and criticisms of the construct validity of the battery. With respect to
the rationale underlying the construction and selection of tests, perhaps
the most telling criticism was leveled by Luria and Majovski, who pointed
out that "the battery lacks grounding in a theoretical formulation of the
brain's organization governing psychological processes affecting behavior" (Luria & Majovski, 1977, p. 961). Noting the development of com-
puter-axial tomography, they observed, "What this technique poses for
the future of neuropsychologists using the Halstead-Reitan battery is how
to go about the systematic study of different kinds of behavior involved
in brain-behavior disturbances without a working theory or a conceptual
scheme of the functional organization of the brain" (Luria & Majovski,
1977, p. 962). Apparently, these authors were either unaware of or rejected the working theory Halstead (1947) used in selection of his tests.
Interestingly, although differing from those of Goldstein and Halstead,
Luria's working theory also described the frontal lobes as playing a critical
role in "higher cortical functions" (Luria, 1966a).

Luria's theories and the Luria-Nebraska battery (L-N)

Korchin and Schuldberg (1981) cited the Luria-Nebraska (L-N)
(Golden, 1981) as the second most widely used neuropsychological battery in this country. However, it was developed only three years ago,

based on the theories of Luria (1966a, 1966b, 1973) and an earlier battery of his tests constructed after consultations and Luria's approval by Christensen (1975a, 1975b, 1975c). In the three years since it was constructed, an astounding number of initial, multiauthored published reports by Golden and his colleagues have described even greater accuracy in diagnosing and localizing diverse types of occult focal and diffuse brain lesions with the L-N than the remarkable accuracy with the HRB initially reported by Reitan (1964). As noted above, Reitan's ability to localize focal lateralized lesions in the frontal and posterior regions of the left and right hemisphere was cited as evidence of the validity and sensitivity of the HRB. Golden (1981), however, reported even more-accurate diagnoses and precise localizations of similarly diverse focal and diffuse lesions in the frontal area, sensory motor area, temporal lobe, and occipital-parietal lobe of each hemisphere with the L-N (Golden, 1981).

The rationale underlying the organization of the first Luria battery of clinical nonstandardized tests by Christensen (1975a, 1975b, 1975c) and the different quantified, standardized version by Golden (1981) was based on assumptions of the scientific validity of Luria's theories and speculations, or in his words, ". . . conceptual scheme of the functional organization of the brain." For Golden, ". . . belief in Luria's procedures depends not so much on observable evidence, but on a trust in Luria's impressive skills. The adoption of procedures based *simply on trust* runs contrary to the psychometric tradition so prominent in American psychology" (Golden, 1981, p. 609, [italics added]). As noted above, Golden (1981) reported greater accuracy not only in diagnosis and more precise localization of focal lesions, but also in differentiations of patients with functional versus organic disorders with the L-N than in those reported for the HRB. It might appear, therefore, that his sanguine "belief" and "trust" in Luria's speculations were not misplaced. Reitan (1976) had criticized Luria's tests, observing that instead of objective studies by disinterested investigators, the only measure of their reliability and validity was Luria's opinion. In answer to this criticism, Golden (1981) could have cited the remarkable accuracy in diagnosis and precise localization of diverse occult focal lesions in several studies he and his colleagues have reported. Of far greater importance than the mutual recriminations, the results of these studies apparently provide seemingly compelling evidence of the validity of Luria's—until now—unverified theories and speculations.

In view of the glittering promise of the L-N indicated in the recent prolific publications by Golden and his colleagues, the uncritical acceptance and use of this battery by some clinical psychologists and neuropsychologists (who have long been hoping and searching for some marvelous breakthrough that would provide an economic sensitive and valid single test or group of tests for neuropsychological assessment) is understandable. However, one should be cautious, in light of the obvious inadequacies of earlier psychometric batteries and single tests of organicity described above, as well as the numerous reports by Reitan and his colleagues describing similarly remarkable accuracy in diagnosis and localization of cerebral lesions which were cited as evidence of the validity of Halstead's theories and led to the earlier similarly uncritical acceptance, use, and promotion of the HRB for neuropsychological assessments.

Almost a century ago, Goltz made the melancholy observation, "*The research into the functions of the various parts of the brain is a very old question. Many have tried and many have erred*" (Goltz, 1888, trans. von Bonin, 1960, p. 130).

The rationale underlying the organization of the first Luria battery of nonquantified clinical tests by Christensen (1975a, 1975b, 1975c) in consultation with Luria, and the standardized, quantified version developed from that battery into the L-N by Golden (1981) is based on Luria's attempts to define the roles of different parts of the brain in different functions (Luria 1966a, 1966b, 1973). According to Luria, human brain functions are products of a complex of different discrete, functional systems that are variously linked and integrated to provide the specific cerebral mechanisms underlying the wide spectra of higher (cognitive) and lower (sensory and motor) human performances. He postulated that such complex functional systems as those involved in mental functions ". . . cannot be localized in narrow zones of the cortex, but must be *organized in systems of concertedly working zones, each of which performs its role in [a] complex functional system,* and which may be located in completely different and often far-distant areas of the brain" (Luria, 1973, p. 31). While all functional systems therefore consist of multiple component subsystems (or neural) elements, those same components may also participate in other functional systems to varying degrees.

Interestingly, this same view had been set forth by Gowers, who noted that combinations of neurons subserving a given function may also serve in a multiplicity of other functions, in which they may participate to different degrees. Although Gowers used the term *center* (explicitly in a physiological and not a topographical sense) instead of functional system, he also noted the cerebral mechanisms mediating a given complex of functions "may consist of elements that are anatomically distant—even situated in different hemispheres" (Gowers, 1885, pp. 4–5).

Luria, therefore, rejected the concept of narrow cortical zones in which specific functions are localized. However, based on his clinical studies of different symptoms resulting from variously situated lateralized lesions, he divided each of the two great cerebral hemispheres into four different, symmetrically distributed regions, in each of which the variously linked but discrete functional systems were maximally represented. Thus, in cases with focal lateralized lesions in one of the four zones in either the left or right cerebral hemisphere, the nature and severity of specific neuropsychological deficits reflect the extent to which the different functional systems are represented in the region of the area destroyed. Conversely, the specific pattern of deficits elicited by Luria's tests (and, presumably, the L-N battery) permit not only the detection of brain damage but also the accurate lateralization and localization of focal lesions in one of the four regions of the right or left hemisphere. Essentially, therefore, Luria's revision of the concept of localization appears to be little more than an expansion of earlier concepts of punctate (or more focal) localization of specific functions to regional localization.

Hit rate for accurate detection in comparison of brain-damaged and nonbrain-damaged subjects with the L-N was reported to be 93 percent (Golden, Hammeke, & Purisch, 1978); for lateralization of lesions, 98 percent (Osman, Golden, Purisch, Hammeke, & Blume, 1979); and for accurate localization of lesions, 88 percent (McKay & Golden, 1979). Golden also reported that, in contrast to generally chance levels in efforts to discriminate between chronic schizophrenics and brain-damaged groups using other tests and batteries, the L-N scales ". . . were able to discriminate 92 percent of the schizophrenic group and 84 percent of the neurological group to yield an overall hit rate of 88 percent. This result is significantly higher than any result with a comparable population in the published literature" (Golden, 1981, p. 623). As noted above, Reitan and others invested in the HRB have sharply criticized the findings reported by Golden and his colleagues, the rationale and validity of the L-N, as well as the assumptions, theories, and clinical studies of Luria (Reitan, 1976; Adams, 1980a, 1980b, Spiers, 1981).

Luria was unquestionably a persuasive, eloquent, and prolific writer with a lively, creative, imagination, and his rich, theoretical speculations and interpretations of his clinical observations are stimulating and highly provocative. However, while current texts on neurology and neuropsychology reviewing the numerous prevailing theories of human brain functions include Luria's theories, there has been no more evidence indicating the scientific validity of his theories than that following the theories of Halstead or the rationale underlying the HRB.

In contrast to the uncritical acceptance and assumptions of scientific validity of Luria's unconfirmed theories by Christensen and Golden, Teuber (1966) described Luria's claims as "bold generalizations." Based on the results of long-term studies (including personal efforts and efforts by others to test some of his claims), the present author would describe the varying formulations of Luria's theories as extravagant overinterpretations and speculations. It is interesting to note that the first three neuropsychological batteries developed by Goldstein, Halstead, and Luria were based on earlier preoccupations and theories emphasizing a special and unique role of the frontal lobes in mental functions. For example, Goldstein cited impairment of the "abstract attitudes" as a characteristic mental defect—more frequent in patients with frontal (especially left) than nonfrontal lesions. Halstead claimed that his new psychological dimension underlying all mental processes was not only concentrated and uniformly distributed in *both* frontal lobes; he also described them as "the organs of civilization—the basis of man's despair and of his hope for the future." Luria's theories were only slightly less extravagant: ". . . *the frontal lobes synthesize the information about the outside world received through exteroceptors and the information about the internal states of the body* and that *they are the means whereby the behavior of the organism is regulated in conformity with the effect produced by its actions"* (Luria, 1966a, p. 233).

This theory was subsequently amplified and modified, with the frontal cortex being later described as "an apparatus maximally adapted to receiving proprioceptive and interoceptive impulses to regulate the state of the several levels of reflex activity, and to undertake the programming and regulation of complex forms of activity" (Luria, 1969, pp. 728–729). Still later, the frontal lobes are described as "tertiary zones for the limbic system on the one hand and for the motor cortex on the other hand . . ." and as important ". . . in the regulation of vigilance and in the control of the most complex forms of man's goal-linked activity" (Luria, 1973, pp. 187–188). Also, the frontal lobes ". . . participate in the regulation of the activation processes lying at the basis of voluntary attention" (Luria, 1973, p. 188); they ". . . *constitute the cortical apparatus regulating the state of activity* and that they thus play a decisive role in the maintenance of one of the most important conditions of *human conscious activity*—the *maintenance of the required cortical tone and modification of the state of waking in accordance with the subject's immediate tasks"* (Luria, 1973, p. 197).

Based on his subjective clinical assessments, Luria also reported that the patient with a frontal-lobe lesion (apparently regardless of laterality) has profound difficulties "when he attempts to understand the meaning of a series of pictures depicting the stages of a story" (1966a, p. 273). With his usual eloquence, he also described the serial-sevens subtraction test as an important neurological test that demonstrated specific error patterns reflecting mental disturbances unique to patients with frontal-lobe lesions. "This test makes particularly high demands on the mobility of the nervous processes at the level of the second signal system. Having done the subtraction, the patient must immediately convert the difference into the starting point for further subtraction and repeat this process over and over again. All these operations must be carried out by memory traces, with constant carrying over from tens to units and intermediate breaking down of numbers, addition of remainders, and so on" (Luria, 1966a, p. 438). He described various error patterns—simplification of the mental operations involved; fragmentation of those operations; substitutions of stereotyped responses such as 100–93–83–73–63, etc.; or aban-

donment of the task completely—as evidence of specific intellectual disturbances unique to patients with frontal lesions.

Interestingly, some of the same error patterns Luria described as characteristic of frontal-lobe lesions in adults were identical with those previously described by Hayman (1942) in normal 8- to 15-year-old children
as well as in adults with diverse psychiatric disorders.

However gradually, reality eventually overtakes rhetoric. Administration of the serial-sevens test to 132 normal adults with above-average
education and socioeconomic status (and including neurologists, psychiatrists, psychologists, and social workers) revealed correct successive sub-
tractions by only 56 (42.4 percent). Of the remaining 76, the error patterns
described as pathognomonic in adults with frontal lesions by Luria and
in others with psychiatric disorders were present in 16 (21.1 percent)
or 12.1 percent of the total population (Smith, 1967).

As the Wechsler Picture Arrangement (PA) subtest taps ability "to understand the meaning of a series of pictures depicting the stages of a
story," the present author also compared weighted scores on this subtest
in 170 adults with verified brain tumors (consisting of 46 with right, left,
or bilateral pre-rolandic or frontal tumors, 40 with overlapping tumors,
and 84 with post-rolandic tumors) tested with the Wechsler scales shortly
before or after surgery. In contrast to Luria's conclusions based on his
clinical observations, the mean weighted PA scores of the 46 frontals
(6.4) exceeded those of the 40 with overlapping tumors (6.0) and showed
the lowest mean value for the 84 with post-rolandic tumors (5.7) (Smith,
1967).

In an investigation of Luria's hypothesis on the nature of frontal-lobe
mental deficits, Drewe (1975) compared 24 patients with lateralized-fron-
tal versus 24 with nonfrontal lesions. His findings differed from those
reported by Luria and also showed no evidence that the type of mental
deficits conformed with Luria's hypothesis.

Reviews of Luria's theories in recent neurological texts (Hecaen & Albert, 1978; Damasio, 1979) noted the absence of normal controls and
of comparisons of patients with frontal and nonfrontal lesions, as well
as the confounding effects of associated pathophysiological reactions in
many of his cases with massive bilateral-frontal tumors that probably extended beyond the frontal lobes (both in depth and on the cortical surface). Moreover, his hypothesis and conclusions were also based on
purely qualitative or subjective assessments rather than objective tests.
As Damasio observed, "The limits of studies performed under such unsatisfactory methods are obvious" (1979, p. 385).

While Luria formulated and expressed his theories in an incisive and
forceful style, some of them were apparently contradictory or underwent
drastic revisions. For example, on the role of the right hemisphere in
mental functions and speech, he first cited studies supporting the view

that, "both hemispheres participate jointly in the performance of complex mental functions (including speech); . . . the higher mental functions, including speech, result from the combined activity of both cerebral hemispheres, with each making its own, though not equal, contribution" (Luria, 1966a, pp. 87–89).

Seven years later, he cited subsequent studies of hemispherectomy by Smith (1966c, 1969; Smith & Burklund, 1966) and studies of commissurotomy as confirming the view that, "any complex mental function is *effected by* the combined activity of both hemispheres, but that each makes its own particular contribution to the construction of mental processes" [italics added]. However, he goes on to describe one of the "facts" regarding the functions of the right hemispheres as ". . . firmly established . . . discovered long ago and there is no question about its validity." Namely, ". . . the nondominant (right) hemisphere, despite its complete symmetry with the left, plays no part in the organization of speech activity . . . The nondominant hemisphere naturally can neither perform complex speech and intellectual functions, nor even participate in the construction of complex motor acts" (Luria, 1973, p. 163).

Luria's claims on the cerebral roles of the frontal lobes in higher mental functions were based on his subjective clinical observations, and his illustrative cases included patients with left, right, or bilateral frontal tumors. However, his conclusions based on such cases were incompatible with those of many earlier neurologists, including equally eminent students of human brain functions. For example, clinical studies by Jackson (1874), Phelps (1897), Dana (1915), Goldstein and Gelb (1918), Dew (1922), Papez (1929), Worster-Drought (1931), German and Fox (1934), Busch (1940), and Goldstein (1948) of the effects of tumors and other focal brain lesions led to the common conclusion that left-frontal lesions had resulted in more frequent and marked mental impairment than similar lesions in the right-frontal or other regions of the brain.

With respect to similar studies using psychological tests, Teuber (1964) cited earlier reports by Rylander (1939, 1943) and Halstead (1947) of maximal intellectual deficits in patients with left- and/or right-frontal tumors. However, in support of his conclusion that frontal lesions have *less* effect on "test intelligence" than nonfrontal lesions, Teuber called attention to studies by Pollack (1955), and Battersby, Krieger, and Bender (1955) reporting greater intellectual impairment in groups with nonfrontal rather than frontal lesions.

Other studies of the initial and later effects of carefully designed bilateral-frontal psychosurgical lesions (Smith & Kinder, 1959; Smith, 1960, 1964) and comparisons of Wechsler intelligence tests of patients with left- versus right-frontal tumors (Smith, 1966b) and other focal-lateralized lesions (Zubrick & Smith, 1978) also failed to support Luria's theories. Instead, with respect to comparisons of left- versus right-frontal lesions, they revealed significantly greater impairment of both verbal *and* nonverbal cognitive functions in patients with left- than right-frontal lesions (Smith, 1966c), as initially reported by Jackson (1874), and subsequently by many others cited above.

Golden noted that his uncritical acceptance of Luria's theories and procedures, "based simply on trust runs contrary to the psychometric tradition so prominent in this country" (Golden, 1981, p. 609). However, as indicated in the studies cited above, Luria's theories and conclusions also run contrary to the findings in similar clinical studies by earlier neurologists as well as the findings based on standardized and objective tests of mental functions.

It is, therefore, not surprising that in contrast to the remarkable accuracy in diagnosis and localization of brain lesions in studies cited by Golden (1981), a recent study of 35 patients with verified brain lesions and 18 normal controls tested with the L-N scales reported less-impressive findings. In fact, Brown, Adams, Rourke, Mehta, and Daly (1981) reported that, when all the L-N scales were considered, the results failed to confirm the hypothesis that the brain-damaged patients would perform significantly more poorly than the normal controls.

The similarly recent rapid development and application of various test batteries for diagnosis of learning disabilities has prompted an observation that is also relevant in evaluation of current neuropsychodiagnosis techniques: ". . . The lack of scientific foundation for the learning disabilities battery, in contrast to ubiquitous recommendations for its use, forces the observation that by replacing science with assertion, analysis with alchemy, and modesty with hyperbole, the learning disabilities battery appears to have sprung full-formed out of the heads of learning disabilities professionals like Athena out of Zeus" (Coles, 1978, p. 319).

Quo Vadis?

Recently, Smith (1981a) observed,

> As in many new disciplines, the current teachings and textbooks of clinical neuropsychology are often uncritically accepted by students. The opinions or conclusions of selected authorities are accepted as facts, and the persisting diverse and often conflicting findings reflecting unresolved historical controversies are ignored (p. 219).

One of the reasons cited by Korchin and Schuldberg for the steady, marked decline in testing by clinical psychologists was, "Psychodiagnosis was initially oversold as well as clothed in an oracular mysticism. Disappointment was bound to follow as negative research results accumulated that failed to support many of the claims of the testers" (1981, p. 1149). In view of the extravagant initial (but later unsubstantiated) claims of Reitan and Golden and their followers, what is past for clinical psychological testing may well be prologue for the future of the HRB and L-N batteries for the same reasons. However, this does not imply a similar fate for the future development of more economic and valid techniques of neuropsychological assessment.

The almost explosive development of the "subspecialty called neuropsychology" (Korchin & Schuldberg, 1981) was not a result of the development of the HRB and the L-N. Quite the opposite: it was the growing realization of the critical need for the development of economic, standardized and objective techniques of neuropsychological testing that prompted the development of these two and other batteries and single neuropsychological tests. Economy precludes even brief reviews of the Michigan Neuropsychological Battery (Smith, 1975, 1981), the Montreal Neurological Institute Battery (Kolb & Whishaw, 1980) or other of the many single or groups of tests currently being used by clinical psychologists and neuropsychologists in diagnostic studies of children and adults with suspected brain damage and in neuropsychological assessments of others with confirmed brain insults. Apart from their obviously important, practical clinical contributions in such studies, increasing refinements in neuropsychological testing are also essential for the continuing elucidation of principles underlying the organization, disorganization, and reorganization of human brain functions reflected in studies of children and adults with insults incurred at different stages in cerebral maturation. They are also critically important to the clinical psychologist in considerations of the problems of treatment of the affective—as well as cognitive and other neuropsychological—disorders in brain-damaged children and adults. The growing appreciation of the important role of the clinical psychologist in neuropsychodiagnosis as well as treatment of brain-damaged children and adults is reflected in the recent successive editions of *Neuropsychodiagnosis in Psychotherapy* by Small (1973, 1980).

As noted above, almost all patients referred to clinical psychologists present with various types and degrees of emotional disturbances. However, many of the same disturbances are also present in children with suspected and unsuspected underlying brain insults. It is, therefore, first important to differentiate patients with underlying organic disorders from others with functional or psychogenic disorders. Moreover, in patients with underlying brain damage amenable to psychotherapy, it is also necessary to further differentiate those emotional disturbances that are due to the patient's reactions to the various cognitive, sensory, and motor defects from associated affective disorders that are organically determined. (The present author's experiences indicate that this is far easier said than done. Repeated neuropsychological studies have shown that therapeutic intervention—especially in children—may result in a significant decrease in the severity of persisting "hard" neuropsychological symptoms—such as specific cognitive, sensory, and/or motor deficits—with gradual diminution of associated affective disturbances).

For psychologists working in mental hygiene or psychiatric settings, the problems of neuropsychodiagnosis are often even further compounded by the fluctuating effects of recently emerging or long-standing affective disorders and/or of differently prescribed psychotropic drugs on the specific tests used. Moreover, as has been previously observed, as psychiatric disorders do not confer immunity from neurological diseases, it is also often difficult to distinguish between the fluctuations of symptoms common in patients with psychiatric disorders from those that gradually emerge as a result of slowly or rapidly developing neoplastic, vascular, and other naturally occurring diseases of the brain to which we are all subject.

Often, the questions prompting referrals of children and adults with relatively innocuous to severe affective or behavioral disturbances are posed in the form of a mutually exclusive dichotomy. "Are the patient's presenting symptoms due to an underlying functional or psychogenic disorder or are they organic in etiology—due to some occult neuropathologic process?" Like many others long ago and some even today, the present author was taught that the severe affective disturbances in patients with chronic schizophrenia and other psychiatric classifications of psychosis were functional disorders. Not surprisingly, therefore, in addition to the selected studies with the HRB and L-N, psychologists and neuropsychologists have attempted to demonstrate the sensitivity and validity of specific batteries or individual tests of organicity in comparsions of performances of groups with diagnoses of psychiatric disorders with those of groups diagnosed as organics. While the persisting assumptions and findings in recent studies bear on historical controversies on the etiology of schizophrenia and other chronic grave psychoses, they also provide contexts for clinical psychologists for "appraising the literature" and for evaluating the reliability and validity of the diverse findings reported with different tests.

COMPARISONS OF FUNCTIONAL PSYCHIATRIC VERSUS ORGANIC PATIENTS

In a recent review, Heaton and Crowley reported, "Among studies published between 1960 and 1978, we found 132 attempts to use neuropsychological tests to distinguish between organics and functional patients." They concluded that when "chronic/process" schizophrenics were excluded, "the median correct-classification rate for attempts involving all other psychiatric groups compares favorably with the diagnostic accuracy achieved by tests with organics and nonpsychiatric controls" (Heaton & Crowley, 1981, p. 516). In assessing the diverse and inconsistent findings, they also called attention to many methodological errors in such studies. Not surprisingly, many of these errors and unwarranted assumptions are also evident in other studies reporting remarkable accuracy (or lack of accuracy) of single tests or neuropsychological batteries in diagnosis, lateralization, and even precise localization and identification of the type of focal and diffuse brain damage cited above. As Smith (1962a, 1962b, 1975, 1979, 1981a,b) has also noted, although the diverse and paradoxical findings in studies of effects of focal-lateralized and diffuse brain insults also reflect similar methodological errors and unwarranted assumptions, the seemingly paradoxical findings in many such studies may be reconciled when such errors and assumptions are taken into account. For example:

1.   Smith (1981) has called attention to a widespread, tacit assumption in comparisons of psychological and neuropsychological test performances of patients with diagnoses of functional psychotic and nonpsychotic psychiatric or affective disorders versus others diagnosed as organics. Namely, ". . . that the various classifications of schizophrenia (e.g., simple, hebephrenic, paranoid, process, reactive) and other severe psychiatric disorders are psychogenic (*or nonorganic*) in etiology, and that the central nervous system is structurally and biochemically normal" (Smith, 1981a, p. 188). In addition to those cited by Heaton & Crowley (1981), numerous other studies of patients with diagnoses of various types of schizophrenia and other prevailing classifications of psychiatric disorders have demonstrated compelling evidence of organic cerebral dysfunction or brain damage in clinical neurological examinations; regional cerebral bloodflow studies; CAT scans, pneumoencephalographic, and other neuroradiological studies; EEG's, neurohistologic, and neuropathologic studies of children and adults described as functionals in comparisons with others described as brain damaged or organics. Although the incidence of reported positive organic findings in such functionals varied according to the psychiatric labels attached (as Heaton and Crowley observed), it was higher in those diagnosed as schizophrenics. Thus, it is not surprising that—*apparently regardless of the nature of the tests used*—the percentages of correct classifications *according to diagnosis* of functionals versus organics in the studies reviewed by Heaton and Crowley systematically decreased as the proportion of schizophrenics in the functional samples increased, with the lowest percentage (54 percent—or chance levels) in comparisons of chronic/process schizophrenics versus organics.

Moreover, as Walsh (1978) has emphasized, the absence of positive evidence in neurological diagnostic studies *cannot be cited as positive evidence of the absence of organic cerebral dysfunction.* As Smith (1975, 1981a,b) has observed, and as illustrated in the earlier studies of Tissenbaum, Harter, and Friedman (1951), many patients may initially manifest or undergo treatment for affective disorders that emerge in the early stages and mask the gradual develoment of insidious neuropathologic processes which may not be detectable for many years later—in some cases, until autopsy.

2.   Paralleling the unwarranted assumptions that patients with diverse

psychiatric disturbances constitute a homogeneous population of non-brain-damaged functionals in comparisons with organics, we may also ask, "What is an organic?"

In support of the claims of the validity and remarkable accuracy in diagnosis, lateralization, and precise localization of focal lesions by various tests, numerous studies have reported comparisons of brain-damaged or organic patients with normals as well as with pseudoneurologic and psychiatric patients. However, the brain-damaged patients, in most such studies, have consisted of varying proportions with traumatic, vascular, neoplastic, congenital, metabolic, toxic, or other early or more recently incurred embarrassments of the brain, including cases with epilepsy of unspecified origins.

As illustrated in documented cases with follow-up studies reported by Smith (1981a,b), the demonstrable effects of the diverse types of brain insults in single studies administered at varying stages in the course of evolving and resolving lesions will vary as a function of the nature of the specific tests. However, the results obtained with any test will also vary as a function of the specific nature, locus, and extent of the underlying lesion, its momentum and dynamics, the age of the patient, the extent to which the specific tests used are sensitive to education and sex differences, *and especially, the particular time in the course of varying evolving and resolving lesions when the patient is tested.*

3. Neuropsychological assessments focus primarily on definitions of the nature and degree of impairment of verbal and nonverbal cognitive and memory functions. However, the critical significance of the status of the modalities involved in perceptions of and in response to tests designed or assumed to measure such functions is often overlooked. In the overwhelming majority of cases, the initial neuropsychological sequelae of resolving brain lesions include varying degrees of overt and convert impairments of sensory, motor, and language (as well as nonlanguage) cognitive functions. The rate and degree of recovery of the various initial neuropsychological sequelae, however, depend on the nature, locus and extent of the underlying lesion, time, age, and other factors cited above. A moment's consideration will suffice to show that subnormal performances in cognitive tests may reflect impairments of the modalities involved in perceptions of and responses to the tests, rather than impairment of the higher verbal or nonverbal cognitive functions the tests were assumed to measure. Moreover, the documented cases in follow-up studies reported by Smith (1981a,b) and Campbell et al. (1981) also demonstrate that the impairments of lower-level sensory and motor functions are more reliable indices of the laterality and even of localization than impairment of verbal and nonverbal cognitive functions.

For example, as Walsh (1978) has pointed out, the presence of a right or left homonymous hemianopia provides more direct and reliable evidence of the presence of a lesion in the posterior region of the contralateral hemisphere. Similarly, in cases with apparent left or right hemipare-sis, the hit rate with respect to the presence and laterality of brain damage by any clinical psychologist without even formal testing would rival and probably exceed even the highest percentages reported in validation studies cited above; and the presence of aphasia—with or without associ-ated right hemiparesis—would yield even higher accuracy in lateralization and localization of lesions in the language zone of the left hemisphere.

In psychiatric diagnostic categories, the classification of Organic Brain Syndrome (OBS) has often been used to indicate the presence of varying degrees and types of damage to the brain. In fact, this diagnosis had also been applied to a 44-year-old man after his entire right hemisphere had been removed because of a malignant tumor (Smith, 1972). More-over, the diagnosis of OBS provides no information of the severity of mental impairment and of associated sensory and motor deficits as well as the nature and extent of the underlying neuropathologic anatomy. It is therefore obvious that the varying hit rates for the different psychological tests reviewed by Spreen and Benton (1965) and in subsequent validation studies cited by Heaton and Crowley (1981) may reflect more critical differences in the clinical populations studied than in the validity and sensitivity of the tests used.

SUGGESTED CONTEXTS AND GUIDELINES FOR EVALUATING NEUROPSYCHOLOGICAL TESTS

In a review of experimental studies of the neural bases of learning, Morrell concluded,

> We have surveyed a field in the throes of almost frenetic experimental activity. Development has been so rapid that there has been little time for stock taking. There are so many things to do, so many facts to gather, so many experiments to be confirmed or which require additional controls that, for the moment, it seems wiser to be wary of far reaching conclusions. Much more has been discovered of what has to be learned than has emerged as fairly established knowledge. (1961, p. 483)

In view of the even more rapid proliferation of theories of human brain functions and the spawning of new individual tests and batteries based on attractive but unverified speculations, the problems of clinical psycholo-gists in evaluating the claims of their remarkable accuracy in diagnosis and localization of brain insults are even more formidable.

"But, doctor, the patient is knocking at my door now!" In efforts to include more refined psychological tests of organicity in initial clinical assessments, some clinical psychologists with little or no previous formal training or experience in neuropsychological assessments have/invested in occasional three- to four-day workshops with the Halstead-Reitan, Luria-Nebraska, or other neuropsychological batteries. Such workshops may

be helpful. However, the chances for acquiring the minimum required neuropsychological skills in one or two such wokshops would probably be comparable to those of experimental or physiological psychologists with no previous training or experience in clinical psychology to practice psychotherapy after one or two similar workshops on specific psychotherapeutic techniques.

This does not mean, however, that there are no current useful psychological tests for detection of brain damage that can readily be incorporated and contribute significantly to the efficacy of diagnostic test batteries used by clinical psychologists. As noted, above, the Wechsler intelligence scales do not provide adequate data or evidence for determining the presence or absence of lateralized or diffuse brain damage. While Wechsler IQs are also of little value for such purposes, each of the 11 subtests provides measures of different abilities that are variously vulnerable to the effects of focal and diffuse brain insults. Thus, when incorporated into a battery of other tests selected according to a definite rationale, the individual subtest scores contribute significant evidence for accurate determination of the presence or absence of brain damage and also to definitions of the nature and degree of impairments in specific mental (as well as sensory and motor) functions (Smith, 1975, 1981a,b; Campbell, Bogen, and Smith, 1981; Rathbun & Smith, 1982). Since the Wechsler scales are reportedly the most widely used measures in clinical psychological and neuropsychological assessments, the underlying rationale and criteria for selection of other psychologcial tests for brain damage are of conceivable interest.

The concept of brain damage as a unitary disorder in a single psychological test function

As noted above, the use of Bender-Gestalt, Hooper Visual Organization, and other single tests of organicity is predicated on the assumption that the specific functions involved in such measures are always (or almost always) impaired by any and all kinds of organic brain pathology. Thus, as in the review of the reported efficacy of different individual or groups of tests by Spreen and Benton (1965), the absence of considerations of the specific locus, nature, dynamics, age, and extent of the lesion suggest that these factors apparently have no effect on the specific functions being tapped by the various tests. Essentially, therefore, such tests reflect the basic assumption of brain damage as a unitary disorder and earlier, outmoded concepts suggesting equipotentiality of all areas of the brain with respect to the specific functions being tapped.

By contrast, the development of the HRB and L-N batteries reflected subsequent but equally outmoded concepts of the localization of biological intelligence by Halstead (1947) or higher mental functions by Luria (1966a, 1966b, 1973) in the frontal lobes, and of other specific language and nonlanguage cognitive, sensory, and motor functions in different regions of the two cerebral hemispheres. Thus, the construction of single tests of organicity or brain damage was based on the rationale of general defects regardless of the specific locus of the lesion, whereas the construction of the HRB and L-N batteries was based on the rationale of specific defects, or impairment of selected functions resulting from destruction of specific areas in either hemisphere in which those functions were either maximally represented or localized.

General versus specific defects

As described previously (Smith, 1975, 1981a; Rathbun & Smith, (1982), the concepts of general versus specific deficits of focal and diffuse brain insults evolved as a result of studies of effects of concealed brain tumors in the 19th century before the development of neurosurgery. Accumulating findings in retrospective studies of patients with verified brain tumors (usually at autopsy) eventually revealed the development of a triad of symptoms (headache, vomiting, and papilledema) that were common and came to be considered as positive diagnostic signs of the presence of a tumor somewhere in the brain. Unlike the frequently associated various specific defects (such as impairments of language, sensory, motor, and visuospatial functions), the triad of symptoms provided no evidence of its specific locus. They, therefore, came to be considered *general* defects. (Subsequently, these symptoms were discovered to be due to increased intracranial pressure resulting from not only tumors but also from other affections of the brain causing increased pressure.)

The locus of the tumor in different parts of the brain, however, was often reflected by other, associated symptoms that emerged at different (often earlier) stages of its development. These varying and less-frequent symptoms were therefore recognized as *specific* defects. Thus, the distinction between general (nonlocalizing) defects and specific defects (indicating embarrassments of cortical regions in either the left or right hemisphere) contributed to increasing accuracy in diagnosis and localization of concealed intracranial lesions.

In light of the continuing subsequent, remarkable increase in accuracy of diagnosis and localization of such lesions by CAT scan and other neurological diagnostic techniques, the implications of this historical tidbit may seem to be academic. However, it also provides an important model and criteria for definitions of the specific or general nature of defects revealed by the various tests of brain damage. More immediately relevant, it also provides criteria for evaluations of the rationales of current tests of organicity and bases for selections of certain tests of general and specific defects to complement the Wechsler scales in routine screening examinations by clinical psychologists.

For example, the rationale for the development of the Symbol Digit

Modalities Test (SDMT) (Smith, 1968, 1973) as an economic neuropsycho-diagnostic test was based on fundamental neuropsychological principles that also underlie the construction and development of the Michigan Neuropsychological Test Battery (Smith, 1975).

1. Since premorbid measures of patients with suspected or confirmed cerebral lesions are usually lacking, the tests should include standardized and objective measures of a broad range of language, verbal, and nonverbal reasoning, and auditory and visual memory functions.

2. Tests should be selected *that permit differentiation of the sensory and motor modalities involved in perception and execution of the task* (or lower-level cerebral functions) *from the mental or cognitive processes* (higher-level cerebral functions) *they were designed to measure.*

Test batteries selected according to these criteria would thus include measures of the same or similar mental functions involving different modalities and of different mental functions involving the same modalities. The SDMT is an example of a test of the same mental functions using different modalities. (Smith, 1975, p. 87)

This simple substitution test requires the subject to substitute numbers for geometric symbols—first in writing the responses—and then in speaking the responses, which the examiner records. Since the same task is performed with both written and spoken responses, comparisons of the two performances reflect the status of the two different response modalities. Although written and oral substitutions are simple responses, they are the end products of the integration of many complex neurophysiological processes underlying visual, motor, speech, and mental functions involved. They, therefore, reflect the efficiency and the integration of functions of many different cerebral mechanisms in the two great cerebral hemispheres. It is therefore not surprising that brain-damaged children and adults will reflect reduced efficiency in one or more of the chains of cerebral mechanisms resulting in subnormal SDMT written and oral performances, despite normal (and even above-normal) Wechsler Verbal, Performance, and Full Scale IQs (Smith, 1981a,b).

Since publication of the SDMT (Smith, 1973), the sensitivity of this simple substitution test to the presence of brain damage in children and adults has been further documented. Several studies comparing the sensitivity of assorted tests of organic cerebral dysfunction in different clinical populations have recently reported the highest hit rate with the SDMT (Watson, Davis, & Gasser, 1978; Whelan, Berker, Campbell, & Smith, 1980; Whelan, Schteingart, Starkman, & Smith, 1980; Watson, Gasser, Schaefer, Buranen, & Wold, 1981; Campbell et al. 1981; Hartlage, in press; Pfeffer, Kurosaki, Harrah, Chance, Bates, Detels, Filos, & Butzke, 1981).

Impaired SDMT written and oral performances provide no evidence of the nature, locus, or even lateralization of the underlying cerebral pathology; *or of the nature of the specific defects in one or more of the different functions involved resulting in subnormal SDMT scores.* However, the demonstrable sensitivity of the SDMT to the presence of highly diverse (reversible or irreversible, evolving or resolving) brain insults and to subsequent´changes in the status of overall cerebral functions is an outstanding example of a test for general deficits of cerebral lesions, regardless of their nature or locus.

The sensitivity and validity of the SDMT as a diagnostic and prognostic indicator has been intensively and extensively evaluated in Michigan Neuropsychological Test Battery studies of initial (and later) effects of almost all types of focal and diffuse, evolving and resolving brain insults (including toxic, anoxic, neoplastic, vascular, infectious, traumatic, metabolic, and other neuropathologic processes), as well as in patients with extracranial systemic or organic disorders that also affect brain functions. Systematic preoperative and continuing long-term post-operative studies of children and adults with hemispherectomy and commissurotomy and of others with resolving focal, resectable cerebral lesions have also revealed changes with time contributing to further definitions of its diagnostic and prognostic value.

For example, the SDMT has proven to be the most sensitive and valid indicator of the presence of acute or chronic brain insults in single studies of children and adults with the MNTB. However, continuing long-term follow-up studies of many patients have revealed a small proportion with gradually improving SDMT performances ultimately approaching (or even exceeding) appropriate age-education norms. Thus, when used as part of a test battery, this pattern contributed to definition of the diagnostic significance of slightly subnormal, normal, or even above-normal SDMT performances. Namely, in cases with normal SDMT performances, "either the subject *is normal*—or, if other tests indicate organic cerebral dysfunction, the underlying pathology is probably of a chronic (and especially in children without recent history indicating brain damage or injury) or long-standing nature" (Smith, 1978b, p. 1).

By contrast, other tests—such as the Visual Organization Test (VOT) devised by Hooper (1958) as a test of organic brain pathology—tap specific deficits. For example, as illustrated in single and in follow-up studies of cases with documented focal-lateralized and diverse types of brain lesions, initial, marked impairment of the specific visual organization or non-motor constructional functions of this test usually reflects damage to the right hemisphere with more marked and persisting impairment in cases with posterior, right-hemisphere lesions (Zubrick & Smith, 1978; Berker & Smith, 1980; Smith, 1981a; Campbell et al., 1981). As described by Rathbun & Smith (1982), these functions are often spared or only mildly or temporarily depressed in patients with right-frontal or left-hemisphere lesions.

This characteristic feature indicates the limitations and differential sensitivity of the VOT to the presence of brain lesions as a function of their specific locus. It also emphasizes the important difference between such tests like the SDMT which are sensitive to the general defects of diverse types of brain damage and others which are sensitive to the specific defects resulting from focal-lateralized lesions. Parodoxically, however, it is precisely the limitations that distinguish tests of specific defects from the SDMT and other tests of general defects that contribute to their value in diagnostic studies. For example, since the specific functions tapped by the VOT are spared (or only mildly or briefly impaired) in cases with right-frontal or left-hemisphere lesions, if SDMT performances are positive (reveal general defects), normal VOT performances indicate that the underlying lesion is not likely to be in—or directly compromise the functions of—the posterior region of the right hemisphere.

SUGGESTED GUIDELINES FOR EVALUATION OF WECHSLER SUBTEST PERFORMANCES

Because the Wechsler scales for children and adults are the most widely used tests in diverse clinical assessments by psychologists, the accumulated findings in studies of initial and long-term effects of various brain insults in children and adults over the past three decades may provide some useful rules of thumb in evaluating performances on specific subtests and various subtest patterns. Earlier studies reflected a primary if not almost exclusive focus on Wechsler Verbal, Performance, and Full Scale IQs. As noted above, initial attempts to diagnose the presence and laterality of brain damage based on V-P IQ differences have proven to be unreliable and frequently misleading.

Similarly, the accumulation of data for large clinical populations has dispelled an earlier widespread notion that intelligence as measured by the Wechsler scales is necessarily and demonstrably depressed by *acute* or *chronic* brain damage. For example, WB tests administered before or shortly after surgery to 147 nonaphasic patients with verified brain tumors (mean age, 47 years, mean education 10.1 years) revealed a mean VIQ of 99.4, PIQ 91.1, FSIQ 94.5; 33 had FSIQs of 110 or above, and 8 had FSIQs of 120 or above. Thus, not surprisingly, 2 college graduates, 35 and 42 years old, with malignant tumors, had FSIQs of 133 and 131, respectively.

In almost all cases referred to psychologists for clinical assessments, interpretations of the diagnostic significance of test performances are qualified by the absence of comparable data obtained in the premorbid stage or before the onset of problems warranting referral. Since IQs are aggregate scores, they often obscure significant pathognomonic diagnostic findings that are revealed by quantitative and qualitative analyses and comparisons of performances on the 11 subtests. Since each of the subtests are variously affected by education (Matarazzo, 1972, p. 373), as well as by age (Wechsler, 1958, p.146), analyses and comparisons of the 11 individual subtests must be evaluated in terms of the subject's age and background. Moreover, in assessing inter-test scatter and the significance of disparities between higher and lower subtest weighted scores, the nature of the specific tests showing such disparities must also be taken into account along with age and education.

Economy and focus permit only limited considerations and illustrations of the various types of inter- and intra-test scatter suggesting the presence of organic cerebral dysfunction. However, the importance of taking the nature of the subtest, as well as age, into account in evaluating the diagnostic implications of inter-test scatter (i.e., whether the marked disparity is pathognomonic or simply normal variability) is amply illustrated in Wechsler's standardization data. For example, the sample of 100 presumably normal men between 55 and 64 years old in the standardization of the WAIS (Wechsler, 1958, p. 146) shows mean weighted subtest scores ranging from 6.11 in Digit Symbol to 10.46 in Information (over 70 percent higher). As noted above, Digit Symbol has been frequently reported to be the Wechsler subtest most sensitive to the effects of brain lesions, regardless of their locus, magnitude, or nature. The marked disparity or abnormal inter-test scatter between Digit Symbol and Information in normal subjects 55 to 64 years old is therefore presumably a reflection of the greater vulnerability of one or more of the complex sensory, motor, and mental functions involved in making simple Digit Symbol written substitutions than the mental functions involved in recall of earlier acquired information to the effects of advancing age in later life.

While the decline of manual motor speed with advancing age is widely recognized, standardization studies of the SDMT have demostrated that oral (as well as written) Symbol Digit substitutions also decline. However, the studies also revealed that both written and oral substitutions also *increase* with *education*. Thus, the development of norms for age and education provides more-reliable bases for evaluating the diagnostic implications of SDMT performances and, by comparisons with concomitant Digit Symbol substitutions, for more-reliable evaluation of the diagnostic significance of markedly lower weighted scores in the Digit Symbol when compared to other Wechsler subtests.

The importance of taking the nature of subtests showing wide discrepancies, as well as the subject's age and educational background, into account was illustrated in a patient this author examined immediately before writing this section. A 63-year-old engineer was referred for differential diagnosis and possible recommendations for therapy, following an episode of brief loss of consciousness. Although a very high blood pressure (200/50) had suggested a tentative diagnosis of a mild stroke, this diagnosis was not confirmed by CAT scan and other neuroradiologic, EEG, and clinical neurological studies. Although the WAIS-R FSIQ (109) was in the normal range, weighted subtest scores ranged from 5 in Object Assembly, 6 in Digit Symbol (approximating the norms for a 63-year-old man), and 7 in Picture Completion and Block Design, to 15 in Comprehension and Arithmetic.

His performances in the Block Design and Object Assembly subtests emphasized the critical importance of qualitative (as well as quantitative) analyses of test behavior. Although he was a consulting engineer and stated that he and his family always had enjoyed "jigsaw puzzles" at home, he was stunned at his inability to copy a simple Block Design (2) immediately after witnessing a demonstration of how to assemble the blocks. Instead of following the simple organization of the square tetrad just demonstrated to him, he *turned all four blocks so that red sides were on top and arranged them in a simple line slanted at the same angle as the stripe on the card* (45 degrees to the right). Similarly, he was deeply perplexed and baffled by his inability to correctly assemble the face or the hand in the Object Assemby subtest. He would try to fit a piece in an inappropriate site. On seeing that it did not fit, he tried another and yet another; and when these did not fit, he attempted to assemble them separately. Then he would return to his initial pattern, repeating the same errors in attempting to fit the same pieces at the same inappropriate sites.

In view of the patient's history as a successful consultant engineer, even allowing for the estimated declines with advancing age in normal adults, his weighted scores in Block Design (7) and Object Assembly (5) were subnormal and in contrast to a weighted score of 10 in Picture Arrangement. However, in addition to subnormal scores, the specific aberrant nature of his test responses to both subtests was also characteristic of patients with constructional dyspraxia, a specific neuropsychological deficit indicating disruption of cerebral mechanisms in the post-rolandic region of the right hemisphere.

The differential sensitivity of the 11 subtests to focal-lateralized lesions in different sites of the two great cerebral hemispheres cannot be considered here. However, beginning with Wechsler (1944, p. 150), the Vocabulary subtest has been described as most resistant to focal or diffuse brain damage and as a reliable reflection of premorbid intellectual capacities. Apart from the subsequent findings in studies of aphasics, the vulnerability of vocabulary skills to left-sided lesions in nonaphasic patients has been documented in our studies of initial and long-term effects of commissurotomy (Campbell et al., 1981). However, just as qualitative analyses of test behavior in responses to the Block Design and Object Assembly (in the case cited above) contribute to the diagnosis, analysis of the responses to the Vocabulary subtest often provides valuable information on the nature and quality of the mental functions involved; the ability to focus and sustain attention in the organization and expression of the underlying verbal-reasoning processes; on the status of the specific cerebral mechanisms involved in articulating grammatic, appropriate, and meaningful responses and in verbal comprehension.

Thus, while the weighted Vocabulary subtest score provides a gross measure of expressive-vocabulary skills, qualitative analysis of the spoken responses may reveal unique clinical features that contribute far more about the patient and diagnosis than the weighted score. For example, frequent requests for repetition and inappropriate responses to relatively common words may reflect erratic lapses in verbal comprehension. Conversely, occasional dysarthric, articulation, or word-finding difficulties in responses may reflect embarrassments of one or more of the cerebral mechanisms required for normal fluent, grammatic, and prosodic speech. Analyses of the responses may reveal erratic or loose associational mental processes: for example, nonaphasic patients with various types of brain damage have given for the word *commence,* "to cease" and "to stop"; for *obstruct,* "to break down", "destroy", "get rid of"; for *fortitude,* "latitude"; for *tangible,* "you can read it."

The accumulated findings in repeated follow-up studies have also indicated the diagnostic significance of intra-test scatter, failures in easier items followed by successes in harder ones in the same test. As noted by Smith (1981a), inconstancy of responses is a common feature in tests of patients with overt or occult brain damage. Generally, such inconstancy reflects erratic fluctuations in cerebral efficiency as a result of the dynamics of the underlying lesion and its effects on the rest of the brain in efforts to cope with the changing pathophysiological process. Thus, in cases with evolving or progressive lesions, repeated tests will show increasing intra-test scatter; whereas in resolving lesions, the intra-test scatter decreases as the brain reorganizes with time.

Finally, the profile of all 11 subtests should be analyzed as a whole, along with other tests that have been administered. As emphasized earlier:

> A cardinal rule in diagnostic studies of children and adults is this: regardless of the sensitivity, validity, and comprehensiveness of neuropsychological testing techniques, and the expertise of the examiner, an eminently normal or even superior-level profile of overall test performances—free of any signs of neuropsychological deficits—does not warrant the firm conclusion that the patient is normal. In patients with evolving or slowly progressive neuropathologic processes, there are almost always intervals in the early course of the disease when the associated lesions may gradually develop without affecting the functions (or underlying neurophysiological mechanisms) tapped by comprehensive neuropsychological or psychiatric examinations. (Smith, 1981a, p. 188)

In many cases, the early, stuttering course of occult, slowly progressive processes may not be apparent in repeated neurological studies including EEG, CAT scans and other neuroradiological diagnostic techniques. (This was dramatically illustrated by one of the author's patients, an attorney, with a long history of gradually increasing short periods of somnolence, mild blackouts, and negative neurological findings in repeated neurological studies—until eventually an intraventricular meningioma became manifest—18 years after initial onset of his short, mild blackout episodes.)

BRIEF SUPPLEMENTAL SCREENING TESTS

In view of the obvious limitations of the Bender-Gestalt, Rorschach, and other earlier developed tests currently used by some general clinical psychologists in screening for brain damage, Editor C. E. Walker recommended suggesting other selected tests that might be added or substituted in routine clinical assessments. The rationales underlying the selection of other brief tests of language, verbal and nonverbal cognitive, memory, motor, and sensory functions to complement the Wechsler scales in continuing refinements of the Michigan Neuropsychological Test Battery (MNTB) are based on economic (as well as theoretical) considerations that are of practical concern to the clinical psychologist. One of the important considerations in test selection is how much each contributes to the accuracy of diagnosis. Moreover, apart from the important question of time required for testing, a positive diagnosis—either by neuropsychologic testing or by a CAT scan revealing a large or small, focal or diffuse, cerebral lesion—*provides no evidence of the patient's functional abilities and limitations for work, school or activities in daily life;* and consequently, *no bases for developing remediation or rehabilitation programs specifically designed to assist the patients in their efforts to compensate or adjust to the various persisting neuropsychological disabilities.*

The tests incorporated in the MNTB for these purposes have been described elsewhere (Smith, 1975, 1981a; Campbell et al., 1981). The criteria and methods for evaluating the individual measures are described in the Guidelines (Smith, 1978b) in the Appendix to this chapter. Unfortunately, the training necessary for the required professional skill in administering, scoring, and interpreting the MNTB cannot be achieved by attendance at one or two three- to five-day workshops, let alone by simply applying the Guidelines described in the Appendix. However, selected tests among those listed may be easily incorporated as screening instruments for brain damage in the various batteries used by clinical psychologists. Before considering the tests suggested below, the present author would first like to emphasize that no current tests—or, for that matter—neurologic diagnostic techniques, including CAT scans, are free from the "haunting spectre" of false positives and false negatives. Moreover, economy—especially of time—is obviously an important practical consideration.

The Symbol Digit Modalities Test (SDMT)

For screening purposes, studies by others cited above and our experiences during the past two decades indicate that the SDMT is probably the most economic, sensitive, valid, and useful single test for differential diagnostic studies and for general clinical assessments. As described above, when used with the Wechsler scales, the development of SDMT norms for age and education contributes to greater definition of the diagnostic implications of written and oral SDMT scores, when compared to scores on the Digit Symbol and other subtests of the Wechsler scales. Moreover, since Symbol Digit substitutions are made in both written and spoken responses, in cases with manual motor difficulties resulting in subnormal written Digit Symbol and Symbol Digit performances, the oral SDMT score provides bases for determining whether or not the subnormal written scores simply reflect manual, motor difficulties. As described in the manual, if both written and oral SDMT scores are more than one standard deviation below appropriate age-education norms, the patient should be referred for more detailed neuropsychological studies and especially for examinations of visual acuity and oculomotor coordination.

Single and Double Simultaneous Stimulation (Face-Hand) Test (SDSS)

In cases with verified brain lesions, the SDSS is a similarly economic (taking less than five minutes) and useful test for determining the presence or absence of somatosensory deficits. The accumulated findings in MNTB studies of initial and long-term effects of diverse-focal and diffuse brain insults in children and adults with and without hemiplegia have revealed that somatosensory deficits occur less frequently than lateralized or bilateral motor deficits. Generally, the severity of associated neuropsychological deficits is greatest in those with bilateral SDSS defects, less in those with lateralized deficits, and least in those with normal SDSS test performances. Moreover, as with the SDMT, follow-up studies with the SDSS also frequently reflect the course of the underlying neuropathological process, i.e., in cases with progressive lesions, increasing lateralized and bilateral errors versus gradual diminution of such errors in others with resolving brain insults. Unlike the Wechsler scales and most other psychological tests of higher (cognitive) functions, the SDSS taps lower-level (somatosensory) cerebral functions and is relatively independent of the effects of education and intelligence.

Purdue Pegboard Tests of Manual Dexterity

The Purdue Pegboard is another brief, simple test (placements of pegs with each, and then with both, hands simultaneously, each for 60-second periods) which is also relatively independent of intelligence and educational background. As indicated in the guidelines, the pattern of performances with each, and with both, hands in most cases with acute cerebral lesions often provides evidence not only of the presence but also laterality or bilaterality of organic cerebral dysfunction.

Benton Visual Retention Test

This test involves visuographic or figure-drawing performances similar to those in the Bender-Gestalt test. However, it is also a standardized test of immediate visual memory with norms for children and adults. This author's experiences in studies of children and adults with hemispherectomy, commissurotomy, diverse focal, and diffuse cerebral insults indicate that, although patients with acute right-hemisphere temporal-parietal lesions show more frequent and marked defects, the specific functions tapped by the BVRT are also vulnerable to the effects of lesions in other parts of the brain.

Other memory tests

The 11 Wechsler subtests tap a wide variety of higher verbal and nonverbal cognitive functions. However, they are insensitive to one of the serious (and often severely disabling) neuropsychologic deficits that may emerge in the early stages of evolving brain insults or persist long after significant improvement or recovery of cognitive functions in patients with resolving brain lesions—namely, memory deficits. Not uncommonly, normal or only slightly subnormal scores in the Wechsler Digit Span subtest may suggest that immediate (and by implication, intermediate or long-term) memory is intact or only slightly subnormal. However, as illustrated in one of the documented cases (WM) by Smith (1981a, pp. 206–207), recovery of Wechsler IQs to normal levels may mask the persistence of a severe Korsakoff-like impairment in intermediate memory. This covert defect is more likely to occur in cases with diffuse cerebral damage (such as that resulting from severe, closed head injuries, anoxic, toxic, or infectious brain insults). Such patients may show increasing recall of earlier learned material (higher scores in the Information subtest) and be able to achieve normal scores in the Digit Span subtest. However, when instructed to repeat and remember a simple name, "Martin Harrison," and then asked after five minutes of interpolated testing, "What was the name I asked you to remember?", the patient will strongly deny that he was ever told or asked to remember any name. After serial repetitions of the same name and continuing failures to recall that name, certain patients become aware (or are able to admit the presence) of impairment of intermediate memory.

Such patients also tend to perform poorly in immediate recall of the two paragraphs of the Logical Memory section of the Wechsler Memory Scale, as well as in delayed recall. The need for the development of more valid, standardized, and sensitive measures of intermediate auditory memory was indicated in a recent review by Russell (1981) of *The Pathology and Clinical Examination of Memory*. Albeit, in cases with diffuse brain damage or with suspected memory deficits, immediate and delayed auditory memory may be evaluated by using the two paragraphs of the Logical Memory section of the Wechsler Memory Scale, as well as by clinical unstandardized techniques such as testing recall of simple names after five-minute periods of interpolated testing activities.

SEX AND BRAIN DAMAGE

Recent studies with the Wechsler scales and other tests have reported that comparisons of male and female adults with lateralized cerebral lesions indicate significant and systematic differences in the degree of hemispheric specialization in verbal and nonverbal functions as a function of sex (Lansdell, 1961, 1962, 1968; McGlone & Kertesz, 1973; McGlone, 1977, 1978; Inglis & Lawson, 1981). Todd, Coolidge, and Satz (1977), however, failed to find the significant sex differences in earlier studies. Since most of the clinical populations reported in such studies consisted of patients with diverse types of evolving and/or resolving lesions randomly distributed in frontal and nonfrontal regions of either hemisphere, the controversial findings are not surprising (Smith, 1979, 1981a). Studies of hundreds of children and adults (including patients with hemispherectomy, commissurotomy, and focal-lateralized lesions) have failed to reveal systematic differences in effects of such lesions on verbal and nonverbal cognitive abilities as a function of sex. However, apart from the theoretical implications of the reported greater hemispheric specialization of males than females in verbal and nonverbal cognitive functions, there is another aspect of sex in brain-damaged men and women that has received little attention and yet is of considerable importance to both the patient and clinical psychologist.

At the beginning of this chapter, attention was called to the frequent association of emotional problems, sometimes described as "change of personality" in brain-damaged patients. Whether because many patients are reluctant or unwilling to discuss them, or because they have somehow been overlooked by psychologists engaged in diagnosis and/or treatment, in contrast to the voluminous and controversial literature on cognitive, memory, and other psychological deficits, the numerous recent texts reflect a remarkable paucity of reported studies on effects of brain insults on libido or sex drive as well as on sexual performance. For example, the voluminous *Handbook of Clinical Neuropsychology* does not even include the word *sex* in the subject index. Blumer and Walker (1975) reported changes in sexual behavior in 35 (70 percent) of 50 temporal-lobe epileptics, with reduced libido in all but 2 of the 35. The present author's studies of initial and long-term effects of hemispherectomy and of other focal and diffuse brain lesions also indicate reduced sexual drive as well as performance (inability to have an erection, ejaculation praecox) in most males as well as loss of interest in females for varying periods following brain insult.

In a 33-year-old man tested before and two years after right-anterior lobectomy with gyrectomies of the frontal opercular regions for relief of recently emerging and uncontrolled seizures, the progressive reduction of libido before and after surgery evoked considerable concern in both the patient and his wife, who perceived his sharply diminished sexual appetite and poor performance as a rejection.

Another with a very severe closed head injury (including multiple skull fractures, requiring wiring to reattach the separated skull bones) showed a quite different change in sexual drive and performance. When seen two years post-trauma, interview with the patient elicited only a casual admission of occasional slight memory lapses since his accident. However, in a separate interview, his wife stated that his sexual behavior and personality changed drastically immediately after the accident. She reported that, shortly after recovering from the anesthetic following neurosurgery, she thought he was joking when he tried to get her to go to the bathroom for "a quickie." Since he was suffering from serious, acute head and associated body injuries, she was disturbed when she realized he was serious. On discharge from hospital, she stated that his hypersexuality had increased so much (three or more times daily), ". . . he drives me bananas. I mean I have my kids, and I can't take it." On follow-up study, the patient reported that, although there had been no diminution in his sexual appetite, he had tempered his attempts to initiate sexual activities because he was aware of his wife's resentment of his excessive demands. However, on being questioned whether he enjoyed sexual relations any more or less than he had before his accident, he was puzzled: "I don't know . . . maybe less."

In summarizing grounds for suspecting possible neurological involvement in neuropsychodiagnostic studies, Small included, "A sudden emotional change has occurred which cannot be ascribed to specific precipitating circumstances, and the change is accompanied by disturbances of sleep, ravenous hunger and/or thirst, metabolic disorders, or changes in sexual appetite" (Small, 1980, p. 307). In the present author's experience, changes in sexual appetite and/or performance have more often been reflections of underlying anxieties, doubts, and emotional problems in patients undergoing psychotherapy. Thus, except in rare cases, it is unlikely that such changes will be the first manifestations of an underlying organic-cerebral disorder. Albeit, the frequency of serious problems of sexual disturbances in the early and often later stages are obviously important considerations not only for the diagnosis but especially for the clinical psychologist's treatment of associated affective disturbances of brain-damaged patients.

SUMMARY

Diagnostic considerations are discussed in relation to neuropsychological assessment for clinical psychologists in screening patients referred for therapy. The evolution of current psychological and neuropsychological testing techniques is reviewed, with emphasis on current tests of organicity.

A discussion of the rationale in constructing and selecting both individual psychological tests and neuropsychological test batteries precedes the present author's suggested guidelines for evaluating these instruments. Specific attention is given to the use of the Wechsler subtest performances as a neuropsychological instrument. Brief screening tests are reviewed as supplemental instruments in clinical assessments.

APPENDIX: GUIDELINES FOR EVALUATION OF INDIVIDUAL MEASURES OF THE MICHIGAN NEUROPSYCHOLOGICAL TEST BATTERY

1. Human Figure Drawing

Clinical judgment for "organicity" using a 5-point scale from 1 (clearly normal), 2 (approaching or just within normal limits), 3 (equivocal), 4 (slightly to moderately abnormal), 5 (grossly abnormal).
   a. A normal drawing does not preclude organicity.
   b. A grossly distorted drawing suggests hypothesis of right hemisphere dysfunction.

2. WAIS or WISC

a.   First check Digit Symbol or Coding subtest. In the overwhelming majority of patients with acute lesions and in most patients with longstanding or chronic lesions, substitution tests are markedly subnormal. A normal or mildly subnormal Digit Symbol/Coding score indicates that either the subject is normal, or, if other tests indicate organic cerebral dysfunction, the underlying pathology is probably of a chronic (and especially in children without recent history indicating brain damage or injury) or long-standing nature.

b.   Check scatter between and within subtests, comparing the subtests that show the highest scores versus those that show the lowest scores. Remember that WAIS IQs are relative, not absolute, measures. Thus, both IQs and individual subtest scores should be evaluated for expected scores in terms of the subject's educational, socioeconomic, and professional background.

3. VOT, RCPM, and VRT

Generally, although lesions in either hemisphere may result in subnormal scores in any or all three of these tests, markedly subnormal scores suggest the greater likelihood of organic involvement of the post-rolandic (temporal and/or parietal) regions of the right hemisphere, which often also results in depressed scores in the Block Design and Object Assembly subtests. The more marked the subnormality in these visual-ideational, spatial-constructional perceptual tests, the greater the likelihood of right post-rolandic involvement.

4. Purdue Pegboard

Check norms for evidence of laterality or bilaterality of indicated cerebral dysfunction. Although normal scores with each and both hands simultaneously reduce the probabilities, like each of the other measures, they do not preclude the possibility of a lesion that spares the specific functions being tested. A borderline normal score should be considered in the "possibly suggestive" category and evaluated in terms of the evidence provided by other tests.

5. Symbol-Digit Written and Oral Substitutions

Of all the individual measures, SDMT scores are usually the most sensitive to the presence of acute or chronic "organic" cerebral dysfunction. Not infrequently, although Digit Symbol/Coding scores may be normal, SDMT written and oral scores will indicate either chronic or long-standing organic dysfunction or, in some cases, provide the first signs of a covert evolving morbid process.

6. Single and Double Simultaneous Stimulations

Evaluate abnormal performances not only in terms of suggested laterality or bilaterality of organic involvement but the severity of somatosensory deficits as indicated by the number of errors. Compare right- versus left-sided errors. Note also the number and patterns of DISPLACEMENT errors as compared to extinction errors.

7. Memory for Unrelated Sentences

In general (or, with occasional exceptions), subnormal scores are usually associated with left hemisphere involvement; the more markedly subnormal score, the greater the likelihood of left hemisphere dysfunction. Exceptions include cases in which early left hemisphere damage (or, more rarely, genetic factors) have resulted in the right hemisphere playing the leading role in language functions.

GENERAL PRINCIPLES AND IMPLICATIONS

Review the overall profile for consistency. If only a single measure is subnormal, how can you explain the normal scores in all other measures? If several measures are subnormal, what is their nature and how do they differ from those that are normal? Does the pattern of impaired versus relatively spared or normal functions indicate right, left, or bilateral cerebral dysfunction? Could the pattern of specific deficits be explained on the basis of nonorganic factors such as impaired hearing, vision, motor functions, motivation, depression, malingering, and the like?

If the findings clearly indicate organic cerebral dysfunction, does the history indicate whether the underlying pathology is evolving or resolving in nature? What would you expect if you reexamined the patient in 6 to 12 months? What are the implications of your findings for immediate treatment, remediation, or rehabilitation? What are the implications for long-term effects with respect to maturation of the different higher- and lower-level cerebral functions in children and the long-term implications for successful adjustment in adults?

Remember that in children, early brain insults often result in different patterns of development and organization of hemispheric mechanisms underlying language, verbal, and nonverbal cognitive functions; also, thanks to the greater plasticity of the younger brain, the potential for reorganization and improvement of functions is considerably greater than that in adults. It is also important to remember that in adults with resolving lesions, the process of reorganization and recovery of functions continues over many years.

In cases with positive signs of organic cerebral dysfunction and equivocal findings with respect to laterality of involvement, "Look to the hands." In other words, the association of right- or left-sided sensory and/or motor defects indicates major involvement of the contralateral hemisphere.

REFERENCES

Adams, K. M. An end of innocence for behavioral neurology. Adams replies. *Journal of Consulting and Clinical Psychology*, 1980, *48*, 522–524. (a)

Adams, K. M. In search of Luria's battery: A false start? *Journal of Consulting and Clinical Psychology*, 1980, *48*, 511–516. (b)

Anderson, A. L. The effect of laterality localizations of brain damage on Wechsler-Bellevue indices of deterioration. *Journal of Clinical Psychology*, 1950, *6*, 191.

Anderson, A. L. The effect of laterality localization of focal brain lesions on the Wechsler-Bellevue subtests. *Journal of Clinical Psychology*, 1951, *7*, 149–153.

Babcock, H. An experiment in the measurement of mental deterioration. *Archives of Psychology*, 1930, No. 117.

/

Battersby, W. S., Krieger, H. P., & Bender, M. B. Visual and tactile discriminative learning in patients with cerebral tumours. *American Journal of Psychology,* 1955, *68,* 562–574.

Bender, L. Gestalt function in visual-motor patterns in organic disease of the brain. *Archives of Neurology and Psychiatry,* 1935, *33,* 300–328.

Benton, A. L. Review of the Visual Motor Gestalt Test. In O. K. Buros (Ed.), *The Fourth Mental Measurements Yearbook.* Highland Park, N.J.: Gryphon Press, 1953.

Benton, A. L. *Benton Visual Retention Test* (Rev. ed.). New York: Psychological Corporation, 1963.

Berker, E., & Smith, A. Specific site and diaschisis in Raven Coloured Progressive Matrices and other performances in 37 adults with acute focal cerebral lesions. *International Journal of Neuroscience,* 1981, *12,* 225–226.

Bigler, E. D., & Ehrfurth, J. W. Critical limitations of the Bender Gestalt Test in clinical neuropsychology: Response to Lacks. *CLinical Neuropsychology,* 1980, *2,* 88–90.

Binet, A., & Simon, T. Méthodes nouvelles pour le diagnostic du niveau intellectuel des anormaux. *L'Année Psychologique,* 1905, *11,* 191–244.

Blumer, D., & Walker, E. A. The neural basis of sexual behavior. In D. F. Benson & D. Blumer (Eds.), *Psychiatric Aspects of Neurologic Disease.* New York: Grune & Stratton, 1975.

Boll, T. J. The Halstead-Reitan Neuropsychology Battery. In S. B. Filskov & T. J. Boll (Eds.), *Handbook of Clinical Neuropsychology.* New York: John Wiley & Sons, 1981.

Bonin, G. von. *The Cerebral Cortex.* Springfield, Ill.: Charles C Thomas, 1960.

Boring, E. G. *A History of Experimental Psychology.* New York: Appleton-Century-Crofts, 1950.

Boyd, J. L. A validity study of the Hooper Visual Organization Test. *Journal of Consulting and Clinical Psychology,* 1981, *49,* 15–19.

Brown, J. *Mind, Brain, and Consciousness.* New York: Academic Press, 1977.

Brown, S., Adams, K., Rourke, B., Mehta, B., & Daly, R. Predictive utility of the Luria-Nebraska Scales in brain-damaged and non-brain-damaged groups. *International Neuropsychologcial Society Abstracts,* December 1981, p. 13.

Bruell, J. H., & Albee, G. W. Higher intellectual functions in a patient with hemispherectomy for tumor. *Journal of Consulting Psychology,* 1962, *26,* 90–98.

Burgermeister, B. *Psychological Techniques in Neurological Diagnosis.* New York: Harper & Row, 1962.

Burt, C. Experimental tests of general intelligence. *British Journal of Psychology,* 1909, *3,* 94–177.

Busch, E. Psychical symptoms in neurosurgical disease. *Acta Psychiatrica,* 1940, *15,* 257–290.

Campbell, A. L., Jr., Bogen, J. E., & Smith, A. Disorganization and reorganization of cognitive and sensorimotor function in cerebral commissurotomy. *Brain,* 1981, *104,* 493–511.

Centofanti, C. C. & Smith, A. *Single and Double Simultaneous (Face-Hand) Stimulation Test (SDSS).* Los Angeles: Western Psychological Services, 1979.

Christnsen, A. L. *Luria's neuropsychological investigation.* New York: Spectrum, 1975. (a)

Christensen, A. L. *Luria's neuropsychological investigation: Manual.* New York: Spectrum, 1975. (b)

Christensen, A. L. *Luria's neuropsychological investigation: Test cards.* New York: Spectrum, 1975. (c)

Coles, G. S. The Learning Disabilities Test Battery: Empirical and social issues. *Harvard Educational Review,* 1978, *48,* 313–319.

Costa, L. D., Vaughan, H. G., Levita, E., & Farber, N. The Purdue Pegboard as a predictor of the presence and laterality of cerebral lesions. *Journal of Consulting and Clinical Psychology,* 1963, *27,* 133.

Cronbach, L. J. *Essentials of Psychological Testing.* New York: Harper & Row, 1960.

Damasio, A. The frontal lobes. In K. M. Heilman & E. Valenstein (Eds.), *Clinical Neuropsychology.* New York: Oxford University Press, 1979.

Dana, C. L. *Textbook of Nervous Diseases* (8th ed.). New York: Wood, 1915.

Dew, H. R. Tumours of the brain: Their pathology and treatment: An analysis of 85 cases. *Medical Journal of Australia,* 1922, *1,* 515–521.

DiChiro, G. How reliable is neurology? *Neurology,* 1962, *12,* 93.

Dimond, S. J. *Introducing Neuropsychology.* Springfield, Ill.: Charles C Thomas, 1978.

Drewe, E. A. An experimental investigation of Luria's theory on the effects of frontal-lobe lesions in man. *Neuropsychologia,* 1975, *13,* 421–429.

Filskov, S. B., & Boll, T. J. (Eds.). *Handbook of Clinical Neuropsychology.* New York: John Wiley & Sons, 1981.

Fitzhugh, K. B., Fitzhugh, L. C., & Reitan, R. M. Effects of "chronic" and "current" lateralized and nonlateralized cerebral lesions upon Trail Making Test performances. *Journal of Nervous and Mental Disease,* 1963, *137,* 82–87.

Flechsig, P. E. (1905) Brain physiology and theories of volition. Rome: Fifth International Psychological Congress. Trans. G. von Bonin. In *The Cerebral Cortex.* Springfield, Ill.: Charles C Thomas, 1960.

German, W. J., & Fox, J. C. Observations following unilateral lobectomies. *Research Publications for Association of Research on Nervous Diseases,* 1934, *13,* 378–434.

Golden C. J. *Diagnosis and Rehabilitation in Clinical Neropsychology.* Springfield, Ill.: Charles C Thomas, 1978.

Golden, C. J. *Clinical Interpretation of Objective Psychological Tests.* New York: Grune & Stratton, 1979.

Golden, C. J. A standardized version of Luria's neuropsychological tests. In S. J. Filskov & T. J. Boll (Eds.), *Handbook of Clinical Neuropsychology.* New York: John Wiley & Sons, 1981.

Golden, C. J., Hammeke, T. A., & Purisch, A. D. Diagnostic validity of a standardized neuropsychological battery derived from Luria's neuropsychological tests. *Journal of Consulting and Clinical Psychology,* 1978, *46,* 1258–1265.

Goldstein, K. *After-effects of Brain Injuries in War.* New York: Grune & Stratton, 1942.

Goldstein, K. *Language and Language Disturbances.* New York: Grune & Stratton, 1948.

Goldstein, K., & Gelb, A. Psychologische Analysen Hirnpathologischer Fälle auf Grund von Untersuchungen Hirnverletzter. *Ztschr. für die gesamte Neurologie und Psychiatrie,* 1918, *41,* 1.

Goldstein, K., & Scheerer, M. Abstract and concrete behavior: An experimental study with special tests. *Psychological Monographs,* 1941, *53,* No. 2.

Goltz, F. (1888) On the functions of the hemispheres. *Pfluger's Archiv fur die Gesamte Physiologie*. Trans. G. von Bonin. In *The Cerebral Cortex*. Springfield, Ill.: Charles C Thomas, 1960.

Gowers, W. R. *Diagnosis of Disease of the Brain and of the Spinal Cord*. New York: William Wood, 1885.

Graham, F. K., & Kendall, B. S. Memory for designs tests. *Perceptual and Motor Skills*, 1960, *11*, 147.

Guertin, W. H., Frank, G. H., Ladd, C. E., & Rabin, A. I. Research with the Wechsler Intelligence Scales for Adults. 1960–1965. *Psychological Bulletin*, 1966, *66*, 385–409.

Guertin, W. H., Frank, G. H., & Rabin, A. I. Research with the Wechsler-Bellevue Intelligence Scale. 1950–1955. *Psychological Bulletin*, 1956, *53*, 235–257.

Guertin, W. H., Ladd, C. E., Frank, G. H., Rabin, A. I., & Heister, D. S. Research with the Wechsler Intelligence Scales for Adults. 1965–1970. *Psychological Record*, 1971, *21*, 289–339.

Guertin, W. H., Rabin, A. I., Frank, G. H., & Ladd, C. E. Research with the Wechsler Intelligence Scales for Adults. 1955–1960. *Psychological Bulletin*, 1962, *59*, 1–26.

Halstead, W.C. *Brain and Intelligence: A Quantitative Study of the Frontal Lobes*. Chicago: University of Chicago Press, 1947.

Hardwick, R. S. Intelligence tests in a case of brain injury. *Psychological Bulletin*, 1927, *24*, 185.

Hartlage, L. C. Neuropsychological assessment of anticonvulsant drug toxicity. *Clinical Neuropsychology*, in press.

Hayman, M. Two-minute clinical test for measurement of intellectual impairment in psychiatric disorders. *Archives of Neurology and Psychiatry*, 1942, *47*, 454–464.

Head, H. *Aphasia and Kindred Disorders of Speech*. Cambridge, Mass: Cambridge University Press, 1926.

Heaton, R. K., & Crowley, T. J. Effects of psychiatric disorders and their somatic treatments on neuropsychological test results. In S. B. Filskov & T. J. Boll (Eds.), *Handbook of Clinical Neuropsychology*. New York: John Wiley & Sons, 1981.

Hecaen, H., & Albert, M. L. *Human Neuropsychology*. New York: John Wiley & Sons, 1978.

Heilman, K. M., & Valenstein, E. *Clinical Neuropychology*. New York: Oxford University Press, 1979.

Hooper, H. E. *Visual Organization Test* (Rev. ed.). Los Angeles: Western Psychological Services, 1958.

Hunt, H. F. *The Hunt-Minnesota Test for Organic Brain Damage*. Minneapolis: University of Minnesota Press, 1943.

Inglis, J., & Lawson, J. S. Sex differences in the effects of unilateral brain damage on intelligence. *Science*, 1981, *212*, 693–695.

Jackson, J. H. (1874) On the nature of the duality of the brain. In J. Taylor (Ed.), *Selected writings of J.Hughlings Jackson*. New York: Basic Books, 1958.

Klebanoff, S. G. Psychological changes in organic brain lesions and ablations. *Psychological Bulletin*, 1945, *42*, 585–623.

Klebanoff, S. G., Singer, J. L., & Wilensky, H. Psychological consequences of brain lesions and ablations. *Psychological Bulletin*, 1954, *51*, 1–41.

Kolb, B., & Whishaw, I. Q. *Fundamentals of Human Neuropsychology.* San Francisco: W. H. Freeman, 1980.

Korchin, S. J., & Schuldberg, D. The future of clinical assessment. *American Psychologist,* 1981, *36,* 1147–1158.

Lacks, P. B. The use of the Bender-Gestalt Test in clinical neuropsychology. *Clinical Neuropsychology,* 1979, *1,* 29–34.

Lansdell, H. The effect of neurosurgery on a test of proverbs. *American Psychologist,* 1961, *16,* 448.

Lansdell, H. A sex difference in effects of temporal-lobe neurosurgery on design preference. *Nature,* 1962, *194,* 852–854.

Lansdell, H. The use of factor scores from the Wechsler-Bellevue Scale of Intelligence in assessing patients with temporal-lobe removals. *Cortex,* 1968, *4,* 257–268.

Lezak, M. D. *Neuropsychological Assessment.* New York: Oxford University Press, 1976.

Luria, A. R. *Restoration of Function after Brain Injury.* New York: Macmillan, 1963.

Luria, A. R. *Higher Cortical Functions in Man.* New York: Basic Books. 1966. (a)

Luria, A. R. *Human Brain and Psychological Processes.* New York: Harper & Row, 1966. (b)

Luria, A. R. Frontal-lobe syndromes. In P. J. Vinken & G. W. Bruyn (Eds.), *Handbook of clinical neurology.* vol. 2. New York: John Wiley & Sons, 1969.

Luria, A. R. *The Working Brain: An Introduction to Neuropsychology.* London: Allen Lane, 1973.

Luria, A. R., & Majovski, L. V. Basic approaches used in American and Soviet clinical neuropsychology. *American Psychologist,* 1977, *32,* 959–968.

Malamud, R. F. Validity of the Hunt-Minnesota Test for organic brain damage. *Journal of Applied Psychology,* 1946, *30,* 271.

Matarazzo, J. D. *Wechsler's Measurement and Appraisal of Adult Intelligence.* Baltimore: Williams & Wilkins, 1972.

Matthews, C. G., Shaw, D. G., & Klove, H. Psychologic test performances in neurologic and pseudoneurologic subjects. *Cortex,* 1966, *2,* 244–253.

McFie, J. Psychological testing in clinical neurology. *Journal of Nervous and Mental Disease,* 1960, *131,* 383–393.

McFie, J. *Assessment of Organic Intellectual Impairment.* New York: Academic Press, 1975.

McGlone, J. Sex differences in the cerebral organization of functions in patients with unilateral brain lesions. *Brain,* 1977, *100,* 775–793.

McGlone, J. Sex differences in functional brain asymmetry. *Cortex,* 1978, *14,* 122–128.

McGlone, J., & Kertesz, A. Sex differences in cerebral processing of visuospatial tasks. *Cortex,* 1973, *9,* 313–320.

McHenry, L. C. *Garrison's History of Neurology.* Springfield, Ill.: Charles C Thomas, 1969.

McKay, S., & Golden, C. J. Empirical derivations of experimental scales for localizing brain lesions using the Luria-Nebraska Neuropsychological Battery. *Clinical Neuropsychology,* 1979, *1,* 9–23.

Morrell, F. Electropsysiological contributions to the neural basis of learning. *Physiological Reviews,* 1961, *41,* 443–494.

Osman, D. C., Golden, C. J., Purisch, A. D., Hammeke, T. A., & Blume, H. The use of a standardized battery of Luria's tests in the diagnosis of lateralized cerbral dysfunction. *International Journal of Neuroscience,* 1979, *9,* 1–9.

Papez, J. W. *Comparative Neurology.* New York: Thomas Y. Crowell, 1929.

Parsons, O A., & Prigatano, G. P. Methodological considerations in clinical neuropsychological research. *Journal of Consulting and Clinical Psychology,* 1978, *46,* 608–619.

Pascal, G. R., & Suttell, B. J. *The Bender-Gestalt Test: Quantification and Validity for Adults.* New York: Grune & Stratton, 1951.

Pfeffer, R. I., Kurosaki, T. T., Harrah, C. H., Jr., Chance, J. M., Bates, D., Detels, R., Filos, S., & Butzke, C. A survey diagnostic test for senile dementia. *American Journal of Epidemiology,* 1981, *114,* 515–527.

Phelps, C. *Traumatic Injuries of the Brain and Its Membranes.* New York: Appleton-Century-Crofts, 1897.

Piotrowski, Z. The Rorschach inkblot method in organic disturbance of the central nervous system. *Journal of Nervous and Mental Disease,* 1937, *86,* 525–537.

Piotrowski, Z. Rorschach studies of cases with lesions of the frontal lobes. *British Journal of Medical Psychology,* 1938, *17,* 105–118.

Piotrowski, Z. Positive and negative Rorschach organic reactions. *Rorschach Research Exchange,* 1940, *4,* 147–151.

Pollack, M. *Effect of Brain Tumor on Perception of Hidden Figures, Sorting Behavior, and Problem-Solving Performance.* New York: New York University Press, 1955.

Rathbun, J., & Smith, A. Comment on the validity of Boyd's validation study of the Hooper Visual Organization Test. *Journal of Consulting and Clinical Psychology,* 1982, *50,* 281–283.

Raven, J. C. *Standard Progressive Matrices.* London: Lewis, 1960.

Raven, J. C. *The Coloured Progressive Matrices Test.* London: Lewis, 1965.

Reitan, R. M. Investigation of the validity of Halstead's measures of biological intelligence. *Archives of Neurology and Psychiatry,* 1955, *73,* 28–35.

Reitan, R. M. Investigation of relationships between "psychometric" and "biological" intelligence. *Journal of Nervous and Mental Disease,* 1956, *123,* 536–541.

Reitan, R. M. Psychological deficits resulting from cerebral lesions in man. In J. M. Warren & K. Akert (Eds.), *The Frontal Granular Cortex and Behavior.* New York: McGraw-Hill, 1964.

Reitan, R. M. The vulgarization that Luria always wanted. *Contemporary Psychology,* 1976, *21,* 737–738.

Reitan, R. M., & Davison, L. A. *Clinical Neuropsychology.* New York: John Wiley & Sons, 1974.

Russell, E. W. The pathology and clinical examination of memory. In S. B. Filskov & T. J. Boll (Eds.), *Handbook of Clinical Neuropsychology.* New York: John Wiley & Sons, 1981.

Russell, E. W., Nueringer, C., & Goldstein, G. *Assessment of Brain Damage.* New York: John Wiley & Sons, 1970.

Rylander, G. *Personality Changes after Operation of the Frontal Lobes: A Clinical Study of 32 Cases.* Copenhagen: Munksgaard, 1939.

Rylander, G. Mental changes after excision of cerebral tissue. *Acta Psychiatrica Neurologia,* Supplement 25, 1943, 1–81.

Small, L. *Neuropsychodiagnosis in Psychotherapy.* New York: Brunner/Mazel, 1973.

Small, L. *Neuropsychodiagnosis in psychotherapy* (Rev. ed.). New York: Brunner/Mazel, 1980.

Smith, A. Changes in Porteus Maze scores of brain-operated schizophrenics after an eight-year interval. *Journal of Mental Science,* 1960, *106,* 967–978.

Smith, A. Ambiguities in concepts and studies of brain damage and organicity. *Journal of Nervous and Mental Disease,* 1962, *135,* 311–326. (a)

Smith, A. Psychodiagnosis of patients with brain tumors. *Journal of Nervous and Mental Disease,* 1962, *135,* 513–533. (b)

Smith, A. Changing effects of frontal lesions in man. *Journal of Neurology, Neurosurgery, and Psychiatry,* 1964, *27,* 511–515.

Smith, A. Certain hypothesized hemispheric differences in language and visual functions in human adults. *Cortex,* 1966, *2,* 109–126. (a)

Smith, A. Intellectual functions in patients with lateralized frontal tumours. *Journal of Neurology, Neurosurgery, and Psychiatry,* 1966, *29,* 52–59. (b)

Smith, A. Speech and other functions after left (dominant) hemispherectomy. *Journal of Neurology, Neurosurgery, and Psychiatry,* 1966, *29,* 467–471. (c)

Smith, A. Talkers and doers, or education, intelligence and WAIS Verbal-Performance ratios in psychiatric patients. *American Psychological Association Convention Proceedings,* 1966, 233–234. (d)

Smith, A. Verbal and nonverbal test performances of patients with "acute" lateralized brain tumors. *Journal of Nervous and Mental Disease,* 1966, *141,* 517–523. (e)

Smith A. The Serial-Sevens Subtraction Test. *Archives of Neurology,* 1967, *17,* 78–80.

Smith A. The Symbol Digit Modalities Test. *Learning Disorders,* 1968, *3,* 61–81.

Smith, A. Nondominant hemispherectomy. *Neurology,* 1969, *19,* 442–445.

Smith, A. Dominant and nondominant hemispherectomy. In W. L. Smith (Ed.), *Drugs, Development, and Cerebral Functions.* Springfield, Ill.: Charles C Thomas, 1972, 37–68.

Smith, A. *Symbol Digit Modalities Test.* Los Angeles: Western Psychological Services, 1973.

Smith, A. Neuropsychological testing in neurological disorders. In W. J. Friedlander (Ed.), *Advances in Neurology* (Vol. 7). New York: Raven Press, 1975.

Smith, A. Appraising the neuropsychological literature. *Bulletin of the International Neuropsychological Society,* August 1978, 3–5. (a)

Smith, A. Guideline for evaluation of individual measures of the Michigan Neuropsychological Test Battery. Ann Arbor: University of Michigan Neuropsychological Laboratory, 1978. (b)

Smith, A. Lenneberg, Locke, Zangwill and the neuropsychology of language. In G. Miller & E. Lenneberg (Eds.), *Psychology and Biology of Language and Thought: Essays in Honor of Eric H. Lenneberg.* New York: Academic Press, 1978. (c)

Smith, A. Practices and principles of clinical neuropsychology. *International Journal of Neuroscience,* 1979, *9,* 233–238.

Smith, A. Principles underlying human brain functions in neuropsychological sequelae of different neuropathological processes. In S. B. Filskov & T. J. Boll (Eds.), *Handbook of Clinical Neuropsychology.* New York: John Wiley & Sons, 1981a.

Smith, A. On the organization, disorganization, and reorganization of language and other brain functions. In Y. Lebrun & O. L. Zangwill (Eds.), *Lateralization of Language in the Child.* Amsterdam: Swets and Zeitlinger, 1981b.

Smith, A., & Burklund, C. W. Dominant hemispherectomy: Preliminary report on neuropsychological sequelae. *Science,* 1966, *153,* 1280–1282.

Smith, A., & Kinder, E. F. Changes in psychological test performances of brain-operated schizophrenics after eight years. *Science,* 1959, *129,* 149–150.

Smith, A., & Sugar, O. Development of above-normal language and intelligence 21 years after left hemispherectomy. *Neurology,* 1975, *25,* 813–818.

Spiers, P. A. Have they come to praise Luria or to bury him? The Luria-Nebraska controversy. *Journal of Consulting and Clinical Psychology,* 1981, *49,* 331–341.

Spreen, O., & Benton, A. L. Comparative studies of some psychological tests for cerebral damage. *Journal of Nervous and Mental Disease,* 1965, *140,* 323–333.

Teuber, H. L. The riddle of frontal-lobe function in man. In J. M. Warren & K. Akert (Eds.), *The Frontal Granular Cortex and Behavior.* New York: McGraw-Hill, 1964.

Teuber, H. L. Alterations of perception of the brain injury. In J. E. Eccles (Ed.), *Brain and Conscious Experience.* New York: Springer, 1966.

Tissenbaum, M. J., Harter, H. M., & Friedman, A. P. Organic neurological syndromes diagnosed as functional disorders. *Journal of the American Medical Association,* 1951, *147,* 1519–1521.

Todd, J., Coolidge, F., & Satz, P. The Wechsler Adult Intelligence Scale discrepancy index: A neuropsychological evaluation. *Journal of Consulting and Clinical Psychology,* 1977, *45,* 450–454.

Walsh, K. W. *Neuropsychology: A Clinical Approach.* New York: Churchill-Livingstone, 1978.

Watson, C. G., Davis, W. E., & Gasser, B. The separation of organics from depressives with ability- and personality-based tests. *Journal of Clinical Psychology,* 1978, *4,* 393–397.

Watson, C. G., Gasser, B., Schaefer, A., Buranen, C., & Wold, J. Separation of brain-damaged from psychiatric patients with ability and personality measures. *Journal of Clinical Psychology,* 1981, *37,* 347–353.

Watson, C. G., Thomas, R. W., Anderson, D., & Felling, J. Differentiation of organics from schizophrenics by use of the Reitan-Halstead Organic Test Battery. *Journal of Consulting and Clinical Psychology,* 1968, *32,* 679–684.

Wechsler, D. *The Measurement of Adult Intelligence.* Baltimore: Williams & Wilkins, 1944.

Wechsler, D. *Wechsler Memory Scale.* New York: Psychological Corporation, 1945.

Wechsler, D. *Measurement and Appraisal of Adult Intelligence.* Baltimore: Williams & Wilkins, 1958.

Weigl, E., Goldstein, K., & Scheerer, M. *Color Form Sorting Test.* New York: Psychological Corporation, 1951.

Whelan, T., Berker, E., Campbell, A. L. Jr., & Smith, A. *Comparative vulnerability of neuropsychological test functions in Huntington's disease.* Paper presented at the 88th Annual Convention of the American Psychological Association, Montreal, September 1980.

Whelan, T., Schteingart, D. E., Starkman, M. N., & Smith, A. Neuropsychological deficits in Cushing's syndrome. *Journal of Nervous and Mental Disease,* 1980, *168,* 753–757.

Williams, M. *Brain Damage, Behavior, and the Mind.* New York: John Wiley & Sons, 1979.

Worster-Drought, C. Mental symptoms associated with tumours of the frontal lobes. *Proceedings of the Royal Society of Medicine*, 1931, *24*, 1007.

Yakovlev, P. I. Vladimir Mikhailovich Bekhterev (1857–1927). In W. Haymaker, (Ed.), *Founders of Neurology*. Springfield, Ill.: Charles C Thomas, 1953.

Yates, A. J. The validity of some psychological tests of brain damage. *Psychological Bulletin*, 1954, *51*, 359–379.

Zubrick, S., & Smith, A. *Factors affecting BVRT performances in adults with acute focal cerebral lesions*. Paper presented at the Sixth Annual Meeting of the International Neuropsychological Society, Minneapolis. February 1978.

15

Writing psychological reports

Walter G. Klopfer*

INTRODUCTION

The present chapter will review some of the recent literature on the subject of psychological report writing. The reader will be reminded of the complex interprofessional and interpersonal issues that are involved in psychological reporting. The report has been described as an important document that may be influenced by and, in turn, influences the examiner submitting the report, the referrer requesting the report, and the client concerning whom the report has been written. In recent years, an emphasis on the collaborative model has become prominent in the literature, and many clinicians now prefer to share their findings with the client either prior to or following submission of the report. The fact that false feedback is readily accepted along with true, makes it necessary for the psychologist to be especially vigilant about the nature of his or her remarks, both in written and in oral form. The safe course is always to be vague, general, universalistic, and generally accurate. It is more hazardous to be specific. However, if the examiner keeps the matter of making clear distinctions between behavioral, self-report, and symbolic levels in mind, and makes no interpretations and predictions not justifiable on the basis of the data collected, then even the specific predictions should be reasonably safe. Some examples of reports will be cited which illustrate what (in the opinion of this author) is a simple, direct, and useful way of providing information. Thus, the psychological report hopefully will continue to be of assistance to those persons who have been examined. They are, after all, the basic consumers of our services.

* Professor of Psychology, Portland State University; Editor, *Journal of Personality Assessment;* Independent Practice, Portland, Oregon.

The author wishes to express his appreciation to Barbara Norcross-Renner for her assistance in the preparation of this chapter.

HOW INFLUENTIAL IS THE PSYCHOLOGICAL REPORT?

The impact of the psychological report has been of interest to several investigators. Dailey (1953) cited 32 important clinical decisions ordinarily made in clinical practice and demonstrated that the psychological report produced important increments over the base level (based on anamnestic data) in the ability of judges to make these decisions with confidence. In a survey by Morrow (1954), it was discovered that psychiatrists found psychologists' reports increasingly useful as they had more experience with them. Psychologists said they were able to be of service if the referral was specific and asked appropriate questions. Certainly, this suggests that mutual training between referrers and examiners boosts the utility and popularity of the report.

In a study concerning strong and weak aspects of psychological reporting, Caudra and Albaugh (1956) discovered that the greatest breakdown in communication occurred in regard to differences in emphases. Vague and universalistic statements produced disagreement between referrers and examiners. In a survey by Tallent and Reiss (1959a, 1959b, 1959c), psychologists agreed with psychiatrists and social workers concerning information desired from reports. However, psychiatrists and social workers were more interested in having IQs than psychologists were in reporting them, and psychologists wanted to furnish more information concerning treatment suggestions than the other two professions were interested in having. In another survey by Tallent and Reiss published in the same year, all three groups agreed that social data (or a mixture of medical, psychological, and social data) should not be included in the psychologist's report. The three groups favored matter-of-fact presentation to literary style and brief, descriptive summary over formal diagnosis. The same group, when surveyed, demonstrated another difference: psychologists wanted to furnish less raw data; psychiatrists wanted them to furnish more. This clearly implies a territorial conflict. Psychologists feel that they themselves are the best interpreters of their data (the "radiologist" model); and psychiatrists feel that they should be the last word in interpretation (putting psychologists in the "x-ray technician" model). Moore, Boblitt, and Wildman, (1968) surveyed 500 psychiatrists and discovered that the average psychiatrist uses a psychological evaluation only 20 percent of the time and that psychiatrists do not view the psychological report as an essential part of patient work-up. The psychiatrists surveyed were kind enough to say that the report had as much validity as a clinical interview conducted by a psychiatrist. Changes that psychiatrists would like to see in psychological reports include the provision of more help with decisions about cases and more-detailed analyses of patients' motivations.

Smyth and Reznikoff (1971) surveyed 57 psychiatrists and found that they considered psychological tests moderately valuable, using them primarily for differential diagnosis. Their major criticisms were stereotyped reporting and lack of separation between objective test reports and subjective interpretations. An interesting study by Affleck and Strider (1971) examined the contribution of psychological reports to management decisions. With data based upon interviews with the referrer, it was discovered that the bulk (59 percent) felt the decisions used the psychological data as a confirmatory measure, whereas 27 percent of them believed that such data contributed new and significant information. Altogether, 52 percent of the reports actually altered management decisions in some direct and significant way. In a study by Adams (1972), the psychological reports studied had little discernible impact on the final psychiatric diagnosis, except in increasing the confidence of the physician. Since this study merely emphasized the final diagnosis and nothing else, it failed to deal with other aspects of the report. Olive (1972) surveyed psychoanalysts in New York City and found that 75 percent of them were generally "satisfied" with reports they received. When they did have criticisms, these dealt with "lack of clarity," "vagueness," "excessive use of jargon," "theoretical bias," "unreliability," and "over-generalization." An interesting methodological note was added in a study by Tidwell (1976), who studied expectancy effects and their relationship to psychological report writing. He discovered that, when examiners have the specific reason for the referral available, they are significantly more likely to address themselves to that reason in their psychological report. When reasons for the referral were known to the examiners, there were no cases in which the referring problem was not discussed. When the reasons were unknown, however, there were 7 (out of 11) cases when the referral problem was not addressed.

During the past two years, the present author has had the opportunity to serve as the psychologist representative on the state of Oregon's Psychiatric Security Review Board. This rather innovative board has jurisdiction over all those individuals found not guilty for misdemeanors and felonies as a result of mental disease or defect. Jurisdiction of the board lasts for as long as the time that the individual would have served if he or she had been found guilty and, therefore, varies anywhere from a year to a lifetime. During the time the board has jurisdiction, it decides where the individual is to be hospitalized, when he or she is to be released, what kind of treatment is to be used, how much freedom is to be allowed, etc. On most of these individuals, a good deal of clinical data is available, usually including psychological tests administered by a number of different psychologists. Therefore, the present author has had the opportunity of seeing at first hand the impact of psychological tests upon important management decisions on the part of a multidisciplinary board.

The conclusion from the above observations is that when psychological reports are well done, they have considerable credibility. For example, they are usually decisive in diagnosing mental retardation. They are also usually decisive in borderline cases involving differential diagnosis between personality disorder and psychosis. The latter is important, because many board members see psychosis as being tantamount to the legal "mental disease" category. Often, the original decision of the judge or jury has been made primarily on the basis of expert testimony by psychologists and their reports. Thus, daily decisions involving life and death are made on the basis of psychological reports in this, and every other, state in the Union. Since psychologists have gone public, been more visible as private practitioners and political animals, and become part of the warp and woof of local government, psychological reports have gained greatly in impact.

At the same time, consumer education has resulted in a more critical attitude toward psychological reports not only among other professionals, but also among members of the general public. Administrators are cautious about proceeding unless the report has credibility with them, and the person writing it is known to be proficient. Persons who are the subjects of psychological reports have access to them in most instances and have the ability and right to challenge them if they feel the information is not appropriate. During the time the present author was chair of the Ethics Committee of the Oregon Psychological Association, there were three instances when individuals in the criminal-justice system made allegations of unethical conduct against psychologists, based upon reports written about them. The conclusion is that psychological reports are important, that they do make a difference, and that, therefore, it behooves us to try to make them as accurate, precise, and defensible as possible.

BARRIERS TO COMMUNICATION AND THEIR RESOLUTION

In their attempts to communicate with one another and with members of other professions, psychologists are sometimes troubled by matters of status and prestige. Occasionally, their efforts to communicate are hampered by excessive hostility or obsequiousness toward the referrent. Also, psychologists are prone to projecting their own characteristics. For example, Filer (1952) discovered that examiners who stressed hostility turned inward in their reports tended to be rated themselves as depressed and intropunitive. Examiners who stressed hostility turned inward and either passive-dependency or inferiority in their reports tended to be rated themselves as submissive. Stress on either inferiority or passive-dependency (but not on hostility turned inward) in reports is associated with ascendant behavior ascribed to the examiner. Those classified as the most ascendant examiners were well above the median on references to hostility in their reports and were also rated as extrapunitive. Appelbaum and Siegal

(1965) deal with the potential influences upon the tester that arise from the social, professional, and interpersonal context in which he or she works. They point out that influences stemming from special characteristics of the patient (such as fame, sensational crimes, etc.) are influential, and that influences stemming from the process of communicating test findings (such as territorial conflicts with other professions) also have an impact. In addition, they mention—as was emphasized by the present author (1960)—that influences stemming from personal or professional motives (such as desire to earn respect and admiration) also influence the tone and nature of the report. Strauss (1968) studied the influence of pretesting information on personality reports. Data suggest that information made available prior to testing may well bias examiners, so that they ignore test data they obtain as well as their own observations of subject behavior. Koscherak and Masling (1972) studied the effect of ascribed social class on the interpretation of identical Rorschach responses. They found no difference in prognosis, but they did find differences in diagnosis. None of the 20 middle-class protocols were classified as "normal," but five lower-class ones were. "Character disorder" was used only once for middle-class but six times for lower-class. "Neurotic" and "psychotic" were chosen most often for middle-class. This again reflects the fact that the testing situation is not independent of the larger social context.

In addition to the biases mentioned above on the part of the examiner, there are, of course, biases on the part of the reader of the report that have been alluded to in a previous section. The credibility of the psychologist writing the report may be established as high or low on the basis of other factors (including territorial struggles between the competing professions of psychiatry and psychology, social work and psychology, education and psychology, etc.). Sometimes, excessive credibility may be ascribed to the psychologist and, therefore, even modestly stated hypotheses in the report may be taken as eternal verities that threaten to have an undue influence upon the further disposition of the case. On the other hand, if the credibility is unduly low, even painfully worked out and very reasonable conclusions may be taken lightly and not influence the outcome to any significant degree.

Ultimately, whether the psychological report communicates well or not depends upon the effectiveness of the examiner. Probably, the written report should be supplemented by verbal discussion with all the relevant parties, with an opportunity for consideration of all of the ramifications of the points covered in the report. A psychologist who acts as if his or her written report were a document engraved on stone rather than a series of probability statements will eventually lose his or her audience. Clinical psychology remains an inexact science, and appropriate humility about our degree of certainty will always be a respectable rather than a weak posture.

IMPORTANCE OF SPECIFYING LEVEL OF
BEHAVIOR

One of the basic fallacies in clinical evaluation is that there exists such a phenomenon as a "basic" or "true" personality. One can view the spectacle of a clinician comparing the results of various tests (projective, objective, observations, and behavioral) together with an analysis of the patient's life history and the results of interviews, trying to decide which of these emerging portraits is correct. This seems to be an inappropriate question. Rather, the present author would like to make the assumption that behavior is always basically consistent, that every piece of information we collect during the process of acquiring data for the clinical case study must be integrated into a conceptual framework concerning the patient in order to ultimately arrive at the truth. This might be referred to as the "six blind men and the elephant" model, after the famous fable by that name. A useful conceptual framework is suggested by Leary in his book, *The Interpersonal Diagnosis of Personality* (1957). These were modified by the present author (1981) to help in organizing data used as part of the clinical case study:

Level I.   Leary called this the "level of public communication." It is operationally defined as the level at which an individual is perceived by significant others, using sociometric ranking techniques. It can also be measured by interviews with significant others, by having significant others fill out checklists on the individual under study, by observing the individual as he or she interacts with other persons, or by the observations of nurses and other caretakers in an institutional setting. This level therefore deals with direct behavioral data and can be interpreted in the same way. Thus, the sources of information referred to above can be interpreted in the psychological report as predictions not of aggressive (sexual, passive, etc.) *feelings*, but rather of aggressive *behavior*. When we try to make important predictions about such socially delicate phenomena as suicide, homicide, rape, fraud, etc., it will be useful to be able to speak in behavioral terms of the likelihood of these events occurring.

Level II.   This level of conscious self-concept is operationally defined as the level at which people describe themselves. This can be measured by interviews, adjective checklists, personality inventories, and other such devices. It is often quite different from the level referred to above, since an individual's view of him/herself may differ a good deal from others' views of him or her. When this kind of material is referred to in a psychological report, it should be clear that we are talking about a patient's statements about him/herself, rather than someone else's description of his or her behavior. Because everyone has a tendency to censor self-descriptions to a certain degree—exaggerating their desirable qualities and modestly disclaiming undesirable ones—self-report is likely to be influenced by this kind of alteration. This is not to say, however, that self-report is useless, as when we are attempting to predict reactions to psychotherapy, the likelihood of being successful in a given area of endeavor, or self-confidence, the individual's conscious reports about his or her own feelings, thoughts, and ideas are certainly to be considered. This is the subject's or client's basis for action that he or she knows about consciously.

Level III. This level of private symbolization is operationally defined by Leary as the level measured by projective tests. This is another one that we have to be careful about. When people tell violent stories on the TAT or see blood on the Rorschach, this does not mean that they behave in a violent way nor necessarily that they perceive themselves as violent persons. It simply means that, in their fantasies, violence is an occurrence. Psychologists have often made themselves vulnerable to criticism by translating fantasy into behavior or into conscious self-concept, without any justification. If we, therefore, refer to projective material on a psychological report, we should specify that it is part of the individual's fantasy or inner life, or that these phenomena occur without any implication that they will be translated into behavior or into conscious self-report.

If the psychological report is to be useful and have credibility, every statement in it should be carefully weighed as to the appropriate level that is being predicted. Psychologists have sometimes made themselves appear foolish, by referring to such phenomena as "latent homosexuality." This could mean that the individual is soliciting sexual favors from members of the same sex without actually culminating the act; it might mean that the individual has thought about doing so but has not translated it into action; it could mean that such fantasies occur strictly at the unconscious level and have never risen to the level of awareness. Certainly, this makes a big difference to whoever is treating the individual; also it makes a big difference to the examiner whether he or she says something that can be checked and validated. It is, therefore, the conclusion of the present author that in a psychological report, particular attention should be paid to the matter of level. Statements in the report, no matter in what section they may reside, should specify whether they are behavioral, self-concept, or fantasy interpretations.

HOW TO WRITE A PSYCHOLOGICAL REPORT

Probably the most comprehensive book on this topic since the author's appeared (1960) is the 1976 edition of the book by Tallent. It is updated from his 1963 book by additional illustrative reports and new material on automatic computer-generated reports and behavioral reports. He rails against inappropriate literary styles, laboratorylike reports, and overly general reports. He warns the reader against the uses of highly technical jargon and a segment format in which test-by-test reports are given. He advocates the *case-focused report,* which is defined as the simple statement answering specific questions posed by the referring person. A book by Hollis and Donn (1973) came out a few years earlier. These authors tried to be exhaustive and ended up telling us much more than we ever needed to know. They become so concrete and specific in their suggestions that the reader is left thinking that one who needs to read this book shouldn't be writing psychological reports at all. It seems to be aimed at a very unsophisticated audience. The latest book was a little volume (93 pages) by Mack (1978) which focused on reports concerning children and aimed primarily at the young audience. In the introduction, he refers to the shopworn division of labor between clinical psychologists, psychiatrists, and social workers. As might be expected from this, he does not emphasize the use of instruments specific to clinical psychology.

In the journals, there have been suggestions about report writing from time to time. Carr (1968) presents a four-page format and emphasizes the delicate balance between being definite, yet playing it safe. Forer (1968) emphasizes the needs to describe persons as individuals and to avoid general statement. One can understand Forer's concern, in view of his research on false feedback described in a later section of this chapter. Appelbaum (1970) describes psychological reports as not solely technical or scientific documents but as political, diplomatic, and strategic persuasions functioning in a complex sociopsychological context. He suggests that the writing of a report should balance data and abstraction. Fischer (1972) was one of the first to advocate sharing results with the client. She justifies this on a humanistic and collaborative basis. She suggests that we address ourselves to particular behaviors, to their interactions, and to the context in which they occur. In her list of recommendations, there are no constructs, causal interpretations, or other jargon; there are only descriptions of assessment behaviors and of life behaviors reported by the person or important others (Fischer, 1973). Craddick (1975) also lines up on the side of sharing information with the client as a further diagnostic device, and Cerney (1978) talks about the use of the psychological report as a facilitative instrument in psychotherapy.

Dana (1970) describes the clinical method as consisting of three levels to correspond with progressively increasing distances from the raw data. He described level 1 as the use of observations of behavior, either descriptive statements or test scores. Level 2 employs concepts, trait adjectives, or summaries to build together and describe the level 1 statements. Level 3 consists of a word picture which integrates the abstractions from level 2 into a personality portrait, a generalized description of the person. Research on Dana's part has determined that agreement on relevant data diminishes from level 1 to level 3. The uniqueness of the content increases as scorer reliability decreases. He believes that a psychological report is an interpretation, a useful work in conceptualization at one point in time, which should make no specific claims for rightness or "truth." Rather, he sees it as a personal, creative experience which enables others to see someone through our eyes.

Hudgins and Schultz (1978) discuss the process of observation and present a systematic approach for incorporating behavioral observations into evaluations and written psychological reports. Their approach is based on R. R. Carkhuff's human resource-development model, which combines the psychologist's attending and responding skills to explore where clients are, personalizing skills to understand where they need to be, and initiating skills to act on these goals.

Some additional points which the present author believes ought to be kept clearly in mind in preparing psychological reports are these:

1. It is important how the client, subject, or patient is referred to. Patronizing statements ("this little girl," "this young gentleman") immediately tend to produce a halo effect and arouse suspicion of bias on the part of the examiner. The individual being studied ought to be referred to respectfully as "the client" or else by appropriate name and title.

2. There seems to be general agreement that giving redundant background information which can be found in the social history or psychiatric work-up is regarded by the readers of the psychological report as unnecessary padding which doesn't serve any useful purpose. When elements of background are supplied, they should be integrated with current consultative data from the psychological examination.

3. Listing tests—but not acting as if each test were for a specific function—is very important. Most pychological tests are molar instruments and not simply designed for a specific purpose. The Bender-Gestalt can do more than screen for organicity, the WAIS can do more than provide an IQ, the Rorschach can do more than indicate whether thought content is bizarre or not. Almost all writers and researchers appear to agree that a description of the personality-integrating information from various sources is more readable and more acceptable. In spite of this, many psychologists are still writing a paragraph on the Rorschach, a paragraph on the Bender, a paragraph on the MMPI, etc. The present author has personally witnessed the fact that this makes a very poor impression on members of other professions. Often, completely inconsistent statements are made in parts of the report without being integrated. Thus, the individual may appear of average intelligence in one paragraph, superior in another, and inferior in the third. He may appear stable in the one instance and unstable in another. This does not add to our credibility.

4. Quantitative statements are dearly beloved by clinical psychologists, but they may not be of equal interest to everyone. Psychological reports in which four or five norms are given for every test result, for high-school seniors, for members of the Rotary Club, for women over 80, begin to lose reader interest rather rapidly. On the one hand, we do not want to make exaggerated claims concerning our accuracy, but it seems unwise to be any more specific than the reader desires. That comes under the heading of answering more questions than we have been asked or than anyone wants answered.

5. It is important that all information from the psychological tests get into the report. In the book by the present author (1960), a system was specified whereby each instrument was thoroughly culled for information, and this information was then integrated into statements unifying the various sources of information. This system was again described in the book by Sundberg and Tyler (1962).

6. We need to be rather careful to see that our conclusions on diagnostic findings have some relationship to the rest of the report. References have been made earlier in this chapter to the political nature of some psychological reports. This becomes especially important when such matters as guilt or innocence, release from an institution, or legal responsibility, hinge upon the psychological findings. The present author has seen reports which describe a personality disorder but end up with a diagnosis of psychosis or the other way around. This does not make a very good impression, since anyone who takes the trouble to read the report would be rather startled at the inappropriate conclusion. Thus, the recommendations are that the report hang together and that the conclusions follow logically from the data.

FEEDBACK: FALSE AND TRUE

False feedback

In one study (which since has become a classic), Forer (1949) discovered that standard feedback, given to a group of college students allegedly interpreting their responses to a projective test, received warm acceptance from members of the group. Statements in the standard report tended to be universalistic, generally applicable, and generally laudatory or mildly critical. This phenomenon of accepting false (positive) feedback was labeled *The Barnum Effect* by Paterson (1957). Such descriptions do possess a good deal of accuracy, but they are not uniquely accurate for specific individuals, rather nearly accurate for all people. This generated a large volume of research, some of which is described below.

Carrier (1963) found that the gullibility of college students accepting false personality analyses of themselves was related to the achievement, deference, and introception variables of the EPPS, among male subjects.

Among female subjects, gullibility was positively related to abasement and introception and negatively related to endurance. Ulrich, Stachnik, and Stainton (1963) repeated Forer's design and found that 53 of his 57 subjects rated the interpretations as good or excellent. He also had subjects give psychological tests to an acquaintance and then give them a standard interpretation. In this case, 59 of the 79 subjects rated the interpretations as good or excellent. This study illustrates a common phenomenon: namely, that experimenter prestige influences acceptance. Mosher (1965) gave his subjects a number of tests and then presented them with three kinds of statements: Barnum (from Forer) and favorable and unfavorable ones (from MMPI items). He discovered that the favorable interpretations yielded the most acceptance, the Barnum interpretations next, and the unfavorable ones least. He further discovered that high scorers on the Marlowe-Crowne social-desirability scale were significantly more accepting of favorable interpretations and less accepting of unfavorable ones than those that scored low on the Marlowe-Crowne. Lattal and Lattal (1967) expanded the information concerning the Barnum effect by showing that it was not influenced adversely by negative information about the test allegedly administered. Merrens and Richards (1970) demonstrated that college students prefer generalized (fake) interpretations to actual ones concerning their test performance. Weisberg (1970) added the finding that even the appeal value of otherwise socially undesirable descriptions may be enhanced if they are properly placed within a list of highly preferred descriptions. Richards and Merrens (1971) demonstrated that their subjects (even though accepting the various Barnum statements quite well) tended to assign them greater credibility when the interpretation was attributed to the Rorschach than when it was attributed to either the Bernreuter or a questionnaire. Dies (1972) discovered that his group of student subjects were unable to discriminate between genuine and fictitious personality feedback. O'Dell (1972) studied the Barnum effect upon computerized printouts. He found that Barnum reports were judged as more accurate than computer-generated ones. He pointed out correctly that Barnum statements (because of their extremely high base-rate) should apply accurately to everyone; hence, they should be perceived as more accurate than statements constructed from "less than perfectly" accurate test scores by a "less than perfect" interpretation program. What is needed in clinical descriptions, therefore, is not simply accuracy, for this can be obtained simply by using statements of high base-rate. The more important goal is that of discovering clinically meaningful ways in which a person differs from others (the ideographic approach).

Dmitruk, Collins, and Clinger (1973) discovered that subjects were equally willing to accept a bogus interpretation from a psychologist and from a student. Also, they tended to accept a negative evaluation as readily as a Barnum, irrespective of whether it were made by the high-prestige or the low-prestige judge. In another study by Merrens and Richards (1970), it was discovered that (along with an overwhelming endorsement of the bogus interpretation) greater efficiency was ascribed to a shorter assessment instrument. The above findings were discussed in 1975 by Snyder and Shenkel, who pointed out that persons have generally accepted universalistic descriptions of personality from astrologists, handwriting analysts, and sometimes, psychologists. Barnum's formula for success was to have a little something for everyone, coupled with the belief that "there's a sucker born every minute." He pointed out that important variables were the favorability of the interpretation and whether it was allegedly prepared for them specifically or true of people in general. The illusion of uniqueness tended to enhance the faith of the individual in the bogus interpretation. Snyder points out that this illusion of uniqueness may be behind the widespread faith in astrology, and experiments have shown that the more specific the information requested by the astrologer, the greater the acceptance of the horoscope.

Schroeder and Lesyk (1976) attempted to put the Barnum report into perspective by comparing the abilities of naive and more-sophisticated judges to evaluate bona fide and Barnum assessment statements. These two groups of judges were asked to rate statements on the dimensions of usefulness, information, social desirability, and typicalness. The two groups of judges were given 10 Barnum statements and 10 genuine statements and were asked to rate the 20 statements for amount of information, degree of usefulness, degree of social desirability, and typicalness in the general population. The sophisticated judges did find the genuine statements somewhat more informative and useful. This was not true of the naive judges. The study tends more to approach the clinical situation and implies that psychological assessments may be more sophisticated than implied in the usual Barnum-type research.

Snyder, Larsen, and Bloom (1976) demonstrated that faith in assessment procedure and perceived diagnostician skill increases significantly from before to after the interpretation has been received. This suggests that those diagnosticians who utilize various assessment procedures should realize that their clients may have more faith in the procedures and in the skill of the diagnosticians as a result of the feedback process, even though the interpretations may not be specifically valid for a given client. After a diagnostician delivers an interpretation, he or she also may expect a halo response on the part of the client in terms of highly consistent views of a positive nature about the assessment procedure. Snyder, Shenkel, and Lowery summarized the review of the literature in 1977 and discovered the following important factors in eliciting acceptance of bogus personality interpretations:

1. Acceptance is higher with a more general interpretation; i.e., subjects perceive a generally fake interpretation as more accurate than ones

actually derived from personality tests. But these fake interpretations have a high base-rate and so should be seen as more likely to be generally accurate than real ones.
2. Acceptance is greater when the interpretations presented are specifically described as being for one person, rather than being presented as true of a group of people in general.
3. Interpretation is more likely to be accepted if it is favorably rooted.
4. It is more likely to be accepted if it is allegedly based on short procedures, especially those with ambiguous stimuli to which the individual is asked to respond in an idiosyncratic way (such as projective techniques).
5. Although favorable ones are more likely to be accepted than unfavorable ones, this can be compensated for, in part, by a high-prestige clinician providing the information.

Other experimenters have interpreted the same data in different ways, e.g., Bradley and Bradley (1977) state that, although the Barnum-effect literature has suggested that situational and interpersonal factors may elicit an individual's acceptance of general personality evaluations, it has failed to demonstrate that the acceptance of genuine test-based interpretations may result from factors in the actual clinical situation. The Barnum studies have used universally valid statements which are inappropriate for three reasons: (a) universally valid descriptions are generally not given in actual test-interpretation situations; (b) the vagueness of universally valid personality statements may serve to enhance their acceptability; and (c) a universally valid interpretation is, by definition, one which is true of nearly everyone. By providing real feedback, the authors discovered that the subjects accepted the interpretations irrespective of the personality of the experimenter or the status of the person providing the feedback.

Green (1977) added the finding that, although students accepted generalized descriptions, they indicated an awareness of their lack of specificity and uniqueness. Thus, he discovered that students can assess the accuracy and the triviality of generalized interpretation, if they are specifically asked to do so.

Layne (1978) discovered that feedback rating and test taking are both instances of a more general behavior, significantly correlated, and equally affected by both descriptive favorability and subject defensiveness.

In another article, Layne (1979) argues that the data does not support the theory that the acceptance phenomenon is caused by a subpopulation of especially gullible people. He further says that the argument that all people and not just the subgroup are gullible is also unsound, because the Barnum effect consists of people rating accurate descriptions of themselves as accurate descriptions of themselves. A rational person would rate such descriptions as accurate, trivial, and reasonably favorable. Thus, the high base-rate accuracy of the Barnum statements (not the gullibility of people) explains the Barnum effect. Since it is known that subjects' opinions are readily changed by high-status, credible communicators, it would seem natural that any sort of feedback would cause a change of view.

By 1979, the whole Barnum-research effort had succeeded in arousing the attention of Richard Dana (1979), who pointed out that the Barnum concept constituted only a consistent minority of personality-descriptive statements in psychological reports. To study Barnum concepts out of context with other concepts descriptive of personality seems to be misleading, antifactual, and fragmentary. Dana and other like-minded individuals have not succeeded in stopping the Barnum research, but they seem to have slowed it down somewhat. Enough questions have been raised about the relevance of these studies to the actual clinical situation to take some of the wind out of the sails of those who have been enthusiastically pursuing this goal. What it seems to boil down to is that statements that are highly favorable, very general, and universalistic, are true of almost everybody. Whether this is or is not relevant to the usual clinical situation or to the literature examining the validity of tests is left up to the reader to decide.

True feedback

Baker (1964) was one of the first to describe the process of interpreting a subject's own test results to him or her. Richman (1967) added to the (then) meager literature on the subject by giving actual examples of test feedback to patients and providing some guidelines as to how this could be done. Aronow and Reznikoff (1971) present an approach for giving feedback which is very cautious and more conservative than the one above mentioned. Brodsky (1972) recommends that psychological files be open to the client. He was the first to go this far, but not the last. Jourard (1972) talked about a "quiet revolution." By this he referred to psychologists allying themselves with their patients and clients in developing a more collaborative and less mysterious style. He felt that this concept would be a challenge to what was then established professional training and practice and that it would take some years to respond as radically as the challenge required. Dana and Graham (1976) viewed the literature and feedback experiments with an emphasis on the importance of using true feedback rather than bogus. They stated the opinion that the usefulness of personality-relevant or true-feedback statements may be more of an empirical issue than researchers using a Barnum paradigm have admitted.

Real versus random statements cannot only be distinguished by college students, but by hospital patients as well. A study which supported the superiority of true over false feedback was conducted by Greene, Harris, and Macon (1979). They gave sophomores, seniors, and graduate students both true and false information about their performances on the California Personality Inventory (CPI). The information provided consisted of the actual profile and a copy of the descriptive adjectives characteristic of high and low scores on all scales taken directly from the manual. For both the seniors and the graduate students, the subjects were able to select the real profile and the real list of adjectives to a significant degree. Dana (1979), in an address before the Society for Personality Assessment, suggested a new model for clinical assessment procedures which would include the following preconditions:

1. Assessment is to be a shared process, which he calls part of the "quiet revolution." This would change assessment from a routine and ancillary service into a consultative one.
2. Honest feedback is a condition of human existence, and assessment practices should reflect this.
3. Honest and meaningful feedback is a clinical act which can be described from the perspective of assessee, assessor, and referral-source person.
4. Feedback to assessors is a critical part of the training and accountability process.

In the opinion of the present writer, the matter of feedback continues to be of the utmost importance. In former days, when psychologists were more willing to play medicine man, they hid behind the mask and behind the torches and pretended that they were engaged in some mysterious rite that would bring about truth and justice in a way too complex and esoteric for the common mind to fathom. We were, thereby, following the old medical example in assuming that our prestige would be enhanced by our incomprehensibility and mysterious posturings. However, time has shown us the fallacy of this assumption. Clients who have been exhaustively examined by means of tests, interviews, and behavioral observations, and then chased out into the cold, cruel world with nary a word as a reward for their efforts, have gone away feeling robbed and invaded. The assumption we have made in doing diagnostic consultations that the referrent will provide appropriate feedback is all too often unwarranted. Because the referrents are often physicians, social workers, and school administrators, etc. (who themselves are not used to giving very much feedback), they are not likely to alter their ordinary procedure in this case. The net effect of our mysteriousness has been to arouse public suspicion and antagonism against psychological procedures and sometimes to actually provoke legislation against our use of such procedures.

The present writer is sympathetic to Jourard and Dana and their concept of collaboration. Any assessment procedure requires the cooperation of the client; for without it, nothing can be discovered of any value. When someone collaborates with you, appreciation and reward is indicated.

Feedback is not only ethically necessary and humanly desirable, it is also clinically valuable. Years ago, George Bach coined the term *theragnosis*. He referred to the continuing diagnostic information available during therapy. However, one might also refer to the therapeutic impact of providing diagnostic information. Certainly a diagnostician can think of some valuable pieces of information that can immediately be used by a client as soon as they are provided. Some judicious selection of data would probably have to be made, as all writers on the subject have pointed out. How far to go in providing information at unconscious (as well as conscious and behavioral) levels remains a matter of clinical judgment. No generalizations about this can be accepted, since we are likely to be dealing with clients of varying degrees of ego strength, intelligence, and protective environments. Thus, the idea of providing clinical feedback remains delicate and a matter of skill. Although the procedures suggested by Dana—providing clients with their own reports—seem reasonable in some instances, the generality of this procedure seems dubious to the present writer. However, some form of feedback always seems to be necessary.

In providing feedback to an individual client, rules generally governing good communication should apply. The words used with an intelligent, sophisticated, and educated client should not be the same as those used with someone who has a more limited vocabulary and lesser ability to conceptualize and abstract. An effort should be made to talk neither up nor down, but rather across. By this time, the examiner should have some information about the conversational style that is most natural with the particular person. Also, he will have discovered in which area the client is sufficiently comfortable for direct statement and in which areas he or she is rather vulnerable and needs to be approached with greater caution. The test interpretation gives an opportunity for the selective reinforcement of strong areas so as to provide some support during this part of the clinical situation, and allusion can be made to problems together with proposed solutions. It is very gratifying to clients to be understood; this makes them feel that the whole situation is worthwhile and productive. Accepting some of the recommendations that the examiner makes in the report (and also articulates to the client during the feedback session) increases their motivation for following-up. If the client asks questions about any of the test materials, the examiner should make some effort to explain the use of the test and should give illustrations of how the client's own test behavior is more generally meaningful and leads to valuable predictions and generalizations. The kind of explanations concerning psychological tests provided to clients might be very similar to the explanations given juries when the psychologist functions as an expert witness. If psychologists can't explain what they are doing in everyday language and in a clear and simple way, then suspicion is raised that their own understanding is rather shallow and tied to buzz words rather than to clear concepts.

Every psychological examination might be construed as having three parts. During the first part, an agreement is made to work together or to establish rapport. This means that one person is to provide information, and the other is to carefully note this information, organize it, integrate it, and use it for the best interests of the examinee. In the second part of the procedure, data is being provided, integrated, and organized. During the third part of the procedure, the examiner summarizes and provides information while at the same time being open to amending and revising his or her findings in line with the client's reactions to the feedback.

The present writer has always recommended to his students that they do the bulk of their interviewing after giving psychological tests and that this be integrated with the feedback process concerning the test results. In line with the "six blind men and the elephant" model, many of the tests we have given will provide us with hypotheses rather than finite results. Certainly, the client's reactions, both overt and covert, will be of value in further modifying, refining, and clarifying the issues under consideration. Therefore, a discussion of the findings as a last aspect of the assessment procedure will be both reassuring to the client and to the examining psychologist.

When clients being examined are under stress (such as being incarcerated, hospitalized, in a difficult family situation, or in a difficult legal situation) they have a special need to know what use is going to be made of the information collected and what will be reported to the relevant decision makers. It seems fair for them to expect this information from the examining psychologist and necessary for the examining psychologist to provide it. Hopefully, this will promote the view of psychologists as allied with their clients rather than in some way using them or acting on their behalf without their knowledge or consent.

ILLUSTRATIVE REPORTS

The first report was submitted by Richard Dana. It was based primarily on the Rorschach and was addressed to the client who has been examined. It is evident that Dana has stayed away from Barnum-like statements and has been rather specific and direct in the interpretations that are being offered. This is part of Dana's system of collaborative sharing of the report with the subject:

> You are essentially a cautious, secretive person who chooses the time and place for encounters with others. You find some sanctuary in things and places that are yours alone, and you are reluctant to share yourself with

other persons. This renders you somewhat detached, distant, and separate from others. When you do engage with others, it is an erratic, sudden, and tentative sociability as if you are more certain of yourself when alone than with others.

And you are very different from other persons, very individualized in the way you see the world and interpret your own experiences. Somehow the world around you is not to your liking, so you often transform it for yourself. Such personal alteration allows for selection from experiences, intensification of selected experiences, and a recreation of the vividness of cherished memories. This way of intellectualizing experience enables control of yourself and of the world.

Behind the self-imposed control and the apparent easy detachment from others there is a person who is mildly dysphoric, stubbornly suspicious of others, and concerned about her feelings about herself, as she tries to make do in the confines of her immediate experience. You are somehow very young and very old simultaneously, with a lacuna in between that remains unfulfilled. It is as if at one time way back in your past you were so hurt by someone close to you that you vowed never again to be defenseless, never to be at risk with other persons. So you remain enmured, in chrysallis, guarding the integrity of your own experiences and possessions, cherishing what you have, but admitting few persons into your secret domain. And yet this domain and its treasures are not enough for you. You often feel inert and helpless, unhappy with who you are, not certain that you can be the person you want to be with only occasional forays out of your sanctuary. And not sure, indeed, that more than even these occasional sorties are tolerable because of the risk of hurt and loss of control over your own experiences.

The next report was submitted by Robert William Davis and is based upon a number of different assessment procedures that are integrated and presented in a highly literary and readable manner. The client really comes to life in Davis's report, and the language is couched in a manner sufficiently complex to do justice to the personality of the client and yet lacks any jargon that would be incomprehensible to the reader, who in this case is an attorney:

> I have seen Mr. L. for evaluation and treatment subsequent to referral by Dr. K., neurosurgeon, and yourself. To date, my contacts with Mr. L. have extended over five visits, on December 13, 20, and 28, 1978, and January 5 and 12, for a total of eight hours. Mrs. L. was also interviewed as part of the psychological evaluation of L. which included two interviews and the following psychological tests: Wechsler Adult Intelligence Scales, Rorschach Psychodiagnostic Technique, Wagner's Hand Test, Thematic Apperception Test, Minnesota Multiphasic Personality Inventory, Strong Vocational Interest Blank, and the Bender Visual-Motor Gestalt Test. Following is a summary of my findings.
>
> Mr. L. is a 50-year-old freight handler for Pan Am Airlines who has been disabled on two occasions since January, 1975 by a back injury which required a laminectomy and two fusions. He has been unable to

work for extended periods, currently since October 1978. He is now manifesting overtly moderate depression, severe anxiety, and accompanying loss of self-esteem. He is seen to worry to extremes and is described by his wife of 23 years as easily upset and emotionally labile to an increased extent since the injury, although he has been "a worrier" ever since she has known him.

Mr. L. has been cast from a very early age in the role of the *one* responsible, the lead worker, and beast of burden. This was true of his relationship with a demanding father who was physically abusive and whom Mr. L. feared in the extreme. His self-concept was forged in an atmosphere of intense, serious labor and accountability for his younger brothers. Independent evaluation seen in test results shows him to be overly conscientious, highly anxious, and a tense person who is very demanding of himself—physically oriented and tends to place extreme pressure on himself to perform to ever higher standards. He is, for example, literally out to set a record almost every time he loads an airplane, and this concern is reflected repeatedly in interviewing about his job. He has never learned or felt it permissible to ease up on himself or allow for any relaxation as long as there is work to be done. For the present, he views his job as setting up very exacting demands for physical strength, agility, and alertness, qualities he has come to doubt in himself. Consequently, he is very fearful of returning to work because he sees doing so as exposing himself to almost certain failure, particularly since he feels he is not a worthwhile person unless he proves himself through physical exertion.

Examination results further reveal an extremely intelligent man (IQ = 127) well into the Superior range, who sometimes functions within the Very-Superior range of intelligence (the top 1 percent of the general population). He also manifests a fairly wide range of interests and abilities, evidencing a good understanding of people, social conventions, organizational and mechanical aptitudes, mathematical skills, and verbal ability, with interests in nature and the out-of-doors. With these abilities, it is likely that his capacity to profit from further educational endeavors is quite high, although there is some interference with these abilities caused by his anxiety and depression. The pain he continues to experience in neck, back, and legs is certainly worsened by the presence of tension and anxiety, as are his hand tremors.

In summary, Mr. L. is a person with a strong predisposing condition who is seriously neurotic at this time and who experiences significant elements of anxiety, depression, and loss of self-esteem relating to his diminished ability to work, held in place by his intense fear of failure at the level of his expectations. This anxiety neurosis is not directly amenable to logic, and medical advice is unlikely, taken alone, to effect a return to work.

As requested, I have undertaken a course of psychotherapy to assist Mr. L. to work through inappropriate and dysfunctional aspects of his self-concept, expect somewhat more relaxed levels of performance and reassure him of a likelihood of success on the job. His pain is surely related to the fears mentioned, which need to be desensitized in treatment. Prognosis is only fair in terms of an early, symptom-free return to work, although it is quite good when considered as long-term potential to resume an active, anxiety-free vocational role in some occupation. When he goes back to the company physician for review, he will require a great deal of reassurance of his fitness and even then will quite likely harbor serious doubts, although this may provide him with sufficient impetus to give it a fair trial. It will be helpful too, if his employer can accept some initial shakiness and tentativeness and cooperate in keeping job pressures at a lowered level.

I expect that Mr. L. will need to continue with psychotherapy over a period of several months or longer, if he is to alter his long-held pattern of excessive demands, pessimism, and over-responsiveness to stress. Over the years, and especially since his injury, he has developed a pattern of excessive alerting toward or apprehension of possible dangers, which he has attempted recently to quell by means of alcohol. He has only occasionally drunk to excess, but since the recent (October) incapacitation he has had less control and drinking has begun to be a problem. The treatment already done has had a significant effect in that he has cut down drastically on the drinking, and it would appear that his depression has lifted considerably.

Thank you for referring Mr. L. Let me know if I can provide further information.

The next report was submitted by Norman S. Mitroff. It deals with a complex assessment question: namely, the suitability of an individual for a particular kind of hazardous and delicate work (law enforcement). Mitroff's report is brief and to-the-point. It is readable and clear and should be easily comprehended by the person making the referral—who, in this case, is a city manager:

Dear R:

On this date, I examined the above-referenced applicant as part of his preemployment screening to become a police officer for the city. Mr. T. arrived for his scheduled appointment early, neatly but casually dressed and groomed. He was noted to be an exceptionally slow and deliberate worker on all of the various tasks presented to him. The rather slow pace that Mr. T. worked at is indicative of some difficulties that will be more elaborately discussed in the report later on.

Mr. T's intellectual abilities were found to range from the bright-normal to the superior level of functioning. This is an applicant, from an intellectual point of view, who clearly has more than sufficient intellectual strengths necessary to undertake the complexities of police work. There were no intellectual deficits to speak of, and he intellectually excels at most tasks that he would undertake. His short-term as well as long-term memory are exceptionally intact and strong assets for him. His general fund of knowledge regarding his environment is well above average and, from an intellectual point of view, Mr. T. would be an individual who would have minimal difficulty expressing his points of view and understanding communications with others.

The current emotional functioning of Mr. T. brought to light some concerns regarding the suitability of his employment with the city. To begin with, as stated previously, Mr. T. works at an exceptionally slow rate of speed. The slowness of his rate of speed is because of a rather strong, obsessive characteristic in his personality. This is an individual who lacks spontaneity and needs to carefully review in his own mind all of the facts and details before responding. He is quite cautious and perhaps even fearful of making errors or mistakes. Because of his anxieties and concerns in this area, his rate of speed for responses is exceptionally slow. As a result, this is an individual who would likely fail to meet deadlines on various assignments that would be given to him, may fail to take full advantage of opportunities that are presented to him because of his inability or time delay in making a decision, and may annoy others because of his worries over irrelevant or uncontrollable events. Additionally, he is likely to be an individual that would take the job "home with him," thereby adding to his overall level of stress and strain.

Mr. T.'s other major personality characteristic is that he tends to be very inflexible and has difficulty modifying his behavior to match the situation. As a result, his inflexibility is likely to present itself in the complexities of police work. He might conceivably be an individual who would exacerbate conditions rather than bring them to a more calm and controllable conclusion. He is likely to have difficulty understanding generalizations made by others because his own thought processes are so narrowly constricted.

It appears from the basis of this evaluation that Mr. T. is an individual who keeps rather rigid and tight controls over his emotions, thoughts, and behavior. He tends to do this because of what appears to be rather strong negativistic feelings that are well ingrained in his personality. He appears to have anxieties and apprehensions about losing control, and one would hypothesize that he fears losing control because he would become enraged. The vast majority of these personality characteristics are not completely understood by Mr. T., and he tends to be not very reflective at looking at his own feelings and behavior. As a result, the probability that he is likely to change any of these major characteristics in the very near future is very minimal.

On the basis of the population with which a police officer for the city must work and the number of officers that he would have to work in close proximity with and have strong relationships with, I am making a prediction that Mr. T. would not be well suited for employment with your department. This psychological evaluation is only one part of his overall screening for employment with your city and should be taken as such. However, it is my recommendation that you not seriously consider Mr. T. for the position of police officer for the city.

I wish to thank you very much for referring Mr. T. to me for this psychological evaluation. If you have any further questions or concerns regarding this evaluation, please do not hesitate to contact me.

In discussing this psychological examination with the client, Dr. Mitroff might very well make an effort to cushion the blow by trying to persuade him that a career in law enforcement would not make him happy or be suitable in terms of his interests and abilities. He might do this by complimenting the client upon his careful and precise manner of working which, in many instances, produces much more orderly and competent results than a more slovenly and haphazard approach. He could point out to the client a number of occupations in which this kind of behavior would be at a premium and would cause him to be approved of and promoted. He could illustrate this by various test and interview behaviors which show how the client weighed every detail and made decisions that took a maximum of data into account. At this point, he could refer to the law-enforcement situation as not allowing for this kind of deliberate, thorough approach, but rather necessitating rapid decisions and behavior which to the client might appear ill-advised, impulsive, and reckless. Hopefully, the feedback session actually might produce a set on the part of the client against pursuing a career in law enforcement, which would make the eventual negative decision much easier for him to bear.

The last report is one of the present author's. It is based upon the Rorschach and a short interview and deals with the specific problem of differential diagnosis. It is directed to a social worker and tries to clearly lay out the parameters relevant to the question asked by the referrent:

Dear Ms. Rogers:

Thank you for referring Mary R. to me for diagnostic consultation. Prior to seeing her, I reviewed the psychological report from Dr. Z. and other attached materials. I examined her in my office on January 28, 1980, where I administered a Rorschach and a short diagnostic interview with the following results:

Ms. R. is most comfortable when provided with maximum structure accompanied by approval, attention, and good humor. She is dissatisfied with her limitations and keeps trying to create the impression that she is more knowledgeable than she is and that she comprehends matters that are really beyond her ability.

When she doesn't fully understand the situation, she tends to extrapolate and guess, and this creates the impression that she is delusional. In fact, she is just filling in the blank spaces because she doesn't like to admit that there are many things she does not understand.

Ms. R. is most severely handicapped in the area of interpersonal relationships. In her fantasies, she is generally admired and approved of, and this contrasts sadly with the fact that she is often criticized, disapproved of, and frustrated. Most people appear to her to be rather monstrous, incomprehensible, ordering her about, and hurting her for reasons that she is unable to understand. When she has control over the situation and understands it, she can be neat, orderly, and good-humored.

She reacts violently to stress, lashing out at the world about her and expressing her outrage at having her routine disrupted and her even flow made tumultuous. For example, she was outraged that her soap operas on television have been interferred with by news about the presidential inauguration and the hostages. She sees this as offensive because it interrupts her routine to which she clings for safety and security.

Ms. R. tends to rationalize a good deal so that she ends up feeling better about herself. When she is excluded from something, she claims she didn't want to participate anyway. When someone dislikes her, she claims that she disliked them first; and she generally tries to make her situation appear better than it really is (like all the rest of us).

Conclusion

The major referral question posed by you is whether or not I believe (on the basis of the Rorschach) that this client is psychotic. In my opinion, based upon the data described above, I believe that calling her psychotic would be an over-interpretation that is unjustified. She is a mildly defective person who is quite unhappy about her limitations and tries to extrapolate with fantasy and defend herself against feeling inadequate in the ways that I have described in the preceding sections. She is aggressive rather than passive, and extrapunitive rather than intropunitive, which gives her a somewhat paranoid personality structure; however, I would not call her schizophrenic, but rather would describe her as immature, explosive, and unsettled when it comes to dealing with her limited abilities.

I hope that the above information will be of value to you. If you have any further questions, please feel free to contact me again.

In discussing this examination with the client, I commended her for her assertiveness and her unwillingness to be passive in a situation which she felt to be unfair. I pointed out to her that when she understood a situation and was being treated well, she was quite efficient and also good-humored. I also acknowledged the fact that it is hard sometimes not to understand things and that she had a good deal of pride, which made it necessary for her to bluster when she felt confused and on the spot. The client admitted as much and seemed to feel good that somebody could understand why she behaved the way she did. She had no particular interest in the inkblots, except that it was fun to look at them and to use your imagination. The examiner pointed out that sometimes other people find it hard to distinguish her being imaginative from her believing the things that she was imagining. The client could see some need for greater caution in this area.

SUMMARY

Psychologists are best known for the reports they write. When a psychologist has credibility and communicates well, his or her report can have great influence upon the life of the person who has been examined.

The psychological report sometimes becomes a shibboleth to be refuted or defended, when it is used as a political instrument for determination of territory, power, or status. In their desire to prove themselves as scientists and academicians, psychologists often rely on jargon, numbers, and broad generalizations. These techniques are usually not effective in impressing other people; rather, brevity, simplicity, and clarity tend to be the virtues that are generally lauded and appreciated.

Suggestions as to how to write a good psychological report are reviewed, and the value of sharing the information with the client as part of the examination is discussed at length. Providing feedback is strongly supported as a means of assisting the client directly and also as a means of being less patronizing and more respectful and collaborative.

REFERENCES

Adams, J. The contribution of the psychological evaluation to psychiatric diagnosis. *Journal of Personality Assessment,* 1972, *36,* 561–566.

Affleck, D. C., & Strider, F. D. Contribution of psychological reports to patient management. *Journal of Consulting and Clinical Psychology,* 1971, *37,* 177–179.

Appelbaum, S. A. Science and persuasion in the psychological test report. *Journal of Consulting and Clinical Psychology,* 1970, *35,* 349–355.

Appelbaum, S. A., & Siegal., R. S. Half-hidden influences on psychological testing and practice. *Journal of Projective Techniques & Personality Assessment,* 1965, *29,* 128–133.

Aronow, E., & Reznikoff, M. Applications of projective tests to psychotherapy: A case study. *Journal of Personality Assessment,* 1971, *35,* 379–393.

Baker, G. A therapeutic application of psychodiagnostic test results. *Journal of Projective Techniques,* 1964, *28,* 3–8.

Bradley, G. W., & Bradley, L. A. Experimenter prestige and feedback related to acceptance of genuine personality interpretations and self-attitude. *Journal of Personality Assessment,* 1977, *41,* 178–185.

Brodsky, S. L. Shared results and open files with the client. *Professional Psychology,* 1972, *3,* 362–364.

Carr, A. C. Psychological testing and reporting. *Journal of Projective Techniques & Personality Assessment,* 1968, *32,* 513–521.

Carrier, N. A. Need correlates of "gullibility." *Journal of Abnormal and Social Psychology,* 1963, *66,* 84–86.

Caudra, C. A., & Albaugh, W. P. Sources of ambiguity in psychological reports. *Journal of Clinical Psychology,* 1956, *12,* 109–115.

Cerney, M. S. Use of the psychological test report in the course of psychotherapy. *Journal of Personality Assessment,* 1978, *42,* 457–463.

Craddick, R. A. Sharing oneself in the assessment procedure. *Professional Psychology,* 1975, *6,* 279–282.

Dailey, C. A. The practical utility of the clinical report. *Journal of Consulting Psychology,* 1953, *17,* 297–302.

Dana, R. H. A hierarchical model for analyzing personality data. *Journal of General Psychology,* 1970, *82,* 199–206.

Dana, R. H. *The communication of psychologists' assessment interpretations.* (Extension of) paper presented at the meeting of the Society for Personality Assessment, Scottsdale, Arizona, March 1979.

Dana, R. H., & Fouke, H. P. Barnum statements in reports of psychological assessment. *Psychological Reports,* 1979, *44,* 1215–1221.

Dana, R. H., & Graham, E. D. Feedback of client-related information and clinical practice. *Journal of Personality Assessment,* 1976, *40,* 464–469.

Dies, R. R. Personal gullibility or pseudodiagnosis: A further test of the "fallacy of personal validation." *Journal of Clinical Psychology,* 1972, *28,* 47–50.

Dmitruk, Z. M., Collins, R. W., and Clinger, D. L. The "Barnum Effect": An acceptance of negative personal evaluation. *Journal of Consulting and Clinical Psychology.* 1973. *41.* 192–194.

Filer, R. N. The clinician's personality and his case reports. Summary of paper presented at 1952 APA meeting. *American Psychologist,* 1952, *7,* 336.

Fischer, C. T. Paradigm changes which allow sharing of results. *Professional Psychology,* 1972, *3,* 364–369.

Fischer, C. T. Contextual approach to assessment. *Community Mental Health Journal,* 1973, *9,* 38–45.

Forer, B. F. The fallacy of personal validation: A classroom demonstration of gullibility. *Journal of Abnormal Psychology,* 1949, *44,* 118–123.

Forer, B. R. Personal validation and the person. *Psychological Reports,* 1968, *23,* 1214.

Greene, R. L. Student acceptance of generalized personality personal interpretations: A reexamination. *Journal of Consulting and Clinical Psychology,* 1977, *45,* 965–966.

Greene, R. L., Harris, M. E., & Macon, R. S. Another look at personal validation. *Journal of Personality Assessment,* 1979, *43,* 419–423.

Hollis, J. W., & Donn, P. A. *Psychological report writing: Theory and practice.* Muncie, Ind.: Accelerated Development, 1973.

Hudgins, A. L., & Schultz, J. L. On observing: The use of the Carkhuff HRD model in writing psychological reports. *Journal of School Psychology,* 1978, *16,* 56–63.

Jourard, S. M. Some reflections on a quiet revolution. *Professional Psychology,* 1972, *3,* 380–381.

Klopfer, W. G. *The psychological report: Use and communication of psychological findings.* New York: Grune & Stratton, 1960.

Klopfer, W. G. Integration of projective techniques into the clinical case study. In A. I. Rabin (Ed.), *A concise introduction to projective techniques in personality assessment.* New York: Springer, 1981.

Koscherack, S., & Masling, J. Noblesse oblige effect: The interpretation of Rorschach responses as a function of ascribed social class. *Journal of Consulting and Clinical Psychology,* 1972, *39,* 415–419.

Lattal, K. A., & Lattal, A. D. Student "gullibility": A systematic replication. *Journal of Psychology,* 1967, *67,* 319–322.

Layne, C. Relationship between the "Barnum effect" and personality-inventory responses. *Journal of Clinical Psychology,* 1978, *34,* 94–97.

Layne, C. The Barnum effect: Rationality versus gullibility. *Journal of Consulting and Clinical Psychology,* 1979, *47,* 219–221.

Leary, T. F. *The interpersonal diagnosis of personality.* New York: Ronald Press, 1957.

Mack, J. *Psychological examination and report writing.* Hicksville, New York: Exposition Press, 1978.

Merrens, M. R., & Richards, W. S. Acceptance of generalized versus "bona fide" personality interpretation. *Psychological Reports,* 1970, *27,* 691–694.

Merrens, M. R., & Richards, W. S. Length of personality inventory and the evaluation of a generalized personality interpretation. *Journal of Personality Assessment*, 1973, *37*, 83–85.

Moore, C. H., Boblitt, W. E., & Wildman, R. W. Psychiatric impressions of psychological reports. *Journal of Clinical Psychology*, 1968, *24*, 373–376.

Morrow, R. S. The diagnostic psychological report. *Psychiatric Quarterly Supplement*, 1954, *28*, 102–110.

Mosher, D. L. Approval motive and acceptance of personality-test interpretations which differ in favorability. *Psychological Reports*, 1965, *17*, 395–402.

O'Dell, J. W. P. T. Barnum explores the computer. *Journal of Consulting and Clinical Psychology*, 1972, *38*, 270–273.

Olive, H. Psychoanalysts' opinions of psychologists' reports: 1952 and 1970. *Journal of Clinical Psychology*, 1972, *28*, 50–54.

Paterson, D. G. Character reading at sight of Mr. X according to the system of Mr. P. T. Barnum. Reprinted in M. D. Dunnette. Use of the sugar pill by industrial psychologists. *American Psychologist*, 1957, *12*, 223–225.

Richards, W. S., & Merrens, M. R. Student evaluation of generalized personality interpretations as a function of method of assessment. *Journal of Clinical Psychology*, 1971, *27*, 457–459.

Richman, J. Reporting diagnostic test results to patients and their families. *Journal of Projective Techniques & Personality Assessment*, 1967, *31*, 62–70.

Schroeder, H. E., & Lesyk, C. K. Judging personality assessments: Putting the Barnum report in perspective. *Journal of Personality Assessment*, 1976, *40*, 470–474.

Smyth, R., & Reznikoff, M. Attitudes of psychiatrists toward the usefulness of psychodiagnostic reports. *Professional Psychology*, 1971, *2*, 283–288.

Snyder, C. R., Larsen, D. L., & Bloom, L. J. Acceptance of general personality interpretations prior to and after receipt of diagnostic feedback supposedly based on psychological, graphological, and astrological assessment procedures. *Journal of Clinical Psychology*, 1976, *32*, 258–265.

Snyder, C. R., & Shenkel, R. J. Astrologers, handwriting analysts, and sometimes psychologists use the P. T. Barnum effect. *Psychology Today*, March 1975, *8*, 52–54.

Snyder, C. R., Shenkel, R. J., & Lowery, C. R. Acceptance of personality interpretations: The "Barnum effect" and beyond. *Journal of Consulting and Clinical Psychology*, 1977, *45*, 104–114.

Strauss, M. E. The influence of pretesting information on Rorschach-based personality reports. *Journal of Projective Techniques & Personality Assessment*, 1968, *32*, 323–325.

Sundberg, N. D., & Tyler, L. E. *Clinical psychology: An introduction to research and practice.* New York: Appleton-Century-Crofts, 1962.

Tallent, N. *Psychological report writing.* Englewood Cliffs, N.J.: Prentice-Hall, 1976.

Tallent, N., & Reiss, W. J. Multidisciplinary views of the preparation of written psychological reports: I. Spontaneous suggestions for content. *Journal of Clinical Psychology*, 1959, *15*, 218–221. (a)

Tallent, N., & Reiss, W. J. Multidisciplinary views of the preparation of written psychological reports: II. Acceptability of certain common content variables and styles of expression. *Journal of Clinical Psychology*, 1959, *15*, 273–274. (b)

Tallent, N., & Reiss, W. J. Multidisciplinary views of the preparation of written psychological reports: III. The trouble with psychological reports. *Journal of Clinical Psychology,* 1959, *15,* 444–446. (c)

Tidwell, R. Expectancy effects and their relationship to psychological case report writing. *Psychology in the Schools,* 1976, *13,* 275–278.

Ulrich, R. E., Stachnik, T. J., & Stainton, N. R. Student acceptance of generalized personality interpretations. *Psychological Reports,* 1963, *13,* 831–834.

Weisberg, P. Student acceptance of bogus personality interpretations differing in level of social desirability. *Psychological Reports,* 1970, *27,* 743–746.

Index

Note: Lightface page numbers are in Volume I; boldface page numbers are in Volume II.

Note: Lightface page numbers are in Volume I; boldface page numbers are in Volume II.

Note: Lightface page numbers are in Volume I; boldface page numbers are in Volume II.

Note: Lightface page numbers are in Volume I; boldface page numbers are in Volume II.

Note: Lightface page numbers are in Volume I; boldface page numbers are in Volume II.

Note: Lightface page numbers are in Volume I; boldface page numbers are in Volume II.

Note: Lightface page numbers are in Volume I; boldface page numbers are in Volume II.

This book has been set CAP/VideoComp, in 10 and 9 point Stymie Light, leaded 2 points. Part numbers and titles and chapter titles are 36 point Stymie Light. Chapter titles are 20 point Stymie Light. The size of the type page is 27 by 47 picas.

Note: Lightface page numbers are in Volume I; boldface page numbers are in Volume II.